SATYA SUDHĀ

A Critical Evaluation of Dr. Satya Vrat Shastri's Creative Works

SATYA SUDHĀ

A Critical Evaluation of Dr. Satya Vrat Shastri's Creative Works

Thesis approved for the D. Litt. Degree
by the Kumaun University,
Nainital

SATYA VRAT VARMA
M. A. Ph. D.,
Head, Department of P. G. Studies in Sanskrit,
Government College,
Sri Ganganagar (Raj.)

Eastern Book Linkers
DELHI :: (INDIA)

Published by :
EASTERN BOOK LINKERS
5825, New Chandrawal, Jawahar Nagar,
Delhi-110007
Phone : 2520287

First Edition : 1993

ISBN : 81-85133-53-0

Printed by :
ORIENT OFFSET
Shahadara, DELHI-32

PREFACE

Despite its traditional moorings, the contemporary Sanskrit literature has emerged, over the years, as a vibrantly distinct entity, well attuned to the changing milieu. While drawing sustenance from the vast mass of earlier literature, which in its totality symbolises the ancient wisdom of the nation, the present-day Sanskritist has been equal to the new horizons and challenges, unleashed by emerging social and political forces, and intimate interaction with diverse languages and literatures. That has happily resulted in broadening the dimensions of the contemporary literature and unravelling the possibilities of the Sanskrit speech to voice the varied contours and nuances of modern thought. The contemporary Sanskrit literature is singularly fortunate to be aborned with a galaxy of stalwarts who would do proud any age and literature.

Because of the varied excellences, inherent in the fusion of creative and critical faculties that he has marvellously achieved, over the years, Dr. Satya Vrat Shastri has carved out for himself a high niche among the Sanskrit colossui of the day. Basically trained as a grammarian, he has flowered into a highly gifted poet and a competent critic, and has thereby debunked the oft-repeated charge that critics hardly make good poets. Dr. Shastri has been instrumental in imparting new horizons to Sanskrit poetry, conditioned by time-worn norms, through the vast array of his creative writings that encompass a mass of five thousand verses, spread over three Mahākāvyas, four Khaṇḍakāvyas, a series of versified letters, besides a host of shorter works, refreshing and interesting in their own way. Almost all aspects of Sanskrit poetry have been enriched by his substantial contributions. The freshness of his themes is matched by their equally fresh treatment. He does not have much of love for the mannerisms, prescribed by theory. Rather, he revels in flouting it on counts, more than one. His flair for innovation has led him to come to grips with the subjects that were frowned upon by the traditionalists. He is perhaps the first Sanskrit poet to make the history and culture of some of the neighbouring countries the bedrock of his poems, besides including in their ambit the sketches of foreign lands and scenic beauties thereof. He is the unquestioned master of Sanskrit language. His lucid expression marked by exceptional sweetness and unusual flow is unmatched in the entire domain of contemporary Sanskrit literature. These virtues, besides much else, have served to establish him as a front-ranking Sanskrit poet, unique in many a respect.

It is, however, surprising that despite high excellences of his poetry, no full-fledged critical evaluation thereof has been undertaken so far, though it would have made an extremely rewarding study at any point of time. The present volume seeks to attempt the onerous task with dispassionate vigour. All of Dr. Satya Vrat Shastri's creative works, including the unpublished corpus of versified letters and shorter texts, have been subjected herein, for the first time, to a sustained and searching scrutiny. No aspect of his poetry has been left untouched. The exercise, though painstaking and tiring at times, has resulted in the emergence of an exhaustive and indepth dissertation on his poetry without which no account or study of the contemporary Sanskrit literature, can be acclaimed as complete. The volume thus purports to be the first sustained and multidimensional study of one of the most eminent poets of the day and thereby adds up to a significant contribution to the interpretation of contemporary Sanskrit literature. The main thrust of the study has been to underscore Dr. Satya Vrat Shastri's contributions towards enriching Sanskrit poetry, which happily are substantial, by all standards.

In order to cope with the formidable mass of material and to ensure homogeneous treatment of the subject coupled with scientific presentation thereof, the dissertation has been divided into six chapters of uneven size. The first chapter forms a prelude to the thesis proper. Entitled "Dr. Satya Vrat Shastri - A Profile", it sets forth, in ringing phraseology, the chequered career of the author, who has been a phenomenon of sorts right from his teens and now struts the stage like a colossus, unchallenged and unmatched. However, the chapter has not been allowed to sink into a bald narration of an eventful career. It seeks to attempt the profile of the author vis-a-vis the steady blossoming of his literary potentialities, with the result it enables one to glance through his career in its totality, in one go. Indeed, the chapter settles down as a comprehensive note on the literary achievements of the author, highlighted in tune with his sequential growth in years.

Chapter Two may justifiably be rated as a *tour de force*, both in worth and girth. Spanning no less than 242 printed pages, more than half the bulk of the volume, it is addressed to an exhaustive evaluation of the author's long poems - the Mahākāvyas. The three Mahākāvyas, studied here threadbare, testify to the author's march from defiance to conformism with the theory. The *Bodhisattvacaritam*, a product of his younger years, is fired with the zeal of the author to establish his credentials as a mighty poet, in one go, by stubbornly defying the time-honoured theory. While it has assuredly invested it with a measure of freshness, the author has stirred the hornests nest by throwing the tradition overboard in respect of theme, hero, sentiment, etc. All these tangled issues have been dispassionately considered in the critique. While there has been no strained effort to straighten the apparent anomalies, what emerges from the honest evaluation is the happy fact that the author's defiance of theory has unwittingly resulted in lending new dimensions to the Mahākāvya-tradition. The *Bodhisattvacaritam* serves to convince the perceptive critic that the unnecessarily demanding tradition could be flouted to yield fruitful results. The apparently isolated episodes of the *Bodhisattvacaritam* lend variety to the poem, and themselves cease to be disjointed, blended as they are by the phenomenon represented by the Bodhisattva, who also has to be accepted as its *nāyaka*, howsoever distasteful it might be to the traditionalist. It is heart-warming to find that almost all the major sentiments have been allowed free, independent play in the poem, to heighten its aesthetic appeal, much against the *aṅgāṅgibhāva* that the theory otherwise seeks to impose upon them. While the didactic tone of the theme lends it a moral aura, its alliterative and vibrant phraseology, and the *padalālitya* emanating therefrom, raise the poem to dizzy heights of elegance. All in all, the *Bodhisattvacaritam* seeks to open new horizons for the Sanskrit Mahākāvya, which was hithertofore held in thraldom by rhetorical injunctions.

However, the author seems to have realised the hazards inherent in persistent defiance of the established norms. With the *Indirāgāndhīcaritam*, he reverts to the traditional groove, though here also his innovative flair tends to protrude, albeit meekly. Worthy as a poem and a biography of Mrs. Indira Gandhi, the *Indirāgāndhīcaritam* does have much to commend itself. It boldly projects a woman, outstanding and bold, as the dominant character. The narrative, though imaginatively carved out of a mass of confusing data, suffers from a few factual anomalies which have been duly noted in the critique.

With *Śrīrāmakīrtimahākāvya (RKM)*, the author's poetic potentialities have reached their culmination. Though written in pursuance of the accepted canons, the *RKM* comes as a whiff of fresh air in a literature dominated by stereotyped writings. It seeks to add new dimension to the vast array of Rāma-literature by exploiting, for the first time, an alien (Thai) version of the Rāma-story, which, notwithstanding its broad concurrence with the general frame-work of Vālmīki's epic, betrays substantial divergences to prompt a comparative analysis of the two epics. The sustained comparison, painstakingly attempted in the body of the work, would reveal how the Thais had effected daring changes in Vālmīki's version to make it square with their social and cultural environment. It is these (new) episodes that form the bedrock of the poem and invest it with a vibrance, seldom encountered elsewhere. However, the Thai incarnation of Vālmīki's epic has unwittingly taken sheen off some of the respected and deified heroes, held in reverence over the ages, and tends to reduce them to lesser, if not petty, persons. It was perhaps inherent in the situation. That apart, the *RKM* represents a synthesis of old and new, alien and indigenous and thereby emerges as an outstanding poem of the contemporary era. Rich in sentiments, it shares with the earlier poems of the author, especially the *Bodhisattvacaritam*, gracefully sweet phraseology, unusual flow, rich imagery and charming *padalālitya*, born of skilful handling of Anuprāsa and the lovely Arthāntaranyāsa. By virtue of its manifold excellences, the *RKM* adds a new dimension to modern Sanskrit literature.

Chapter Three is devoted to the study of the poems, known as Khaṇḍakāvyas in the jargon of the poeticians. The author's abhorrence for banal inhibitions manifests itself tellingly in these poems, as well. All the four Khaṇḍakāvyas, evaluated here, bespeak the author's zeal to invest Sanskrit poetry with new contours by pressing into service the hitherto unexplored themes and subjecting them to an equally unconventional treatment. The *Bṛhattaraṁ Bhāratam* thus addresses itself to capture, in a tiny frame, the glory of Southeast Asia, popularly known as Greater India, that served for ages as the cultural outpost of Bhārata. Though conceived as Śataka, it differs from the earlier works in being thematic in character. In a similar tone but with added trappings, the *Thaideśavilāsam* seeks to describe the history of Thailand, the ancient Śyāmadeśa, one of India's cultural outposts in Greater India. It is a tribute to the author's grasp of Thai history and his poetic talents that all that stands for history in Thai conception, has come to life in the slim tract. With the alien theme, skifully executed, the *Thaideśavilāsam* serves to introduce what had been a taboo in Sanskrit poetry. Besides being intended to perpetuate the Śataka-tradition, the *Śarmaṇyadeśaḥ sutarāṁ vibhāti* seeks to enrich Sanskrit poetry with travelogue, which in essentials it is.

The *Gurugovindasiṁhacaritam* (*GGSC*), however, stands on a different footing. Though rated as a Khaṇḍakāvya, with the connected and sustained account of the Guru that it presents in delectable verse, it has a legitimate claim to be treated as a Prabandhakāvya. However in view of its slim girth and somewhat hasty disposal of the theme, it would not be possible to admit it as a Mahākāvya. Even with its limitations, it makes as worthy a poem as readable it is as a biography of the great Guru. Concerned with the Sikh history, its contribution in lending variety to the historical Kāvyas can hardly be overemphasised.

Chapter Four, supplemented by the Sixth forms perhaps the most interesting part of the dissertation. It deals with a mass of poetry that can hardly be brought under the umbrella of any known genre. Herein are subjected to searching scrutiny the host of versified letters that the author wrote to his Sanskritist friends and acquaintances, both Indian and foreign. It is heartening to find how the matter of fact writings, when handled by a gifted poet, acquire, winsome poetic charms. Like some of the ancient inscriptions, they have been conceived as mini-kāvyas, embellished with the trappings that impart them grace and excellence. These have been discussed threadbare in the body of the critique. One is simply enthralled by lovely descriptions, poetic flourishes, judicious application of different *alaṁkāras*, measured touches of sentiments, charming phraseology marked occasionally by learned grammatical forms that pulsate throughout these letters.

Chapter Five is addressed to the appraisal of the author's miscellaneous works which include four elegant poems besides the humorous skit, *Napuṁsakaliṅgasya Mokṣaprāptiḥ*. While the skit is a novel experiment and, as such opens up new vistas in Sanskrit dramatics, the tiny poem *Ko'ham* merits pointed attention in view of the way the Sanskrit speech has been skilfully exploited to garb the varied contours of modern thought.

It has been a painstaking job to prepare an exhaustive dissertation on a formidable literature. While the difficulty was compounded by my indifferent health, an inalienable appendage of old age; the unstinted help that I received from various quarters went far to mitigate the rigours. Dr. Satya Vrat Shastri whose creative works form the subject of the dissertation, has been a perennial source of inspiration in prosecuting my studies and researches. But for his ungrudging help and guidance the volume could have been anything but faultless. To him I owe a deep debt of gratitude. Dr. H.N.Dikshit, Professor and Head of the Department of Sanskrit, Kumaun University, Nainital has been a pillar of strength to me. I express my sincere thanks to him for all that he has done for me. He is an embodiment of kindness and nobility. The contribution of my wife, Smt. Vimla Varma in carrying the work to conclusion has been substantial. She struggled hard to keep me free from domestic worries and persistently enthused me to complete the volume on time. My brilliant pupil Ramandeep Kaur gladly took upon herself the onerous task of preparing the final transcript. She did the job with efficiency and devotion. May God bless her !

I have done my best to make the volume thoroughly scientific and readable, though I am acutely conscious of its shortcomings. For that I crave the indulgence of the scholarly community.

7/34, Purani Abadi, SATYA VRAT
Sri Ganganagar (Raj.)

CONTENTS

CHAPTER ONE

DR. SATYA VRAT SHASTRI

A PROFILE

DR. SATYA VRAT SHASTRI

A PROFILE

Born at Lahore (now in Pakistan) on 29th of September, 1930, Dr. Satya Vrat Shastri was an heir to enviable greatness. His father, Professor Charu Deva Shastri, who, even as a young scholar, had earned the proud sobriquet of *Abhinava Pāṇini* for his profound equipment in Sanskrit grammar and semantics, worked hard to fashion him into a grammarian, a replica of himself. It is a measure of the insight he had acquired in the intricacies of grammar quite early in his career, that he came to be looked upon as a phenomenon, a wonder-boy for his grasp and handling of the Sanskrit language. He could take wind out of the sails of the elderly Sanskritists by his chaste and racy phraseology. Once, when encountered by Pandit Nathu Ram, a Pandit of Lahore while moving about the Gol Bagh when he was just 12 with the intricate frequentative form in *kutra caṅkramyate*, he shot back *atraiva bambhramyate.* When the Pandit out to test his knowledge of Sanskrit grammar which was the talk of the town (and which was a source of jealousy to many) reeling under the impact of the jaw-breaker hurled at him could only say *kim*, what, the young boy hurled at him yet another jaw-breaker : *atraiva dandramyate* making him leave the place in quick steps. His innocuous retort *nāyur veda, vedmi vayaḥ* to the query *kin te āyuḥ* by one of his father's friends made him (the friend) look small. The education and training that he received from his great father laid the foundation of what was to flower subsequently into multidimensional erudition.

The first tangible proof of his equipment came into evidence when at the age of fourteen he passed the Shastri examination, an admirable feat by any standards, even before he had entered the portals of the school. It was followed by a series of distinctions that he won as a brilliant student, over the years. When after the partition of the country, his father migrated to Ambala, he joined the Gandhi Memorial National College there and did the nascent institution proud by getting record marks in B.A. Sanskrit (Honours) examination. The medal awarded by the University was only a small recognition of the scholarship he embodied. By that time his father had retired from the service of the D.A.V. College. In order to enable the son to pursue his studies with single-minded devotion, he shifted to Jullundur, where functioned the Sanskrit Department of the Punjab University after it was uprooted from Lahore. Dr. Shastri kept up his wont and bagged the first position in M.A. Sanskrit as well. That brought him another medal from the University. Concurrently with his formal education, Dr. Shastri was prosecuting his grammatical studies with his father. Now that he was poised to establish his credentials with the scholarly world, Dr. Shastri decided to work on the highly complicated subject of "Time and Space with special reference to Bhartṛhari's *Vākyapadīya*", the text his father had edited with great competence, for his doctoral dissertation. He went over to Varanasi and worked with the eminent scholar, Dr. Suryakant for his research degree which he secured within the stipulated period of two years. While at Varanasi, he came into contact with some of the most learned scholars of the day. It were they – Pandit Shuk Deo Jha , Mahamahopadhyaya Gopinath Kaviraja and Pandit Dhundhiraja Shastri who initiated him into the mysteries of Vyākaraṇa, Navya Nyāya and Vedānta. It was this exposure at Varanasi that Dr. Shastri cherishes fondly to this day. His literary potentialities had blossomed beyond measure. Thus the ancient seat of Sanskrit learning marked the acme to his formal education.

His training and education under a host of eminent scholars including his father, had equipped him fully to meet the challenges that lay ahead. After a brief stint at Hans Raj College, Delhi, Dr. Shastri achieved the first important break-through when he was called upon to give shape to the Sanskrit Department in the University of Kurukshetra, basically conceived as a Sanskrit University but subsequently expanded into a multifaculty institution. However, Kurukshetra could not hold him long. The Year 1959 brought him to the premier centre of learning, the University of Delhi which he has served for over three decades in various capacities. He started his career at the Delhi University with a bang. Soon after he joined it, Dr. Shastri published his first full-fledged Mahākāvya, the *Bodhisattvacaritam*[1] which took the Sanskritists, round the world by storm and served to establish him, in one go, as a front-ranking poet of modern times. With the *Bodhisattvacaritam* he came to be rated as a highly talented poet and thus belied the oft-repeated charge that the grammarians do not make good poets. In Dr. Shastri scholarship and poetry have attained a happy fusion. It might have been a sheer coincidence though, his critical and creative writings seem to alternate at measured intervals. The *Bodhisattvacaritam* was followed by the *Essays on Indology*,[2] a collection of his research papers, published, over the years, in prestigious journals of the land, which attest to the wide range of his scholarship in various disciplines. The next year witnessed the appearance of his remarkable dissertation on Vālmīki's epic, *The Rāmāyaṇa–A Linguistic Study*[3]. It purports to be the first sustained evaluation of the language of the *Rāmāyaṇa* and opens new vistas of linguistic studies because of its refreshing

---

1. First edition, Delhi, 1962, Second edition, 1973.
2. Meharchand Lachhmandas, Delhi, 1963.
3. Munshiram Manoharlal, Delhi, 1964.

approach to the subject. He was subsequently invited by the authorities of the Guru Gobind Singh Foundation, Patiala to compose a Kāvya on the Guru on the occasion of his tricentenary. It resulted into the delectable biography of the Guru *Śrīgurugovindasiṁhacaritam*[4] in elegant verses.The poem was adjudged as the best creative writing and earned Dr. Shastri the prestigious Sahitya Akademi Award in 1968. The interregnum of next seven years led to the composition of two poems, a Khaṇḍakāvya *Śarmaṇyadeśaḥ Sutarāṁ Vibhāti*[5] and a hefty Mahākāvya, *Indirāgāndhīcaritam*[6]. While the former is an account of the author's visit to Germany, the latter seeks to describe, in twenty five cantos, the life of Mrs.Indira Gandhi who presided over the destiny of the country for more than fifteen eventful years. His first assignment as a Visiting Professor in the Chulalongkorn University, Bangkok yielded him two Works– one creative, the other critical. While the *Thaideśavilāsam*[7] a Khaṇḍakāvya in 121 verses, is the first poem in Sanskrit language to deal with the history and culture of the beautiful country of Thailand, the ancient Śyāmadeśa; Dr. Shastri's studies on the same subject, published in various journals, form the sister volume *Studies in Sanskrit and Indian Culture in Thailand*[8]. His second assignment in Thailand has been all the more fruitful. It, in a way, marks the realisation of Dr. Shastri's cherished dream. As a devout student of Vālmīki's epic he has produced the *Śrīrāmakīrtimahākāvyam*[9] which seeks to present, in twenty five cantos, the Thai version of the Rāma story as described in the Thai classic the *Ramakien*. The Hindu temples and Sanskrit inscriptions of Thailand have also engaged Dr. Shastri's attention. He hopes to deal with them in two separate volumes. Of his two volumes on Kālidāsa, the first, *Kālidāsa in Modern Sanskrit Literature*[10], has been recently released. The second volume, *New Experiments in Kālidāsa* will be out soon. His creative and critical works have thus kept pace with each other, down the years. It is this 'combination of critical scholarship and creative composition' in him that distinguish him as the most notable figure among the Sanskritists of the day. A complete list of his works is as follows:

---

4. First edition, Patiala, 1967, second edition, Meerut, 1984.
5. Akhila Bharatiya Sanskrit Parishad, Lucknow, 1976.
6. Bharatiya Vidya Prakashan, Delhi, 1976.
7. Eastern Book Linkers, Delhi, 1979.
8. Parimal Prakashan, Delhi, 1982.
9. Moolamall Sachdev Foundation and Amar Nath Sachdeva Foundation, Bangkok, 1990.
10. Eastern Book Linkers, Delhi, 1991.

(a) Creative Writings

1. *Śrībodhisattvacaritaṁ*
2. *Indirāgāndhīcaritam*
3. *Śrīrāmakīrtimahākāvyam*
4. *Bṛhattaraṁ Bhāratam*
5. *Śrīgurugovindasiṁhacaritam*
6. *Thaideśavilāsam*
7. *Śarmaṇya deśaḥ Sutāraṁ Vibhāti*
8. *Corpus of Letters*
9. *Ṣaḍṛtuvarṇanam*
10. *Napuṁsakaliṅgasya Mokṣaprāptiḥ*
11. *Kālidāsāṣṭakam*
12. *Ko'ham*
13. *Jaya devi svatantrate*

(b) Critical Works

1. *Essays on Indology*
2. *The Rāmāyaṇa- A Linguistic Study*
3. *Studies in Sanskrit and Indian Culture in Thailand*
4. *Kālidāsa in Modern Sanskrit Literature*
5. *New Experiments in Kālidāsa* (in the Press)
6. *Studies in the Yogavāsiṣtha* (in the Press)

(c) Translation

Vaidika Vyākaraṇa : Hindi translation of A.A. Macdonell's "A Vedic Grammar for Students".

Besides these works, Dr. Shastri has contributed over the years, a large number of research papers and articles to a host of leading journals, both foreign and Indian. While some of them have been included in the author's *Essays on Indology*, an overwhelming majority of them were written after the publication of the volume. *Studies in Sanskrit and Indian Culture in Thailand* includes some of the author's studies on the history and culture of Thailand. The papers cover such diverse fields as grammar, semantics, poetics, culture, epigraphy, classical literature, Purāṇas, and epics. It would be worthwhile, to list them here to drive home the depth and range of Dr. Shastri's equipment.

Articles Published in Research Journals :

1 Punjabi Bhaṣa Ke kuch ek Tatsama Śabda, *Hindi Sandesh*, Journal of the Punjab Provincial Hindi Sahitya Sammelan, published serially in two

issues, one in January, 1954, and the other in March-April, 1954.

2. Śabdoṁ ke Vikāsa Kī Bahumukhī Dhārā, *Sapta Sindhu*, Department of Languages, Govt. of Punjab, Patiala, Vol.I, No.9. Oct,1954.
3. Mahābhārata meṁ Yajña, *Akhaṇḍa Jyotiḥ* , Mathura, Vol. XXVII, No.1, January, 1956.
4. Saṁskṛtasāhitye Hāsyarasaḥ, *Bhāratī,* Jaipur, Vol. IX, No.5 Saṁvat 2010.
5. Surabhāratyā Laukike Vaṁmaye Prayogaḥ, *Sanskrit Ratnākaraḥ* , Journal of the All India Sanskrit Sahitya Sammelan, Delhi, Vol. XVII, No.12, March, 1956.
6. Indian Culture in the light of Sanskrit Language, *The Poona Orientalist,* Poona, Vol. XXI, Nos.1-4, 1956.
7. The Story of Udayana and Vāsavadattā through the Ages, *Bhāratīya Vidyā,* Bombay, Vol. XVI, Nos.2,1956.
8. Conception of Space (Dik) in the Vākyapadīya, *Journal of the Asiatic Society,* Letters, Calcutta, Vol. XXIII, No.2, 1957.
9. Bhoodan in Ancient India, *Bhāratīya Vidyā* , Bombay, Vol. XVII, Nos. 1-2, 1957. Also published in the Tribune, Ambala.
10. The Concept of Fate in the Rāmāyaṇa, *The Poona Orientalist,* Poona, Vol. XXIII, Nos 1-2, 1958.
11. Notes on the Language of the Yogavāsiṣṭha, *Annals of the Bhandarkar Oriental Research Institute*, Poona, Golden Jubilee Volume, 1958.
12. The Concept of Time according to Bhartṛhari, *Annals of the Bhandarkar Oriental Research Institute,* Poona, Vol. XXXIX, Parts 1-11, 1958.
13. Studies in Sanskrit Semantics, *The Poona Orientalist,* Poona, Vol.XXIII, Nos. 3-4, 1959.
14. Advaitavādaḥ, *Sārasvatī Suṣamā* (Journal of the Sanskrit University, Varanasi), Vol. XII, Nos. 3-4, Saṁvat 2014.
15. Vāmaṇapurāṇa meṁ Kāvyacchaṭā, Saptasindhu, Patiala, Vol. V, No. 11, Nov. 1958.
16. Iṁdudūta of Vinayavijayagaṇi – Textual study, *The Poona Orientalist,* Poona, Vol. XXIV, Nos. 3-4, 1959.
17. Prāgaitihāsika Bhārata meṁ Jātiya Sammiśraṇa, *Nāgarī Pracāriṇī Patrikā,* Varanasi, Vol. LXXV, No.1, Saṁvat 2016.
18. Saṇskrit aur Hindi Uccāraṇa, *Jāgṛti,* Chandigarh, October, 1961.
19. Unpāṇinian Forms in the Yogavāsiṣṭha *Vishveshvaranand Indological Journal,* Hoshiarpur, Vol I, Part II, Sept. 1963.

20. Sanskrit Bhāṣā Vic Latāvācaka Śabda (Words for creeper in Sanskrit – article in Punjabi), *Ālocanā*, Ludhiana, Vol. XI, No. 3, 1965.
21. On the Words Lāvaṇya, Kirāṭa and Kāhalā, *Transactions of the Linguistic Circle of Delhi,* 1966.
22. Conception of Time in the Mahābhāṣya, published serially in the *Mysore Orientalist,* Vol.I, No.1, 1967 (Inaugural Number in Commemoration of the Golden Jublilee of the University of Mysore) and Vol.I, No.2, 1968.
23. Neglected Fields in Sanskrit Research, Paper read at Seminar on Modern Sanskrit Research, Aligarh Muslim University, Aligarh, November, 1965. Since published in the *Calcutta Review,* Calcutta, Vol.190, No.1, July 1966.
24. Prepositional Verbs in the Yogavāsiṣṭha, Paper read at the Grammar and Linguistics Section of the Golden Jubilee Celebrations of All India Sanskrit Sahitya Sammelan, Delhi, October, 1966. Since published in the *Journal of the Asiatic Society,* Calcutta, Vol.IV, No.1, 1967.
25. Macdonell-kṛta Vaidika Vyākaraṇa (Chātra saṁskaraṇa), kā Hindī Anuvāda – Samasyāeṁ aur *Samādhāna*, *Anuvāda*, Bharatiya Parishad, Delhi, Vol.III, No.4, May, 1967.
26. Yogavāsiṣṭha meṁ Kāla kā Svarūpa, *Viśvabhāratī Patrikā,* Santiniketan, Vol. VII, No.4, 1967.
27. Delhi's Contribution to Sanskrit Literature, Published in Gujarati Translation, *Souvenir Volume,* Annual Session of the Gujarati Sahitya Parished, Delhi, 1967.
28. Guru Gobind Singh -- The Apostle of Human Brotherhood, *Guru Gobind Singh Ji Tricentenary International Celebrations Committee* Volume, Delhi, 1968.
29. Onomatopoeia in the Yogavāsiṣṭha, *Transactions of the Linguistic Circle of Delhi,* 1968.
30. Synonyms in the Bhāgavatapurāṇa, *Annals of the Bhandarkar Oriental Research Institute,* Poona, Vol. II, 1971.
31. Dr.Raghavan : The Poet, *Dr. V. Raghavan Shashtyabdapurti Felicitation Vol.,* Madras, 1971.
32. Haryana Ke Ādhunika Sanskrit Sāhityakāra, Halwasia Commemoration Volume, Calcutta, 1971.
33. Kṛ in its Various Meanings, *Pandit Kunji Lal Dube Commemoration Volume*, Jabalpur, 1972.
34. Descriptive Poetry in the Yogavāsiṣṭha. *Journal of the Department of*

Sanskrit, University of Delhi, Vol. I, No.1, December, 1971.

35. Some Popular Etymologies in the Yogavāsiṣṭha, *Journal of the Department of Sanskrit, University of Delhi,* Vo.I, No.2, July, 1972.
36. Jaina Meghadūta of Merutuṅga, *Adhyayana–Anusandhāna,* Institute of Higher Studies and Research, Jaipur, February, 1974.
37. The Plan of the Yogavāsiṣṭha, *Studies in Indology,* Institute of Indology, Delhi, 1973.
38. Some Thoughts on Onomatopoeia, *Journal of the Ganganath Jha Kendriya Sanskrit Vidyapeetha,* Allahabad (Ganganath Jha Centenary Volume), Vol. XXIX, Parts 1-4, 1973.
39. Sanskrit meṁ Kārakoṁ kī Vivakṣādhīnatā, Institute of Indology, Delhi, 1973.
40. Samāsavicāraḥ, *the Rajasthan University Studies in Sanskrit and Hindi,* Vol.5, 1973-1974. Also published in M.M.Parameshwaranand Shastri Smṛti Grantha, 1974.
41. Dhātvarthavicāraḥ, *M.M. Parameshwaranand Shastri Smṛti Grantha,* New Delhi, 1974.
42. Saṁskṛte Paryāyavācinaḥ Śabdāḥ, ibid. Also published in English under the title : Synonyms in Sanskrit, *Indologica Taurinensia,* Torino, Italy, Vol.III, 1977.
43. Shalokas of Baba Farid – A Study in Imagery, The Sikh Review, Calcutta, Vol. XXIII, February - March, 1975.
44. Kumārasambhavacampū – A Study, *Indologica Taurinensia,* Torino, Italy, Vol. III, 1977.
45. The Sanskrit Usage, ibid.
46. Mahābhārate Nirvacanāni, *Ṛtam* (Prof. K.A.S. Iyer Felicitation Volume), Lucknow, Vols. II, VI, July 1970, January, 1975.
47. Sanskrit Grammar, *Cultural Heritage of India,* Calcutta, Vol. V, 1977.
48. The Contribution of Muslims to Sanskrit, Institute of Indology, Delhi, 1977.
49. A Note on *Ka (Kan)*-ending Words in the Yogavāsiṣṭha, *Annals of the Bhandarkar Oriental Research Institute,* Poona, Diamond Jubilee Volume, 1977-78.
50. Thailand kī Ayodhyā, Gagananchal, Indian Council for Cultural Relations, New Delhi, Vol.I, No.2, 1978.
51. Sanskrit in Thailand, *Indologica Taurinensia,* Torino, Italy, Vol.V, 1978.

52. Thailand - Dharmoṁ aur Saṁskṛtiyoṁ kā Saṅgama, *Gaganachal*, Indian Council for Cultural Relations, New Delhi, Vol.II, No.I, 1979.

53. A New Sanskrit Inscription from Thailand, *Indica*; Father Esteller Felicitation Volume, Heras Institute of Indian History and Culture, Bombay, 1979.

54. Thailand kī Muslim Sanskrit Vidūshiāṁ , *Navabharat Times*, New Delhi, September 2, 1979.

55. Thailand ke tīn Prachin Hindu Mandir, *Gagananchal*, Indian Council for Cultural Relations, New Delhi, Vol. III, No.3, 1979.

56. Sanskrit Studies in Thailand, *Bulletin of the IV World Sanskrit Conference*, Weimar, G.D.R.,1979.

57. Indo-Thai Relations – Cultural Perspective, *Prācyavāṇī*, Delhi, Vol. IX, 1979.

58. Poland kā Ek Vayovṛddha Bhāratīyavidyāviśeṣajña, Ludwik Sternbach, *Ludwik Sternbach Felicitation Volume*, Lucknow, Part I, 1979.

59. Thoughts on Gītā, *Ludwik Sternbach Felicitation Volume*, Part I, Lucknow, 1979.

60. Mahimabhaṭṭa's Criticism of the Concept of Dhvani, *Bhāratīya Vidyā*, Bombay, Vol. XXXIX. No.1, 1979.

61. Putreṣṭi in the Rāmāyaṇa --Was it really necessary? *Indologica Taurinensia*, Torino, Italy, Vol. VI, 1979

62. Taddhita Formations in Yogavāsiṣṭha, *Brahmavidyā*, Adyar Library Bulletin, Dr. K.K. Raja Shashtyabdapurti Felicitation Volume, Madras, 1980.

63. A Note on Jinendrabuddhi's Contribution to Sanskrit Grammar, *Ancient Indian Culture and Literature*, Pt. Gangaram Commemoration Volume, Eastern Book Linkers, Delhi, 1980.

64. The Yogavāsiṣṭha– A Study in Vocabulary, *Indologica Taurinensia*, Torino, Italy, Vol. VII (1979), 1980.

65. Panom Rung Shrine of Thailand, *Recent Studies in Sanskrit and Indology*, Prof. Jagannath Agrawal Felicitation Volume, Ajanta Publications, Delhi, 1982.

66. Brahmins in Thailand, *Abhinandana Bhāratī*, Prof. Krishna Kanta Handiqui Felicitation Volume, Gauhati, 1982.

67. Hinduism in Thailand, *Amṛtadhārā*, R.N. Dandekar Felicitation Volume, Ajanta Publications, Delhi, 1984.

68. Hungarian Verse Rendering of Sanskrit Poems, *Journal of the Department of Modern European Languages*, University of Delhi, Delhi, Vol.I, No.1, March, 1984.
69. Fate in Kālidāsa, *Jñānāmṛtam,* Dr. A. C. Swain Felicitation Volume, Bhubaneswar, 1985.
70. New Panom Rung Sanskrit Inscription of Thailand, *Mañjūṣā,* Dr. S.R.Rao Felicitation Volume, Bangalore, 1985.
71. Kālidāsa's Philosophy of Life, *Prof. M. P. L. Sastry Felicitation Volume*, Bangalore, 1985.
72. Review article on Sindhukanyā, the Sahitya Akademi Award Winning Book, *Indian Literature*, New Delhi, Vol.109, Sept-Oct,1985.
73. Kālidāsa's Ṛṣis, *Ṛtam*, Lucknow, Gopal Chandra Sinha Commemoration Volume, 1986.
74. The Ramakien and the Vālmīki Rāmāyaṇa : A study in Comparison, *Souvenir Volume*, Second International Rāmāyaṇa Conference, Bangkok, Thailand, 1986.
75. Śapathas in Ancient Sanskrit Texts– A Material Source for Culture, *India and the Ancient World,* Prof. P.H.L. Eggermont Jubilee Volume, Leuven, Belgium, 1987.
76. Vedic Sacrifices in Kālidāsa, *Bhāratīya Vidyā,* Bombay Prof. J.H. Dave Felicitation Volume, 1987.
77. The Date of the Yogavāsiṣṭha, *Modern Researches in Sanskrit,* Dr. Veermani Prasad Upadhyaya Felicitation Volume, Indira Prakashan, Patna, 1987.
78. Vaideśikaviduṣāṃ Saṁskṛtaracanāḥ, *Pūrṇatrayī* Journal of Sri Ravi Varma Granthavali, Tripunithura (Kerala), Vol. I, No.1, 1988.
79. The Concept of Death in the Upaniṣads, *Malattia Morte* (Volume of Proceedings of the International Workshop on Health and Illness: A Comparison of the Concept in India and Europe), Venice, Italy, 1991.
80. Modern Christian Literature in Sanskrit, *Rama Kant Shukla Felicitation Volume*, Devavani Parishad, New Delhi, 1992.
81. Pāṇini's Regard for Usage, *Studies in Sanskrit and Musicology* (Shrimati Kamlesh Kumari Kulshreshtha Memorial Volume), Eastern Book Linkers. Delhi, 1992.

Articles Published in General Magazines :

1. Bīj bone kī Katipaya Prathāyeṁ, *Dharma Yug,* Bombay, Vol. I, No.9, Oct.,1954.

2. Puñjābī Grāmya Jīvan ke Vichitra Vishvāsa aur Prathāyeṁ, *Viśva Jyoti,* Hoshiarpur, Vol.II, No.10, Dec.1954.
3. Scientists Athinking, *Varsity Mirror,* Journal of Benaras Hindu University Youth Forum, 1955.
4. Vṛkṣoṁ, se Vivāha, *Dharma Yug,* Bombay, Vol.VIII, No.42. Feb.2 1955.
5. Writing in old India, *Deepak,* Ambala, Vol.VIII, No.3, Nov.-Dec.1955.
6. Democracy in Ancient India, *Deepak,* Ambala, Vol. VIII, No.3 Nov.-Dec. 1955.
7. Pañcabāṇas tu Bāṇaḥ, *Bhāratī,* Jaipur, Vol.VIII, No.7. Saṁvat 2012.
8. Sanskrit– A Great Unifying Force, *The Tribune,* Ambala, Jan.10, 1957.
9. Ātmā, *Divyajyotiḥ*, Simla, Vol.XIII, Nos. 1-2, Oct.-Nov. 1957.
10. Kurukshetra through the Ages, *The Tribune,* Ambala, April,16, 1958.
11. Deepavali in Legendary Lore, *The Tribune,* Ambala, Nov.10, 1958.
12. Reform in Our Present Examination-Ridden Educational System, *The Tribune,* Ambala, Nov. 25, 1958.
13. What is Wrong with Teaching Profession ?, *The Tribune,* Ambala, Dec.4, 1958.
14. Food and Agriculture in Ancient India, *The Tribune,* Ambala, Jan. 16,1959.
15. Spring Festival in Historical Perspective, *The Tribune,* Ambala, Feb.15, 1959.
16. Research in Indian Universities, *The Calcutta Review,* Calcutta, Vol. 153, No.2, Dec. 1959.
17. Sanskrit Puñjābī Kā Ādisrota, *Viśva Jyoti,* Hoshiarpur, Vol.III, No.3, May. 1984.

Dr. Shastri has addedly contributed Foreword to as many as thirty books. The volumes deal with almost all branches of literature, from Veda to such secular subjects as Śyainikaśāstra,the art of hunting. TheForewords, quite a few of them very detailed and exhaustive,[11] are noted for the keen perception and lucid exposition of the subject and thus bear further testimony, if it was needed, to Dr.Shastri's wide scholarship. The enviable equipment of such an outstanding scholar was bound to percolate to his students in prosecuting research on a variety of knotty problems. Seventeen of them have already secured the degree under him. Some of the more interesting topics dealt by his students may be noted here :

---

11. As an instance could be mentioned the Foreword to Ram Krishna Sharma's play *Baṅgladeśodayam* which runs into sixteen pages in print.

1. *Patañjali as a Critic of Katyāyana and Pāṇini*
2. *Unpāṇinian Sandhi and Syntax in the Mahābhārata*
3. *A Study of Padamañjarī*
4. *The Carakasaṁhitā – A Literary Study*
5. *A Study of Nyāsa*
6. *Stage-Directions, Properties and Stage Setting in Sanskrit Dramas (from beginning to 10th Century A.D.)*
7. *Modern Sanskrit*

Dr. Shastri is an heir to the great ancient tradition. He has been liberal in sharing his equipment with younger scholars in the country and in guiding them in their literary and academic pursuits. Literary conferences and symposia provide ideal ground for disseminating the results of one's researches and studies. Dr. Shastri has been a popular figure in these *Jñānasatras,* right from the beginning of his career. The large number of conferences,seminars and symposia he has attended, over the years, speak volumes for his zeal to exchange notes with other scholars and thereby perpetuate knowledge in the best traditions of the country. The following list of the conferences and seminars attended by him would give an idea of his zestful participation in literary activities, be they in the country or abroad.

Important Conferences :

1. International Congress of Orientalists, New Delhi, January 4-10, 1964.
2. All India Sanskrit Sahitya Sammelan, Delhi, Silver Jubilee Session, 1965.
3. Sanskrit Vishva Parishad, Bangalore, May 27-29, 1966.
4. Bharatiya Darshan Parishad, University of Delhi, Delhi.
5. All-India Oriental Conference, Silver Jubilee Session, Jadavpur, Calcutta, October 29-31, 1969.
6. Kālidāsa Samāroha, Vikram University, Ujjain, November, 9-15, 1970.
7. Vishva Sanskrit Sammelan, Allahabad, February 5-7, 1971.
8. Writer's Camp (Regional) of National Book Trust of India, Poona, Aug. 1-7, 1971. Writer's Camp (National), New Delhi, March 25 – April 1, 1972.
9. First World Sanskrit Conference, New Delhi, March 25-31, 1972.
10. Second World Sanskrit Conference, Torino, Italy, June 9-15, 1975.
11. All India Oriental Conference, XXVIII Session, Dharwar, Nov. 1976, presided over the Classical Sanskrit Section.
12. Third World Sanskrit Conference, Paris, France, June 20-25, 1977.
13. International Gitā Conference, Kuala Lumpur, Malaysia, August 9-10, 1978.
14. XIV Congress, International Association of the History of Religions

Winnipeg, Canada, August, 17-22, 1980. Presided over the Concluding Session of the Indian Religions Section.

15. IV Conference, International Association of Buddhist Studies, Winnipeg, Canada, August 22, 1980.
16. All India Oriental Conference, XXX Session, Santiniketan, October, 1980.
17. V World Sanskrit Conference, Varanasi, October 21-26, 1981.
18. All India Sanskrit Conference, Sanskrit Sansad, Lucknow, December 31, 1981 – January 2, 1982.
19. All India Oriental Conference, XXXI Session, Jaipur, October 29-31, 1982, Presided over the Southeast Asian Studies Section.
20. International Gītā Conference, Bangkok, Thailand, Dec. 27-28,1982.
21. XXXI International Congress of Human Sciences in Asia and North Africa, Tokyo and Kyoto, Japan, August 31-September 7. 1983. Presided over the Section III of the above in Kyoto on September 5, 1983.
22. III World Hindi Conference, New Delhi, October 28-30, 1983.
23. International Conference on Reorganization and Reorientation of Education, New Delhi, February 25-26, 1984.
24. Sixth World Sanskrit Conference, University of Pennsylvania, Philadelphia, U.S.A., Oct., 13-20, 1984. Was Chairman of the Symposium on Modern Sanskrit.
25. Was Chairman of the First European Conference on Vedic Science, Vlodrop, Holland, March 22-24, 1985.
26. All India Oriental Conference, XXXII Session, Ahmedabad, Nov.6-8, 1985. Was President of the Indian Linguistics Section at the above conference.
27. Maṇḍaliya Śanskrit Sammelan, University of Gorakhpur, Feb. 13-15, 1986.
28. Second International Rāmāyaṇa Conference, Bangkok, Thailand, April 8-11,1986. Presided over one of its Sessions and presented a paper in connection with Rāma story in Thailand.
29. All India Oriental Conference XXXIII Session, Calcutta, Oct. 24-26, 1986. Addressed the Southeast Asia Section of the above conference.
30. Third International Rāmāyaṇa Conference, Toronto, Canada July 9-12 1987. Presided over one of the Sessions of the above.
31. Seventh World Sanskrit Conference, Leiden, Holland, August 23-29, 1987. Was Chairperson of the Workshop on Modern Sanskrit Literature at the above conference.

Seminars and Symposia :

1. Buddhism through the Ages, University of Delhi, Delhi, March 28-30, 1967.
2. Sanskrit Learning through the Ages, University of Mysore, May 1-3, 1968.
3. The Style and Technique of Ahiṁsā, University of Delhi, Delhi, October 11-15, 1969.
4. Seminar on Ādiśaṅkarācārya and his Works. Sringeri, (Mysore State), May, 5-12, 1970.
5. Seminar on the Contribution of Jainism to Indian Culture with Special Reference to Ahiṁsā, University of Delhi, May 25- June 8, 1974.
6. Seminar on Bhagavān Mahāvīra and his Heritage, Jainological Research Society, New Delhi, December 30-31, 1973.
7. Summer School on Jainism, University of Delhi, May 25- June 8, 1974.
8. Seminar on Jain Studies, Jain Vishwa Bharati, Ladnun, November 2-4, 1974.
9. Seminar on the Influence of Pali and Sanskrit on Thai Language, Chiangmai, Thailand, October 24-27, 1979.
10. Seminar on Yoga and Equanimity, New Delhi, November 16, 1980.
11. Seminar on Bhāratīya Saṁskṛti ke Vikās meṁ Prākrit Evam Jaina Kaviyoṁ kā Avadāna (Contribution of Prākrit and Jainism to the Development of Indian Culture), Sampurnanand Sanskrit University, Varansi, March 14-16, 1981.
12. International Seminar on Pāṇini, Poona, July 9-14, 1981.
13. First International Symposium on the Sanskrit Language, Mexico, February 14-21, 1982.
14. Seminar on Inter-Religious Perceptions of Hindus and Muslims in India, Indian Institute of Islamic Studies, New Delhi, April 23-25, 1985.
15. Seminar on the New Education Policy and the Role of Sanskrit, University of Gorakhpur, Gorakhpur, Feb.13-15, 1986.
16. International Seminar on Rāmāyaṇa Traditions and National Cultures in Asia, Lucknow, Oct. 2-6, 1986. Presided over one of its sessions.
17. Seminar on Vyutpatti and Arthanirdhāraṇa, M.M.H. College, Ghaziabad, Nov. 6, 1986.
18. Seminar on Relevance of Sanskrit Poetics to the Study of Modern Aesthetics, Utkal University, Bhubaneswar, Dec. 26-30, 1986. Delivered Keynote Address at it on the 'Making of a Poet'.
19. Seminar on the Concept of Lokasaṅgraha, Punjab University,

Chandigarh, Feb. 25-28, 1987.

These literary gatherings besides his multifocal output have been instrumental in bringing him widespread fame, which overstepped the confines of the country. While at home, he was invited by a number of universities to guide them in various projects or deliver talks on some of the toughest problems of Sanskrit grammar and literature, some of the foreign Universities vied with each other in appointing him a Visiting Professor in their departments of Sanskrit, Religion and Indian/Oriental Studies. His assignment as Visiting Professor of Indian Studies was in the Chulalongkorn University, Bangkok (Thailand). It was followed by his appointment as Guest Professor of Sanskrit in the University of Tübingen, Tübingen, West Germany (Nov.7, 1982-July 31, 1983). The Catholic University, Leuven, Belgium invited him subsequently as Visiting Professor from Feb. 1 to May 31, 1985. Still later the University of Alberta, Edmonton invited him as Visiting Professor in its Department of Religious Studies (March 15- April 7, 1988). Till Jan. 7, 1991 he was with the Silpakorn University, Bangkok. At home, he has been a Visiting Professor with the Jodhpur University. This widespread recognition culminated in his elevation as Vice-Chancellor of Shri Jagannath Sanskrit University, Puri, Orissa, the assignment he held with dignity and poise. He has travelled almost all over the world in response to invitations from various universities and has taught or delivered lectures there on a wide variety of subjects which evoked instant acclaim from the orientalists and other scholars. He visited at different points of time, the Universities in Germany, England, the U.S.A., Canada, Italy, Hungary, Belgium, Poland, Japan, Holland, Nepal, Mexico, Thailand, etc. and gave talks or held discussions with scholars and creative writers in them on Indian Studies. There is hardly any notable university in the country that has not had the benefit of his illuminating lectures. The lectures that he delivered at home and abroad reflect, in ample measure, his versatility and depth. It would be interesting to record the topics that he covered in his talks.

Prominent Lectures : National

1. "Sanskrit and Hindi Phonetics" delivered in the Staff Training School, All India Radio, New Delhi, on 16.3.1961, 20.3.1961, 23.3.1961, and 6.4.1961.
2. "Prepositional Verbs in the Yogavāsiṣṭha" delivered in the Asiatic Society of Bengal, Calcutta, in April, 1968.
3. "Sanskrit Semantics" delivered in Jadavpur University, Calcutta, in April, 1968.
4. "Epigraphy and Sanskrit" delivered in the Government of India Epigraphy Office, Mysore, in June, 1968.
5. "Synonyms in Sanskrit" delivered in Centre of Advanced Study in Sanskrit,

University of Poona, Poona, in January, 1969.

6. Delhi's Contribution to Modern Sanskrit Literature" delivered in the Prācyavāṇī, New Delhi in November, 1971.
7. "Indian Culture in the Light of the Sanskrit Language" delivered in the University of Jammu, in February, 1970.
8. "Kālidāsa ke Kāvya meṁ Śabdaparipāka", delivered in Indore University in November, 1970.
9. "Contribution of Haryana to Modern Sanskrit Literature" delivered in the Kurukshetra University in January, 1972.
10. "Kālidāsa kā Kāvyasauṣṭhava" delivered in the University of Jabalpur, Jabalpur, in January, 1971.
11. "Synonyms and Homonyms in Sanskrit" delivered in Vikram University, Ujjain in January, 1972.
12. "Modern Sanskrit Writers in Delhi" delivered in the Seminar on Twentieth Century Sanskrit Literature, Bharatiya Vidya Bhavan, Bombay, in September, 1972.
13. "Modern Sanskrit Literature" delivered in the University of Bangalore, in September, 1972.
14. "Synonyms in Sanskrit" delivered in Osmania University, Hyderabad, in September, 1972.
15. "Dhātvarthavicāraḥ" delivered in Shri Lal Bahadur Shastri Kendriya Sanskrit Vidyapeetha, New Delhi, in January, 1974.
16. "Sphoṭavicāraḥ" delivered in Shri Lal Bahadur Shastri Kendriya Sanskrit Vidyapeetha, New Delhi, in January, 1974.
17. "Saṁskṛte Paryāyavācinaḥ Śabdāḥ" delivered in Shri Lal Bahadur Shastri Kendriya Sanskrit Vidyapeetha, New Delhi, in February, 1974.
18. "Contribution of Muslims to Sanskrit" delivered under the auspices of the Institute of Indology, New Delhi, on May 5, 1977, (Shri B.D.Jatti, Acting President of India presided).
19. A series of three Lectures on the "Language of the Yogavāsiṣṭha" delivered in the Ganganath Jha Kendriya Sanskrit Vidyapeetha, Allahabad, March 25-27, 1976.
20. "Kālidāsa Retold" delivered in the Kendriya Sanskrit Vidyapeetha, Tirupati, in February, 1976.
21. "Kārakāṇāṁ Vivakṣādhīnatvam" delivered in the Sanskrit College, Calcutta, in March 30-31, 1976.

22. "Some Modern Adaptations of the Works of Kālidāsa" delivered in the South Gujarat University, Surat, on January 27-29, 1977.
23. "U.G.C. Extension Lectures", delivered in the University of Bhagalpur, on March 11-13, 1981.
24. Dr. A.D. Pusalkar Memorial Lecture on the Rāmāyaṇa in Thailand, delivered in Bharatiya Vidya Bhavan, Bombay on September 25, 1981.
25. "Saṁskṛte Paryāyavācinaḥ Śabdāḥ" delivered in Shri Sadasiva Sanskrit Vidyapeetha, Puri, on August 23, 1983.
26. Inaugurated the Students Union of the Berhampur University, Berhampur, on January 18, 1984.

Prominent Lectures: International

27. "Sanskrit Synonyms" delivered in the University of Tübingen, on June 17, 1975.
28. "Modern Sanskrit Literature" delivered in the University of Heidelburg on June 20, 1975.
29. "Modern Sanskrit Poetry with Special Reference to My Own Poetry" delivered in the University of Tübingen on June 27, 1977.
30. "Kālidāsa's Philosophy of Life" delivered in the University of Munich on June 28, 1977.
31. "Vedic Verb Forms" delivered in the University of Erlängen on June 29, 1977.
32. "Sanskrit Synonyms" delivered in the Free University of Berlin on June 1,1977.
33. "Contribution of Muslims to Sanskrit" delivered in the University of Hamburg on July 4, 1977.
34. "Contribution of Muslims to Sanskrit" delivered in the Alexander Von Humboldt University, Berlin (G.D.R.), on July 4, 1977.
35. "Concept of Time in Ancient Indian Thought" delivered in the Koresi Csoma Society, University of Budapest on July 26, 1977.
36. "Kāvya Elements in Sanskrit Literature" delivered in the Columbia University, New York, on Oct. 11, 1978.
37. "Contribution of Muslims to Sanskrit" delivered in the University of Pennsylvania, Philadelphia, on October 17, 1978.
38. "The Philosophy of the Upaniṣads and the Law of Karman" delivered in the Mc Gill University, Montreal, on October 18-19, 1978.
39. "The Upaniṣads and the Gītā" delivered in the Concordia University,

Montreal, on October 18, 1978.

40. "Sanskrit in Thailand" delivered in the University of Toronto, Toronto, on October 23, 1979.
41. "Aspects of Sanskrit Literature" delivered in the Brock University, St. Catherines, on October 25, 1978.
42. "Thai Words in Relation to Sanskrit" delivered in the University of Wisconsin, Madison, on October 26, 1978.
43. "Sanskrit Semantics" delivered in the University of Chicago, Chicago, on October 27, 1978.
44. "Sanskrit Culture" "Sanskrit Poetry", and "Indian Culture in the Light of Sanskrit Language" delivered in the University of Calgary, Calgary, on October 30-31,1978.
45. "The Concept of Time in Ancient Indian Thought" delivered in the University of Edmonton, Alberta, on Nov. 1, 1978.
46. "Modern Sanskrit Literature" delivered in the British Columbia University, Vancouver, on Nov. 3, 1978.
47. "Contribution of Muslims to Sanskrit" delivered in the University of California, Los Angeles, on Nov. 6, 1978.
48. Addressed the Royal Nepal Academy, Kathmandu, on May 4, 1979.
49. "Sanskrit Studies in India", delivered in the University of Tokyo, on September 29, 1980.
50. "Sanskrit Studies in India and Thailand" delivered in the University of Kyoto on September 30, 1980.
51. "Origin and Development of Sanskrit Drama" delivered in the University of Venice on May 30, 1982.
52. "Modern Sanskrit Drama" delivered in the Catholic University, Leuven, Belgium, on March 26, 1985.
53. "Modern Hindu Society" delivered in the Catholic University, Leuven, Belgium, on March 26, 1985.
54. "Essentials of Hinduism" delivered in the Faculty of Comparative Religion, Antwerp, Belgium, on May 8, 1985.
55. "Ṛṣis of Kālidāsa" delivered in the University of Tübingen, Tübingen, West Germany, on June 8, 1986.
56. "Kālidāsa's Philosophy of Life" delivered in the University of Bonn, West Germany, on June 18 and 20, 1986 and the University of Torino, Torino, Italy, on June 2, 1987.

57. "Indian Culture and its Influence on Southeast and East Asia" delivered in the Catholic University, Leuven, Belgium, to mark the Golden Jubilee of the setting up of the Oriental Institute on May 11, 1987.
58. "Indian Culture in the Light of Sanskrit Language" delivered in the University of Torino, Torino, Italy, under the auspices of CESMEO on June 3, 1987, and in the University of Alberta, Edmonton, Canada, on 6.4.1988.
59. "Rāma Story in Thailand" delivered in the University of Torino, Torino, Italy, under the auspices of CESMEO on June 4, 1987, and in the University of Alberta, Edmonton, Canada, on 5.4.1988.
60. "Vedic Sacrifices in Kālidāsa" delivered in the University of Torino, Torino, Italy under the auspices of CESMEO on June 5, 1987.
61. "Modern Hindu Society" delivered in the University of Alberta, Edmonton, Canada on 21.3.1988 and the University of Calgary, Calgary, Canada, on 25.3.1988.
62. "The Concept of Time according to Bhartṛhari" delivered in the University of Alberta, Edmonton, Canada, on 22.3.1988.
63. "The Cult of Jagannath in Historical Perspective" delivered in the University of Lethbridge, Lethbridge, Canada, on 24.3.1988.
64. "Sanskrit Studies in India" delivered in the University of Calgary, Calgary, Canada, on 25.3.1988.
65. "Hindu Marriage" delivered in the University of Alberta, Edmonton, Canada, on 22.3.1988.
66. "Death in the Upaniṣads" delivered in the University of Alberta, Edmonton, Canada, on 29.3.1988.
67. "Māyā and the Ethics of Hinduism" delivered in the University of Alberta, Edmonton, Canada, on 30.3.1988.

Awards and honours were bound to flow to such a mighty scholar. Besides the Sahitya Akademi Award, one of the country's highest awards in creative writing in Sanskrit, in 1968, Dr. Shastri was honoured by the Sahitya Kala Parishad, Delhi Administration for Sanskrit scholarship in 1974, got the President of India Certificate of Honour in Sanskrit in 1985, was honoured by the Catholic University, Leuven, Belgium with a Medallion of Honour for contribution to Sanskrit and Indology in 1985, was conferred the title Shiromani Sanskrit Sahityakar by the Language Department of the Govt.of Punjab for outstanding literary output in 1985 and was honoured by the Uttar Pradesh Sanskrit Academy, Lucknow, with the Vishishta Sanskrit Sahitya Puraskara. He is associated with a number of academic and literary bodies both in the country and abroad. He was nominated honorary Member of the Italy- India Association, Venice, Italy, presided four times over the different sections of the All India Oriental Conference, was President of the Symposium on Ancient and Modern Sanskrit at the Sixth World Sanskrit Conference, Philadephia, U.S.A., in 1984 and the Workshop on Modern Sanskrit at the Seventh World Sanskrit Conference, Leiden, Holland, 1987. In addition to that, he had the honour to be the Chairman of the first European Conference on Vedic Science, Vlodrop, Holland (1985), of the Concluding Session of the Hinduism Section at the Fourteenth Congress, International Association of the History of Religions, Winnipeg, Canada (1983), of Section III of the Thirty-first International Congress of Human Sciences, Kyoto, Japan (1983), of a section in each of the three International Rāmāyaṇa Conferences, Bangkok, Toronto and New Delhi (1986,1987, 1988).

It is a tribute to the quality of his poetry that some of Dr. Shastri's Kāvyas have already become subjects of research. While a scholar got the M. A. degree on his *Śrīgurugovindasiṁhacaritaṁ* from the Punjabi University, Patiala, Indira Kant Pathak's exhaustive thesis on *Indirāgāndhīcaritam* earned him the degree of Ph.D. from the Bhagalpur University in 1989.

Such is thus the phenomenon that Dr. Satya Vrat Shastri is. He was trained as a grammarian but flowered into a highly talented poet, unmatched in certain respects. Grammar and poetry have worked out a happy blend in him. Though there is no dearth of intricate grammatical forms in his poems yet nowhere the grammarian in him is allowed to overpower the poet. Poetry to him is "very much a thing of the heart than of the brain". His poetry is distinguished by pleasing directness and lucidity besides unusual flow and rich imagery, all of which he owes to the two great epics, the *Rāmāyaṇa* and the *Mahābhārata*. He has deservedly earned rich encomia from worthy critics and scholars. To quote Dr. K. Krishnamoorthy, the eminent literary critic: "Dr. Satya Vrat's limpid flow of the verse is unparalleled today. It is a case of inborn genius coupled with complete learning– *pratibhā* competing with *vyutpatti*" .

A critical evaluation of his creative writings follows in subsequent pages.

CHAPTER TWO

MAHĀKĀVYAS

(I) ŚRIBODHISATTVACARITAM
(II) INDIRĀGĀNDHĪCARITAM
(III) ŚRĪRĀMAKĪRTIMAHĀKĀVYAM

ŚRĪBODHISATTVACARITAM

The *Śrībodhisattvacaritam* (*SBSC*)[1] has the proud distinction of being the first full-fledged poetical work of Dr. Satya Vrat Shastri. It seeks to offer in fourteen cantos, composed of one thousand verses, the Sanskrit version of some of the most elevating and instructive *avadānas* (meritorious deeds) of the Bodhisattva, as detailed in the Jātaka stories. The Bodhisattva is the soul struggling, in a variety of ways, to attain Buddhahood, which is the state of perfect enlightenment (Bodhi). Bodhisattva, is thus a state prior to the attainment of the Bodhi *par excellence* that the Buddha represented. As a Bodhisattva, he is born in a plethora of forms, from the lowly dog to the learned Brāhmaṇa. Whatever form he assumes, it is intended to uphold, through varied actions, human values that unfold themselves in different contours of conduct. It is these ideals that successively entitle the Bodhisattva to attain the denouement of perfect enlightenment. The *avadānas* of the Bodhisattva thus exercise ennobling influence on society and thereby purge it of all that debases human dignity. The Bodhisattva may, therefore, be construed as a phenomenon that has been instrumental in improving the health of the society through a series of idealistic behaviour.

Dr. Shastri has laid the Sanskritists under a debt of gratitude by reducing the Bodhisattva's *avadānas,* hitherto available in Pali, to mellifluous Sanskrit verses. He thus emerges as a peer to Āryaśūra, who had rendered the Jātaka stories into Sanskrit prose. Rather, the poetic medium entitles him to a higher rung. Viewed from this angle, the *SBSC* opens up new vistas in literature that has been rather parsimonious in dealing with the Buddhistic themes in poetry, stray efforts notwithstanding. Besides freshness of the subject-matter, the *SBSC* represents a *tour de force* on the part of the poet to establish himself as a notable poet in one go. And the Kāvya does it with a vengeance.

SUMMARY

Though somewhat fragmented in nature, the *SBSC* has a broad canvas, spanning fourteen cantos of uneven size.

The portrayal of the Bodhisattva as a tactful trader characterises the First Canto.

When king Brahmadatta was ruling over it, the Bodhisattva was born as a son to a wealthy merchant of Vārāṇasī. As he grew rich in worldly dealings and grasped

---

1. Mehar Chand Lachman Das, Delhi, Second Edition, 1973.

the intricacies of business, the young Bodhisattva decided to make fortunes by intraland trade. That would yield financial dividends besides pleasure born of visiting unknown lands, he mused. He therefore prepared himself to leave with a large convoy of five hundred bullock-carts laden with a variety of merchandise, for greener, though unexplored, pastures. Right then, another young trader of the town, Śāntabuddhi by name, decided to pursue the same course for similar purposes, with an equally large caravan. The Bodhisattva rightly viewed it as an impediment to his venture. Detailing the hazards, not precluding the loss of life and equipment, of a simultaneous journey along a comparatively narrow and inhospitable course, he impressed upon the young trader the lack of feasibility of the proposition, and offered him the option to precede or succeed him in the venture (*bhavān pruastād vrajatu prakāmaṁ yāyām ahaṁ veti viviṅgdhi bandho*, I.18). The reckless trader saw much merit including the fabulous return for the merchandise, in stealing thunder over his rival and lost no time in leaving first (*puro gamiṣyāmy aham eva nūnaṁ dravyaṁ tato me bhavitā hy anūnam*, I.22). On the other hand, the Bodhisattva was convinced of the abundant advantages that were to flow from following the young man, at a subsequent date (24-29).

The itinerary of the trader brought him, ere long, in the heart of a massive desert, sixty yojanas in expanse.He had equipped himself with an adequate store of food and water. Soon he found himself surrounded by a demon and his pack with wet hair and clothes, masquerading as a king with his retinue. He had conjured up a host of chariots yoked with sturdy bullocks. The wheels of the carts were apparently sullied with mud. They themselves wore garlands of lotuses and were feasting on their stalks (40-44). Projecting all this as indicative of torrential rains in the vicinity and consequent availability of abundant water, the deceitful demon counselled Śāntabuddhi against carrying back-breaking stores of water. The uncanny trader moved into the trap skilfully laid by the demon and dispensed with the massive jars then and there (*sarvān upādhvaṁsayad āśu kumbhan, na toyaleś 'opi yato' vaśiṣṭaḥ*, I.57). But as they proceeded in the searing winds, they did not obtain a drop of water and perished, unsung and unwept, of hunger and thirst (*sarve 'py abhūvan vigatāsavas te,* I.61). The demon and his bands, who were on the prowl nearby, reduced them all to a heap of bones (*asthnām avāśiṣyata tatra rāśiḥ*, I.63).

It was after more than a month that the Bodhisattva embarked upon the perilous, though otherwise productive, venture, well-prepared and well-equipped (65), with firm advice to his people to be hyper-cautious while negotiating the mighty desert. He was also accosted by the same demon, who did his utmost to dupe him into his trap. The Bodhisattva, who had seen through his wile (*ajñāyi vijñena mayā tvadīyaṁ durdhīpsitam*, I.77), berated him severely much against the wishes of his concourse, and the poor fellow vanished in the thin air (*antarhitaḥ san svapadaṁ prayātaḥ*, I.79).

His logical arguments convinced them of the deceit that the demon wanted to play on them. They were convinced that the young trader lost his life because of lack of shrewedness and foresight. Nearby, the Bodhisattva found the remains of Śāntabuddhi's expedition. He immediately mounted guard to meet any eventuality (*daityopaghātārtham upāttaśastraḥ*, I.97). With his vision, honesty and firmness, the Bodhisattva made a neat fortune. So did his caravan. Armed with multiple wares and huge profits, the Bodhisattva returned home (*guṇyaḥ svadeśaṁ nyavṛtat svapuṇyaiḥ*, I.100).

The lively encounter of Śrīkumāra with Mailika, the ruler of Kosala, forms the contents of the Second Canto. Born to Brahmadatta, the king of Kāśī, the Bodhisattva was aptly named Śrīkumāra. He equipped himself in various śāstras at Takṣaśilā, the ancient seat of learning. On the death of his father, he assumed the reins of the kingdom and carried on the administration in accordance with the precepts of ancient theoreticians. His predilection for the *śāstras* and solicitude for his people left their imprint on the entire administrative set-up. His reign was singularly free from disease, fear and such other calamities with the result the people enjoyed heavenly bliss on the earth itself. Thus feeling assured on all counts, he launched upon the mission of self-purification. With a view to acquainting himself of his vices, if any, he enquired about them of people from different strata of society, but his courtiers and commoners all had nothing but unstinted acclaim for his abundant excellences. He jaunted right up to the border region in search of his *doṣas* but met with little success (*nāpa kañcid api doṣavādinam*, II.26). While he was all set to return home frustrated in a way, he met the ruler of Kosala, Mallika by name. He was also on the mission of self-discovery that had brought Śrīkumāra also there. In the course of journey back to their respective countries, they stumbled upon a narrow and uneven strip that ill-afforded them simultaneous passage (*kiṁ karotu viṣamā rathoddhatā*, II.31). While each of the charioteers claimed precedence for his master on the basis of certain undefined qualities, it was eventually decided that superior merits should resolve the issue (*yogyatātiśayito mahattaraḥ*, II.37). On closer scrutiny it was found that both the rulers were equal in respect of age, wisdom, glory, high caste, administrative skill, wealth and might (42-43). However, Śrīkumāra carried the palm due to the sublimity of character. While Mallika believed in the policy of 'tit for tat' that invited derision from the rival charioteer (*prākṛtā api samācaranti tāṁ yā śaṭheṣu śaṭhatopapāditā*, II.51), the Kāśirāja was liberal to a fault as he did no harm even to the wicked and won over the arrogant with humility (*niruddhatam prati sadaiva śāmyati*, II.58). This aspect of Śrīkumāra's character filled the ruler of Kosala with wonder and admiration, and he alighted from the chariot to concede him the right to proceed ahead first.

Cantos Three and Four form one unit. Here again the ruler of Kāśī is pitted against the king of the Kosala kingdom. The battle is fought on the mundane plane but is won on the spiritual one.

The Bodhisattva, born to Brahmadatta, the ruler of Vārāṇasī, was given the most appropriate name of Śīlavān (*anvarthasaṁjñās tasyāsan*, III.10). While the astrologers predicted prosperity and fortunes for him, he mastered the secrets of the Śāstras including statecraft at the tender age of sixteen. He left no stone unturned to ensure the happiness of his subjects (*prajānām iṣṭam ādadhyau*, III.18). As if out of malice for his prosperous rule, Kali (Yuga) misled his minister into misbehaving with the ladies of the harem that brought about his instant expulsion from the kingdom, (*sapady eva tvayāmātya padyānyādya prapadyatām*, III.31). The minister sought shelter with the ruler of Kosala, and with his wordly wisdom soon became his trusted lieutenant. In order to wreak vengeance on Śīlavān, he instigated his new master to capture the Kāśī country, which, to him, was no stronger than the soft butter and fresh wine (*navanītasamaṁ mṛdu, asty adya madyam ādyam*, III.39). The king of Vārāṇasī would not only not resist the attack, he would actually welcome it, the minister confided. The test skirmishes into the border and middle regions were extremely encouraging for him. The benevolent ruler of Kāśī was the least perturbed at the loss, he rather honoured the marauders with handsome guerdon (*na manāg api cukṣubhe*, III.64; *dhanaṁ dattvāmucat sarvāṅs tān upadravakāriṇaḥ*, III.65). The queer behaviour of Śīlavān prompted the king of Kosala to strike at the capital itself (—*abhyaṣeṇayat*—*kāśīrājyajighṛkṣayā*, III.67) and reached in his expedition as far as the city-gate. Śīlavān overruled his doughty troops who had expressed themselves in favour of punishing the enemy. He also discounted such counter-measures as the ministers contemplated to retrieve the lost ground (*ādeśam anurudhyantaḥ pratirodhaṁ na cakrire*, III.99). The benevolent Śīlavān rather asked them to compensate the Kosalarāja for the losses he might have suffered in the operation (..*dātavyas cārthasampadaḥ*, III.79). And to shun the horrors of war, he offered his kingdom to the ruler of Kosala, on a platter (*rājyaṁ madīyam ādatsva bhogān bhuṅktvā ca nirvṛṇu*, III.91). The Kosalarāja occupied the royal throne. Vārāṇasī was overwhelmed by the hostile hordes but Śīlavān was unconcerned like a recluse (*sthiradhīr munirāḍ iva*, III.104). In the fit of victory, the king of Kosala perpetrated all sorts of atrocities on the people.

He had the ruler of Kāśī and his ministers buried in deep pits in a manner that their necks remained jutted out to be eaten away by the jackals, at night. The leader of the jackals charged at the king with ferocity but suffered unbearable pain when skilfully pressed by the king between his chin and neck. The poor jackal scratched the ground violently. That resulted in the loosenintg of the sand around the king and he managed to release himself and the ministers from the death-pit (*niṣkrāntaḥ sa svayaṁ gartāt----sacivān apy ajījivat*, IV.38). In return of the favour that the king did them in justly dividing a dead body for them, the two Yakṣas conducted him to the sleeping chamber of the king of Kosala. Śīlavān told him (the king) that he had expelled him from Kāśī and buried in a pit to meet miserable end. He withstood the adversities with forbearance and fortitude because nothing can match or surpass *titikṣā* in its effect (*titikṣām avalambyāhaṁ vipadas tā visoḍhavān*, IV. 89). The king of Kosala was instantaneously disarmed by his nobility and greatness (*bhavān atimahān mataḥ*, IV.92). He became poignantly aware of his pettiness also (*ahaṁ narādhamo nūnam*, IV.96). He returned the kingdom of Kāśī to its rightful owner and accepted his servitude. As a finale to the episode, he punished the wicked minister who had brought havoc to the two kings.

Canto Five, in a way, amounts to a tribute to fraternal affection.

Unable to apprehend the real culprits, the police-officials brought to Brahmadatta, the king of Vārāṇasī, three persons in chains, who were actually tilling their land, unconcerned with the goings on in the town. In the meanwhile, a woman arrived there, crying for their release. She told the king that they were her husband, brother and son respectively. She was offered to seek the release of one of them since they all could not be freed in one go (*pradeyā na sarve mayaite bhavanti*, V.16). With her options closed, she requested the king to release her brother from thraldom. In order to reinforce her claim she argued that while husband and son can be had easily, brother is difficult to attain. In fact, in comparison to brother, all relations and possessions pale into insignificance. That was why she craved for the release of her brother in preference to husband and son (*na me bhartṛkāmyā na vā putrakāmyā, tathāsti prakṛṣṭā yathā bhrātṛkāmyā*, V.21). The king was so impressed by her fraternal affection that he ordered forthwith the release of all the three. Brahmadatta henceforth came to understand the importance of brother in human life (*aho, bhrātur atrāstri kīdṛṅ mahattvam* V.28). As that woman secured the release of her brother in the present birth, in earlier life also she had been instrumental in ending the bondage of others through securing the release of her brother.

In Canto Six is related the story of a young monk, who, while returning from alms-round had chanced to see a lovely maiden at Śrāvastī and fell headlong, in love with her (*nālaṁ manaḥsaṁyamane babhūva*, VI.4). Smitten with love, he was reduced to the state of a deer harrowed by the hunter's arrows. The terrible agony that he suffered rendered him a physical and emotional wreck (*mlānaṁ mano 'bhūn malinā manīṣā, tejo 'khilaṁ cājarad indriyāṇām*, VI.7). He also lost interest in religious studies (*dharmopadeśo'py arucan na cāruḥ*, VI.8). On persistent inquiries from fellow mendicants he confided to them the cause of the sea-change that had abruptly overtaken him (*na sāsti śāntir muditā na kāntiḥ*, VI.10). "A youthful maiden of ravishing beauty has captured my heart. Unless I get her, now so dear to me (*rāmāṁ svamano 'bhirāmām*, VI.14), I am unlikely to regain normalcy or return to religious studies. I am simply unable to divert my heart from her (*tasmād aniśo 'smi manonirodhe, kathaṁ, pravarteya ca dharmabodhe*, VI. 18)", he whispered. The fellow monks cautioned him against straying into this perilous course. "Only the unlucky turns to sensual pleasures in preference to the elevating message of the Master. Apparently attractive, the material objects are dreadful in end." All this fell on deaf ears. They therefore conducted him to the Bodhisattva, who, underlining the hollowness of sensual enjoyments, impelled him to desist from them (*tvaṁ cāpi cittaṁ viṣaye prasaktaṁ, nirundhi dhīro bhava sādhuśīlaḥ*, VI.43). And in order to illustrate how great men resist the onslaughts of Cupid, he relates the story of Śibi that forms the subject matter of the succeeding canto.

At Ariṣṭapura in the Śibi kingdom there ruled a king Śibi by name. His queen gave birth to the Bodhisattva who, being a peer of Kārttikeya, was named Kumāra. To the wife of Śibi's Commander (*senāpati*) was born just then, a son. He was given the name Ahipāraka. After completing their training at Takṣaśilā, they assumed their hereditary duties. Kumāra ascended the throne, Ahipāraka was made the general of his forceṣ. Almost simultaneously, the wealthy merchant Tirīṭavatsa had got a daughter. She was the very replica of Lakṣmī, almost angelic (*jātāpsarastulyamanojñarūpā*, VII.12). As she maddened everybody with her exquisite charms she was given the most appropriate name of Unmadantī. Tirīṭavatsa offered his lovely daughter to the king in case she met his approbation. The king despatched the learned Brāhmaṇas to determine if she was worthy of him. But the Brāhmaṇas themselves fell victim to her ravishing beauty. Those who came as doctors, returned as patients (*parīkṣaṇaṁ kartum itāḥ kumāryāḥ parīkṣaṇīyāḥ svayam eva jātāḥ*, VII.23). Their unseemly behaviour infuriated Unmadantī to the extent that she had them booted out unceremoniously. With a view to settling scores with her, the Brāhmaṇas misled the king into believing that Unmadantī was shorn of all that could have made her an apt match to him (*durlakṣaṇatvād bhavato 'nurūpā naivāsty ato drāk parivarjanīyā*, VII.29). He turned down the merchant's proposal (*tadaṅgīkaraṇābhilāṣaṁ jahau*, VII.30). Tirīṭavatsa subsequently married her to Kumāra's Commander Ahipāraka, who tasted in her the heavenly bliss. What invested her with matchless beauty and affable character, is related in the subsequent canto (VIII).

In one of the previous births, Unmadantī was the daughter of poor parents at Vārāṇaṣī. Unable to provide her the saffron robe she had taken fancy for, they allowed her to undertake a petty job with a wealthy merchant– that would enable her to secure the garment of her liking. The merchant was so pleased with her performance that he presented her the saffron apparel besides other pieces, even before the expiry of the stipulated three years. However, she made it over, first half, then the whole, to a needy monk who was clad in barks only (*paṭasyāvaśiṣṭam apy ardham adad vinamra,* VIII.22) and sought his blessings so that she might be born, in the next birth, as a matchless beauty, equipped with an exuberance of excellences. It was thus that she was born as a daughter to the rich Tiriṭavatsa and acquired uncommon charms. That also accounted for her happy marital life with Ahipāraka.

While out at night to view the dazzling Ariṣṭapura, tastefully decorated on the occasion of Kaumudīmahotsava on the full-moon night of Kārttika, the king chanced to see Unmadantī, perched behind the latticed window. No sooner did he see her lotus-like face than a fierce volley of Cupid's arrows descended upon him (*abhūc ca dṛṣṭeḥ samakālam eva kāmasya cāpād api bāṇavṛṣṭiḥ*, VIII.44). That lacerated his heart and he suffered unbearable pangs of separation. Nothing but union with her would restore his calm. As a faithful minister, Ahipāraka decided to redeem the situation. At the supposed intercession of the sylvan Yakṣas, he offered him his wife so that his agony is ended and emotional equilibrium returns to him (*svayaṁ prayacchāmy aham ātmakāntāṁ, tantāṁ manovṛttim apāsya śāntām*, VIII.104). The king was sorry to find that his love for Unmadantī had gained currency. The feeling of guilt coupled with Ahipāraka's breath-taking offer threw him into mental turmoil (*katham adharmam imaṁ tanuyāṁ sakhe na hi tathā patito bhavitāsmy aham*, VIII.110).

Canto IX is couched, for the most, in conversational style. Herein the king (Kumāra) is locked in a lively conversation with his minister (Commander) Ahipāraka. Ahipāraka musters strong arguments to ask Kumāra to accept Unmadantī as his wife to regain emotional tranquillity. With equally powerful logic, the king rebuts his arguments. The mental conflict of the king finds powerful poetic expression here. The minister is bent upon making over his wife to the king. The latter politely declines the despicable proposal. The dialogue between the two is characterised by dramatic overtones. Ultimately it is *dharma* (righteousness) that triumphs over baser instincts and the king emerges as *mārajit* (*mārajit—. preṣṭhatamo 'sy abhīṣṭaḥ*, IX.33). The canto closes with a lengthy discourse on kingly duties by none else than the king himself (*pitāsmi netāsmi...na jātu kāmasya vaśaṁ gataḥ syām*, IX.45).

Canto X and XI set forth a story, split into two parts, and thus form a well-knit unit. Here the Bodhisattva appears as a monk. As he went to the palace of the king of Kosala to obtain alms, he found him estranged from his lovely queen Mallī following a petty love-quarrel. With a view to correcting the aberration, the Bodhisattva relates to them the story of Bhallāṭiya, the king of Vārāṇasi. Once intent upon eating the fresh meat of a deer, Bhallāṭiya set out for hunting in the Himālayas. There he encountered a Kinnara-couple that was behaving mysteriously in alternately making love and crying piteously. On close enquiry, the king discovered that the couple had, in distant past, suffered separation for one night, when a strong current of the river had swept the male Kinnara to the other bank, leaving the female one alone. Whenever they remembered the agonising experience they wept and wailed bitterly (*garīyāṁsaṁ tāpaṁ janayati,* X.25), praying for the non-recurrence of the frightful night (*triyāmā sā māgāt punar iti,* X.25). This they had been doing for the past seven hundred years and were destined to undergo the agony for another three hundred years. But the Kinnarī was convinced that nothing calamitous would happen to them in view of their mutual devotion. Profound love is itself the best antidote to the string of pangs and miseries (*mataḥ premasthemā jagati paramaṁ bheṣajam iha,* XI.3). In comparison to it all else is hollow (*taditarad asad vastu sad api,* XI.5). Their unflinching devotion and prolonged wailings at so much as separation for a solitary night put the king to shame for his unseemly behaviour with his wife (*adhanyo 'haṁ rājā dhṛtanaravapuḥ,* XI.10). He was so moved by the mutual love of the Kinnara -couple that he worked out, forthwith, a compromise with his offended queen .

The identity of the dramatis personae is also revealed by the Bodhisattva. He himself was Bhallāṭiya in the previous birth and the Kinnaras were none else than the king and the queen of Kosala.

The next story, brilliantly detailed in Canto XII emerges as the most moving and elevating piece in the poem. The birth of the Bodhisattva in the regime of Brahmadata, the righteous ruler of Vārāṇasī, was attended upon by widespread prosperity. Here the Bodhisattva appears as a simple, indigent farmer devoted to higher values of life and averse to physical comforts or pleasures. His family composed of, besides himself, his wife, son, daughter, daughter-in-law and a maid-servant gifted to her by her parents. Perfect happiness and harmony prevailed in the family (*ṣaṭ prāṇinaḥ praṇayino gṛhiṇo virejuḥ,* XII.7). In view of the transitory nature of the worldly objects and inevitability of death, he always urged his family to strive for spiritual attainments in preference to mundane pleasures (*preyo vihāya paramārtharatāḥ prakāmam,* XII.13). Once while working in the field with him, his young son died of snake-bite. The Bodhisattva (farmer) took the loss with amazing poise. He placed the dead body under a tree and continued his operation in the field, unperturbed (*tattvavid avāsthita nirvikāraḥ,* XII.21). He sent for the other members of the family with meals for one person (since the other had died) besides flowers and scents. The wife of the Bodhisattva had already known of her son's death through her mental power (*manaḥsamādher jñātam,* XII.30). With the other members she arrived at the fields. Though their dear one lay dead before them, they stood self-composed, unaffected by the disaster that had overtaken them (*dṛṣṭvā vinaṣṭam api te 'nvabhavan na kaṣṭam,* XII.34). The Bodhisattva first took his midday meals beside the dead body of his son and then consigned it, duly adorned with flowers and scents, to the sacred flames. That was certainly a challenge to Indra, the lord of gods. Apprehending loss of seat, he descended upon the earth and subjected the members of the family, in succession, to embarrassing questions about the reason of their composure in the face of the worst disaster. Details apart, they concurred in their response to the query. In view of the fact that the dead is reduced to ashes and attains to the course determined by his actions in the present birth, it is useless to wail for him or subject one to other mortifications (*yādṛṅ mṛto vyadhita karma, gato gatiṁ tām, kuryāṁ tadartham aham atra kathaṁ nu cintām*, XII.50). Indra was overwhelmed with their sense of detachment from worldly life and bestowed upon them jewels and other riches, besides blessings in abundance.

In Canto XIII the Bodhisattva assumes the form of a wealthy merchant Saṁgha, at Rajgir in the country of the Magadhas. Endowed with modesty and the will to serve the people, he was said to own the astronomical amount of eighty crores. He had an equally affluent and loving friend in Pīliya at Vārāṇasī. So intimate was their friendship that though physically distant, they were close to each other's heart (*...sthānato viprakṛṣṭam, sad api satatam āsīc cetasā sannikṛṣṭam*, XIII.5). By a queer quirk of fate, Pīliya suffered heavy losses, and was reduced to pitiable indigence (*naṣṭaniśśeṣavitta*, XIII.9). The poor fellow had to undergo terrible agony, both physical and mental. Ultimately, he decided to seek the help of his rich friend Saṁgha in the hour of turmoil. He was greeted at Rajgir with affection and courtesy. On learning of the adversity that had overtaken his friend (*vipadam adhigato 'haṁ hy āgamaṁ tvatsakāśe*, XIII.17), Saṁgha readily decided to relieve his misery to the best of his capacity. He happily shared with Pīliya not only half of his cash but also other possessions including clothes, jewellery and pet animals. He also gifted some of his servants (*upahṛtanijabhṛtyaḥ*, XIII.24). Pīliya was thus restored to his earlier affluence and happiness. He left Rajgir with a heart full of gratitude to his noble friend (*vividham abhidadhat taṁ śreṣṭhinaṁ sādhuvādam, śamitahṛdavasādaṁ lambhitātmaprasādam*, XIII.25).

As ill-luck would have it, Saṁgha was also subsequently reduced to the fate that Pīliya had suffered earlier. Man is after all a helpless pawn in the hands of fate. He could not have thought of any one else but Pīliya to bail him out of this impasse. Friends do not tend to forget the good gesture, he rightly mused (*na ca kṛtam upakāraṁ bandhavo vismaranti*, XIII. 29). To his utter amazement, Pīliya was not only curt, but patently insulting in behaviour to his former benefactor. He had the temerity to ask him to seek refuge elsewhere (*padam itarad upehi*, XIII. 38). To compound the affront, he offered him a gourdful of chaff, so ungrateful was he. He, whom he thought to be his friend, turned out to be a swindler (*paradhanamuṣi nīce kāmam āśās tv adhanye*, XIII. 47). But in the larger interest of friendship Saṁgha decided to submit to the insult inherent in accepting the chaff. However, he was crest-fallen, confronted with ingratitude in its naked form. Saṁgha's wife, who was in the wings, was also cut to the quick by the ingratitude of the supposed friend (*tam aham atinikṛṣṭam...nābhinandāmi mitram*, XIII.53).

A former servant of Saṁgha, now gifted, to Pīliya, in concert with others of his tribe, decided to take up cudgels against the thankless Pīliya, with the king. On hearing the two, the king ordered Pīliya to surrender all his riches to Saṁgha. Saṁgha protested against the blanket order. He would not accept anything beyond what he had made over Pīliya in the hour of need (*yad aham alam adāṁ tad dāpaya tvaṁ madīyam,* XIII.95). Greed spells doom, he firmly averred (*bahulobhāt sarvatheha praṇāśaḥ*, XIII.96). The king was surprised at his generosity, and ordered Pīliya accordingly.

The last canto (XIV) projects the Bodhisattva as a preceptor (Ācarya) who instructed thousands of pupils in various lores. In view of the despicable overtones inherent in his name, one of his pupils Pāpaka requested the Bodhisattva to change his name in favour of an auspicious and pleasing one. All efforts of the Bodhisattva to impress upon him the irrelevance of the name beyond a point, and potency of actions as an instrument of greatness, fell on deaf ears (*nāmno nāsti mahattvam atra karmaiva mukhyaṁ matam*, XIV.6). Attractive names do not always reflect the virtues that are supposedly associated with them, advised the Ācarya (*syur nāmānuguṇā guṇā iha nṛṇām etad dhy anaikāntikam*, XIV.7). Allegedly ignoble names acquire lustre in the virtuous whereas the so-called noble names earn contempt with the unworthy, he further added. All these arguments left Pāpaka cold and he insisted on the change. The Ācārya, noticing his insistence asked him to find out an appropriate name so that he might rechristen him accordingly. Pāpaka wandered in three towns, only to discover, that names, more often than not, do not accord with the sense that they are supposed to echo. Jīvaka succumbed to death, Dhanapālikā was a poor maid-servant and suffered indignities including physical punishment from her master and Pānthaka lost his path in the forest. It awakened Pāpaka to the merit in the Guru's advice. He decided not to discard his name (*nākhyāyāḥ, parivartanam ca bhagavan svasyāḥ punaḥ kāmaye*, XIV.34). He was convinced that it was the actions that accorded one greatness. Name was merely a convenient mode of addressing and distinguishing a person (*saṁsiddhiḥ khalu karmaṇaiva kathitā syān nāmadheyena kim*, XIV.35).

OBSERVATIONS ON THE SIGNIFICANCE OF THE STORIES INCLUDED IN THE BODHISATTVACARITAM

The Jātaka stories chosen for versified rendering in the *Bodhisattvacaritam* are invariably intended to uphold certain human virtues and values. The author has sought to sum up the moral at the close of each story. However, the didactic message that they convey goes beyond the pithy abstract, attempted by the poet. It should be rewarding to elucidate, at some length, the significance of the various stories.

This is what is sought to be attempted in the subsequent lines.

Canto I

The story of the two traders aspiring to make fortunes, related in Canto One, is intended to illustrate the superiority of foresight and patience over avarice and impulse. In contradistinction to the Bodhisattva, the young trader Śāntabuddhi had the vision that did not go beyond his nose. He had persuaded himself to believe that success rested in brow-beating the Bodhisattva. And all material gains would gush forth from undertaking first the trade-expedition along unbroken paths. He landed himself into disaster, and his mission ended in a fiasco. The maturity and vision of the Bodhisattva, on the other hand, not only thwarted the evil designs of the deceitful demon and his cohorts but brought him rich dividends as well. Thus similar trade expedition brought widely divergent results to the wise Bodhisattva and the greedy Śāntabuddhi.

Canto II

In accordance with the wont of the Jātaka stories, the encounter that the Kāśirāja had with the ruler of Kosala, as detailed in the Second Canto, also seeks to heighten the character of the Bodhisattva (Kumāra). The king of Kosala was almost a match to the young Kumāra in varied qualities like prowess, polity and political acumen (*balanītikauśalādy apṛcchyata*, II.42). However, the totality of character decided the issue in favour of Kumāra. The Kautilyan policy of *śaṭhe śāṭhyaṁ samācaret* proved the undoing of the king of Kosala. Kumāra's generosity even to the wicked entitled him to greatness (*sadapakāriṣv api copakārād dravanamanā yo 'sti, mahān sa eva,* II.66).

Cantos III-IV

The sublime character of the Kāśirāja is again brought into focus in the unit represented by the two successive cantos. The story exemplifies the profundity of equanimity that man is capable of. The detachment of the Bodhisattva from power and pelf is total. He views the havoc wrought to his kingdom by the king of Kosala with a poise of a recluse. He also suffers the agony of the death-trap with a smile. His composure and sufferings ultimately bear fruit. He regains his kingdom and addedly the king of Kosala submits to his greatness (*adyaprabhṛti he rājan bhavadrājyasya sevakaḥ*, IV.108).

Canto V

Canto Five immortalises the sister's love for her brother and establishes its supremacy over all other relations. Arrested for no fault of theirs by the crude cops, the husband, son and brother of the grief-stricken woman stood condemned, but her sound arguments resulted into their instant release. The story highlights the sanctity of fraternal affection as much as the highhandedness of the police.

Cantos VI-IX

The story detailed in the segment formed by the next four cantos, serves to lift yearnings for carnal pleasures to philosophic heights. It is the sublimation of *kāma* (sex) that is skilfully attempted here. Uncontrolled passion of overindulgence in sex brings about ruin of the social order. It has to be disciplined to ensure the health of the society. The young monk's headlong fall for the dame paralleled by Kumāra's cravings for Unmadantī, the wife of his own minister, were serious aberrations that the story seeks to correct in its own way.

Cantos X-XI

Some of the tenderest human emotions have found expression in the story, related in the garb of mutual devotion of the Kinnara-couple. Conjugal love forms the corner-stone of happy life. This is what sustains human life in all the vicissitudes that one has to undergo, willy-nilly. LIfe acquires meaning only in the company of one's sweetheart, Even momentary separation leaves deep scars on the sensitive mind (*manaḥ sīdaty eva kṣaṇam api viyukte priyajane*, XI.6). This has been beautifully illustrated by the touching story of a compromise between the estranged king and the queen of Kosala. The story may be rated as an undying ode to the glory of love.

Canto XII

The story of the humble farmer (Bodhisattva), described in Canto Twelve is the most sublime and moving piece. The divine character of the Bodhisattva, distinguished by deep abhorrence for worldly pleasures and rare devotion to spiritual life, fills one with wonder. He represents the dizzy heights which man is capable to attain. We all are caught in the vortex of mundane affairs and carnal enjoyments to the extent that we hardly strive to realise the sublimity of the self. As an humble farmer, the Bodhisattva illustrates by his actions that voluminous disquisitions fail to disgorge. There is definitely something godly about man. The story exemplifies the truth enshrined in the Upaniṣadic dictum : *na mānuṣāc chreṣṭhataraṁ hi kiñcit.*

Canto XIII

The story of Saṁgha and Pīliya in Canto Thirteen unfolds a noble aspect of human character. It is intended to uphold the ideals of true friendship. This it does by underscoring the contrast represented in the behaviour of two friends, Saṁgha and Pīliya. Two conflicting sets of forces are at work in the story. Saṁgha is an embodiment of goodness that is reflected in his attitude to Pīliya. He goes out of the way to part with half of his total assets to ward off the adversity that had engulfed his friend Pīliya. This he viewed neither as an act of favour nor was he sorry, in any way, for the stupendous loss that was involved therein. It was actuated by an eagerness to maintain the standards of true friendship (*samadhikavibhavasyākhitta naivāsya cittam, parigatasuhṛdicchāpūrtir iṣṭācakāsīt,* XIII.23). The same idealism is demonstrated in his accepting the humiliating gourdful of chaff.

Pīliya exemplfies the other extremity of human character. He is greed and ingratitude incarnate. His greed makes him blind to the favour that Saṁgha had done to him. In his (Saṁgha's) hour of need, Pīliya has no qualms in heaping slights on him. He almost boots him out of his house. To him friendship is a marriage of convenience. Perhaps, chaff is projected here to symbolise his worthlessness both as a friend and as a man. However, Pīliya's ingratitude has not been void of purpose. It heightens the intensity of goodness that Saṁgha exemplifies in his character.

Canto XIV

The story of Pāpaka in the last canto underlines the efficacy of action. Mere attractive/highsounding names do not lead us anywhere. Actions and virtues alone are the stepping stones to success (*satkarmaṇā siddhim upaiti nūnam, na nāmadheyena yatas tad ūnam*, XIV.43).

CRITIQUE :

The *Bodhisattvacaritam* seems to have been conceived as a Mahākāvya. The bulk of the poem and its anxiety, howsoever feeble, to conform to theory lends credence to the belief. Its format distinguished by a string of stories connected with the earlier births of one of the greatest apostles of peace and compassion that human histroy has known, its well-chiselled, graceful language, brook-like swift cadence of its diction combined with a tendency to set certain ideals that shape the destiny of society are actuated to claim for the *SBSC*, the high status of Mahākāvya. However, the *Bodhisattvacaritam*, as it stands, confronts the critic with a plethora of problems that have to be resolved with dispassionate precision.

THEME :

Even when measured by the liberal yard-stick of Bhāmaha[2], the *SBSC*, it has to be admitted, leaves much to be desired. According to the norms, laid down by ancient and medieval poeticians, that have percolated down to the present day, the

---

2. सर्गबन्धो महाकाव्यं महता च महच्च यत् ।
अग्राम्यशब्दमर्थ्यं च सालङ्कारं सदाश्रयम् ।।
मन्त्रदूतप्रयाणाजिनायकाभ्युदयैश्च यत् ।
पञ्चभिः सन्धिभिर्युक्तं नातिव्याख्येयमृद्धिमत् ।।
चतुर्वर्गाभिधानेऽपि भूयसार्थोपदेशकृत् ।
युक्तं लोकस्वभावेन रसैश्च सकलैः पृथक् ।।
नायकं प्रागुपन्यस्य वंशवीर्यश्रुतादिभिः ।
न तस्यैव वधं ब्रूयादन्योत्कर्षाभिधित्सया ।। *Kāvyālaṅkāra*, I.19-22.

theme of a Mahākāvya should emanate from the established sources (*itihāsa*) like the epics and the Purāṇas or should be connected with high personages[3]. Bhāmaha was not much enamoured of the ancient source-books (*upajīvyagranthas*) and admitted a story worthy enough for a Mahākāvya if it revolved round a noble character and was itself ennobling in effect[4]. The theme of the *Bodhisattvacaritam*, as noticed earlier, is doubtless connected with a worthy personage, the Bodhisattva, the Buddha in the making, and may as such, be rated as *sajjanāśraya*. However, it suffers from a nagging lack of cohesion that should form the hallmark of a Mahākāvya. It does not centre round a single individual but hinges upon a variety of characters, both noble and ignoble. It may be tempting to explain away this diversity by resorting to the ethereal argument that the solitary soul of the Bodhisattva pervades the whole spectrum of characters and that serves to impart unity to the separate strands of stories[5].

The argument loses force, whatever one may muster for it, in view of the fact that the Buddhistic conception of soul is wide apart from the postulation of the nondualistic Vedānta as a single, indivisible and lasting entity. The fact remains that the various stories, as detailed in the poem, stand in apparent isolation from each other. The situation is not dissimilar from what obtains in the *Raghuvaṁśa*, where also different threads of various stories have been manoeuvered to form the warp and woof of the Kāvya. The attempt is evidently, far from satisfactory. And the *Raghuvaṁśa*, as observed by a modern critic[6], in all essentials, resembles an art-gallery adorned with a series of paintings, which, howsoever attractive, are after all disconnected from each other. The stories in the *Bodhisattvacaritam* are also apparently detached. What resemblance the story of the lovely Unmadantī or noble farmer bears with that of Pīliya or the reckless young trader, passes comprehension. Evidently the author has not chosen a well-knit single but multi-dimensional theme for the work that he is eager to project as a Mahākāvya. However, broadly speaking, the apparently isolated stories of the *Bodhisattvacaritam* may be taken to be bound together by the phenomenon that the Bodhisattva represents. That is precisely why the various characters of the poem, despite the divergent functions that they perform with diverse results, invariably end up with something noble. This characteristic of the theme of the poem is both its strength and weakness. While it invests the poem

---

3. इतिहासोद्भवं वृत्तमन्यद्वा सज्जनाश्रयम् । *Sāhityadarpaṇa*, VI. 318.
4. *Kāvyālaṁkāra*, I.19.
5. Dharmendra Kumar Gupta: Śrībodhisattvacarita : Eka Ālocanātmaka Adhyayana, *Śrībodhisattvacaritam*, Delhi, 1973, pp. xiv-xv.
6. Bhola Shankar Vyas : *Saṁskṛta-kavi-darśana*, Benares, V.S.2012, p.90.

with the dimensions of a Mahākāvya and enhances the dignity of the story, it, on the other hand, results in reducing the variety and interest of the theme and comes in the way of the poetic possibilities of characterisation and depiction of sentiments in the poem[7].

HERO (NĀYAKA) :

Equally baffling is the problem that the *Bodhisattvacaritam* poses about its hero. Bhāmaha seems to be non-committal on the issue. He is content to prescribe that the Mahākāvya should revolve round great characters who should not be divorced from nobility. Shorn of verbal jugglery, it means that the hero of a Mahākāvya should be both a great and noble personage[8]. Unfortunately greatness and nobility are not always co-existent. The later poeticians like Viśvanātha have been rigorous in closing the options of the authors of the Mahākāvyas with respect to the choice of the hero (*nāyaka*). Viśvanātha is specifically assertive that a Mahākāvya would have one *nāyaka* – a god or kṣatriya of the famed race – endowed with virtues like bravery and noblemindedness. Alternately, he does not hesitate to admit more than one person of the same race as *nāyakas* of a Mahākāvya[9]. Evidently the latter provision has been made to bring poems like the *Raghuvaṁśa* into conformity with the rhetorical injunctions. To be sure, the *Bodhisattvacaritam* has no pivotal figure to sustain the various stories that have been woven into its body. Each story deals with diverse characters who, as enjoined upon by Bhāmaha, are not invariably great and noble. They rather present a study in contrast. While the Bodhisattva commands greatness and nobility both, the other characters like Kosalarāja, the young monk and Piliya are banal in essentials. The *Bodhisattvacaritam*, like the *Raghuvaṁśa*, stands in an unenviable position for its hero. The *nāyaka* of the *Bodhisattvacaritam* cannot therefore be said to be one as the Bodhisattva appears in different stories in different garbs, nor can it be believed to have a multiety of heroes as a single thread runs through the various characters to bind them together, howsoever vulnerable the knot may be. In the *Raghuvaṁśa* also one is confronted with the similar problem. In view of the fact that it is dominated by several towering personalities, all attractive in their own way, the *Raghuvaṁśa* has been indirectly divided by a modern critic into three well-defined segments – the Raghu-khaṇḍa, Rāma-khaṇḍa and Khila-khaṇḍa, though all bound together by

---

7. Dharmendra Kumar Gupta : Śribodhisattvacaritam : Eka Ālocanātmaka Adhyayana, op.cit.,p. xix.
8. *Kāvyālaṁkāra*, I.19.
9. सद्वंशः क्षत्रियो वापि धीरोदात्तगुणान्वितः ।
   एकवंशभवा भूपाः कुलजा बहवोऽपि वा ॥ *Sahityadarpaṇa*, VI.316.

dynastic affinities[10]. The *Bodhisattvacaritam* is not enlivened by such dynamic diversity. However, the *dharmavīratā* of the Bodhisattva is not a poor match to the varied exploits of Raghu and Rāma. After all, both seek to uphold and fight, in their own way, for certain human values that add to the dignity of society. While, as hinted in the title itself, Raghu seems to have been intended by Kālidāsa as the hero of his poem, it should be more appropriate to treat the *Raghuvaṁśa* as a Mahākāvya with a plurality of heroes. How Rāma falls short of his distinguished predecessor Raghu or how Aja and Daśaratha suffer by comparison, defies imagination. Rāma, is as much equipped to be the hero of the *Raghuvaṁśa* as Raghu is. The situation is paralleled by Puṇyakuśala's *Bharatabāhubalimahākāvya* and Hemavijaya's *Vijayapraśastimahākāvya* wherein Bāhubali and Hīravijayasūri cannot in anyway be robbed of the status of *nāyaka*, so thoroughly do they pervade the length and breadth of the respective poems. The position of the *Bodhisattvacaritam* is quite distinct. It is not encompassed, in its different stories, by the Bodhisattva as an individual. He appears in different forms to perform varied functions. Therefore the Bodhisattva as an individual cannot be said to run through the texture of the poem. It is the Bodhisattva as a phenomenon that has to be viewed as the *nāyaka* of the peom. And herein the poet makes a bold departure from the established norms. While it might have infringed the theory, it introduces a new element in the concept of a Mahākāvya that hitherto had been taken to be the preserve of gods or personages of the Kṣatriya race. Why a worthy Brāhmaṇa or Vaiśya should not be assigned the coveted position of *nāyaka?* This is precisely what some of the Jaina poets have sought to do.

RASA :

In the delineation of Rasa also, the *Bodhisattvacaritam* does not wholly submit itself to theory. But interestingly more than any other poetician, it seems to stand somewhat closer to Bhāmaha's injunction on the issue. To Bhāmaha, a Mahākāvya should be rich in sentiments. He appears to accord equal status to all the sentiments to have free, independent play in a Mahākāvya.[11] In recommending the preponderance of one of the sentiments Ānandavardhana has evidently abridged the freedom allowed by his predecessor. This, he asserts, serves to heighten the effect of other sentiments.[12] Viśvanātha is illogically harsh in narrowing down the

---

10. Bhola Shankar Vyas: *Saṁskṛta- kavi-darśana*, op.cit., p.90.
11. युक्तं लोकस्वभावेन रसैश्च सकलैः पृथक् । *Kāvyālaṁkāra*, I.21.
12. प्रसिद्धेऽपि प्रबन्धानां नानारसनिबन्धने ।
    एको रसोऽङ्गीकर्त्तव्यस्तेषामुत्कर्षमिच्छता ।। *Dhvanyāloka*, III.21.

choice of the dominant from the trinity of Śṛṅgara, Vīra and Śānta.[13]

Frankly speaking, the *Bodhisattvacaritam* is not rich in sentiments. In view of the nature of its stories, loosely strung to form an integrated texture, it could not have been so. However, by sheer coincidence, the sentiments depicted here do not stand in the relationship of dominance and subservience (*aṅgāṅgibhāva*). To be sure, not many sentiments are fostered in the poem, certainly not with the vehemence that would raise one of them to the high status of the *aṅgīrasa*. Unlike the conventional themes beset with an abundance of situations, in their diversity and complexity, the episodes in the *Bodhisattvacaritam* do not admit of many an emotion of human breast that could have been exploited by a sensitive poet to release a spring of *rasa*. However, within its narrow limits, the *Bodhisattvacaritam* affords ample opportunities to analyse the varied emotions of its characters which invariably result into the emergence of *rasa* in its various hues.

Roughly, Tranquil (*Śānta*) may be taken to be the major sentiment of the *Bodhisattvacaritam*. *Śama* (tranquillity) or *nirveda* (detachment) is held by the poeticians as the lasting feeling (*sthāyibhāva*) of the Śānta–rasa. And it is *nirveda*/tranquillity (*Śama*) that breathes through the length and breadth of the poem. The *nirveda* that characterises the behaviour of Kāśirāja Śīlavān in not only not repulsing, despite his greater equipment and resources, but also rewarding the marauders and the equanimity with which the farmer Bodhisattva conducts himself in the face of the disastrous death of his young son is as sublime as it is super-human. Elsewhere also in the poem, not unoften, the reader is poignantly reminded of the ephemeral nature of the world and its objects, inevitability of death, hollowness of sensual pleasures and bliss of ultimate emancipation from human bondage. The rebuke that the fellow-mendicants administer to the erratic monk in Canto Six, emanates from this strand of logic. Aversion to worldly pleasures is what commands acclaim (*prītyādṛtā ca viṣayeṣv aniśaṃ viraktiḥ*, XII.83). The carnal pleasures, though *prima facie* attractive, invariably end in revulsion. The wise should not indulge in them beyond a point. They are worthless like a mass of bones, dreadful like the expanded hood of a serpent, dream-like in nature and leave a trail of adversity. Yet like thorny bushes laden with flowers, they invite and repel one and all :

आपातरम्या विषयाः स्फुरन्तः
समन्ततोऽन्ते परितापयन्ति ।

---

13. शृङ्गारवीरशान्तानामेकोऽङ्गी रस इष्यते । *Sāhityadrapana*, VI.317.

न बुद्धिमांस्तेष्वधिकं रमेत
सुदुस्त्यजांस्तान् न च रोचयेत ।।
विभान्त्यमी मांसलपेशलाश्च
कङ्कालवत् कीकसनीरसाश्च ।
विभीषणाः सर्पफणोपमाश्च
प्रभ्रष्टशाखोटफलोपमाश्च ।।

ज्वलत्स्फुलिङ्गाः प्रदहन्ति कामं
तृणोल्मुका यान्त्यचिरादपायम् ।
स्वप्नोपमाः सन्ति घनान्धकाराः
कामादयोऽनिष्टकरा विकाराः ।।

सुपुष्पिताः कण्टकिनः सदैते
विमोहयन्ति व्यथयन्ति लोकम् ।
आपामरं सर्वगता विसिन्व-
न्त्यर्थाः स्वनर्था जनयन्ति शोकम् ।। VI.27-30

Convinced of the amazing equanimity of the farmer Bodhisattva and his family in the face of heart-rending death Indra, the lord of heavens, doles out to them rather undeservedly for him, a lengthy lecture on the impermanence of life contrasted with the permanence of *mokṣa*. Blessed are those who successfully combat the onslaughts of carnal pleasure. That alone ensures the immortal state, beyond death (*mṛtyoḥ paraṁ tad amṛtaṁ ca padaṁ labhadhvam*, XII.85) :

धन्या भवन्ति भुवनेषु भवादृशा ये
नैवासजन्ति वितते प्रकृतेर्निकाये ।। XII.84

संस्मर्यतां च परतत्त्वमिहाविरामम् ।। XII.86

अनित्यमेतत् क्षणदृष्टनष्टं कष्टं जगत् सारविहीनमस्ति ।
ज्ञात्वा तदेकं स्थिरमात्मतत्त्वं भवन्तु सर्वेऽप्यमृताः शमित्योम् ।। XII.92

This aversion from mortality and devotion to immortality combined with yearning to achieve the blissful state through a variety of deeds, culminate in quietism, which, to the Bodhisattva forms the quintessence of human endeavours and aspirations.

Though not intended as ancillary or anti-climax to quietism, erotics, in both its aspects, finds impressive expression in the *Bodhisattvacaritam*. Allpervasiveness of *kāma* is frankly admitted (*sādhāraṇaḥ kāmavikāra eṣaḥ*, VI.26). Greatness of love is not lost on the author. To him, love (*preman*) forms the highest essence of life. Without the comforting touch of love, life has no meaning, no purpose. It is one's dear one that lends relevance to human life (*...sukhadaṁ prema paramaṁ paraṁ tattvaṁ jñeyam... /.... Vinā preyāṅsaṁ kaḥ prabhavati pumān jīvitum api,* XI.5).

In the description of Unmadantī, the charming daughter of the wealthy merchant Tirīṭavatsa, the Vibhāvas, in both the varieties, come out prominently to form the basis of the Śṛṅgārarasa. While the erotic sentiment has Ālambana in her person, her charms form the Uddīpana Vibhāva. The refulgence of her person waxed like the crescent. She strew beauty and sweetness like a *cakorī*. She was tenderness incarnate. In youth she emerged as a match to the heavenly nymphs and thus captivated the heart of one and all :

सौन्दर्यमाधुर्यकिरा चकोरी
स्फुरच्छरच्चन्द्रमुखी किशोरी ।
सौभाग्यवत्युत्पलकोमलाङ्गी
विलक्षणा सोत्तमलक्षणाऽभूत् ।। VII.10

प्रवर्धमाना सुतरां सुशीला
सा षोडशीराप्य समाः कुमारी ।
स्वं मानुषं वर्णमुदस्य दैवा-
ज्जाताऽप्सरस्तुल्यमनोज्ञरूपा ।।

तदोन्मदन्ती कलिकाग्रदन्ती
रतिं हसन्ती हृदयं हरन्ती ।
सर्वाञ्जनान् कामवशं नयन्ती
देवाङ्गनेवाऽऽस्त विमोहयन्ती ।।

तामुज्ज्वलां वञ्जुलमञ्जुलाङ्गीं
समुच्छलद्यौवनचञ्चलाक्षीम् ।
आलोकमालोकमलं विमुग्धाः
सर्वेऽपि कामोपहता बभूवुः ।।

तदङ्गलावण्यमवेक्ष्य लोका
मैरेयपीता इव मोहमापुः ।
भृशं प्रमत्ता बत नष्टचित्ताः
कामोपसृष्टा न किमप्यवापुः ।। VII. 12-15

Śṛṅgāra also finds expression in the amorous description of Kumāra after love had wounded his heart. He was so smitten with the charms of his general's wife, Unmadantī that he sank into deep darkness, lost circumspection and forgot everything including himself. Although indefensible, on all counts, his attatchment to Unmadantī serves to stir tenderest emotions in his bosom :

राज्ञः सपद्यूर्ध्वमुखस्य तस्या
मुखारविन्दे निपपात दृष्टिः ।
अभूच्च दृष्टेः समकालमेव
कामस्य चापादपि बाणवृष्टिः ।।

दृष्ट्वोज्ज्वलां चञ्चललोचनां तां
सुवर्णवर्णां रमणीं महीपः ।
प्रपीडितः कामशरप्रहारै-
र्मङ्क्षु न्यमाङ्क्षीद् गहनान्धकारे ।। VII. 44-45

हृद्युन्मदन्तीमवधाय रम्यां
गम्यामगम्यामपि न व्यजानात् ।
कामाहतो हन्त विमूढचेताः
सद्यो विसस्मार निजस्वरूपम् ।। VII. 47

The sting of Vipralambha (love in separation) is felt more acutely in the poem. It is first encountered in the torment that the young monk undergoes after he is confronted with the lovely damsel of Śrāvastī. Her mere sight throws the youthful mendicant virtually out of gear. Self-restraint, composure, serenity and even physical firmness deserted him instantly. He was reduced to an emotional wreck :

विलोक्य तां लोचनलोभनीयां
मनोज्ञरूपां तरुणीमकस्मात् ।
गृहीतशिक्षोऽपि परं स भिक्षु-
र्नालं मनःसंयमने बभूव ॥

विक्षिप्तचेताः स्वनिकेतनस्थः
कामातुरोऽसौ बुबुधे न किञ्चित् ।
प्रमुग्धगीतध्वनिलुब्धशल्य-
प्रविद्धसारङ्ग इवावतस्थे ॥

निरन्तरं चिन्तयतोऽस्य योषां
सुभूषिताङ्गीं नवयौवनस्थाम् ।
अह्नाय नष्टद्युति पीतवर्णं
वक्त्रं वपुश्चैदतिदुर्बलत्वम् ॥

म्लानं मनोऽभून्मलिना मनीषा
तेजोऽखिलं चाजरदिन्द्रियाणाम् ।
रागातिरेकेण तदेकवृत्ते-
र्ध्वस्ता समस्ताऽऽत्मपवित्रतापि ॥ VI. 4-7

More touching is the description of the memories of separation that the Kinnara-couple had suffered for merely one night but that continued to torment them for a thousand years. Though the dramatis personae are simple demi-humans, the depiction of their emotions echo the most tender and sacred sentiments of human heart. The Viraha-rātri hung so heavily on the loving couple that even a passing thought of the dreadful night was sufficient to throw them into turmoil that reflected itself into their successive weeping and laughter :

वियोगोऽसह्योऽसौ स्मृतिपथमुपेतो मनसि नो
गरीयांसं तापं जनयति च सम्मोहयति च ।
त्रियामा सा माऽऽगात् पुनरिति सचिन्तौ सकरुणं
विलापैरालापै रहसि गमयावः स्वसमयम् ।। X.25

नितान्तं तान्तौ तां रजनिमखिलां सान्धतमसां
सकृच्चावां हासं व्यतनुव सकृच्चापि रुदितम् ।
वियुक्तानामेषा भवति विवशानामिह दशा
मनस्ताम्यद् भ्राम्यद् क्वचिदपि रतिं नैव लभते ।। X.37

The imporper love that Kumāra, the ruler of Ariṣṭapura, entertains for the wife of his general Ahipāraka and the consequent sharp pangs of separation that he undergoes, present a different aspect of Vipralambha. It was the debased form of love. The poet has sought to purge it to sublimity in a unique way. The king who had fallen headlong for Unmadantī turns, as he experiences catharsis in virtuosity, averse to her coveted beloved and consequently regains mental and emotional equanimity. The poet has captured the ravages of this storm and the emotional lull that follows it with charming effect. This is how the storm breaks upon the king following his brief encounter with the angelic Unmadantī :

सुकोमलाङ्गीं मृगलोचनां तां
साक्षात् सुरस्त्रीमिव चन्द्रकान्ताम् ।
दृष्टाममुष्यां निशि पौर्णमास्यां
लब्ध्वाऽहमानन्दमितः कदा स्याम् ।। VII.64

सुहासिनी सुन्दरभाषिणी सा
सुभूषणा कोमलबाहुपाशैः ।
कदा परिष्वङ्क्ष्यति मां कृशाङ्गी
मुदा रसालं नवमल्लिकेव ।। VIII.69

कदा प्रियां प्राणसमां मनोज्ञा-
मालिङ्ग्य दोर्भ्यां नवनीतमृद्वीम् ।

कथाः प्रकुर्वन् रमणीयरूपा-

स्तृप्तो भविष्याम्यधरामृतेन ।। VIII.71

यदा प्रभृत्येव मया व्यलोकि

सा चारुसर्वावयवोन्मदन्ती ।

मनस्तदारभ्य न शान्तिमेति

निवर्तते मे हृदयान्न सा च ।। VIII.73

By its very nature, the *Bodhisattvacaritam* is not amenable to the depiction of Vīrarasa that is otherwise prescribed by the poeticians as one of the dominant sentiments of a Mahākāvya. The whole poem is permeated with values and ideals that run counter to the armed bouts which form the corner-stone of Vīra-rasa. The Bodhisattva is once said to have taken up arms to meet the suspected depredations of the deceitful demon, but it turns out to be an exercise in futility, as the attack never came about :

रात्रौ च सत्रा कतिभिर्मनुष्यैर्दैत्योपघातार्थमुपात्तशस्त्रः ।

युग्यान् निबध्य स्वजनौघमध्ये यामत्रयं जागरितोऽवतस्थे ।। I. 97

However, it is the exalted form of heroism, the chivalrous piety (*dharmavīratā*), that abounds in the poem. The *Bodhisattvacaritam* rather opens up new avenues for the aggressive heroism to flow along placid pastures. Śīlavān meets the forays and the subsequent full-fledged attack of the ruler of Kosala not with force but with the unfailing weapon of renunciation that brings him down to his knee, his earlier vaunts and atrocities notwithstanding :

भूयः पुलकितो भूत्वा शीलवन्तं जगाद सः ।

नाहं वेद महत्त्वं ते भवानतिमहान् मतः ।। I.92

नातः परतरं श्रीमन् त्वामभिद्रोहितास्म्यहम् ।

प्रत्यहं भावयिष्यामि गुणानेव तवाद्भुतान् ।।

श्रीमान् धीमान् मया ज्ञातो वस्तुतः शीलवान् भवान् ।

अहं नराधमो नूनं मन्ये त्वां पुरुषोत्तमम् ।। I.95 96

The virtuous heroism reaches its zenith in the conduct of the farmer Bodhisattva. His pious chivalry had equipped him to the extent that he could throw gauntlet to death itself. He took the death of his young son with equanimity as if nothing disturbing had happened to him. This composure in the face of the worst disaster earned him applause even from the Lord of heavens. His *dharmavīratā* thus put death also to shame :

तत्र स्थिताः समुदिताः सकलाः स्वमिष्टं
दृष्ट्वा विनष्टमपि तेऽन्वभवन् न कष्टम् ।
नाक्रन्दिषुर्न रुरुदुर्न च मृत्युभीताः
संजज्ञिरे विधिवदात्मनि सम्प्रतीताः ।। XII.34

पुत्रो मृतस्तरुतले निहितस्तदासीद्
यत्र द्विजः समुपविश्य स भोज्यमाशीत् ।
सर्वैस्ततः समुदितैर्मुदितैश्च तस्य
काष्ठान्युपाधिषत तत्र तनौ मृतस्य ।। XII.36

Elsewhere also the pious deeds of the Bodhisattva touch the high water-mark of resignation and result in the sublimation of human values. All the stories of his deeds have been developed to the highest possibilities and they reflect his chivalrous piety with a vengeance. Saṁgha overcomes ingratitude with gratitude (XIII), selfishness combined with lack of vision submits to the Bodhisattva's catholicity (I), superior virtues of the Kāśirāja steal thunder over fragmented excellences (II), fraternal affection the Bodhisattva rewards with unexpected bonanza (V), sensual cravings for other's wife are sublimated into detachment (VIII) and name gets a back seat in comparison with the purity of action (XIV) . All these episodes serve to establish the Bodhisattva as a *dharmavīra, par excellence.*

CHARACTERISATION :

The *avadānas* of the Bodhisattva as they are described in the poem, with tenuous nexus with each other, have evidently narrowed down the possibilities of effective characterisation. For most of the characters who form the 'dramatis personae' in the play as it unfolds itself on the canvas of the *Bodhisattvacaritam*, we do not have more than skeletal sketches. They hardly come out of their shell, peeping out at best and concealing themselves at worst. But once it is remembered that the leading characters of the stories are but different facets of the same phenomenon (the Bodhisattva), they cease to be fragmented or enigmatic. The author has evolved a novel method of projecting the character of the Bodhisattva. He has sought to depict him by working up constrast from the ordinary characters of the stories. He places the Bodhisattva beside the humble fold and by a few masterly strokes, intelligently aimed at his vital aspects, he elevates him far above the ordinary rut. This process results into lively description of two contrasting attitudes–sublime on the one hand, banal on the other. This study in the conflicting behaviour of two sets of characters invests his characterisation with charm and force.

Of the male characters, the humble but devoted farmer (XII) emerges as the stoutest figure. His is undoubtedly the most attractive and sublime character in the poem. He was the Bodhisattva born as a Brāhmaṇa. His greatness had been obvious from the very start. His birth was attended by widespread prosperity (XII.3). He was endowed with charming complexion besides virtues like truthfulness, compassion, tolerance and civility. Soon he mastered various lores. As a Brāhmaṇa he was versed in various *śāstras*, but he opted for cultivation even though he was unmindful of the bodily sustenance (*kṛṣiparaḥ sa śarīrayātrām*, XII.5). As he bloomed into youth, he flowered in stature. Even before his latent supernatural qualities demonstrated themselves with exuberance, he was in search of heavenly pastures. While instructing his family in what forms the *summum bonum* of life, he enjoins upon his kinsmen to observe good conduct, desist from sinfulness, resist the onslaughts of carnal enjoyments taking the worldly objects to be sorrowful in the end, because life itself is short-lived and death is always on the prowl (*dhyeyaṁ samastajagataḥ kṣaṇabhaṅguratvam,* XII.13). Quietism and chivalrous piety *par excellence!*

The best in him, however, is brought out by the untimely death of his young son. As a man of God, the Bodhisattva (farmer) takes it in his stride with unprecedented equipoise. He not only does not disturb his schedule in the field (*kartuṁ kṛṣiṁ pravavṛte sa punar halena*, XII.22), with divine composure he takes his meals besides the dead body of his son. Convinced of the instability and untenability of human life neither he nor the members of his family wept or wailed for him (*nākrandiṣur na rurudur na ca mṛtyubhītāḥ*, XII.34). And with dry eyes they consigned him to the flames (*naivāśrubindur api kasyacana*, XII.37). Even Indra could not help acclaim their fortitude. Their arguments in favour of keeping poise even against calamities like death filled the lord of heaven with wonder (*dhanya bhavanti bhuvaneṣu bhavādṛśā ye*, XII.84). In fact, the farmer had discovered the true essence of life. He was therefore unperturbed, free from shock, sorrow and grief (*tattvavid avāsthita nirvikāraḥ* XII.21). It is unwise to mourn the loss of what, afterall, is perishable (*kuryāṁ tadartham aham atra kathaṁ nu cintām,* XII.50).

No less attractive is Saṁgha. His character is marked by acute mental conflict and is contrasted from that of his friend Piliya, who is ingratitude incarnate. Saṁgha represents the highest ideals of friendship. He not only relieves the misery of his friend Piliya when he was struck by poverty, but restores to him his earlier affluence and dignity by equally sharing with him the fabulous eighty crores besides the vast paraphernalia of assets (*svam itarad api sarvaṁ sāmyadāyy unnatena,* XIII.22). Though subsequently driven to indigence, he is singularly free from avarice. He touches the highest watermark when despite the royal order in his favour, he refuses to accept anything more than what was his share in Pīliya's property (*nṛpa laghum api rāyaṁ kāmaye nānyadīyam, yad aham alam adāṁ tad dāpaya tvaṁ madīyam*, XIII.95). It is his firm belief that greed invariably leads to destruction. *Mā gṛdhaḥ* is the basis of his philosophy of life (*phalati bahulalobhāt sarvatheha praṇāśaḥ, manasi mama sadāste 'mā gṛdhaḥ' vākprakāśaḥ* , XIII.96).

Contrarily, Pīliya represents the nadir in human relationship. He is a wretched being who meets generosity with ungratefulness. Though his friend Saṁgha had treated him with kindness and had gone out of the way to release him from the impasse, he, in turn not only cold-shouldered him but also heaped abundant slights on him. And to compound the humiliation, he had the audacity to offer him a gourd of chaff. This was something that he should have declined outright. However, the goodness in Saṁgha throws him into terrible conflict. Saṁgha certainly rises in stature by contrast. It is not the author's wont to catalogue the details of the contrast. With a few controlled daubs, he has painted, in black and white, the picture that reflects the two friends respectively. In his anxiety to preserve the values of friendship he suffers the gourdful of chaff and thereby highlights the difference between greatness and meanness, and friendship and selfishness :

यदि बुसमहमेतन्नाददीयैतदीयं
झटिति विघटयेयं मैत्र्यमत्र स्वकीयम् ।
अत उचितमिदं मे, स्वीकरोम्यस्य वस्तु
यदपि लघु, तथाप्यव्याहतं सख्यमस्तु ।। XIII.48

विरहयतु मुधाऽयं बुद्धिहीनः सुहृत्त्वं
न कथमनुभवेयं साध्वहं तन्महत्त्वम् ।
प्रकटयतु च कामं वित्तमत्तो लघुत्वं
कथमहमभिरामं संत्यजेयं गुरुत्वम् ।। XIII.49

The ruler of Kāśi, Śīlavān, though apparently meek and docile, presents an excellent study in contrast. He meets violence with non-violence, avarice with munificence and *asuravijaya* with *dharmavijaya.* And the attitude yields instant dividends. The Kosalarāja who came to win remained to surrender – (*adyaprabhṛti he rājan bhavadrājyasya sevakaḥ*, IV.108).

The mental conflict that the characters in the poem undergo only spurs the development of characterisation in the *Bodhisattvacaritam*. This conflict is found in its extreme intensity in Kumāra, the ruler of Ariṣṭapura. He entertains improper love for his minister's wife. The very sight of Unmadantī maddens him to the extent that he loses his poise, but when confronted with the arguments of the general, he undergoes catharsis. His attachment to Unmadantī is replaced by detachment from her and he suffers volumes of shame at his unworthy behaviour (*bhṛśaṁ vivicyoccākulaṁ svakīyam, na jātu kāmasya vaśaṁ gataḥ syām*, IX.45). The conflict of Pāpaka also does not leave us cold. His endeavours to find out for himself a more meaningful name only turn out to convince him of the greatness of action. (*satkarmaṇā siddhim upaiti nūnam, na nāmadheyena*, XIV.43).

Thus in contrast to the classical Mahākāvyas, the characterisation in the *Bodhisattvacaritam* is brief, almost skeletal, but does not thereby lose either lustre or effect. Rather the mental conflict of its characters distinguishes the *Bodhisattvacaritam* from the bulk of the stereotyped poems.

DESCRIPTIONS :

The *Bodhisattvacaritam* is not beset with the type of digressive descriptions that the poeticians have prescribed as an essential ingredient of a Mahākāvya (*SD*, III.322-324). The author is not enamoured of the conventional descriptions of sun-set, moon-rise, watersports, sexual orgy, etc.,which, their poetic worth notwithstanding, invariably hinder the flow of them and thereby transport the reader to the non-essentials. However, alert to the well-entrenched Mahākāvya-tradition, he has occasionally broken, in the body of his poem, into such descriptions as neither spill wide nor seem to have been deliberately flung in the midst of the narrative. His descriptions are invariably brief and are interwoven in the texture of the poem with such finesse that they form pretty patterns that, often, lend it added charm. The *Bodhisattvacaritam* betrays a wide spectrum of descriptions. The reader is simply thrilled to see on the scroll of the poem, brilliant sketches alternating in quick succession. With incisive insight coupled with matchless competence to muster accordant phraseology, the author has the expertise to enliven the object under description in its entirety. And it is merely a statement of fact that these brief sketches are more impressive and in tune with modern taste than the exhaustive descriptions that abound in the ancient Mahakāvyas. The range of the author's descriptions is amazing. From the traditional beauties of nature and physical charms, it covers in its sweep the rigours of the desert, the bravery and skill of the armed troops, and some of the finest and meanest emotions of human heart.

The mighty desert that the young trader Śantabuddhi had to negotiate in his itinerary could have provoked any other poet into describing its endless ruggedness and nerve-wracking inhospitality with extravagant imagery. But true to his style, the author has eschewed extravagance both in size and imagery. Instead, he has highlighted its ferocity in just two Svabhāvoktis with such precision that the awesome terrain with searing and blinding storms comes to life with its grotesqueness :

मरुस्थली धूलिपरिप्लुताशा-
ऽऽकाशास्त विष्वङ्मुषितप्रकाशा ।
हा ! शान्तबुद्धेरपि तत्र नाशा-
त्लब्धावकाशास्तु कथं सुखाशा ॥

ऊष्मायमाणो बहुतीव्रवेगात्
पृष्ठात् पुरस्ताच्च मरुत् तदैर्त ।
तथापि याति स्म वणिग् रथेष्ठा
भृत्यैः समेतो बहुभिः स्वकीयैः ॥ I. 45- 46

As remarked earlier, lengthy descriptions that create hurdles in the smooth flow of the theme are conspicuous by their absence in the *Bodhisattvacaritam*. The descriptions that we have in the poem are, despite their brevity, effective and powerful. As a counter-weight to the arid desert, may be reproduced the tiny sketch of the hilly tract, conjured up by the fraudulent demon. Covered with lush green frost groove, it was drenched in torrential rains. The hill was dotted with caves full of water and lotus-ponds that heightened the beauty of the entire region. With emphasis on the specifics, the poet has succeeded in drawing an integrated picture of the hilly tract, which though pithy, is shorn of neither effect nor beauty :

एषा विलोक्या हरिता वनाली
तद्भूविभागो ऽस्त्यतिवृष्टिशाली ।
गुहा गिरीणां सलिलस्य पूर्णा
विभान्ति पद्मानि विकासभाञ्जि ॥ I. 51

The depiction of nature (*prakṛti-citraṇa*) is not confined to these flashes alone. The Hemanvati river, as detailed in Canto Ten, also bears testimony to the author's equipment in capturing the beauties of nature, in measured terms. Such is the keenness of the poet's observation and so powerful is his language that the

Hemanvatī, even if it is imaginary, emerges with its lovely surroundings in full glory:

पवित्राम्भःपूर्णा सफलदलपुष्पैः परिवृता
द्रुमैः स्निग्धच्छायैर्वततिततिभिश्चाप्युपचिता ।
तटप्रान्तैर्हृद्या विहगमधुरध्वानमुखरै-
स्तरङ्गैरुत्तुङ्गैररमयदमुं सा सरिदपि ।।
सदा पेयं यस्याः कमठमकराद्यैर्विलुलितं
समन्तात् पूर्णाया अपि जलमुरोदघ्नमभवत् ।
तटे स्वच्छे रेजुः श्रितरजतभासश्च सिकताः
तथा शुभ्रा कारण्डवततिरभूत् क्रीडनपरा ।।
दधाना हेमाभां परमरमणीयां च सुषमां
सरित् सा हेमन्वत्युचितमभिधानं श्रितवती ।
स्थितस्तस्याः पार्श्वे गिरिरतिगुरुर्गन्धमदनो
लतागुल्मै रम्यः सुरभितदिगन्तश्च शुशुभे ।। X. 12-14

The description also serves to testify to the fact that the movable scenes fascinate the author more than their immovable counterparts. Even while detailing the movable panorama, he seems to have special liking for the expanses of the landscape. The delineation of Hemanvatī has precisely been instrumental in spotlighting the vast landscape in its totality.[14]

The following stanza highlights the vastness of the landscape in a slightly different form. Despite the paucity of details, it leaves deep impact on the reader :

पुरस्ताद् दृश्या ते तरुपरिवृतेयं गिरिणदी
स्थिता मध्येशैलद्रुममविरलाम्भोरयवती ।
तटिन्यामेतस्यामनुभवितुमानन्दमधिकं
कदाचिन्मद्भर्ता किल दयितयायात् सह मया ।, X. 27

14. Dharmendra Kumar Gupta : *Bodhisattvacarita : Eka Ālocanātmaka Adhyayana*, op. cit., p.xxii.

An altogether distinct portrayal is found in the description of Ariṣṭapura which was colourfully decorated on the occasion of Kaumudīmahotsava. The town, specially spruced up for the festival, with its streets sprinkled with scented water and its orchards trimmed to beauty, claimed more than casual attention :

प्रमार्जिता पल्लवपुष्पवाटी परिष्कृता गन्धजलावसिक्ता ।
प्रशस्तवस्तूपहिता समस्ता सुशोभिता भूमिरभून्नगर्याः ।। VIII. 32

As a part of the occasion was the description of the festival proper. With the full moon smiling from the heaven above and the infinite strings of lamps imparting the town an aura of fairy-land, the Kaumudīmahotsava was more than a festivity :

अस्तंगते भास्वति, चन्द्रबिम्बे
पूर्णे निशायामुदिते च पुर्याः ।
समन्ततो दीपकदीपितायाः
शोभां शुभां प्रेक्षितुमैन्महीपः ।। X. 39

The palatial house of the commander, Ahipāraka is very much germane to the festival. As a matter of fact, under the garb of the festival, it was to form the cynosure of the king. It is, however, a different matter if it served to inflame his passions, beyond measure. Its pleasing appearance, heaven-kissing *aṭṭālikās* and mighty rampart captivated every heart :

सेनापतेस्तस्य विशेषरम्यः
प्रासाद आसीत् स मनःप्रसाद : ।
अभ्रंलिहाट्टालकदर्शनीयो
मनःशिलाचारुविशालवप्रः ।। III. 41

Troops of Śīlavān, the king of Kāśī, have also claimed the author's attention. His keen perception has enabled him to project them as warriors *par excellence.* In the body of mere four verses, their valour and agility in the battefield, devotion to their master and their steadfastness have been depicted with commendable clarity and precison :

काश्यधीशस्य सेनान्यो वाहिन्याममितौजसः ।
आसन्नासन्नसाहस्रा योद्धारः समराङ्गणे ।।

संमुखापतदुद्दाममत्तवारणवारणाः ।
स्वराष्ट्रस्वामिरक्षार्थं विहितप्राणधारणाः ।।

अपृष्ठदर्शिनो वीरा वज्रपातेऽप्यनाकुलाः ।
क्षेपीयांसो महाप्राणा मनोवाक्कायनिस्तुलाः ।।

विद्युदुद्द्योतवद् दीप्ताः स्वाम्यादेशवशंवदाः ।
जम्बूद्वीपजये शक्ताः शूराः सर्वेऽप्यकद्वदाः ।। III. 68-71

Besides the rather gross descriptions, though drawn with sensitivity worthy of a gifted poet, the author has depicted some of the tenderest emotions on the canvas of his poem. The anguish of the lovelorn Kumāra has already been underlined (VIII.44-48). So have been highlighted the pangs that the young monk suffered at the first onslaught of love (VI.4-8). The admission of his love for the young maiden of Śrāvastī and his yearning for her vicinity have been depicted in swiftly flowing verses that effectively bring out his agony and helplessness in the situation. Every line here exudes the monk's pangs that have done havoc to him :

मया ऽभिदृष्टा रमणी प्रकृष्टा
विशिष्टलावण्यवती प्रहृष्टा ।
अविप्रकृष्टेऽत्र पुरे निविष्टा
सैवास्त्यभीष्टा हृदि मे प्रविष्टा ।। VI. 12

शिरोमणिं तां पुरसुन्दरीणां
चिराय रामां स्वमनोऽभिरामाम् ।
गाढं परिष्वज्य रमेय भूय-
स्तदङ्गसंस्पर्शसुखं लभेय ।।

इतीयमिच्छाद्य वरीवृतीति
दुःखासिकां चेतसि तन्तनीति ।
अतो विवर्णं वदनं ममेदं
यूनोऽपि दूना च कृशाङ्गयष्टिः ।। VI. 14-15

निरस्तधैर्योऽहमुदीर्णरागः
स्मरामि तामेव पुरः स्फुरन्तीम् ।
कामी स्वतां पश्यति सत्यमुक्तं
कामातुराणां न भयं न लज्जा ।। VI. 17

The *Bodhisattvacaritam* is one of the few poems that make bold departure in grappling with subjects that were deemed taboo in the aristocratic milieu of the classical Mahākāvyas. It is here that one comes to grips with such social problems as poverty and ingratitude that in the poem, are curiously interlinked. A set of circumstances conspires to rob the wealthy Pīliya, the resident of Vārāṇasī of his affluence. He is reduced to a financial wreck. With humane susceptibilities the poet has captured Pīliya's tormenting miseries in two Mālinī stanzas :

अथ गतवति काले दैवयोगात् कदाचिद्
विपदमुपगतोऽभूत् पीलियोऽसौ कुतश्चित् ।
प्रियमनशदशेषं तस्य सम्पत्तिजातं
मुखकमलमपि द्राङ् म्लानतां सम्प्रयातम् ।।
रजनिरजनि कष्टा द्रव्यनाशादनिष्टा
दिवसमसुखमिष्टा सा प्रतिष्ठापि नष्टा ।
हतविधिघटितत्वात् संकुचद्भागधेयः
प्रविततमथ तापं प्राप वाराणसेयः ।। XIII. 7-8

In describing Saṁgha's indigence, on the other hand, he has been more rigorous. With brief but extremely appropriate vocables, he has drawn a vivid picture of Saṁgha's poverty. Arthāntaranyāsa thickens the misery further :

विपुलविभवराशेराशु नाशाद् दरिद्रः
समजनि स तदानीं चिन्तया वीतनिद्रः ।
न च परमुपकर्तुं वित्तहीनः शशाक
बलवति सति दैवे पूरुषः को वराकः ।। XIII. 27

The cadence of charming poetry does not in any way attenuate the hardships of the two friends. It rather serves to multiply its poignancy.

As a man of culture, Saṁgha represents the pinnacle of friendship. He was beside himself with joy in greeting his friend with the warmest courtesies. The way he welcomed Pīliya and went the whole hog to restore him to his earlier glory speaks volumes for his kind generosity. The poet has focussed on the godliness of his character with gusto :

स्वसुहृदमवलोक्य श्रेष्ठिनं तं सदारं
सदकृत बहु सङ्गोऽप्येतमारादुदारम् ।
पुलकिततनुरुच्चैः सम्परिष्वज्य कण्ठे
प्रमुदितमनसोपावीविशच्चोपकण्ठे ।। XII.14

किमिति च भवतेदं गेहमभ्यागतेन
मृदुपदकमलाभ्यां भूषितं सम्मतेन ।। XIII.16

वचनमिदमुदीर्य प्रीतिमान् सत्यसन्धः
कृतसुहृदनुकम्पः स्फीतसौहार्दबन्धः ।
स्वयमनुपधि चत्वारिंशतं वित्तकोटी-
र्व्यतरदयममुष्मै सद्य आपन्निमित्तिम् ।। XIII. 21

The Antyānuprāsa marked by lovable *padalālitya* goes far in raising the stature of Saṁgha.

Perhaps the most touching description is reserved for the worst of all the emotions–ingratitude. Pīliya, who had been earlier elevated by Saṁgha from the abysmal poverty to the apex of affluence and dignity had the audacity to rain slights on him, when he approached him for help in trying circumstances. Contrary to the courtesies, verging on deference, that he had received from Saṁgha, Pīliya subjected him to a series of curtness, insults and worse. Even in the tender Mālinī metre, the poet has come down heavily on Pīliya for not only what he had done to his friend but for what he symbolised as the worst specimen of human being :

परमिदमतिचित्रं वीक्ष्य लब्धोपकारः
किमपि न सुहृदस्य स्वागतं व्याजहार ।

न च समुदमुदस्थान्नैव वाऽभ्युज्जगाम

गलितविभवमेनं प्राप्तमप्यात्मधाम ।। XIII.34

तदभिहितमवेक्ष्य त्यक्तसन्मित्रकार्यः

कुटिलमतिरवादीत् पीलियोऽसावनार्यः ।

पदमितरदुपेहि, त्वत्कृते स्थानमत्र

न भवति मम गेहे श्रूयतामङ्ग मित्र ।। XIII.38

अपि शृणु निकटस्थं तत् पुरो वेश्म गत्वा

लघु महदपि किञ्चिद् देयमेवेति मत्वा ।

प्रवितर बुसमस्मै सम्यगालोक्य तुम्बी-

परिमितमिह दूरादागतोऽयं कुटुम्बी ।। XIII.40

स्वयमयमुपलभ्याशीतिकोट्यर्धमर्थं

त्यजति निजसहायं सङ्गमद्यासमर्थम् ।

कथमिव स कृतघ्नस्तस्करः स्यात् प्रशस्यः

क्व च भवतु कदर्यस्तादृशो वा यशस्यः ।। XIII.44

However, when administered rebuff by the king, Pīliya broke down like a neo-criminal. He was stung with shame and repentance. Vivacity deserted him. He was a picture of grief and muteness. With mild but telling touches the poet has drawn a lively profile of the ungrateful creature :

इति तु वचनमाकर्ण्योत्तरं न प्रपेदे

मलिनमजनि वक्त्रं चेतसा न प्रसेदे ।

अनवहितपरार्थाः स्वार्थमेवाश्रयन्तः

कथमिह न सुशोका लज्जिताः सन्त्वसन्तः ।। XIII.86

हृदयनिहितशोकान् मन्दधीः पीतिमानं

परमभजत तत्र स्वार्थिकश्चापमानम् ।। XIII.88

The poet is equally at home in describing the physical charms of his characters. Originating in Kālidāsa (*Kumāra*, I.31-49), the depiction of human beauties had established itself, down the ages, as a poetic convention that the writers of the Mahākāvyas exploited with gusto. The convention degenerated to the level that the poets took to delineating the beauties of the human form with meticulous details, from top to toe, in the true *nakhaśikha* style. In consonance with his balanced approach to the form of poetry, our poet does not relish these prolixities which, not infrequently, are marked by tautology at worst and sparse poetic flashes at best. He has sought to depict the inviting charms of the female person without taking recourse to complicated sketches or gaudy colours. It is in this style that he has drawn beauties of Unmadantī and the lass of Śrāvastī who had cast their spell on the king and the monk, respectively. Their beauties have already been detailed as Vibhāvas of Śṛṅgāra or as part of the Vipralambha (VII.9-10, 12-15; VIII. 44-45; VI.4-7). However, some of the verses, setting forth, Unmadantī's irresistible charms brook repetition. The following portrayal of her ravishing beauty, though attempted in a simple style without extravagant poetic flourishes, enthralls the heart down to its moorings, and serves well the purpose for which it is intended. Unmadantī was the very angel on the earth. The two verses, combined together, project her as a beauty *par excellence,* captivating everyone with her amours and putting to shame the totality of womenfolk including the matchless Rati :

तदोन्मदन्ती कलिकाग्रदन्ती रतिं हसन्ती हृदयं हरन्ती ।
सर्वाञ्जनान् कामवशं नयन्ती देवाङ्गनेवास्त विमोहयन्ती ।। VII.13

रूपप्रकर्षेण समुज्ज्वलन्तीं सुवासिनीं चारुविलासिनीं ताम् ।
अलोकसामान्यगुणाभिरामां क्षणं निरीक्ष्यैव समे व्यमुह्यन् ।। VII. 21

The verses reproduced below betray a different approach to the detailing of her charms. Here she is not the simple adolescent girl, unconcerned to the worth of her blossoming youth, but a seasoned *nāyikā* (*prauḍhā*), who though the legally married wife of Ahipāraka, wins the king into submission. He who had repudiated her on misinformation, now pines for her proximity :

कपोतपादारुणवस्त्रभासा प्रकाशिताशा विकसद्विलासा ।
चन्द्रोदये चन्द्रमुखीं विलोक्य चन्द्रावहो विस्मयमभ्युपेतः ।।

अनङ्गरङ्गस्थलमन्तरङ्गं तरङ्गयन्ती कुटिलैः कटाक्षैः ।
असौ विशालायतपक्ष्मलाक्षी मनोऽहरन्मे वनकिन्नरीव ।।

मणिप्रभोद्भासितकुण्डलश्रीर्हैमद्युतिर्विद्युदिवोल्लसन्ती ।
मुग्धा विदग्धोचितलीलया मां व्यलोकयत् सा चकिता मृगीव ।। VIII. 65-67

By bringing into play the figures of speech like alliteration and simile, embedded with sweet phraseology distinguished by attractive *padalālitya*, the author has depiced a very lovely picture of the flowering beauty of the merchant's daughter.

The king of Kāśī represents the other pole to his sweetheart. With a masterly stroke of the author's pen, the hefty lover disfigured with pot belly and protruding teeth deservedly claims derision (*yas tundilaḥ sthūlatanur gariṣṭho rathasthito 'dṛśyata danturaś ca,* VIII.79).

CONVERSATIONS :

Besides these lively descriptions that afford an insight into the poet's deep understanding of human behaviour and the emotions that criss-cross him under conflicting and differing situations, the *Bodhisattvacaritam* vouches for his skill in conducting the narrative in a conversational style that invests his poem with dramatic effect. Taking cue from the young ascetic's confabulations with Umā in the fifth canto of the *Kumārasambhava*, the subsequent generations of poets have sought to exploit the device with uneven results.[15] In the *Bodhisattvacaritam* the dialogue is conducted not between the hero and the heroine, in overt or covert form, but between other characters of the poem. It not only serves to enliven the poem but with its dramatic touches leaves deep imprint on the reader also. Occasionally these dialogues bring into relief the mental conflict that rages in different sets of characters.

The parleys that the Bodhisattva (merchant) carries on with his caravan in the First Canto, forms the first illustration of the device. In a lovely homely way, he convinces his bands of the deceit, that the demon had conspired to play upon them (*pratārakaḥ ko 'pi tu daitya āsīt*, I.92).

The encounter between the charioteers of the rulers of Kāśī and Kosala, in Canto II, is also, conducted in the form of dialogue. The device not only invests the rather prosaic comparison of virtues of the two rulers with dramatic overtones, it forcefully drives home the lasting truth that what is complete is esteemed more than what is not so complete . More than anything else, it applies to ethical values (II.32-35, 39-60).

It is, however, in the Canto IX that the device unfolds its utmost possibilities. The conversation, strengthened with stout arguments and counter arguments,

---

15. *Jaina Kumārasambhava,* VIII.9-67

between the king of Ariṣṭapura and his general, with one pining for the general's wife and the latter determined to gift her out to his master, is touching to the extreme. The dialogue is distinguished by such buoyancy, effectiveness and unimpeded flow that it may well form part of a worthy play. More than the imbecility of Ahipāraka, it brings into focus the sublimity of the king's character, who triumphantly tides over the storm that threatened to impair him beyond redemption. It is not the ferocity of his unmitigated yearnings for Unmadantī but the lull that follows them, that is engagingly attractive. The conflict catapults the king to unprecedented greatness.

A similar conflict of sorts grips Pāpaka in the Fourteenth Canto. However, it does not take long to resolve itself. The greatness of action in preference to all else is established beyond question.

LANGUAGE :

The greatest asset of the *Bodhisattvacaritam* is its language which is distinguished by exceptional sweetness and chastity. Seldom does one come across such phraseology, pregnant with infinite possibilities of Sanskrit speech. Though it is as old as Pāṇini and as pure as his precepts would like it to be, it is a dynamic medium for a plethora of situations, ideas and emotions. And never does it fall short of the diversity and complexity that they symbolise with their subtle nuances. The language of the *Bodhisattvacaritam* is adorned with a variety of *alaṁkāras* and is addedly marked by pleasingly smooth evenness. There is hardly anything rugged about it. It is invariably competent to give lovely expression to all sorts of ideas. The loveliness of its expression emanates from the rhythmic effect of phraseology. The cadence has been fostered with cautious effort. In a limited sense it may be taken to exemplify the author's predilection for the *citra-kāvya* which in essentials it is not. The poet is always alive to the sound effect of his language. He has so moulded his verses or parts thereof that they enchant the reader with their musical flow and sweetness. The grace that his language imparts to the varied contours of his descriptions has been duly noticed earlier.The pen-picture of the forms that the deceitful demon and his hordes assume to dupe the uncanny Śānta-buddhi, vibrates with liveliness, thanks to the refined and lovely phraseology :

विचिन्त्य दैत्याधिपतिर्यथोक्तं मायाविधाने बहुशः पटीयान् ।
श्वेतान् महोक्षान् रमणीययानेष्वायोजयामास तदा स्वकीयान् ॥

तूणीरचर्मेष्वसनासिरूपाण्यादत्त चत्वारि स आयुधानि ।
मिथ्याजलक्लेदितकेशचैलो ललास नीलोत्पलमालभारी ॥

तद्भृत्यवर्गोऽपि तथार्द्रवासाः क्लिन्नालकः शुक्लसरोजमाली ।
पङ्कोदबिन्दून् विसृजन्नुपायात् मृणालमूलं रसयन्नुपायात् ।।

सकैतवप्रेष्यगणः समेतं जलाशयापन्नमिवोन्नगात्रम् ।
विलोक्य दैत्याधिपतिं तदानीं न्यमज्जदाश्चर्यमहोदधौ सः ।। I. 40-44

Though the focus on alliteration– it has been whipped up to yield unbounded results– will be turned later it should suffice to observe here that it forms the bedrock of both the loveliness and liveliness that the language of the *Bodhisattvacaritam* emits profusely. The judicious use of Anuprāsa has enabled the poet to spin out the spectacularly winsome phraseology that, in turn, ushers in extreme lucidity in the poem. It is to the credit of the author that his cautiously chiselled and polished phraseology has nowhere impaired the naturalness and sweetness of the language, nor has it retarded its smooth, graceful movement. It would be rather an extravagant claim to make that the language in the *Bodhisattvacaritam* measures well up to the complicated situation. However, there is no gain-saying the truth that it rises to the variety of the functions it is called upon to discharge. Rather, it performs them with beauty and effect. But these varied situations have not been instrumental in disturbing the evenness of the rhythm. And this accounts for the naturalness of flow which is doubtless the hallmark of the author's phraseology. The lucidity of the language combined with rhythmic sweetness and elegant flow has resulted in the emergence of the phenomenon which, in the poetician's jargon, is happily called *padalālitya*. It can be confidently asserted that the *padalālitya* in the *Bodhisattvacaritam* compares favourably with that of the ancient masters like Daṇḍin and Śrīharṣa. Some of the telling illustrations of the phenomenon may be reproduced here to acquaint the reader with the amazing possibilities the Sanskrit language is capable of :

1. मरुस्थली धूलिपरिप्लुताशाकाशाऽऽस्त विष्वङ्मुषितप्रकाशा । I.45
2. सन्तु मन्नृपगुणास्तवागुणाः
   कीदृशास्तु भवदीशितुर्गुणाः ।। II.55
3. रमणी रमणीयाङ्गी रममाणा चिरं मुदा ।
   सम्पन्नापन्नसत्त्वा सा ब्रह्मदत्तेन भूभृता ।। III.4
4. सपद्येव त्वयामात्य ! पद्यान्याद्य प्रपद्यताम् । III.31
5. अस्त्यद्य मद्यमाद्यं ते क्षुद्रं क्षौद्रमिवानतम् ।। III.39

6. अथ बुद्धौ विरुद्धायां युद्धमद्धा विधीयताम् ॥ III.88

7. इति स्पष्टमाख्येयमार्ये ! निवार्ये
विचार्ये च कार्ये भवेन्नैव दोषः ॥ V.12

8. न सास्ति शान्तिर्मुदिता न कान्तिः ॥ VI.10

9. तस्मादकस्मादुदितादमुष्मात्
पापात्समस्ताद् विरमाशु भिक्षो ॥ VI.32

10. इभ्यस्य सभ्यस्य मतस्य तस्य ॥ VII.9

11. नाहं विमूढा न च दुर्दुरूढा । VII.32

12. क्षणे क्षणेऽयं क्षण ईक्षणीयः । VIII.61

13. मया निरुद्धाऽपि कथं विरुद्धा
जाताऽभिजाताऽपि मुधा वियाता । VIII.83

14. मल्लीमतल्लीमिव कामवल्लीम् । IX.27

15. रुचिरा रुचिरारचिता न चिरात् । IX.56

16. क्षणो न स्याद् यस्यां क्षणमपि तया किं क्षणदया । X.38

17. वयोवृद्धैः सिद्धैर्निगमपरिशुद्धैरविकलम् ।
तथादिष्टं दिष्टं सुखमयमभीष्टं च सकलम् ॥ XI.2

18. स्त्रीतल्लजाया निजवल्लभायाः श्रीमल्लिकायाः प्रणयी बभूव ॥ XI.22

19. स्फुरदुपकृतिरिभ्यस्तादृशः क्वेह लभ्यः । XIII.24

20. व्यथितमृदुलचित्ता रोदितुं सा प्रवृत्ता । XIII.52

21. स धनिकमनिकेतं सर्वथाऽर्थादपेतं
परनगरमुपेतं वीक्ष्य भार्यासमेतम् । XIII.72

22. सन्दीप्तः शुशुभे शुभंयुरभितः श्रेयोंऽशुभिः प्रांशुभिः । XIV.2

23. नामान्विच्छ महेच्छ वाञ्छितम् । XIV.10.

The poet has unmistakably expressed himself in favour of the language, adorned with graceful poetic qualities and figures of speech. (*śubhaguṇālaṁkāra-yuktaḥ sadā,* XIV.35). Although it does not need much of ingenuity to trace out from the poem the poetic virtues prescribed by the poeticians, their number notwithstanding, the *śubhaguṇa* espoused by the author is undoubtedly *prasāda*, the clarity of style. Perspecuity, as observed earlier, proceeds from well-laid phraseology. In the *Bodhisattvacaritam* it has resulted from the sweet medium that invariably shuns complex or inverted construction. Recondite grammatical forms apart, there is hardly any passage in the poem which may be rated as abstruse. Clarity of expression, its sweetness and limpid flow combine together to raise the poem to an enviable stature. *Prasāda* in the poem performs in full measure the function that the poeticians expect for it . The excerpts quoted earlier in various contexts betray amply, the felicity of expression abounding in transparent simplicity. A few more may be added to highlight this aspect of the poem, rather prominently. The following couplet goes the whole hog to project the superhuman character of the Kāśirāja :

शान्तिपूर्वकमयं प्रयस्यति क्रोधमेष सुतरां निरस्यति ।
साधुवद् व्यवहरन्नसाधुनाप्युद्धतं प्रति सदैव शाम्यति ।। II.58

How effectively the simple alliterative phraseology characterised by *prasāda* drives home the lady's love for her brother in preference to her husband and son, is beautifully summed up in the verse that follows :

न वाञ्छाम्यहं कान्तमेकान्तकान्तं
न वा पुत्रमिच्छामि मत्स्नेहपात्रम् ।
प्रियं भ्रातरं सोदरं प्राप्य राजन्
सुखं प्राप्नुयां भ्रातृमत्येव भूयः ।। V.18

The whole of Canto Nine, concerned with logical wrangling of sorts, is brimming with limpid expression. The first major argument which the king musters to counter his general's plea brings home a lasting truth in terms that serve to raise its appeal to dizzy heights :

पापं प्रकुर्वन् मनुते मनुष्यो
मद्दुष्कृतं वेद न कश्चिदन्यः ।

किन्तु स्थिता देवगणास्तदीयं

जानन्ति सर्वं ह्यशुभं शुभं वा ।। IX.5

The thrust of his arguments leads Kumāra to enunciate the ideals of a king and commoner in happy phrases :

प्रशस्यते धर्मरुचिर्महीपः

प्रज्ञान्वितः पुण्यपथप्रदीपः ।

विश्वासघाताज्जनितानुतापात्

पापाज्जुगुप्सुश्च जनः प्रशस्यः ।। IX.35.

The restrained, rather divine, reaction of the Bodhisattva (farmer) to the death of his young son and his consequent incredible composure, take wind out of Indra's sails :

शोचाम्यतो न खलु, रोदिमि नैव चाहं

स्वस्थः स्थितोऽस्म्यनुभवामि न दाहदुःखम् ।

यादृङ् मृतो व्यधित कर्म, गतो गतिं तां

कुर्यां तदर्थमहमत्र कथं नु चिन्ताम् ।। XII.50

Besides other excellences that mark these illustrations, *prasāda*, uninvolved straight expression, lends them added elegance and attraction.

While waxing eloquent on the chastity and clarity of expression in the *Bodhisattvacaritam*, one cannot afford to be blind to the plethora of complicated grammatical forms which one meets with in the poem. Unlike in his other writings, the author's predilection for grammar here is not confined to the strings of aorist forms or those ending in *kvasu*. He has sought to embed his language with the subtle nuances of Sanskrit grammar. He seems to be so determined to overawe the reader with his profound equipment in the semantics of Sanskrit language that he seldom desists from transplanting learned grammatical forms in the body of his poem. These intricate forms might or might not have lent his poetry 'unusual splendour', it is however undeniable that the author's *vyutpatti* and *pratibhā* are both grammar-oriented. His love for Sanskrit grammar is as deep as for the Sanskrit language itself. To him therefore, the language in the *Bodhisattvacaritam* is wedded to grammar. It may be unkind to compare his recondite forms with the phenomenon that obtains in Bhaṭṭi's *magnum opus*, the multiety of grammatical forms in the poem, however, pose challenge even to the specialist in grammar. The neo-grammarian would be better advised not to burn his fingers with them. To him, they present insuperable hurdles in resolving their complexities. It is indeed amazing how the author has worked out co-existence between simplicity and complexity.

The *Bodhisattvacaritam* may be said to be a sort of thesaurus of recondite forms in grammar and their usages, as prescribed by Pāṇini. To be sure, the author has deferential regard for the master grammarian *(sūkṣmā matiḥ pāṇineḥ, XIV.16)*. It is therefore no wonder that he has incorporated in his poem a host of intricate grammatical forms, sanctioned by equally abstruse aphorisms. While the aorist in all its hues steals the thunder, the poem abounds in the wide spectrum of complex formations including desideratives, causals, frequentatives, denominatives, compounds besides subtleties of syntax and forms ending in intricate suffixes, both primary and secondary, and complex perfect, imperfect and first future forms. The number of such forms adds up to about four hundred precluding the simpler *liṭ* forms.

Some of the formations that were hitherto buried in the disquisitions on grammar or seldom employed elsewhere, but have been exhumed in the poem, may be detailed here- चञ्चूर्यमाणः (I.64), बम्भ्रम्यते (I.73), समयाकुर्यात् (III.13), सौहृदय्यम् (III.19), अटाट्यमानः (III.35), जीविकाकृत्य (III.56), आसन्नसाहस्राः (III.68), रोरूयांचक्रे (IV.22), भ्रातृकाम्यामि (V.21), वरीवृतीति, तन्तनीति (VI.15), मा पप्तत् (VIII.36), आर्थि (VIII.98), शोशुभति (X.22), अपपारम् (X.36), अवास्थिष्वहि (XI.36), अखित्त (XIII.23), राजीचिकीर्षुः (XII.97), मा तमः (XIV.6), अशीलि, सममीलि (XIII. 100).

The *Bodhisattvacaritam* abounds in various types of aorist forms. The author has used them both in *kartṛ* and *karman*. He also revels in using the aorist with *māṅ* without the augment *aṭ*. Its frequency defies all limits. The author's grasp of the intricate *sūtras* that lead to their formation is doubtless astounding :

अवालोचत् (I.7), अभ्यधायिषत (II.24), समगत (II.29), अचिच्यवत् (III.19), अन्वशिषत् (III.82), ऐक्षि (III.101), प्रापिपन् (IV.10), आहसत् (IV.12), अबीभयन् (IV.23), अचकलन् (IV.27), निरक्रमीत् (IV.36), अयासिष्टाम् (IV.44), आह्वषाताम् (IV.56), आक्रमीः (IV.85), न्यमाङ्क्षीत् (IV.91), असूसुपत् (IV.97), अशयिष्ट (IV.98), अपूरि (IV.103), आर्पिपत् (V.26), अमूमुचत् (V.30), मा---उत्पीपतत् (VIII.83), सम्प्रैषिषत् (VIII.97), अपीप्यत् (X.3), अपप्तत् (X.5), ऐषि (X.7), अपिनषम् (X.34), अकथि (XI.23) उपाधिषत (XII.36), मा शंकि (XII.44), उदपिपीडत् (XII.73), अक्रुधत् (XII.75), सम्प्रैक्षि (XII.81), अज्ञास्त (XIII.39), मा स्म भाजि (XIII.56), अचकथत् (XIII.65), समजनिषत (XIII.71), अध्यापिपत् (XIV.2), अलप्सि (XIV.32), अभ्यार्चिचत् (XIV.36).

Quite a few of the forms ending in various primary and secondary suffixes also engage attention. Some of the more interesting of them bear reproduction :

Secondary suffixes (Taddhitas) : अलंकरिष्णुः (I. 2), काशिकानि (I.52), युग्यान् (I.58), सर्वपथीना (III.14), गत्वरैः, विजित्वरैः, सृत्वरैः (IV.15), अदसीयम् (V.8), वाराणसेयः (XIII.8), आढ्यम्भविष्णुः, अलङ्करिष्णुः, चरिष्णुः (XIII.73).

Primary suffixes (Kṛdanta) : अभ्रंलिहम् (I.4), लोकव्यवहारदृश्वा (I.6), ईप्सुः (I.10), प्रयास्यन्तम् (I.12), भोज्यम् (I.15), उपेयिवान् (I.47), अधीती (II.7), ऊचुषि (II.38), क्रममाणः (III.13), अधिजग्मुषी (III.14), संचक्ष्या (III.33), जीवग्राहम्, श्वनाशम् (III.76), हस्तबन्धम् (IV.1), चोरङ्कारम् (IV.16), उपस्कृतम् (IV.63), अवस्कन्तुः (IV.64), शय्योत्थायम् (IV.83), कथंकारम् (IV.86), वशंवदः (VII.3), स्मारं स्मारम् (X.40), इत्थंकारम् (X.40), शुभंयुः (XIV.2).

Of the forms that owe themselves to special rules of grammar, but have been employed in the poem with not unpleasing results, mention may be made of the following : अविसंष्ठुला (I.25), विशंकटम् (I.34), मध्येऽटवि (I.36), ऊष्मायमाणः (I.46), बिभरांबभूविरे (II.9), राजनीत्यामधीती (III.12), सौहृदय्यम् (III.19), तद्राजः (III.40), अनलम्भूष्णुः (III.48), अशब्दायन्त (IV.25), कामुका ---स्वस्य पत्युः (V.9), भ्रातृकाम्या (V.21), कुमारश्रमणः (VI.3), दुःखासिका (VI.15), अन्धङ्करणी (VI.18), कर्मन्दिन् (VI.19), मल्लीमतल्ली (IX.27), प्रशाधि मां चापि तमेव (IX. 33), पूनम् (IX. 30), आत्मनीनम् (IX. 54), अटाट्याम् (XI.9), भूजानिः (XI.16), रोरुद्यते (XII.47), बोभवीषि (XII.73), कडङ्गर्यः (XIII.42), अमृत (मृतोऽभूत्) (XIV.13), माणवीनम् (XIV.34), अकपूयः (XIII.98).

In the zeal to parade his equipment in grammar, the author has gone to the extent of illustrating in Canto XIV the formation of word Jīvaka by two *sūtras* of Pāṇini (आशिषि न, III.1.150; कुत्सिते, V.3-74) that lend it the diametrically opposite connotations.

Some of the formations in the *Bodhisattvacaritam* bear the stamp of Vedic phraseology. तृष्णक् (I. 38), रथेष्ठा (I.46), सत्रा (I.16,97), तोक (XII.35) and अपचिति (XIII.87) may be cited as illustrations thereof. These bespeak the author's anxiety to impart serenity to his language, no matter what devices he employs.

He has not been miserly in demonstrating his control on Sanskrit vocabulary. This is what seems to have prompted him into inducting in his poem words that either adorn the lexica alone or have been used, if at all, very sparsely. The words that fall in this category may be listed below: अविसंष्ठुला (I.25), विशंकटम् (I.34), कौसृतिकः (I.53), उपशल्यम् (II.26), सौहृदय्यम् (III.19), मङ्क्षु (III.51, III.45, XIV.30), अकद्वदाः (III.71), आभीलम् (III.90), दुःखासिका (VI.15), कृष्टि (VIII.48), वियाता (III.83), भावुक (III.102), पूनम् (I.40), याप्यपथ (IX.56), निर्ल्वयनी (XII.48), अकपूय (XIII.68).

It should be evident by now that the author has decided predilection for well-turned phraseology. He has mustered his equipment in varied disciplines to achieve the intended purpose. That is precisely what accounts for the proclivity to incorporate in his mellifluous verses elegant expressions from ancient masters. There is nothing surprising about it as choice clauses from the ancient texts naturaly suggest themselves to a modern writer. However, the author has been rather extravagant in admitting such expressions or ideas represented by them. The number of such borrowals, direct or indirect, is not negligible. The *Bodhisattvacaritam* echoes ideas from the Upaniṣads, the *Bhagavadgītā* and the two great epics besides, of course, the classical authors. It is interesting that the direct borrowals in the *Bodhisattvacaritam* are minimal. Whatever the nature of his indebtedness to ancient texts, the borrowed clauses or ideas melt out completely in his poem and thereby add lustre to its expression. The fusion between the two is almost complete and smooth. And that is no mean achievement for the poet. A complete list of such borrowals alongwith their original sources is appended below to facilitate a comparative evaluation :

1-2. मूढः परप्रत्ययनेयबुद्धिः (I.57) and कामी स्वतां पश्यति (VI.17) are bodily lifted from Kālidāsa's *Mālavikāgnimitra* (I.2) and *Abhijñānaśākuntala* (II.2).

3. वीतरागभयक्रोधः स्थिरधीर्मुनिराडिव ।
तटस्थः सन्नवैक्षिष्ट कोशलेश्वरचेष्टितम् ।। III.104
दुःखेष्वनुद्विग्नमनाः सुखेषु विगतस्पृहः ।
वीतरागभयक्रोधः स्थिरधीर्मुनिरुच्यते ।। *Gītā*, II.56

4. एक आत्मैव सर्वत्र मन्तव्यः सततातत: ।
द्रष्टव्यः श्रवणीयश्च विज्ञेय इति मे मतम् ।। IV.18
अविनाशि तु तद्विद्धि येन सर्वमिदं ततम् । *Gītā*, II.17
नित्यः सर्वगतः स्थाणुरचलोऽयं सनातनः । ibid., II.24

5. सच्चिदानन्दरूपत्वादस्य शत्रुर्न विद्यते ।
एक एवायमस्मासु देहोद्भेदस्तु भिद्यते ।। IV. 19
सर्वभूतस्थमात्मानं सर्वभूतानि चात्मनि ।
ईक्षते योगयुक्तात्मा सर्वत्र समदर्शनः ।। *Gītā*, VI.29

6. संभिन्नमात्मनात्मानं मत्वा तस्मादनारतम् ।

उदासीनवदासीनैः कार्यं कार्यं विचक्षणैः ॥ IV.20

7. वशीकृते चेतसि सर्वकालं

शान्तः स्वयं मोक्ष्यसि मोहजालम् । VI.44

यदा ते मोहकलिलं बुद्धिर्व्यतितरिष्यति ।

तदा गन्तासि निर्वेदं श्रोतव्यस्य श्रुतस्य च ॥ *Gītā*, II.52

8. शक्यं न विज्ञैरपि वासनानां

समूलमुन्मूलनमत्र कर्तुम् ॥ VI.40

चञ्चलं हि मनः कृष्ण प्रमाथि बलवद् दृढम् ।

तस्याहं निग्रहं मन्ये वायोरिव सुदुष्करम् ॥ *Gītā*, VI.34

असंशयं महाबाहो मनो दुर्निग्रहं चलम् । ibid., 35

9. विवेकतः संयमतश्च नित्यं

दुर्वासनानां व्यदधुर्निरोधम् । VI.41.

अभ्यासेन तु कौन्तेय वैराग्येण च गृह्यते । *Gītā*,VI.35

10. व्युत्पन्नोऽपि विपद्यते विधिवशात् मृत्युर्ध्रुवः प्राणिनाम् । XIV.17

उत्पन्नस्य मृतिर्ध्रुवा । XIV. 18

जातस्य हि ध्रुवो मृत्युर्ध्रुवं जन्म मृतस्य च । *Gītā*, II.27

11. संसिद्धिः खलु कर्मणैव कथिता । XIV.35

सत्कर्मणा सिद्धिमुपैति नूनम् । XIV.43

कर्मणैव हि संसिद्धिमास्थिता जनकादयः । *Gītā*, III.20

उद्यमेन हि सिध्यन्ति कार्याणि न मनोरथैः । *Hito.*, I.37

12. आततायिनमायान्तं किं न हन्याम तं वयम् । III.74

आततायिनमायान्तं हन्यादेवाविचारयन् । *Manusmṛti*, VIII. 358

यादृशी भावना यस्य सिद्धिर्भवति तादृशी।*Pañcatantra* V. 98

ये यथा मा प्रपद्यन्ते तांस्तथैव भजाम्यहम् । *Gītā*, IV.11

13. यादृशी भवति यस्य भावना

तादृशीं स खलु सिद्धिमृच्छति । II.47

यादृशी भावना यस्य सिद्धिर्भवति तादृशी। *Pañcatantra*, V.98

ये यथा मां प्रपद्यन्ते तांस्तथैव भजाम्यहम्। *Gītā*, VI.32

14. आत्मोपमं दुःखसुखं परेषामीक्षते यः स महान् मनुष्यः । IX.15

आत्मौपम्येन सर्वत्र समं पश्यति योऽर्जुन ।
सुखं वा यदि वा दुःखं स योगी परमो मतः । *Gītā*, VI.32

आत्मौपम्येन भूतेषु दयां कुर्वन्ति साधवः । *Hito.*, p. 75, V.12

15. न तितिक्षासमं किञ्चिदस्ति साधनमुत्तमम् । IV.90

न तितिक्षासममस्ति साधनम् । *Kirāta*, II.43

16. कामातुराणां न भयं न लज्जा । VI.17

well – known Subhāṣita.

17. विकारहेतौ न विकुर्वते ये धन्यास्त एवात्र समुल्लसन्ति । VI.43

विकारहेतौ सति विक्रियन्ते येषां न चेतांसि त एव धीराः ।

Kumāra, I.59

18. विपन्निमग्ना अपि धर्मवीरा-
स्त्यजन्ति कर्त्तव्यपथं न धीराः ।। IX.9

विघ्नैः पुनः पुनरपि प्रतिहन्यमानाः
प्रारब्धमुत्तमजना न परित्यजन्ति । *Nītiśataka*, 27

न निश्चितार्थाद् विरमन्ति धीराः । ibid.,81.

अद्यैव वा मरणमस्तु युगान्तरे वा
न्याय्यात् पथः प्रविचलन्ति पदं न धीराः । ibid.,84

19. विना विचारं मतिमान् मनुष्यः
कदापि कार्यं सहसा न कुर्यात् ।
विनिन्द्यमुक्तं विपदां पदं तत्

दुःख्यत्यवश्यं ह्यविमृश्यकारी ।। IX.37

सहसा विदधीत न क्रियामविवेकः परमापदां पदम् ।

वृणते हि विमृश्यकारिणं गुणलुब्धाः स्वयमेव सम्पदः ।। *Kirāta*, II.30

20. जगच्छून्यं भाति प्रदहति च सत्प्रेमरहितम् । XI.6

शून्यं मन्ये जगदविरतज्वालमन्तर्ज्वलामि । *Uttara*, III.38

21. प्रलोभिता भूरि सुखैषणाभिः

कष्टैरनिष्टैः परिवेष्टिता वा ।

कल्याणहेतुं सुविनिश्चितार्थं

धीराः स्वमार्गं न परित्यजन्ति ।। IX.10

निन्दन्तु नीतिनिपुणाः----न्याय्यात् पथः प्रविचलन्ति

पदं न धीराः । *Nītiśataka*, 84

प्रारब्धमुत्तमजना न परित्यजन्ति । ibid.,27.

22. यज्जन्मना सर्वदिशः प्रसेदुर्ववुः सुखा गन्धवहाश्च भूयः । I.51

दिशः प्रसेदुर्मरुतो ववुः सुखाः । *Raghu*, III.14

23. वियोगोऽसह्योऽसौ स्मृतिपथमुपेतो मनसि नो

गरीयः सन्तापं जनयति च संमोहयति च ।। X.25.

विकारश्चैतन्यं भ्रमयति च संमीलयति च । *Uttara*., I.35

घनीभूतः शोको विकलयति मां मूर्च्छयति च । ibid., II.26

24. संचक्ष्या ह्यसुखोदर्का सदा दुर्जनसङ्गतिः । III.33

हीयते हि मतिस्तात नीचैः सह समागमात् । *Hito., p*.30,V.44

किमसुखं प्राज्ञेतरैः सङ्गतिः । *Nitiśataka*,103

25. उपकर्ता भवेत्साधुः सदैवापकृतावपि । III.59

अपकारिषु यः साधुः स साधुः सद्भिरुच्यते । *Hito*., 2

26. श्लाघ्यमक्रोधनस्येह क्षमा वीरस्य भूषणम् । III.85

शक्तानां भूषणं क्षमा । *Vṛddhacāṇakyaśataka*, XIII. 22

27. किं स्यान्मृते पुनरिहौषधसम्प्रयोगात् । XII .31

प्रोद्दीप्ते भवने च कूपखननं प्रत्युद्यमः कीदृशः । *Vairāgya.*,82

28. प्रबलविधिविधानं को नरो रोद्धुमीष्टे । XIII.26

बलवति सति दैवे पूरुषः को वराकः । XIII.27

दैवं त्वप्रतिरोध्यम् । XIV.14

दैवमेव हि नृणां वृद्धौ क्षये कारणम् । *Nītiśataka*, 85

विधिरहो बलवानिति मे मतिः । ibid., m 91

लिखितमिह ललाटे प्रोज्झितुं कः समर्थः । *Hito.*,p. . 52,V.21

29. सदा गुणानां ग्रहणं विधेयं ।

गुणाः प्रधानं न तु नामधेयम् । XIV.41

गुणप्रकर्षे यतनं विधेयम् । XIV.42

गुणाः पूजास्थानं गुणिषु न च लिङ्गं न च वयः । *Uttara.*, IV.11

30. कदाचिन्नोपेक्ष्या भवति कमनीया हि रमणी । IX.4

कः सन्नद्धे विरहविधुरां त्वय्युपेक्षेत जायाम् । *Megahduta*, 8

DIDACTIC MATTER :

Being didactic in character with special emphasis on human conduct and behaviour the *Bodhisattvacaritam* seeks to instruct the reader, in sublime values of life, which combine to impart it dignity and grace. It is however a different matter if in the process the poet occasionally tends to sound pedagogic. To the poet, it is the purity of conduct that makes life worthwhile. One who is generous even to the wicked is a truly great person. In comparison to good conduct all else, including riches, pales into inferiority All human accomplishments emanate from pure conduct (*sadācara*) :

विना सदाचारमहं विलोके न जीवनं किञ्चन जीवलोके ।
सदाऽपकारिष्वपि चोपकाराद् द्रवन्मना योऽस्ति महान् स एव ।। II. 66

तथा महत्त्वं न धनस्य विद्यते वृथार्जनात् तेन मनश्च खिद्यते ।

यथेह शीलं सदलङ्करोत्यलं महोज्ज्वलं मानवजन्म निर्मलम् ।। II. 67

The concept of non-violence that forms the cornerstone of the Buddhistic way of life, is tellingly set forth in the following verses. Violence cannot root out violence. It rather breeds more violence. The effective way to checkmate violence is non-violence. Fire is after all extinguished with water :

हिंसैव वर्धते बह्वी हिंसकं प्रति हिंसया ।
सुखमात्यन्तिकं लब्धुमहिंसैव गरीयसी ।। III.80
शान्त्या प्रशमयेत् क्रोधं सलिलेनेव पावकम् ।
चित्तं प्रसादयेद् धीमान् सर्वभूतानुकम्पया ।। III. 81

अहिंसैव गरीयसी (Non-violence *par excellence),* सर्वभूतानुकम्पा (compassion to all) and शान्ति (peace, tolerance) in fact represent all that is the best in Indian culture. To the Indian mind, it is simply despicable to rob some one of his life to ingratiate the other's baser instincts (IV.15).

On the philosophic plane, the world with its perplexing diversity and enigmatic loveliness, is but shortlived. The fulfilment of human endeavours lies in the realisation of the self. That alone ensures immortality :

अनित्यमेतत् क्षणदृष्टनष्टं कष्टं जगत् सारविहीनमस्ति ।
ज्ञात्वा तदेकं स्थिरमात्मतत्त्वं भवन्तु सर्वेऽप्यमृताः शमित्योम् ।। XII 92

One encounters lengthy didactic passages also in the poem. However, they are skilfully interwoven in the texture of the narrative so that they do not seem to have been foisted on the reader to overwhelm him with moral instructions. The way the fellow mendicants seek to divert the young monk from the snares of charms of the pretty damsel, by emphasising the transitoriness of human life and pseudo-attractions of sensual pleasures, has already been noticed (VI.27,29).

The following verses that are again intended to wean away the young monk from worldly objects remind one of Kṛṣṇa's sublime message to the similiarly vacillating Arjuna and what the *Yoga-sūtra* presents in the situation :

अतो मनश्चञ्चलमस्थिरं सद् यदापि यस्मिन् विषयेऽपि यायात् ।
तदा ततस्तत्प्रसभं निरुध्य समादधीतात्मनि सर्वदैव ।। VI.42

चञ्चलं हि मनः कृष्ण प्रमाथि बलवद् दृढम् । *Gītā,* VI.34

कामस्य वेगं बलवन्निगृह्य त्वं नित्यसत्त्वस्थ इहाश्रमे स्याः ।

वशीकृते चेतसि सर्वकालं शान्तः स्वयं मोक्ष्यसि मोहजालम् ।। VI.44

निर्द्वन्द्वो नित्यसत्त्वस्थो निर्योगक्षेम आत्मवान् । *Gītā,* II.45

तत्रैकाग्रं मनः कृत्वा यतचित्तेन्द्रियक्रियः । VI.12

FIGURES OF SPEECH :

Another prominent feature of the *Bodhisattvacaritam* is its elegant, polished style. That doubtless rests on its embellished and graceful phraseology. The poet is confidently cautious of the role the *Alaṁkāras* play in enriching the expression (*śubhaguṇālaṁkāra-yuktaḥ sadā* XIV. 35). The figures of speech, however, are not to him a contrivance to air his equipment in rhetorics. They are intended to strengthen as well as clarify the ideas that were otherwise likely to suffer haze.

As attested by his other works also, the author has pronounced fondness for Anuprāsa. In the *Bothisattvacaritam*, his predilection for it has assumed fabulous dimensions. It is so minutely woven in the poem that the *Bodhisattvacaritam* may well be regarded as an imposing store house of Anuprāsa with its tremendous possibilities and advantages. How in the poem it has resulted into loveliness of phraseology (*padalālitya*) has been duly noticed earlier. The Anuprāsa, as it has been employed in the *Bodhisattvacaritam*, lends itself to two broad divisions. The first evidently adheres to the traditional norm (*anuprāsaḥ śabdasāmyaṁ vaiṣamye 'pi svarasya yat, SD*. X. 3. It has been handled so ingeniously by the author that the expression that thus flows is stately in movement and superb in sweetness. Most of the *padalālitya* in the poem owes itself to these salient features of the most innocuous of the *alaṁkāras*. Besides those quoted earlier, a few additional illustrations should bring into relief the expertise of the poet in working up the Anuprāsa :

1. त्वमच्छ गच्छेह यथेच्छमग्रे । I.29
2. भवन्ति वर्षाः प्रकटप्रकर्षाः । I.50
3. अहिंसाया इवादर्शं दर्शं दर्शमनुत्तमम् ।। III.102
4. दृष्ट्वाभिजातां कनकावदाताम् । VII.16
5. वयोवृद्धैः सिद्धैर्निगमपरिशुद्धैरविकलं
   तथादिष्टं दिष्टं सुखमयमभीष्टं च सकलम् ।। XI.2

6. श्रीबुद्धस्तु विशुद्धबुद्धिरभितो बुद्ध्वा प्रवृद्धोदयम् ।। XIV.36

The other variety of alliteration, the Antyānuprāsa has been exploited in the poem to its farthest imaginable possibilities. Ours is perhaps the solitary poet to have used it on such a massive scale to churn out soothing rhythmic notes that virbrate throughout the poem . The device has reached its zenith in the Twelfth and Tthirteenth Cantos where there is barely any stanza that is not characterised with rhythm. The two cantos, in a way, betray a set pattern of the use of this lovely form. The verse herein appears to have been treated as a unit composed of two halves. The two sets of quartets rhyme among themselves, i.e., the first quartet rhymes with the second and the third with the fourth The resultant cadence simply enthralls the reader. Apart from several such verses reproduced under different sub-heads, some of the more imposing may be listed below to provide an idea of the excellence which gushes from Antyānuprāsa :

1. त्वदीयसौन्दर्यमतीव हारि
सर्वस्य लोकस्य विकारकारि ।
भूपः स मा पप्तदभिन्नरूपे
भूयोऽभिरूपे तव रूपकूपे ।। VIII. 36

2. पुत्रोऽस्ति मे प्रियतरोऽयमनिन्द्यवृत्तः
क्षेत्रे स्वयं यमिह दग्धुमहं प्रवृत्तः ।
प्राणाधिकः प्रियतमो बहुधा हितोऽयं
यस्मिन् मृते पितृषु मेऽवसितं हि तोयम् ।। XII.46

3. प्राप्तोत्तमप्रकृतिचारुविशिष्टदेवाः
सत्यव्रता विहितवृद्धजनोपसेवाः ।
विद्यागमं स्थिरसुखप्रदमाश्रयध्वं
मृत्योः परं तदमृतं च पदं लभध्वम् ।। XII.88

4. इति तु वचनमाकर्ण्योत्तरं न प्रपेदे
मलिनमजनि वक्त्रं, चेतसा न प्रसेदे ।
अनवहितपरार्थाः स्वार्थमेवाश्रयन्तः

कथमिह न सशोका लज्जिताः सन्त्वसन्तः ।। XIII.86

5. न हि मम परकीये स्वापतेयेऽभिलाषः

फलति बहुललोभात् सर्वथेह प्रणाशः ।

मनसि मम सदाऽऽस्ते मा गृधो वाक्प्रकाशः

किमु निबिडतमःस्थः स्यामहं प्राप्तपाशः ।। XIII.96

The number of such mellifluous verses can be multiplied *ad infinitum.*

In a bid to obviate the abstruseness that invariably creeps in from fearsome Yamaka, the poet has resorted to it with extreme reluctance. That is what is expected of a champion of Vaidarbhi (lucid style). Whenever it occurs on its own, it is happily shorn of complexities. His Yamaka is as sweet as his alliteration, and, not unoften, it heightens the musical effect like the Antyānuprāsa, he has so effectively handled in the poem. The best of illustrations of Yamaka in the poem is provided by IX.55, that he has fondly transplanted into his *Śrīgurugovindasiṁhacaritam* as well ((I.89). Its text would be reproduced in the critique on *SGGSC*. The following hemistich repeats *upāyāt*, in the same sequence with different meanings attached to them. While the second *upāyāt* is the imperfect first person singular form of *upāyā*, the first is the ablative singular of *upāya*. It therefore meets the norm laid down by Viśvanatha :

सत्यर्थे पृथगर्थायाः स्वरव्यञ्जनसंहतेः ।

क्रमेण तेनैवावृत्तिर्यमकं विनिगद्यते ।। *S.D.* X.8.)

पङ्कोदबिन्दून् विसृजन्नुपायात्

मृणालसूत्रं रसयन्नुपायात् ।। I. 43

In रमणी रमणीयाङ्गी रममाणा चिरं मुदा III. 4

the second *ramaṇī* is void of sense. So is the *śodhanataḥ* in the second quartet of IX.57.

स पुनः स्वमनःक्षतशोधनतः

श्रमणोचितपुण्ययशोधनतः ।। IX.57

For other illustrations of Yamaka one may refer to I.22, 34, 102, II.31, 55, III.27, 46, 68, IV.84, XII.7, XIII.8.

Of the *Arthālaṁkāras*, the author seems to have special fancy for the Arthāntaranyāsa. Next to the alliteration, it is this figure that may be claimed to abound in the poem. The author has effectively used it to strengthen the varied situations. The Brāhmaṇas sent by Kumāra to ascertain the worthiness of Unmadantī as his prospective spouse, themselves fell victim to her charms. Their predicament has been supported by the general statement that lovesickness afflicts even the discreet :

नष्टो विवेकः सकलोऽपि तेषां द्विजन्मनां कामवशं गतानाम् ।
उन्मादयत्येव विवेकिनोऽपि कष्टो विकारः खलु कामजन्यः ।। VII.22

Here again a general statement has been pressed into service to highlight the helpless situation of the king after Unmadanti's charms had overwhelmed his heart. Even though he was in *śuddhānta*, the harem (lit. a place of purity, hence the contrast in mentioning him *aśuddhāntara*), the king's heart was smitten with impurity, surely the assault of love defiles the mind :

नृपस्तु शुद्धान्तगतोऽपि रागादासीदशुद्धान्तर एव हन्त ।
वृद्धिं गते रागमलानुषङ्गे बुद्धेर्विशुद्धेर्हि कुतः प्रसङ्गः ।। VIII.100

The phenomenon has given rise to a host of beautiful *subhāṣitas* in the poem, a few of which are reproduced below by way of illustration :

1. अनर्थमेकः कुरुते तदीयं फलं तु तत्पृष्ठचरोऽपि भुङ्क्ते। I.59
2. आकारचेष्टादिभिरभ्युपायैः किं नोहतेऽनुक्तमपीह धीमान् । I.77
3. गुणाधिकरणे क्व दूषणम् । II.22
4. क्रममाणा मतिः स्वच्छा न वयःक्रममीक्षते । III.13
5. यतां विकारं त्यजतां विचारं
   धिक्कार एवास्तु कुतोऽधिकारः । VII.27
6. मतः प्रेमस्थेमा जगति परमं भेषजमिह । XI.3
7. स्मरति सुहृदमर्थी ह्यर्थवन्तं विपन्नः । XIII.30
8. न भवति हि कृतागाः क्वापि कस्याप्यभीष्टः । XIII. 30

As would be borne out by his other writings, except the latest one, the *Śrīrāmakīrtimahākāvyam*, the author is not much enamoured of Simile though that is where his favourite classical authors Vālmīki and Kālidāsa excel. The illustrations of the Simile in the *Bodhisattvacaritam* hardly exceed a score. It is resorted to in order to impart clarity to the subject under description that in turn hinges on the aptness and freshness of the *upamānas*. Most of the *upamānas* used are conventional but they are not shorn of beauty because they have been invested with new shades of connotations. When seated on the throne Śīlavān shone forth with his qualities as the moon perched on the orient-hill shines with its cool rays (III.16). The lord of Kāśī, attended upon by thousands of his generals, is compared with the full orb of the moon surrounded by a host of stars (III.103). The description of Unmadantī though based on four traditional *upamānas*, depicts the totality of her charms :

सौदामनीवाश्रितचन्द्रशाला
लावण्यवत्युत्पलिनीव बाला ।
प्रसन्नपूर्णेन्दुमतीव राका
समुज्वलद्दीपशिखेव सा का ।। VIII.50

It is, however, the adroitly chosen unconventional standards of comparison that serve to infuse new life into the author's expression and contribute to its clarity beyond measure. To the wily minister of Kosala, the Kingdom of Kāśī is vulnerable like butter and enjoyable like wine and honey :

देव वाराणसीराज्यं नवनीतसमं मृदु ।
अस्त्यद्य मद्यमाद्यं ते क्षुद्रं क्षौद्रमिवानतम् ।। III.39

The king of Kāśí, buried in the sandpit, emerges from the mass of sand like the moon from behind the cloud, wafted by a strong gust of wind. The swiftness of the emergence of the king should be clear from the abruptness with which the moon breaks asunder the thick clouds :

गर्तस्योपर्यवष्टभ्य हस्तयुग्मं महाबलः ।
न चिरात् पवनध्वस्तमेघाच्चन्द्र इवोद्गतः ।। IV.37

Elsewhere the poet has likened the young monk, bewitched by a maiden's form, with a deer injured with the hunter's shafts :

विक्षिप्तचेताः स्वनिकेतनस्थः

कामातुरोऽसौ बुबुधे न किञ्चित् ।
प्रमुग्धगीतध्वनिलुब्धशल्य-
प्रविद्धसारङ्ग इवावतस्थे ।। VI.5

Ahiparaka's proposed gift of Unmadanti to the king has been emphasised by inviting comparison with *dakṣiṇā* given to a Brāhmaṇa in a sacrifice (IX.24). Following the onslaught of Unmadanti's charms, the king had lost sleep like a gambler groaning under heavy debt. The heavily indebted gambler to explain the miserable plight of the king is indeed a forceful *upamāna.* :

ततः प्रभृत्येव लभे न निद्रा-
महं सहस्रर्ण इवाक्षशौण्डः ।। VIII.74

For other examples of Upamā reference may be made to III.81, 103, 104, IV.8, 37, VI.5, VII.9, VIII.19,69. IX.53, 67, 77, etc.

The *Bodhisattvacaritam* has received sizable sprinkling of the Svabhāvoktis. The rationale of the Svabhāvokti lies in projecting the object under description in details condign enough to present it with life-like precision. Cantos XI, XII and XIII are replete with several illustrations of Svabhāvokti. The Svabhāvokti untinged by any other *alaṁkāra* is rated best by the poeticians. The portrayal of shame brought on Piliya by the king's rebuke is depicted in its totality, in the following verse :

इदमपि च निशम्यावास्थितावाङ्मुखस्तु
न च किमपि जगाद प्राप्तकालार्थवस्तु ।
हृदयनिहितशोकान् मन्दधीः पीतिमानं
परमभजत तत्र स्वार्थिकश्चापमानम् ।। XIII.88

The verse reproduced below graphically describes the hunting expedition of Bhallāṭiya that yielded him the choicest dishes :

भ्रमन् नद्यास्तीरे बहलजटिलायां वनभुवि
बहून् दृष्ट्वा सोऽहन् विपिनशरणान्.मुग्धहरिणान् ।
प्रदीप्तेष्वङ्गारेष्वकृत विधिना मांसपचनं

प्रकामं प्रत्यग्रं मृगपललमास्वादयत च ।। X.10

The Svabhāvokti coloured with elegant alliteration emerges perhaps as the best piece in the poem. Though cited earlier, it brooks repetition :

मरुस्थली धूलिपरिप्लुताशा-

ऽऽकाशास्त विष्वङ्मुषितप्रकाशा ।

हा शान्तबुद्धेरपि तत्र नाशा-

ल्लब्धावकाशाऽस्तु कथं सुखाशा ।। I.45

As against the down to earth description in Svabhāvokti, the Sahokti hinges on the simultaneity of two actions in violation of their natural sequence. Dṛṣṭi and *bāṇavṛṣṭi* descended on the king without the least inter-regnum.

राज्ञः सपद्यूर्ध्वमुखस्य तस्या

मुखारविन्दे निपपात दृष्टिः ।

अभूच्च दृष्टेः समकालमेव

कामस्य चापादपि बाणवृष्टिः ।। VIII.44

The *Bodhisattvacaritam* cannot boast of much of imagery. Utprekṣā has been used very sparingly. The charms of Unmadantī's person had sent the people into swoon. The poet imagines the phenomenon to have occurred from their tasting the choicest wine :

तदङ्गलावण्यमवेक्ष्य लोका

मैरेयपीता इव मोहमापुः । VII.15

The erstwhile servant of Saṁgha was pained to find his master maltreated by the ungrateful Piliya. His distress is fancied to have resulted from the poison as it were :

स गरलमिव पीत्वाऽभूत्तदाऽत्यन्तमार्तः । XIII.65

Rūpaka in essentials, amounts to a veiled Simile. Herein the *aprakṛta* is sought to be imputed on the *prakṛta* to drive home the covert similarity between the two. While underlining the efficacy of forbearance, boat and stream have been imposed respectively on endurance and adversity :

तितिक्षानावमारुह्य तीर्यास्त्वं विपदापगाः ।। IV.90

Other examples of the Rūpaka in the poem are found in VIII.36, IX.53 and XIV.11.

In III.23 may be seen the figure of speech called Paryāyokta. The implied idea that the king Śilavān ruled righteously unchallenged by any rival has been expressly stated in the following words :

अधर्मश्चारिवर्गश्च न पुरे पदमादधौ । III.23

The stanza that follows is intended to describe the bands of attendants conjured up by the deceitful demon to bamboozle Śāntabuddhi. Here the Yamaka is interspersed with the Parikara. All the adjectives in the verse are meaningfully employed to convince the trader and his concourse of the supposedly torrential rain that had drenched them to the skin :

तद्भृत्यवर्गोऽपि तथाऽऽर्द्रवासाः
क्लिन्नालकः शुक्लसरोजमाली ।
पङ्कोदबिन्दून् विसृजन्नुपायात्
मृणालमूलं रसयन्नुपायात् ।। I.43

Virodhābhāsa has been exploited effectively at several places to draw contrast between what it should have been and what it actually is :

The young monk, who had fallen for the beauty of the pretty maiden, though well-grounded in righteous conduct was unable to restrain his restive mind, aspiring impatiently for her proximity. Contradiction is evidently involved in his behaviour :

गृहीतशिक्षोऽपि परं स भिक्षु-
र्नालं मनः संयमने बभूव।। VI.4

Contradiction is perceptible in the way the king was situated and the unseemly manner in which he conducted himself. Even while he enjoyed the comforts of the *śuddhānta* (harem), he was tormented with impure thoughts about Unmadantī (*aśuddhāntara*) :

नृपस्तु शुद्धान्तगतोऽपि रागा-

दासीदशुद्धान्तर एव हन्त ॥ VIII.100

METRES :

The canvas of the *Bodhisattvacaritam* affords wider avenues to the author to unfold his skill in handling a variety of metres with equal ease. In the use of metre, he has meticulously adhered to theory. While one metre preponderates, in obedience to theory, it varies towards the close of the canto. (*ekavṛttamayaiḥ padyair avasāne 'nyavṛttakaiḥ, Sāhityadarpaṇa*, VI.320).

In view of the fact that they tarnish the flow of narrative and additionally tend to distract the reader from poetic niceties, the author has wisely dispensed with the multiety of metres in one of the cantos. (*nānāvṛttamayaḥ kvāpi sargaḥ kaścana dṛśyate, SD.*, VI.321).

The author is equally at home in handling metres of all sorts, from the tiny Anuṣṭup to the mighty Śārdūlavikrīḍita. However, he has pronounced fondnes for medium sized metres like Upajāti, Rathoddhatā, Vaṁśastha. Interestingly Upajāti is the dominant metre in four (I, VII, VIII, IX) of the fourteen cantos. Canto One has the distinction of being uniformly composed in Upajāti. In Canto VII and VIII, the last verse has claimed Svāgatā (37) and Drutavilambita (110) respectively. Canto IX closes with Vasantatilakā (52-54), Drutavilambita (55) and Toṭaka (56-57). The Rathoddhatā, which on the poet's own admission is Viṣama (*kim karotu viṣamā rathoddhatā*, II.31) forms the major metre of the Second Canto ((1-60). The next four stanzas claim Mālinī (61-64), while the closing three are in Upajāti (65), Upendravajrā (66), and Vaṁśastha (67) respectively. Cantos III and IV are dominated by the lovely Anuṣṭup. Canto III ends up with Bhujaṅgaprayāta. In Canto IV the last three verses are composed respectively in Drutavilambita (110), Anuṣṭup (111) and Toṭaka (112). Canto VIII is the only one wherein the Bhujaṅgaprayāta, based on four *yakāras,* preponderates. However, it closes with the equally elegant Mālinī (37). Whereas verses 43 and 44 are in Upajāti and the concluding 45 claims Toṭaka, the Vaṁśastha rules canto VI (1-42).

In the next five cantos, the author turns to longer metres as if to deter the sceptic from entertaining apprehensions about his capacity to handle Śikhariṇī, Śārdūlavikrīḍita and others of their tribe. Cantos X and XI have Śikhariṇī as their chief metre. In the Tenth, it varies to Vasantatilakā in the last stanza (42), while the eleventh shares its four concluding verses between Indravajrā (22) and Upajāti (20-21,23). Vasantatilakā (1-88) in the Canto XII is followed by Śārdūlavikrīḍita (89-90) and Upajāti (91-92) towards the close. Mālinī, with fifteen syllables has been adopted as the main metre for the better part of Canto XIII (1--98). Next two verses claim Svāgatā, while verses 101 to 105 are in the Śārdūlavikrīḍita. It reigns supreme in the last (XIV)

Canto, with two stanzas (37-38) in the Mandākrantā and the closing six (39-44) in Upajāti.

Despite the constraints imposed by an incohesive theme, fragmented into isolated episodes, coupled with the daring departures that he has made from the established norms, the author has given in the poem, powerful expression to some of the highest moral values and ideals that sustain society. By dint of his poetic talents, smooth and polished language, refined style, perceptive imagination, profound grammatical equipment and the didactic and ethical values that he espouses in the *Bodhisattvacaritam*, the author, has ensured for himself, a high niche in the galaxy of modern stalwarts. Indeed the *Bodhisattvacaritam* establishes him as a front-ranking poet.

INDIRĀGĀNDHĪCARITAM

Notwithstanding the unkind charge that "India has no historians and no historical sense", the tradition of writing versified biographies of eminent personages is rooted in antiquity, the earliest such attempt being the *Buddhacarita* of Aśvaghoṣa, which despite its defective text, seeks to detail the life account of Lord Buddha, the matchless apostle of peace and non-violence, in its entirety, from his birth to the attainment of enlightenment. Padma Gupta Parimala's *Navasāhasāṅkacarita*, Bilhaṇa's *Vikramāṅkadevacarita* and others of their ilk combine to perpetuate the tradition, though they are primarily intended as Kāvyas embellished by all the trappings sanctioned by theory, with the result it is the form that dominates the narrative and historigraphy, not unoften, is pushed into cussed oblivion. Contrary to these versified *carita-kāvyas*, the *Harṣacarita* of Bāṇa addresses itself to detail the chequered career of Harṣavardhana with the gimmicks that Sanskrit prose admits in ample measure. It, however, concurs with them in making the narrative a handmaid of the flamboyant medium. This is precisely what accounts for the failure of these so-called ancient biographies to meet the purpose they are intended to serve. They are essentially Mahākāvyas or prose romances, far removed from the modern concept of biography, their nomenclature (*carita-kāvya*) notwithstanding.

The tradition of the *carita-kāvya* has happily percolated down to the present age. And some of the contemporary Sanskritists have been quick to exploit it, with certain modifications, to fruitful results, While attempting biographies of such stalwarts as Tilak, Gandhi and Nehru the modern Sanskritist has been chary of avoiding the pitfalls that stalked his predecessors. He is acutely alive to the requirements of modern biography that invariably insists on the measured but elegant presentation of the narrative. Outer trappings are relevant to him to the extent they serve to enliven the otherwise insipid narrative. The cautious effort to strike balance between the form and content has resulted in the emergence of a number of *carita-kāvyas* that come close to the modern concept of biography. They are distinguished by a full-fledged depiction of the *carita* of the person concerned without overburdening it with such embellishments as combine to turn history into fiction. Dr. Satya Vrat Shastri's *Indirāgāndhīcaritam (IC)*, that purports to be his second Mahākāvya and forms an important link in the long chain of *carita-kāvyas*, is as lively a biography as noteworthy it is as poem. It is indeed refreshing to find a whole lot of celebrities of recent history strutting the stage in the poem with dignity and poise, with Indira Gandhi, the cental figure, overshadowing all others in political sagacity and a host of virtues including unrivalled administrative competence.

SUMMARY

The *Indirāgāndhīcaritam* (*IC*)[1] purports to be the first full-fledged biography in Sanskrit verse of Mrs. Indira Gandhi, the Ex Prime Minister of India, who, but for a brief interlude, presided over the destiny of the country for about two decades and steered it to safe harbours in many a nerve-wrecking crisis. Consisting of 879 verses in different metres, the *IC* is divided into twenty five cantos of uneven size. It not only details the variegated career of Indira Gandhi, from her birth at Allahabad to the tumultuous days of 1975 that drove her, as Prime Minister, to clamp down Emergency in the country to save it from chaos and possible distintegration, it also forms authentic record of the freedom-struggle that culminated in the achievement of independence in 1947 and the phenomenal strides it registered in all walks of life thereafter.

The Pūrvapīthikā, which, though conceived as a part of the First Canto but forms, true to its name, a prologue to the poem, is marked by a rounded resume of the plethora of virtues that served to establish Indira Gandhi as a towering leader wedded to the welfare of her people and country. The canto proper begins with a graphic description of Prayāga, the sacred *saṁgama*, revered, down the ages, for its efficacy to bestow divine bliss on the devout (*svargāpavargasya nimittabhūtam,* I.9). It was here that Pandit Motilal Nehru established himself as a legal luminary and quickly earned, besides wide recognition, a staggering fortune. The vast house he had purchased from an Englishman somehow did not meet his rich tastes. He therefore constructed a new palatial building and tastefully decorated it with the choicest upholstery. In view of the comforts it was to impart to its inmates, it was appropriately named Anand Bhawan (*ānandapūrvaṁ bhavanaṁ cakara,* I.22). The grandeur of the house filled everbody with wonder. In this Anand Bhawan lived happily Motilal with his wife, son Jawaharlal, two daughters Krishna and Vijaya Lakshmi and a brigade of servants.

In deference to Motilal's wishes, the daughter of Jawahar was conducted, as soon as she was born, to his faithful clerk (Munshi) Mubarak Ali who aspired to see Jawahar's son before his imminent end. With his failing sight Mubarak Ali mistook the child for a son and blessed 'him' to be worthy of 'his' great father (*Javāharas te 'sti yathā suputras tatputrako 'py esa bhavet tathaiva,* II.8). The controversy about naming the child that arose between Jawahar and his mother who respectively favoured Priyadarshini and Indira, was skilfully resolved by Kamala. At her suggestion the daughter was given the happy name of Indira Priyadarshini. She was indeed the peer of Lakṣmī (Indirā) and her lovely mien richly deserved the sobriquet of Priyadar-

1. Bharatiya Vidya Prakashan, Delhi, October, 1976.

shini. Her birth was atttended by prolonged festivities. Endless streams of friends and relations poured in to greet Motilal and to bless the child. Motilal showered lavish gifts on the occasion. In the midst of gaity, Jawahar's mother Sarup Rani was a bit dismayed at the birth of the grand-daughter. In order to assuage her ruffled feelings Motilal prophetically assured her that this daughter of ours would outshine the best of sons (*putrī varā putraśatebhya eṣā*, II. 23) and what she was destined to do none would equal or surpass (*nānyena kenāpi kṛtaṁ purā tat*, II.24). Thus composed, she showered abundant blessings on the child (II).

While all vied with each other to shower affection on her, Indira was specially the darling of her grandfather. She imbibed highmindedness and refined tastes from him. From her father she inherited passion for study and indomitable courage. Her grandmother inculcated in her strands of religious fervour. She was an heir to her mother's tenderness and devotion to the country's rich heritage. That was the time when India was groaning under the foreign yoke. Mahatma Gandhi appeared on the horizon like a shooting star and gave the clarion call to oust the cruel Britishers who had sapped the country dry. He evoked wide following and among others Motilal Nehru opted for the rigours of freedom struggle under his banner in preference to the comforts of the luxurious life. So did his son Jawaharlal. Soon the imposing Anand Bhawan was turned into a hub of political activities and people flocked to it in endless streams to conduct political parleys. Motilal invariably kept Indira beside him during those days, While she was too young to grasp the intricacies of what transpired there, she picked up words like Revolution (*krānti*) and Satyagraha, which unfolded their import to her ere long. That spurred her to envision how she, even as a child, could address herself to the service of the country (*kathaṁ deśakārye pravṛtyaṁ mayeti* , III.20). It was at this juncture that she read the story of Joan of Arc, the French girl, who had sacrificed herself at the gallows in a bid to free her country from the British domination (III). Under her stewardship the French succeeded in driving away the alien rulers. But, she was overpowered and hanged by the British (*te ca tāṁ śūlam āropya tad adho 'gnim adīpayan*, IV.5). The story had a tremendous impact on the child Indira. Is it beyond me to accomplish what Joan of Arc had done?, she mused restlessly. Once she actually enacted the sacrifice of the French girl, in her own way. She clasped a column with her arms and with eyes closed imitated the scene at the gallows, feeling the heat of the leaping flames underneath. As she did all this, her face brightened with pride.

On the other hand, the freedom struggle was gaining momentum and the British subjected the Indian people to untold atrocities to break their spirit (*paśutāḍam atāḍayat*, IV. 16). The Satyagrahis from Anand Bhawan were also accorded the same treatment. It caused immense pain to Indira. Her agony exhibited itself in her play as well. She would arrange mock fight between the tin-toys representing the police and Satyagrahis and the latter would invariably emerge victorious. She greeted the triumph of the Satyagrahis with applause and slogans (*bhāratamātā jayatu*, IV.26). Seeds of patriotism were sown in the child, who was mature beyond her years (*bālā 'py abālamativaibhavaśālinī sā,* IV. 29).

The year Indira was born was marked by some of the most momentous events in the world-history. The holocaust of the First World War ended, Russia underwent a unique revolution and, at home, the British rulers had unleashed an unabashed reign of terror on the people that culminated in the brutal carnage at Jallianwala Bagh, Amritsar. While the first two influenced Jawaharlal favourably and he travelled through the length and breadth of the country to apprise himself of the miserable conditions of his own people, the Jallianwala massacre stunned the conscience of the country. Jawaharlal was filled with anger at the brutality of the British rulers and he decided to organise resistance against their atrocities. He urged the people to oppose the heartless rule of the British and the indignities they heaped on the country because the motherland was no different from mother (*jananī nijajanmabhūr mātā*, V.11). He evoked tremendous response from the people. They charted for themselves a well-thought out course of action. Apart from denouncing the British rulers at public rallies, they would form small groups to urge the traders to bycott everythihg that was not indigenous. Soon massive heaps of costly foreign clothes were consigned to flames. The whole country was galvanised to fight the British out. Nehru's aged mother, two sisters and his wife also joined him in the mission. The Nehrus had thus dedicated their all to the cause of the country (V). The sudden upsurge of the people worried the rulers. In a bid to break the backbone of the movement they, in their wisdom, incarcerated the whole lot of top leaders including Motilal and his son Jawaharlal. While the arrest of the Nehrus made Anand Bhawan forlorn, it did not break the spirit of the women-folk now left alone . They donned the mantle of the stalwarts. Clad in hand-made Khadi dress, they continued the mission of the elder Nehrus with zeal and devotion. They rather extended their activities to the educational institutions and impressed upon the student community to dispense with the so-called education because it bred nothing but slavery (*dāsyāya bho nūnam iyam bhaved vaḥ*, VI.15) and thus imbued it with patriotic fervour. Indira was flowering all along into an intelligent child (*bālāpy abāleva,* VI. 21).

As a child of four Indira, alongwith her father, went to Gandhiji's famed hermitage on the bank of Sabarmati. She immediately attuned herself to the culture of the *āśrama*. Like other inmates, she personally performed all the daily chores including cooking and sweeping. She was deeply impressed by Gandhiji's magnetically simple personality. After a brief stay there, she returned to Allahabad. The freedom movement was gaining momentum day by day. So was the people's passion for the Swadeshi. Once Indira, saw near her house, a mass of foreigh clothes, burning in leaping flames. She wanted to dance round the fire to express her joy at the people's resolve to do away with all that was foreign. But she was firmly stopped by her father. She took it to heart. Soon thereafter Jawaharlal was arrested. While in prison, he was always worried about Indira's education and well-being . He asked her to come to the prison to meet him, which she readily did (VII).

In order to join the elderly Congressmen in the service of the country, Indira went to the Swaraj Bhawan to seek the membership of the organisation. Its refusal on the ground of her young years caused her dismay (*svecchāvighātena manāg viṣaṇṇā*. VIII.8).Though firm in her resolve to acquire the membership after six years, Indira decided to serve the country, for the present, outside the umbrella of the Congress. Her resolve to form a children's organisation evoked instant response. Students from schools and colleges besides other children flocked to her on the specified day. She spelled out to them her line of action. She emerged as the undisputed leader (*tām anugatāś ca bālāḥ*, VIII. 25). The children came to perform a variety of important functions. They not only acted as innocuous couriers, they emerged as an intelligence service of sorts. Thus they could pre-empt the impending arrests of the elderly leaders by conveying them intelligence before-hand. They picked up other important secrets as well. They thus did what was impossible for others to do. The police would ignore them as ignorant folk (*sarvathopekṣitā rakṣibhiḥ,* IX 5). The dedication of the children to the cause of the country impressed the elders very favourably. Motilal and others showered unqualified praise on the organising capabilities of Indira. Kamala Nehru named the organisation as Monkey Brigade after the Vānarasenā of the *Rāmāyaṇa*, which rendered vital help to Rāma in his fight against the demons. Indira's Brigade was also engaged in a fight against the monster of imperialism. The fame of the Brigade spread far and wide. It acquired the knack to hoodwink the security guards as and when it suited its purpose. The leader of the organisation, Indira drew much comfort from the service it was doing to the country, in its inimitable way. She was well set on the path of her elders. Qualities like firm resolve, sharp intelligence and organising skill began to manifest themselves in her in abundant measure (IX).

Kamala's arduous schedules coupled with equally demanding political activities reduced her to a physical wreck. She fell victim to tuberculosis. With Indira in attendance, she was promptly shifted to Badenweiler in the picturesque Black Forests of Germany to rest and convalesce. Paradoxically she suffered further deterioration there. She was all a bundle of bones. Indira telegraphically apprised her father of the gravity of the situation and requested him to reach forthwith. Jawaharlal was releasd on parole and he instantly rushed to Germany. Noticing no improvement, he decided to shift her to Switzerland. Kamala's stay at Lausanne in the comforting company of her loving husband brought her substantial relief. His company proved extremely rewarding to Indira also. In India Nehru's frequent detention and Kamala's preoccupations had pushed the daughter into virtual isolation. Switzerland presented to her a refreshintg contrast. It provided her some sort of stable company of her parents. Nehru embarked upon a unique programme to educate Indira. Through a string of stories he acquainted her with the rise and fall of ancient civilisations of the world and celebrated rulers like Aśoka and Akbar (X).

Kamala's disease had stemmed from excessive exertion. Once while she had gone to a college to wean away the students from the worthless education that was doled out there, she swooned under the scorching sun. In contrast to the other students who greeted the mishap with derisive laughter, a handsome Parsi boy, Firoz fondly revived her and escorted her to Anand Bhawan. His frequent visits thereafter to Kamala made him a favourite of the Nehrus. Gradually Indira came into contact with him. When her mother was taken to Switzerland for convalescence, he proceeded to England for higher education. He regularly visited Kamala and Indira in Switzerland. And the contact that Indira and he had formed at Allahabad ripened into love. Leaving Kamala and Indira in Switzerland Nehru returned to India only to be arrested (*sa nigrahaṁ prāpita āsta sadyaḥ* XI.25).

After considerable cerebration Nehru sent Indira to Gurudeva's Santiniketan for regular studies, which had been hitherto on uneven keel. There she belied the apprehensions of the fellow students about her capacity to adapt herself to the life at the hermitage. She identified herself with the *āśrama*. Like other students she used to arise on time, put on the prescribed dress and herself broom her hut. Once while preparing for the Manipuri dance, to be presented on Bengal's new year day to the accompaniment of Tagore's famous song. "Whence traveller have thou come here?", she received a telegraphic message from her father to return home to attend upon her seriously ill mother (*balavad asti rujā paripīḍitā,* XII.22). Santiniketan was plunged into grief at her sudden departure. Her formal education ended but her father's vicinity was a constant education for her. He would take her with him on foreign visits. It was in one such visit to Europe that she met the famous litterateur Roman Rolland. In the meantime, on slight recovery, Kamala returned from Switzerland (*pratigatā Kamalā paradeśataḥ,* XII.33). But she soon had a relapse and died of prolonged illness, leaving everyone aghast. At the time of Kamala's death, Nehru was under detention (*babhūvādhikṛtair niruddhaḥ,* XII.36). He was released to return home, grief-stricken (*śokākulaḥ svaṁ gṛham āsasāda,* XII. 36).

On the completion of Kamala's obsequies, Jawaharlal again plunged into hectic activities. Though engrossed in the service of the country he constantly cherished the fond memories of Kamala. And to symbolise his unflinching love for her, he retained with him a part of her ashes. After her death, he developed, perhaps as a measure of his added duty towards her, greater fondness for Indira (*sutottamāyāṁ prabalo 'nurāgaḥ*, XIII. 10). In order to arouse the people he visited every nook and corner of the country. His masterly call resulted into mass upsurge which shook the alien rule to its moorings (*durdharṣarūpaṁ janavātacakraṁ tathātra deśe pracacāla vegāt*, XIII.15). Whenever he got respite from his arduous schedule he spent some time with Indira which gave her immense joy (*āsannatāsyā atata pramodam,* XIII.18). By now Nehru was convinced of the acuteness of Indira's insight. With a view to ascertain her reaction to it, he once asked her to read aloud the write-up that was to be repeated subsequently on the bank of the Ravi. He noticed that while reading it, Indira's eyes lit up with joy and she was thrilled to the extreme. Since the Charter of Oath was to be announced on the 26th of January every year, the date came to be known as Independence day (Republic day) (XIII).

Because of her father's frequent arrests Indira's education could not proceed systematically. Moreover, there was a difference of opinion between Motilal and Jawaharlal whether she should be educated in India or abroad. The controversy was resolved by Gandhiji's intervention. Once Jawaharlal had to undergo prolonged incarceration. Unable to send any conventional gift from the four walls of the prison, he sent to Indira, on her thirteenth birthday, a unique present in the form of a lengthy letter (*tena patram upadām adhigaccha*, XIV.20) It was a virtual treasure of knowledge for her. He followed it up with a series of 195 letters, which, taken together, set forth, in an inimitable way the history of the world from its inception to the present day besides an account of various noted rulers, artists, thinkers and the various wars the world witnessed, down the ages. This was Nehru's novel method to instruct his daughter in various disciplines (*evam adbhutam avartata tasyāḥ śikṣaṇaṁ svapitur eva sakāśat* XIV. 32). The letters, one hundred ninety six in number, were subsequently published in the Glimpses of World History (XIV).

The love that Indira had come to entertain for Firoz matured in youth. She decided to marry him and expressed her resolve to her father. In view of the wide difference in their nature and background, Jawaharlal advised her to reconsider her decision. Moreover, it attracted sharp opposition from the orthodox Hindus, who went to the length of blashphemy. However, all this hullabaloo could not deflect Indira from her determination. Gandhiji advised Nehru to bless her decision to nail the wild rumours that had been set afloat for extraneous considerations. The marriage was ultimately solemnized in March, 1942 according to Vedic rites, to the delight of one and all. Her wedding garment was made of the thread Jawahar had spun for her in the prison. After Kamala's death, Indira had been his mainstay. While she was unhappy at leaving him alone, he took it as a part of the game (*sūkṣmā praharṣasamaye 'pi viṣādarekhā* XV.25, *prādāt prasannamanasā sa parigrahītre*, XV.27). Immediately after their marriage, Indira and Firoz left for Kashmir (XV).

After a memorable honeymoon in Kashmir they came back to Allahabad to the delight of their kinsmen. In Indira, Firoz had a devoted and intelligent wife who invested him with added confidence. With a view to leading independent life he came to Lucknow and took up a job with the National Herald. There he built an elegant house which was tastefully decorated by Indira. They lived happily in their new house. Indira was a source of delight to Firoz (*taccitte paramam asikta harṣam eṣā,* XVI.14). Meanwhile they attended the historic 1942 session of Congress at Bombay. It was there that the 'Quit India'slogan was raised first. The British rulers responded by arresting almost all the prominent leaders including Jawaharlal. On hearing her father's arrest, Indira came back to Allahabad, dejected (XVI).

Soon thereafter her aunt Vijaya Lakshmi was also put under detention. That was an added blow to Indira (*tasyā bhṛśaṁ duḥkham avātatāna* (XVII.2). She returned to Lucknow to be with her husband. The police wanted to arrest Firoz also but he continued to dupe it for several days. Once the students of Ywing Christian College invited Indira to join them in raising the national flag on the College campus. No sooner had a brave student raised the flag, the police rained *lathi* blows on him. He fell on the ground, injured. But before the flag could fall, Indira held it aloft with alacrity to the chant of 'High up will unfurl our dear flag' (*sadaivordhvagatiḥ priyo naḥ,* XVII.13). That electrified the students to cordon her like a wall. The guards persisted with the blows but she stood firm like a rock. It further infuriated the policemen. They now aimed the lathis on her hands (*krūraṁ prahāraṁ karayoḥ pracakruḥ,* XVII 16). She suffered the pain with enviable courage. Even when she fell on the ground, she did not leave the flag though she was constantly hit with *lathis* and shoes (*niṣpiṣṭagātrāpi padatrajātair dhavajaṁ priyaṁ sā na mumoca dhīrā,* XVII.18). She did not confide even to her husband the ordeal she withstood so bravely . But her injuries were more eloquent than her words. Her father sent her a message to communicate it to the people in the town (XVII).

Indira organised a large meeting to apprise the people of what Jawaharlal expected of them. The police personnel also descended on the scene. Hardly had she started with her speech than a British official threatened her to shoot down in case she did not stop. With lightning speed Firoz pounced upon him from the crowd. Firoz's courage filled Indira with pride. To him too, she was an embodiment of boldness and firmness (*garvonnatā taṁ ca dadarśa patnī*, XVIII.10). While the guards strove hard to drag her to the waiting van, the crowd resisted them tooth and nail. Thus being pulled in different directions by two different sets of people, Indira was subjected to torrid test. Her clothes were torn and her body was *kṣatavikṣata* (*babhūva devī kṣatavikṣatāṅgī,* XVIII.15). In the meanwhile additional force arrived. They drove Indira, Firoz and hundreds of others to the Naini jail near Allahabad. Indira and Firoz were kept in separate wards. In the prison, Indira met her aunt Vijaya Lakshmi. She was released after nine long months. On recouping healtlh, she again devoted herself to the service of the country. It was through the endeavours of Gandhi, Nehru and other stalwarts that millions and millions of people from all parts of the country dedicated themselves to the freedom struggle, caring not an iota for their comforts or safety. The British rulers were by now convinced that it was impossible to stem the spate of upsurge of the Indian people. But they wilely sowed the seeds of dissension to drive permanent wedge between the Hindus and the Muslims, the two dominant communities in the country (XVIII).

Consequently the Muslims, under the leadership of Mohammad Ali Jinnah, put forth the pernicious Two Nations Concept, disclaiming any bonds whatsoever, with the Hindus (*pṛthaktā, sarvātmanā no 'sti tataḥ prasiddhā* XIX 2); and raised demand for a separate country with Islam as its sole religion. Since it squared with the evil designs of the British to bifurcate the country, they readily accepted the demand (*vaideśikānāṁ svamano 'nukūlānity abhyupāyuḥ khalu tāni te ca,* XIX.7). Though deeply perturbed at the vivisection of the country, the Indian leaders accepted it as a price for freedom, entertaining the hope that the Muslim opposition would wear down subsequently (*kālena śānto bhavitaiva satyam*, XIX.12). India emerged as a free country on 15th August, 1947. On the same day came into existence Pakistan consisting of the Muslim majority parts of Bengal and Punjab and Sindh, Baluchistan and the North West Frontier province. Jawaharlal Nehru became the first Prime Minister of independent India. Claiming Pakistan to be meant for the Muslims only, the non-Muslims (Kafirs) were asked to disgorge themselves out of the country. In a trice the Hindus and Sikhs became aliens in their own land (XIX).

Carried by communal frenzy, the Muslims in Pakistan perpetrated abominable atrocities on the Hindus. They burnt down their houses, abducted their women, looted and killed them like so many cattle. The country was turned into a virtual bedlam. It invited equally heinous retaliation in india against the Muslims. The Hindus had to seek safe sanctuary in India. This mindless carnage filled Nehru with anger and sorrow. In order to lend them a helping hand in the stupendous task that awaited him, Indira came to stay with her father, almost permanently, and took a deeper plunge into public activities. She relieved him of considerable burden to enable him to concentrate on vital issues (*ātmani kṛtyaṁ bahu sādadhau svayam*, XX.13). The refugees from Pakistan received her immediate attention. She put up a massive awning in her father's house itself to provide them shelter and personally looked after their boarding. She also took it upon herself to welcome the visiting dignitaries. Soon she found herself, not unlike her father, immersed in multifarious works (*na hi sā kṣaṇam apy akarmakṛt samavātiṣṭhata*, XX.20). Whenever Nehru went abroad on official visits, Indira invariably accompanied him. Thus devoted to her father, she did not care for her comfort, nor did she long for any reward (*nahi sā svakṛte tu kiñcana cakame tātasukhe ratāniśam,* XX.22). Only once during her father's regime was she made President of the Indian National Congress. She held the office for two years with poise and application (XX).

Worn out by strenuous work and old age and addedly feeling cheated by China's perfidy, Nehru died (On May 27,1964). Robbed of her fond father, Indira was extremely forlorn. One of his trusted lieutenants, Lal Bahadur Shastri succeeded Nehru as Prime Minister. He had unfortunately a brief tenure of eighteen months. During his stewardship, Indira was Minister of Communication and Broadcasting. After Shastri's death, Indira defeated Morarji Desai in a straight contest to assume the coveted office of Prime Minister. While she was carrying on the administration with admirable efficiency, she was confronted with a complex problem. Differences arose between her and the old guard of the Congress over the choice of the candidate to succeed Zakir Hussain, who had died suddenly of heart-attack. While the old guard supported Sanjiv Reddi for the office, her choice fell on V.V. Giri, the Vice -President who was all too eager to be elevated in accordance with the practice (*uparāṣṭrapatir yaḥ syāt syāt sa rāṣṭrapatiḥ kila*, XXI.29). Giri contested, apparently as an independent candidate and won convicingly. Indira had marshalled all her resources to ensure his victory. Giri thankfully attributed his triumph to Prime Mnister Indira (— —*so 'py etad avāpya tasyā ayam jayo' bhūd iti manyate sma,* XXI.4). Unable to pull on with the elderly leaders, actuated by selfish considerations Indira formed a new Congress which soon eclipsed the old organisation and emerged as the real Congress (*tatra nūtnā vyaśiṣyata*, XXI. 42).

Indira was not only an ideal daughter, she was an equally fond mother. To her, motherhood represented the fulfilment of a woman. She gave birth to a lovely son In 1944. Two years later, another son was born to her. They were respectively named as Rajiv and Sanjay. Despite her heavy preoccupations, she invariably spent some time in their company. Rajiv subsequently married an Italian girl Sonia. While Sanjay wedded Menaka, a lovely Sikh girl. The birth of the grand children brought Indira immense joy . Even as she shouldered the onerous office of Prime Minister, she played with her grandchildren, whenever she got the slightest opportunity to do so. Although she could not stay with her husband, he always resided in her heart. Firoz visited her off and on. Loneliness and weakness combined to overpower Firoz and he was struck with cardiac trouble (*hṛdroga āskandad imaṁ balena,* XXII.39). Fortunately he responsed to the treatment. His stay in Kashmir with Indira brought him tremendous relief, but he relapsed soon thereafter and this time could not be saved despite best possible treatment (*prāṇān priyān eṣa mumoca dhīraḥ*, XXII.44). Indira was thrown into grief, but she maintained her poise (*dhairyaṁ na sā dhairya-dhanā mumoca*, XXII.46).

Giri's election as President immensely raised the Prime Minister in stature and consolidated her position beyond measure. After five years of fruitful rule, she had to contend with a grim situation in the east. Pakistan was ruling over its eastern wing, carved out of Bengal, like a colony. It not only sapped it of its wealth and resources, but also foisted Urdu on the unwilling Bengalis. The resentment that was brewing, over the years, ultimately burst out in the formation of Awami League which was essentially projected as a counterweight to Bhutto's Party. In the election to the Lower House of the Parliament, the Awami League, under Mujib, made a clean sweep. However, at the instance of his wily foreign minister Bhutto, President Yahya Khan refused to hand over power to the democratically elected leader Sheikh Mujib (*na śāsituṁ svaṁ hy adadāt sa deśam,* XXIII.24). Not only that, he ordered his arrest which was executed on the night of March 23, 1971. That was the last straw in Bengal's wind. The Awami League responded by declaring East Bengal as an independent country, free from the clutches of Pakistan (*deśaḥ svatantro bhuvi no 'stu*, XXIII.34). And the Pakistani army let loose virtual hell on East Bengal. They massacred the innocent people, abducted and ravished the women, burnt their houses and destroyed all that they could. This orgy of violence continued for several days. Lakhs of people poured into India to save their life and honour. Within the space of eight months, their number swelled to one crore. That was a severe strain on India's security and resources. Those who stayed back formed Mukti Vahini (Liberation Force) and despite poor training put up stiff resistance to the Pakistani army. Taking it all to have been manouvered by India, Pakistan launched full-fledged attack on the country (*ākrāntavān bhāratabhūpradeśān,* XXIII.47). Though Pakistan had the support of the two giants, China and America, Indira faced the war with rare courage and foresight (XXIII).

She ordered the army to frustrate the enemy in its misadventure. Soon the Indian forces were locked in a terrific war in Sindh and Chamb besides the eastern and western sectors. While forces of India wrested large chunks of Pakistani territory in Sindh, Bangladesh (Eastern Pakistan) was liberated with clock like precision. One lac Pakistani troops surrendered to the Indian Commanders at Dhaka. The prisoners of war were brought to India to be repatriated subsequently to Pakistan. Indian forces suffered some reverses in Chamb. After the Indian forces had accomplished their allotted mission, Indira Gandhi ordered ceasefire, delighted like Caṇḍī at the annihilation of the demons (*caṇḍīvogrā jagati viditā daityasaṁhāratuṣṭā* XXIV.7). She made it plain to the world that India did not covet anybody's territory. And as a measure of her sincerity, she signed the Simla Agreement with her Pakistani counterpart Z.A. Bhutto in 1976 (?). The two countries exchanged the territories occupied in the war. Diplomatic relations and trade were restored with Pakistan. Relations with Nepal and Srilanka were put on even keel. A series of remarkable works were accomplished during her regime. A nuclear device was exploded in 1974 at Pokhran. At the request of the people groaning under the misrule of Chogyal, Sikkim, a protectorate of India was integrated with the country as its twenty third state. Aryabhata was sent into the orbit. The sattelite alongwith the nuclear device established India as a major regional power. In order to channelise their resources to more profitable use, fourteen leading banks were nationalised. The Punjab problem that had been hanging fire since long was resolved by creating a new Sikh Majority state (?). With equal skilfulness she entered into a settlement with Sheikh Abdullah to restore peace in Kashmir. A twelve year treaty of peace and friendship was signed with Russia. The leadership that Indira provided to the country in many a crisis was unrivalled. As a token of the nation's gratitude, President Giri honoured her with the highest award of the land, Bharata Ratna, on Dec. 18, 1971 (?). Despite her manifold achievements, some of the selfish people wanted to humble her. The war with Pakistan resulted in price-spiral. There was a drought in the country. Essential commodities became scarce. Blackmarketing increased. Bribery flourished. Smuggling escalated dangerously. Strikes, agitations and indiscipline in educational institutions threatened to paralyse the country. Violence erupted. The Railway Minister, L.K. Mishra was murdered. Attempt was made on the life of Chief Justice Ray. A state of anarchy prevailed. In order to save the country from disintegration and restore order she boldly clamped Emergency in the country. Six political parties were banned and their leaders were put under arrest. Smugglers and unsocial elements were also hauled up (XXIV).

Indira was convinced that without allround economic development, independence was a mere slogan (*vinārthaṛddhim na samagram asmatsvātantryam ity eted iyaṁ prapadya,* XXV.3).For those who have been groaning under abominable indigence for generations, with no food, shelter and clothes, freedom has no meaning. With a view to ensuring economic progress In the country, she identified twenty such areas as demanded immediate attention. The means she suggested to meet these formidable challenges are summed up in her twenty point programme. Her energetic son Sanjay added his own five to complement his mother's twenty. With the declaration of Emergency the drift ended and calm was restored in the country. Profiteering, blackmarketing and adulteration stopped. Discipline descended upon schools and colleges. Seven lac hutments were allotted to the poor. Bonded labour became a thing of the past. Loans were written off. Prices of almost all the commodities fell considerably. The Emergency turned out to be an era of discipline (*anuśāsanaparva*). The people wondered whether it was Emergencly or some mysterious spell that was at work (*māyā kim eṣā kimu vendrajālam,* XXV.75). In order to arouse the people into fruitful action, she gave them a set of slogans: Hard work, Farsightedness and Firm determination. Indira envisioned a strong, stable and affluent India.

CRITIQUE

Contrary to the *Bodhisattvacaritam*, which as noticed earlier, makes mainly a daring departure from the norm, the *Indirāgāndhīcaritam* (*IC*) conforms closely to theory. Though that has not deterred the poet from introducing, in keeping with his wont, certain innovations in the poem that combine to mark it out from the common lot of the stereotyped Mahākāvyas. Despite its undoubted poetic merits and ethical undertones, the *Bodhisattvacaritam*, in ultimate analysis, is limited in its sweep. The *IC* notwithstanding its onesided approach to the subject, on the other hand, commands a broad spectrum with the wealth of contents which concern themselves with one of the most eventful periods of contemporary history and encompasses a wide variety of locales, each of them contributing to the richness of the poem. Unlike the *carita-kāvyas* of old which seem to view the fulfilment of the historical narrative in its extravagant execution in highflown language with little regard/care for the contents and thereby tend to turn history into fanciful myth, the outer trappings in the *IC* have met the poet's approbation only to the extent they relieve the monotony of the historical narrative without overshadowing it in any way whatsoever. It is a measure of the poet's anxiety to be faithful to the narrative that even his language is attuned to the genius of the poem and never for once does it blow out of proportion to overburden the mass of events that form the texture of the poem. It is from this conscious moderation that the *IC* emerges as a faithful *carita-kāvya* which is as lively and readable as any modern biography in any language could be. Rather the poetic medium has enabled it to steal march over others of the kind.

THEME

There can hardly be any doubt about the genre of poetry the *IC* represents. Perhaps to debunk the misgivings that the *Bodhisattvacarita* had raised on certain counts, the *IC* closely adheres to the precepts of a Mahākāvya as they have been evolved down the ages, from Bhāmaha to Viśvanātha. While Bhāmaha[2] is liberal to admit any elevating theme as worthy of Mahākāvya, his successors, Daṇḍin and Viśvanātha in particular, insist, perhaps in order to avoid strain on the reader, on the known character of the theme. It must emanate from such celebrated sources as *itihāsa* and *purāṇa* or alternatively it should concern itself with high personages[3]. The theme of the poem with such wide canvas as Mahākāvya should indeed be dignified enough to exercise ennobling effect on society. The theme of *IC* meets the rhetorical requirements with a vengeance. Being concerned with the character who had the unique distinction of being the only woman in history to have ruled over a vast country like India for more than fifteen years, it is both historical and *sadāśraya*.

2. सर्गबन्धो महाकाव्यं महतां च महच्च यत् । *Kāvyālaṁkāra*, op. cit. I. 19
3. इतिहासकथोद्भूतमितरद्वा सदाश्रयम् । *Kāvyādarśa*, I. 18
   इतिहासोद्भवं वृत्तमन्यद्वा सज्जनाश्रयम् । *Sāhityadarpaṇa*, VI. 318

In mathematical terms the epoch that forms the bed-rock of the poem does not stretch beyond half a century (1919-75). However, it is not the length of years but their importance as an era which decided the fate of the country that marks it out as perhaps the most remarkable period of Indian history, the chequered freedom struggle was followed by an equally stromy phase that witnessed several vicissitudes including three wars, Nehru's death, and a power-struggle of sorts culminating in the imposition of Emergency. This eventful era which shaped Indira in early stages and was subsequently shaped by her, provides the poem with a vast canvas marked by bewildering complexity. It was a severe strain on the ingenuity of the poet to sift relevant events out of a mass of confusing data, that could form an apt backdrop to the poem. It was much more so in the case of the earlier phases dominated by stalwarts like Mahatma Gandhi, Motilal and Jawaharlal Nehru. It is gratifying to find that the poet has come out of the ordeal with remarkable credit. He has wisely chosen such of the events as have direct bearing on Indira or are otherwise connected with her. The astute handling of the heterogeneous events that characterise the freedom struggle and the post-independence era has resulted in a smooth homogeneous theme that forms the warp and woof of the *Indirāgāndhīcaritam*. It is a tribute to the author's skill in weaving out the well-knit texture of the poem that the reader is attuned, right from the beginning, to the main narrative. Hardly does he realise that he is passing through the most tumultuous period of freedom struggle, nor does he ever fall out of step with it. As a matter of fact, the struggle forms, fascinating backdrop, to the career of the central figure of the poem. Indira is rather a child of the movement. The dramatis personae in the struggle are none else but her own kinsmen, parents and grandparents. As she blossoms, she finds herself closely involved in it. In fact, she grows with the movement.

The career of Indira Gandhi, as attemped in the body of the poem, reaches its zenith through three distinct stages. Cantos I-XVI form the first stage. It was essentially the formative period of her life. Her formal education got repeatedly interrupted as and when prison claimed her father who, perforce turned out to be her most trustworthy teacher. She graduated, in this period, from an inquisitive child to a pretty bride with strong will and patriotism that later came to be the hall mark of her character. The second phase is represented by Cantos XVII-XX. Though overshadowed by the greatness of her father, she was all poised for a major breakthrough. While her tenacity in raising the national flag on a college-campus at Lucknow in the face of physical violence unfolds, in ample measure, her patriotism enlivened by indomitable courage, her stint as Congress President and minister in Shastri's cabinet had all but brought her to the threshold of the highest office of the land. In Cantos XXI-XXV she is firmly entrenched in the saddle. It was the most eventful part of her career, full of mighty challenges and grave crises. She was not only equal to the challenge, it found her rising taller and taller. It was her role as Prime Minister in guiding the country to safe shores through many a crisis that ensured her a place in history.

Though meticulously conceived as a well-knit theme out of a mass of confusing accretions, the execution of the theme leaves much to be desired. The author's ingenuity in discarding what could have overlaid the kernel doubtless merits acclaim, nevertheless there are certain inaccuracies which perhaps owe themselves to his defective source material . The most glaring relates to the death of Kamala Nehru. The author would have us believe that on slight recovery, Kamala returned from Switzerland where she had been convalescing after she was struck with tuberculosis. It was at Allahabad that she died after a relapse. At the time of her death, Nehru was in the prison and he was released on parole to attend to her obsequies. This is how Kamala's death is described twice in the body of the poem[4]. It runs counter to the known facts. Kamala is known for certain to have died and cremated at Lausanne in Switzerland on the morning of 28th February, 1936. Nehru and Indira were beside her when she breathed her last[5]. Her ashes were all that Nehru brought to Allahabad to consign them to the holy Ganges[6]. Equally untenable is the statement that Indira was recalled from Santiniketan to attend upon her mother at Allahabad[7]. Both Kamala and Indira were not in the country at the time. While Kamala had shifted from Badenweiler to a Sanatorium near Lausanne in Switzerland, Indira was at School at Bex nearby[8]. The allusion to Indira's foreign trips with her father, soon after her alleged return from Santiniketan is also odd[9].

---

4. अथ कथञ्चिदवाप्तसुखस्थितिः
प्रतिगता कमला परदेशतः।
निजगृहान् न चिरं प्रकृतौ स्थिता
क्षयमुपैदिव चान्द्रमसी कला ॥ *IC.*, XII. 33.
विलपतः परिहाय निजान् प्रियान् स्वसुकृतार्जितलोकमियं ययौ । XII. 34.
पिता जनन्याः किल मृत्युकाले तस्या बभूवाधिकृतैर्निरुद्धः ।
मुक्तः पुनस्तैरधिगत्य वृत्तं शोकाकुलः स्वं गृहमाससाद ॥ XII. 36.
Also XIII. 1,4,5.
5. *Discovery of India*, p.46
6. *ibid*, p.48
7. *IC.*, XII. 22-23
8. *Discovery of India*, pp. 45-46
9. *IC.*, XII. 30-31

The anomalies do not stop here. The sterling role that Prime Minister Indira Gandhi played in leading the country to victory in the 1971-war imposed on an unwilling nation is now a part of history. The grateful nation honoured her with the highest award of the land. The Bharata Ratna was conferred on her not on 18th December, 1971, as recorded in the poem[10], but on the Republic Day, next year. Since the war had ended on the 17th December the following day could not have been the appropriate occasion to honour her with the award.

In order to restore peace and resolve the bilateral issues the countries signed an agreement at Simla. According to the *IC* the agreement was concluded between Indira Gandhi and the Chief Secretary of Pakistan in 1976[11]. It is historically unsound. The agreement was in fact reached in 1972 as a result of long deliberations between Indira Gandhi and her Pakistani counterpart Z.A. Bhutto who was a signatory to the accord.

Likewise the creation of the new Sikh majority state of Punjab is listed as one of the achievements of Indira's regime[12]. The post-partition undivided Punjab was actually split up in twin states of Punjab and Haryana in 1965, during the tenure of Lal Bahadur Shastri.

Some of the events are sequentially indefensible. The description of Kamala Nehru's public activities including her visit to a college that incidentally ended in her swoon, and also of the intimacy that Firoz developed with the Nehru family which culminated in his love with Indira [13], in Canto XI after her departure to Badenweiler[14] offends the sequence.

Canto XXII seems to have been positioned at an inappropriate place. Some of the events described therein belong to the period that is certainly anterior to what has been detailed in the preceding canto. While reference to the marriage of Rajiv and Sanjay might have been necessitated to project the Prime Minister as a fond mother, it violates sequence to describe their birth and the death of Firoz at this juncture [15]. Firoz had died in the life-time of Nehru, much before Indira assumed the

---

10. शशाङ्कसप्तिग्रहचन्द्रवर्षे
    दिशाम्बरेऽष्टादशवासरे ताम् । *IC*., XIV. 54
11. *IC*., XXIV. 9, 13
12. *IC*, XXIV 45-47
13. *IC*, XI. 1-13
14. *IC*, X.1-7
15. *IC*. XXII.6-12, 36-46

office of Prime Minister. And it is Nehru's death and her elevation as PM that occupy the Twenty first Canto.

Similarly reference to the Indo-Soviet Treaty of Peace and Friendship and the moral and material support extended by Russia in the 1971 war with Pakistan[16], after setting forth in some detail, the conclusion of Simla Agreement, in the earlier part of Canto XXIV[17], reverses the sequence of the two events.

These avoidable lapses, however, do not detract from the merits of the theme. Despite the pitfalls it encounters in these oddities, the theme of the poem flows, for the most, with calm serenity, seldom ruffled in its course.

SENTIMENT (*RASA*)

Of the three characteristics—*vastu* (theme), *netā* (hero) and *rasa* (sentiment) that, more than anything else are deemed to distinguish a Mahākāvya, from other genres of poetry, it is *rasa* that contributes the most to its aesthetic pleasure[18]. It is because of its contribution in ensuring poetry wide acceptance as a source of pleasure that *rasa* has been equated by no less than the seers of the Upniṣads with the ultimate truth of life, the Brahman, the fountainhead of all bliss (*ānanda*)[19].

While the earlier poeticians favoured full, independent play to all the sentiments on the vast canvas of Mahākāvya with none undermining the intensity of the other[20], Ānandavardhana was the first to postulate a relationship of dominance and subservience (*aṅgāṅgibhāva*) between various sentiments, which, in his view, goes far to heighten the effect of the poem[21]. The ancillary sentiments do not, in anyway, detract from the eminence and grandeur of the main *rasa*, so thoroughly does it pervade the length and breadth of the poem[22], but he is chary to caution that the secondary sentiment, whether going well or not with the *aṅgī rasa*, should not be stretched

---

16. *IC, .XXV. 50-52*
17. *IC*, XXIV. 9-13
18. Suryakanta : *Sanskrit Vāṅmaya kā Vivecanātmaka Itihāsa*, Orient Longman, New Delhi, 1972, p.170
19. रसो वै सः । *Taittirīyopniṣad,* II.6
20. युक्तं लोकस्वभावेन रसैश्च सकलैः पृथक् । (Bhāmaha), op. cit. I. 21
    रसभावनिरन्तरम्, *Kāvyādarśa*, I. 18
21. *Dhvanyāloka*, op. cit., III. 21 and *Vṛtti* thereon
22. स्थायी यो रसस्तस्य सकलप्रबन्धव्यापिनो रसान्तरैरन्तराल-
    वर्तिभिः समावेशो यः स नाङ्गितामुपहन्ति । *Vṛtti on Dhvanyāloka, III. 22*

beyond moderation. Otherwise it was bound to overwhelm it into *submission*[23]. While Ānandavardhana championed the *aṅgāṅgibhāva* for better resuts, Viśvanātha has delimited, rather unkindly, the choice of the principal sentiment from among Śṛṅgāra, Vīra and Śānta[24]. And it is his injunction that has been accepted as a gospel truth.

Being concerned with the chequered career of one who is celebrated for indomitable courage and iron will, emerging stronger from each crisis, erotics or quietism could not simply have any locus standi as a dominant sentiment in the *Indirāgandhīcaritam*. Kings and rulers, who are excessively addicted to carnal pleasure or are averse to wordly affairs like recluses, invite revulsion rather than respect. The *IC* bristles with a series of heroic deeds of its characters. The whole life of its heroine, Indira Gandhi, is an elevating story of heroism. Though weak in body, she is endowed with funds of fortitude which remains unshaken under even worst odds. It is this fortitude (*utsāha*), in its various hues, that pulsates through the poem. Its depiction as a *sthāyī bhāva* (lasting feeling) invariably results in the emergence of the Vīrarasa which may be admitted its principal sentiment. It is however true that in view of the character of the poem, dominated by the narrative, the Vīrarasa as it unfolds itself in the *IC*, is rather unconventional. The poet has sought to project the *utsāha* of his characters in a manner that with a few judicious strokes in the situation, it culminates into Vīrarasa.

The signs of heroism began to show themselves in Indira right from her childhood. She picked up words like Revolution and Satyagraha even while she was on the lap of her grandfather and aspired to do something to free her country from foreign domination (III. 19-20). The story of the brave French girl Joan of Arc provided a turning point to her life. The nerve-chilling enactment of her sacrifice by Indira was the first flash of heroism of the child that unfolded itself with telling effect.

Even as she stood against a column with closed eyes, feeling, like Joan, the heat of the flames below, her eyes brightened up with a sense of fulfilment. Under shadow of 'gallows', she was a perfect picture of fortitude. It was heroism *par excellence :*

जोनफार्केति नाम्न्या यत्कृतं कर्म विलक्षणम् ।
किं तत्कर्तुमनीशास्मि देशो मेऽपि प्रियो यतः ।। IV.7

---

23. अविरोधी विरोधी वा रसोऽङ्गिनि रसान्तरे ।
परिपोषं न नेतव्यस्तथा स्यादविरोधिता ।। *Dhvanyāloka*, III.24.

24. *Sāhityadarpaṇa*, VI.317

एकदा धात्र्यपश्यत्तां मीलिताक्षियुगां शुभाम् ।
स्तम्भमेकं समाश्रित्य बाहुभ्यां परिवेष्टितम् ।।

स्थितामव्यक्तवचनां शूलारोहणमुद्रया ।
अनुकुर्वतीं वीरकन्यां जोनफार्केतिनामिकाम् ।।

भास्वरो मुखवर्णोऽस्याः सुतरां पर्यलक्ष्यत ।
पद्युगं शिखिनो ज्वाला विशन्तीरिव सान्वभूत् ।। IV. 9-11

It is the heroism of Jawaharlal that is prominently projected in the Fifth Canto. The pogrom at the Jallianwala Bagh provoked him to mobilise his countrymen to resist the ruthlessness of the mighty rulers. His fortitude quickly percolated to the people and they displayed it in a variety of ways. Foremost among the protestors, Nehru was an embodiment of electricity and firmness (*sphūrti*) :

इति कृत्यविधौ स्वदेशिनां
सकुटुम्बः स हि मूर्धनि स्थितः ।
जननेतृवरो जवाहरो
हृदये स्फूर्तिमधादलौकिकीम् ।। V. 22

By substituting *sphūrti* for *utsāha* in the verse , the poet has ingeniously steered himself clear of what otherwise could have been an egregious *rasadoṣa*. The poeticians frown upon the use of sentiment and the primary and secondary feelings by name[25].

Canto VI serves to unfold the Vīrarasa with greater vigour. The Nehru ladies forcefully prove their mettle in the face of heavy odds following the arrest of both Motilal and Jawaharlal. Though dismayed, they neither lost heart nor did they conduct themselves like lesser persons who tend to break down under adversity. They rather donned the mantle of the elder Nehrus and dedicated themselves to enthuse the people in the service of the country. They maintained their *utsāha* undisturbed, which when highlighted, expresses itself into Vīrarasa.

वीरद्वये बन्दिगृहं गतेऽपि
पर्याकुलत्वं हृदये गतेऽपि ।

25. व्यभिचारिरसस्थायिभावानां न शब्दवाच्यता । *Kāvyaprakāśa*, VII. 60

न स्त्रीजनस्तत्र जहौ स्वधैर्यं
स्वदेशरक्षादृढबद्धबुद्धिः ।। VI.10

न स्त्रीजनः प्राकृतवत्कदाचिच्
चेष्टेत नैवाप्रतिमस्वभावः ।। VI.11

Perhaps the most impressive depiction of the Vīrarasa is in Canto XVII. The seemingly innocuous incident of hoisting of the national flag in the Christian College (Lucknow) brought out the best in Indira. It was her first encounter with violence over which she bravely triumphed with rare courage and composure born thereof. Despite injuries and pain, she held the flag aloft with tenacity, unmindful of lathi–blows rained on her. She was firmly established as a brave woman with manly courage :

क्षणं प्रजाता भृशविह्वलापि
पीडां कथञ्चित् प्रविषह्य देवी ।
ध्वजं करान्नो विमुमोच तत्र
भूमिं गताऽप्यार्तिवशं गताऽपि ।। XVII.17

एवं गतायामपि तत्र देव्यां
प्रहारवर्षो निपपात तस्याम् ।
निष्पिष्टगात्रापि पदत्रजातै-
र्ध्वजं प्रियं सा न मुमोच धीरा ।। XVII. 18

The orthodox type of Vīrarasa finds powerful expression in description of India's war with Pakistan. Yahya's misadventure was retaliated with hard punch. Indian forces displayed rare valour to frustrate the evil designs of the enemy. They not only liberated what was East Pakistan then but also secured the surrender of one lac Pakistani soldiers. They dealt an equally hard blow on the western front :

पूर्वस्मिंश्चावृतदथ तदा पश्चिमे देशभागे
बङ्गे छम्बे च तुमुलतरः सङ्गरश्चापि सिन्धौ ।
योधास्तत्र प्रथितयशसो भारतीया विवव्रुः
शौर्यं दिव्यं रिपुभटवरान् पाकदेश्यान् विजेतुम् ।। XXIV.2.

पाकिस्थानात्समुपगतवान् बङ्गदेशो विमुक्तिं
जातोऽरीणां मनसि भयदो भारते हर्षवर्षः ।
ऊर्ध्वं तस्माद्विरतिमगदत् सङ्गरस्येन्दिरा द्राक्
चण्डीवोग्रा जगति विदिता दैत्यसंहारतुष्टा ॥ XXIV.7

While the victory of the Indian forces bespeaks the quality of their training and heroism, the declaration of the ceasefire immediately after East Pakistan was liberated and formed into Bangladesh, symbolises the magnanimity of the PM. Her moral courage also exhibited itself in the firmness she maintained in the face of American and Chinese support to Pakistan (*naivābhūd Indirāyāḥ kṣaṇam api hṛdayaṁ kampitaṁ sattamāyāḥ*, XXIII.49). The same firmness is witnessed in the hard decisions she took, despite reservations by many, to improve the lot of the country.[26]

The exalted form of heroism is found in the chivalry of Motilal Nehru. He not only provided shelter to his devoted Munshi Mubarak Ali and bestowed on him care that a seriously ill person merits, he also respected his desire by conducting to him Nehru's child as soon as she was born. This raises heroism to heroic compassion (dayāvīratā) :

वार्धक्यमस्मिन् समुपेयिषि स्व-
भक्ते प्रिये जर्जरदेहयष्टौ ।
रोगैरनेकैः किल कैंसराद्यै-
र्ग्रस्ते वराके कृपणे कृशे च ॥
श्रीमोतिलालः करुणार्द्रचेता
आनाययत्तं निजगेहमेव ।
तत्रैव चैकत्र कुटीरकेऽसा-
वकल्पयत्तद्वसतिं वदान्यः ॥ II.2-3

The Vīrarasa in its varied manifestations is thus fostered in the *IC* with such vigour that all other sentiments tend to sink into subservience, though they are negligible neither in number nor intensity. Of the subordinate sentiments, Karuṇarasa

26. *IC.*, XXIV. 78, XXV. 1, 84, 88, etc.

stands out prominently by reason of its profundity and the severity of its sting. There are many a situation in the poem to occasion its description. While the great sacrifice of the brave French girl Joan of Arc is chilling in its effect[27], the Karuṇarasa expresses itself with vehemence in the depiction of Kamala's death.

After many a brush with agony in distant Sanatorium Kamala, reduced to a mere bundle of bones, died of tuberculosis, leaving every body aghast. The tragedy is made all the more poignant as, according to the poet's version Indira had to cut short her studies at Santiniketan[28] and Nehru was in the prison, away from Kamala when she needed him most[29]. Kamala's pathetic end and the wailings of her kinsmen combine to stir pathos deeply. It was a severe blow to Indira. Though lost in grief, she did not lose her poise :

प्रतिदिनं क्षयमेवमुपेयती
कृशतनुः क्षयरोगवशं गता ।
विलपतः परिहाय निजान् प्रियान्
स्वसुकृतार्जितलोकमियं ययौ ।।

मात्रा वियोगोऽभवदिन्दिराया
वज्रप्रहारोपम एव तावत् ।
शोकार्णवे घोरतरेऽपि मग्ना
धैर्यं न सा धैर्यधना मुमोच ।। XII.34-35

Nehru was equally broken and forlorn. Inspite of his heavy preoccupations, he fondly cherished the sweet memories of Kamala. It is a measure of his devotion to her that though a highly rational person, he retained a part of Kamala's ashes with him till his death :

---

27. वीरकन्या तु सा हन्त रिपूणां वशमागता ।
ते च तां शूलमारोप्य तदधोऽग्निमदीपयन् ।।
यत्र सा दीप्तवदना कृतकार्या मनस्विनी ।
भस्मशेषा बभूवाथ पुण्यांल्लोकाञ्जगाम च । IV.5-6

28. *IC.*, XII.22-23

29. *IC.*, XII.36,XIII.1.

कार्यान्तरासक्तमना अपि स्व-

पत्नीस्मृतिं स्वस्य दधौ स चित्ते ।

किञ्चिच्छरीरस्य च भस्म तस्या

असौ दधारात्मनि यावदायुः ।। XIII.7

Pathos is again acutely evident in the pall of gloom that Nehru's death cast on the nation. Though it was a national tragedy, his death was a personal loss to Indira. She tried to compose herself but felt lonely and the whole world appeared to her a mere void[30]. The people however were shattered to their moorings. Struck with deadly blow, they wept and wept bitterly :

तादृशे तु महावृक्षे कालेन विनिपातिते ।

हाहाकारः प्रवृत्तोऽभूद्दिक्षु चापि विदिक्षु च ।।

तुल्यं वज्रप्रहारेण घोरं नियतिचेष्टितम् ।

अश्रुपूर्णमुखा लोकाः कथञ्चिदेव सेहिरे ।। XXI.4-5

Śṛṅgāra may not be in tune with a poem dominated by Heroic. But its development as an ancillary sentiment on the vast canvas of a Mahākāvya, is beyond reproach. Otherwise also Śṛṅgāra does not occupy much of place in the *IC*. It is confined to the description of the post–marital enjoyments of the newly-weds Indira and Firoz in the enchanting backdrop Kashmir provides with its bracing climate and picturesque beauty. With the natural phenomena acting as an inflaming agent (*uddīpana-vibhāva*) they were lost in the bliss of love. It is not the poet's wont to delve into details. Couched in the Praharṣiṇī metre; its name eminently suiting the subject matter, that is the author's sense of discrimination; the description enlivened by studied phraseology, emits joy so appropriate to the occasion :

कश्मीरेष्वतिकमनीयसौरभाढ्या

वासन्ती कुसुमसमृद्धिरद्वितीया ।

उद्भेदास्तरुषु हिमात्यये च हृद्या

दम्पत्योः प्रसभमहार्षुरन्तरङ्गम् ।। XVI.1

---

30. आबाल्यात्तातसङ्गे सा स्थिता तेन च लालिता ।

तद्वियोगे जगत्सर्वं तस्याः शून्यमिवाभवत् ।। XXI.11

कुर्वन्तौ मधुरतराः प्रियाः कथास्तौ
विस्रब्धं खलु मधुयामिनीषु तुष्टौ ।
आनन्दं परममुपागतौ रसज्ञौ
स्वं कालं क्षणमिव निन्यतू रसेन ।। XVI.5

Vrīḍā as a subsidiary feeling of the erotic sentiment is mentioned by its synonym *lajjā* in describing the beauties of the new bride Indira (*lajjāvanamravadanātitaraṁ cakāśe*, XV.30).

Hāsya is traditionally believed to have its genesis in Śṛṅgara. The *IC* is enlivened by some of the pleasing touches of the many forms of laughter. Viśvanātha favours *smita* (smile) and *hasita* (controlled laughter) for high personages[31]. The author seems to have followed the prescription with devotion. It is the gentle *hāsya* that is traded between the daughter and the father. To Indira's offer to send the cool breeze from Kashmir, Nehru shot back," Shall I send you a basket of mangoes ?"

तत्रस्थौ मृदुपरिहासकौतुकेन
सन्देशं चपलमती जवाहरं द्राक् ।
कस्मिंश्चिद्दिवस इमावहारयेतां
'सम्प्रेष्यः पवन इतोऽतिशीतलः किम्' ।। XVI.6

वातः स्याच्छिशिरतरः प्रियश्च तत्र
नाम्राणां कथमपि वर्तते तु सत्ता ।
सन्देशं निजगुरुतोऽधिगम्य रम्यं
संहृष्टाविति नवदम्पती अभूताम् ।। XVI.8

Though not universally recognised as sentiment, Vātsalya with affection as its permanent feeling has a far better claim to be admitted as a *rasa* than some of the

---

31. ज्येष्ठानां स्मितहसिते । *Sāhityadarpaṇa* , III. 217
ईषद्विकासिनयनं स्मितं स्यात्स्पन्दिताधरम् ।
किंचिल्लक्ष्यद्विजं तत्र हसितं कथितं बुधैः ।। ibid., III. 218

conventional sentiments. Viśvanātha has indeed favoured it with approval[32]. The *IC* is punctuated by several tender pictures of the Vātsalyarasa.

The description of the childhood pranks of Rajiv, Sanjay, and their children[33] stir the tenderest emotions in the heart of their parents and thereby enrich the poem with the exuberance of the Vātsalyarasa. However, its most powerful expression is found in the depiction of Indira, the child. While she filled every heart with joy, her grandfather was especially fond of her. He was so enamoured of the tender, lovely child that in her he seemed to have achieved a rare treasure :

निभाल्याननं मुग्धमस्या मनोज्ञं
मनो मोतिलालस्य भूयो ननन्द ।
अलभ्यः पदार्थो मया कोऽपि लब्धः
सुखं तावदस्यैवमाविर्बभूव ॥

कृशाङ्गी तथा काञ्चनीं देहयष्टिं
दधाना प्रफुल्लाब्जनेत्रेन्दिराऽसौ ।
समस्य स्वबन्धोर्हृदि स्नेहमिश्रं
प्रहर्षप्रकर्षं ववर्षाशु भूयः ॥ III.1-2

There can be little scope for *krodha* in a poem dominated by Heroic, therefore Raudrarasa is not much in evidence here. However, the threat that the English police official administers to Indira in Canto XVIII emanates from anger (XVIII. 3). Likewise the atrocities unleashed on the hapless people of East Pakistan filled the Awami League with anger (XXIII. 32).

The atrocities done to the innocent people of Bangladesh by the occupation forces of Pakistan, turned the country into hell. The description of murder, loot and worse struck terror in the people down to their spine, which finds culmination in the Bhayānakarasa :

---

32. स्फुटं चमत्कारितया वत्सलं च रसं विदुः ।
स्थायी वत्सलतास्नेहः पुत्राद्यालम्बनं मतम् ॥ ibid., III. 251
33. *IC., XXII.7, 11-12,23 ,27, 29*

रात्रिर्यदैषा व्यगमत्सुदीर्घा
घोरेव सत्यं प्रलयस्य रात्रिः ।
हिंसानटीताण्डवनर्तनेन
रोमाञ्चिताः प्रव्यथितान्तरङ्गाः ।। XXIII.3

Thus the *IC* can legitimately boast of richness in sentiments. The various sentiments have been ably depicted to relieve the tedium of the historical narrative. While Indira Gandhi is the central figure in the fulfilment of the main *rasa*, others emanate from various situations ingeniously exploited by the poet to yield the desired results. In view of the wealth of *rasa* that characterises the poem it would be unfair to claim that it is character rather than *rasa* that dominates the *IC*.[34]

CHARACTERISATION

Netā, one of the chief distinguishing features of a Mahākāvya, manifests himself in the author's skill in portraying the dramatis personae with the *nāyaka* occupying the highest rung. Unlike the restricted avenues of characterisation in the *Bodhisattvacaritam*, occasioned by the peculiar nature of its theme, the cohesive narrative in the *IC*, worked out of a plethora of diverse events, offers abundant scope for the poet to turn focus effectively on at least some of his chief characters. It is however Indira Gandhi who emerges as the most colourful figure with all her prominent traits perceptibly in view. In making her the focal character the poet has oddly defied the tradition which unreasonably insists on a divine figure or male Kṣatriya to don the role of the hero[35]. True to his penchant for innovation, the author has rightly accorded the high status of the 'hero'(ine) to the lady who presided over the destiny of the greatest country for more than fifteen years with rare vision and firmness. While shunning the theory, the poet has interestingly sought to highlight in his heroine almost all the virtues that the theory expects the 'hero' to embody. The *IC* is crowded with a variety of characters including the shortsighted Yahya Khan, his wily foreign minister Z.A. Bhutto and Sheikh Mujib, an unfortunate victim of the worst conspiracies. However, most of them are represented by occasional flashes. Besides Indira Gandhi, her parents, grandfather and husband Firoz, are the only characters who have engaged the poet's attention.

---

34. Pathak Indira Kant, *Indirāgāndhīcaritam: Ek Samīkṣātmaka Adhyayana* (Typed Ph.D. Thesis), p.190
35. --- तत्रैको नायकः सुरः ।
सद्वंशः क्षत्रियो वापि धीरोदात्तगुणान्वितः ।। *Sāhityadarpaṇa*, VI.315-316

INDIRA GANDHI

The qualities of the hero summed up by Daṇḍin in the pithy phrase *caturodātta–nāyakam*[36], but blown into details by the later poeticians[37] are represented by his mental, moral and physical equipment. He should in essence, be an ideal man whom the society may follow with profitable results. This is how Indira Gandhi is sought to be projected in the poem. The way she is depicted leaves little doubt that to the poet she is an ideal specimen of humanity, a paragon of virtues. Born in an aristocratic family, Indira was an heir to enviable greatness. She inherited highmindedness and refined tastes from her grandfather. From her great father she acquired devotion to books and dauntless courage. While her grandmother inculcated in her firm resolve and liking for religion, her lovely mien and regard for heritage she owed to her mother (III.6-7). Whatever was worthwhile anywhere, she received it zealously, but it was the milieu, more than anything else, that exercised the most powerful influence in shaping her (*svakālaprabhāvas tu sarvātiśāyīti sādatta tasmāt tu sarvādhikaṁ hi,* III.8). The noble impressions (*saṁskāras*) of patriotism that she imbibed in early childhood, especially after Anand Bhawan had become the centre of political activities, following Motilal's plunge into the Freedom Movement under the spell of Gandhiji, not only enabled her to quickly grasp the connotation of such profound terms as Revolution and Satyagraha but also manifested themselves in her childhood-play that invariably culminated in the Satyagrahis routing the police in the mock fight she arranged between the two sets of her toys (IV.22-25). The applause with which she greeted the victory of the Satyagrahis (IV.27-28) was as much an expression of her innocence as her reaction to the atrocities the alien rulers had unleashed on the harried people, engaged in a grim fight against their might. Thus she was gradually coming under the influence of the milieu. It was because of that impact that even her play was turned into a replica of the freedom struggle. The elevating story of the French girl Joan of Arc was another milestone in her formative era. It inspired her to resolve to do for the country what Joan had bravely done for hers[38]. And perhaps in a bid to establish her credentials, she went to the extent of gleefully re-enacting Joan's martyrdom. It marked tremendous upliftment of her patriotic conscience. This facet of her *saṁskāras* may plausibly be detected in the way she laid down her life for the country. The unruffled courage and zeal with which the Nehru-women carried on the fight after the arrest of both Motilal and Jawaharlal,

---

36. *Kāvyādarśa*, I.15
37. *Sāhityadarpaṇa*, III. 32
38. जोनफार्केतिनाम्न्या यत्कृतं कर्म विलक्षणम् ।

instilled into her self-reliance coupled with unshakable courage. It is no wonder that her inner urge led her to the male *khadi* garments, like a volunteer (*tadveṣadhṛc cāpi bhṛśaṁ pratītā,* VI.21). She rather longed to accompany her mother on the mission, she had embarked upon (*nijāmbayā gantum iyeṣa sākam*, VI.22). Her brief sojourn at Gandhiji's hermitage on the Sabarmati alongwith her father, was for her a unique lesson in discipline and dignity of labour. She was so thoroughly overwhelmed with Gandhiji and the simplicity and self-reliance at the *āśrama* that, forgetting her aristocratic moorings, she personally performed at the hermitage, all the chores including cooking and brooming (VII.6-7). Thus her inheritance, training and environment had combined to put the perceptive child on the right track that led her, steadily and assuredly, to the dizzy heights of greatness. She was indeed much wiser than her years (*bālāpy abālamativaibhavaśālinī sā*, IV.29). The poet has lavished choicest epithets on her to highlight her equipment.[39]

The adolescence saw her blossom tremendously. While her father's action in inhibiting her from dancing round the bonfire of foreign clothes near Anand Bhawan, had damped her in the childhood, the denial of membership of the Congress party at the age of twelve, though a source of dismay, only initially, spurred her to canalise her organisational capabilities in forming the Childrens' Brigade, which popularly came to be known as Vānarasenā. With its adolescent and therefore unsuspect members, it turned out an intelligence service of sorts besides being an effective agency to carry errands. The Brigade had been instrumental in thwarting the arrest of some of the elderly people by conveying them beforehand the almost certain information of their planned detention. It was the first assured expression of the organisational skill and quality of leadership of Priyadarśini. The acclaim that they earned from stalwarts like Motilal and others was a modest recognition of what was to take the world by surprise subsequently. The organisation of the Vānarasenā and its attendant activities also went after to project the firmness of her resolve and sharpness of intellect[40].

It is ironic that such a brilliant child wth perceptible signs of greatness could not get systematic education. Her brief stay at Santiniketan and elsewhere was invariably interrupted by her father's frequent arrests and mother's illness. Ultimately her father emerged as her educator. Though even his vicinity was repeatedly denied to her

---

39. नानाविधैर्दिव्यगुणैरुपेता ।
बालाप्यबालेव विवृद्धसत्त्वा
कुशाग्रधीः स्फूर्तिमती प्रदीप्ता ॥ *IC.*, VI.21
40. दृढता सङ्कल्पस्य पटुता बुद्धेश्च कौशलं कृत्ये च ।
एते गुणाः समस्ता आविरभवन् कुलक्रमागता अस्याम् ॥ *IC.*, IX.24

yet in the interludes when he was with her and even when he was in jail, Jawaharlal, through a series of conversations and writings, equipped her eminently well to break through all the challenges and crises to the top. While in earlier stages she learnt a lot from the stories and events skilfully related by her father, the celebrated letters written by him from the prison were an elevating experience of its own type for her. Equally rewarding were the meetings she had in the company of her father with the celebrities of the world. Thus it was from the book of life that she learnt the most.

As she entered youth, her various traits, particularly the sense of judgement and firmness of resolve, had ripened beyond measure. All the protests against her decision to marry the Parsi boy Firoz and her father's advice to reconsider it in view of the wide disparities between the two, could not deflect her fom the course; 'I have already accepted him as my husband. There is therefore no question of my having second thought on the issue', she argued convincingly (---*mayakā manasā vṛto 'yam,----(nahi) vṛṇvīya kañcid aparam patim ity avehi*, XV.5). Patriotism and firmness, besides unbounded capacity to suffer for the sake of the country, are tellingly underscored by her rare act of bravery in not surrendering the national flag even under the volley of lathi-blows (XVII. 17). Taking it as a part of her inheritance to face odds boldly, she withstood the ordeal admirably (XVII.19-20). The influence of this inheritance was again evident when she underplayed the gravity of the incident to her husband (*svalpo virodho 'jani rakṣibhir no*, XVII.23). She was by now fully initiated into the intricacies of the freedom movement. It was precisely because of this that she took with a smile the police official's threat to shoot her down in case she persisted with her speech. That earned her the first incarceration. Soon thereafter Indira alongwith her husband participated in the historic 1942-session of the Congress party. Her involvement with history was by now complete.

In the midst of these tumultuous events, Indira established herself as a loving wife, always conscious of her duties. She was devoted to her husband as Śacī was to Indra (*śakraṁ taṁ satatam anuvratā śacīva*, XVI.14). Her competence as a housewife also manifested itself in the way she decorated her new house at Lucknow (XVI.15).

The first phase of her career thus ends in her rising to the status that contained, in an embroynic form, the seeds of her future stature.

The next phase of Indira's career as depicted in Cantos XVIII, XIX and the earlier part of the XX, entirely belongs to her father. The independence of the country brought in its trail partition and the orgy of communal carnage. Nehru's problems as PM were greatly compounded by the influx of millions of refugees from Pakistan. Indira, as a devoted daughter, rose to the occasion to lighten the burden of her father so that he might concentrate on the vital issues that confronted the nascent State.

She stayed with him, almost permanently and addressed herself to solve the stupendous problem of rehabilitating the refugees. She did all that could be done to alleviate the miseries of those unfortunate victims of bigotry. She also took upon herself the duty of welcoming the foreign dignitaries. All this she did with unbelievable self-effacement. Only once during the regime of her father, she was made president of the All India Congress. She held the office with skill and dignity.

Indira Gandhi flowered into her fullest self on her elevation as Prime Minister of the country. The long tenure witnessed her rising higher and higher. That doubtless marked acme to her political sagacity, undaunted courage, unfailing foresight and her innate capacity to prove not only equal to each crisis but emerge stronger out of it. Her first acid test as Prime Minister came when she was locked in conflict with the old guard of the Congress over the choice of the candidate for the office of the President after the sudden death of Zakir Hussain. In opposition to their choice, she backed V.V. Giri, an independent candidate, and marshalled all her resources to ensure his success. And in order to purge the organisation of the dead wood, she did not hesitate to create schism in it. She was vindicated in her stand by the overwhelming support she evoked from the people. The old Congress was eclipsed ere long (*tatra nūtnā vyaśiṣyata*, XXI.42). The influx of swarms of refugees following the crackdown of the Pakistan army on its eastern wing was the gravest crisis of her career, but that only served to bring out the best in her. The courage and foresight with which she led the country to victory in the war imposed by Pakistan in 1971 evoked world-wide acclaim. At home, she was hailed as Caṇḍī, the goddess of might (*caṇḍīvogrā jagati viditā daityasaṁhāratuṣṭā*, XXIV.7). The two bouts established her as the tallest leader in the country. When the country slid to the brink of disaster, she, sure of herself, stemmed the rot by imposing Emergency which restored peace and order overnight. The Emergency enabled her to embark upon multipronged measures to rejuvenate the country.

Indira Gandhi thus represents an embodiment of patriotism, foresight, firmness tempered with total dedication to the welfare of the people. To the poet, she was a rare character far above the lesser mortals (*alaukikānāṁ khalu sarvam eva hy alaukikam*, IX.25). He has drawn a long catalogue of her virtues that entitle her to the status. The *Pūrvapīṭhikā* is intended as an index of her personality endowed with a plethora of uncommon qualities :

यस्या ध्रुवं विविधचारुविचारवीचि-

व्यावल्गितो लसति मानसराजहंसः ।

या चापि दिव्यधिषणा परिकल्पनाभिः

स्वाभिः करोति धिषणं सुतरामधस्तात् ।। Pūrva;1-

नेत्री जनानां हृदयस्य जेत्री
भेत्त्री रिपूणामपि दुर्मदानाम् ।
सौम्याकृतिः सौम्यगुणाभिगम्या
यत्राकृतिस्तत्र गुणा वसन्ति ।।

देशो मदीयः सुतरां समृद्धो
भवेदितीच्छा परमा यदीया ।
न कोऽपि दीनो न च वा दरिद्रो
न व्याधितो वा न च पीडितः स्यात् ।। 3.

The poet is so enamoured of her manifold excellences that he is often disposed to deify her, far above the mortals. And he is not alone in the belief[41].

Motilal's prediction about her turned out to be literally true. Indira indeed put to shame hundreds of sons[42] What she did would seldom be equalled or excelled[43].

JAWAHARLAL NEHRU

Though overshadowing all else including the heroine of the poem, and a colossus in his own right, Jawaharlal Nehru, Indira's father, would be rated as an ancillary character of the Kāvya. A wise son of a wise father, Jawaharlal's exceptionally unique education in foreign land equipped him to emerge as a multi-dimensional man, the like of whom are a rare species. A loving and devoted husband, who, despite his highly scientific temper, retained, till his death, a part of ashes of

---

41. Compare शिवा यासि साक्षात् शिवस्य त्वमेव । *Indirāvijayapraśastiśatakam* , 71
त्वमाद्यासि शक्तिर्ह्यनादिरीश्वरस्य । ibid. 19
सुश्रीन्दिरे त्वमसि सा परमेशशक्तिः । *Śrīmatīndirāgāndhīcaritāmṛtam*, 79
विविधदेवतातत्त्वसंयुता । *Indirākīrtiśatakam*, 9
All Quoted in *Sanskrit Vāṅmaya meṁ Indira Gandhi* (Typed Ph. D. Thesis), by Kanak Mathur, p. 299.
42. पुत्री वरा पुत्रशतेभ्य एषा । *IC.*, II.23
43. सत्यं हि तत्कर्म करिष्यतीयं
नान्येन केनापि कृतं पुरा यत् । *IC.*, II.24

his wife[44], he was equally a fond father. He loved to be with his daughter, though his incarcerations frequently detached him from her. He wanted Indira to bloom into her full. Jawahar was worried about the frequent interruptions that Indira's education suffered due to one reason or the other. When he was convinced that formal education may ultimately be denied to her, he, in his inimitable way, evolved the novel method of instructing her through informative stories, besides the thorough impact of his personality which she imbibed quickly. The process culminated in the famous letters, that he wrote to her from the four walls of the prison. What started as a birthday gift[45], in place of the conventional present, ended in a series of 196 letters. That was Indira's first full-fledged lesson in world history and civilisation. Besides being a scholar and farsighted person, he was a man of indomitable courage. This was the quality that percolated to his daughter with a vengeance.

Jawaharlal was drawn into the freedom struggle quite early in life. He was a patriot *par excellence.* He was greatly inspired by the Russian revolution. It was its impact that led him to every nook and corner of the country to see for himself the miserable life of the people. Their poverty combined with the atrocities that the British rulers had unleashed on them provoked him to organise resistance against their cruelties (*niścikāya sa pratirodham*, V.7). The last straw came with the massacre at Jallianwala Bagh. Thereafter, there was no looking back for him. He bravely called upon the people to throw away the British yoke as it was a sin to tolerate the pack of heartless rulers, impervious to their cause[46]. His call evoked instant response from them to the extent that they bycotted everything that was foreign and openly made bonfire of costly British goods (*navavāsāṁsy analāya te daduḥ*, V.21). He mobilised the people into an upsurge that shook the foundations of the British rule. Since he was foremost in the movement (*iti kṛtyavidhau svadeśināṁ sakuṭumbaḥ sa hi mūrdhani sthitaḥ,* V.22), he was arrested. That started the story of his incarcerations which continued with unending frequency. He was established as the unquestioned leader of the masses.

When India achieved independence in 1947 after a long struggle, Jawaharlal became the Prime Minister of the country. He had accepted the partition of the country as the price for independence (XIX.9). But the large scale massacre that

---

44. किञ्चिच्छरीरस्य च भस्म तस्या
असौ दधारात्मनि यावदायुः ।। *IC.*, XIII.7

45. केवलं स्वहृदयं प्रहिणोमि पत्रकेण तदुरीकुरु पुत्रि । *IC.*, XIV.23

46. अयि ! शासनमाततायि भोः
सहते क्रूरमिदं भवान् कथम् ? *IC.*, V.10

followed filled him with anguish (*iti tena kadarthitaṁ mano*, XX.12). He was torn between mental agony and tremendous responsibilities of the high office. He quenched the flames of communal frenzy and took immediate steps to rehabilitate the refugees from Pakistan. He was not only a Prime Minister, he was the darling of the people. His death, hastened by the Chinese perfidy, left the people aghast. They never imagined that he would leave them one day, so enamoured they were of him[47] He was a fascinating figure (VII. 27).

OTHER CHARACTERS

MOTILAL NEHRU

The other characters have been disposed of hastily. Even Jawaharlal himself had not received his due. His father Motilal, a sharply intelligent person, established himself as a legal luminary. His roaring practice brought him wide recognition and equally fabulous wealth (I.17). Extremely personable, he was known for eloquence (*vāgvilāsena hṛdyo*, I.26) and refined tastes. It is a measure of the richness of tastes and likings that when the house he had purchased from an Englishman did not meet his approval, he built a palatial house with a vast garden attatched to it. He not only imaginatively named it as Anand Bhawan but also tastefully decorated it with rich furniture, curtains, carpets, etc. It elicited acclaim from one and all (*sarvo jano vismayam ājagāma*, I.21)

A kind-hearted man, his solicitude expressed itself in alleviating the sufferings of others. The care bestowed by him on his cancerous clerk Mubarak Ali speaks volumes of his magnanimity (II.3). Equally touching was his gesture to Mubarak Ali in conducting to him Jawahar's newly–born child on whom he showered blessings (*tatputrako 'py eṣa bhavet tathaiva*, II. 9).

Like all great men, Motilal was fond of children. He celebrated Indira's birth with festivities and rich gifts to friends and relatives. She was indeed his darling. As a legal celebrity, he had an unfailing insight. The prophecy that he made about Indira came out literally true.

Though fabulously rich and given to fine things of life, Motilal was imbued with the spirit of patriotism. Under the spell of Gandhiji he plunged deep into the freedom movement (*tam evānugantuṁ manaḥ svaṁ babandha*, III. 14). He had to suffer incarceration.

---

47. न हि प्रधानमन्त्र्यासीत्केवलं स महाजनः ।
पूजनीयश्च वन्द्यश्च प्रियश्चापि बभूव सः ।।
तादृशेन महापुंसा कदाचिद्विरहो भवेत् ।

FIROZ

Firoz, the handsome Parsi boy, came into contact with the Nehru family, in a dramatic manner. His kind gesture to Kamala Nehru, when she swooned outside a college, resulted into intimacy with Indira, which subsequently climaxed into their marriage. Firoz was self-respecting individual and considered it against his ethos to crutch on others. In order to lead an independent life, outside the umbrella of his father-in-law, he took up a job with the National Herald and built a house at Lucknow[48]. Even as a member of Lok Sabha, he stayed in a separate house. He participated in the freedom struggle and underwent imprisonment, alongwith his wife. He was a skilful person and evaded his arrest for quite some time (XVII.4). He was an eloquent speaker (*vāggmivaraḥ*, XXII.36). Despite his no mean equipment, Firoz, in the poem, appears to be overwhelmed by his wife, though it would be unkind to rate him as her appendage.

KAMALA

A brilliant woman, Kamala was not merely Nehru's wife. She was on the right track, when death cut short what promised to be a fruitful life.

YAHYA KHAN AND BHUTTO

Yahya Khan and his wily foreign minister Zulfiquar Ali Bhutto may be taken as villains of sorts. They had been instrumental in dismembering their country and subjecting it to a humiliating military defeat.

MUJIB

Sheikh Mujib was a victim of the conspiracy deceitfully hatched by Bhutto in collusion with Yahya Khan, the President of Pakistan. It is ironic that though he made a clean sweep of the first ever democratically contested election, he was not only denied Prime Ministership of the country, he was thrown behind the bars. It is a different matter that it nailed the fate of Pakistan. Its eastern wing was liberated with Mujib as its first PM.

DESCRIPTIONS

The varied descriptions, prescribed by the poeticians, as an inalienable feature of a Mahākāvya, were primarily intended to lend diversity to the narrative and thereby relieve the tedium that was otherwise bound to overwhelm it . It was more so in a historical poem, which by its austere devotion to facts, scarcely lends itself to tender poetic niceties. In order to avoid distraction or disruption to the theme, the descriptions by their very nature had to be moderate in size. Unlike the later classical poets who had blown them out of proportions to the extent that they threatened to convert

---

48. *IC.*, XVI.12.

the Mahākāvyas into a mass of unwieldy descriptions, the poet true to his wont, has admitted in the *IC* only such of the descriptions as emanate from the narrative itself. The poem is doubtless dotted with a number of perceptive accounts of diverse phenomena but they are so smoothly woven in the warp and woof of the poem that they form its inextricable parts. Never do they seem to have been forced upon the narrative or glued at a place where they do not stick. They rather emerge as oases in the rugged historical narrative, though, in itself, the latter is not shorn of charm. Their variety is as admirable as their freshness. It is refreshing to find the time-worn descriptions of sun-set, moonrise, water-sports, etc. replaced in the poem by graphic accounts of such contemporary social evils as casteism, dowry, population explosion, bonded labour and environmental pollution besides the gorgeous portrayal of scenic beauties of foreign lands. The *IC* has the rich distinction of being the solitary Mahākāvya to cover in its ambit such unorthodox descriptions as those of Black Forests of Germany and the Alps of Switzerland. It is indeed laudable that the ingenuity of the author does not sag under the diversity of descriptions. He is admirably equal to the task. It is a tribute to his keen observation and poetic talents that the descriptions in the *IC* have to vibrate with liveliness, their diversity and complexity notwithstanding. With measured strokes backed by unfailing insight and lucidly sweet phraseology, the poet goes the whole hog to capture the essence of the objects under description, within the parametres determined by him.

It is a measure of the importance the descriptions have been accorded in the *IC* that the poem, preliminaries apart, opens with a graphic account of the sacred confluence at Prayāga, celebrated down the ages, in history and mythology. Its sanctity has aroused many a poet, including Kālidāsa, into poetic flourishes. The cynosure of crores of people of all times and climes, Prayāga is celebrated for its efficacy in purging the devotees of their sins and thereby ensuring them liberation from bondage. The Saṁgama there derives its name conformable to its meaning from the confluence of two of the most sacred rivers, the Gaṅgā and the Yamunā. The conjunction of the two currents, one white and the other black, imparts it beauty that can be best illustrated by the mingling of the darkness of dense forests with the rays of the moon. The current is so pure and purifying that a mere sip of its water invests one with fulfilment. Within the tiny frame of six verses, the poet has captured the greatness of this renowned centre of pilgrimage. Sweet alliteration and Simile, besides lucid language, combine to invest the description with poetic tenderness and charm :

पुण्यात्मभिः सेवितमात्मविद्भिः
सद्भिः सदाचारविचारवद्भिः ।

स्वर्गापवर्गस्य निमित्तभूतं
प्रयागतीर्थं प्रथितं पृथिव्याम् ॥ I.9

यदीयमाहात्म्यविमुग्धभावा
दिग्भ्यो विदिग्भ्यः समुपेयिवांसः ।
प्रक्षाल्य पापं कलिकल्मषोत्थं
जना गृहान् स्वान् प्रतियान्ति हृष्टाः ॥ I.10

यत्र स्फुटं भाति विभिन्नरूपं
गाङ्गं जलं यामुनमेव चापि ।
श्यामासु शुभ्राः शशिनः प्रविष्टाः
पादा यथा सान्द्रवनस्थलीषु॥ I.12

पुण्यानि हृद्यानि च शीतलानि
यदीयतोयानि सुपावनानि ।
स्नानेन चैवाचमनेन चापि
कुर्वन्ति लोकं कृतकृत्यरूपम् ॥ I.14

Hardly had the narrative taken a step, that it is punctuated by a lively, though pithy, description of Motilal Nehru's palatial house imaginatively named as Anand Bhawan, built after the old house failed to satisfy his rich tastes. Anand Bhawan with its elegant structure, rich upholstery and expansive garden filled everybody with wonder. Based on Svabhāvokti, the description serves to bring into relief the grandeur and affluence of the imposing building :

नूत्नैः कुथैरास्तरणैस्तथा च
नूत्नैस्तथाऽऽसन्दिवरैरुपेतम् ।
पीठैश्च नूत्नैरथ रम्यरूपै-
र्विराजितं नूतनपारिणाह्यैः ॥
विस्तारिशोभेन सुपुष्पितनो-
द्यानेन नीराजितमद्वितीयम् ।

श्रीमोतिलालस्य निरीक्ष्य वेश्म

सर्वो जनो विस्मयमाजगाम ।। I.20-21

The vibrance of the Anand Bhawan has been sought to be contrasted, in Canto VI, with the desolation that had overtaken it after the arrest of both Motilal and Jawaharlal. With their removal to the prison, the Anand Bhawan was divested of *ānanda* (joy). It turned colourless, as if it were untenanted. Without them, it was no better than the sky without sun and moon . One pined thereafter for Motilal's loud laughter and Jawahar's graceful and thoughtful figure. It ceased to be the centre of political activities, nor were now heard the heated discussions. It appeared to be a big void. The brief description adds up to a perceptive pen-picture of the Anand Bhawan under a different set of circumstances :

आनन्दनाम प्रथितं पृथिव्यां

विलक्षणं यद् भवनं विरेजे ।

आसीत्तदानन्दविहीनमेव

विच्छायमेवापि च शून्यमेव ।। VI.6

नैवागमच्छ्रोत्रयुगं तदानीं

श्रीमोतिलालस्य शुभोऽट्टहासः ।

न वा तदाऽलक्ष्यत भव्यमूर्ति-

र्जवाहरश्चिन्तनदत्तचित्तः ।। VI.8

न तज्जनाकीर्णमभूत्तदानीं

न वा नवाऽजायत तत्र चर्चा ।

शून्यं जनस्थानमिवाबभौ तत्

स्त्रीलोकनाथं भवनं तदानीम् ।। VI.9

The same Canto (One) is embedded with a brilliant sketch of Motilal Nehru. A sharply intelligent and handsome person, he was known for his eloquence . His legal attainments had won him wide recognition and astronomical affluence. With his effective expression, the author has highlighted the colourful personality of Motilal in just three verses:

कुशाग्रबुद्ध्या च परिश्रमेण
चोपार्ज्य विद्यां विधिशास्त्रगम्याम् ।
न्यायालयेऽसौ विबभौ भृशं प्राड्-
विवाकरूपेण विदां वरेण्यः ।। I.16

अत्यल्पकालेन बभूव तस्य
यशोऽतिशुभ्रं प्रथितं पृथिव्याम् ।
अतः श्रिया तं युयुजे मुदा श्री-
'र्भवन्ति भव्येषु हि पक्षपाताः' ।। I.17

कीर्त्या दीप्रो वाग्विलासेन हृद्यो
वक्त्राम्भोजं रम्यरूपं दधानः ।
ख्यातो लोके कोविदाग्रेसरोऽयं
कालं हृष्टो मोतिलालो विनिन्ये ।। I.26

A contrast of sorts is represented by Indira, who, even in her childhood-innocence, was aiming at dizzy sublimities. The impressions of patriotism that she had imbibed from the milieu, found their first expression in the chilling enactment by her of the supreme sacrifice that Joan of Arc had made to liberate her country from foreign domination (IV. 9-11). The incident at the Christian College, on the other hand represents a far developed stage in Indira's march to patriotism and firmness which have been depicted with appropriate Svabhāvokti. The event has been described with such precision and force that while reading it one may well feel the lightning speed with which Indira dashed to hold the national flag and the tenacity she displayed in not surrendering it despite the worst blows showered on her :

उच्चैश्च चुक्रोश ध्वजो भविष्य-
त्ययं सदैवोर्ध्वगतिः प्रियो नः । XVI.13

एवं गतायामपि तत्र देव्यां
प्रहारवर्षो निपपात तस्याम् ।
निष्पिष्टगात्राऽपि पदत्रजातै-
र्ध्वजं प्रियं सा न मुमोच धीरा ।। XVII.18

(XVII.12–18):

As observed earlier, the author is not enamoured of banal prolixities. This aversion to needless details has led him to discard the orthodox descriptions that continue to evoke esteem till the present day. That is why the *IC* is shorn of extravagant descriptions which are worked up to indulge in poetic flourishes, even if they do not accord with the character of the theme. More than anything else, the author revels in depicting the tender emotions of the human heart. He is at his best in dealing with the conflicting emotions that tend to overpower man in various situations. While Indira's joy at her marrige was deeply tempered with the sorrow caused by her mother's departure, the thought of impending separation from her father was equally chilling.Torn between these contradictory feelings, her eyes were perceptibly tinged with despondency, the jubilations on the occasion notwithstanding :

प्रीतिः परा पतिसमागमनेन तस्या
आसीत् स्वमातुरनुपस्थितिजं च दुःखम् ।।
एवं परस्परविरोधिविचारवृन्दै-
रान्दोलिताऽतिसुकुमारवयाः कुमारी ।
सम्पत्स्यमानमचिराद्विरहं पितुः सा
सञ्चिन्त्य न क्षणमपि क्षणमाससाद ।।

हासप्रहासनिरते स्वसखीजनेऽपि
हर्षाप्लुते परिजने परितः स्थितेऽपि ।
आलक्ष्यताक्षियुगले भृशमायतेऽस्याः
सूक्ष्मा प्रहर्षसमयेऽपि विषादरेखा ।। XV. 23-25

The description comes within an ace of Karuṇarasa. The last line *sūkṣmā praharṣasamaye 'pi viṣādarekhā* is marked by infinite pathos. It may well compare with the immensely pregnant description of Rāma after Lakṣmaṇa had apprised him of Sītā's plight in the jungle :

babhūva Rāmaḥ sahasā sabāṣpas tuṣāravarṣīva sahasyacandraḥ, Raghu. XIV. 84.

The serene but lively description of the bride presents a refreshing contrast to the gripping depiction of human emotions. Adorned with choice ornaments and sobre wedding garments but overcome by an onrush of feelings, not precluding modesy (vriḍā), Indira was a perfect figure of an Indian bride. The deep understanding of the emotions that characterise an Indian bride coupled with a liberal dose of alliteration has enabled the poet to draw a faithful replica of the bride :

शाटीमिमां च परिधाय मनस्विनी सा
रक्तान्तकां प्रियतमे हृदयेन रक्ता ।
आरक्तवर्णकमनीयकपोलकान्तिः
कम्रा वधूरतितरां सुषमां प्रपेदे ।।

दत्ताङ्गरागरुचिरा स्वसखीभिरेषा
मुग्धा वृताऽतिकमनीयशरीरयष्टिः ।
नानाविधाभरणभूषितहृद्यरूपा
लज्जावनम्रवदनाऽतितरां चकाशे ।। XV. 29-30

These pithy sketches of some of the tenderest emotions are again intened to be brought into vivid contrast with the description of fierce indignation, preceded by helpless dejection, of Bengalis or East Pakistanis at the loot of their land by Pakistan and the imposition of a different language and culture on them. The sweet Mālini metre, apt phraseology attuned to the helplessness of the people and figures of speech like alliteration and Arthāntaranyāsa join hands to highlight the plight of the people, groaning under alien domination :

विपुलविभवशाली सत्यमस्मत्प्रदेशो
विभवमपहरन्ति त्वन्यभागस्थलोकाः ।
इत इति भृशमासन्नत्र लोका विषण्णा
जननभुव उपेक्षां मानिनो नो सहन्ते ।। XXIIII.12

नहि विभवमहार्षुः केवलं पश्चिमस्था
अपि तु बलवदेवारोपयंस्तत्र धृष्टाः ।
भुवि जननिवहस्यासंस्तुतां वाचमुर्दू
मधुरमधुररूपां बङ्गभाषामपास्य ।। XXIII.13

इति मनसि विचिन्त्य प्राप्तरोषा हि बाङ्गाः

कथमपि जनसङ्घा आत्ममुक्तिं लषित्वा
क्षणमपि नहि लब्ध्वा निर्वृतिं शिश्रियुस्ते
बहुतरकमुपायं कृत्यजाते प्रवीणाः ।। XXIII.16

Besides the many laurels the *IC* has to its credit, it is perhaps the first Mahākāvya to grapple with issues which were frowned upon by the classical and contemporary writers alike. It is here that social evils like dowry, casteism, bonded labour, etc. are duly noticed and denounced. This is how the victim of the pernicious system of dowry is described in the solitary verse :

विद्धा वचोभिर्बहु यावदायु-
रुन्तुदैः कष्टमियं प्रपन्ना ।
भस्त्रेव दीर्घं श्वसती कथञ्चित्
स्वजीवितं संक्षपयत्यभाग्या ।। XXV.47

While caste-system is reviled as an affront to human dignity (XXV.52), forestration is recommended as an antidote to ecological imbalance (XXV.56).

As the *Indirāgāndhicaritam* concerns itself with recent history, both succeeding and preceding the attainment of independence, it deals with a wide range of political problems that plagued the country at different points of time, and the phenomenal progress that it made in its march to a new era. The imposition of Emergency on the country in 1975 was by far the most crucial, though unpleasant, step that Indira Gandhi was constrained to take to stem the burgeoning rot. The circumstances that culminated in the proclamation of Emergency have been forcefully, albeit briefly, described in the poem with dispassionate faithfulness. Those who have been witness to the stormy days and the near anarchy that had overtaken the country, would unhesitatingly vouch for their veracity :

पाकिस्थानेन युद्धेन महार्घत्वमजायत ।
दौर्लभ्यं चापि वस्तूनां सर्वं कालप्रचोदितम् ।। XXIV.59
उत्कोचादिप्रदानं च तदादानमनिष्टकृत् ।
सर्वत्र प्रसृतं देशे महारोग इवाभवत् ।। XXIV.64
वृत्तपत्राण्यनेकानि वृत्तमुच्छृङ्खलं बहु ।

स्वैरं प्रकाशयामासुः शासनप्रतिरोधकृत् ।। XXIV.65

अन्यदेशेभ्य आनैषुः पदार्थान् बहुमूल्यकान् ।
देशस्य घातकाः केचित् तास्करीं वृत्तिमाश्रिताः ।। XXIV.66

आन्दोलनादिवृत्तिश्च विनिवृत्तिश्च कर्मणाम् ।
नैकेषु व्यवसायेषु विद्याशालेष्वसंयमः ।। XXIV.67

राजकीयनिकायेषु सर्वत्रैवाभ्यदृश्यत ।
याथाकामी प्रवृत्तेव सर्वलोकस्य दुःखदा ।। XXIV. 68

देशोऽयं न भवेच्चापि खण्डितोऽन्योन्यविग्रहैः ।
अचिरोपार्जितं चास्य स्वातन्त्र्यं नापगच्छतु ।। XXIV.73

एतत्सर्वं समालोच्य कृतबुद्धिर्विदां वरा ।
आपत्स्थितेः समुद्घोषं स्वदेशे निर्भया व्यधात् ।। XXIV.74

No less challenging were the developments in East Pakistan (now Bangladesh) that threatened to throw the country into turmoil. The mindless atrocities unleashed on the Bengalis and their resultant resolve to throw away the yoke of Pakistani domination are vividly described in a manner that the gory scenario comes alive :

घोरं जनानां कदनं प्रचक्रु-
स्तद्वस्तुजातस्य विनाशनं च ।
नानादिनान्येवमभूत्प्रवृत्त-
मनागसां हिंसनमेव हन्त! ।। XXIII.28

रात्रिर्यदैषा व्यगमत्सुदीर्घा
घोरेव सत्यं प्रलयस्य रात्रिः ।
हिंसानटीताण्डवनर्तनेन
रोमाञ्चिताः प्रव्यथितान्तरङ्गाः ।। XXIII.30

नाशं स्वदेशस्य विधीयमानं

स्वदेशजैरेव निशाम्य घोरम् ।
पदाहताशीविषतुल्यरूपा
आहारयन्नात्मनि मन्युमुग्रम् ।। XXIII.31

देशः स्वतन्त्रो भुवि नोऽस्तु पाकि-
स्थानस्य पाशात्सुदृढाद्विमुक्तः ।
अद्यावधीति प्रविनेदुरेते
सिंहोरुसत्त्वा भुवि सिंहनादम् ।। XXIII.34

The explosion of the nuclear device at Pokhran was a landmark in the country's rapid march to self-reliance. However, it caused apprehensions in the neighbouring countries. The PM sought to allay the unfounded fear by emphasising the tradition of peace and universal brotherhood that the country has espoused, down the ages. These ideals are beautifully set forth in the following stanzas :

शमप्रधानः खलु देश एष
नाशं न कस्याप्यभिरोचयेत ।
एतादृशी नाम परम्पराऽत्र
न प्राणिहिंसाऽभिमताऽत्र पुंसाम् ।।

मैत्री समैरत्र जनैरभीष्टा
कल्याणबुद्धिः प्रसृताऽत्र साध्वी ।
अत्रैव पूर्वे ऋषयोऽभ्यवोचन्
कुटुम्बमेकं वसुधां समग्राम् ।। XXIV. 22-23

The *IC* is not wanting in the gorgeous descriptions of the scenic beauties as well. If anything , the descriptions transcend the narrow barriers and turn focus on the beauties of nature that characterise the alien lands. However, in accordance with his predilection for the unconventional, the author does not relish to depict the type of hackneyed phenomena that the poeticians have been at pains to prescribe for a Mahākāvya. He has sought to depict only those facets of nature which accord with his theme, and therefore form its essential ingredients. HIs aversion to trite details has equipped him to opt for pleasing brevity. The descriptions of nature in the *IC* are distinguished by a proclivity to highlight the phenomena in their totality without running after inconsequential details. It is a measure of the author's skill that even the lengthiest description in the *IC* does not extend beyond four verses. The description of the expanses of the Black Forests of Germany (X.4-6), though transplanted from the author's Khaṇḍakāvya *Śarmaṇyadeśaḥ sutarāṁ vibhāti* (89–91), is marked by natural beauty and resoundingly swift alliteration comparable respectively to their own verdour and brooks. Based on Svabhāvokti the brief depiction of Switzerland (X.18–23) tellingly captures the essence of its gorgeous charms that lead one to forget everything including oneself. The lucid language, marked by *mādhurya*, serves to heighten them further. No wonder, it has been compared with the mythical Nandana forest :

यदीयसौन्दर्यमतीव हारि
　　यद्वैभवं लोचनयुग्मलोभि ।
योरूपभूमण्डलमध्यवर्ती
　　यो भात्यहो ! नन्दनतुल्यरूपः ॥ X.18

दिव्या यदीया सुषमाऽद्वितीया
　　नेत्रद्वयासेचनिका चकास्ति ।
जना हृतान्तःकरणा ययाऽहो !
　　स्वस्यैव सत्तां ननु विस्मरन्ति ॥ X.22

Kashmir, that is intended to form backdrop to the post-marital enjoyments of the newly-wedded Indira and Firoz, appears in all its glory as *uddīpanavibhāva* (exciting agency). Barely running into four verses, the beauty of Kashmir with its hilly brooks, chirping birds, wide green expanses, snow-covered peaks and house-boats comes to vibrate with life (XXI. 1-4).

The best description is however reserved for Gurudeva Tagore's cultural and academic hermitage, Santiniketan, which, as one of the few centres of learning that Indira attended for a brief spell, forms an attractive design in the texture of the poem. With its sylvan surroundings lending an ideal aura for the prosecution of literary and artistic pursuits, Santiniketan spurred the poet to break into emotional rapture. In the ecstatic moment, he has tenderly viewed it as a poem, a sculpture, rather a whole philosophy. In view of its poetic merits, it would be appropriate to reproduce the description in its entirety. The Anuprāsa and the Drutavilambita metre combine to lend it a peculiar cadence :

प्रकृतिसुन्दरमक्षियुगप्रियं

विहगसङ्घनिनादितदिक्तटम् ।

विविधशाखियुतं कुसुमोत्करैः

सुरभितं सुमनोहरमद्भुतम् ॥

द्रुमलतापरिशोभि समन्ततो

भ्रमरसन्ततगुञ्जितकुञ्जकम् ।

उदितकोकिलपञ्चमनिःस्वनं

रुचिरकेकिकलापमनोहरम् ॥

तरुतले क्वचनाध्ययने रतै-

र्बटुजनै रुचिरं प्रियवादिभिः ।

क्वचन नृत्यविधिप्रसिताङ्गना-

चरणनूपुरनिक्वणनाकुलम् ॥

सुकविता सुकवेरिव कस्यचित्

सुघटिता प्रतिमेव सुशिल्पिनः ।

सुरमणीयमृषेरिव दर्शनं

लसति शान्तिनिकेतनमद्भुतम् ॥ XII.2-5

LANGUAGE

Every work, great or small, aims at effective communication with the reader. It is acheived through the medium of expression – language which enables the author to strike responsive communion with the reader and thereby serves as a meeting ground for the two. The *IC* is intended to acquaint in elegant verses, the cultured Sanskritist with the inspiring life of the iron lady and the milieu whereform it sprang, serving as an apt backdrop to it. By its very nature it could ill afford the luxury of involved or abstruse language. The *IC* concurs with the *Bodhisattvacaritam* in the lucidity and simplicity that breathe through its language. But while in the *Bodhisattvacaritam* the lucid medium has been consciously whipped up to yield *padalālitya* and musical cadence inherent in it, the down-to-earth narrative in the *IC* does not lend itself to such tender niceties. It rather calls for the matter-of-fact approach to come to terms with what is intended to be conveyed in the poem. However, it is a measure of the author's equipment and commitment to his aim that the language in the *IC* has neither sunken into a pedestrian exercise nor is it weighed down with his unquestioned erudition. It is marked by heart-warming moderation. While its lucidity and chastity are beyond dispute, it cannot boast of the kind of flourishes that distinguish the *Bodhisattvacaritam*. It may suffer by comparison but no better contours of language could have been conjured to enclothe the historical poem that the *IC* essentially is. The elevating episodes in the *Bodhisattvacaritam* indeed needed the sublime language to accord with the idealism that they seek to uphold, the prosaic narrative in the *IC*, on the other hand, could hardly have claimed an extravagant medium. The language fostered in the poem is perfectly in tune with the genius of the factual theme. It is marked by natural flow and sweetness and is addedly enlivened by extreme perspecuity. All these have combined to make the *IC* an immensely readable poem.

Since it spans one of the most fateful periods of recent history, the *IC* abounds in a wide range of events and situations that join to form is warp and woof. Exceptions apart, all of them constitute parts of the same texture. The common thread of patriotism binds them together. As such they differ in degrees, not in basic substance. But even in their perceptible similarity some distinguishing layers peep out unmistakably. It is a tribute to the poet's insight in Sanskrit semantics that every situation has evoked corresponding phraseology to echo it in all its lucidity. It doubtless has the vitality to keep abreast of the shifting phenomena. While it is vibrance mingled with sweetness that marks the depiction of scenic beauties and mirthful occasions, the language swiftly assumes serenity in dealing with serious matters and sedate situations. As noticed earlier, the description of the Black Forests, Switzerland and Santiniketan are marked by buoyancy and sweetness. They also vouch for the poet's regard for proportion. None of the descriptions, that could have provoked the lesser poets into endless imageries, extends beyond four verses. The prediction that Motilal makes to allay his wife's apprehensions about Indira's worth as a daughter has its appeal heightened by the firm tone in which it is couched :

मैवं शुचे दा स्वमनः शुभे ! त्वं
पुत्री वरा पुत्रशतेभ्य एषा ।।
सत्यं हि तत्कर्म करिष्यतीयं
नान्येन केनापि कृतं पुरा यत् ।
निशम्य पत्युर्गिरमेवमर्थ्यां
स्वचेतसो ग्लानिमसावहासीत् ।। II.23-24

Whatever the situation, the poet aims to give it effective expression in accordant phraseology. The doubts that the inmates of Santiniketan entertain about Indira's capacity to adapt herself to the hard life there have been expressed in limpid language which serves to project in relief the contrast between her tender age and rigours of the life there. The Viṣama *alaṁkāra* goes far to compound the severity :

क्व नु कठोरमिहाश्रमजीवनं
क्व नु सुखैः सकलैः सह वर्धनम् ।
कृशतनुः सुकुमारवया इयम्
इति जना विविधं प्रबभाषिरे ।। XII.9

Likewise the way Indira's resolve to return to seek the membership of lthe Congress after six years has been detailed serves dual purpose. On the one hand it bespeaks the firmness of her commitment, on the other, it underscores the streak of dejection that was tormenting her deeply :

साऽऽकर्ण्य तस्याधिकृतस्य वाचं
स्वेच्छाविघातेन मनाग् विषण्णा ।
भवन्तमेतास्मि पुनस्तथैव
षड्हायनानन्तरमित्युवाच ।। VIII.8

Touching situations are sought to be highlighted in the correspondingly moving language. Kamala's attenuation caused by tuberculosis and her resultant death are described in serene terms that verge on pathos. The comparison with the digit of moon adequately captures the frailty of her blighted figure :

निजगृहान् न चिरं प्रकृतौ स्थिता
क्षयमुपैदिव चान्द्रमसी कला ।।
प्रतिदिनं क्षयमेवमुपेयती
कृशतनुः क्षयरोगवशं गता ।
विलपतः परिहाय निजान् प्रियान्
स्वसुकृतार्जितलोकमियं ययौ ।। XII.33-34

The commitment of the author to the lucidity of language is so deep that even in the description of war it does not lend itself to harshness. His aversion to rough and rugged phraseology is total. The hemistich that follows would bear it out in ample measure. So does the excerpt quoted earlier :

बङ्गान् कृत्वा सपदि वशगान्ख्यातशौर्यातिरेका

हर्षोत्कर्षाज्जयमुपगता भारतीया विरेजुः ।। XXIV.3

Despite the uninterrupted flow of lucidity in the poem, two distinct trends seem to distinguish the quality of its language. The subjects or situations that admit of leisurely treatment are invested with lively language characterised by happy alliteration. The parts of narrative that have to be dealt with swifty, on the other hand, claim a peculiar type of medium that comes quite close to prose. The events described in Cantos XXI and XXV bear it out in large measure. It could not have been otherwise in describing the quickly shifting scenario that followed the proclamation of Emergency in the country :

नो चेद् भवेत्तस्य बलात्स्वयं वा

शल्यक्रिया, येन भवेदशक्तः ।

जनः प्रजाया जनने यतश्च

जनाभिवृद्धिः खलु वारिता स्यात् ।। XXV.65

In keeping with his wont, the author has sought to invest the *IC* with dramatic overtones by marshalling a series of elements that rightfully belong to the domain of drama but are not alien to the broad canvas that the Mahākāvya commands. The poem may suffer by comparison, on this count, with the *Bodhisattvacaritam*, which as noticed earlier, unravels the tremendous possibilities of Sanskrit language to convey the dramatic effect. However, while in the *Bodhisattvacaritam*, it is only the conversations, conducted between different sets of characters, that have been pressed into service to lend dramatic flavour to the poem, the *IC* can deservedly boast of much else besides dialogues that serves to imbue it with dramatic touches. The vastness of narrative provides the author with abundant opportunities to conceive and execute some of the episodes or parts thereof with the skill of a dramatist. The mock enactment by Indira of the supreme sacrifice made by the valiant French girl Joan of Arc, in Canto IV, may well form part of a play by virture of the representation (*abhineyatā*) inherent in it, so can be the violent scene staged on the campus of the Christian College in the Canto VII. The way Indira dashed to grasp the national flag before it could have tumbled down and the unshakable fortitude with which she withstood the relentless blows but did not surrender the flag are characterised by swiftness and abruptness that the events in the drama take to unfold themselves. The highest drama, however, is witnessed in the meeting that Indira intended to address to apprise the people of the course of action, chalked out for them by her father. Even as with the police official training his gun at her and the people shielding her with equal tenacity, Indira seemed to be a helpless victim, Firoz sprang up from nowhere to try with the petty policeman. The pride with which Indira and Firoz looked at each other is as heart-warming as it is dramatic in appeal and effect :

गर्वोन्नता तं च ददर्श पत्नी
प्रियेन्दिरा साहसिकं पतिं स्वम् ।
स चापि धैर्यस्य च साहसस्य
मूर्तिं प्रियां स्वां पुरतो ददर्श ।। XVIII.10

Two sets of actors may well be detected in the formations in which Indira as a child arranged her toys. While the victory of the Satyagrahi formation, might have been occasioned by the impact of the milieu, it may be construed with equal force as the victory of good over evil that the drama symbolises (IV, 21-27).

The device of dialogue has been effectively exploited in Canto XV to impart it an aura of a play. The conversation between youthful Indira and her father, reinforced with telling arguments, with the father advising restraint and the daughter firm in her determination, not only serves to enliven the issue but contributes to its happy resolution as well. In view of the lucidity and vibrant logic that mark it, the conversation may be reproduced to bring home its effectiveness :

वृद्धिं गते च सुतरां प्रणयप्ररोहे
तं बालमित्रमसकौ पतिमाचकाङ्क्ष ।
इच्छां निजां च जनकं निजगाद धीरा
स त्वाह तामिह विचारय पुत्रि ! भूयः ।।

कन्यापिताऽस्मि हितमित्यवधार्य वच्मि
कार्यं विचार्य करणीयमिह त्वयाऽत्र ।

सङ्कल्पमात्रवशगो न विनिर्णयोऽयं
पूर्वं परं च तनये ! प्रविचारयेह ॥

भेदोऽस्ति कश्चिदुभयोः प्रकृतौ च पृष्ठ-
भूमौ च हन्त ! युवयोरनुपेक्षणीयः ।
एवं विधेहि सुखिता भवितासि येन
नातः परं खलु भवेन्मम किञ्चिदिष्टम् ॥

तं पुत्र्युवाच मयका मनसा वृतोऽयं
स्वस्थो युवा च पतिरित्यवधारणीयम् ।
वृत्वा सकृच्च नहि तात ! कथञ्चिदेव
वृण्वीय कञ्चिदपरं पतिमित्यवेहि ॥

तस्या दृढां मतिमवेक्ष्य पिता स्वपुत्र्या-
श्छन्दस्तवास्तु तनये ! इति तामुवाच ।
नेच्छाविघातमहमाचरितास्मि ते, त्वं
प्राणैः प्रियाऽसि गुणवत्यसि मे तनूजे ॥ XV.3-6

The author's keenness to ensure grace and effect to his expression has led him, as attested by the *Bodhisattvacaritam* as well, to incorporate in the body of the *IC* such of the phrases or ideas represented by them from ancient texts as suited his purpose. The practice seems to have settled as a sort of motif with him. As elsewhere, the borrowals fall into two categories. While some of the expressions have been physically borrowed from the earlier authors, a vast majority of them echoes their ideas in a thinly garbed language. It is however to the credit of the author that these borrowals, whether direct or indirect, almost dissolve their identity in his verses and do not appear to have been forcibly glued. It is pertinent to point out that the range of his sources in the *IC* is not as wide as in the sister poem, *Bodhisattvacaritam*. Most of the phrases owe themselves to the classical writers. Both classes of the borrowals are listed here to gauge the quantum of debt the author owes to his predecessors in the matter :

1. यत्राकृतिस्तत्र गुणा वसन्ति ।[49]

---

49. Purvapiṭhika, 2, *Pañcatantra*, I. 208

2. भवन्ति भव्येषु हि पक्षपाताः ।[50]

3. परस्परेण स्पृहणीयशोभं
तद् द्वन्द्वमायोजितमास्त धात्रा ।[51]

4. अविवेकः परमापदां पदम् ।[52]

5. अधृष्यश्चाभिगम्यः (स) भीमकान्तैर्गुणैरभूत् ।[53]

6. आत्मकर्मक्षमं देहं क्षात्रो धर्म इवाश्रितः ।[54]

7. मृत्युर्वै प्राणिनां ध्रुवः ।[55]

8. मूढः परप्रत्ययनेयबुद्धिः ।[56]

9. प्रवर्तितो दीप इव प्रदीपात् ।[57]

(b) Borrowals that echo the earlier expressions:

1. आगन्तुकानां रमयन्ति चेतः । X.20
रमयति जनो यत्र बन्धूनभिज्ञः ।

Meghadūta, Additional verse after 31.

2. श्रुतिकर्मीकृतवाननेकशः । V.12
गमिकर्मीकृत (नैकनीवृता) *Naiṣadhacarita*, II.40.

3. शय्यां गता धूसरवक्त्रकान्तिः
प्रभातकल्पा रजनीव साऽऽभात् । X.10

---

50. *IC.*, I.17; *Kirātārjunīya*, III.12
51. *IC.*, XV. 6; slightly modified version of–
परस्परेण स्पृहणीयशोभं न चेदिदं द्वन्द्वमयोजयिष्यत् । *Raghuvaṃśa*, VII.14
52. *IC.*, XX. 11; *Kirātārjunīya,* II.30
53. *IC.*, XXI. 8; *Raghuvaṁśa*, I.16
54. *IC.*, XXI. 8; *Raghuvaṁśa*, I.13
55. *IC.*, XXI. 9; part of an old *subhāṣita* –
अद्य वाऽब्दशतान्ते वा मृत्युर्वै प्राणिनां ध्रुवः ।
56. *IC.*, XXII. 23; *Mālavikāgnimitra*, I. 2
57. *IC.*, XXV. 40

शरीरसादादसमग्रभूषणा मुखेन सालक्ष्यत लोध्रपाण्डुना ।

तनुप्रकाशेन विचेयतारका प्रभातकल्पा शशिनेव शर्वरी ।। *Raghu.*, III.2

4. सम्बन्ध आभाषणपूर्वकोऽभूत् । XI.11

सम्बन्धमाभाषणपूर्वमाहुः । *Raghuvaṁśa*, II.58

5. अनन्यसामान्यविभूतिकानि

तेषां चरित्राणि भवन्ति लोके । XIII.9

लोकोत्तराणां चेतांसि को नु विज्ञातुमर्हति । *Uttararāmacarita*, II.7

6. वाते महत्यपि महागिरयो भवेयु-

र्निष्कम्परूपरुचिरा इति नात्र चित्रम् । XV.12

प्रवातेऽपि निष्कम्पा गिरयः । *Abhijñānaśākuntala*, p.152.

7. तामर्थ एव परकीय इति प्रपद्य

प्रादात्प्रसन्नमनसा स परिग्रहीत्रे । XV.27

अर्थो हि कन्या परकीय एव

तामद्य सम्प्रेष्य परिग्रहीत्रे । *Abhijñānaśākuntala* , IV. 22

8. फ़ीरोज़ः प्रयतपरिग्रहद्वितीयः । XVI.11

अध्यास्य, प्रयतपरिग्रहद्वितीयः । *Raghuvaṁśa*, I.95

9. सा वाग्मिनीनां धुरि कीर्तनीया । XVIII.6

अपांसुलानां धुरि कीर्तनीया । *Raghuvaṁśa*, II.2

10. यावद् गिरस्तस्य मुखाच्चरन्ति

क्रूरा इमा आंग्लभटाधमस्य ।

तावत्सभाया उदगात्तरस्वी

फ़ीरोज़गान्धी महता जवेन ।।XVIII.8-9

क्रोधं प्रभो संहर संहरेति यावद् गिरः खे मरुतां चरन्ति ।

तावत्स वह्निर्भवनेत्रजन्मा भस्मावशेषं मदनं चकार ।।

Kumārasambhava, III.22

11. बीजोपक्षेपमादावतनिषत । XVIII.33
कार्योपक्षेपमादौ । *Mudrārākṣasa*, IV.3

12. न हि सा क्षणमप्यकर्मकृत् समवातिष्ठत कोविदाग्रगा । XX.20
न हि कश्चित् क्षणमपि जातु तिष्ठत्यकर्मकृत् । *Bhagavadgītā*, III.5

13. मित्रभावमिवापन्नैर्विषकुम्भैः पयोमुखैः । XXI.2
परोक्षे कार्यहन्तारं प्रत्यक्षे प्रियवादिनम् ।
वर्जयेत्तादृशं मित्रं विषकुम्भं पयोमुखम् ।। Famous *subhāṣita*

14. ----जगत्सर्वं तस्याः शून्यमिवाभवत् । XXI.11
शून्यं मन्ये जगत् । *Uttararāmacarita*, III.38

15. सुताविमौ यौवनभिन्नशैशवौ । XXII.18
रघुः क्रमाद्यौवनभिन्नशैशवः । *Raghuvaṁśa*, III.32

16. प्रविनेदुरेते सिंहोरुसत्त्वा भुवि । XIII.34
सिंहोरुसत्त्वं निजगाद सिंहः । *Raghuvaṁśa*, II.33

17. अत्रैव पूर्वे ऋषयोऽभ्यवोचन् कुटुम्बमेकं वसुधां समग्राम् । XXIV.23
उदारचरितानां तु वसुधैव कुटुम्बकम् । *Hitopadeśa*, I.73

18. हिमालये नाम नगाधिराजे
विराजते सिक्किमनामधेयः । XXIV. 26
अस्त्युत्तरस्यां दिशि देवतात्मा
हिमालयो नाम नगाधिराजः । *Kumārasambhava*, I.1

19. गुणा भवन्त्यादरभाजनानि
लोके न लिङ्गं न वयश्च सत्यम् । XXIV.55
गुणाः पूजास्थानं गुणिषु न च लिङ्गं न च वयः ।
Uttararāmacarita, IV.11

20. शान्तमित्यभवच्चित्रं चित्रोल्लिखितमूर्तिवत् । XXIV. 75

अहो रागबद्धचित्तवृत्तिरालिखित इव सर्वतो रङ्गः ।

Abhijñānaśākuntala, p.8

21. आहारनिद्राभयमैथुनानि

येषां समेषां पशुभिः समानि । XXV.57

आहारनिद्राभयमैथुनानि

समानमेतत् पशुभिर्नराणाम्। *Hitopadeśa*, Preliminary Verses, 26

22. स्वर्गापवर्गस्य निमित्तभूतम् । I.9

देशोऽस्मदीयः सुतरां प्रकृष्टः स्वर्गापवर्गस्य निमित्तभूतः । XXV.85

स्वर्गापवर्गस्य च हेतुभूते भवन्ति भूयः पुरुषाः सुरत्वात् ।

Viṣṇupurāṇa, II.3.24

23. अस्मादशिक्षन्त पुरा मनोज्ञात् स्वं स्वं चरित्रं भुवि सर्वलोकाः ॥

XXV.85

एतद्देशप्रसूतस्य सकाशादग्रजन्मनः ।

स्वं स्वं चरित्रं शिक्षेरन् पृथिव्यां सर्वमानवाः । *Manusmṛti,* II.20

While there is no conscious effort to enrich the language in the *IC* with various trappings, it has received, not unlike the *Bodhisattvacaritam*, considerable sprinkling of learned grammatical forms. It was neither unnatural nor unexpected in the work of a grammarian that the author basically is. An overwhelming majority of these or cognate forms occurs in his other writings and as such may not have been altogether unknown but they merit notice because of their diversity and complexity. the author has unmitigated fascination for the aorist forms of all hues which are interspersed throughout the body of the poem. The plethora of other recondite forms cover the whole gamut of grammar, namely, causatives, desideratives, frequentatives, compounds, syntax, primary and secondary suffixes, euphonic combination, etc. It is, however remarkable that contrary to *Bodhisattvacaritam*, these forms have occurred naturally to the poem and do not seem to have been forcibly thrust to parade the author's equipment. Some of the more glaring forms may be listed here to drive home the depth of the author's grasp of Sanskrit grammar and semantics.

Aorist Froms : अवर्धिष्ट (II.25), व्यतानीत् (III.23), समध्यगीष्ट (VI.24), उपायंस्त (XIII.8), अचकात् (XV.8), अकार्ष्टाम् (XVI.10), निरचैषीत् (XXI.40), निरवोढ (XXII.14),

व्यधिषत (XXIII.6), अतनिष्ट (XXIII.9), अचकलन् (XXIV.4-5), अध्यक्षैप्सु: (XXIV.58), आनैषु: (XXIV.66).

Aorist Forms with *ṇic:* आर्पिपत् (III.5), आपिपन् (IV.4), अचीकरत् (IV.23), प्राबूबुधत् (VI.15), संम्रैरिरत् (XV.7).

Potential Forms : the potential forms that owe themselves to the Pāṇinian rule *śaki liṅ ca* (III.3.172) deserve attention :

बाला: स्वदेशस्य हितं विदध्यु:, VIII.9, विदध्यु: = विधातुं शक्नुयु: । कथमिहाश्रमवृत्तिमुपाश्रयेत् XII.8, उपाश्रयेत्= उपाश्रयितुं शक्नुयात्। पीडां कथं नाहमलं सहेय XVII.20, सहेय=सोढुं शक्नुयाम्।

Primary Suffixes : Though the *kvasu* and the *kānac* suffixes are substituted optionally for *liṭ* vide the aphorisms *liṭaḥ kānaj vā* (III.2.106) and *kvasuś ca* (III.2.107), their use is basically restricted to the Veda but the poet loves to use them especially the *kvasu*, frequently [58]. Besides the aorist, *kvasu* is his forte. The forms ending in *kvasu* have been used in the *IC* quite often. Some of them merit attention:

उपेयिवान् (I.23), समुपेयुषि (II.2)[59], प्रतिपेदुषी (XII.13), सम्प्रतिपेदिवांस: (XV.8), ऊचिवान् (XIII.13, XV.7), उपसेदिवांस: (XVII.7)[60], ऊचिवांस: (XVII.8).

Other forms ending in Primary Suffixes :

ṇamul : पशुताडम् (IV.16), पशुमारम् (V.5, XX.1), विचायं विचायम् (XVII.29)[61]

inuṇ : सांराविणम् (VIII. 16) [62]

ḍāc : दु:खाकरम् (XXIV. 48) [63]

Secondary Suffixes :

akac : पिता चास्यकै पुत्रिकायै । III.4

दीपितोऽतितरकां च भस्मसात् , VII.11

---

58. क्वंसुकानचावपिच्छान्दसाविति त्रिमुनिमतम् । कवयश्च बहुलं प्रयुञ्जते ।

Bhaṭṭoji on Pāṇini, III.2. 106-107

59. उपेयिवाननाश्वाननूचानश्च । Pāṇini, III.2. 109

60. भाषायां सदवसश्रुव: । Pāṇini, III.2. 108

61. कर्मणि च । Pāṇini, III.4.45

62. अभिविधौ भाव इनुण् । Pāṇini, III.3.44

अणिनुण: । Pāṇini, V.4.15

63. दु:खात् प्रातिलोम्ये । Pāṇini, V.4.64

पिता कदाचित् तयका सहैव । X.27

कदाचन तत्सहितैषका । XII.30 [64]

kan in svārtha : प्रियतरकैः (XV.10), अतितरकम् (XXIV.1)

aṇ in svārtha : विलक्षणप्रातिभनेत्रवल्या : (XIV.36)[65], प्रतिभैव प्रातिभम् ।

cha : अथ जन्म यदाभवददसीयम् । V.1 [66]

ini : हार्दी स्वयं बभूव तेषु । XI.10[67]

ḍhak : नादेयवारीण्यधिकृत्य चापि । XXIV.49 [68]

Compounds : पाठशालम् (XIV.3)[69], बालसभम् (VIII.11).[70]

अनवाप्तकांग्रेससदस्यताकाऽनि[71] (VIII.24), विषमस्थितिकस्य[71] (XIV.20), हतभाग्यकानाम्[71] (XXV.4,8),[71] स्त्रीपुंसयोर्भेदवशात् (XVIII.18).[72]

The author thus seems to have mustered all the reasonable avenues to ensure an elegant medium marked by *prasāda* that eminently corresponds with his narrative.

FIGURES OF SPEECH

Notwithstanding their deep espousal by a band of devoted champions, the figures of speech (*alaṁkāras*) are essentially the outward trappings of poetry. This is not to deny the fancy the Sanskrit poets have entertained for them, down the ages.

---

64. अव्ययसर्वनाम्नामकच् प्राक् टेः । Pāṇini, V.3.71
65. प्रज्ञादिभ्यश्च । Pāṇini, VI.4.68
66. त्यदादीनि च । Pāṇini, I.1.74
    वृद्धाच्छः । Pāṇini, IV.3.114
67. इनिठनौ । Pāṇini, V.2.15
68. नद्यादिभ्यो ढक् । Pāṇini, V.3.97
69. सेनासुराच्छायाशालानिशानाम् । Pāṇini, II.4.25
70. अशाला च । Pāṇini, II.4.24
71. शेषाद्विभाषा । Pāṇini, V.4.154
72. अचतुरविचतुरसुचतुरस्त्रीपुंस -- । Pāṇini, V.4.77

Even the Vedic seers could not resist the fascination that the *alaṁkāras* exercised on them, though they had not evolved by then as an independent discipline. However, the *alaṁkāras* purport to be at best the means to ensure clarity and force to the expression.[73] Even a prosaic idea, when clothed in the garb of *alaṁkāra,* strikes responsive chord in the heart of the reader. As attested by his works, the author is not much enamoured of the figures of speech as such. To him they form an effective device to dispel the haze that otherwise threatens to overpower the muse.

Of the two types of *alaṁkāras*, those based on words occupy a lower rung. Ingenious formations of words or syllables constitute the bedrock on which the edifice of the *śabdalaṁkāras* is sought to be raised. The author has special fondness for alliteration which runs through his writings like the spinal chord. Based on the similarity of syllables (consonants), the Anuprāsa lends rhythm and musical effect to verse. The author's expertise in spinning out unending strings of alliteration is astonishing. While the *Bodhisattvacaritam* is brimming with an overabundance of Antyānuprāsa, it has been used sparingly in the *IC*. Perhaps the nature of the narrative does not lend itself to such finesse. Other varieties of the alliteration, however, have been exploited in the poem with gusto. Some of the more interesting illustrations from the *IC* may be listed here :

1. यस्या ध्रुवं विविधचारुविचारवीचि -
   व्यावल्गितो लसति मानसराजहंसः ।
   या चापि दिव्यधिषणा परिकल्पनाभिः
   स्वाभिः करोति धिषणं सुतरामधस्तात् ।। Pūrvapīṭhikā, 1
2. सर्वेऽत्र सम्भूय सुखं वसन्तु प्रियं वदन्तु प्रियमाचरन्तु । ibid.,4
3. दिशि दिशि विशदयतां सेन्दिरा स्वामभिख्याम् । ibid.,6.
4. प्रहर्षप्रकर्षं ववर्षाशु भूयः । VII.15
5. इत्यभून्मनसि हन्त नितान्तं तान्तिरेव विदुषः पितुरस्याः । XIV.1
6. कार्यं विचार्य करणीयमिह त्वयाऽत्र । XV.3

---

73. अङ्गीकरोति यः काव्यं शब्दार्थावनलङ्कृती ।
    असौ न मन्यते कस्मादनुष्णमनलङ्कृती ।। *Candrāloka,* I.8

7 देशे मानं परमुपगते मानवा मानभाजः । XXV.88

8. सन्तो भवन्तो बहुशक्तिमन्तः । XIII.13

The Antyānuprāsa, as it has been used in the *IC*, is no match to what adorns the *Bodhisattvacaritam*. A few may be taken up below by way of illustration :

1. पुण्यानि हृद्यानि च शीतलानि
   यदीयतोयानि सुपावनानि । I.14
2. उपायनानां प्रददौ शतानि
   स्वबन्धुवर्गाय तदीप्सितानि ।। II.19
3. दीर्घाणि दीर्घैस्तरुभिर्युतानि ।। X.4
4. प्रधानमन्त्री विदितो जनाना-
   मादर्शभूतो भुवि सज्जनानाम् । XIX.22
5. एवं विनीता विविधं विनीता
   कथादिकैर्ज्ञानचये, प्रतीता । X.38

While the Anuprāsa involves repetition of consonants, the Yamaka is based on both consonants and vowels (words) repeating themselves in the corresponding sequence, with or without meaning attached to them. Like Anuprāsa it doubtless contributes to the rhythmic effect, but, more often than not, it tends to rob poetry of charm and freedom. In view of the ambiguity it seeks to inflict on the verse. The author has resorted to it sparingly almost reluctantly. Even when he has pressed it into service, it does not deprive his muse of its clarity and simplicity. The following illustrations would bear it out beyond cavil :

1. क्षणमपि क्षणमध्यगमन्नहि । XI.26
2. रसमयं समयं गमयन्त्यसौ । XII.15
3. अतोऽनुरोधादयमस्य विद्वान्
   रुग्णां स्वपत्नीमपि साधु विद्वान् । XI.24
4. विद्वानपीदं सुतरामविद्वान् । XXIV. 31

5. रक्तान्तकां प्रियतमे हृदयेन रक्ता ।। XV.20

6. परं परं व्याजमुपेयुषी सा । XXIII.31

In view of his commitment to *viśuddhokti*[74], Śleṣa or double entendre could not have met the poet's approbation. Perhaps *mānasa* in *lasati mānasarājahaṁsaḥ* (Pūrvapīṭhikā, 1), is the solitary example. It means in the context, both heart and the Mānasa-lake.

Variously described as *śailūṣī* and source (*mātā*) of the figures of speech in view of its vital role in providing corner-stone to the *alaṁkāras* based on similarity (*sādharmyamūlaka*), Upamā dominates the *arthālaṁkāras* that have been mustered in the *IC*. Besides the Arthāntaranyāsa, Simile is indeed the author's favourite *alaṁkāra*. In comparison with his other works it has been used in the present poem with greater vigour and frequency. The author has been alert in culling appropriate *upamānas* wherein lies the relevance of the Simile. Most of the standards of comparison have been marshalled from natural phenomena and day-to-day life. Ocean (III.13), river-current (IX.21,XVIII.28), hilly-stream (IX.21), moonshine (I.12), digit of the moon in both the ascending and descending order (III.3, X.2), whirlwind (XV.9), rock (XVII. 15, VI.11), furious serpent (XVIII.4, XXIII.19), moth-eaten necklace (XXV.50) are some of the notable *upamānas* that serve to facilitate a better understanding of the *upameya* in the poem. A few illustrations would suffice to uphold the point. Even in the early phases of the freedom struggle people were attracted to Gandhiji as the rivers rush to the ocean (III.13). While Indira grew in her loveliness like the digit of moon in the bright fortnight (III.3), her mother Kamala wore out with tuberculosis like its attenuating counterpart in the dark half (*kṣayam upaid iva cāndramasī kalā*, III.3). After Jawahar's arrest, the Nehru ladies conducted themselves firmly like a rock (VI.II). Indira's firmness in the face of lathi-blows also invited comparison with the rock (*śileva sākṣāt sudṛḍhāvatasthe*, XVII.15).

As the freedom movement neared its climax, the British rulers were convinced that the upsurge of the people was as difficult to be contained as it was to arrest the mighty current of the Ganges (XVIII.28). The gravity of disaster that had overwhelmed East Bengal was comparable to the surging conflagration (XXIII.4). In the pre-Emergency era the evil of bribery had broken out like an epidemic (XXIV. 64). Not wholly original, the following verse forms probably the best illustration of Upamā. The lovely spectacle of the intermingling of the currents of the Gaṅgā and the Yamunā at Prayāga has been happily compared with the penetration of the dark

---

74. विशुद्धोक्तिः शूरः प्रकृतिमधुरा भारविगिरः ।

Saduktikarṇāmṛta (Punjab Sanskrit Book Depot, Lahore, 1935), 5.26.5. Quoted in Indirakanta Pathak's thesis, op. cit., p. 301, F.N. 2.

expanses of the forest by moonshine :

यत्र स्फुटं भाति विभिन्नरूपं
गाङ्गं जलं यामुनमेव चापि ।
श्यामासु शुभ्राः शशिनः प्रविष्टाः
पादा यथा सान्द्रवनस्थलीषु ॥ I.12

The injuries on Indira's person, despite her persistent effort to underplay them, sent Firoz into a fit of frenzy like a furious serpent :

आकर्ण्य तस्या गिरमेवमर्थ्यां पतिः क्षतैर्ज्ञातसमस्ततत्त्वः ।
क्रुद्धः श्वसन् सर्प इव प्रकोपात् यथागतं प्रत्यगमत् प्रवीरः ॥ XVII.24

Arthāntaranyāsa has also been employed with equal zeal and frequency in the *IC*. It consists of two statements, general, and specific, with one alternatively serving to strengthen the other[75]. Arthāntaranyāsa not only contributes to the clarity of the subject or idea under description, it invariably results in the emergence of pretty *subhāṣitas* that subsequently settle down as wise sayings among the cultured. The *IC* abounds in a series of Arthāntaranyāsas. The three stanzas reproduced below have particular statements upheld by the general expression. After marriage, Firoz did not deem it proper to be a burden on his kinsmen or move under the umbrella of his father-in-law. It has been sought to be reinforced by the general statement that the highminded persons always conduct themselves in an independent manner :

न स्वानामकृत समाश्रयं कथञ्चित्
नैवाथ श्वसुरसमाश्रयं गतोऽयम् ।
वृत्त्यर्थं स्वयमकृत प्रयत्नमेष
मानेच्छोर्भवति परावलम्बिता नो ॥ XVI.12

Although the British rulers were convinced of the futility of stemming the spate of mass upsurge with force, yet they did not take the right course. Indeed the wily are seldom guided by reason :

75. उक्तिरर्थान्तरन्यासः स्यात्सामान्यविशेषयोः । *Kuvalayānanda*, 122

परं परं व्याजमुपेयुषी सा
बुद्धिर्न तान् प्रैरिरदत्र सम्यक् ।
प्रवर्तितुं, वक्रधियः कदाचि-
दृजुं न पन्थानमुपाश्रयेयुः ।। XVIII.31

The plunder of their country by Pakistan left the Bengalis dejected. No self-respecting person can brook the slights heaped on one's motherland :

विपुलविभवशाली सत्यमस्मत्प्रदेशो
विभवमपहरन्ति त्वन्यभागस्थलोकाः ।
इत इति भृशमासन्नत्र लोका विषण्णा
जननभुव उपेक्षां मानिनो नो सहन्ते ।। XXIII.12

For other examples one may refer to III.9, VII. 26, VIII.20, IX.25, XV. 12, XXII. 45, etc.

tādṛśe tu mahāvṛkṣe kālena vinipātite (XXI.4), exemplifies the variety of Atiśayokti wherein *prastuta* fuses into *aprastuta* to dissolve its identity[76]. The verse seeks to describe the death of India's first Prime Minister, Pt. Jawaharlal Nehru. The *mahāvṛkṣa* used in the hemistich symbolises Pt. Nehru. Atiśayokti of ordinary type may also be detected in *putrī varā putraśatebhya eṣā*, II. 22.

Apahnuti is illustrated by the description of Nehru's greatness : *atiśubhraṁ yaśa ānanena vahann atigauravamiṣeṇa buddhimān* (V.14). The *yaśas* on his face is sought to be concealed by his *gaurava*.

Viṣama consists of the combination of two discordant objects[77]. This is what is sought to be done in the apprehensions that the inmates of Santiniketan entertained about Indira's capacity to measure up to the hard life there :

क्व नु कठोरमिहाश्रमजीवनं
क्व नु सुखैः सकलैः सह वर्धनम् ।

---

76. रूपकातिशयोक्तिः स्यान्निगीर्याध्यवासनतः । ibid., 36.
77. विषमं वर्ण्यते यत्र घटनाऽननुरूपयोः । ibid., 88

कृशतनुः सुकुमारवया इयम्

इति जना विविधं प्रबभाषिरे ।। XII.9

Apparent paradox between various objects, on the other hand, results in Virodhābhāsa[78] The author has resorted to it in a number of verses. The following lines form its fit examples :

प्रबुद्धापि बाल्यान्न साऽबुद्ध चर्चाम् ।। III.18

आनन्दनाम प्रथितं पृथिव्यां

– – – – – – – – – – – –

आसीत्तदाऽऽनन्दविहीनमेव । VI.6

स्थितिं पृथक् स्वां कलयन्त्यपीयं

स्वस्मात्पतिं नैव पृथक् चकार । XXII.34

विद्वानपि सुतरामविद्वान् चोग्यालराजोऽत्र --- । XXIV.31

Rūpaka is one of the *arthālaṁkāras* that have been sparsely employed in the *IC*. Herein is sought to be obliterated the apparent difference between the *prastuta* and *aprastuta* by imputing the latter on the former[79]. Some of the more noteworthy examples of it may be reproduced here :

तस्या इति प्रासरदन्तरङ्गसरोवरे मोदतरङ्गभङ्गः । IX.25

ज्ञानभानुरुदितो हृदयेऽस्याः । XIV.25

विस्मयाम्बुधिमगाधमुपायुः । XIV.34

हर्षप्रकर्षस्य बभूव वर्षः । XIX.16

जना इहाज्ञानतमोनिमग्नाः शक्ता न किञ्चित्करणे जडाश्च । XXV.42

Svabhāvokti accords most with the genius of the narrative. As a majority of the situations, events and episodes in the poem are factual in character, no better figure of speech could have been imagined to deal with them. Svabhāvokti has been chiefly instrumental in investing the poem with life-like precision. Most of the descriptions, as illustrated earlier, emanate from the judicious use of this *alaṁkāra*.

---

78. आभासत्वे विरोधस्य विरोधाभास इष्यते । ibid., 76

79. विषय्यभेदताद्रूप्यरञ्जनं विषयस्य यत् । ibid., 17

A few more would effectively project its role in the poem. The schedule of the Satyagrahis is described with Svabhāvokti in the following verse :

समुपेत्य च पण्यवीथिका
लघुसङ्घाः प्रतिवासरं दृढाः ।
बहुधा पणिकानवारय-
न्नथ वैदेशिकपण्यविक्रयात् ॥
यदि नोऽभ्युपयन्ति सद्वचो
न भवन्तः स्थितिरत्र नो भवेत् ।
इति वाचमुदीर्य ते दृढां
नहि ताभ्यः कथमप्यपाययुः ॥ V.18-19

METRE

Metre like the figure of speech is evidently an outward trapping of poetry though it is vital to its character. Shorn of metre, it sinks into prose. The onrush of emotions invariably breaks into the frame of metre. Metre not only ensures effective communication, it also lends grace to poetry. The *IC* bears testimony to the author's ingenuity in handling a variety of metres. Against 15 in the *Bodhisattvacaritam*, he has employed no less than twenty two metres in the *IC* which are as follows : Upajāti, Anuṣṭup, Vaitālīya, Svāgatā, Bhujaṅgaprayāta, Praharṣiṇī, Mālinī, Rathoddhatā, Vaṁśastha, Mandākrāntā, Pañcacāmara, Śālinī, Toṭaka, Puṣpitāgrā, Śārdūlasvikrīḍita, Sragdharā, Vidyunmālā, Śikhariṇī and Indirā. The last – Indira claimed to be a new metre in fact represents an adaptation of Pañcacāmara excluding the last syllable from the scheme. It seems to be a metre made of two quarters having fifteen letters each with the scheme ra, ja, ra, ja, ra. the author has broken each quarter into two comprising eight and seven syllables respectively. Otherwise also Indirā, a metre of eleven syllables in each line (*na, ra, ra, la, ga*), is noticed by Bhānukavi in his *Chandaprabhākara*[80]. In this motley crowd of metres Upajāti stands out prominently, being the dominant metre in the poem.

The metres, as employed in the *IC*, faithfully stick to theory. While each canto is dominated by a solitary metre which changes towards the close, Canto XXII is marked by plurality of metres. Upajāti predominates in twelve (I, II, VI, VII, X, XI, XIII, XVII, XVIII XIX, XXIV, XXV) out of the twenty five cantos. The First Canto is couched besides the Upajāti, in Vasantatilakā, Mālinī, Āryā, the last verse being in Śālinī which

80. *Indirāgāndhicaritam : Eka Samīkṣātmaka* Adhyayana, op. cit., 283-284

is replaced in Canto II by Bhujaṅgaprayāta. The last stanza in other cantos dominated by Upajāti has successively claimed Rathoddhatā, Āryā, Toṭaka, Drutavilambita, Puṣpitāgrā, Mālinī, Śārdūlavikrīḍita, and Vaitālīya. Cantos III, IV, V, VII and IX have respectively Bhujaṅgaprayāta, Anuṣṭup, Vaitālīya, Rathoddhatā and Āryā as their major metre. They close with Anuṣṭup, Vasantatilakā, Upajāti, Svāgatā (24-27) and Upajāti. The Canto XII is composed for the most part in Drutavilambita. The last two verses (35-36) have claimed Upajāti. Svāgatā, Vasantatilakā, Praharṣiṇī and Vaitālīya form the dominant metres in Cantos XIV, XV, XVI, and XX. They end with Upajāti (35-36), Praharṣiṇī, Upajāti, and Anuṣṭup (28-29) respectively. Canto XXI is overwhelmed by tiny Anuṣṭup; the last two verses are respectively in Upajāti and Mālinī. Though the next canto (XXII) is distinguished by a number of metres, it is dominated by Upajāti, having claimed 15 out of 47 stanzas with Vaṁśastha coming a close second with twelve. Like the *Bodhisattvacaritam* the author has tried his hand on longer metres in the next two cantos (XXIII, XXIV). While the first twenty one stanzas in Canto XXIII are in Mālinī, it closes with Mandākrāntā (49). The remaining stanzas (22-48) have the ubiquitous Upajāti. It is again Upajāti that claims most of the verses in Canto XXIV (14-15,17-55). The first thirteen verses are couched in Mandākrāntā, the sixteenth has Sragdharā. While Anuṣṭup has been pressed into service for verses 56-78, the canto is wrapped up by Vidyunmālā (79). The last canto (XXV) has also Upajāti as its chief metre (3-86). It opens with Pañcacāmara (1-2) and ends with Indirā (90). The other three stanzas are in Mandākrāntā (87-88) and Śikhariṇī respectively.

The use of metres in the *IC* is distinguished by certain notable trends. Some of the cantos are dominated by the metre which concludes the preceding canto. The metre, as it has been employed in the poem seems to accord with the subject under description. While Upajāti as a cosmopolitan metre competent enough to come to grips with a variety of situations, is best suited to descriptive poetry. That probably accounts for the eminence it has been accorded in the *IC*. It has been aptly used to deal with a wide spectrum of situations. Anuṣṭup is the ideal vehicle for situations that demand hasty disposal. It has been exploited in Canto IV and parts of Cantos XXI and XXIV that abound in rather prosaic details. Indira's marriage with Firoz, which was solemnized in the month of March, when it is the season of *Vasanta*, Spring, in India, has been described appropriately in Vasantatilakā while the joy of the honeymoon is detailed in Praharṣiṇī.

The *Indirāgāndhīcarītam* differs widely from the author's *Bodhisattvacaritam*. While it adheres to the norms more faithfully, it, in a way, represents a pole apart from that lively Mahākāvya which flouts them with impunity. The *Bodhisattvacaritam* is actuated by a keeness of the author to establish himself as an eminent poet. The objective of the *Indirāgāndhīcaritam*, on the other hand, is to spin out a faithful biography of the lady who wielded unchallenged power for long as PM of the largest democracy, in elegant verse. The poet has eminently succeeded in the mission that he had set before himself.

It is no wonder then that the work has won its author warm plaudits from critics. It has become a subject for research. The degree of Ph.D. was awarded on its critical appraisal by the University of Bhagalpur in 1989.

ŚRĪRĀMAKĪRTIMAHĀKĀVYAM

यावत्स्थास्यन्ति गिरयः सरितश्च महीतले ।

तावद्रामायणकथा लोकेषु प्रचरिष्यति ॥

Ages have gone by since this above prediction was made about the vitality of the appeal of his immortal song that had sprung up from the depths of Vālmīki's heart when it was touched by an experience which a lesser poet could have dismissed as inconsequential. The *Rāmāyaṇa* is not a mere poem. It symbolises all that has sustained mankind in its joys and sorrows, down the ages. Unlike Kṛṣṇa of the Song Celestial, Rāma did not leave to posterity learned disquisitions or mystic doctrines. He himself was an embodiment of the virtues that have guided humanity, through centuries to higher goals. The message of "love, pity, fidelity and self-abnegation", handed down by Vālmīki is as fresh today as it was when it was first delivered. There is hardly any other work that has exercised so powerful an influence on the " life and thought " of the Indian people. This work has been a perennial source of raw-material which the successive generations of poets have drawn upon with fruitful results.

The appeal of the *Rāmāyaṇa* has been truly universal. While it is woven inextricably in the texture of the Indian society, the neighbouring countries have not lagged behind in drinking at its nectar-founts. Almost all the countries of South and Southeast Asia, notwithstanding the religion they profess and the political system they espouse, have come under its spell. They have recast it to suit their varied milieus and traditions, invested it with new moral and ethical contours and ultimately adopted it as their own, blissfully ignorant of its original source and creator. The alacrity with which the Thais have assimilated the epic into their social fabric is as heart-warming as it is surprising. They have not just adopted it smugly. With their religion, tradition and folklore forming an apt backdrop, they have changed the very genius of the story almost beyond recognition. The *Ramakien* has thus come to represent an independent version of the Rāma-story. Dr. Satya Vrat Shastri's *Śrīrāmakīrtimahākāvyam* (*RKM*) seeks to describe, in twenty five cantos, the main episodes of the Thai version, with such connecting links as were necessary to make it a cohesive entity. The changes that the Thais have made in the epic story tend to take much of the sheen off its heroes and thereby reduce them to lesser persons, shorn of the idealism that has inspired the millions in India.

SUMMARY

Canto One, which is primarily intended to introduce the poem, opens with a graphic description of Thailand. Its capital, a place of beauty and pleasure (*aiśvaryasaundaryavilāsadhānī*, I.5), shines forth as if it were a pearl necklace round the neck of the earth. Though uniformly known as Bangkok, the world over, the Thais themselves have no fascination for the appellation. They prefer to call it Krungthev, which represents a queer mixture of Sanskrit and Thai languages. While *theva* is evidently a corrupt form of Sanskrit *deva*, *krung* in Thai means 'abode'. Taken together, the compound means 'an abode of gods'. The capital was founded, some two hundred years ago by the founder of the ruling Chakri dynasty, Buddha Yod Fah. A sound scholar and a gifted poet, he composed the burly poem, *Rāmakīrti*, based on the Rama-story, in several thousand elegant verses (I.14). His successor Buddha Nai Lert La reduced the story to dramatic form. Because of its brevity, his work is best suited for stage-presentation. It is his version that is widely presented, till date, by talented Thai actors, who, dressed in rich raiments and masks present it so skilfully that even its minute nuances are effectively unravelled. (I.20-22).

One of his successors, Maṅkut, subjected it to extensive researches. He ably elucidated, many a thorny problem connected with the story which has invested his work with great significance. Prior to that, the Thais did not at all know that Vālmīki was the original author of the *Rāmāyaṇa*. They took it to be their own preserve. Most of the places like Ayodhyā, connected with the Rāma-story, are located in Thailand. The hill which yielded the famed Sañjīvanī herb to Hanumān is also taken to be there. Lopburi bears the imprint of the name of Lava, the son of Rāma. A rock there is supposed to have turned green with Rāma's arrow. The Thais also believe that Rāma's battle with Rāvaṇa took place in their country (I.27-35).

The devotion of the Thai people to the *Rāmāyaṇa* is so deep that a large number of scenes from the epic are found depicted in ancient temples and monasteries. Their predilection for the Rāma-story has led them to introduce in its framework a number of such episodes as are not found in any other version. Some of these are related in the present work, in Sanskrit verses, to highlight the contribution the Thais have made to enrich the story.

Canto Two may be taken to mark the beginning of the poem proper. The episode of the birth of Anomatan forms the contents of the canto.

Oppressed by Hirantayakṣa, foremost among the wily demons, the host of deities waited upon Īśvara (Śiva) to relieve them of the misery. Even before they could recount their woes, Lord Śiva, reliever of calamities as he is (*vipadāṁ nirāsam*, II.4), decided to obtain the services of Nārāyaṇa for he alone was competent to meet the menace. At his behest (*ato bhavān yātu ca hantu cainam*, II.9), Nārāyaṇa engaged the mighty demon on mount Cakravāla, his abode, and after a fierce encounter, killed him with his unfailing weapons. As he returned to his retreat, the milky ocean, he found there a lotus and a child encased in its petals. He immediately forayed to Kailāsa to dedicate the child to Īśvara according to whose injunction the child, named Anomatan, was to be the first king of he world (*rājā bhavatv eṣa śiśuḥ śubhāṅga ādyaḥ pṛthivyā iti cādideśa*, II.14). His capital Ayodhyā was laid for him by Indra at the behest of Īśvara and was named on the first letters of the four sages he met on the way, Achangavī, Dāha, Yugāgra, and Yāga.

In Daśaratha, Anomatan had a brave and disciplined son. His son Rāma was adorned with a plethora of virtues (*guṇagaṇamaṇḍitaḥ*, II.18) and was therefore adorable for the whole world (*akhilajagannamasyabhūtaḥ*, II.18). It is his divine character that has been reverently sung in the *Rāmakīrti.*

In Canto Three is related the story of Rāma's birth (Rāmajanmopākhyāna).

As Daśaratha did not beget son on any of his queens, he decided to perform the *Putreṣṭi* sacrifice with the help of the sage Kalaikoṭi. Before embarking on the sacrifice, the sage went to the mount Kailāsa to apprise Lord Śiva of the havoc the demons, under boons from the three major gods, were playing with the three worlds. The menace, he averred could be averted if Nārāyaṇa were to be born as son to Daśaratha, the ruler of Ayodhyā. In deference to the wishes of the sage, the god requested Nārāyaṇa to incarnate himself as the son of Daśaratha (*bhavān daśarathāpatyaṁ bhavatv iti matir mama*, III.10). Nārāyaṇa agreed to do the bidding provided his conch, disc and mace, besides Ananta and Lakṣmī, accompany him to the earth, in human form. Śiva asked the sage to return to Ayodhyā and conduct the sacrifice for the king. He assured him that a divine figure with four rice balls would emerge from the flames of the sacrifice. Two of them would be appropriated by someone from the southern quarter. The remaining two balls the three queens should be made to eat (*piṇḍanām avaśiṣṭau dvau bhojayer mahīṣīr ṛṣe*, III.17) whereby they would conceive ere long and give birth to four sons. Everything happened as bidden by the Lord. Nārāyaṇa was born as Rāma from Kausalyā. The disc assumed the form of Bharata from the womb of Kaikeyī. Ananta and Conch were born as Lakṣmaṇa and Śatrughna respectively as sons of Sumitrā.

The first segment, formed by verses 1-20, of Canto Four seeks to recount the story of the previous birth of Rāvaṇa, the lord of Laṅkā. As a demigod, Nandaka by name, he was charged to wash the feet of the deities who came to Kailāsa to wait upon the great god. Nandaka turned out to be a source of entertainment to them (*vinodabhāṅ nirjarasāṁ babhūva*, IV.4). They made fun of him by plucking tufts of hair from his head. As an humble attendant, he brooked the humiliation till the time he turned bald. Unable to suffer slights any more, he requested Lord Śiva to grant him miraculous power to avert the menace. In view of the services he had rendered to him, the Lord condescended to grant him the desired boon. Thereafter any deity, who, unaware of Nandaka's newly acquired powers, dared to take liberties with him, fell dead the moment he pointed out his finger at him (*petuś ca devā vyasavaḥ kṣaṇena*, IV.10). The deities were reduced to such straits that they had to seek the help of Lord Śaṅkara. The Lord requested Nārāyaṇa to bail the gods out of the impasse by killing Nandaka. Nārāyaṇa assumed the form of a heavenly nymph and tried to seduce Nandaka. In the course of the dance, the nymph touched the lower part of her body with her finger. The short-sighted Nandaka followed suit. That resulted in the disintegration of his lower body. Nārāyaṇa took it the most opportune moment to strike. Nandaka, however, charged him with deceit. In order to reassure him Nārāyaṇa promised to invest him, in the next birth, with ten heads and twenty arms while himself retaining the normal body. As he said this, he killed Nandaka. It was this Nandaka who was born as Rāvaṇa in the next birth.

The episode of Sītā's birth occupies the remaining part of the Fourth Canto.

Of all his queens, Rāvaṇa entertained exceptional love for Mandodarī. Once she smelt the sweet scent of the rice-balls, wafted by the air and expressed the desire to eat them. Rāvaṇa immediately ordered the demoness Kākanā to bring the balls. She assumed the form of a crow and snatched back from the northern Kosala half of the balls the divine figure had emerged with, from the sacrificial fire. On eating them Mandodarī became pregnant and gave birth to a beautiful girl. Vibhīṣaṇa and others versed in astrology predicted that the girl was born to spell doom to Laṅkā and Rāvaṇa. That sent shudder down to the spine of Rāvaṇa. He asked Vibhīṣaṇa to dispose of the child in the manner he deemed best. Vibhīṣaṇa put the girl in a jar and bade a servant to throw it in the river (*taraṅgiṇyāṁ ghaṭo 'yaṁ bhoḥ satvaraṁ kṣipyatām iti*, IV.32). The girl was in fact an embodiment of Lakṣmī, the goddess of affluence and beauty. Therefore, instead of any harm to the child, a divine lotus emerged in the river to steer the jar safe to the bank (*tasyās taṭaṁ tat samupājagāma*, IV.35). King Janaka, who in the dress of a sage, was practising austerities nearby came just then, to have ablution in the river. As soon as he opened the jar, he was wonder struck to find therein a new-born girl (*tāvad dadarśāntar amuṣya kanyāṁ, sadyaḥ-prasūtām ativismitaḥ saḥ*, IV.37). Maṇimekhalā, the presiding deity of the river was convinced of the divine character of the girl which, she believed, enabled her to survive the captivity in the jar (I.39). The king deposited the jar in a pit under a tree wherein a lotus had cropped up to sustain it (*kumbhaṁ tadātiṣṭhipad atra padme*, IV.43) and returned to prosecute his austerities unhindered. He persisted with the penance for sixteen long years but did not achieve the fulfilment. Before returning to the capital, he asked his servant to retrieve the jar from under the tree. When all his efforts failed to locate the pitcher, the king ordered the servant to bring from Mithilā his army equipped with ploughs and spades. The operation of the army also ended in a fiasco. Thereupon the king himself decided to till the land. No sooner did he launch upon the operation, than there emerged the jar with a pretty girl perched on the bed of lotuses therein. As she had emanated from the furrows worked out by the king, the girl was given the appropriate name of Sītā. He returned to his kingdom with the girl. When she attained the marrigeable age, he arranged *svayaṁvara* for her with the stipulation, that whosoever strings the mighty bow of Śaṅkara would win her hand. Rāma strung the bow with ease. He married Sītā according to Vedic rites and returned to Ayodhyā.

When Rāmāsura, the demigod, came to know that Rāma had broken the bow unceremoniously, he challenged him to an encounter. Rāmāsura, the wielder of axe (*paraśu*), however, had to suffer the ignominy of defeat. Finding that it was Nārāyaṇa who had manifested himself there, Rāmāsura in order to win him over, presented him with the bow that Śiva had made over to him earlier (*dhanur maheśaḥ pradade purā yat,* IV.62). Rāma accepted the bow with great pleasure but threw it in the void to stay as a deposit with Varuṇa and to return to him whenever summoned.

Canto Five addresses itself to detail Rāma's banishment and the interesting story of the demon Jihva.

On Rārna's return to Ayodhyā, Daśaratha, his father decided to consecrate him as the new king. One of his queens, Kaikeyī did not relish the prospect of Rāma's occupying the throne in preference to her son, Bharata. At the instigation of her hump-backed maid, who wanted to settle scores with Rāma for his subjecting her to indignity by removing and recreating her hump by two successive shots, she demanded of the old king the fulfilment of the two boons he had granted her for her services on the battle-field. The boons would be met if Rāma was sent into exile for fourteen years and Bharata was put on the throne. Thc king, all too worn out by age, could not withstand the shock. Rāma alongwith his wife Sītā and younger brother Lakṣmaṇa repaired to the forest, though calamities stalked him there also (*tatrāpi kaṣṭam nahi taṁ mumoca*, V.18).

Once Rāvaṇa left Laṅkā, in the charge of Jihva, the husband of her sister Śūrpaṇakhā and went to jungle for some momentous work. Jihva guarded the town so conscientiously that he did not have even a wink of sleep for seven nights. Ultimately, as if to revenge 'her' humiliation, sleep (*nidrā*) overwhelmed him. He rightly thought it impossible to protect the town in sleep. He therefore stretched his tongue so wide as to cover the whole Laṅkā (*dīrghīcakārāsura eṣa jihvāṁ, tayāvṛṇoc cāpi samastalaṅkām*, V.23). That plunged the town into blinding darkness. On return, Rāvaṇa found all entrances to Laṅkā blocked. Incensed at Jihva's action, he cut his tongue to gain entry into the town. Jihva fell dead with this. Rāvaṇa was full of remorse when he came to know of the actual position. He performed the obsequies of his brother-in-law in accordance with the prescribed rites.

After the death of her husband Śurpaṇakhā was forlorn (*patyur vihīnā katham atra dīnā*, VI.2). On the pretext of seeking comfort with her son Kumbhakāśa but in fact to find out another husband for herself (*nijārtham anyaṁ patim ācakāṅkṣa*, VI.3), she reached the forest where Rāma had taken up abode. The moment she saw Rāma, she fell for him smitten with love. With her guile she assumed the form of a pretty maiden and launched upon the perilous course of making advances to him. She was stunned to find him averse to her because of his devotion to his wife (*sadaikapatnīvratam ādadhānaḥ*, VI.7). She took her to be the prime impediment in winning him over and therefore decided to dispose her off. She charged at her with the ferocity of a tempest but was stoutly held back by Lakṣmaṇa. He reprimanded her severely and chopped off her ears and nose as punishment for her misadventure. Thus deformed, she provoked her brothers Khara and Dūṣaṇa to wreak vengeance on Lakṣmaṇa. They stormed the two brothers with a large contingent but were vanquished and killed by Lakṣmaṇa single-handed. Frustrated Śurpaṇakhā apprised Rāvaṇa, her brother, of her miserable plight and instigated him to avenge the insult by abducting his charming wife Sītā, the veritable elixir to the eyes. She herself wanted to gift her (Sītā) to him but she confided, was foiled in her attempt by Lakṣmaṇa (*matto 'cchinat tāṁ Janakasya putrīm*, VI.16). Lured by Sītā's charms detailed by her dear sister, Rāvaṇa asked the deceitful Mārīca to assume the form of a golden deer to seduce Rāma into wilderness. Soon the golden deer was found hopping in the vicinity of Rāma's cottage. Though she knew it fully well that the *hemamṛga* was an utter impossibility, Sītā fervently longed to possess it. Rāma did his best to convince her of the stratagems the demons were capable to conjure, but she persisted in her demand. The crafty Mārīca drew Rāma deep into the forest and while dying of his shot, let off the desperate cry 'Oh Jānaki'. Sītā interpreted it to signal Rāma's hopeless predicament, and in a trice despatched Lakṣmaṇa to bail his brother out of the impasse (*tadīyāgrajarakṣaṇāya*, VI.25). In the meanwhile Rāvaṇa descended upon the cottage in the guise of a sage and carried the helpless Sītā away to Laṅkā.

Daśaratha's friend Jaṭāyu, though worn out by age, encountered the demon with unexpected vehemence. With fierce strikes of his mighty beak and wings, he reduced the demon to a hopeless state but invited his end by bragging out the secret of his death which was the hit by the ring in Sīta's finger. Rāvaṇa thereupon took out the ring from Sītā's finger and struck Jaṭāyu with it. That transported him to the heavenly regions.

On their return to the cottage, Rāma and Lakṣmaṇa found it empty with no trace of Sītā anywhere. They launched upon a vigorous search for her in the course of which they met the divine eagle (Jaṭāyu). Though killed, his divine soul had not deserted him as yet (*hate 'pi yasmin na samatyajad yaṁ viśeṣakāryāntarito yadātmā*, VI.35). He told Rāma of Sītā's abduction by Rāvaṇa and made over to him, her ring before relapsing into peace (*kṛtī viśaśrāma sukhaṁ sa ātmā*, VI.36). After performing his obsequies, Rāma left for the southern quarter to track down the demon.

Canto Seven is devoted to describing Rāma's meeting with Hanumān and the consequent friendship with Sugrīva.

As Rāma in the course of his journey, rested under a tree, he lapsed into sleep. Lakṣmaṇa mounted the guard to ward off any eventuality. In the meanwhile, a burly monkey descended upon the tree. In order to attract Lakṣmaṇa's attention he shook it violently (*śākhamṛgo 'dhūnayad atra śākhām*,VII.5), and persisted with the exercise for quite some time. Lakṣmaṇa took it as an affront and took up his bow to punish the monkey . But to his dismay and amazement, the monkey snatched away both and darted to the tree with surprising agility. Thereafter he reverted to shaking the tree (*śākhāmṛgas taṁ dhavituṁ pravṛttaḥ*, VII.9). Lakṣmaṇa felt small and awakened his elder brother to apprise him of all that had transpired there. As soon as Rāma looked upwards he recognised the cognizances of the monkey. Hanumān was equally quick in concluding that the person who had recognised the cognizances could have been none else but Nārāyaṇa himself (*janaṁ sa nārāyaṇam eva sākṣāt*, VII.11). He reverently approached Rāma and vowed, henceforth, undying allegiance to him (*adyaprabhṛty asmi tavāṅga dāsaḥ*, VII.13). He requested him to favour him with a command for service. Rāma sought his help in tracing out his wife, abducted by the demon Rāvaṇa. Hanumān conducted him to Sugrīva. Their friendship born of mere conversation ripened progressively (*pragāḍhatāṁ yā kramaśaḥ prayātā*, VII.16). Sugrīva pledged all help in securing the release of Sītā. Rāma, on his part, established his credentials with Sugrīva by killing Vālin, who, though his elder brother, had turned enemy by a strange quirk of fate.

The assassination of Vālin forms the main contents of the Eighth Canto.

The demon Nandakāla was appointed to guard one of the entrances to Mount Kailāsa. His misdemeanour to one of Śiva's concubines earned him instant imprecation from the Lord to be condemned as a *mahiṣa* (bison), Darabha by name, which was so stipulated as to end at the sight of his son. It was also ordained that he would meet his end at the hands of one of his sons (*haniṣyate 'sau tanujena*, VIII.5). He therefore killed several of his sons as soon as they were born. His wives, aghast at his demonic violence, decided to save somehow the next son. When one of his wives subsequently conceived, she hid herself in a cave, somewhere in the jungle. She gave birth to a son in due course and apprised him of his father's diabolic designs (*taṁ cāha tattātanṛśaṁsakṛtyam*, VIII.8). The child was named Darabhī. She left the son in the cave and herself departed to happy pastures. At the appropriate time, he escaped from the cave to challenge his father and killed him in the duel. Emboldened by the initial victory, he dared even Lord Śiva to fight it out. Convinced as he was of his (Darabhi's) imminent end, Śiva deputed Vālin to meet the arrogant Darabhī. The first combat ended in a fiasco. Vālin asked him to try conclusions in a hilly cave. He deputed his younger brother Sugrīva at the entrance to deduce the result of the combat by the colour of the blood of the contestants. The red blood was to indicate his own death whereas the dark colour of that of the demon. As the duel proceeded, it began to rain in torrents which resulted in diluting the colour of blood of the demon beyond recognition. Sugrīva erroneously concluded the defeat and the death of his elder brother, and in a bid to check the demon's escape blocked the entrance of the cave with a colossal boulder. Vālin somehow removed the boulder to emerge out of the cave. He became suspicious of Sugrīva's bonafides in plugging the entrance. Thinking that Sugrīva was plotting to overthrow him and usurp the throne (*syān nāma rājye mama gṛdhnur eṣaḥ*, VIII.24), Vālin banished him from the kingdom for no fault of his (*pṛthak kṛto 'sau sutaraṁ nirāgāḥ*, VIII.27). Sugrīva requested Rāma to kill his brother for his offence. At his suggestion Sugrīva engaged Vālin in a combat. While they were locked in a duel, Rāma killed Vālin from behind a tree (*śareṇa vṛkṣāntarito jaghāna*, VIII. 30) and consecrated Sugrīva on the throne. Sugrīva renewed his pledge to help Rāma in tracing out Sītā. He secured the help of Aṅgada, Nīlaphad and others, and with his army reached the sea-shores that were to serve as a spring board to annex Laṅkā.

Hanumān flew across to Laṅkā and gave to Sītā the ring Rāma had sent to reassure her of his (Hanumān's) credentials. While returning, he burnt down Laṅkā with his tail that the demons had set ablaze. There were piteous wailings all around as the golden city was reduced to ashes (*dadāha hāhākṛtam āsta yena, svāhākṛtañ cāpi samastapuryām*, VIII.35). As Hanumān posted Rāma with all that had occurred there, he (Rāma) geared himself for the strike.

Once while in restful sleep, Rāvaṇa saw in dream two falcons locked in fierce fight. The white falcon, charged at its black adversary with vehemence and killed it in the fight. In the subsequent dream he saw a coconut-shell placed on his palm. He himself poured oil in it but as soon as he put the wick, an unknown woman appeared from nowhere and lit the wick. That resulted in the burning of the shell. Thereafter the fire entered into his palm and soon his whole body experienced the heat of the fire. He asked his younger brother Vibhīṣaṇa to dispassionately interpret the dreams. Vibhīṣaṇa warned that the dreams were extremely inauspicious and spelt disaster for him: *svapnāv etau subhṛśam aśubhau kaṣṭasaṁsūcakau* te, IX.9). The black and white falcons, according to his interpretation represented him (Rāvaṇa) and Rāma respectively. The death of the black falcon brought about by the white one meant his own end. The coconut was the symbol of Laṅkā. The woman who lit the lamp was none else but their sister, the root cause of all dissensions (*sakalakalahad-vārabhūtā svasaiva*, IX.11). And the flame that burnt his palm symbolised Sītā, the embodiment of chastity, who was destined to bring about his ruin (tvadvināśaik-ahetuḥ, IX.12). If the Rākṣasa race was dear to him, he would do good to return her to her husband, Vibhīṣaṇa advised him wisely.

The arrogant Rāvaṇa took it as an affront to his supposedly unmatched might. He reviled Vibhīṣaṇa for the temerity in suggesting Sītā's return. There was no comparison, he bragged, between him and Rāma whom he could pulverize like a mosquito with incredible ease (.......*maśakam iva.......niṣpīḍyāhaṁ karatalagataṁ helayaiva prasannaḥ*, IX.16). He went to the length of ridiculing him as Vibhīṣaṇa only in name with his dreadfulness having already deserted him (*vigatam iva te bhīṣaṇatvam*, IX.17). That is what drove him to treat Rāma as the cause of his death. With such like rantings, Rāvaṇa bundled him out from the kingdom unceremoniously. He sought refuge with Rāma which he readily granted. With a view to allay Vibhīṣaṇa's apprehensions about their capacity to withstand the ferocity of Rāvaṇa's hordes, Sugrīva ordered the monkeys to convincingly demonstrate their might. Some of them uprooted trees and mountains, others enveloped the sun that threw the world into darkness. While still others churned up terrific tempests with their velocity and dried the oceans. Vibhīṣaṇa was amazed to see the might of the monkey-hosts, who, he was now convinced, were well-equipped to take on the Rākṣasa-hordes (*yat satyaṁ te kapivarabhaṭā rākṣasair yoddhum arhāḥ*, IX.28). The terrific sound produced by the breath-taking feats of the monkeys, pervaded all the quarters. Its ferocity stunned Rāvaṇa as well who decided to gather intelligence through his spies.

At his bidding Śukrasara entered Rama's camp in the guise of a falcon and soon converted himself into a monkey. Vibhīṣaṇa did not err in recognising him. Śukrasāra was overpowered by Hanumān. He was severely beaten with lashes, branded on all parts of the body and ignominously bundled out. He reported back to his master all that he had undergone and cautioned him against the might of the monkeys (*śauryaṁ kapīnāṁ tam abodhayac ca*, IX.39). After the failure of Śukrasāra's mission, Rāvaṇa himself slipped into Rāma's camp in the guise of an ascetic like a shark into the ocean (*duṣṭābhisandhir makaro yathābdhim*, IX.40). He also did not escape Vibhīṣaṇa's Argus eye but he kept silent under the influence of the *mantras*. Unaware of his deceit, Rāma first extended him a respectful welcome (*taṁ pūjayāñcakre*, IX.42). But as the ascetic advised him not to burn his fingers with Rāvaṇa for he was no match to him (*trailokyajetā kva nu rākṣasendraiḥ parivṛtas tvaṁ kva ca vānarair bhch*, IX.47), he got suspicious of his motives. He saw through his wile and in a bid to browbeat him unequivocally expressed his resolve to punish Rāvaṇa for his misdemeanour in abducting his wife. Humiliated and confused, Rāvaṇa, fell back to the safe sanctuary of Laṅkā and decided to employ an alternative device to frustrate his mission.

The episode of Beñjakayī occupies the Tenth Canto.

In a bid to overwhelm Rāma with grief and thereby throw him out of gear, Rāvaṇa drafted the services of dreadful girl Beñjakayī. In obedience to the demon's behest she assumed the form of Sītā's corpse and floated in the river near Rāma's camp where he usually took his bath every morning. Rāvaṇa was convinced that when confronted with the dead body of his wife, Rāma would not be able to stand the shock (*khinnāntarātmā viramet sa yuddhāt, prāṇāṁs tyajed vā vanam āśrayed vā*, X.4). True to the demon's calculations, on seeing Sītā's corpse Rāma fell into mourning. Lakṣmaṇa who had joined his brother was equally aghast (*duḥkhasya koṭiṁ paramāṁ jagāma*, X.8). Perturbed at the delay in Rāma's return, Sugrīva and Hanumān reached the river only to find the two brothers immersed in grief. Hanumān was sure that Sītā could never have committed suicide like lesser persons. After all, the daughter of the earth was firm in her resolve like the earth itself (*bhūmeḥ sutā bhūmivad eva tasyā dhairyaṁ bhaved dhairyadhanā matā sā*, X.12). In order to ascertain the genuineness of the corpse when Hanumān put it on the burning pyre, the girl leapt into sky in her true form. Hanumān dragged her down to Rāma.

In the meanwhile Vibhīṣaṇa also reached there in search of the two brothers. He told Rāma that the girl who had attempted to beguile him was none else but his daughter Beñjakayī. She deserved the extreme penalty of death (*sutā mameyaṁ vadham arhatīti*, X.20). Rāma magnanimously condoned her offence, she being his friend's daughter . He asked his dutiful friend Hanumān to escort her to Laṅkā. While he was conducting Beñjakayī to it he fell in love with her, which resulted in the birth of a son, Asuraphad. After enoying himself with Beñjakayī for some time, Hanumān came back to Rāma. With his stratagem to vanquish Rāma thus having gone awry, Rāvaṇa geared himself up for the battle. So did Rāma.

Canto Eleven concerns itself with the quarrel between the monkey chiefs Hanumān and Nīla whom Rāma had charged to build a causeway to Laṅkā to enable his army to cross the mighty ocean. They dutifully addressed themselves to the task. It was so stipulated that while one of them would pass on the rocks, the other would set them in position to facilitate the quick disposal of work. Nīla deemed it the opportune time to avenge the maltreatment that Hanumān had meted out to his uncle Jambū. He threw the rocks with such rapidity that Hanumān could not keep pace with him, his strenuous efforts notwithstanding. Evidently, the respective tasks required substantially differing durations to accomplish them. However, in keeping with the command of the master, their functions were subsequently reversed. Hanumān felt slighted at the change but decided to utilize the occasion to turn tables on his rival. He tied a stone each to his hair on his body and angrily threw them in the ocean with bewildering frequency. Despite the brave efforts that he made, Nīla could not position them with matching efficiency. He felt insulted.

Rāma did not approve of their behaviour. He rightly decided to punish them for the indiscipline which was otherwise bound to filter down to the troops. Nīla was sent to Kiṣkindhā as Sugrīva's regent and was asked to make addedly suitable arrangements for the provisions for the army. Hanumān, on the other hand, was ordered to complete the causeway within seven days. Both proceeded to carry out the orders.

Hanumān embarked upon his work in right earnest. With hosts of monkeys he hurled thousands of rocks and stones to build the causeway on schedule. As he came to continue the work the next morning, he was surprised to find that all the rocks they had positioned the previous day, had mysteriously vanished. Unable to determine the cause thereof he plunged into the work (*prakrantavyaṁ punaḥ kāryam,* XII.5). His astonishment knew no bounds when he found that his strenuous exercise had again góne waste and there was no trace whatsoever of the mass of rocks that they had assembled earlier so meticulously. If their endeavour were to go up in smoke thus, he feared it would be impossible to complete the causeway within the stipulated time *(evaṁ sthite setunibandhanaṁ syād aśakyam eveti mahān anarthaḥ*, XII.10). He therefore during the night decided to mount guard on the seashore to see for himself how the rocks were removed so persistently. As he dived into the ocean, what he saw there was simply unbelievable. He found thousands of fish engaged in removing the rocks under the orders of their mermaid queen Suvarṇamatsyā. She herself had been deputed by her father Rāvaṇa to thwart the monkeys in their mission of constructing the causeway, which, if completed, would spell doom to the demons. And the order of the parents is beyond question. Hanumān assured her that while he esteemed her devotion to her father, it was circumspection that distinguished man from the animal. Despite his erudition, her father had earned scandalous ignominy by his outrageous behaviour in abducting the legally married wife of Rāma. And if a father were to conduct himself despicably, he too has to be shunned like rotten food (*varjyo bhaved eva kadannavat saḥ,* XII. 33). It therefore did not behove her to obey her evil-minded father. After all, she was a sane woman (*vivekinām agrasarā matāsi*,XII.33). After some hard cerebration, she saw merit in what Hanumān had impressed upon her so logically. She ordered her hosts to desist from the destructive operation. As Hanumān looked at the pretty mermaid after the heady argument, he fell for her. Soon they were locked in the bliss of love for the night. The result was that before Suvarṇamatsyā returned to Laṅkā 'fully contented', she had become mother to Hanumān's son Macchānu whom she left on the sea-shore for fear of her father. He grew into a powerful being like his father.

The next two cantos (XIII-XIV) are encompassed by the absorbing episode of

Maiyarāba.

Having thus failed to abort the construction of the causeway that brought Rāma and his hosts to the doorsteps of Laṅkā, Rāvaṇa in a bid to outmanoeuvre him now deputed his devoted friend Maiyarāba, the king of Pātāla, to take on Rāma effectively. Maiyarāba went to his camp and with the help of.a soporific powder sent everybody there to sleep (*nidrāvaśaṁ tatra gatā akasmāt*, XIII.9). He kidnapped unconscious Rāma to Pātāla to throw him, at the opportune moment, in the boiling water. As the effect of the powder wore out, his companions were astonished to find Rāma missing. "How could the sun that Rāma was set mysteriously" (*śrīrāmasūryo 'stam upāgato 'sti*, XIII.4), they pondered restlessly. Vibhīṣaṇa applied his mind to it and with his divine power born of the divine crystal in his possession, discovered that Rāma had been carried away by Maiyarāba, the invincible friend of Rāvaṇa. He had to be retrieved to avoid harm to him that Maiyarāba was determined to do (*prāptavya evāsti sa deśa āśu, yāvat sa taṁ hanti raghupravīram*, XIII.16). And Hanumān alone was competent to reach his abode in the Pātāla. In the course of his journey he (Hanumān) arrived at a lake that was guarded by his own son Macchānu, born of Rāvaṇa's daughter Suvarṇamatsyā, who had discarded him, as soon as he was born, on the sea-shore to avoid her father's wrath. Maiyarāba had taken fancy for him to the extent that he had adopted him as his son. Macchānu, surprised to see a fascinating figure, Hanumān, who, as he persisted to intrude, arrongantly despite warning to the contrary, sprang up, like a porvoked serpent, to obstruct his course (*Macchānur enaṁ nyaruṇat tadānīm*, XIII.35). That resulted into a fierce fight between the two. When, despite the use of all the weapons in their respective armours, neither of them could subdue the other, they deemed it saner to cease the bout. Hanumān discovered to his astonishment and pleasure that the young one who had withstood his might, with equally hard punch in retaliation, was none else but his son (*vāyos tanūjasya suto 'smy ahaṁ bhoḥ*, XIII.44), born of Suvarṇamatsyā and thus represented the mix of the prowess of Vāyu and Daśānana (*śaktī sthire sto mayi viddhi tāvat*, XIII. 45). Hanumān was now prompted to disclose his identity. Macchānu begged his pardon for his misdemeanour in engaging him in a combat (*kṣamām imañ cāpi bhṛśaṁ yayāce* XIII. 53). The father and the son were thrilled to meet under mysterious circumstances. When the onrush of emotions subsided Macchānu enquired of him of the purpose of his visit. Hanumān told him that he had to retrieve Rāma, deceitfully kidnapped by Maiyarāba, and therefore wanted to know the road to the region. Macchānu was torn between two loyalties. However, he adroitly indicated the source by putting the query "is it not possible for him (Hanumān) to go through the same way through which he had come to the place where he now was. Hanumān took the hint and made himself enter into a lotus stalk and proceeded ahead.

He was immediately encountered by a fiery mountain. Rightly treating it as the enemy's ruse to deflect him from his mission, Hanumān crossed it with ridiculous ease. The mighty tusker that subsequently dared to obstruct him, was despatched to Yama's abode with typhonic velocity (*Vāyoḥ suto vāyujavena cainaṁ, samprāpayāmāsa Yamasya lokam*, XIV.5). As he proceeded a little further, he was surrounded by a swarm of menacing mosquitoes. Though bitterly harassed and his visibility seriously impaired, Hanumān churned the swarm with his mighty arms and emerged like the sun from the hell it had inflicted on him (*chittvā ca tāṁ sūrya ivodgataḥ san*, XIV. 11). On ultimately reaching the Pātāla, he found a woman crying piteously. When consoled by Hanumān with an assurance of help, she told him that she was Maiyarāba's sister, Vīrakvanā by name, and was crying at the impending end of her son, who, alongwith Rāma, was soon going to be roasted alive in the boiling couldron by her cruel brother. Hanumān assured her that it could be averted if she conducted him to Maiyarāba, who was bound to perish at his hand (*durdāntaṁ enaṁ nikaṣāntakaṁ svaśaktyā 'payiṣyāmy acireṇa bhadre*, XIV 24). It was after outwitting the ruthless guards at the gate which involved Hanumān's converting himself into a lotus-filament that she succeeded in taking him to the place where Rāma was incarcerated. He challenged the demon king to a combat. To Maiyarāba's vaunt that he did not want to sully his immaculate fame, born of many a victory over powerful warrior, by killing a petty monkey, Hanumān administered resounding rebuff. He reminded the demon that he was son of the wind-god, firm like thunderbolt and was bound to pound him as does a tusker the lotus-stalk (*mṛṇāladaṇḍaṁ dvirado yathaiva*, XIV. 58). His actions, he added, spoke more than his words. With his anger inflamed by Hanumān's biting retort, the wicked demon pounced upon him but was himself hurled headlong on the ground (*sampātayāṁ bhūmitale babhūva*, XIV.62). The fight that ensued between the two was unprecedented, unheard and unseen before. Vīrakvanā advised Hanumān to kill Maiyarāba's soul on Trikūṭa mountain positioned in the form of a black-bee. As he was knocked out, Maiyarāba rolled down dead on the earth. Having thus killed the demon, Hanumān secured the release of Rāma and brought him back to his camp to the delight of his friends (*taṁ nināya śibiraṁ svam athaiṣaḥ*, XIV.76).

After the supposedly invincible Maiyarāba had been killed by Hanumān, Rāvaṇa in his wickedness twined his thought to the great warrior Kuṁbhakarṇa. Though Rākṣasa by brith, Kumbhakarṇa was not so by conduct. He did not approve of Rāvaṇa's despicable conduct in abducting Sītā. However, he consented to undertake an operation against Rāma to retrieve the honour of his family and motherland. Considering him irresistible like a swollen river, Vibhīṣaṇa decided to deal with him diplomatically. Kumbhakarṇa was terribly worked up to see him. He berated him severely for his perfidy to his kinsmen and country (*jñātidrohāt parataraṁ deśadrohāt tathā ca na*, XV. 21). Vibhīṣaṇa's attempt to pacify him by telling him that Rāma was an incarnation of Nārāyaṇa, provoked him to pose four questions that Rāma could not answer.

Kumbhakarṇa charged at Rāma's force with vehemence but was stopped by the monkey-chief Sugrīva. On finding a powerful rival in him, the demon decided to wear him down through a strategy. He invited Sugrīva to fight with him with the mighty tree, Raṅga by name, found in the Himālayas. The tree was fetched speedily. However, the journey to the far away Himālaya and to return from it put a severe strain on the monkey-chief. He was overpowered and arrested. Hanumān immediately launched measures against the demon and secured his release. Kumbhakarṇa returned to Laṅkā, humbled and ashamed.

He decided to arouse his missile, Mokṣa by name, to avenge the humiliation and thereby save the demons from the terror that Rāma represented (*mokṣopāyo dānavānāṁ rāmākhyavipadas tadā*, XV.55). However, Hanumān and Aṅgada combined to frustrate him in his attempt at propitiating its presiding deity. That, however, did not deter him from starting an operation against Rāma. In his fierce encounter with Lakṣmaṇa, Kumbhakarṇa hurled the missile at him. Struck hard, Lakṣmaṇa fell unconscious (*Saumitrir āsīt patito visañjñaḥ*, XV.71). Vibhīṣaṇa asked Hanumān to bring from the Sarvaya Mountain the divine herb before sun-rise, whereafter it would be ineffective in reviving Lakṣmaṇa. Soon after he left, he was bewildered to find daylight all around. The moment he attempted to turn away the chariot of the sun, he was parched by its rays. However, the sun was filled with remorse at the stern measures against one devoted to Rāma. He was not only brought to his own, the sun hid itself behind the clouds and thus turned the day into night to facilitate the completion of his mission. After some nagging equivocation on the part of the herb, Hanumān located and procured it according to his lights. And in order to meet the condition, he rushed to Ayodhyā to consecrate it with the sacred waters of the five rivers. Its use brought Lakṣmaṇa back to consciousness.

After Kumbhakarṇa had gone the way of Maiyarāba, Rāvaṇa elevated his son Indrajit as head of his forces. He had fettered Rāma's concourse with the noose of serpents (*nāgapāśa)*, though Garuḍa had subsequently scared them away. His manifold bravery notwithstanding, he too met the fate of Kumbhakarṇa. Thus demon after demon fell to superior power of Rāma or Hanumān. Rāvaṇa was overwhelmed with grief at the heavy losses. In order to avert effacement of his army, he decided to persuade Malivaggabrahmā or Malīvarāja Brahmā, the lord of three worlds, to punish Rāma for his indefensible act of invading his country. If the Lord could curse Rāma, he chuckled, he would be robbed of his virility and his army would become rudderless. He sent two of his envoys for the purpose. Malivagga descended on the neutral territory between the two forces. He declared that he had come there to pronounce judgement on the dispute. He could not do so unless he had heard Rāma and Sītā as well, with the deities standing witness to the judgement. On hearing the two, he found Rāvaṇa guilty and cursed him to be killed by Rāma's weapon. This filled Rāvaṇa with shame.

As the stratagems employed to vanquish Rāma off the field failed successively, Rāvaṇa decided to take the bull by the horn. Rāma and Rāvaṇa got locked in a fierce battle. Though their might was equally balanced, Rāma displayed unusual valour. But to his surprise he found that Rāvaṇa was immune to the barrage of arrows that he rained on him (*vivyathe nahi ca rākṣasarājaḥ*, XVII.6). Rāvaṇa's heads and arms were all chopped off successively but to the chagrin of Rāma they joined the body soon thereafter. Vibhīṣaṇa knew that it could go on like that endlessly unless Rāvaṇa's soul retained in a receptacle (*pañjara*) with the sage Goputra, the latter's preceptor, in his hermitage was destroyed first. Hanumān offered to accomplish the task but cautioned Rāma that he might be constrained to resort *inter alia* to many a stratagem in the process and that should not drive him to doubt his integrity. Together with Aṅgada he left for Goputra's Āśrama. He told the sage that he had been subjected to indignities by Rāma and therefore wanted to desert him (*tyāga eva khalu tasya tu sādhuḥ*, XVII.16) to join Rāvaṇa who is known for his solicitude for his allies (*sevayā sukṛtino 'dya kṛtī syām*, XVII.20). The knave sage took him at his word and waxed eloquent on the advantages that were to flow from allying with Rāvaṇa (*saphalayiṣyati sa tvām,* XVII.28). However, Hanumān expressed the apprehension that if he went to him on his own, that might provoke Rāvaṇa to finish him off. After all, he was an ally of his enemy. He therefore requested the sage to intercede on their behalf which he readily agreed to do. At Hanumān's caution that Rāma might steal away in his absence, the receptacle that housed Rāvaṇa's soul, the sage took it along with him. At the city gate cropped up a problem. If the receptacle were to be taken into the town, the soul might escape to Rāvaṇa to meet him (*taṁ draveta tam anu praviśec ca*, XVII. 44). At Hanumān's suggestion, it was decided to leave the receptacle with Aṅgada. Hanumān and Goputra entered Laṅka. After a while Hanumān on the pretext of giving instructions to Aṅgada came back to him, created with his miraculous power a feint of the soul and put it in the receptacle to replace the original which Aṅgada, at his behest, buried beneath the sea-shore (*samudratīre nyakhanad yena nāvirbhaved ayam*, XVII. 57). With Rāvaṇa's soul buried, there was no difficulty for Rāma in killing the demon. In the duel that ensued Rāvaṇa was finished off with ease.

Unaware of the disaster that had overtaken Rāvaṇa, his friend Mahīpāladevāsura, king of Cakravāla, came to visit him. When he came to know that Vibhīṣaṇa had been instrumental in bringing about the end of his friend, he became furious and decided to punish him for his outrageous conduct. He besieged the city of Laṅkā which was now being ruled by Vibhīṣaṇa under the new name of Daśagrīvāṁśa. Vibhīṣaṇa, who did not possess the miraculous powers of Rāvaṇa, was perturbed at the sudden turn of events (*mahān vyākulībhāva āvirbabhūva*, XVIII.8). He was suddenly reminded of the arrangement that Rāma had made at the time of his enthronement that he would send every week an arrow to him and the latter should return it with a note appended to it in case he felt threatened or otherwise insecure. As the city was under the siege now, Vibhīṣaṇa attached a note to the arrow and shot it back to Rāma (*śare lekham ekaṁ nibadhyāsrjat tam*, XVIII. 13). Rāma immediately deputed his eternal devotee (*ananyabhakta*) Hanumān, who was then ruling over the city of Navapurī under the new name of Phya Anujit to bail his former ally out of the impasse. Hanumān challenged Mahīpāladevāsura. In the fierce encounter that followed, Hanumān tore him into two. But to his amazement, the two pieces were miraculously united (*kṣaṇenaiva bhūyaḥ sa yukto 'janiṣṭa*, XIII.30). At the suggestion of Vibhīṣaṇa, Hanumān rent asunder his (*Mahīpāla's*) chest and the latter fell dead (*vidīrṇamātre tadurasy apāsuḥ, papāta bhūmau daśakaṇṭhamitram*, XVIII.33)

When Mandodarī became one of the wives of Vibhīṣaṇa after Rāvaṇa's death, she was already pregnant. She gave birth to a son, who was named Vaiṇāsuravaṁśa. As he came of age, he was apprised by his governor, Varaṇisura, of what Vibhīṣaṇa, in league with the enemy, had done to his father (Rāvaṇa). He felt pained at Vibhīṣaṇa's perfidiy and decided to wreak vengeance on him. He sought the help of his father's friend Cakravartī, the king of Malivan, who treated him as his son. He pledged to teach a lesson to Vibhīṣaṇa, who, he thought, was primarily responsible for the destruction of his friend (*sa eva daṇḍyaḥ svajanāpakārī*, XIX.12). Cakravartī invaded Laṅkā and put Vibhīṣaṇa behind the bars. Asuraphad, Hanumān's son from Beñjakayī, who was in attendance on Vibhīṣaṇa quietly escaped to obtain his father's help in foiling the evil designs of the enemy. After vigorous search, he discovered Hanumān practising austerities, in the garb of man, on the peak of a mountain and was convinced of his identity after initial disbelief (*mameṣṭadevo'si pitā mama tvam*, XIX. 39). Hanumān discontinued the penance and went to Kiṣkindhā with his son. They collected the army and proceeded to Ayodhyā where Bharata and Śatrughna also joined them. The combined army crossed over to Laṅkā. In the encounter that ensued after the failure of peace talks, Vaiṇāsuravaṁśa was killed and Vibhīṣaṇa released. Then they turned their fire to Malivan. Cakravartī was killed by Bharata with his Brahmāstra. Bharata also consecrated Hanumān's son Macchānu as the king in his place with Cakravartī's daughter Ratnamālī as his chief queen.

Canto Twenty is devoted to the banishment of Sītā.

On his return to Ayodhyā, Rāma was consecrated the new king, much to the delight of his people. Atulā the wicked daughter of Śūrpaṇakhā, was thirsting for revenge for the deformation that Lakṣmaṇa had inflicted on her mother. The opportunity presented itself to her when Rāma departed to a forest for a brief sojourn and Sītā repaired to a river to quench the fire of separation. Atulā, in the garb of a maid, served Sītā faithfully, without in any way, arousing her suspicion. The simple-hearted Sītā unwittingly moved into her trap by consenting to draw, on a block of stone, the portrait of Rāvaṇa. The moment it was completed, the demoness vanished into thin air (*kṛtakāryā gatavaty adarśanam*, XX.19). She entered into the picture, with the result the harder Sītā endeavoured to erase it to obviate the suspicion that Rāma might entertain about her fidelity to him on seeing it, to her utter chagrin, the brighter it became (*atisphuṭatā 'sya jāyate*, XX. 24). As Rāma reclined on the bed for rest, he was bewildered to feel heat all over the body (*mahad uṣṇatvam ihānvabhūd asau*, XX.28); *sutarāṁ samabhūc ca viklavaḥ*, XX, 29). Lakṣmaṇa ultimately found the cause in the portrait of Rāvaṇa which Sītā candidly admitted to have drawn in deference to the wishes of her servant (*kṛtam asti mayeti jānakī mama ceṭī-vacanānusārataḥ*, XX.36), and to have concealed it there to eschew her husband's wrath (*apahartum idaṁ svabhartṛtaḥ*, XX. 27). Rāma was aghast at the discovery. He was now convinced of her extramarital wanderings (*nanu saiva jane 'apare ratā*, XX. 40). Equally confident of her chastity, Sītā did her best to allay the ill-founded apprehensions of her husband (*uditas tava mānase bhramaḥ*, XX.46), but to no avail (*nahi pratyayam ādadhāt prabhuḥ*, XX.47). Agog with indignation Rāma charged Lakṣmaṇa to put her to death in the wilderness and bring back her heart to assure him of having carried out his orders. Lakṣmaṇa was torn between two loyalties. Finding him hesitant in executing the brother's order Sītā went to the length of provoking him with unkind utterances (*adhicikṣepa padair anargalaiḥ*, XX.59). In order to avoid the ignominy that was otherwise sure to stick to him. Lakṣmaṇa saw much merit in killing her. But to his amazement, all his shots failed to do her any harm (*kṣatim asyā vidadhe na kāñcana*, XX.71). Rather, Lakṣmaṇa himself fell unconscious. It was after much effort on Sītā's part that he was brought to his own. Overwhelmed with shame, he returned to Ayodhyā with the heart of a deer to reassure his brother of his obedience. His condemnation of 'her' heart as despicable as that of a beast notwithstanding, Rāma could not erase from his mind the feeling of guilt on Sīta's part (*na tasya bhāvaḥ pariśuddhim āgāt*, XX-83).

As Sītā cried piteously at her predicament and toyed with the idea of ending her life (*na jīvanasyāsti mamābhilāṣaḥ*, XXI.6), Indra, in the form of a bison, came to lead her to the hermitage of the sage Vajmṛga, who was a veritable repository of compassion. The sage took pity on her for the harsh treatment accorded to her, notwithstanding her innocence (*tyaktāpi bhartrā sutaraṁ nirāgāḥ*, XXI.15). He lodged her in a cottage in his āśrama where in due course of time, she gave brith to a child, the peer of sun (*prācīva kālena sahasraraśmim*, XXI.17). The sage himself performed his birth-ceremonies and blessed him with the name of Maṅkuṭa. He was the only solace to Sītā in the hopeless situation (*yo 'syā abhūt sāntvanam ekamātram*, XXI.17). Once while the sage was engrossed in meditation, Sītā left the child beside him and proceeded for bath in a river. On the way she met a group of monkey mothers, hopping from tree to tree, with their offsprings clung to their bosoms. Sītā's unsought caution to them to ensure the safety of their young ones brought her the cold retort that they, like her, did not consign their children to the care of the sage who might not cast even a glance on them because of his preoccupation with meditation. She was cut to the quick. She rushed back to the sage to retrieve the child quietly. The sage, on the other hand, was surprised and pained, as he rose from meditation, to find the child missing (*cintām anantāṁ sa tadā prapede*, XXI.39) presuming that Sītā's sufferings would be compounded enormously by the mysterious disappearance of her son (*Sītāntaraṅgam śakalāni kuryāt*, XXI.42). He decided to compensate her for the loss by creating a new child by his miraculous power. He drew on a slab the portrait of a child resembling in appearance the son of Sītā, and as he was pondering over as to how to invest the drawing with life, he was astonished to find Sītā with the child. She apprised the sage of all that had happened while he was in meditation. The sage now saw no point in persisting with the exercise (*....asmi tato viraktaḥ*, XXI.52). However in deference to Sītā's wishes, he infused life in the portrait and there arose a lovely child, the creation of his yogic power. The sage named him Lava and made him over to Sītā, who brought up the two with fond care.

In a bid to test the velocity of his arrow, Maṅkuṭa once shot down a burly tall tree. The terrific noise produced by its fall shook the earth to its moorings (*sarvā pṛthvī vyakampata*, XXII.7). Rāma also heard the noise in Ayodhyā. He took it as a challenge to his godhood and was therefore extremely perturbed (*sutarām udvig-nātmā babhūva saḥ*, XXII. 10). In order to track down the arrogant culprit, he decided to perform the Aśvamedha sacrifice. With Hanumān, Bharata and Śatrughna in attendance, he let loose the horse with the edict strung to its neck that whosoever resisted or mounted it in defiance of the royal force would be treated a traitor inviting suitable punishment. As Maṅkuṭa read the inscription, he took it as an aberration of a haughty person. With his anger inflamed, he, to the chagrin of the guards, mounted the horse and drove it away to the forest. As Hanumān tried to resist him, he (Maṅkuṭa) rendered him unconscious with a shot of an arrow (*sasarja bāṇaṁ niśitaṁ niḥsañjñaṁ yaś cakāra tam*, XXII. 31). Hanumān's subsequent attempt, on coming to his own, to punish the errant boys, only earned him chains (*sandānitaṁ vidadhatus taṁ tau śūraśiromaṇī*, XXII. 36). Notwithstanding his proud descent and fabulous might, he was reduced to dire straits. He was shackled like an ordinary monkey by the two teenagers in a manner that none but his master could unfetter him (*svasvāminam ṛte nainaṁ śakto mocayituṁ janaḥ* XXII.37). Licking his wounds, he flew to Ayodhyā in order to secure his release. Hanumān apprised Rāma of all that had been done to him by the two tiny warriors. Rāma immediately proceeded to the forest to bring them to book. His beratings to them only resulted in inflaming their anger. Charging him with arrogance, Maṅkuṭa challenged Rāma to settle it in a combat in case he had the capacity for it or return subdued (*yady asti śaktir bhavatāṁ yoddhavyaṁ vā mayā saha / nivartitavyaṁ deśaṁ vā svaṁ prahīṇa-parākramaiḥ*, XXII.66). The *śarabhas* do not brook the rumblings of cloud, he thundered. His powerful arrow invited an equally mighty shot from Rāma. The two arrows surprisingly missed their respective marks and joined together to fall on the earth. Not only that, Maṅkuṭa's arrow, mysteriously clothed in flowers, descended at Rāma's feet to pay him obeisance (*parivṛttaḥ puṣparāśasu Rāmapādāv apūjayat*, XXII. 72). Rāma's joy knew no bounds when he learnt on an enquiry after the happening that Maṅkuṭa was the son of Sītā, who was currently living in Vajmṛga's hermitage. What could have been a greater blessing than his sudden meeting with his son whose birth he did not know and wife whom he had discarded. Maṅkuṭa led Rāma to the āśrama and told his mother of how the union had been brought about.

Initial euphoria (*yayau naiva ca tṛptim eṣā*, XXIII.2) tempered with embarrassment (*sthātuṁ na śaktā na ca vā prayātum*, XXIII.1) apart, the sight of Rāma provoked the harried Sītā into an outburst against the maltreatment he had unkindly meted out to her. Overwhelmed with shame, Rāma cursed himself repeatedly for his odious behaviour towards her and begged her pardon. After all, everyone, howsoever enlightened, was liable to err (*loke 'tra ko nāma na nāparādhyet,* XXIII.14). His submission that he had come to take her back to Ayodhyā so that his life, which had ceased to interest him, may acquire relevance, only served to inflame her into denouncing him as petty-minded, suspicious and malicious (*kṣudraṁ tavātīva mano mataṁ me, śaṅkāgrahagrastam asūyakaṁ ca,* XXIII.27). She expressed her resolve to spend the rest of her life alone, away from him, the cruel killer of his wife (*patnyā nihantuḥ savidhe kathañcit, mayā na vastavyam avaśyam eve*, XXIII.35), reminding him at the same time that he had now a stronger reason to suspect her. As an alternative, Rāma suggested to her to send her sons with him. She subordinated her interest to those of her sons and sent them with Rāma in the belief that they would be brought up and educated better at Ayodhyā.

The warrior-sons of Rāma were a delight to people of Ayodhyā. As they went to visit their mother in Vajmṛga's hermitage, Rāma sent through them the message that in case she did not return, he would weep out to death (*mamāśrujalaṁ mama prāṇahṛt syāt*, XXIV. 7). She did not submit herself to emotional upsurge on hearing the terrifying threat. She rather told them to convey it to him that in case, it happened, she would come for his last 'darśana' (*eṣyāmy ahaṁ te 'ntimadarśanārtham*, XXIV.11). When it was subsequently conveyed to Rāma by Maṅkuṭa and Lava, on their return to Ayodhyā, Rāma underwent extreme agony. He then employed a ruse to bring back Sītā. He charged Hanumān to go to the hermitage of Vajmṛga to tell Sītā that unable to stand the pangs of separation, Rāma had died (*divaṁ gataḥ samprati Rāghavendraḥ*, XXIV.17). Despite her hardened heart Sītā was plunged into grief on hearing the dreadful news . She returned to Ayodhyā with Hanumān and immediately went to the palace. As she was cursing her wretched lot and wailing bitterly, Rāma appeared from behind the curtain, where he had concealed himself (*tiraskariṇyāḥ prakaṭaś chalena*, XXIV.30). She now discovered to her chagrin that she had been duped into visiting Ayodhyā by her deceitful husband (*matprāptiheto racitātra māyā māyāvinā matpatinā nṛśaṁsā*, XXIV.34). She rebuked Rāma for his mean trickery. As she started to leave for the hermitage, Rāma decided to block her departure. When the entreaties (*dayāpara 'sādhum imaṁ kṣamasva,* XXIV.39) invited greater rebuff from Sītā (*pravañcakeneha na me 'sti karyam*, XXIV.40), he threatened her with dire consequences and closed the doors all around She was taken aback by his conduct and prayed for divine help. Just then the earth burst open and Sītā went through it to the Pātāla where ruled king Nagaviruṇ. Rama fell unconscious on seeing the amazing spectacle.

Lord Śaṅkara organised a large assembly of gods on the Kailāsa mountain. The deities told him that while peace reigned supreme all over the world following the destruction of the Rākṣasas by Rāma, he himself was suffering agony of separation from his wife, Sītā. A solution had to be found to the situation. Śaṅkara sent for Rāma. Sītā was also brought from the distant Pātāla. Knowing well the rigid postures they had struck, the lord thought it prudent to handle the delicate issue with caution (*vyacintayad yad yadi kauśalena, varte' ham*, XXV. 11). He first reprimanded Rāma on three counts. He was guilty of ordering Sītā's execution, cheating her through Hanumān by the false news of his death and impeding her exit after she had come to Ayodhyā for his supposedly last 'darśana'. Śaṅkara bade him to beg her pardon for his acts of omission and commission, which Rāma promptly did. Sītā complied with the behest of Iśvara but not before expressing her serious reservations about his (Rama's) fickle-mindedness and consequent unpredictable behaviour (*an-gīkaromy eva tavājñayāhaṁ, patiṁ punaḥ*, XXV.25). Thereafter Rāma lived happily with Sītā, performing many a *yajña* that brought him immaculate fame (-- *vimalatamām avāpa kīrtim*, XXV. 31).

CRITIQUE

The *Rāmakīrtimahākāvyam* (*RKM*) marks the fulfilment of the author's march to conformism. While the *Bodhisattvacaritam* boldly defies theory on many a count and the *Indirāgāndhīcaritam*, notwithstanding its adherence to tradition, seeks to introduce innovation in elevating a woman to the high status of the heroine, the *RKM* has been written in deferential obedience to the rhetorical texts, though the author's penchant for freshness protrudes convincingly in a variety of ways. The epic story that forms the bedrock of the poem, despite its indigenous moorings and concurrence with the general framework thereof, makes departures from Vālmīki 's narrative to the extent that it has come to assume a new aura. It represents the version of the Rāma-story, as it is depicted in the Thai classic the *Ramakien*. By its very nature the narrative commands a wide canvas, enriched by a wealth of contents which emanate from the breathtakingly innovative episodes that dominate the Thai version. The author has sought to highlight the peculiarly differing strands of the Rāma story that indeed is the rationale of the *RKM*. He admits only such of the episodes as harmonise with the main narrative and unfold, in the process, their relevance to the epic. The episodes might have divested the narrative of substantial amount of its idealism, but have invariably resulted in lending it fascinating richness of contents. The freshness of the narrative is matched by the diversity of descriptions with subjects that are otherwise pushed into oblivion claiming added attention. The penetrative depiction of the differing emotions has culminated into the emergence of a wide variety of sentiments that are held to form the quintessence of poetry. The alliteratively lucid phraseology, which as evidenced by the author's other works, forms distinctive characteristic of his poetry, has reached its acme in the *RKM*. Rarely does one come across elsewhere such chaste and sweet language. It is a measure of the author's commitment to *viśuddhokti* that even the situations that ought to claim involved language are couched in incredibly simple and lively phraseology. All these combine to establish the *RKM* as a worthy Mahākāvya that has the proud distinction of presenting in elegant verse, an hitherto unkown version of the epic story. Despite his adherence to theroy, the author has no fascination for extravagant embellishment.

The outer trappings are admissible to him to the point they do not overburden the poem and contribute to enliven it without turning it into a *tour de force* like some of the other poems based on the story. It is moderation that breathes through the length and breadth of the poem.

THEME

The theme of the *RKM* accords with the injunctions Daṇḍin and Viśvanātha who contrary to their predecessor Bhāmaha, admit , perhaps to ensure effective communication, only a known narrative as worthy of a Mahākāvya[1], that, by its very character, has the potential in influencing society in various repects. Since it concerns itself with the epic-hero Rāma it is both *itihāsodbhava* and *sajjanāśraya*. As an inexhaustible store-house of raw material, the *Rāmāyaṇa* has led to the emergence of a vast mass of worthy literature. However, strictly speaking, the theme of the *RKM* does not owe itself to Vālmīki's epic. It has been admittedly adopted from the Thai classic the *Ramakien*. As such it represents an alien version of the Rāma story. No poet, howsoever gifted and industrious, can afford to deal with the epic story in its entirety, within the narrow limits of a Mahākāvya, its bulk notwithstanding. To strive to do that is to burn one's fingers with the impossible. The author has wisely picked up for treatment some of those episodes as are found neither in Vālmīki's epic nor in the *Rāmacaritamānasa* of Tulsīdās. That has added a new dimension, rather a new character, to the poem. But left to themselves, these episodes could have formed an incoherent jumble of heterogenous events hardly worthy of serving as the theme of a Mahākāvya. It could have been a severe strain on the ingenuity of any poet to spin them out in a coherent texture. The author has risen to the occasion to deftly provide the connecting links, which the two epics often share, to bind the apparently disjointed episodes together. The device has resulted into the emergence of a well-knit narrative that could do any poem proud. It has also enabled the author to turn spotlight on the *Ramakien*-episodes, which, in essentials, form the warp and woof of the poem. The theme thus resembles a fine piece of drapery with prominent patterns in full view. The *RKM* turns out to be the sole Mahākāvya to relate an alien (Thai) version of the Rāma story in a medium that serves to enrich and heighten its appeal, beyond measure.

The theme however may appear to an Indian rather unusual. The treatment of the characters he has been made to adore all through may even hurt him, but such is the story. The author could not have taken liberty with it. The theme, as it is, shows some of the respected and deified heroes of Vālmīki or other authors of India into lesser, if not petty, persons. Notwithstanding the divinity associated with him, Rāma is reduced to a scheming hero, not averse to cruelty and untruth, something frowned upon by tradition. Sita, likewise is shorn of virtuous idealism. She smacks of a heartless and ill-tongued woman. And gone is celibacy of Hanumān. He struts about like a dandy. This apart, the *RKM* is distinguished by remarkably vibrant narrative. It owes its vivacity to the genius of the episodes which the local tradition and

---

1. इतिहासकथोद्भूतमितरद्वा सदाश्रयम् ।
इतिहासोद्भवं वृत्तमन्यद्वा सज्जनाश्रयम् ॥

folklore seem to have joined to inspire. Motifs like the change of form[2], kidnapping[3], journey to the nether regions[4], propitiation of weapons to acquire greater power[5], invocation of divine curse for one's adversary[6], encasement of one's soul[7] belong to the domain of folklore rather than serious literature. The Thai milieu has asserted itself forcefully to cast the epic story in its queer mould. As conceived out of a mass of available data, the theme represents an admixture of indigenous and alien traditions.

While it is a tribute to the poet's sense of judgement to weave out a homogeneous theme out of a bewilderingly diverse data, its execution bears the imprint of a sober mind with no fascination for extravagant detalis or worthless accretions that combine to turn even some of the celebrated classical poems into an arena for misplaced display of one's equipment in a variety of disciplines. It is a measure of the author's commitment to the uninterrupted flow of his theme that he has skilfully pruned it of all avoidable accretions, though he could have occasionally afforded the luxury, without impairing the effect of the poem. In order to ensure the smooth flow of his theme, the author seems to have devised a happy pattern. While he has been quick in disposing of the events that are rather well-known and serve to act as cohesive agents, the peculiarly alien *upākhyānas* have been accorded fuller treatment. However, it is not the author's wont to blow anything out of proportion. Those of the episodes that are infested with abundant details have been sought to be dealt with rapidly in the accordant Anuṣṭup metre. The episode of Kumbhakarṇa (XV) and Rāma's meeting with his sons (XX) bear testimony to the author's skilfulness in handling the plethora of details. Even the core episodes have not been allowed to overstep the bounds of moderation. In keeping with his aversion to unnecessary details or overstretching the events, the author has been wisely economical in describing such brief episodes as that of Anomatan. The self-born child in Canto Two could have occasioned a description of his physical traits or beauties. But the author has discreetly avoided it. Nārāyaṇa is described to have carried the child to Śiva who, without the least delay or query, named him as Anomatan and proclaimed him as the first ruler of the earth. The swiftness with which Īśvara is described to have deputed Nārāyaṇa to meet the menace of Hirantayakṣa, even before the deities

2. *RKM.*, X.3,XIV.31,XV.65
3. ibid., XIII. 15
4. ibid., XIV
5. ibid., XV. 58
6. ibid., XIV
7. ibid., XIV.72, XVII.8

could recount their woe, has emanated from the author's anxiety to ensure unhindered flow of the narrative. The way the abundant details in Cantos Thirteen, Fourteen, Fifteen and Twenty-two have been treated by divesting them of the potential to fling spanner in the narrative, speaks volumes of the author's sense of proportion. He fully understands the psychology of the reader. Before a description tends to strain his patience, the narrative is carried forward to resume its serene flow.

RĀMAKIRTIMAHĀKAVYAM AND THE RĀMĀYAṆA : A STUDY IN CONTRAST

Since the *Rāmakirtimahākavyam* seeks to relate the Thai version of the epic story, as detailed in the *Ramakien*, it shows substantial divergences from the *Rāmayaṇa* . The story in the *RKM* differs from that of Vālmiki in two respects. While, on the one hand, it introduces some altogether new episodes which do not occur in the *Rāmayaṇa*, on the other, even when the incidents are identical, they differ in details. The differences have evidently stemmed from the alien version that forms its basis.

The new episodes that relate to Anomatan (II), Nandaka (IV.I), Birth of Sitā (IV-II), Jihva (V), Beñjakayī (X), Suvarṇamatsyā (XII), Maiyarāba (XIII-XIV) Malivaggabrahmā (XVI), Rāvaṇa's soul (XVII), Mahipāladevāsura (XVIII), Insurrection in Laṅkā (XIX), Birth of Lava (XXI), Reconciliation of the estranged couple (XXV) have been described in detail earlier and do not, therefore, brook repetition. It is, however, pertinent to note that more than anything else, it is these episodes that have invested the epic story with a distinct character and divested the adorable heroes of the idealism that makes them what they are in the *Rāmāyaṇa*.

The other differences are equally glaring. It is imperative to turn focus on them to understand the extent to which the Thais have reshaped the epic story to bring it in tune with their way of life.

MAJOR DIFFERENCES :

Of the episodes which the *RKM* shares with the Vālmiki *Rāmāyaṇa* but differs in details, Sitā's banishment merits foremost attention because of the wide divergences in the way the two versions have been dealt with. According to the *RKM*, Atulā, the daughter of Śūrparṇakhā infiltrated as a maid into Sitā 's palace and in order to settle score with her for the wrong done to her mother by Lakṣmaṇa, duped her, in the absence of her husband, into drawing a portrait of Rāvaṇa, who had held her in captivity for long. As soon as the picture was completed, the demoness vanished into thin air. Sitā got suspicious of the evil design. In a bid to avoid the wrath of her husband she strove hard to obliterate it from the slab. Not succeeding in it because of the trick of Atulā who had made herself enter into it and had it in her magic grip, Sitā concealed it under the bed. As Rāma reclined on the bed, he experienced burning sensation all over the body. Lakṣmaṇa traced the cause of it to the picture hidden under the bed. Rāma lost faith in Sītā's fidelity.[8] He charged Lakṣmaṇa to execute her in the forest and bring back her heart as a proof thereof. Despite the unequivocal order of his brother and Sītā's provocative taunts he could not summon the courage or the will to commit the ghastly act. He left her to fate and brought the heart of a deer to convince Rāma of the successful execution of the assignment. Sītā was mysteriously led to the hermitage of the sage Vajmṛga where she continued to live[9]. In the *Rāmāyaṇa* also Sītā had to undergo the agony of expulsion. But she was banished, according to the epic version, not because Rāma doubted her faithfulness to him but because of his inability to withstand the public calumny. Lakṣmaṇa took her to the forest but did not leave her to perish. He directed her to Vālmīki's hermitage[10]

The account of Lava's birth, as set forth in the *RKM* and Vālmīki's epic, is distinguished by total variation. The *RKM* would have us believe that while living in the hermitage of Vajmṛga during her exile, Sītā gave birth to one son only. He was named Maṅkuṭa and was trained and brought up under the Argus eye of the sage, who subsequently created the second son through his yogic power to compensate Sītā for the supposed loss of the other son. The boy was given the name of Lava.[11]

It is interesting to find that the *Ānandarāmāyaṇa* has much the same version of the birth of Sītā's sons. It mentions that Sītā had only one son Kuśa, named so by Vālmīki because of the sprinkiling of the holy water on him with the kuśa grass. Once she left the child to the care of Vālmīki. On her way to the river she saw a monkey-mother carrying its litter of five on its person. She cursed herself for indiscretion in leaving the child with the sage while he was in meditation. She dashed to the āśrama. As Vālmīki had gone out, she brought back the son with her. When, on return, the sage did not find the child he created anoher one for fear of Sītā's

---

8. A Bundelkhandi folk song provides interesting parallel to the version of the incident. After Sītā was united with Rāma, she visited the forest. There, says it, her friends persuaded her, in order to satisfy their curiosity, to draw Rāvaṇa's portrait which she did with the cow-dung. As she had sketched the figure up to the waist, there appeared Rāma. He recognised the figure and came to suspect her fidelity and therefore ordered her expulsion.
   Dr. Satya Vrat Shastri,*Studies in Sanskrit and Indian Culture in Thailand*, Parimal Publications, Delhi, p.69.
9. *RKM.*, XX. 1-83
10. *Rāmāyaṇa* (Gita Press Edition), VII. 45.1-20, 47.1-18
11. *RKM., XXI. 1-56*

curse. He offered it to her who readily accepted it. He gave it the name Lava created as he was by Lavas (wool or quails). Both the children grew together as brothers in the hermitage[12].

The *Kathāsaritsāgara* differs slightly in its version of the children's birth. According to it, Sītā had given birth to Lava and it was Kuśa who was created by Vālmīki as he suspected the other child to have been carried away by a wild animal.[13] It appears that there was a story in circulation in India, at some point of time, which believed that Sītā had only one son, the other having been created by Vālmīki to make up the supposed loss of the other. It was this version which seems to have travelled to Thailand.

The Vālmīki *Rāmāyaṇa*, on the other hand, unequivocally states Sītā to have given birth to two sons, named respectively as Kuśa and Lava,[14] leaving no scope for the sage to demonstrate his miraculous power.

The events that led to the entombment of Sītā are radically different in the two poems. According to the Thai version, as told in the *RKM*, Rāma, as he got suspicious of her fidelity following the recovery of Rāvaṇa's portrait drawn by her, unceremoniously expelled her from the kingdom and ordered her execution which, however, was never carried out by Lakṣmaṇa. Rāma presumed her dead and felt lonely without her. When he discovered that she was alive he, stung with remorse for his harshness, begged her pardon and requested her to bury the hatchet and return to Ayodhyā to embalm his wounded life. She was too wronged to forget or forgive. All the subsequent overtures were also turned down by her with equal contempt. Rāma felt humiliated. With no alternative left, he duped her through none else but Hanumān, into believing that Rāma had died. Sītā came to Ayodhyā but was furious to find that she had been a victim of a mean conspiracy and Rāma was alive. Rāma added salt to her injury by attempting to block her return to the hermitage. Thus cornered and insulted, she requested Mother Earth to take her into her bosom. The earth erupted and Sītā went to Pātāla[15].

This wealth of details is conspicuous by its absence in the *Rāmāyaṇa*. In the epic, as Sītā stood to convice the assembly of her chastity, a throne emerged from

---

12. *Ānandarāmāyaṇa*, Janmakāṇḍa, IV.21-86
13. *Kathasaritasagara*, IX.86-93
14. यामेव रात्रिं शत्रुघ्नः पर्णशालां समाविशत् ।

    तामेव रात्रिं सीतापि प्रसूता दारकद्वयम् ॥ *Rāmāyaṇa*, VII.66.1
15. *RKM*. XXIV.1-48

the earth and she disappeared seated thereon, to the nether region, never to return.[16]

Another prominent difference between the *RKM* and the Vālmīki *Rāmāyaṇa* concerns the denouement of the story. The Thai version ends in the reconciliation of the estranged couple, brought about by Śaṅkara, as a reward to Rāma for his services in ridding the earth of the menace of the demons. Rāma pleads gulity and tenders unequivocal apology to Sītā for the wrong done to her for no fault of her. Sītā, brought from Pātāla, is fastidious but relents at the behest of the Lord. They lead a happy conjugal life thereafter.[17]

This is in stark contrast to Vālmīki's epic which ends on a tragic note, with Sītā entombed in earth for ever.[18]

However, it is in reducing the main characters of the epic strory to lesser, down to-earth persons that the alien milieu has asserted itself with a vengeance. As observed earlier, Rāma, the divine darling of the masses since ages, is turned into a heartless, scheming hero. Sītā has come to bear resemblance with an ill-tongued lady. And Hanumān has been pushed fom the high pedestal of adoration to a level where he is no different from a gallant, making love to many youthful women and begetting sons on them.

MINOR DIFFERENCES

Besides the new episodes that distinguish the *RKM* as a distinct version and the other glaring variations that mark some of the episodes and events which it shares with the *Rāmāyaṇa*, some minor differences can also be noticed in quite a few other incidents. While the *Ramakien* reveals such divergences in a large number of incidents the author has admitted only a few of them in his poem.

The account of Rāma's birth, as related in the *RKM* betrays slight differences from Vālmiki's version. While unlike the Thai *Rāmāyaṇa*[19] but obviously under Vālmīki's influence, the name of the sacrifice which Daśaratha performs for

---

16. भूतलादुत्थितं दिव्यं सिंहासनमनुत्तमम् । *Rāmāyaṇa,* VII.97.17
    तामासनगतां दृष्ट्वा प्रविशन्तीं रसातलम् । ibid.,97.20
    रसातलं प्रविष्टायां वैदेह्यां सर्ववानराः । ibid.,VII.98.1
17. *RKM.*, XXV. 1-31
18. अपश्यमानो वैदेहीं मेने शून्यमिदं जगत् ।
    शोकेन परमायस्तो न शान्तिं मनसागमत् ।। *Rāmāyaṇa,* VII.99.4
19. *Studies in Sanskrit and Indian Culture in Thailand*, op.cit., p.68

begetting sons, is given as Putreṣṭi, the *ṛṣi* who performs it is Kalaikoṭi in the *RKM*[20] whereas it is Ṛṣyaśṛṅga in the epic. Likewise against *pāyasa* in the *Rāmāyaṇa*,[21] the divine food intended for the queens is rice-balls, two of which are mysteriously intercepted midway.[22] The *RKM* seeks to associate different colours with the four brothers. Thus Rāma is green in colour, Bharata red, Lakṣmaṇa is golden and Śatrughna purple[23]

As seen earlier, the birth of Sītā is also differently described in the *RKM*. There she is shown as the daughter or Rāvaṇa, one single most glaring departure form the Vālmīki's narrative. As said earlier, at the son-sacrifice (Putreṣṭi) a divine being emerges from fire with a tray of four rice-balls. On eating two of the balls stolen by the demoness Kākanā, from Uttarakosala for her, Mandodarī, the chief queen of Rāvaṇa, conceives and subsequently gives birth to a daughter. Because of her quaint behaviour at the time of birth in declaring Rāvaṇa's death, she is thrown in a jar to perish in the river. Janaka retrieves the jar and buries it deep underneath. As he ploughed it out from a furrow, the girl was given the apt name of Sītā (IV.27-52).

Paraśurāma is called Rāmāsura in the poem. He like his prototype in the Vālmīki *Rāmāyaṇa*, tastes defeat at the hands of Rāma, but tries to win his favour by gifting him a divine bow[24] which he (Rāma) assigns to the custody of god Varuṇa.

The story of Vālin's fight with Darabhī (Māyāvin) is identical in both the *Rāmāyaṇa* and the *RKM* upto the point where Sugrīva is placed at the entrance of the cave wherein the fight takes place. The *RKM* gives a slightly different turn to the story when it introduces the element of rain. Vālin, before entering the cave, had told Sugrīva that if he saw thinner blood coming out, he should take it to be his (Vālin's) and presume him dead. If instead, he saw thicker blood gushing out of the cave, it should be construed to mean the end of Darabhī. However, the rain played havoc with the scheme. On account of it Darabhī's blood became lighter. when Sugrīva saw it, he thought that Vālin had been killed. And in order to prevent Darabhī's escape he blocked the cave with boulders and left. Vālin could come out of the

---

20. *RKM.*, III.3
21. दिव्यपायससम्पूर्णां पात्रीं पत्नीमिव प्रियाम् । *Rāmāyaṇa*, I.16.15
22. *RKM., III.15-16*
23. ibid., III. 20-23
24. तस्यानुकूल्याय समार्पिपत्तद्
धनुर्महेशः प्रददे पुरा यत् ॥ ibid., IV.62

cave with great difficulty. He was enraged at Surgrīva's behaviour and came to suspect his loyalty. [25]

The episode of Kumbhakarṇa also reveals some differences. Vibhīṣaṇa's meeting with him and the four questions that he poses to him for Rāma to answer are unknown in Vālmīki's epic. Some of the feats like propitiation of the missile and the injury to Lakṣmaṇa that necessitated the divine herb sañjīvanī, attributed to him, were actually performed by Indrajit. [26]

SENTIMENTS (RASA)

Rightly viewed as the soul of poetry,[27] and the single most potent factor to distinguish a Mahākāvya as a source of aesthetic pleasure,[28] the concept of *rasa* suffered progressive abridgement in its function at the hands of the subsequent generations of poeticians. While the early rhetoricians unequivocally expressed themselves in favour of uninhibited role for all the sentiments to contribute to aesthetic pleasure and thereby ensure for it wide acceptance, it was Ānandavardhana who first applied closure to their independent functioning and cast them in the relationship of principal and subsidiary though he was wary to prescribe that the subsidiary sentiment should not be carried beyond a point, otherwise it was bound to detract from the eminence of the principal one, the *aṅgī rasa.* Ānandavardhana had postulated the relationship to enhance the cumulative impact of poem[29]. The later theroriticians have been more rigorous in restricting the choice of the principal sentiment from among Śṛṅgāra, Vīra and Śānta.[30] With subsequent generations of poets meekly submitting to it, the injunction continues to hold the field, its weak premise notwithstanding.

It is interesting to find that with the years the author has shed his aversion to theory in the depiction of sentiments as well. While in the *Bodhisattvacaritam*, the various sentiments have been allowed independent play with quietism commanding an edge over the others, the *Indirāgāndhīcaritam* attests to his anxiety to elevate the Vīrarasa to the dominant position. The same is true of the *RKM* as well, though it is

---

25. *RKM.*, VII.14-24
26. *RKM.*, XV.58-67, 71-87
27 वाक्यं रसात्मकं काव्यम् । *S.D.*, I.3(1)
वदन्ति काव्यं रसमेव यस्मिन् निपीयमाने मुदमेति चेतः । *Hammīramahākāvya*, XIV.35
28. *Saṁskṛta Vāṅmaya kā Vivecanātmaka Itihāsa*, op.cit., p.170
29. *Dhvanyāloka*, op. cit., III., 21,24
30. *SD.*, VI. 317

much more pronounced than in the former. The Rāma-story, as executed in the poem in pursuance of its Thai version is frequently punctuated by a string of fierce encounters among mighty contestants, each violently determined to maul the adversary to death, besides Rāma's final combat with Rāvaṇa. The imaginative delineation of these duels among heady heroes has raised the Vīrarasa to a new high. However, the actual duel in the poem is preceded, almost invariably, by a wordy bout that serves to unfold the personal prowess of the intrepid combatants involved therein. The exposition of their valour by them, designed to browbeat the respective rivals, exudes heroism. Full of confidence in their infallible might, they mean to pour scorn on their opponents. Hanumān's dauntless verbal duel with Mahīpāladevāsura, though a replica of the corresponding bout with Maiyarāba (XIV.50-60), emerges as the best illustration of the wordy warfare that seems to have settled as a motif of sorts of the Heroic sentiment, as it is treated in the *RKM*. Mahīpāla treats Hanumān with the contempt that he as a supposedly unequal adversary, deserves. The combat with him, the demon brags, would only expose him (Mahīpāla) to ridicule and tarnish the fame that he had earned by his countless victories over famed warriors. He therefore deserved pity, not fight because that would entail his pounding to dust. The caustic rebuke provokes equally harsh, though succinct, retort from Hanumān. Bravery is not determined by birth nor is it tested by hollow vaunt, the monkey thundered. All this tantamounts to an expression of *utsāha*, admitted by poeticians as the lasting feeling (*sthāyibhāva*) of Vīrarasa :

समालोक्य वीरं कपिं सम्मुखे स
तृणायैव तं मन्यमानो बभाषे ।
अपेह्याश्वितो नैव वाञ्छामि युद्धं
त्वया दर्शितं हन्त ! कापेयमत्र ।।

अहं चक्रवालाधिपो भूमिपालो
दिशां चक्रवाले प्रसिद्धिं गतश्च ।
त्वया वानरेणास्तु मे चेन्नियुद्धं
परीहासपात्रत्वमेष्यामि सत्यम् ।। XVIII.21-22

दयाया वशात्त्वां विमुञ्चामि शाखा-
मृग त्वं पलायस्व रक्षापि च स्वम् ।

मदीयेन हस्तेन निष्पीडिताङ्गो
दशां भाग्यदिष्टां प्रयातासि नो चेत् ।।
समाकर्ण्य तस्यासुरस्योग्ररूपां
गिरं स प्रवीरोऽशनिध्वानवाचा ।
कपिः प्राह तं नैव जात्याऽस्ति कश्चिद्
बली वाऽबली वेति बाढं गृहाण ।।
कपित्वान्न मे वीर्यहानिर्भवेद्वा
ऽसुरत्वादथो तेऽस्तु भो ! वीर्यवृद्धिः ।
परीक्षा नियुद्धे भवेदावयोर्द्राक्
न कस्यापि वीर्यं परीक्ष्यं गिरैव ।। XVIII.24-26

Even otherwise some of the doughty heroes in the poem are prone to indulge in the boasting of their supposedly unmatched valour that often leads them to underrate their rivals, unmindful of the disaster that is to overtake them subsequently. Vībhiṣaṇa's prudent advice to Rāvaṇa to release Sītā to ensure the safety of the Rākṣasa-race provoked him into waxing eloquent on his prowess, which, he reminds him, has been instrumental in routing even the proud regents of the quarters. He would crush Rāma like a mosquito, Rāvaṇa ranted. Whatever their worth, these vauntings exude heroism :

शक्तिं न्यूनां गणयसि कथं राघवान्मे विजेतु-
र्दिक्पालानां सकलभुवनस्पृह्यकीर्तेर्विमूढ !
क्वाहं वीरो जगति विदितो राक्षसानामधीशो
राज्याद् भ्रष्टो वनमधिवसन् राघवो वा पुनः क्व ।।
तं तादृक्षं मशकमिव भोः स्वेच्छयैवोपपन्नं
निष्पीड्याहं करतलगतं हेलयैव प्रसन्नः ।
मामाक्रान्तुं कृतपरिकरं स्वस्य मृत्युं यथैव
रामं रामाविरहजरुजं प्रापयिष्याम्यनन्ताम् ।। IX.15-16

The rebuff that Rāma administers to Rāvaṇa, disguised as an ascetic, who had sought to overawe him with his (Rāvaṇa's) might entails exposition, albeit subdued, of his valour and his unshakable faith therein. While the ascetic threatened that Rāvaṇa would crush him like a moth, Rāma retorted with equal vehemence that he would sever his ten heads like balls of cards with incredible ease. It is *utsāha par excellence*:

त्वां राम तस्मात्परिबोधये मा
दशास्यवह्नौ शलभायितो भूः ।
त्रैलोक्यजेता क्व नु राक्षसेन्द्रैः
परीवृतस्त्वं क्व च वानरैर्भोः ।। IX.47

भार्या हृता मेऽधमराक्षसेन
ततोऽस्ति मे दण्ड्यतमो मतोऽयम् ।
वृत्तोऽहमस्मादभिषेणनेऽस्य
प्रयोजकोऽन्यो नहि मेऽत्र हेतुः ।।

चापद्वितीये मयि युध्यमाने
स्थातुं ममाग्रे न भवेदलं सः ।
एकैकशः कर्तयिताऽस्मि तस्य
तीक्ष्णैर्दशास्यानि शरैरहं द्राक् ।। IX.50-51

Against this form of heroism, which, in ultimate analysis, is aimed at belittling and harming others, stands, almost as an opposite pole, the Heroic compassion (*dayāvīratā*) that unfolds itself in the ennobling magnanimity of some of the leading characters of the poem. It touches its zenith in the way Rāma condones the grave offence of Beñjakayī, the demon girl charged by Rāvaṇa to inflict anguish on Rāma by feigning Sītā's corpse. Contrary to the extreme penalty her father Vibhīṣaṇa had recommended for her, Rāma liberally pardons her and addedly deputes Hanumān to escort her safely back to Laṅkā. A lesser person would have executed her then and there :

नृशंसमस्या अतिनिन्दनीयं
कर्मेति तावद् धृदि सम्प्रधार्य ।

त्वां वच्म्यहं मित्रमिति प्रपन्नः

सुता ममेयं वधमर्हतीति ।।

एवं सखे ! नैव भवेत्कदाचिद्

हन्यां कथं मित्रवरस्य कन्याम् ।

यथा तवेयं हि तथा ममापि

क्षम्यो मयाऽस्याः प्रथमापराधः ।। X.20-21

The depiction of the duels in which Hanumān is engaged as one of the contestants occasions vigorous expression of the Heroic sentiment. His encounters with Maiyarāba and Mahīpāla, which do not differ in essentials, may justifiably be rated as the most telling illustrations of the Vīrarasa. The treatment of the dominant sentiment in the poem happily adheres to the norm, as it manifests itself in theory and practice. The author seems to lay down certain ground-rules for the combatants. Unequal encounters do not meet his approbation[31]. That is what led Maiyarāba and Mahīpāla to scoff at the monkey (Hanumān) as a poor rival to them, the fight with whom would entail ignominy (*mā bhūt parivādanavāvatārah*, XIV.54; *parihāsapātratvam eṣyāmi satyam,* XVIII.22). It is a measure of the author's anxiety to respect the tradition that he has not hesitated to whip up some of the accepted motifs in delineating the Vīrarasa: the intemperate verbal exchanges between the opponents, the war cries, trembling of the earth under the impact of the fierce combat, the descent of the divine beings to witness the clash, the use of sticks, fists, teeth, etc. With no holds barred are some of the mannerisms that the author has pressed into service to demonstrate his adherence to tradition in giving expression to the Heroic sentiment. Hanumān's breath-takingly terrific combat with Maiyaraba, the king of Pātāla,is characterised by all these features and results in the emergence of Vīrarasa, with the vigour and intensity of the dominant sentiment. With the final charge by the 'monkey' the 'invincible' demon rolled down to dust :

पातालराजो निशितैः समन्ताद्

हनूमतो वाग्विशिखैः प्रविद्धः ।

---

31. नियुद्धं समेनैव तावत् समस्य
प्रशस्यं भवेन्नेतरेण प्रमादिन् ।। *RKM.*, XVIII.23

क्रोधेन जज्वाल तदाज्यधारा-
सारैः समिद्धो हुतभुग्यथैव ।।
ततः समादाय कपिं स दोर्भ्यां
बलाद्विनिष्पेष्टुमियेष दुष्टः ।
कपिस्तरस्वी तरसा च तं द्राक्
सम्पातयां भूमितले बभूव ।।
समारुरोहाथ च तस्य वक्षो
विनिष्पिपेषाथ च तत्समन्तात् ।
नखैश्च तीक्ष्णैर्नखिनां वरेण्य
'उरोविदारं प्रतिचस्करे च' ।।
उन्मोच्य हस्ताद् दृढया स्वशक्त्या
हनूमतो दानवराजमुख्यः ।
कोपारुणाक्षः पुनरेव तावत्
तमभ्यधावद्विनिहन्तुकामः ।।
ततोऽतिभीमं ववृते नियुद्धं
दुर्दान्तयोस्तत्र परस्परेण ।
नैव श्रुतं वा न च वा कथञ्चिद्
दृष्टं भवेल्लोमविहर्षणं यत् ।।
दण्डादण्डि मुष्टीमुष्टि दन्तादन्ति कचाकचि ।
हनुमन्मैयराबौ तौ न्ययुद्ध्येतां परस्परम् ।।
सर्वं पातालंलोकं तन्नियुद्धं समकम्पयत् ।
द्रष्टुं भूतगणाः सर्वे नानादिग्भ्यो यदागताः ।। XIV.61-67
तस्मिन्पिष्टे मैयराबो निःसञ्ज्ञो भूतलेऽपतत् ।
अलुठद् दीनवच्चापि दशकण्ठसखः शठः ।। XIV.74

Rāma's clash with the hermit-boy Maṅkuṭa, though not so fierce, is notable for the latter's intrepidity in taking up cudgels with Nārāyaṇa himself, and the sublimity it undergoes in the submission of the irrepressible son to his great father and the resultant meeting with Sītā, whom he (Rāma) had given up as dead since long. Maṅkuṭa scornfully reminds Rāma that his edict was offensive to the extreme as the earth was not yet void of the Kṣatriya-warriors. He, on his part, refused to take his command lying down and challenged him to try conclusion on the battle-field if he were capable of doing that or slip back subdued. The Śarabhas do not sleep over the rumblings of the cloud. Within the few verses, the Heroic sentiment, breaks through forcefully though not many arrows were exchanged :

दोषस्तु भवतामेव यल्लेखो दृप्तभावतः ।
अतिसृष्टो भवद्भिर्यं मादृशो विषहेत नो ।।

नहि निःक्षत्रिया राजन् ! पृथिवी सचराचरा ।
अहमत्र प्रतीरोधं भवतां कर्तुमुद्यतः ।।

यद्यस्ति शक्तिर्भवतां योद्धव्यं वा मया सह ।
निवर्तितव्यं देशं वा स्वं प्रहीणपराक्रमैः ।।

न मेघगर्जनं सह्यं शरभाणां कथञ्चन ।
युद्धं मे दीयतां राजन्नहं शरभशावकः ।।

इत्युक्त्वा स शरं घोरं रामप्रभुमवासृजत् ।
जाज्वल्यमानः क्रोधेन स चापि प्राहिणोच्छरम् ।।

एतावुभौ शरौ हन्त लक्ष्यभ्रष्टौ बभूवतुः ।
परस्परेण संश्लिष्य पेततुश्च महीतले ।। XXII.64-69

मङ्कुटस्य प्रवीरस्य सायको निशितः क्षणात् ।
परिवृत्तः पुष्पराशौ रामपादावपूजयत् ।। XXII.72

Thus the Vīrarasa has been fostered in the poem so vigorously that there could be fear that the other sentiments would have been relegated to the background with inconsequential role to play. It is however notable that the *RKM* has received heavy sprinkling of some of the ancillary sentiments. Of these, the Marvellous sentiment, which in its intensity and frequency, tends to equal the *aṅgī rasa*, has been treated with admirable tenacity. While in view of the restrictions imposed by theory, it may not be justified to raise it to the pinnacle of the *aṅgī rasa*, it is pertinent to recall that some of the ancient poeticians viewed it as the sole sentiment worthy to be admitted as the chief sentiment. The narrative, as executed in the *RKM,* indeed abounds in a host of events and situations that fill one with wonder. These have been skilfully exploited by the poet to occasion the emergence of the Adbhutarasa which may well dare the principal sentiment by its profundity, its ancillary status notwithstanding. It is interesting that in delineating the Wonderous sentiment, the author has often felt tempted to use its lasting feeling (*vismaya*) by name[32]. It is permissible in case it serves to heighten the intensity of the sentiment[33]. This is precisely the function it performs in the poem.

Though, as remarked earlier, there are occasions galore in the poem for the Adbhutarasa to bloom, its first impressive depiction is met in the Fourth Canto which is marked by several marvellous situations. Rāvaṇa's daughter as soon as she was born, uttered thrice, to the surprise of all, the words "kill Rāvaṇa , kill Rāvaṇa , kill Rāvaṇa".[34] When discarded in a river to perish, a lotus mysteriously appeared to sustain the jar which floated safe to the bank.[35] As Janaka opened it out of curiosity, he was filled with wonder to find a newly-born girl happily encased there[36]. He buried the pitcher under the earth. As soon as the king decided to launch upon the ploughing operation to retrieve it after sixteen years, following the failure of his forces, there emerged the jar and the beautiful girl seated on a bed of lotus petals therein. Everybody was struck with wonder at the sudden appearance of the pitcher and the captivating charms of the girl :

तत्कालमेव प्रकटो घटोऽभूत्

तन्मध्य आसीच्च विलोभनीया ।

---

32. दृष्ट्वा दृश्यं तदखिलमभूद्विस्मयाविष्टचेताः । IX.27
विस्मयाविष्टबुद्धेः । IX.29
शब्दो भीमो जनित इह यो विस्मयं नस्तनोति । IX.30
विस्मितः कपिपुङ्गवः । XII.4
यद्विस्मयं तस्य भृशं ततान । XII.16

33. व्यभिचारिरसस्थायिभावानां शब्दवाच्यता । *Kāvyaprakāśa*, VII.60

34. जातमात्रैव सा कन्या रावणो हन्यतामिति ।
त्रिरवादीद्वचो नो च पित्रोस्तच्छ्रोत्रमापतत् ।। IV.28

35. पद्मं यदात्मन्यधि कुम्भमाधात् । IV.34.

36. तावद्ददर्शान्तरमुष्य कन्यां
सद्यः प्रसूतामतिविस्मितः सः ।। IV.37

अध्यासती पङ्कजपत्रपङ्क्तिं
दिव्यस्वरूपा खलु कन्यकैका ।।
गण्डच्छविन्यक्कृतपुण्डरीका-
ममूं विशालायतपक्ष्मलाक्षीम् ।
हेमद्युतिं चन्द्रमरीचिगौरीं
दृष्ट्वा जना विस्मयमभ्युपायन् ।। IV.50-51

The Wonderous sentiment is again perceptible in Rāma's encounter with Rāmāsura of divine origin. After he had subdued Rāmāsura, Rāma immediately revealed his true form of Nārāyaṇa. Already feeling small, Rāmāsura's surprise was heightened as he found himself face to face with the Lord. His hair stood on end and he made a childish bid to win him over by presenting him Śiva's bow :

पराजितः शस्त्रभृतां वरेण
प्रदर्शितश्चापि निजस्वरूपम् ।।
नारायणोऽयं प्रकटः पुरस्ता-
न्मद्भागधेयादिति हृष्टरोमा ।
तस्यानुकूल्याय समार्पिपत्तद्
धनुर्महेशः प्रददे पुरा यत् ।। IV. 61-62

The interesting episode of Suvarṇamatsyā also serves to unfold the Adbhutarasa in substantial measure. Entrusted with the building of the causeway to Laṅkā Hanumān devoted himself to the work alongwith his companions, in right earnest. But he was wonderstruck to discover one morning that the rocks that he had positioned the previous day, had mysteriously disappeared. He plunged into work with added vigour. His surprise knew no bounds when he found his endeavours go waste, next morning, in a similar manner. There was no trace of the stones he had set so assiduously. The enigmatic disappearance of the rocks has been ingeniously exploited to result into the emergence of Wonderous sentiment :

दिनमेकं स बलवान् शतशः कपिभिः सह ।
अनारतं शिला अब्धौ प्रक्षिपन् व्यापृतोऽभवत् ।।

अपरस्मिन् दिने प्रातः स्वकार्यार्थमुपस्थितः ।
अदर्शनं गतास्तत्र समवालोकयच्छिलाः ।।

केयं मायेति सुतरां विस्मितः कपिपुङ्गवः ।
विनष्टा रात्रिमात्रेण शिलाः कुत्र गता इति ।। XII.2-4

स स्वयं कपयश्चापि तदादिष्टाः समन्ततः ।
शिलौघान् प्राक्षिपन् वार्धौ स्वस्य कर्मण्यतन्द्रिताः ।।

प्रातर्यदाऽऽगाद्धनुमान् परेद्युः
समुद्रतीरे कपिभिः समेतः ।
नालोकयन् क्षिप्तचरं समुद्रे
विसिष्मिये पूर्वदिने शिलौघम् ।। XII.6-7

In a bid to obviate the recurrence of loss, Hanumān mounted guard on the sea-shore. As he heard strange noises, he dived into the ocean to see for himself what was going on there. What he witnessed there took him by surprise. It was a wonderous spectacle, the like of which was never heard or seen before. He found thousands of fish engaged in removing the rocks under orders of their queen Suvarṇamatsyā, herself a miraculous lady, half woman, half fish. The unique scene served to stir his wonder (*vismaya*), that constitutes the bedrock of Adbhutarasa :

अवप्लुतः संस्तरसा तदन्त-
र्विचित्रदृश्यं समवालुलोके ।
अभूतपूर्वाश्रुतपूर्वमेव
यद्विस्मयं तस्य भृशं ततान ।
अकल्पनीयं सुतरां बभूव
यत्तेन साक्षात्परिदृष्टमास्त ।।
मत्स्यांश्च मत्सीश्च सहस्रशोऽसौ
युक्तान् शिलानां व्यपरोपणाय ।
ददर्श राज्ञीमपि तत्र तेषा-
मासन्निमे यद्वचनात् प्रवृत्ताः ।।

सुवर्णमत्स्येत्यभिधानिका सा
दशाननस्यास्त सुता सुबुद्धा ।
अर्धं शरीरेण बभूव मत्सी
बभूव सार्धेन मनुष्ययोनिः ।। XII.15-18

However, the most vigorous expression of the Wonderous sentiment is found in the manner the monkeys set about to exhibit their phenomenal powers to dispel the apprehensions that Vibhīṣaṇa entertained about their capacity to meet the might of Rāvaṇa (*sākṣāt dṛṣṭe bhavati sutarāṁ pratyayo nātra śaṅkā*, IX.24). They virtually let loose hell in the forest. They not only uprooted the trees and the mountains, they also lept high to withhold the wind and envelope the sun in their sweep and dived low to dry up the oceans. These breath-taking feats thrilled Vibhīṣaṇa to the extent that he was covered with horripilation and could not simply believe his eyes. He shed his scepticism and was convinced of Rāma's victory. The terrific noise stirred by the monkeys pervaded the universe. The quarters resounded with its vehemence. Despite the bold face, Rāvaṇa also was taken aback by its ferocity. The furiousness of the monkeys and the destruction unleashed by them as detailed in the poem, struck all with wonder :

तच्छ्रुत्वा ते वचनममलं यूथमुख्यस्य दीप्ताः
शक्तेः स्वस्याः परिचयविधौ स्वं मनो दत्तवन्तः ।
वृक्षान् केचिद् विपुलतरकान्केचिदेवापि चाद्रीन्
मूलोच्छेदं करतलगताञ्चक्रिरे साऽहसेन ।।

अन्ये तावद् दृढतरधियः सूर्यमावव्रिरे द्राग्
जातं विश्वं प्रबलतमसाऽऽच्छादितं येन विश्वम् ।
केचिच्चाथो पवनमबलं तेनिरे स्वस्य वेगा-
दन्ये चाथो जलधिमतुलं शुष्कतां नीतवन्तः ।।

दृष्ट्वा दृश्यं तदखिलमभूद्विस्मयाविष्टचेता
हृष्यद्रोमा निजनयनयोर्विश्वसन्नो महात्मा । IX.25-27

ते तं प्रोचुः कपिवरभटै राघवस्यैष चम्वा
शब्दो भीमो जनित इह यो विस्मयं नस्तनोति ।। IX.30

Śṛṅgāra may not square with the character of the narrative, dominated alternately by the Heroic and Wonderous sentiments, but, as Rasarāja it commands eminence that none can afford to ignore or downgrade. Even when cast in the subordinate role, its contribution in reinforcing the principal sentiment and thereby investing the poem with beauty is beyond question[37]. Notwithstanding the constraints inherent in the ancillary status, it is bound to assert itself on the wide canvas of such a massive form of poetry as Mahākāvya. Contrary to the author's earlier Mahākāvyas, the Śṛṅgāra has not only received greater notice in the *RKM*, it tends to conform in its depiction to the norms as they are laid down by the poeticians. Almost all the feelings associated with Śṛṅgāra not precluding the inflaming agents (*uddīpanavibhāvas*) and manifestations thereof (*anubhāvas*) have been assiduously mustered to ensure its vigorous expression. The happy tendency to philosophise on the irresistible pervasiveness of Kāma tends to lift the affair to sublime heights. Love doubtless encompasses one and all in its sweep (*sādhāraṇaḥ prāṇiṣu bhāva eṣaḥ,* XII.40). One has to submit to its might at one point or the other (*kusumāyudhaśaktir aho amitā*, X.27). Even the wise recluses have no answer to the onslaughts of love. It is as natural to life as the union of a creeper with a tree and of a river with an ocean.[38] Strangely enough, it is Hanumān's romantic forays that culminate in the emergence of Śṛṅgāra in the poem. Evidently the Thai milieu has asserted itself in turning the celibate demigod into a gallant, out to make love with any beautiful girl that comes his way. While his affair with Beñjakayī tends to be a wee general, its effectiveness notwithstanding[39], it is his love-making with Suvarṇamatsyā, the charming daughter of Rāvaṇa, that is exhaustively detailed to yield the Erotic sentiment in its profundity and intensity. Once convinced of the unequivocal response to their mutual advances,

---

37. रसोऽस्ति यः कोऽपि परं स किञ्चिन्नास्पृष्टशृङ्गाररसो रसाय ।

Hammīramahākāvya, XIV. 36

38. *RKM.*, X.25,28

39. कुसुमायुधशक्तिरहो ! अमिता
हनुमानपि यद्वशमाप कृती ।
असुरीमपि स प्रणयं प्रबलः
समयाचत तत्सहितो रहसि ॥
अथ साऽपि शशाक विधातुमिमं
बलिनं प्रविलोक्य विलोक्यतमम् ।
स्वमनो न मनोजवशात्स्ववशे
मुदिता समरंस्त च तेन समम् ॥ X.26-27

they fall headlong for each other and are lost in the bliss of love with all that leads it to culmination, where both virility and beauty are amply rewarded. It is here that the author, lavishes, much against his wont, his regard for details. The treatment is indeed methodical. The Vasantatilakā metre joins the sweetly lucid and alliterative phraseology to heighten the tenderness of the delicate emotions :

दृष्ट्वैनमत्र मनसः सुतरामनीशा
जाने न किं खलु मया करणीयमत्र ।
पर्याकुलेव लुलितेव सुविह्वलेव
वल्लीव पौरुषतरुं श्रयितुं लषामि ।। XII.42

चिन्तापरा विविधचारुविचारवीचि-
प्रेङ्खोलिता न वचनं किमपि प्रपेदे ।
वायोः सुतोऽपि कमनीयतमाङ्गयष्टिः
पश्यन्न तां स्वमनसः प्रबभूव वीरः ।। XII.44

धीरं विलोकयति विस्फुटमन्दहासा
वाचं न मिश्रयति वानरवीरवाचा ।
आविष्करोति दृढभूमिमुपेयिवांसं
निःश्वासवायुमिषतः स्मरदाहमेषा ।।

अन्योन्यमेवमवितृप्ततयोपपन्नौ
गाढोपगूहनसुखाकुलितान्तरङ्गौ ।
वायोः सुतश्च रमणी च सुवर्णमत्स्या
गाढं बभूवतुरुभौ मदनेषुविद्धौ ।।

आनन्दमापतुरुभौ च गिरामगम्यं
संमीलिताक्षियुगलौ परिलुप्तधैर्यौ ।
रागाङ्कुरस्फुरणताम्रकपोलयुग्मौ
वक्षोनिपीडमधरामृतपानमग्नौ ।।

रोमोद्गमप्रकटरागविशेषवृत्ती
विद्धौ समं मनसिजासमपुङ्खपत्रैः ।
आबद्धबाहुयुगलौ परिनिःश्वसन्तौ
स्वेदाम्बुजालजटितालकजालकाली ।।
अन्योन्यचुम्बनपरौ रतिकर्मसक्तौ
सम्प्रापितौ मनसिजेन दशां विचित्राम् ।
आनन्दसागरतरङ्गपरम्परासु
प्रेङ्खोलितौ सममुभौ रजनीं व्यनैष्टाम् ।। XII.46-50

Not unlike the *IC*, the *Rāmakīrtimahākāvyam* is also enlivened by the Vātsalyarasa, doubtless the tenderest and the most ennobling sentiment, though it has not met unqualified acceptance as such, its universal appeal notwithstanding. Viśvanātha merits unstinted esteem for his vision in according it the status it richly deserves[40]. Hanumān again has been central to the exuberance of the Vātsalyarasa in the poem. It is the dramatic meetings with his (unknown) sons that serve to stir affection beyond measure and have therefore been instrumental in enriching the poem with the loveliest of the sentiments. When Hanumān came to know that the young man who had been locked with him in a fierce combat a short while before, was none else but his son Macchānu, begotten on Suvarṇamatsyā, he was overwhelmed with blissful Vātsalya. He felt as if he had attained all that was worthwhile to have in life. He deemed himself the worthiest and luckiest father under the sun. He was convinced of the wisdom enshrined in the Vedic dictum that a son is the very soul of his parents. Tears welled up in his eyes. The intensity of his Vātsalya manifested itself in repeated kisses and caresses. The expression of affection earned him sincere regards and apologies from the son[41]. Almost the same scenario is witnessed in his meeting with his other son, Asuraphad who had come to seek his help in bailing Vībhīṣaṇa out of the impasse. While in the earlier meeting affection outweighed the expression of respect by the son, in the latter the two seem to be evenly balanced. Hanumān was overpowered by a plethora of emotions. Overjoyed at the meeting, he viewed it as no less than the sudden discovery of treasure. To Asuraphad, it represented the fulfilment of a long-cherished dream. This individualised

---

40. *Sāhityadarpaṇa*, III.215
41. *RKM*, XIII. 42-51

Vātsalya strikes responsive chords in every breast. On generalisation it culminates in expression of Vātsalyarasa :

उत्थाप्य दोर्भ्यां हनुमांस्तनूजं
गाढं परिष्वज्य च साश्रुनेत्रः ।
पुत्रस्य लाभात्परमप्रतीतो
ऽकस्मादमुं वाचमिमामुवाच ।। XIX.34

अतर्कितं रत्नमिवास्ति पुत्र-
रत्नं मया लब्धमिहाद्रिशृङ्गे ।
सद्यःफलं मे तप इत्यनेन
हर्षप्रकर्षो हृदि मे न माति ।।
वचोऽतिहृष्टोऽसुरफद् बभाषे
श्रुत्वा वचस्तज्जनकस्य हन्त !
तृप्तं चिरायाथ मदीयनेत्र-
युगं समालोकयतस्स्वतातम् ।।
''अद्य क्रियाः कामदुघाः क्रतूनां
सत्याशिषः सम्प्रति भूमिदेवाः ।''
चिराय यद्दर्शनमीप्सितं मे
स एव साक्षात् पुरतो ममास्ति ।। XIX.36-38

Similar expression of intense Vātsalya enlivened by delight is found in Canto XXII where Rāma, like Hanumān, comes to know that the boy pitted against him was his son Maṅkuṭa. He was beside himself with joy at the unexpected meeting and he manifested his affection for the son by kisses and embraces :

तच्छ्रुत्वा रामभद्रस्य हृदये न ममुर्मुदः ।
असम्भावितसम्प्राप्तिः कस्य मोदाय नो भवेत् ।।
ममैवायं सुत इति तं स द्रुतमुपागमत् ।
प्रहर्षनिर्भरश्चापि समालिङ्गत्पुनः पुनः ।। XXII.76-77

शिरस्यजिघ्रदेनं स हर्षाश्रुभरितेक्षणः ।
सविग्रहं स्थितं पार्श्वे मनोरथमिवात्मनः ।। XXII.79

It is heartening that the author's penchant for Hāsya manifests itself in the present poem also, which otherwise does not afford many opportunities for this most lively sentiment. Contrary to the *IC*, the *RKM* is not content with the gentle form of Hāsya such as exchanged between Indira and Nehru. It is the full-throated laughter that is stirred in the drama enacted by Rāma with Kubjā the hunch-backed maid of Kailkeyī. While one shot of his arrow removed the hump of the maid, the second one soon thereafter, resulted into its reappearance. Kubjā's funny plight sent the spectators into peals of laughter. Here the permanent feeling is nursed to blossom into the Hāsyarasa. It is however a different matter that what was intended as a playful prank of the adolescent age subsequently invited calamitous retaliation from the scheming maid :

क्रीडारसादल्पवयाः कुमार-
स्तत्कुब्जपृष्ठं तरसा जघान ।
कुब्जत्वमस्या यत आश्वपागात्
सत्सङ्गमेनेव कुबुद्धिदोषः ।।
क्रीडारसाद् दाशरथिः पुनश्च
किञ्चित्क्षणानन्तरमेव रामः ।
बाणेन तस्यां प्रजहार येन
कुब्जत्वमस्यां प्रकटीबभूव ।।
सर्वेऽपि पार्श्वस्थजना अनेन
दृश्येन तावद्धसितुं प्रवृत्ताः । V.3-5

Terror is inherent in the way the people conducted themselves on hearing the terrific sound kicked up by the fall of the colossal tree. As the tree tumbled down, cut into two, by the fearsome shot of Mankuṭa's arrow, the earth shook violently under its impact. Struck by terror, people ran helter skelter. Some of them took refuge in the caves. Even Rāma was deeply perturbed (*sutarām udivignātmā*) by the mind-boggling sound, the peer of *pralayavāta* :

प्रजहार स वेगेन विशिखं लक्ष्यवेधिनम् ।
द्रुमः प्रहृतमात्रोऽसौ द्विधा येन व्यभज्यत ॥

तादृशे तु महावृक्षे द्विधा भग्ने विलक्षणे ।
सांराविणमभूद्येन सर्वा पृथ्वी व्यकम्पत ॥

भयार्ताः प्राणिनश्चापि सर्वे चेरुरितस्ततः ।
शिश्रियुस्तेषु केचिच्च गहनाः कन्दरा गिरेः ॥

द्रुमभञ्जननिर्घोषो घोषः प्रलयवातवत् ।
सर्वैरपि जनैस्त्रस्तैः शुश्रुवे पृथिवीगतैः ॥

रामस्यापि स निर्घोषोऽयोध्यायां श्रोत्रशष्कुली ।
पस्पर्श येन सुतरामुद्विग्नात्मा बभूव सः ॥ XXII.6-10

Pathos has also bared its sting in the *RKM* though, unlike the *Indirāgāndhīcaritam*, its position is somewhat tenuous. There are doubtless several situations to occasion it, but it seems to proceed from a weak premise. It is sought to be distinguished from its *vipralambha* variety by the permanence of separation, which is invariably caused by death. The separation brought about by death is also taken to come in purview though some of the rhetoricians like Viśvanātha are inclined to view the miraculous revival and the consequent union after certain death as Karuṇavipralambha.[42] Interestingly, it is the feigned death that has been sought to be exploited to stir Karuṇarasa in the poem though that does not in any way diminish its poignancy. Strictly speaking, it could not have formed the basis of Pathos but the *āśraya* suffers no illusion about the actual occurrence.To him, it is as shocking as the real death, though he has been maliciously duped into the belief. In a bid to frustrate Rāma in his mission, Beñjakayi, at the behest of Rāvaṇa, feigned Sītā and floated dead to Rāma. On seeing the dead body of Sītā in the river, Rāma wept bitterly. His fortitude sagged and he swooned under the weight of emotions. His wailings, though occasioned by a despicable stratagem, form the *sthāyibhāva* of Karuṇarasa that is moving in its sincerity :

---

42. यूनोरेकतरस्मिन्गतवति लोकान्तरं पुनर्लभ्ये ।
विमनायते यदैकस्तदा भवेत्करुणविप्रलम्भाख्यः ॥ *Sāhityadarpaṇa* , III.209

मृतं शरीरं जनकात्मजाया
नदीप्रवाहेण समुह्यमानम् ।
तदैव संमोहमुपागतोऽभू-
दमुञ्चदश्रूणि च लुप्तधैर्यः ।। X.7

It was again mean trickery on the part of Rāma, neatly executed by his unfailing friend Hanumān, that drove Sītā to presume her husband dead. Despite her revulsion for him for his cruelty in ordering her execution, she rushed back to Ayodhyā and wailed at his supposed death as sincerely as a wife in the situation would do. "The woman who outlives her husband is the most cursed being on the earth. I suffered long separation during the life-time. How it is that you did not unite me in death as well", she bemoaned pathetically. The Karuaṇarasa expresses itself with tantalizing acuteness in her wailings (*vilāpa*). It is a different matter if she turns violent when Rāma reveals himself soon thereafter :

प्राप्ता च तत्सा विललाप धीरा
ऽप्यधीरवद् बाष्पमवासृजन्ती ।
कुत्रासि मे नेत्ररसायन ! त्वं
कुतो न मां त्वं सह नीतवांश्च ।।

त्वं जीवने मह्यमदा वियोगं
वर्षाणि नाना नयनाभिराम ।
न मृत्युकालेऽपि समागते ते
सङ्गो मया सार्धमभीप्सितोऽभूत् ।।

विहाय किं त्वं त्रिदिवं गतोऽभू-
रेकाकिनीं मामिह जीवलोके ।
स्वभर्तृवर्त्मप्रतिपन्नतैव
स्त्रीणां विधात्रा विहिता जगत्याम् ।।

पतिं तु या नार्यतिजीवतीह
नान्या ततोऽधन्यतमाऽत्र लोके ।

एवंविधाया हतजीविताया

न जीवनं हा मम जीवनं स्यात् ॥

न जीविता वा न मृता च वापि

स्वकर्मभोगार्थमहं श्वसन्ती ।

यथाकथञ्चिन्निजमायुषोऽहं

शेषं प्रभो ! यापयिताऽस्मि कृच्छ्रात् ॥ XXIV.25-29

Raudrarasa protrudes vehemently in the reprimand that Vālin and Rāvaṇa administer to their respective brothers, Sugrīva and Vibhīṣaṇa for their questionable loyalty. They charge them with motives for their enigmatic behaviour and pour angry rebuke on them[43]. The streak of quietism, on the other hand, is perceptible in the realisation of impermanence of life[44].

Besides its richness in sentiments the *RKM* is marked by an happy interplay of *bhāvas* in their multiple forms. Defined as *rati* intended to gods and others including parents[45], it is manifestly inherent in the deferential regards that Asuraphad and Macchānu tender to their father Hanumān in their respective meetings with him :

व्रीडावनम्रः स च तं विनम्र-

भावेन भूयो विनिबद्धभावः ।

अतर्किताव्याप्ततदीयसङ्गः

समालिलिङ्ग प्रणनाम चापि ॥ XIII.55

ममेष्टदेवोऽसि पिता मम त्वं

'मनोरथानामतटप्रपातः' । XIX.39

While the emergence of *bhāva* is found in joy that Hanumān experiences on meeting Asuraphad, his son,[46] its cessation is evident in the way *udvega* cools down

43. *RKM.*, VIII.25-26, IX.13

44. किञ्चिन्नैव स्थिरमिह जगत्यस्ति सञ्चारशीले । ibid., IX.4

45. रतिर्देवादिविषया व्यभिचारी तथाऽञ्जितः । भावः प्रोक्तः । *Kāvyaprakāśa*, IV.35

46. *RKM.*, XIX. 36

in Hanumān and Macchānu following their meeting in unexpected circumstances[47]. Loss of peace and humiliation combine in Rāvaṇa to form the conjunction of two unhappy *bhāvas (bhāvasandhi)*[48]. And *bhāvaśabalatā* may be detected in the variety of feelings that Suvarṇamatsyā undergoes on hearing the logical plea of Hanumān[49].

A number of prominent sentiments thus join hands to contribute to the richness of aesthetic pleasure in the poem. While the Heroic sentiment, in its varied manifestations, has been accorded the enviable status of *aṅgī rasa*, in view of its depth and frequency the Adbhutarasa occupies an equally high rung though it may not be possible to glue the similar label to it.

CHARACTERISATION

Effective depiction of the mental, moral and physical traits of the dramatis personae with the hero claiming maximum esteem, forms the quintessence of the phenomenon symbolised by *netā,* deemed to be one of the characteristics that invests a Mahākāvya with a distinct personality. The *RKM* marks acme to the successive widening of the avenues which the author's poems, especially the Mahākāvyas, offer for characterisation. While it represents a pole apart from the constricted possibilities of characterisation as they hesitatingly unfold themselves on the disjointed canvas of the *Bodhisattvacaritam*, the *RKM* has a cohesion of the narrative and variety of characters that strut the stage with dignity. The author's defiance of the tradition in characterisation, besides much else, was what distinguished the earlier poems, in the *RKM* it is his faithful adherence to theory that engages attention. Here neither an ethereal phenomenon nor a heroine is sought to be projected as the leading character. It is Rāma, the darling of successive generations of poets, who has been accorded the highest rung. In making Rāma the hero, the author has manifested his regard for tradition which requires a divine figure or a Kṣatriya of noble lineage to assume the pivotal role in a Mahākāvya[50]. It is indeed reassuring to find the time-honoured characters, who have exercised ennobling influence on society, down the ages, grace a modern poem. The possibility of their slipping into pre-determined grooves has been effectively warded off by assigning them substantially different roles that they are expected to play in obedience to the milieu from which they have stemmed. This deliberate conditioning might have turned them into more attractive figures, some of the characteristics that have come

---

47. *RKM.*, XIII.52
48. ibid.,IX.19
49. ibid.,XII.34
50. *Sāhityadarpaṇa*, VI.316

to enrobe them infringe upon the elevating idealism that they symbolise in the Indian mind. They are essentially Thai figures transplanted on Indian soil with the oddities that are inherent in the situation. The *RKM* seems to have been conceived as a rendezvous for a vast array of characters, drawn from diverse cultural backgrounds. Though not intended as the pivotal figure, Hanumān is doubtless the most colourful character in the poem, strutting the stage like a colossus. Everyone else, not precluding Rāma, seems to have been overshadowed by his phenomenal might and resourcefulness that prove equal to the toughest challenge.

RĀMA

Of all the colossui in Indian tradition, Rāma represents the embodiment of the plethora of excellences that have combined to turn him into ideal, rather divine, figure whom society has revered, down the ages. He is the fountainhead of the virtues that the poeticians have prescribed for the hero of a Mahākāvya[51]. As drawn in the *RKM*, he may be taken to broadly square with the rhetorical prescriptions. He has indeed been an ideal hero through the ages. But since the *RKM* is intended to offer the Rāma-story as related in the *Ramakien*, It is the Thai version of Rāma that one encounters in the poem. While he concurs with his Indian counterpart in substantial measure, some of the contours of his character are breathtakingly queer. In view of the fact that the coincidences have been relegated to the background, it is these aspects of his character that protrude prominently in the poem.

The divinity of Rāma is beyond dispute. He is doubtless Nārāyaṇa who had incarnated as the son of Daśaratha to release the world from the oppression of the demons (*kausalyātaḥ prajāto 'bhūt svayaṁ Nārāyaṇaḥ prabhuḥ*, III.20). He was not to be viewed as an ordinary person. Vibhīṣaṇa was convinced that it was the most pious deed to attend upon him with reverence[52]. Rāma himself was conscious of his divine origin. He took Maṅkuṭa's conduct as an offence to Nārāyaṇa[53]. Equipped with a host of virtues (*guṇagaṇamaṇḍitaḥ*, II.19), his divinity evoked widespread reverence (*akhilajagannamasyabhūtaḥ*, II. 19.). It was deemed the fulfilment of one's dreams to sing his sacred *caritra* (II.19).

There is not much to distinguish him till his return from Laṅkā. His sincerity as a friend had unfolded itself in settling scores with Vālin on behalf of his ally and friend

---

51. *Kāvyādarśa*, op. cit., I. 15
 Sāhityadarpaṇa, III. 32
52. न पृथग्जनवद्रामो द्रष्टव्यो येन केनचित् ।
 भूलोकमवतीर्णोऽयं साक्षान्नारायणः प्रभुः ।। XV.23
53. कोऽयमेतादृशं घोषं मयि नारायणे स्थिते ।। XXII.11

Sugrīva. His achievements on the battle-field remain subdued in view of the restricted avenues to which his combat with Rāvaṇa is reduced. Though the battle has been evaluated in poetic terms as 'fierce' (*ghora*) and 'unprecedented' (*na śruto na hi ca vā paridṛṣṭaḥ*, XVI.2), but for Hanumān's stratagem in having his (Rāvaṇa's) soul, buried underground, the demon might have frustrated Rāma in his mission. It was only after Hanumān's trickery succeeded that Rāma could kill him on the battlefield[54]. While his encounter with Maṅkuṭa, whom he had not yet known to be his son, underwent sublimation, he could neither brow-beat the boy into submission nor humble him in the battle[55]. If carried further, the combat could well have ended into stalemate.

It is the alien component of his character that puts Rāma on a different footing. And unfortunately that is not something to do him proud. As conceived in the Thai tradition and depicted, under its impact, in the *RKM*, Rāma, his divine origin apart, is indistinguishable from a common man. He seems to suffer from infirmities that could well be associated with a lesser person. These may justifiably be taken to rob him of the excellences that make a hero *dhīrodātta* [56].

The stratagems cunningly employed by Rāvaṇa to humble him off the field might not have served their purpose to the desired extent, they have certainly been instrumental in exposing him to awkward situations, unworthy of the equanimity that otherwise is his forte. It is surprising that he was duped with incredible ease into presuming Sītā dead on seeing so much as her figure floating in the river, blissfully forgetting the deceit the demons were capable of. It was Hanumān's alertness occasioned by unfailng vision that saved Rāma from what might have been a sure disaster[57]. The ordeal, however, served to bring into prominence his compassion (*dayāvīratā*) that manifested itself in granting reprieve to the culprit, Beñjakayī, despite advice to the contrary.[58] His brush with Maiyarāba shows him in still poorer light. It is a measure of the lack of alertness against the possibility of the enemy's depredations that he was thrown into swoon by such a cheap device as magic

---

54. *RKM.*, XVII.58-60
55. *RKM.*, XXII.68-72
56. *SD.*, III. 32

57 आकृष्य तां तत्र समार्पिपच्च ।
श्रीरामचन्द्राय विदां वराय ।। X.17

58. *RKM.*, X.20

powder and carried, unnoticed, to Pātāla to be encaged there like a petty criminal[59]. It was again Hanumān, guided by Vibhīṣaṇa, who rescued him after a longdrawn struggle, at great peril to himself[60]. If Rāvaṇa had the audacity to invoke divine verdict against him, he could not be absolved of the responsibility. It was the fairness of Mallivaggabrahmā that turned the tables on Rāvaṇa and made him bite dust. Rāma cannot be credited to have averted the divine wrath, on his own. He rather seems to be a helpless victim of a variety of conspiracies with no capacity or power to thwart them.

The way he conducts himself vis-a-vis his devoted wife is patently reprehensible. He emerges from the exercise as a suspicious and scheming husband with no qualms to employ the worst trickery and deceit. Though endowed with funds of fortitude and equanimity, he loses his equipoise the moment he experiences burning heat all over the body on his cosy bed[61]. And notwithstanding his firm belief in her chastity, he sights many a phantom rising from the **portrait** of Rāvaṇa that innocent Sītā was tricked into drawing by Śūrpaṇakhā's daughter Atulā to wreak vengeance on her for the wrong done to her mother because of her (Sītā). He comes to suspect her fidelity and in a fit of rage orders Lakṣmaṇa to execute her in the forest[62] and bring back her heart as a proof thereof. That was unmitigated cruelty[63] that ill behoves the hero of the poem, much less of the stature of Rāma . No wonder Sītā, doubtless under impact of the milieu that has fashioned her, pelts him, at different points of time, with such epithets as suspicious, cruel (XXIII.5), petty-minded, jealous (XXIII.27), wife-killer (XXIII.35), wicked (XXIV.36), deceitful (XXIV.40-41), fickle (XXV.19) and evil-minded (XXV.20), so deep were the scars he had inflicted on her.

---

59. पातालभूमिं वधकाम्यया तं
सम्प्रापयामास च हेलयैव । XIII.6
उपस्थितस्तत्र बभूव यत्र
सन्दानितो दाशरथिर्बभूव ।। XIV.46

60. एवं निहत्य तं दैत्यं रामं मुक्तं विधाय च । XIV.75

61. स तु धैर्यधनोऽपि सन्नभूच्
च्युतधैर्यो रघुनन्दनस्तदा । XX.29

62. किमियं दनुजानुरागिणी । XX.37
जहि चापि न जीविता चिरं
स्थितिभाक् स्यात् प्रमदा प्रमादिनी ।। XX.42

63. शङ्कालुना क्रूरतमेन चापि । XXIII.5

His behaviour following the unexpected meeting with Sītā, after ten long years, is all the more enigmatic. In moments of remorse, he humbly pleads guilty[64], begs her pardon [65], touches her feet[66], expresses his unequivocal devotion to her[67], rates her as the summum bonum of his life[68] and respectfully entreats her to return to Ayodhyā to lend relevance to his meaningless life, simultaneously asking her to kill him in case she decides to stay on because his survival without her would be a mere exercise in futility[69]. Perhaps in a bid to somehow sustain himself without her comforting company, he requests her to send Maṅkuṭa and Lava with him which she does in the larger interests of her sons. Obviously they could not fill the void in his life. He, in a way, continues to pine for her with no respite in sight.

These tender sentiments and honest pleadings, evidently emanating from a chastened heart, however, yield place to despicable schemings soon thereafter. He certainly appeals to her softer feelings. He seems to serve on her a notice of sorts in conveying to her, through the young boys, his resolve to weep to death in case she was firm in her determination not to return.[70] What followed was the negation of all that Rāma stands for. When he finds Sītā unrelenting, he decides to cheat her into believing that he (Rāma) had ended his life because of his inability to stand the pangs of separation.[71] Sītā does move into the trap. However, when on discovering the truth, she tries to leave for the hermitage after some sharp exchange with Rāma, he not only blocks all possible routes, he even goes to the length of threatening her[72]. This was something which even Śaṅkara could not condone. He rather reviled him for this. His (Rāma's) reconciliation with her was as mysterious as the

---

64. कृतागसि त्वं मयि यद् दधासि कोपं । XXIII.,16
65. क्षमां त्वामहं याचे । ibid.
66. पस्पर्श पादावपराधचण्ड्याः । XXIII.19
67. त्वदेकचित्तोऽस्मि । XXIII.15
68. त्वमेव सर्वस्वमसि । XXIII.34
69. उवाच सीतां यदि नो प्रयासि,
    मया समं त्वं जहि तर्हि मां त्वम् । XXIII.33
70. नो चेत्त्वमायासि पुरीमयोध्यां, ममाश्रुजलं मम प्राणहृत्स्यात् । XXIV.7
71. त्वद्विप्रयोगार्तिविदीर्णचेता, दिवं गतः सम्प्रति राघवेन्द्रः । XXIV.17
72. --- गन्तुमितो न शक्ताऽसि कथंचिदेव ।
    न त्वादृशाः स्युर्विनयेन शक्या :
    कर्तुं वशे नानुनयेन वापि ॥

estrangement. The couple lived happily after all the bitterness that had turned its life into virtual hell. As depicted in the *RKM*, Rāma, seems an unpredictable person with inconsistent conduct which is again evident in his cheer to Lakṣmaṇa for his not killing Sītā in obedience to his bidding[73]

SĪTĀ

In Sītā the *RKM* has its heroine. While the *IC* thwarts the norms in elevating a woman as the central figure, the *RKM* is the author's solitary Mahākāvya to have claimed, like a play, the heroine as well. Unlike her husband, she represents the fusion of the indigenous and alien components. Whereas the former is too well-known to arouse curiosity, it is the elements introduced by the land of her adoption that distinguish her from what we have known of her, down the ages. She is indeed the child of the new enviornment, having not much in common with what made her the paragon of moral and idealistic values in the *Rāmāyaṇa*.

Born as Rāvaṇa's daughter of his chief-queen Mandodarī as a result of her partaking the divine rice-balls, she, as soon as born, enigmatically pronounced thrice the death of her father. In order to avert the catastrophe that she, as the soothsayers interpreted it, was bound to invite for Rāvaṇa, the child was thrown in a jar to float to end in a river. Janaka retrieved the jar and buried it deep. She was ploughed out after sixteen years by him. She was befittingly named as Sītā and he came to be known as her father[74].

Alien elements assert tellingly in her behaviour after her return from Laṅkā. Her encounter with Atulā, projects her as gullible young woman, shorn of vision to frustrate the designs of scheming adversaries. In order to settle scores with her, Atulā, Śūrpaṇakhā's daughter, dupes her into drawing the portrait of Rāvaṇa which marked the prelude to a series of sufferings that she had to undergo for no fault of her. While her readiness in outlining the figure might be taken to have emanated from innocence and a friendly gesture, her subsequent attempts to efface and conceal it attest to her nervousness compounded with a sense of guilt. Thus what could have been dismissed as an aberration turned out to be her undoing. Unsure of her faithfulness, Rāma not only banishes her but also orders Lakṣmaṇa to put her to

---

73. *RKM* ., XXIV. 43

74. यतोऽभवल्लाङ्गलकृष्टसीता-
समुद्भवोऽस्या अत एव नाम ।
सीतेति तस्या अभवत्पितेति
ख्यातश्च पृथ्व्यां जनको बभूव ॥ *RKM*., IV.52

sword as a punishment for her 'breach of fidelity' and bring back her heart to convince him of her execution[75]. This was too much for her to pocket. Cut to the quick by unfounded accusation despite her fire ordeal, she, not unlike her counterpart in Vālmīki, decides to end her life[76]. With Lakṣmaṇa vacillating with indecision, she, perhaps in a bid to prove her credentials, charges him with evil intentions in not carrying out the order of his elder brother. Even the recluse, she asserted, lose restraint with woman in private[77]. Whatever the cause of the outburst, her behaviour with Lakṣmaṇa, who was to her as good as a brother, is indefensible.

The way she grills Rāma after he was conducted to her by Maṅkuṭa, marks the negation of what is believed to distinguish her to Indian mind as the perfect specimen of virtuous womanhood. Her behaviour tends to project her as a champion of the present-day movement for women-liberation. Despite Rāma's pleading guilty and his unqualified apology for his misdemeanour, she decides to give him the taste of his own medicine. She berates him as a cruel and suspicious person who revels in maltreating his innocent wife. She rejects his sincere plea to return to Ayodhyā to end his tribulations[78]. She can have no truck with a woman-killer, she thunders[79]. It would be wiser and safer for her, she adds, to perish in wilderness than to stay with a petty-minded, jealous man who could question her chastity on so fragile a pretext as a portrait that she had been tricked to draw unsuspectedly[80]. She taunts him to enjoy the comforts in his mansion leaving her to suffer her fate to which she had become accustomed after undergoing agony for ten long years[81]. Otherwise also she bitingly remarks, she is as good for him as dead.

Her caustic tongue did not stop there. She became more aggressive. She not only rejected Rāma's subsequent plea, conveyed through the sons, to bury the past. She was unmoved by his threat to end his life in case she refused to return. She

---

75. *RKM.*, XX.44-48
76. *RKM.*, XX.6
77. *RKM.*, XX.60
78. तेनास्ति मे किं करणीयमद्य, शङ्कालुना क्रूरतमेन चापि ।
कठोरतां मां प्रति यो बिभर्ति, न स्यादहं तं प्रति किं कठोरा ? ।। *RKM.*, XIII.5
79. पत्न्या निहन्तुः सविधे कथञ्चित्, मया न वस्तव्यमवश्यमेव । ibid., XXIII.35
80. क्षुद्रं तवातीव मनो मतं मे, शङ्काग्रहग्रस्तमसूयकं च ।
कृतां दशास्याकृतिमेव दृष्ट्वा, क्रोधेन सद्यो भ्रमितं बभूव ।। ibid., XXIII.27
81. स्वकीयहर्म्ये सुखितस्त्वमासीरहं पुनः काननमध्यवात्सम् ।। ibid., XXIII.25

breathtakingly proclaims her resolve to visit Ayodhyā only for his last *darśana*[82]. And when as a result of the most heinous conspiracy she actually did come for his supposedly last *darśana*, she was on terra firma to fly into a frenzy of rage. On discovering that she had been cheated by her husband by the fake news of his death, she vehemently reproached him with such devastating epithets as wicked, deceitful, merciless executioner. She was unequivocal in condemning him for his despicable action and declared her determination not to give credence to him under any circumstances[83]. She had lost faith in Rāma to the extent that Lord Śaṅkara had to strain hard to bring about rapprochement between the two. Her submission to the Lord had been preceded by some harsh speaking by her for what Rāma had done to her. It was not before Īśvara had held Rāma guilty on several counts and she herself had reviled him for his fickle-mindedness and unjust behaviour that she agreed to terminate the estrangement[84]. It is indeed surprising that she could lead smooth life with her 'dear' husband thereafter free from rancour whatsoever.

Sītā as depicted in the poem, thus suffers, like Rāma, from infirmities of the worst type. She seems to have shed her idealism that accorded her the most enviable status. She has the unmistakable imprint of a highly modernised woman.

HANUMĀN

Though intended as an ancillary character Hanumān emerges as the most colourful figure in the poem. He is the driving force behind all that transpires between the dramatis personae. Shorn of him, the poem would sink into an insipid exercise. Notwithstanding his subsidiary status, the poet has turned focus on him with zealous tenacity with the result the various layers of his character have unfolded themselves so convincingly that he may unhesitatingly be rated as a strong contendor for the highest position of the hero. It is interesting that he too has largely shed his moorings and owes his character to the milieu that has adopted him with verve. However, he has retained some of his basic characteristics. The poet has highlighted both the aspects. He seems to have captured the various features of his character in a solitary verse :

---

82. एष्याम्यहं तेऽन्तिमदर्शनार्थं पुरीमयोध्यामिति मे प्रतिज्ञा । XXIV.11

83. अहो जघन्याऽस्य विचाररीतिः
कृत्यं जघन्यं च ततोऽपि भूयः ।। XXIV.32
पुनर्न विश्वासमहं कदाचिद् गिर्यस्य यास्यामि शठोत्तमस्य । XXIV.36
हन्ताऽसि पत्न्या अनुदारभावः प्रवञ्चकोऽस्युत्पथमाश्रितोऽसि । XXIV.41

84. पतिर्ममैषोऽस्थिरचित्तवृत्तिः । XXV.19
असाधुवृत्तिर्मयि ------ XXV.20

वज्राङ्ग एष तरुणः शुभदर्शनश्च
धीरः पराक्रम इवाश्रिततत्स्वरूपः ।
सुश्लक्ष्णवाक् परहिते निरतो वदान्यो
लोकातिगैर्गुणगणैः परिभूषितश्च ।। XII.41

Peer of wind in impetuosity, he is its son . He is proud of his origin and misses no opportunity to underline it with enthusiasm[85]. He is an embodiment of valour, as if he were made of thunderbolt. A young being with lovely appearance, he is devoted to the well-being of others. His lovely mein is matched by his sweet tongue. He is generous to a fault. He is indeed endowed with a large variety of excellences which are hard to come across elsewhere. Like his original, he is the supreme friend, devotee and ally of Rāma. His devotion to Rāma is proverbial[86]. He may well lay down his life for the sake of his master. And he has always been equal to the trust reposed in him.

What strikes as the most wonderful characteristic of Hanumān is his boundless energy. He is valour incarnate. Because of the unbounded funds of power, Hanumān emerges as Rāma's trusted trouble shooter. Howsoever grave the task, he comes out with flying colours. He built the causeway to Laṅkā within the stipulated seven days, and frustrated, in the process, the concerted efforts of Suvarṇamatsyā to destroy it. He had to be traced out for giving rebuff to Mahīpāladevāsura and to secure Vibhīṣaṇa's release. The gravest of the challenges to him was posed by Maiyarāba in deceitfully kidnapping Rāma to Pātāla. There too he (Hanumān) proved his mettle. He not only overcame the grave difficulties in the journey, but also killed the demon on his homeground and retrieved Rāma from abominable thraldom[87]. The credit for freeing Sugrīva from the clutches of Kumbhakarṇa also rests with him. [88].

It is, however, not the brute force alone that he embodies. His prowess is deeply tempered with discretion and resourcefulness. His farsight has been chiefly in-

---

85. सुतः प्रभञ्जनस्याहं प्रभञ्जनसमो जवे । XXII.40
86. श्रीरामस्य परो भक्तः । XVII.60
हनूमत्समाख्यं निजानन्यभक्तम् । XVIII.14
87. एवं निहत्य तं दैत्यं रामं मुक्तं विधाय च । XIV.75
88. परापतद् दानवेन्द्रं सुग्रीवं च व्यमोचयत् । XV.52

strumental in revealing the true identity of Beñjakayī who had otherwise thrown Rāma out of gear. He does not hesitate to take recourse to stratagems and tricks to accomplish his mission. At times he seems to believe that ends justify the means. He thus had no qualms in assuming the form of a dead dog to foil Kumbhakarṇa in propitiating his lethal missile[89]. It was again through the neatly executed stratagem that he disposed of Rāvaṇa's soul, encaged in Goputra's hermitage and thereby enabled Rāma to kill the demon who hithertofore was defying all his attempts with surprising ease[90]. With equal ease he browbeat the gate-keepers converting himself into a tissue of lotus stalk[91]. But for his resourcefulness, the outcome would have been disastrous to his master. While he frustrated these adversaries through trickery, he employed powerful logic to wean away Suvarṇamatsyā from wrecking the causeway[92]. It is surprising that such a resourceful, wise and intrepid hero had to eat an humble pie in his encounter with the hermit-boys Maṅkuṭa and Kuśa[93].

Thai folk-lore seems to have been instrumental in turning the Indian demigod, celebrated down the ages, for celibacy and high idealism, into a gallant, who is out to fall for any beautiful girl who comes his way. The warmth with which his love-making with Beñjakayī and Suvarṇamatsyā is described can only serve to send shudder down to the spine of the devout Indian.

Notwithstanding his reckless heroism and gallantry, Hanumān emerges as a fond father. His chance meeting with his sons Asuraphad and Macchānu stirred his Vātsalya so deeply that even ceaseless kisses and caresses could not satiate him, so overwhelmed with joy he was. He behaved almost like an innocent child in consenting to repeat his feats of devouring sun, moon and stars to convince Asuraphad of his identity[94].

According to the *RKM* version Hanumān seems to have been conceived as a

---

89. हनूमता युक्तिरियं पूजाविघ्नार्थमाश्रिता ।
शुनः शवस्य रूपं स एव नद्यामुपाश्रयत् ।। XV.65

90. दशग्रीववधे तावद् धनूमान् युक्तिमास्थितः । XVII.60

91. कार्येऽभ्युपेते प्रमना हनूमान्
अम्भोजतन्तुप्रतिरूपकोऽभूत् । XIV.31

92. XII. 28-38

93. मङ्कुटेन स वीरेण हतप्रायत्वमापितः । XXII.33
करुणां च दशां स्वस्य नैराश्यं च परं गतः । XXII.46

94. XIX.-31-32

complete man, a phenomenonally powerful warrior, a lover, a fond father and an astute tactician.

RĀVAṆA

Rāvaṇa, the demon king of Laṅkā, is also enclothed in an alien garb, though, like other characters some of his basic features are intact. He is the mightiest king the Rākṣasa-race has ever produced. His very name strikes terror in the heart of his enemies. His skill in warfare is matchless (IX.1). He has earned widespread fame by his victories over the three worlds (XVII.23). His repeated triumphs and the resultant fame have combined to compound his inborn arrogance (IX.1). This hauteur has landed him in miserable situations. It has emboldened him to turn deaf ear even to sane and well-meaning advice. Vibhīṣaṇa's honest interpretation of his dreams and the wise advice to release Sītā to save the Rākṣasas from utter destruction, was disregarded by him. Vibhīṣaṇa's unceremonious dismissal [95] as a sequal to his sane advice in ultimate analysis proved his undoing. It is again this arrogance that led him to underestimate the might of Rāma[96] which proved a grave miscalculation. His erudition in Veda is emphasised in the poem (IV.1).

While all this is what Rāvaṇa traditionally stands for, he appears in the *RKM* a mere shadow of his real self. He seems to be unsure of himself, almost diffident of the success of his might. He is keen to avoid headlong collision with Rāma. It leads him to try various devices to humble him off the ground. The mission of Beñjakayī, Suvarṇamatsyā, Maiyarāba, etc. are intended to serve the purpose. It is however a different matter if all of them end in smoke. Even the contrivance of keeping his soul away from Laṅkā does not work. Nowhere in the poem is he seen to be eager or enthusiastic for trying conclusions with Rāma. He meets his end as a result of the strategy chalked out by Vibhīṣaṇa and executed by Rāma and Hanumān.

MAṄKUṬA

Though no more than a footnote to the poem, Maṅkuṭa is a lively character. Son of Rāma, he was born in Vajmṛga's hermitage while Sītā was in exile. He was trained under the Argus eye of the sage who equipped him in the art of warfare in a manner that he could humble the mightiest warrior. He treated Rāma's vaunt inherent in the edict attatched to the sacrificial horse with derisive contempt. He was convinced that the earth could not be presumed to be devoid of Kṣatriyas, till he was alive. The havoc that he played with Rāma's forces including his younger brothers and Hanumān, is simply unbelievable. He had all but killed Hanumān. He did not spare

---

95. स्वाङ्गं चेत्स्याद् वपुषि गलितं तद् बहिष्कार्यमेव । IX.18
96. राज्याद् भ्रष्टो वनमधिवसन् राघवो वा पुनः क्व । IX.15

even Rāma and challenged him to fight it out or return with injured pride[97]. He was instrumental in bringing about Rāma's meeting with Sītā, though he could not unfortunately work out rapprochement between them, the role he played as a courier notwithstanding.

VIBHĪṢAṆA

Vibhīṣaṇa plays a pivotal role in the poem, though he is seen in occasional flashes only. As a devoted younger brother, he tenders sincere advice to Rāvaṇa to release Sītā to ensure the safety to the Rākṣasas. In a fit of anger the demon banishes him from the kingdom. That however turned out to be the beginning of his end. He joins Rāma and acts as a guiding spirit in a host of frustrating situations. It was because of his guidance that Rāma could be retrieved from Pātāla and Maiyarāba and Rāvaṇa were done to death. He is convinced of the divine character of Rāma, Kumbhakarṇa's rantings to the contrary notwithstanding. He is consecrated as the king of Laṅkā after Rāvaṇa's death.

DESCRIPTIONS

The *RKM* is dotted with a host of descriptions, imaginatively positioned at measured intervals, which combine to impart vibrance to the poem and thereby serve to relieve the tedium that a long narrative would otherwise mean. As testified by his other poems as well, the author does not have undue predilection for the conventional subjects, detailed by the poeticians, as worthy of description in the body of a Mahākāvya. He revels in the descriptions that defiantly depart from the norm. The vast canvas of the *RKM* affords him abundant scope to work up in the poem a string of descriptions that are notable as much for their variety as for the novelty. He does not hesitate to deal with the subjects that did not engage the attention of the ancient poets. The current milieu seems to assert itself in inspiring such descriptions. The traditional descriptions are few in the poem. The author does not seem to relish them, beyond a point. That accounts for their scarcity and brevity. He is at his best in dealing with the various emotions that criss-cross the human heart in differing situations, prompting him into a psychological analysis to determine the rationale behind specific behaviour. It is these that steal thunder in the poem which throws up quite a few of the interesting psychological descriptions, prompted by both noble and ignoble emotions that drive man to peculiar conduct. Besides the descriptions of alien lands and scenic beauties thereof it is these sketches that settle down as the author's contribution to the Mahākāvya tradition.That, however, should not be construed to detract from the undoubted merits of the plethora of other descriptions that embellish the long narrative and eminently reflect the various situations that

---

97. *RKM.*, XXII.33, 43-46, 64-67

imbue the poem with refreshing variety and gaity. Brevity and diaphanous lucidity are the characteristics that the descriptions in the *RKM* share with those in the two sister poems, the *Bodhisattvacaritam* and the *Indirāgāndhīcaritam*. Rather, contrary to them, the *RKM* represents neither conscious chiselling nor effort in its varied descriptions. It is its refreshing lucidity and limpid as well as unhindered flow that breathe through the poem which is further distinguished in its descriptions in the admirable capture of the subject under depiction in all its hues and contours, resulting in the emergence of an integrated whole.

The study of human behaviour under a variety of emotional stresses is the author's forte in some of his descriptions. It is deep understanding of the human mind and its responses to bewildering situations, that has enabled him to turn spotlight on the most imperceptible contours of emotions which give rise to otherwise inexplicable conduct. How a person, howsoever humble, with bruised ego, strains at the leash and reacts violently as soon as he can, is beautifully illustrated by the indignities Nandaka (the precursor of Rāvaṇa) suffered helplessly at the hands of the deities and the havoc he consequently wrought on them on acquiring miraculous power from Śaṅkara, whom he had served so devotedly. Considering him as an humble attendant, the deities took liberties with him to the extent that they turned him bald by plucking the tufts of his hair at regular intervals. Ashamed of himself and unable to bear the humiliation any more, he obtained a boon from Śaṅkara that not only rendered him unassailable but also enabled him to turn tables on his adversaries. His tormentors, the deities, were made to bite dust the moment he pointed his finger at them. Those who came to ridicule the poor attendant, now fell dead at the fall of his hat. The author has beautifully summed up the situation in following verses :

स सेवकत्वेन नियुक्त एवं
विनोदभाङ् निर्जरसां बभूव ।
उपाहसंस्ते समुपेयिवांस-
स्तं शीर्षकेशोद्धरणक्रमेण ।।

क्रमेण तेनाभवदेष केश-
हीनोऽतिदीनस्त्रिदशौघसेवी ।
हीनत्वबुद्ध्याऽऽत्मनि चाप दुःखं
ययौ महेशं च स तन्निवृत्त्यै ।।

बद्धाञ्जलिः प्रार्थयतैनमाशु-
तोषं निजं तोषमभीप्सुरेषः ।
तादृग् वरं देहि विभो ! भवेयं
भूयो न येन ह्युपहासपात्रम् ।।

युगानि नाना मयका विसोढा
ऽवमाननादुःखपरम्परा भोः ।
नातः परं सोढुमहं क्षमस्तां
तद् देहि मे शक्तिमनन्तशक्ते ! ।।

यमेव तावत्स्वकराङ्गुलेन
विनिर्दिशेयं स भवेत्प्रमीतः ।
तथास्त्विति प्रत्यवदन्महेशः
सेवां तदीयां गणयन् पुरस्तात् ।।

ततोऽनु देवाः समुपेयिवांसः
कैलासशैलं प्रभुदर्शनार्थम् ।
समाचरन्पूर्ववदेव तस्मि-
न्नबुध्यमाना नवशक्तिमस्य ।।

तदाऽङ्गुलं तद्दिशि सोऽकरोद् द्राक्
पेतुश्च देवा व्यसवः क्षणेन ।
तदेषु भूयो भयमाततान
जग्मुः प्रभुं ते च समे जवेन ।। IV.4-10

It is again the hurt ego that manifests itself in the way the hump-backed maid poisoned the mind of Kaikeyī to administer rebuff to Rāma, poised for coronation. Determined to settle scores with him for the insult he had done to her in alternately removing and recreating the hump on her back, Kubjā, the pampered servant of Kaikeyī, got the opportunity when Daśaratha decided to consecrate him on the throne. Her lacerated ego spurred her to subject Rāma to crushing insult, inherent in his banishment, by conjuring up the disaster that was to befall to Kaikeyī, once her step-son ascended the throne. The stratagem worked. Kubjā's approach had been psychological. Her jibe at the shortsightedness of her mistress in not safeguarding her interest and the stress on the gains that were bound to flow from Rāma's banishment combined to tempt Kaikeyī in attempting the indefensible. The caustic offer of the Kubjā to lend Kaikeyī her vision in case she lacked her own (*no cet matis te sphuratīha bhadre, matiṁ mama tvaṁ samupāśrayasva*, V.12) could have provoked even the most fastidious diehard into action. It is chilling to find that Kubjā's reaction to her supposed humiliation had been as deadly in its effect as that of Nandaka. It is a tribute to the author's poetic genius that he has detailed the situation beset with an interplay of revenge and trickery with malice and hatred, in the body of mere six verses :

पूर्वापकारप्रतिशोधनाय
दन्दह्यमाना हृदयेन कुब्जा ।
मत्वोपयुक्तावसरं जगाम
सा सत्वरं केकयराजपुत्रीम् ।।
उवाच चैनां तनयः सपत्न्या
राज्येऽभिषिक्तो भवतीति वृत्तम् ।
ज्ञात्वापि किं त्वं न कमप्युपायं
विचिन्तयस्यद्य विचारमूढा ।।
रामेऽभिषिक्ते नृपतौ पुरेऽत्र
का ते दशा वा भरतस्य वा स्यात् ।
अकालहीनं तत आश्रयस्व
कमप्युपायं न चिरं विधेहि ।।
दन्दह्यमाने भवनेऽग्निना स्यात्
कूपस्य तावत्खननं वृथैव ।
न चेन्मतिस्ते स्फुरतीह भद्रे !
मतिं मम त्वं समुपाश्रयस्व ।। V.9-12
याचस्व तौ सम्प्रति त्वं वरेण्ये
तदीयकालः समुपस्थितोऽद्य ।

नैवं यदि त्वं प्रविधास्यसि द्राक्

काल: पिबेत्तद्रसमेव नूनम् ।। V.14

While Nandaka and Kubjā, both thirsting for revenge for the insults heaped on them, give expression to their injured psyche in an abominable way to deal with their adversaries, Rāma's anticipated reaction on seeing the feigned corpse of Sītā, floating in the river, stands on a different footing, though that too has been brought about by a stratagem to turn tables on the enemy to escape his wrath in the battle-field. Rāvaṇa was convinced that the mere sight of Beñjakayi, masquerading as Sītā, would drive Rāma to swoon or suicide :

मायावशेनैव तथा स्वरूपं

धृतं मृताया जनकात्मजाया: ।

येनावगाहार्थमुपागत: स-

न्नालोक्य तां मुह्यतु रामभद्र: ।।

नष्टा प्रिया मे किमु जीवितेन

कार्यं ममेति प्रतिपन्नबुद्धि: ।

खिन्नान्तरात्मा विरमेत्स युद्धात्

प्राणांस्त्यजेद्वा वनमाश्रयेद्वा ।। X.3-4

The *RKM* is characterised by opposing emotions. Contrary to the outrageous instincts that resulted into the fall of adversity to venerable personages, some of the tenderest emotions also have full play here . And they have been analysed with equal skill and penetration. Hanumān's encounter with Suvarṇamatsyā in the depths of ocean ultimately served to stir love in the two hearts. The youths, who were brought face to face, by the queer mission, though unknown, were instantly drawn to each other. With one as the embodiment of manly power and the other of ravishing beauty, their fall, however, was not headlong. Though overpowered by the other, each entertained mysterious apprehension about the other's response. The conflict between the two persists till they dissolve their distinct identity in the vast ocean of love. The poet has captured the conflict, its subsequent resolution and the culmination of their love with admirable sensitivity. After all, none can defy the pervasive sweep of love (*sādhāraṇaḥ prāṇiṣu bhāva eṣaḥ*, XII.40). The lucid language, the Vasantatilakā metre and the Vaidarbhi style join to heighten the tenderness of love still further :

एवं तदाऽऽलोकयमानयोस्तु
मिथोऽनुरागोऽङ्कुरितो बभूव ।
बभूवतुस्तद्वशगावुभौ च
साधारणः प्राणिषु भाव एषः ।। XII.40

दृष्ट्वैनमत्र मनसः सुतरामनीशा
जाने न किं खलु मया करणीयमत्र ।
पर्याकुलेव लुलितेव सुविह्वलेव
वल्लीव पौरुषतरुं श्रयितुं लषामि ।।

किं नाम चेतसि भवेच्छुभदर्शनस्य
भावः स एव हृदयं मम यो धुनोति ।
एषोऽपि किं कुसुमचापशरौघविद्धो
गाढं भवेदहमिवेति सुवर्णमत्स्या ।।

चिन्तापरा विविधचारुविचारवीचि-
प्रेङ्खोलिता न वचनं किमपि प्रपेदे ।
वायोः सुतोऽपि कमनीयतमाङ्गयष्टिः
पश्यन्न तां स्वमनसः प्रबभूव वीरः ।। XII.42-44

अन्योन्यमेवमवितृप्ततयोपपन्नौ
गाढोपगूहनसुखाकुलितान्तरङ्गौ ।
वायोः सुतश्च रमणी च सुवर्णमत्स्या
गाढं बभूवतुरुभौ मदनेषुविद्धौ ।। XII.47

Suvarṇamatsyā emerged from the affair extremely contented. The description of her return to Laṅkā, though limited to a solitary verse, is very suggestive. The phrase *paraṁ nirvṛtim īyuṣī* is pregnant with infinite suggestion, liable to sizable exegesis :

विनिर्गतां समुद्राच्च मत्स्यकन्याऽपि सुन्दरी ।
लङ्कां प्रत्याजगामाथ परां निर्वृतिमीयुषी ।। XII.52

Hanumān's fierce encounter with the doughty guard of the tank ended in the revelation of the latter's identity as Macchānu, his own son begotton on Suvarṇa-matsyā and therefore an embodiment of the twin powers of Vāyu and Rāvaṇa. Hanumān virtually burst with joy on meeting his dear son in unusual circumstances. That affords the poet an excellent opportunity to describe with gusto the sacred feelings that a father entertains for his gifted son. On finding his son, though discarded by his mother right at the time of his birth, developed into a brave and handsome young man fully worthy of him, Hanumān underwent unique experience. His hair stood on end. He felt as if he had found an inexhaustible treasure. Even repeated caresses and kisses did not bring him full contentment. Unable to control the onrush of feelings, he burst into tears of joy. The truth of the Vedic precept that son was no different from one's soul was now fully realised by him. He considered himself the luckiest person under the sun. It is Vātsalya *par excellence*, that encompasses even the lowliest being in its sweep and stirs in his breast the tenderest of emotions. The rhythm of alliteration besides other judiciously chosen Alaṁkāras, lucid and effective phraseology and the warmth of the poet's own feelings serve to invest the description with pervasive appeal :

श्रुत्वैतदूर्जस्वि वचः सुतस्य
संहृष्टरोमा हनुमांस्तदानीम् ।
अवाप्तसर्वस्व इवातितृप्तो
मच्छानुमूचे वचनं प्रहृष्टः ॥
त्वं मे सुतो वीर ! पिता तवाहं
लोके हनूमानहमेव पुत्र !
त्वद्दर्शनेनैव सुतृप्तमेहि
मह्यं परिष्वङ्गसुखं प्रदेहि ॥
सत्पुत्रिणां धन्यतमोऽस्मि पुत्र!
यत्त्वादृशो मेऽस्ति गुणी सुपुत्रः ।
आलोकमालोकमहं न तृप्तिं
त्वां यामि कल्पद्रुफलं यथैव ॥
आत्मैव नामात्मज उक्तपूर्वः
श्रुतौ, ममात्मैव ततोऽसि वीर !

शौर्यं यथा मे त्वयि तत्तथैव
तथैव रूपं च गुणास्तथैव ॥

प्रभो ! विचित्रैव तवाऽस्ति माया-
ऽकस्माद्यया सङ्गमिताविह स्वः ।

इत्येवमुक्त्वा स बभूव तूष्णीं
कपिः प्रहर्षाश्रुभराविलाक्षः ॥ XIII.46-50

Hanumān's Vātsalya immediately evoked filial regards from Macchānu. He was caught, for a trice, in the vortex of opposing feelings of delight and guilt. However, he braved the onslaught to shed the complex of guilt. His heart melted to the marrow and he made ample amends for the blows he had rained on his father by closing him in warm embrace. Not only that, he touched his feet, begged his pardon and thus effectively dismantled his misplaced bravery to emerge as a respectful son. His conflict that ultimately yielded to deferential reverence is happily described in the following verses :

मच्छानुरप्येनमथो विदित्वा
वायोस्तनूजं पितरं प्रियं स्वम् ।

अप्रार्थितावाप्तफलो विधानाद्
विधेर्बभूवातितरां प्रहृष्टः ॥

याभ्यां भुजाभ्यामभवन् प्रहाराः
सम्पातिता येन भृशं कठोराः ।

ताभ्यां गलच्चेतन एष तात-
मालिङ्गने गाढतमे बबन्ध ॥

पादौ च पस्पर्श गुरोः प्रवीरः
क्षमामिमं चापि भृशं ययाचे ।

अज्ञानहेतोर्बहु कर्म लोके
ऽनौचित्यपूर्णं क्रियते जनेन ॥ XIII.51-53

The two descriptions are imaginatively intended to release the tension generated by the fierce duel between the irrepressible heroes, each straining hard to establish his superiority.

Kāma is the common characteristic of human life. The irresistibility of Kāma is happily described in the poem in simple terms. Even Hanumān was smitten with love. As a matter of fact, it is hard to withstand the onslaught of the charms of woman, gold, lotus and Lakṣmī. They captivate every heart. It is driven by Kāma that the creeper clings to the tree, river merges into ocean and Prakṛti joins Puruṣa :

तरुणी कनकं कमलं कमला
नहि कस्य हरन्ति मनोहरिणम् ।
न विवेकिजनोऽपि निवर्तयितुं
प्रभवेदिममित्यमृषोद्यवचः ।। X.25

यदि याति लता स्वयमेव तरुं
यदि याति नदी च तथा जलधिम् ।
नहि तत्र विचित्रमिति प्रकटं
प्रकृतिः पुरुषं स्वयमेति यतः ।। X.28

As remarked earlier, the author has not much of liking for the conventional subjects in theory to form the basis of descriptions in Mahākāvya. These descriptions are therefore minimal. While the description of Thailand which marks the beginning of the *RKM* has been transplanted from the author's *Thaideśavilāsam*, the physical beauties and the moon-rise (XIV.14) have been disposed of in a solitary verse each. It is to the credit of the poet that he has succeeded in drawing in a single verse an integrated sketch of the girl, subsequently named as Sītā, that serves to project her as a charming figure. Such pithy sketches, worked up with masterly strokes, have a better claim to attention than the time-worn burly descriptions :

गण्डच्छविन्यक्कृतपुण्डरीका-
ममूं विशालायतपक्ष्मलाक्षीम्
हेमद्युतिं चन्द्रमरीचिगौरीं
दृष्ट्वा जना विस्मयमभ्युपायन् ।। IV.51

Needless to say her charms contributed as much as her mysterious discovery to arouse the people's wonder.

It is however, the non-conventional descriptions coupled with the depiction of varied emotions, detailed earlier, that do the *RKM* proud. The range of such descriptions in the poem is indeed astounding. They cover in their ambit such diverse subjects as frightful dreams, demonstration of powers or bragging thereof, anxious conjectures, wailings on various counts, spirited responses to differing situations and pen-sketches occasioned by a variety of individuals. The character of the narrative, distinguished by many a vicissitude, indeed lends itself to the diversity inherent in the descriptions. And the poet has been more than equal to demanding variety. It is a measure of his rich equipment that the subjects under description have been clothed in such an appropriate phraseology marked by matching imagery that they come to project themselves in totality with telling effect.

The disturbing dreams that Rāvaṇa saw following the burning of Laṅkā by Hanumān, filled him with fear to the extent that he apprehended himself to have been sawed apart in two pieces. The dreams were doubtless quaint. He saw two falcons locked in bitter fight wherein the dark bird was torn asunder by its white adversary. The dream that followed was still more perplexing. He visioned himself pouring oil in the shell of coconut placed on his palm. The moment he added wick to it, an unknown woman descended there from nowhere. She instantly lighted the wick which burnt down the shell. The fire entered into his hand and soon the whole body was in flames. Couched in accordant phraseology, the description conjures up the fear that such dreams cause. The complexity of the Mandākrāntā metre serves to heighten the perplexity :

अस्मिन्स्वप्नेऽतितुमुलतया युध्यमानौ ददर्श
श्येनावेकोऽभवदिह ययोः कृष्णवर्णस्तथा च ।
आसीदेकोऽतिधवलरुचिर्येन कृष्णो हतोऽभूत्,
प्रत्यग्दिग्भागत उपगतः पूर्वकाष्ठागतेन ।।

तत्पश्चात्स स्वककरगते कोटरे नारिकेले
तैलासेकं विदधतमहो स्वं ददर्शातिमुग्धः ।
वर्तिं तस्मिन्निदधतमसौ स्वं यदा पश्यति द्राग्
योषा तत्रापतति सहसाऽदृष्टपूर्वा कुतश्चित् ।।

वर्तिं सा प्रज्वलयति तदा येन तत् कोटरं द्राक्

दग्धं वह्निः करतलमनु प्राविशच्चापि तस्य ।

सर्वः कायस्तदनु सुतरामन्वभूद्वह्निदाहं

तस्मिन्काले झटिति शयनादुत्थितोऽभूद् दनूजः ॥ IX.5-7

The interpretation of the dreams, dutifully attempted by Vibhīṣaṇa, was as revealing as it was frightening. The black and white falcons represented, according to him, Rāvaṇa and Rāma respectively. The end of the black bird heralded his (Rāvaṇa's) violent death. The coconut shell symbolised the city of Laṅkā. The oil poured in it was nothing else but his family, the woman who lighted the wick was their sister Śūrpaṇakhā, the root-cause of all dissensions. And the fire that seemed to burn his body stood for the fire of chastity with which Sītā was destined to destroy him and whose release therefore, Vibhīṣaṇa wisely recommended :

कृष्णः श्येनस्त्वमसि धवलश्चास्ति रामोऽभिरामो

हिंसा कार्ष्णी धवलविहिता तेऽन्तसंसूचिकाऽस्ति ।

लङ्कापुर्या विगणय विभो नारिकेलं प्रतीकं

तत्तैलं ते कुलमविकलं वह्निसाद्यद् भवेन्नु ॥

योषा स्वप्ने नयनविषयं या गता ते बभूव

दीपं यावज्ज्वलयति पुरां कोटरं नारिकेलम् ।

सा नौ भ्रातः सकलकलहद्वारभूता स्वसैव

वह्निज्वालाऽतिकुटिलधिया दीपिता भोस्तयैव ॥

ज्वाला भ्रातर्निजकरतलं याऽनुभूता दहन्ती

सैषा साध्वी जनकतनया त्वद्विनाशैकहेतुः ।

तां त्वं शान्त्या दशरथसुतं द्राग् विनिर्यातयस्व

रक्षाथो च प्रियमिह कुलं राक्षसानां समस्तम् ॥ IX.10-12

Vibhīṣaṇa's honest interpretation of the dreams and his well-intentioned advice only served to inflame the arrogant Rāvaṇa, who did not hesitate to impute motives on his faithful younger brother. He reviled him as a traitor, inclined towards his enemy, in preference to him. He, in his hauteur, threatened to spell doom for Rāma, a mere forester, divested of his kingdom by his own kinsmen. The author has skilfully turned the spotlight on Rāvaṇa's complexes that had led him to suspect even his well-wishers and to underestimate the might of his enemy. The diaphanous language used to describe the ignoble emotions like anger and hauteur, far from being a defect, serve to reinforce the impact of the description :

निर्यात्या मे जनकतनयेत्येवमात्थात्र यत्त्वं
तत्ते नूनं कलुषहृदयं स्पष्टमाविष्करोति।
भ्राता मे त्वं कथमिव नु मे राघवान्नाशमात्थ
लङ्कायां त्वं निवससि परं शत्रुपक्षे स्थितोऽसि ।। IX.14

तं तादृक्षं मशकमिव भोः स्वेच्छयैवोपपन्नं
निष्पीड्याऽहं करतलगतं हेलयैव प्रसन्नः ।
मामाक्रान्तुं कृतपरिकरं स्वस्य मृत्युं यथैव
रामं रामाविरहजरुजं प्रापयिष्याम्यनन्ताम् ।। IX.16

The description of their latent powers by the monkeys to assure Vibhīṣaṇa of their capacity to meet the might of Rāvaṇa, stands on a different footing. Occasioned by humility, provoked by worst suspicions (*śaktāḥ kiṁ syur danujakulajair yoddhum ete kapīndrāḥ*, IX.23), it represents a pole apart from Rāvaṇa's arrogant vaunt. Contrary to Rāvaṇa, the monkeys seemed to trust the time-tested dictum that actions spoke louder than the words. Within moments Vibhīṣaṇa was wondering at the havoc they had unleashed on forests, mountains, seas and sun and wind themselves. The tiny depiction in merely two verses serves to highlight the might of the monkeys with deftness :

तच्छ्रुत्वा ते वचनममलं यूथमुख्यस्य दीप्ताः
शक्तेः स्वस्याः परिचयविधौ स्वं मनो दत्तवन्तः ।
वृक्षान् केचिद् विपुलतरकान्केचिदेवापि चाद्रीन्
मूलोच्छेदं करतलगताञ्चक्रिरे साहसेन ।।

अन्ये तावद् दृढतरधियः सूर्यमावव्रिरे द्राग्
जातं विश्वं प्रबलतमसाऽऽच्छादितं येन विश्वम् ।

केचिच्चाथो पवनमबलं तेनिरे स्वस्य वेगा-

दन्ये चाथो जलधिमतुलं शुष्कतां नीतवन्तः ।। IX.25-26

Hanumān's fight with Maiyarāba, the king of Pātāla to secure the release of Rāma, fraudulently kidnapped by him, is preceded by an equally fierce verbal encounter. Brimming with arrogance Maiyarāba treats Hanumān with contempt. The intrusion of the monkey in his guarded domain and his audacity in challenging him to a combat (*tam āhvayāmāsa niyoddhukāmaḥ*, XIV.49) provoked him to break into an ode to his valour, which, he brags, would consume him in its flames like a moth. Maiyarāba not only derides the 'humble' origin of the monkey but also deems it below his dignity to fight with him as that would only serve to sully his widespread fame, emanated from countless victories over mighty warriors. Hanumān contends the demon's hauteur with rare poise and firmness. While he reminds Maiyarāba that birth was a matter of chance, and therefore not a cause to gloat over, he draws a frightening picture of his power and threatens to pulverize him like a lotus-stalk. Unlike lesser poets the author has not succumbed to the temptation of describing the wordy duel with frustrating gimmicks like *citra-kāvya*. His description, is couched in sweetly simple language and is marked by life-like precision with the result the reader, while browsing through it, seems to sight the two heroes locked in encounter before his eyes :

हसन् बभाषे कपिमेष मे त्वं

कोपाग्निमेतः शलभो यथैव ।

भस्मीभविष्यस्यचिरेण तेन

मच्छक्तिसंज्ञापरिशून्यकत्वात् ।। XIV.51

किं मादृशा वीरवराः कदाचित्

प्रत्यर्थिसार्थं प्रविजेतुकामाः ।

नियुध्य तावत्कपिना विशुद्धां

कीर्तिं स्वकामाविलयन्ति लोके ? ।।

पातालराजेन दिगन्तराल-

विश्रान्तिमद्विश्रुतकीर्तिभाजा ।

कपिर्नियुद्धे हत इत्ययं मे

'मा भूत्परीवादनवावतारः' ।।

अपेहि तत्त्वं प्रददामि तेऽहं
भिक्षामसूनां नहि मे प्रियास्ते ।
पात्रं दयाया असि नैव तिर्यग्-
योनिं गता मे प्रतिरोधमर्हाः ।।

श्रुत्वादसीयं वचनं विहस्य
कपिर्बभाषे किल मैयराबम् ।
विकत्थसे त्वं बहु मैयराब !
विकत्थना नैव भवन्ति शूराः ।। XIV.53-56

प्रभञ्जनस्यास्मि सुतः प्रसिद्धो
लोकेषु वज्राङ्गबली हनूमान् ।
भङ्क्ष्यामि ते संहननं विशालं
मृणालदण्डं द्विरदो यथैव ।।

सञ्जातमात्रोऽपि सहस्ररश्मे-
रास्वादनायोत्प्लुत आसमद्धा ।
फलाभिसन्धिं प्रविधाय तस्मिन्
शौर्यस्य गाथां विवृणोति मे तत् ।।

अलं बहूक्तैरथवाऽत्र शक्तिं
नियोधने त्वं मम विद्धि साक्षात् ।
हस्ते स्थिते नैव हि कङ्कणे स्यात्
कस्याप्यपेक्षा मुकुरस्य तावत् ।। XIV.58-60

When Lakṣmaṇa mysteriously failed to carry out the order of his elder brother to execute Sītā for her supposed leanings towards Rāvaṇa, as revealed by the discovery of his portrait drawn by her, he left her in the jungle infested with wild beasts. Sītā curses her lot for her miserable life. The author has drawn a moving description of her wailings which because of their intensity could rend the mounts and drive stones to tears. She was sore at her banishment at an advanced stage of pregnancy, on ill-founded suspicion, which was more painful than the unimplemented execution. She wanted to kill herself but was deterred by her love for the child she expected soon. It was indeed a quirk of fate that she was discarded like an orphan, her noble lineage notwithstanding. She was reduced to a helpless state to undergo unendling sufferings. To her now the whole world was a mighty void. Thus drawn to the wall, Sītā cried piteously. With his readily responsive mind and poetic skill, the author has so highlighted the pathos, inherent in the situation that it strikes a responsive chord in the reader. Nay, he is moved to tears at her predicament :

कठोरगर्भाऽप्यहिवद् वनेऽस्मिन्
त्यक्तास्मि शङ्कालुहृदा स्वभर्त्रा ।
बाढं निरागा अपि सर्वथाऽह-
मकिञ्चना दैवगतिर्विचित्रा ।। XXI.4

त्यागो न भर्त्रा तुदते तथा मां
मिथ्या यथा लाञ्छनमेतदस्मात् ।
न जीवनस्यास्ति ममाभिलाष-
स्त्यागस्तु तस्याभिमतो मतो मे ।।

त्यागाय यद्यप्यहमुत्सुकाऽस्मि
निरर्थकस्यास्य तिरस्कृताऽहम् ।
प्रजानिषेको मयि वर्तमानो
भर्तुर्भवत्यत्र ममान्तरायः ।।

शून्या दिशो मे सकला विभान्ति
शून्ये वने कोऽपि न मे सहायः ।
किं वा करोम्यत्र क्व वा च यामि
कं वाऽऽह्वयाम्यत्र च मेऽस्ति नायः ।।

वधू रघूणां भुवि विश्रुतानां
ब्रह्मज्ञराजर्षिविदेहपुत्री ।
दैवस्य तावद्विपरीतभावाद्
दशामहं भोः ! करुणां गताऽस्मि ।।

इत्थं सबाष्पं विललाप सीता
तस्मिन् वने श्वापदसङ्कुले सा ।
विदारयेद् दीर्घतरं यदद्रिं
विलापयेद् यत्सुतरामयोऽपि ।। XX1.6-10

The author has drawn some brilliant pen-pictures in the poem. Of these the sketch of the two hermit-boys emerges as the most engaging. Rāma's reprimand to them for what they had done to Hanumān only serves to stir them into action. With their anger inflamed, they let out a terrific cry as do the cubs at the sight of a lordly elephant. Incensed like a provoked serpent, Maṅkuṭa tried to scare him away with the twang of his bow. With reddened eyes he invited comparison with the sun. The judicious use of Simile with telling *upamānas* has enabled the poet to project a realistic account of the powers of the little warriors :

तस्य निर्भर्त्सनं तावत्तयोर्बालकयोस्तदा ।
क्रोधाग्निं दीपयामास घृतधारेव सन्तता ।।
सिंहनादः प्रादुरासीत्सिंहशावकयोरिव ।
गजेन्द्रालोकने तावन् नृपेन्द्रालोकने सति ।।
आस्फालयन् घोरघोषां धनुर्ज्यां मङ्कुटो मुहुः ।
अवसृजंश्च फूत्कारं पदा स्पृष्ट इवोरगः ।।
प्रज्वलत्क्रोधताम्राक्षो बालसूर्य इवापरः ।
ओजस्विनीं तदा तत्र गिरमेवं समाददे ।। XII.59-62

LANGUAGE

Language, the only sure medium of expression, is an index to the genius of the poem, as of an individual. Sweetness and lucidity that form the hallmark of the author's poetry have reached their zenith in the *RKM*. While lucidity in the *Bodhisattvacaritam* has been consciously worked up by sustained chiselling to yield a variety of happy results and the down-to-earth narrative of the *Indirāgāndhīcaritam* has shorn it of much of its sheen, it has bloomed into full in the *Rāmakīrtimahākāvyam*. The author has not only drawn the theme, albeit enclothed in an alien garb, from the fountainhead represented by the *Rāmāyaṇa,* he has also been an heir to much of what Vālmīki has espoused to emerge as an immortal poet. The unusual flow besides smooth evenness and winsome mellifluousness that distinguish the language of the *RKM*, evidently owe themselves to Vālmīki. It is a measure of the influence that the epic has exercised on the author, that, not unoften, his well-turned phraseology tends to reflect the serenity and sweetness that breathe through its language. Otherwise also, the *RKM* has received a heavy sprinkling of the master's phraseology. Whatever the influences working on it, the language in the poem has graduated into a medium, tender though forceful, that breaks through, like a cascade, unimpeded in its flow, unmindful of the terrain it has to encounter. It would not be an extravagant claim to make that the epic calm and sweetness reign supreme in the poem. The language in the *RKM*, in essence, is distinguished by natural ease, enlivened by a happy blend that it has struck between smoothness and liveliness that it exudes in profusion which have, in ultimate analysis, emanated from the lucidity that runs, like the vital breath-air, throughout the length and breadth of the poem.

Because of his commitment to *śubhaguṇa* (*prasāda,* perspicuity), the author could ill afford the luxury of highflown or abstruse language in a poem, that is intended to project him as a champion of epic-like felicity. As a poem that seeks to set forth the epic story, the *RKM* abounds in a large variety of differing situations, miraculous incidents marked by a plethora of emotions, both noble and ignoble, and breath-taking combats. Reinforced by alien tradition and folk-lore, an endless spectrum seems to have overwhelmed the poem. It indeed requires varied state of language to come to grips with the unending contours of thoughts and feelings inherent in overabundance of data that melt to form the homogeneous poem. In keeping with the ideal that he seeks to realise in , the author has uniformly fostered lucidly pleasing language, strengthened by suggestive import and clarity of expression.[98] However, even, in this apparent uniformity, minute layers of diversity may be detected, though they differ in degrees only. All the situations, irrespective of their character and worth, seem to have claimed not much dissimilar language which in the poem is equal to the varied functions it has been assigned to perform. It may be difficult to claim that every situation has evoked accordant phraseology to convey the different contours in which it unfolds itself on the canvas of the poem, it can be asserted with confidence that the language in the poem does not fall out of step with it. While tender emotions, as noted earlier, have been depicted in vibrantly sweet phraseology, it tends to don a new garb to come to grips with harsher situations like duels, both wordy and physical. Occasionally, it is seen to be invested with psychological overtones. As seen in the preceding section, the well-laid lucid

98. अर्थ्यं च हृद्यं च वचस्तवेदं
सुवर्णमत्स्ये ! स्फुटवर्णशोभि । *RKM.*, XII.27

phraseology has contributed richly to heighten the effect of the reaction that wounded pride evokes from Nandaka and Kubjā. The *dayāvīratā* of Rāma in forgiving Beñjakayī inspite of the havoc she had done to him, emerges stronger in the terms it has imaginatively been clothed. A trend of sorts may be detected in the styles two sets of situations have been dealt with in the poem. The commonplace subjects, replete with a profusion of details, have been disposed of in the Anuṣṭup metre in the language, not much of a match to the charm and buoyancy of its counterpart that has been mustered to deal with the subject or events that admit of leisurely treatment.

It is in dealing with the other class, which dominates the poem, that the language unfolds its tremendous potential. It may broadly be said to accord with the subjects under description. It is here that the author has shed his aversion to longer descriptions though nowhere do they overstep the bounds of moderation. The *RKM* is the only poem of the author that carries a full-fledged exposition of the Śṛṅgārarasa with all the details that are believed to carry it to culmination. The description of Hanumān's love with Suvarṇamatsyā, the mermaid daughter of Rāvaṇa, is more exhaustive and meets the precepts of the theoreticians in an abundant measure. A part thereof may be reproduced to drive home the intensity with which it has been drawn and the quantum of contribution that the correspondingly tender and sweet phraseology has made to strengthen its impact :

आनन्दमापतुरुभौ च गिरामगम्यं
संमीलिताक्षियुगलौ परिलुप्तधैर्यौ ।
रागाङ्कुरस्फुरणताम्रकपोलयुग्मौ
वक्षोनिपीडमधरामृतपानमग्नौ ।।
रोमोद्गमप्रकटरागविशेषवृत्ती
विद्धौ समं मनसिजासमपुङ्खपत्रैः ।
आबद्धबाहुयुगलौ परिनिःश्वसन्तौ
स्वेदाम्बुजालजटितालकजालकाली ।।
अन्योन्यचुम्बनपरौ रतिकर्मसक्तौ
सम्प्रापितौ मनसिजेन दशां विचित्राम् ।
आनन्दसागरतरङ्गपरम्परासु
प्रेङ्खोलितौ सममुभौ रजनीं व्यनैष्टाम् ।। XII.48-50

Rāvaṇa's amazement at the terrific sound caused by the havoc the monkeys had done to the forests, mountains, and oceans besides the celestial bodies in a bid to allay Vibhīṣaṇa's apprehensions about their might to meet the demon-hordes, has evoked amazingly simple and lucid phraseology shorn of such compounds as mark the preceding description. The language is ingeniously framed to highlight the measure of surprise inherent in the abrupt eruption of the noise. With its ease and lucidity, it captures the demon's state of mind in the situation. The sonorous Mandākrāntā has joined the accordant language to reinforce the cumulative effect :

योऽभूत् शब्दस्तरुगिरिशतव्रातसन्दारणोत्थो
व्याप्नोत्सोऽयं सकलभुवनं नादयन् दिग्दिगन्तान् ।
लङ्कापुर्यामपि गतवता राक्षसेन्द्रस्य तेन
सृष्टास्तावच्छ्रवणकुहरा विस्मयाविष्टबुद्धेः ।।

कोऽयं शब्दः कुत इत इतः किङ्कृतो वा किमर्थं
वाऽयं लोके जनित इति स स्वाञ्जनानन्वयुङ्क्त ।
ते तं प्रोचुः कपिवरभटै राघवस्यैष चम्वा
शब्दो भीमो जनित इह यो विस्मयं नस्तनोति ।। IX.29-30

Serious situations, on the other hand, are sought to be delineated in sombre terms. Rāma's agony at the supposed infidelity of Sītā, apparently confirmed by the discovery of Rāvaṇa's portrait drawn by her, is set forth in a language that amply reflects the intensity of his pain at the stunning betrayal. Complete absence of compounds and swift flow combine with *prasāda* to lend the description a pathetic shade. It is however a different matter if it simultaneously serves to bring into limelight the recklessness of Rāma as well. However, it is Vaidarbhī *par excellence* :

अथ यत्कृत एव सन्ततं
गतवान् कष्टपरम्परामहम् ।
ननु सैव जनेऽपरे रता
किमु मे दुःखमतः परं भवेत् ।।

अधुना नहि वस्तुमालये
क्षणमप्यर्हति मामकेऽधमा ।
वधमर्हति चाश्विति क्रुधा
समुवाचावरजं स लक्ष्मणम् ।।
अपनेष्व ममाप्रियामथो
वनमेनां च नय त्वमाश्वितः ।
जहि चापि न जीविता चिरं
स्थितिभाक् स्यात् प्रमदा प्रमादिनी ।। XX.40-42

Similar tenderness of language marks the description of Sītā's wailing at her spiteful expulsion on unfounded suspicion. She curses her fate for the predicament that had overtaken her. More than the banishment, it was the stigma attached to it that caused her anguish, which she thought death alone would end. The transparently simple language reinforced in its appeal by the judicious application of Upamā and Anuprāsa, serves to project in relief the misery that had overwhelmed the hapless lady. It also goes to highlight the efficacy of Upajāti to meet the plethora of situations :

विदेहजां शून्यवने विहाया-
योध्यां सुमित्रातनये निवृत्ते ।
एकाकिनी दुःखभरार्दिता च
चक्रन्द सीता कुररीव भीता ।।
तस्यास्तदा दुःखभरो बभूव
बहिर्गतो ह्यश्रुभरच्छलेन ।
शून्या दिशः सम्प्रविलोकयन्ती
'स्वमेव सा दुष्कृतिनं निनिन्द' ।। XXI.1-2
कठोरगर्भाऽप्यहिवद् वनेऽस्मिन्
त्यक्ताऽस्मि शङ्कालुहृदा स्वभर्त्रा ।
बाढं निरागा अपि सर्वथाऽह-

मकिञ्चना दैवगतिर्विचित्रा ।। XXI.4

त्यागो न भर्त्रा तुदते तथा मां
मिथ्या यथा लाञ्छनमेतदस्मात् ।
न जीवनस्यास्ति ममाभिलाष-
स्त्यागस्तु तस्याभिमतो मतो मे ।। XXI.6

The author has exploited all possible avenues to make his language as lively a medium as it should be to voice the diversity and complexity inherent in a burly poem like a Mahākāvya. It is with this end in view that he has kept up his wont to impart to his language an aroma of drama through the device of catchy dialogues, which alongwith the *subhāṣitas* and borrowals, have settled down as a motif in his longer poems. Herein it concurs with the *Bodhisattvacaritam* but the two differ from the sister poem the *IC* in the fact that the dramatic elements in them are confined to conversations alone whereas, as seen earlier, there is much more besides the dialogues in the *IC* that tends to turn some parts thereof into befitting scenes for the stage. It is a measure of the author's fascination for the device that he has exploited it with alacrity in at least seven of the cantos. The dialogues conducted between the respective characters not only serve to enliven the poem, they have the added merit of advancing the narrative with a swiftness which otherwise might have been denied to it. If backed by logic, they unfold their tremendous potential in highlighting or resolving the issues under discussion. As mustered in the *RKM*, the device has forcefully brought into focus some of the vital aspects of the story that could have suffered obscurity, if not oblivion. After he failed to gather intelligence through the spy, Rāvaṇa himself intrudes into Rāma's camp, disguised as an ascetic. Unaware of the demon's vile, Rāma greets him with courtesy. What follows is a substantially lengthy dialogue between the two. With the saint masquerading as his well-wisher by advising him to desist from the perilous course of taking on Rāvaṇa and Rāma, who had by now seen through his game, sticking to his guns, the dialogue serves to bring into bold relief the demon's cunning and Rāma's determination to punish him for the despicable act of kidnapping his wife :

श्रुतं मया यद्दशकन्धरं त्व-
माक्रान्तुकामः कपिसेनयाऽसि ।
सोऽयं न कामोऽस्ति तवाभिरामो
नाशोऽत्र ते स्यात्परिणाम एव ।। IX.46

दुःसाहसं त्वं त्यज, याहि चापि

भ्रात्रा समं काननमेव भूयः ।

विवेकिनो नो सहसा क्रमन्ते

पथा ध्रुवं येन भवेद्विनाशः ॥

आकर्ण्य तस्याप्रियवाक्यजालं

तान्तान्तरङ्गोऽपि बहिः प्रशान्तः ।

काल्यं वचश्छद्मतपस्विनि द्राक्

प्रावर्तयद् दाशरथिर्महात्मा ॥

भार्या हृता मेऽधमराक्षसेन

ततोऽस्ति मे दण्ड्यतमो मतोऽयम् ।

वृत्तोऽहमस्मादभिषेणनेऽस्य

प्रयोजकोऽन्यो नहि मेऽत्र हेतुः ॥

चापद्वितीये मयि युध्यमाने

स्थातुं ममाग्रे न भवेदलं सः ।

एकैकशः कर्तयितास्मि तस्य

तीक्ष्णैर्दशास्यानि शरैरहं द्राक् ॥ IX. 48-51

The conversation between Hanumān and the sage Goputra who had with him the soul of Rāvaṇa in a cage, forms by far the longest piece in the poem (XVII.14-51). The lively encounter represents two opposing forces at work. While, in the face of well-conceived strategy, the sage is reduced to a simpleton, Hanumān comes out as a crafty diplomat. By his skilful overtures and astute logic he accomplishes, with ease, even the seemingly thorny assignment. The dialogues in which the father is locked in an argument with his son, whose identity he does not know, stand on a different footing. With each conscious of his bravery that brooks no rival, they invariably culminate in a fierce combat which has a happy denouement in the haughty young warriors surrendering to their elderly fathers.The anti-climax is indeed heart-warming. Macchānu was proud of the prowess that he inherited from Hanumān and Rāvaṇa's mermaid daughter

Suvarṇamatsyā[99] and Maṅkuṭa was arrogance incarnate.[100] He was confident that with him alive, the earth could not be presumed to be devoid of the Kṣatriyas. Both, however, are subsequently overwhelmed with remorse on discovering the identity of their rivals who were none else but their rspective fathers.

It is, however, Hanumān's intimate conversation with Suvarṇamatsyā in the deep ocean that emerges as the most vital wordy engagement conducted by the author in any of his works, with tremendous bearing on the outcome of the narrative. Though on different wavelengths, both are determined to uphold the validity of their stand with stout arguments. To the mermaid her father's order was beyond question and that was what had led her to foil the construction of the causeway. With powerful logic Hanumān meets her arguments, appealing at the same time to her innate goodness to convince her of the futility of the venture she had embarked upon vigorously. It is a measure of the soundness of his arguments that the daughter of Rāvaṇa, otherwise devoted to him, sees merit in not doing the bidding of her reckless father. The dialogue not only serves to underline the triumph of the good over evil, it also yields rich dividends to the youthful dramatis personae. A part of the dialogue is reproduced here to bring into focus the sobriety of the logic that enabled Hanumān to achieve the impossible :

एते मदादेशवशात्प्रवृत्ताः
पितुर्ममादेशवशादहं च ।
कुर्वे तथाऽहं स यथाऽऽदिशन्माम्
'आज्ञा गुरूणां ह्यविचारणीया' ॥
बद्धो भवेत्सेतुरपांनिधौ चेच्
चमूरुपेयाद् भवतां नु लङ्काम् ।
मा भूदिदं, तत्परिहारहेतो-
स्तातोऽत्र मां कर्मणि संन्ययुङ्क्त ॥ XII.20-21

---

99. न मे पुरः स्थातुमिहात्र शक्तः शक्तोऽपि लोके क्व भवान् पुनस्तु ।
वायोर्दशास्यस्य च भीषणे द्वे शक्ती स्थिरे स्तो मयि विद्धि तावत् ॥ *RKM.*, XIII.41

100. न मेघगर्जनं सह्यं शरभाणां कथञ्चन ।
युद्धं मे दीयतां राजन्नहं शरभशावकः ॥ ibid., XXII.67

तदेव तावद्विदधामि भद्र !
रक्षात्मनो नो भृशमेषणीया ।
स्वरक्षणान्नास्ति परो हि धर्मः
स एव तावत् परिपाल्यतेऽत्र ॥ XII.25

'सम्बन्धमाभाषणपूर्वमाहु-
र्वृत्तः स नावत्र समुद्रमध्ये' ।
ब्रवीमि यत्त्वां हितकाम्ययाऽहं
सम्बन्धिनो मे श्रृणु देवि ! तत्त्वम् ॥ XII.28

सत्यं वचस्तद् भवती यदाह
मान्याः सदा नो गुरवो जगत्याम् ।
तथाऽप्यनौचित्यकृतं कदापि
कर्मादसीयं न समर्थनीयम् ॥

श्रीरामपत्नीमहरत् पिता ते
छलेन साध्वीं धृतसाधुवेषः ।
अधर्म्यमाचारविवर्जितं च
कार्यं कृतं तेन जघन्यमेतत् ॥

पिताऽपि यद्युत्पथमाश्रयेत
वर्ज्यो भवेदेव कदन्नवत्सः ।
साहाय्यमस्य प्रविधेहि न त्वं
विवेकिनामग्रसरा मतासि ॥ XII.30-32

श्रुत्वैतदूर्जस्वि वचः कपेः सा
ऽभवत्क्षणं गूढविचारमग्ना ।
आन्दोलिताऽथो विपरीतभावै-
र्वातेरिता नौरिव निम्नगायाम् ॥ XII.34

सज्जाऽस्मि कर्तुं वचनं त्वदीयं
सर्वेऽनुगा मे विरता भवन्तु ।
स्थाने स्थिताः सन्तु शिलास्तवैताः
सिद्धोऽस्तु ते भद्र ! मनीषितोऽर्थः ॥ XII.38

In order to invest the expression with added effect, the author has not hesitated to admit into the body of his poem quite a few of the telling phrases or ideas they embody from ancient texts. As observed earlier, it has established itself as a mannerism with him. These excerpts from a variety of sources indeed lend lustre to his phraseology. As elsewhere, the borrowals belong to two categories. While some of them have been bodily lifted, others represent the ideas in the author's own language, which, because of its close affinity with the original, does not take long to detect. Contrary to the phenomenon that obtains in his other works, the two classes are evenly balanced in the *RKM*. it is to the credit of the poet, that these borrowals, irrespective of the class, have melted into the texture of the poem. While some of them are met in the author's other works also, others are new occurrences. The two classes of borrowals may be listed here alongwith their original sources to get an idea of the fascination the ancient masters have exercised on the author.

(a) Excerpts physically borrowed from ancient texts :

Excerpts	Original Sources
1. आसीन्महीक्षितामाद्यः प्रणवश्छन्दसामिव । II.1	*Raghuvaṁśa*, I.11
2. परित्राणाय साधूनां विनाशाय च दुष्कृताम् । II.10	*Bhagavadgītā*, IV. 8
3. छिद्रेष्वनर्था बहुलीभवन्ति । V.18	*Pañcatantra*, II.186,192
4. एकत्र सौन्दर्यदिदृक्षयेव । VI.15	*Kumārasambhava*, I.49
5 असम्भवं हेममृगस्य जन्म तथापि सीता (रामो) लुलुभे मृगाय ॥ VI.21	*Hitopadeśa*, I.28
6. अन्यथावृत्ति चेतः । IX.4	*Meghadūta*, 3
7. महाजनो येन गतः स पन्थाः । IX.19	*Mahābhārata*,Vana,313.117
8. आज्ञा गुरूणां ह्यविचारणीया । XII.20	*Raghuvaṁśa*, XIV.46
9. सम्बन्धमाभाषणपूर्वमाहुर्वृत्तः स (नावत्र समुद्रमध्ये) XII.28	*Raghuvaṁśa*, II.58
10. आचारहीनं न पुनन्ति वेदाः । XII.32	*Vāsiṣṭhasmṛti*, VI.63
11. रुदितानुसारी XIV.13, XXI.14	*Raghuvaṁśa*, XIV.70

12. तुषारवर्षीव सहस्यमेघः (चन्द्रः) XIV.47 — *Raghuvaṁśa*, XIV.84

13. मा भूत्परीवादनवावतारः । XIV.54 — *Raghuvaṁśa*, V.24

14. उरोविदारं प्रतिचस्करे च । XIV.63, XVIII.32 — *Śiśupālavadha*, I.47

15. सुप्तमीन इव ह्रदः । XV.58 — *Raghuvaṁśa*, I.73

16. सर्वथाऽनिष्टचिन्तानां परदारापहारिणाम् ।
अभिप्राया न सिध्यन्ति तेनेदं वर्तते जगत् ।। XVI.27 — A well-known subhāṣita

17. अद्य क्रियाः कामदुघाः क्रतूनां
सत्याशिषः सम्प्रति भूमिदेवाः । XIX.38 — *Kirātārjunīya*, III.6

18. मनोरथानामतटप्रपातः । XIX. 39 — *Abhijñānaśākuntala*, VI.10

19. विललाप सबाष्पगद्गदं
सहजामप्यपहाय धीरताम् । XX. 74 — *Raghuvaṁśa*, VIII. 43

20. उपोषिताभ्यामिव लोचनाभ्याम् । XXIII. 13 — *Raghuvaṁśa*, II.19

21. विशुद्धामपि यत्समक्षम् । XXIII. 13 — *Raghuvaṁśa*, XIV. 61

22. सूर्ये तपत्यावरणाय दृष्टेः
कल्पेत लोकस्य कथं तमिस्रा । XXV. 7 — *Raghuvaṁśa*, V. 13

(b) Expressions that represent earlier ideas:

1. काव्यामृतरसज्ञानां नैव तृप्तिः प्रजायते । — I. 17
कादम्बरीरसज्ञानामाहारोऽपि न रोचते । — well-known sūktī

2. दन्दह्यमाने भवनेऽग्निना स्यात्
कूपस्य तावत्खननं वृथैव ।। — V. 12
प्रोद्दीप्ते भवने च कूपखननं प्रत्युद्यमः कीदृशः ।। — *Vairāgyaśataka, 82*

3. कालः पिबेत्तद्रसमेव नूनम् — V. 14
क्षिप्रमक्रियमाणस्य कालः पिबति तद्रसम् । — *Hitopadeśa,* Suhṛdbheda, verse 146; Sandhi, verse 94

4. सेवां तदीयां गणयन् पुरस्तात् ।। — IV. 6
तां भक्तिमेवागणयत् पुरस्तात् ।। — *Raghuvaṁśa,* V. 20

5. विचारमूढा — V. 10
विचारमूढः (प्रतिभासि मे त्वम् ।। — *Raghuvaṁśa,* II. 47

6. प्रायः समासन्नपराभवाणां
धियो विपर्यस्ततरा भवन्ति । VI. 21
प्रायः समापन्नविपत्तिकाले
धियोऽपि पुंसां मलिना भवन्ति । *Hitopadeśa*, I. 28

7. अद्यप्रभृत्यस्मि तवाङ्ग दासः । VII. 13
अद्य प्रभृत्यवनताङ्गि ! तवास्मि दासः । *Kumārasambhava*, V. 86

8. सम्बन्ध आभाषणपूर्वकोऽभूद् VII. 16
सम्बन्धमाभाषणपूर्वमाहुः । *Raghuvaṁśa*, II. 58

9. रज्जुच्छेदे घटमिव नु को धारयेत् सद्वचोऽज्ञः । IX. 13
रज्जुच्छेदे के घटं धारयन्ति । *Svapnavāsavadatta*, VI. 10

10 क्षम्यो मयाऽस्याः प्रथमापराधः । X. 21
भगवन् प्रथम इति प्रेक्ष्याविज्ञाततपःप्रभावस्य दुहितृजनस्य
भगवतैकोऽपराधो मर्षयितव्य इति । *Abhijñānaśākuntala*, p. 89

11. अङ्गीकृतान्नैव कथञ्चनापि
धीराः स्वकार्याद्विरता भवन्ति । XII.13
न निश्चितार्थाद्विरमन्ति धीराः । *Nītiśataka*, 81

12. न्ययुङ्क्त मां योजनकर्मदक्षः XII.24
योजकस्तत्र दुर्लभः ॥ *Subhāṣita*

13. मोहोऽस्ति नष्टो वचनैः स मेऽद्य । XII.37
नष्टो मोहः स्मृतिर्लब्धा त्वत्प्रसादान्मयाच्युत । *Bhagavadgītā* , XVIII.73

14. वाचं न मिश्रयति वानरवीरवाचा । XII.46
वाचं न मिश्रयति यद्यपि मद्वचोभिः। *Abhijñānaśākuntala*, I.18

15. स्ववाग्मितायाः परमं प्रमाणं
मितं च सारं च वचो ऽभ्युवाच ॥ XIII. 60
मितं च सारं च वचो हि वाग्मिता ॥ *Naiṣadhīyacarita*, IX. 8

16. परेङ्गितज्ञानफलाढ्यबुद्ध्या
तदाशयं द्राग् बुबुधे हनूमान् ॥ XIII. 65
परेङ्गितज्ञानफला हि बुद्धयः । *Pañcatantra*, I. 44

17. घनान्धकारेष्विव दीपहीनः । XIV.9
घनान्धकारेष्विव दीपदर्शनम् *Mṛcchakaṭika*, I. 10

18. अभूत्तदा तद्रुदितानुसारी XIV. 13

	तामभ्यगच्छद्रुदितानुसारी	*Raghuvaṁśa*, XIV. 70
19.	जन्मादि दैवेऽधि न पौरुषं तु	
	तन्मय्यधीत्येव गृहाण तावत् ।	XIV. 57
	दैवायत्तं कुले जन्म मदायत्तं तु पौरुषम् ।	*Veṇīsaṁhāra*, II. 37
20.	श्रीरामकार्यैकपरायणं तम् ।	XV. 78
	राम काज करिबै को आतुर	*Hanumān Chālīsā*
21.	न्याय्यात्पथः प्रच्यवनं सहेत	XVI. 13
	न्याय्यात्पथः प्रविचलन्ति पदं न धीराः ।।	*Nītiśataka*, verse 84
22.	चयस्त्विषामित्यवभासमानः ।।	XVI. 16
	चयस्त्विषामित्यवधारितः पुरा	*Śiśupālavadha*, I. 3
23.	न विश्वसेदविश्वस्तं विश्वस्तेऽपि न विश्वसेत् ।	XVII. 62
	न विश्वसेदविश्वस्ते विश्वस्तं नाति विश्वसेत् ।	*Pañcatantra*, II. 45
24.	तेजो दशास्याहितमादधाना ।	XIX. 2
	दुष्यन्तेनाहितं तेजो दधानां भूतये भुवः ।	*Abhijñānaśākuntala*, IV. 4
25.	कपिस्तुषारस्रुतिधौतवर्णः ।।	XIX. 20
	पदं तुषारस्रुतिधौतरक्तं ।	*Kumārasambhava, I. 6*
26.	परिवादोऽवतरेन्नवो मम ।।	XX. 63
	मा भूत्परीवादनवावतारः ।	*Raghuvaṁśa*, V. 24
27.	चक्रन्द सीता कुररीव भीता ।।	XXI. 1
	चक्रन्द विग्ना कुररीव भूयः ।।	*Raghuvaṁśa*, XIV. 6
28.	नूनं मया पूर्वतनेषु जन्म- स्वतीव घोरं कृतमस्ति पापम् । यत्तस्य साक्षात्परिणामरूपं समश्नुवे कष्टमिदं कठोरम् ।।	XXI. 3
	ममैव जन्मान्तरपातकानां विपाकविस्फूर्जथुरप्रसह्यः ।	*Raghuvaṁśa*, XIV. 62
29	प्रजानिषेको मयि वर्तमानो भर्तुर्भवत्यत्र ममान्तरायः ।	XXI. 7
	प्रजानिषेकं मयि वर्तमानं (सूनोरनुध्यायत चेतसेति)	*Raghuvaṁśa*, XIV. 60
	स्याद्रक्षणीयं यदि मे न तेजस्त्वदीयमन्तर्गतमन्तरायः ।	ibid., 65
30.	स्वमेव सा दुष्कृतिनं निनिन्द ।	XXI. 2 ,
	आत्मानमेव ----दुष्कृतिनं निनिन्द	*Raghuvaṁśa*, XIV. 57

31. विदारयेद् दीर्घतरं यदद्रिं, विलापयेद् यत्सुतरामयोऽपि । XXI. 10
अपि ग्रावा रोदित्यपि दलति वज्रस्य हृदयम् । *Uttararāmacarita*, I. 28

32. नैकस्य कष्टस्य हि यावदन्तस्तावद् द्वितीयं समुपस्थितं हा । XXI. 41
एकस्य कष्टस्य न यावदन्तं गच्छाम्यहं पारमिवार्णवस्य ।
तावद् द्वितीयं समुपस्थितं मे छिद्रेष्वनर्था बहुलीभवन्ति ।। *Pañcatantra*, II. 186, 192

33. नहि निःक्षत्रिया पृथ्वी गीरेवं यत्समादृता ।
यो वा को वा भवेदेष दर्शयिष्यामि पौरुषम् ।। XXII. 25
भो भोः तत्किमक्षत्रिया पृथ्वी यदेवमुद्धोष्यते । *Uttararāmacarita*, p. 124
यदि ते सन्ति सन्त्येव केयमद्य विभीषिका ।
किमुक्तैरेभिरधुना तां पताकां हरामि वः ।। ibid., IV. 28

34. स्थातुं न शक्ता न च वा प्रयातुं
गता तरङ्गेष्विव राजहंसी । XXIII. 1
सोऽनिश्चयान्नैव ययौ न तस्थौ तरंस्तरङ्गेष्विव राजहंसः । *Saundarananda*, IV. 42

35. किमस्य राज्ञः सदृशं कुलस्य । XXIII.7
श्रुतस्य किं तत्सदृशं कुलस्य । *Raghuvaṁśa*, XIV. 61

36. तथापि लावण्यमयी न छाया
विमुञ्चतीदं नयनाभिरामम् । XXIII. 11
छाया तु लावण्यमयी मुमोच । XXIV. 13
केवलं लावण्यमयी छाया त्वां न मुञ्चति । *Abhijñānaśākuntala*, p. 69

37. शून्या दिशो भान्ति जगच्च शून्यं
शून्यस्य मे सर्वत एव शून्यम् । XXIII. 19
शून्यं मन्ये जगदविरतज्वालमन्तर्ज्वलामि । *Uttararāmacarita*, III. 38

38. वाच्यः पिता मद्वचनाद् भवद्‌भ्याम् । XXIV. 11
वाच्यस्त्वया मद्वचनात्स राजा । *Raghuvaṁśa*, XIV. 61

39. निमन्त्रयामास कपिं स्वभक्तं
सदा स्वकार्यार्थसमुत्सुकं सः । XXIV. 15
राम काज करिबै को आतुर । हनुमान् चालीसा

40. स्वभर्तृवर्त्मप्रतिपन्नतैव XXIV. 27
प्रमदाः पतिवर्त्मगा इति । *Kumārsambhava*, IV.33

41. क्षमस्व सीते ! पतिमर्हसि त्वं
नैवास्य तावत् प्रणयं विहन्तुम् । XXV. 18

तद्भूतनाथानुग ! नार्हसि त्वं
सम्बन्धिनो मे प्रणयं विहन्तुम् ।। *Raghuvaṁśa*, II. 58

42. सर्वत्र वार्तं भगवन्नवेहि । XXV. 4
सर्वत्र नो वार्तमवेहि राजन् । *Raghuvaṁśa*, V.13

43. रुष्येत्कदाचित्त्वथवा प्रसीदेत्
कदाचिदित्यस्मि नितान्तभीता । XXV.19
सत्यं प्रसादोऽपि भयङ्करः स्यात्
लोके जनस्यास्थिरचित्तवृत्तेः । XXV.21
क्षणे रुष्टः क्षणे तुष्टो
रुष्टस्तुष्टः क्षणे क्षणे ।
अव्यवस्थितचित्तानां
प्रसादोऽपि भयङ्करः ।। *Subhāṣita*

44. आज्ञा प्रभूणां ह्यविचारणीया । XXV.24
आज्ञा गुरूणां ह्यविचारणीया । *Raghuvaṁśa*, XIV.46

Occasionally the author permits himself a few of the Sanskritized Hindi proverbs. एक म्यान में दो तलवारें नहीं रह सकतीं, he puts in his Sanskrit as नैकत्र कोशेऽसियुगं सह स्यात् VI.9. Similarly, हाथ कंगन को आरसी क्या he puts in his Sanskrit as हस्ते स्थिते नैव हि कङ्कणे स्यात्कस्याप्यपेक्षा मुकुरस्य तावत्, XIV. 60. The Hindi word बजरंग बली going with Hanumān he adroitly puts back in Sanskrit from where it must have come in the form वज्राङ्गबली. He uses it as a qualifying epithet for the great monkey at a number of places. It is a tribute to his skill in the use of words that he always couples वज्राङ्ग with बली As an individual word वज्राङ्ग means in Sanskrit 'serpent'.

The author has thus taken pains to explore and press into service the various devices to ensure elegant and vibrant expression. But as a grammarian, he could hardly resist the temptation of inducting into the poem a host of complicated grammatical forms which bear testimony to his insight in Sanskrit semantics. He has gone to the extent of weaving skilfully into his expression technical grammatical terms like *prayojako hetuḥ* (IX.50), *karmavyatihāra* (XI.14), *kṛt* and *taddhitavṛtti* (XIII.6) though in their literal sense. The intricate forms, as handled in the *RKM*, cover in their sweep almost all the prominent sections of Sanskrit grammar. His fascination for the aorist of various hues remains unabated. However, the whole corpus of forms is not peculiar to the poem. Since most of them are met elsewhere in the author's works, it would suffice to notice some of the more prominent of the forms only.

By ओमाङोश्च (6.1.95) Pāṇini enjoins a single substitute of the form of the subsequent in place of the preceding अ and ओ of the following ओम्. The author resorts to this more than once in the course of his work, e.g.,

1. एवमुक्तो महेशेनोमित्युवाच रमापतिः । III.11
2. उवाच भद्रोमिति तं कपीन्द्रम् । XIV.30
3. तेनोमिति सति प्रोक्ते । XXII.88

A र् followed by र् is dropped while the preceding vowel, if short, is lengthened. This is the import of the Pāṇini sūtras रो रि (8.3.14) and ढ्रलोपे पूर्वस्य दीर्घोऽणः (6.3.111). The work furnishes quite a few examples of it :

1. जनी रामस्य सीतायाश्चात्रैवाजन्यसंशयम् । 1.31
2. नार्यशीलं विदू राक्षसनार्य आर्यम् । VI.7
3. कपिः प्रभू रुद्र इवान्तकाले । XIV.48
4. मूर्खो यती राम एव । XV.37
5. निशाचरा भूमितले निपेतू रक्तं वमन्तो लुलुठुश्च दीनाः । XVI.8

The author follows Pāṇ. भो भगो अघो अपूर्वस्य योऽशि (8.3.17) when he substitutes in the following instance the *visarjanīya* of भो by य् : भोयाश्रितो भवति, XVII. 12.

A peculiar Sandhi form सैष is justified by Pāṇ. सोऽचि लोपे चेत् पादपूरणम् (6.1.134) which enjoins the elision of the case affix *su* of *sas* when a vowel follows it and when by the elision the verse can be completed. The work furnishes an example of it in एनं विधिं सैष समाश्रितः सन्, IX. 36.

KĀRAKAS

Apart from the normal use of the *vibhaktis* going with respective *Kārakas*, Pāṇini has made a special case for their use under special conditions. The author has the knack of keeping in mind those conditions and making use of the *vibhaktis* enjoined under them.

DVITĪYĀ-VIBHAKTI

The second case, the *dvitīyā-vibhakti*, is enjoined to the words denoting the site of वस् with the prepositions *upa, anu, adhi* and *āṅ*. The *RKM* has the uses of the above with *adhi* only :

1. लङ्कापुरमध्युवास ।। V.19
2. वनमधिवसन् । IX.15

There are a number of instances when the *dvitīyā-vibhakti* is used with the words समया and निकषा enjoined by the Vārttika अभितःपरितःसमयानिकषाहाप्रतियोगेऽपि :-

1. स्थास्यामि रात्रावतिसावधानो विहाय निद्रां समया समुद्रम् । XII.11
2. मां प्रापय त्वं समया च तं द्राक् । XIV.24
3. दुर्दान्तमेनं निकषान्तकम् । ibid.
4. विभीषणं यः समया न्यवात्सीत् ।। XIX.14
5. समया तं समाययौ । XXII.21

The work has a number of examples of the *dvitīyā-vibhakti* going with the roots याच्, अर्थ्, प्रच्छ्, ब्रू or their synonyms, the second dvtiiyā-vibhakti appearing on account of the कर्मसञ्ज्ञा enjoined by अकथितं च (1.4.51) :

1. याचस्व तौ सम्प्रति तं वरेण्ये । V.14
2. भरतस्य चापि ....राज्येऽभिषेकं पतिमर्थयस्व । V.15
3. रामं दशास्येन शठेन तावद्विदेहजाया हरणं स ऊचे । VI.36
4. तं चाह तत्तातनृशंसकृत्यम् । VIII.8
5. स्वप्नव्याख्यां स निजमनुजं पृष्टवान् । IX.8
6. असुरीमपि स प्रणयं प्रबलः
   समयाचत तत्सहितो रहसि ।। X.26
7. क्षमामिमं चापि मृशं ययाचे ।। XIII.49

The *dvitīyā-vibhakti* is enjoined by the sūtra कालाध्वनोरत्यन्तसंयोगे (2.3.5) to a word for time or distance when denoting full duration. The work furnishes an example of it in

सुदुःखितास्तत्र समा बभूवुः
समा महिष्यः सुतहिंसयाऽत्र । VIII.6

TṚITIYĀ-VIBHAKTI

Pāṇini enjoins this *vibhakti* in अपवर्ग by the sūtra अपवर्गे तृतीया (2.3.6) after the words denoting the duration of time or place to express the accomplishment of the desired object. The *RKM* furnishes an instance of this in दिवसैः केवलं सप्तभिर्बुधः, IX.23.

CATURTHĪ-VIBHAKTI

A noteworthy instance of this in the *RKM* is राध्यन्तोऽस्यै कन्यकायै IV.29. Pān. राधीक्ष्योर्यस्य विप्रश्नः (1.4.39) assigns the nature of Sampradāna to the word denoting the person about whose good or bad fortune questions are asked in the case of the verbs राध् 'to propitiate' and ईक्ष् 'to look to'.

It is due to Pān. नमः स्वस्तिस्वाहास्वधाऽलंवषड्योगाच्च (2.3.16.) that there is *caturthī-vibhakti* in ते in स्वस्ति तेऽस्तु, XXIII.30

PAÑCAMĪ-VIBHAKTI

A noun joined with आरात् gets this *vibhakti* by Pāṇ. अन्यारादितरर्तेदिक्शब्दाञ्चूत्तर-पदाजाहियुक्ते (2.3.29). The poet follows this in at least two places in his work :

1. स्थेयं मयाऽऽराज्जलधेर्निशायाम् । XII.8
2. मच्छानुरारात्सरसः स्थितः सन् । XIII.28

प्रति which is कर्मप्रवचनीय in the sense of representative by प्रतिः प्रतिनिधिप्रतिदानयोः (1.4.92) is the cause of *pañcamī-vibhakti* after a word which it governs by Pān. प्रतिनिधिप्रतिदाने च यस्मात् (2.3.11). This is what explains the use of this *vibhkakti* after सुग्रीवात् in सुग्रीवात्प्रति तत्रास्तु , XI.21.

ṢAṢTHĪ-VIBHAKTI

Of its many uses one refers to the disregard shown to something, vide, Pāṇ, षष्ठी चानादरे (2.3.38). It is in this very sense that it is used in

----- सर्वेषां पश्यतामहम् ।

बालाभ्यां गमितस्तावद्दयनीयामिमां दशाम् ॥ XXII.39

According to Pāṇ. अधीगर्थदयेशां कर्मणि (2.3.52.) the object of अधि+इक् and its synonyms (the roots meaning remembering) takes the *ṣaṣṭhī-vibhakti.* The poet follows this in

1. स्मरन् स्वमातुर्वचनस्य चापि VIII.9
2. प्रभोः स्मरन् X.32

SAPTAMĪ-VIBHAKTI

The *RKM* furnishes a number of instances of what goes by the name of *bhāvalakṣaṇā* or *sati-saptamī* which is common enough in Sanskrit literature. The more scholarly use of this *vibhakti* he resorts to in आत्मन्यधि कुम्भमाधात् IV.34, आत्यन्यधि सम्प्रधार्य VI.9, जन्मादि दैवेऽधि XIV.57. अधि assigned the कर्मप्रवचनीयसञ्ज्ञा by अधिरीश्वरे (1.4.97) is the cause of it by Pāṇ. यस्मादधिकं यस्य चेश्वरवचनं तत्र सप्तमी (2.3.9).

COMPOUNDS

The work has typical instances of the different types of compounds in Sanskrit, of *Avyayībhāva* in विभक्त्यर्थ in अधिलोकम्, I.15, vide Pāṇ. अव्ययं विभक्तिसमीप.... (2.1.6), of Tatpuruṣa in मध्येपुरि, I.34, मध्येनदि, IV.34, vide Pāṇ. पारेमध्ये षष्ठ्या वा (II.1.17), देहभाजाम्, VII. 2, मयाऽतिकष्टश्रितया, XXII.10, मया कष्टश्रितेन, XXII. 51, vide Pāṇ. द्वितीया

श्रितातीतपतितगतात्यस्तप्राप्तापन्नैः (8.1.24).

Pāṇini enjoins the addition of certain suffixes at the end of compounds, of टच् in Tatpuruṣa and कप् in Bahuvrīhi ending in words like उरस् vide, उरःप्रभृतिभ्यः कप् (5.4.151). The poet resorts to many a formation with these, e.g.,

1. कल्याणकृत् स स्वसखस्य तस्य XIII.6
2. विंशतिबाहुकः IV.8
3. प्राप्तलङ्कापुरीकः X.31
4. सेवनवृत्तिकस्य XX.17
5. दनुजाऽतुलसंज्ञका XX.19
6. आहितभूरियत्नका XX.22
7. कृतापराधकः XX.71

In the sense of reciprocity of action इच् is the समासान्त enjoined in Bahuvrīhi by Pāṇ. इच् कर्मव्यतिहारे (V.4.127) a chain of beautiful instances of which is met with in the verse

दण्डादण्डि मुष्टीमुष्टि दन्तादन्ति कचाकचि ।
हनुमन्मैयराबौ तौ न्ययुध्येतां परस्परम् ।। XIV.66

A particularly noteworthy instance of a compound in the work is देवसभम् XXV.2 where the Tatpuruṣa ending in सभा being preceded by a word not signifying a human being gets the neuter gender by Pāṇ. सभा राजाऽमनुष्यपूर्वा (2.4.23).

In the context of the compounds it may not be out of point to record the poet's predilection for the compound formations ending in पति where the peculiarity lies in the restriction of the घिसञ्ज्ञा to पति in compound only by Pāṇ. पतिः समास एव (1.4.8.) with all the functions of the said सञ्ज्ञा available to it. Such formations in the work are :

1. स्वपतेर्वियुक्ताऽप्येषा X.12
2. प्रपतेदथ मत्पतेरिह XX.21
3. स्वपतेरन्यजनो मया क्वचित् XX.51
4. मया विना मत्पतिना नृशंसा XXIV.34

Before discussion on the compound formation in the *RKM* is brought to a close, it would be worthwhile to notice a typical form. It is तापसचेल where after adding the word चेलट् in the sense of कुत्सा by चेलड्ब्रुवगोत्रमतहताः the Tatpuruṣa compound is resorted to by Pāṇ. कुत्सितानि कुत्सनैः (2.1.53).

PRONOUNS

An eye-catching peculiarity in the case of the use of the pronouns in the work lies in the use of स्व in the sense of kinsmen where pronominality is forbidden by the गणसूत्र-स्वमज्ञातिधनाख्यायाम् which the poet follows strictly :

छिद्राणि येनापरपक्षपातात्स्वानां परेभ्यः प्रकटीकृतानि ।। XIX.11

Another eye-catching peculiarity is in the use of the suffix अकच् permited by Pāṇ. अव्ययसर्वनाम्नामकच् प्राक् टेः to Indeclinables and pronouns with no addition to sense, e.g.,

1. उषिता ...... दशवक्त्रालय एषका चिरम्, XX.38
2. स विवेकात्त्वयकाऽपनीयताम्, XX.46
3. मयकैव समं समागता, XX.63
4. हनने त्वहमस्यकाः, XX.64
5. नयने पततोऽस्यकां ततः, XX.69
6. त्वं मयका प्रयातुं सह, XXI.36
7. असकौ समतप्यत, XXII.38

KṚT FORMATIONS

Of the more noteworthy of such formations are those with the suffix णमुल्. This is added to roots in the sense 'again and again', vide Pāṇ. आभीक्ष्ण्ये णमुल् (3.4.22) as in पाठं पाठं च तत्काव्यं पायं पायं च तद्रसम् I.17, उद्धारमुद्धारमपाकरोमि XII. 22 or to rootrs meaning 'to strike' when their object is the object of the main verb and when the noun with which it is compounded ends in the Third case, vide Pan. हिंसार्थानां च समानकर्मकाणाम् (3.4.48) :

उरोविदारं प्रतिचस्करे च, XIV. 63, XVIII.32

मुष्टिनिष्पेषं निष्पिपेष, XIV. 63, XVIII.32

By ल्यपि लघुपूर्वात् (6.4.56) Pāṇini enjoins the substitution of णि (णिच्) by अय् when it is preceded by a short vowel. The author follows this when he uses such forms as निशमय्य, IV.17 and सम्पचय्य, XIV.21. Of the other notable Kṛt forms mention may be made of अलम्भूष्णु, XIII.55 formed with ग्स्नु by pāṇ. ग्लाजिस्थश्च ग्स्नुः (3.2.139) (च

of the sūtra carrying forward भू from the preceding sūtra भुवश्च (3.2.138)), निराकरिष्णु formed with इष्णुच् by Pāṇ. अलंकृञ्निराकृञ्वृतुवृधुसहचर इष्णुच् (3.2.136) and अजीवनि, XXIII. 7 with अनि by Pāṇ. आक्रोशे नञ्यनिः (3.3.112).

TADDHITA FORMATIONS

The Taddhita suffix रूपप् added to a stem denoting प्रशंसा, praise, by Pāṇ. प्रशंसायां रूपप् (5.3.66) the author uses in पद्यरूपैः, I.15, बन्धुरूपैः, XIX.10, which mean 'praiseworthy stanzas' and 'praiseworthy kinsmen' respectively.

The word आत्मनीन which has the suffix ख (change of it to ईन by Pāṇ. आयनेयीनीयियः फढखछघां प्रत्ययादीनाम् (7.1.2) enjoined by Pāṇ. आत्मन्विश्वजन-भोगोत्तरपदात्खः (5.1.9) in the sense 'good for that' with आत्मन् remaining intact by Pāṇ. आत्माध्वानौ खे (6.4.169) the author uses in तस्यात्मनीनस्य चिकीर्षयैव, VI. 37, इत्थङ्कारं वचनरचनां संविरच्यात्मनीने -------, IX.13.

Pāṇ. enjoins the suffix पाशप् by याप्ये पाशप् (5.3.47) in the sense 'condemnable' which the author uses with पितृव्य-पितृव्यपाशः XIX.6. The word कापेय formed with ढक् to कपि by Pāṇ. कपिज्ञात्योर्ढक् (5.1.127) in the sense 'nature' or 'action thereof' the author uses in कापेयमेतन्मम यत्पुरस्त्वं स्थितो नियुद्धं ननु याचसे माम्, XIV. 52, त्वया दर्शितं हन्त कापेयमत्र, XVIII. 21. The word काल्य meaning 'timely' with यत् by Pāṇ. तत्र साधुः (4.4.98) the author uses in काल्यं वचश्छद्मतपस्विनि द्राक् प्रावर्तयद्दाशरथिर्महात्मा, IX.49. The word कार्ष्णी with the suffix अण् by Pāṇ. तस्येदम् (4.3.120) in the sense 'belonging to' he uses in हिंसा कार्ष्णी धवलविहिता, IX.10.

VERBAL FORMS

Some of these forms depict twofold peculiarity, one, the author's fondness for Aorist and the other, his use of some typical Ātmanepada-Parasmaipada formations. To the first category belong such forms as प्रास्तौषीत्, I.18, अशिश्रियत्, I.19, प्रार्तथत, IV.6, अशिषत्, IV. 21, समजीगणन्, IV. 29, न्यास्थत्, IV. 32, आधात्, IV.34, उदपादि, ibid., साम्प्रार्तथत, IV.43, VIII.28, संन्यवृतत्, IV.53, न्यवृतत् IV.59, अयुद्ध, IV.60, अपागात्, V.3, अशयिष्ट, V.22, व्यतनिष्ट X.2, अभ्युपागात्, XIV.24, समागात्, XVIII.1, असोष्ट, XIX.2, पर्यचारीत्, XIX.3, न्यवात्सीत् XIX.14, अधात्, XIX.22, XX.27, XX.62, अवोढ, XXI.18, अक्षमिष्ट, XXII.27, अदाः, XXIV.26 in Simplex and प्रत्यपीपदत्, I.26, प्रत्यबूबुधत्, I.29, अतिष्ठिपत्, IV. 43, न्यवीविदत्, IV.47, IX.39, समार्पिपत्, IV.62, X.17 and अचिचिन्तत्, XV.18 in Causative and to the other such forms as समगंस्त,[101] IV.9, XXII.89, आह्वत,[102] IV.60, VIII, 10-II, आह्वयस्व,[103]

---

101. Ātmanepada by समो गम्यृच्छिभ्याम् (1.3.29)
102. Ātmanepada by स्पर्धायामाङः (1.3.31)
103. ibid.

VIII.29, (अध्वनोंऽशं) क्रमते[104] IV.1, क्रमन्ते[105] XI.48, (अध्वानमेष) क्रमते[106] XIV.1, उत्कुरुते,[107] XIV.37, (परस्परेण) व्यतिजघ्नतुः (तौ),[108] XIII.37.

In the context of Ātmanepada it may be pertinent to notice some of the शानजन्त forms. शानच् is the substitute in आत्मनेपद of लट् enjoined in specific cases, the more noteworthy of those in the work being : क्रममाणः (पथा स्वेन),[109] IV.5, सङ्क्रीडमानः,[110] XXII.19-20, सङ्क्रीडमानौ (अन्योन्यम्),[111] XXII.57.

He has also used the aorist forms with माङ् alone or along with स्म, e.g., मा चिचिन्तः, XIV.29, मा स्म चूचुरत्, XVII.,38, मा स्म दाः, XVII.49, मा गमः, XXI.15, मा क्रुधः, XXIV.38, मा कृथाः, XXV.22.

Apart from the causal verbs noticed above in the treatment under Aorist, the *RKM* has a number of secondary verbal forms too in an odd case or two with शानच्, e.g., अजिघांसत्, V.11, पुत्रीचकार, XIII.26, प्रविवृत्सति, XIVX.18, जिघासति, XIV.21, बम्भ्रम्यमाणः, V.18.

Pāṇini enjoins the use of present tense, लट्, with the use of यावत् and पुरा, vide यावत्पुरानिपातयोर्लट् (3.3.4). The author resorts to this in :

मध्येपथं यावदसौ प्रयाति सूर्यप्रभास्तं स्नपयन्ति तावत् । XV.7

यावत्स तं हन्ति रघुप्रवीरम् ॥ XIII.16

ṢATVA OR THE ABSENSE OF IT

In this category could be mentioned forms where षत्व is done or not done as per the specification of Pāṇini. The example of the first is प्रादुःष्यात् V.27 where षत्व is done by Pāṇ. उपसर्गप्रादुर्भ्यामस्तिर्यच्परः (8.3.87) and the example of the second is विसोढाः, XIII. 38, विसोढा, XXIII. 23, where it is not done by Paṇ. सोढः (8.3.115).

Miscellaneous usage :

वमाननायाः प्रतिकारवेलाम् (V.7)

नद्या वगाहं व्यतनिष्ट [112] (X. 2)

104–106. Ātmanepada in the sense of वृत्ति, continuity, by Pāṇ वृत्तिसर्गतायनेषु क्रमः (1.3.30).

107. Ātmanepada by Pāṇ गन्धनावक्षेपणसेवनसाहसिक्यप्रकथनोपयोगेषु कृञः (1.3.32). The sense here is that of अवक्षेपण = भर्त्सन, rebuke, reprimand.

108. Ātmanepada is barred here by Pāṇ न गतिहिंसार्थेभ्यः (1.3.15).

109. Ātmanepada by वृत्तिसर्गतायनेषु क्रमः (1.3.38).

110–111. Ātmanepada by क्रीडोऽनुसम्परिभ्यश्च (1.3.21) .

112. वष्टि भागुरिरल्लोपमवाप्योरुपसर्गयोः ।

FIGURES OF SPEECH

Orignally intended to lend beauty to the expression,[113] the *alaṁkāras* exercised fascination for the successive generations of poets to the extent that they ceased to be mere outer trappings and settled down as an independent discipline, vigorously championed by a devoted band of theoreticians as an inalienable characteristic of poetry.[114] However, their excessive use that, not unoften, tended to degenerate into verbal jugglery, evoked equally sharp disapproval.[115] Obviously, the *alaṁkāras* are not an end in themselves, though their contribution in dispelling the insipidness that might have otherwise overtaken poetry can hardly be overemphasised.

As evidenced by his writings, the author has no undue insistence on the figures of speech. It is their judicious application that has met his approbation.[116]

That precisely accounts for the happy phenomenon that nowhere in his works do they overburden his muse or inflict obscurity thereon. The *RKM* bears out the fact in abundant measure. Alliteration stands out as one of the favourite *alaṁkāras* of the author. His penchant for Anuprāsa uniformly unfolds itself in all his works. It protrudes more prominently in the *RKM* after suffering unintended slid in the preceding poem, the *Indirāgāndhīcaritam*. Based on the ingenious arrangement of consonants, it imparts musical cadence to the verse and leads to pleasing *padalālitya* with which the poem happily abounds. The different varities of Anuprāsa, imaginatively used in the poem, exude sweetness. Some of the more interesting examples of its different types deserve notice hereunder :

छेकानुप्रास

1. रामायणे रामकथाऽभिरम्ये ।। I. 39
2. जनयेयुः सुतांश्चापि चतुरश्चतुराञ्शुभान् । III. 18
3. खर्वीकृतस्वाखिलवीर्यगर्वः ।। VII. 9
4. क्रोधानलोद्दीप्तमना मनस्वी ।। VIII. 25

---

113. Compare– सालङ्कारः कवेः काव्यसन्दर्भ इव व्यभात् । *Pārśvanātha-mahākāvya*, III.156

114. *Candrāloka*, op.cit., I. 7

115. अनलङ्कृती पुनः क्वापि । *Kāvyaprakāśa*, I. 1
शब्दार्थयोरस्थिरा ये धर्माः शोभातिशायिनः । *Sāhityadarpaṇa*, X.1
किं कर्णतर्णर्णसुपर्णभ्यर्णादिवर्णार्णवडम्बरेण । *Hammīramahākāvya*, XIV. 35

116. Compare- यथौचित्यमलङ्कारान् स्थापयामास पार्थिवः । *Pārśvanāthacarita*, IV. 291

5. रामं रामाविरहजरुजं प्रापयिष्याम्यनन्ताम् । IX. 16
6. विद्धौ समं मनसिजासमपुङ्खपत्रैः । XII. 49
7. विभीषणो भीषणशोकमेषां । XIII. 13
8. न मे पुरः स्थातुमिहात्र शक्तः शक्तोऽपि लोके । XIII. 41
9. व्रीडावनम्रः स च तं विनम्रभावेन भूयो विनिबद्धभावः । XIII. 50
10. आत्मानमात्मप्रतिपन्नरूपः ।। XIV. 45
11. हनूमत्समाख्यं निजानन्यभक्तं ।
स भक्तानुरक्तः प्रभुः सन्दिदेश ।। XVIII. 14
12. अयं विन्दन् भिन्दन् जनमनसि मोहान्धतमसं XX. 22
13. इति कारणमार्गणाकुलो बहुमार्गां स्वमतिं व्यधादयम् । XX. 68
14. तमसा मलिनो गिरिर्यथा मलिनाभां बिभराम्बभूव सः ।। XX. 77
15. तस्यां तदेवाभरणं तदाऽऽसीत् । XXI. 29
16. शक्तोऽस्मि प्रतिविधातुं विधातुः शासनादहम् ।। XXII. 41
17. कृत्स्नमायुर्मया याप्यमहो याप्या मम स्थितिः ।। XXII. 52
18. विमुञ्चतीदं नयनाभिरामं मोदं परं सिञ्चति चान्तरङ्गे ।। XXIII. 11
19. प्रासादशोभा भव मे पुनस्त्वं मम प्रसादं च विवर्धयस्व ।। XXIII. 17
20. त्वया विना भामिनि कल्पकल्पा । XXIII. 18
21. तच्चित्रमाभाति वचस्त्वदीयं चित्राऽस्ति पुंसा मनसो गतिर्नु ।। XXIII. 24
22. संरक्षिताया दशकण्ठहर्म्ये पुरा सुरक्षापुरुषैरनेकैः XXIII. 25
23. कष्टान्यनिष्टानि सहेत नारी । XXIV. 23
24. रामे भुवं शासति सर्वथाऽत्र
रक्षःकुलस्यास्ति विराम एव ।। XXV. 6
25. अङ्गीकुरुष्वात इमं प्रसादा-
न्मत्वात्र सीते खलु मत्प्रसादम् । XXV. 23
26. शुद्धबुद्धिरसकावचकासीत् ।। XXV. 29

श्रुत्यनुप्रास

1. जनी रामस्य सीतायाश्चात्रैवाजन्यसंशयम् । I. 31
2. दशास्यसम्मार्गणसम्प्रयुक्तः स दक्षिणाशां प्रति सम्प्रतस्थे । VI. 39
3. अहं गुहायां विलयं प्रयायाम् । VIII. 24
4. अजेयो मैयराबोऽपि केनाप्यन्येन हन्यते । XV. 1
5. श्रुत्वादसीयं वचनं गरीयः । XV. 74
6. उवाच चैनामपराधभीरुर्भीरु क्षमां त्वामहमद्य याचे । XXIII. 6

वृत्त्यनुप्रास

1. रामरूपेण हरितवर्णो वर्ण्यो विपश्चिताम् । III. 20
2. रक्तवर्णो भृशं रक्तः स्वभ्रातुः पादपङ्कजे ॥ III. 21
3. वीर्येण वीरानपि योद्धृवर्यः । IV. 2
4. विवेद सा साधुतयाऽति साध्वी । IV. 39
5. अयुद्ध तेनाथ च घोरयुद्धम् । IV. 60
6. रामे न कस्याभिरमेत दृष्टिः ॥ VI. 5
7. रामं सकामाऽभिससार रामा ॥ VI. 6
8. तच्चित्रमस्याः कृत आस्त नार्य -
   शीलं विदू राक्षसनार्य आर्यम् ॥ VI. 7
9. तद्रामरामारमणं विधेहि ॥ VI. 17
10. रामो जगन्नेत्रयुगाभिरामः ॥ VII. 5
11. ददाह हाहाकृतमास्त येन
    स्वाहाकृतञ्चापि समस्तपुर्याम् ॥ VIII. 35
12. इत्थङ्कारं वचनरचनां संविरच्यात्मनीने । IX. 13
13. कोऽयं शब्दः कुत इत इतः । IX. 30
14. तदर्थमात्मानमतस्ततान
    वितानरूपं पवनस्य पुत्रः ॥ IX. 34

15. सोऽयं न कामोऽस्ति तवाभिरामो
नाशोऽत्र ते स्यात्परिणाम एव ॥ IX. 46

16. तान्तान्तरङ्गोऽपि बहिः प्रशान्तः । IX. 49

17. इत्यस्तसमस्तकार्ये । X. 9

18. तरुणी कनकं कमलं कमला
नहि कस्य हरन्ति मनोहरिणम् । X. 25

19. नितान्तं च तान्तान्तरङ्गो बभूव ॥ XI. 10

20. निचिक्षेप तं सन्ततं तान्तचित्तः । XI. 15

21. त्वत्तो न मे विप्रतिपत्तिरस्ति ॥ XII. 35

22. चिन्तापरा विविधचारुविचारवीचि-
प्रेङ्खोलिता न वचनं किमपि प्रपेदे ॥ XII. 44

23. कष्टैरनिष्टैरपि वेष्टिताङ्गाः । XII. 20

24. स्वेदाम्बुजालजटितालकजालकाली ॥ XII. 49

25. एवं स्थिते किं करवाणि किं वा
ब्रवाणि किं वा खलु चिन्तयानि । XIII. 59

26. धैर्यं स नो धैर्यधनो मुमोच । XIV.7

27. यस्या विलापावलिवाक्प्रपञ्चः । XIV.12

28. प्रभञ्जनापत्यवरो हनूमान्
वेगेन तत्पञ्जरमाबभञ्ज । XIV.45

29. बलाद् बली बालिशबुद्धिमेनम् । XIV.49

30. पातालराजेन दिगन्तराल-
विश्रान्तिमद्विश्रुतकीर्तिभाजा । XIV.54

31. कपिस्तरस्वी तरसा च तं द्राक् । XIV.62

32. हर्षवर्षमतुलं परिवर्षन् । XIV.76

33. अकालहीनं कार्यार्थी कुम्भकर्णं विभीषणः । XV.16

34. तत्सर्वमालोक्य बभूव चिन्ता-
चान्तान्तरङ्गो दनुजाधिनाथः । XVI.8

35. विच्छायवक्त्रोऽर्क इवोपरक्त-
श्चिन्ताचिताध्वस्त इवाबभासे ।। XVI.26

36. पादपङ्कजरजोऽस्य मम स्यादङ्गराग इति मे हृदि रागः ।। XVII.18

37. विपद्वारिराशौ निमग्नं विदित्वा
सहायं पुराणं स्वकीयं सुदुःख्यन् ।
हनूमत्समाख्यं निजानन्यभक्तं
स भक्तानुरक्तः प्रभुः सन्दिदेश ।। XVIII.14

38. उरःपेषमेतौ नियुद्धे प्रवृत्तौ
तलाभ्यां भुजाभ्यां कराभ्यां च वीरौ । XVIII.28

39. सद्यःफलं मे तप इत्यनेन
हर्षप्रकर्षो हृदि मे न माति । XIX.36

40. श्रुत्वाभवद्यत्सुतरामशान्तस्तान्तान्तरङ्गश्च कपिप्रवीरः ।। XIX.4

41. पदं सीता राज्ञ्या इह जगति वीताखिलभया
विनिन्ये सुप्रीता निजसमयमत्यन्तसुखिता ।। XX.4

42. मम भृत्यजनस्य गीर्ध्रुवं
परिपाल्याऽस्ति मयेति भावतः ।। XX.17

43. गहनां रुजमावहन्नहो
विमले हन्त विदेहजाहृदि ।। XX.43

44. हन्तू रिपूणां जगतां नियन्तुः । XXI.23

45. पतेद्यदीदं प्रसभं पृथिव्याम् । XXI.33

46. आदाय तं च प्रययौ प्रतीता
सीता ऋषेः पादयुगं प्रणम्य ।। XXI.55

47. शक्तोऽस्मि प्रतिविधातुं विधातुः शासनादहम् ।। XXII.41

48. किन्तु सीता प्रमीतेति लक्ष्मणः प्रोक्तवान् पुरा । XXII.83

49. कष्टैरनिष्टैः परिवेष्टितां मां । XXIII.8

50. तन्मेऽपराधं सुमुखि क्षमस्व
क्षमाधना त्वं सुतरां क्षमेव । XXIII.14

51. शून्या दिशो भान्ति जगच्च शून्यं
शून्यस्य मे सर्वत्र एव शून्यम् ।। XXIII.19

52. त्वं शङ्कितान्तःकरणो नितान्तम् । XXIII.25

53. कष्टैरनिष्टैः परिवेष्टिता च । XXIII.40

54. कष्टानि नाना नयनाभिराम । XXIV.26

55. तस्यैव राजधानीं सा सीता माता गताऽभवत् । XXIV.47

56. विदेहजासङ्गमसम्प्रहृष्टः । XXV.26

The alliteration attains culmination in its loveliest variety, popularly known as Antyānuprāsa, which rests on the skilful formation of the last words of its various quarters (*pādāntaga*) or the finals of the individual words in a line (*padāntaga)*. It is met with in the poem in both these varieties. It is chiefly instrumental in investing it with delightful rhythm, almost lilting in effect. While it forms the corner-stone of the edifice represented by the *Bodhisattvacaritam*, it was mysteriously pushed into oblivion in the author's *IC*. In the *RKM* it has been restored to the glory it richly deserves. Not unoften, it is only two of the quarters that concur in rhythm. Seldom do the bouts extend to the whole verse. It occurs the maximum number of times in Canto XVII where it goes very well with the 'heaving' rhythm of the Svāgatā metre. Of all its two scores and odd occurrences as many as thirteen are found in this canto itself. Because of the limitations of space only a few are reproduced below by way of specimen :

1. स्वयंवरे शार्वमसौ न्यधत्त
शार्ङ्गं तदर्थं च विधिं व्यधत्त । IV.55

2. अविरतगमनाच्छ्रमं प्रपन्नो
दशरथवंशधरो भृशं विपन्नः ।। VI.40

3. अथ सापि शशाक विधातुमिमं
बलिनं प्रविलोक्य विलोक्यतमम् ।

स्वमनो न मनोजवशात्स्ववशे
मुदिता समरंस्त च तेन समम् ॥ X.27

4. प्रसूतमात्रं किल सा तनूजं
दशास्यरोषं परिहर्तुकामा ।
समुद्रतीरे विससर्ज वामा
प्रीताऽपि पुत्राप्तिवशेन भीता ॥ XIII.24

5. त्वद्दर्शनेनैव सुतृप्तमेहि
मह्यं परिष्वङ्गसुखं प्रदेहि ॥ XIII.47

6. तत्समीक्ष्य सकलस्थितिविद्वान्
रावणानुज उवाच सुविद्वान् ॥ XVII.7

7. तेन मान्यवर ! विप्रकृतोऽस्मि
धिक्कृतोऽस्मि बहु चापकृतोऽस्मि ।
न क्षणं क्षणमपि प्रतिपन्न-
स्त्वां शरण्यमहमस्म्युपपन्नः ॥ XVII.15

8. नाममात्रमपि यस्य रिपूणां
मानसं वितनुते भयकम्प्रम् ।
सोऽखिलस्य भुवनस्य विजेता
रावणोऽस्ति यशसां भुवि चेता ॥ XVII.23

9. पृथ्वी विदीर्णा स्वयमेव जाता
विदेहजाता च ततः प्रयाता । XXIV.45

10. कीर्तिरास्त प्रसृताऽस्य जगत्याम्
इन्दुकान्तिधवला, न च मत्याम् । XXV.29

Other examples of the above Anuprāsa can be marked at II,3,4,6,8, IV. 10, 13, VI.2, VII.49, VIII.36, IX.54, X.15, XII.14, XIII.2,15, 24, 43, XIV. 19, XVI.4, XVII.6, 8, 9,10, 11,14,15,16,23,27,36,37, XVIII.6, XIX.14, XIX.46, XXI.8, 26, 33, XXIV.45, XXV.8, 29, 30.

The author has used Yamaka also quite often. It is not like fearsome Yamaka that one meets with in some of the classical poems. As used in the *RKM*, it is shorn of ambiguity, being almost as transparent as Anuprāsa. The examples noticed here would attest to the fact :

1. तत्पीडिता देवगणा उपायन्नुपायमन्यं नहि वीक्षमाणाः । II.4
2. नारायणो लोकपरायणोऽसौ । II.10,24
3. सतीष्वपि सतीष्वस्य । III.2
4. येन लोकस्य कल्याणं भविष्यति भविष्यति । III.18
5. बद्धाञ्जलिः प्रार्तथतैनमाशुतोषं निजं तोषमभीप्सुरेषः ।। IV.6
6. रामोऽभिरामोऽपि युवत्वमाप्तः । IV.57
7. एवं रामासुरे पूर्वं निर्जिते निर्जितेन्द्रियः । IV.65
8. कृत्वा विरूपामथ मां स मत्तो
   मत्तोऽच्छिनत्तां जनकस्य पुत्रीम् ।। VI.16
9. हनिष्यतेऽसौ तनुजेन तेने-
   त्येवं प्रभुस्तत्र विधिं वितेने । VIII.5
10. सुदुःखितास्तत्र समा बभूवुः
    समा महिष्यः सुतहिंसयाऽत्र । VIII.6
11. रामोऽभिरामो . . IX.10
12. स्वप्नव्याख्याविधिविधिवशात् IX.19
13. विवेकिनो नो सहसा क्रमन्ते IX.48
14. सञ्चिन्तयामास च सोऽन्यमेवो-
    पायं ततो रोद्धुमना अपायम् ।। IX.53
15. अथ साऽपि शशाक विधातुमिमं
    बलिनं प्रविलोक्य विलोक्यतमम् ।
    स्वमनो न मनोजवशात्स्ववशे
    मुदिता समरंस्त च तेन समम् ।। X.27
16. नवसृष्टिरभूत्प्रकटा विकटा ।। X.29

17. प्रयत्नजाते विफले प्रजाते । X.33

18. क्षणं नापि रामः क्षणं प्राप वीरः ।। XI.12

19. शिला इतः कोऽपनयत्यकस्मात्

कस्मादिति ज्ञातुमशक्नुवानः । XII.8

20. निशम्य वाचोऽस्य तदा प्रवाचो । XIII.39

21. अल्पेन कालेन च वातवत्सो घनावलीं वात इवाच्छिनत्ताम् ।। XIV.10

22. शक्तेर्जागरणं शक्तेर्भवेद्दैवतपूजया । XV.56

23. सैन्यानि येन प्रययुः सुखेन पारेसमुद्रं प्रयतानि तानि ।। XIX.43

24. दधानैका रक्षःस्त्री विकृतकृतरूपा शठतमा । XX.9

25. प्रपतेदथ मत्पतेरिहा ------- XX.21

26. इति चिन्तयमानमानसा । XX.22

27. हनने त्वहमस्यका गुरु गुरुवाक्यं परिपालयञ्जनैः । XX.64

28. असिमुद्धृतवानयं बलादबलायां विनिपातनाय हा । XX.66

29. बलवत्पतितेन तेन नो । XX.72

30. अयि वत्स कुतो ऽकुतोभयो XX.75

31. प्रकृतिं गतवान् स नाददे

वचनं ग्लानमना मनागपि । XX.76

32. समयं गमयन्नधोमुखः । XX.77

33. कृतदुष्कृतदुःखभावना-

व्यथितः स्वं पुरमेव लक्ष्मणः ।। XX.78

34. न जीवनस्यास्ति ममाभिलाष-

स्त्यागस्तु तस्याभिमतो मतो मे ।। XXI.6

35. न चैव गीतानि पिकस्वनीभि-

र्गीतानि नारीभिरमन्दहर्षात् ।। XXI.25

36. दयामयी वाचमिमामुवाच ।। XXI.32

37. सम्पन्नमात्रे च विधौ कुमारः समुत्थितोऽभूत्सुकुमार एकः ।। XXI.54

38. हन्तुं प्रदिष्टा ननु मन्ददिष्टा । XXIII.3

39. ऋषेः कुटीरे निवसामि कष्टा-
तपस्विनीवाद्य तपस्विनी भोः ।। XXIII.6

40. सा मानिनी वाचमिमामुवाच ।। XXIII.20

41. कुमारयोस्तं सुकुमारयोः सः । XXIV.6

42. प्रियोऽसि मे त्वं कुरु तत्सखेदं
कुरु प्रसन्नं ननु मां सखेदम् । XXIV.19

43. पुनः पुनर्वाचमिमामुवाच । XXIV.40

Interestingly, Upamā, Simile, is the dominant figure of speech in the *RKM*. Because of its contribution in raising the *alaṁkāras* based on similarity to fulfilment, the Simile doubtless occupies an enviable status. More than any other *alaṁkāra*, it serves to dispel ambiguity from the expression and has therefore evoked wide esteem. The validity of Upamā rests on appropriate *upamānas* that go far to impart clarity to the idea. The standards of comparison mustered by the author in the *RKM* are marked by refreshing variety. They vouch as much for his rich equipment and keen observation as for his anxiety to make his expression felicitous and forceful. His repertoire includes among others such interesting *upamānas* as streak of evil deeds, fell disease, alligator, lotus-stalk, tempest, rudderless boat, massive tree, mass of clouds, stream of ghee, wild fire, mouse and the legendary wish-granting tree (*kalpataru*). The author has resorted to Simile with quite some frequency. There is hardly any canto which is not enlivened by its imaginative touch. In some of the cantos it is found used successively in a string of verses (XIV.6-11). The author is evidently under the spell of the primeval bard Vālmīki in using Upamā in the poem with exuberance. The way the Upamā has contributed to the richness of his expression in the poem should be obvious even from stray instances. The first shot of Rāma's arrow resulted in removing Kubjā's hump as the evils of the perverted mind are destroyed by noble company[117]. The mighty tongue of the demon Jihva, stretched to block entry into Laṅkā, plunged the town into darkness like the string of evil deeds.[118] The ferocity with which

117. कुब्जत्वमस्या यत आश्वपागात्
सत्सङ्गमेनेव कुबुद्धिदोषः ।। V.3

118. दुष्कर्मरेखा विततेव जिह्वा
तां पातयामास तमस्यनन्ते । V.24

Śūrpaṇakhā charges at Sītā has been sought to be brought into bold relief by inviting comparison with storm[119]. Alienated by Rāvaṇa's despicable behaviour towards him, Vibhīṣaṇa parted company with him in the manner the doctor discards the patient with fell disease.[120]. Rāma makes it clear to the fake ascetic that he could not be deflected from his resolve to punish Rāvaṇa like rock whom even the worst tempest cannot toss[121]. While propitiating his trusted missile, Kumbhakarṇa sat in meditation motionless like the tank with the fish in sleep[122]. Rāvaṇa was convinced that once Malivagga Brahmā cursed Rāma, his forces would perish like a ship without captain[123]. But when he himself was pronounced guilty by the Lord, he turned pale like the sun under eclipse[124]. Rāma's order to Lakṣmaṇa to execute Sītā for her supposed unfaithfulness to him, struck her like the thunderbolt at the destruction of aeon[125]. In his chance meeting with Sītā, after ten long years, Rāma did not feel contented on repeatedly seeing her sorrowful face as a thirsty person is not satisfied even if he drinks large quantity of sweet water[126]. Besides these worthy illustrations some more telling instances are :

1. मोघे प्रयत्ने प्रणिधेः प्रजाते
स्वयं दशास्यः कृतसाधुवेशः ।

---

119. वात्यामिवाभ्यापतितां विलोक्य । VI.10

120. याप्ये रोगे भिषगिव रुजाक्रान्तकायं नरं स
सन्त्यज्यायादवमतिशिखिज्वालया दह्यमानः । IX.19

121. न मामतश्चालयितुं समर्थो
भवाञ्शिलौघं पवनो यथैव ।। IX.52

122. मोक्षशक्तिं निधायासौ सम्मुखे स्वस्य निश्चलः ।
सम्मीलिताक्षियुगलः सुप्तमीन इव ह्रदः ।। XV.58

123. तस्मिंश्च नष्टे सकलाऽस्य सेना
दिशो द्रवेन्नौरिव नेतृहीना । XVI.14

124. विच्छायवक्त्रोऽर्क इवोपरक्तः XVI.26

125. प्रलयाभ्राशनिसंनिभा इमाः ।
गहनां रुजमावहन् गिरो
विमले हन्त ! विदेहजाहृदि ।। XX.43

126. पुनः पुनर्नैव जगाम तृप्ति-
मुदन्यितः स्वादुतमाम्बुनेव ।। XXIII.10

रामस्य सेनामनुसम्प्रविष्टो
दुष्टाभिसन्धिर्मकरो यथाऽब्धिम् ॥ IX.40

2. सीतेव वह्निं परिदीप्यमानं
वीरक्वना तत्र तुलां रुरोह ॥ XIV.35

3. प्रभञ्जनस्यास्मि सुतः प्रसिद्धो
लोकेषु वज्राङ्गबली हनूमान् ।
भङ्क्ष्यामि ते संहननं विशालं
मृणालदण्डं द्विरदो यथैव ॥ XIV.58

4. पातालराजो निशितैः समन्ताद्
हनूमतो वाग्विशिखैः प्रविद्धः ।
क्रोधेन जज्वाल तदाज्यधारा-
सारैः समिद्धो हुतभुग् यथैव ॥ XIV.61

5. रावणे यद्यपि स्नेहश्चेतस्यस्यास्ति सुस्थिरः ।
नैषोऽभिभूतस्तेन स्याद्वातेनेव महाद्रुमः ॥[127] XV.15

It is a measure of the author's fascination for it that he has used more than one Simile in some of his verses. It is actuated by a keen desire to ensure added clarity to the idea under description. Canto Fourteen, which forms a mini-thesaurus of Similes, yields one such instance. As the unending swarm of mosquitoes surrounded Hanuman, his visibility was so reduced that he could see nothing like a person without lamp in pitch darkness. But he immediately churned it with his mighty arms like a brimful river :

द्रष्टुं समर्थोऽपि न किञ्चिदेष
घनान्धकारेष्विव दीपहीनः ।
आलोडयामास भुजद्वयेन
जलप्रपूर्णामिव तां स्रवन्तीम् ॥ XIV.9

---

127. For other interesting examples of Simile in the *RKM* one may refer to VIII. 18, XII.33, XV.7, XXI.17, XXII.61-62, XXIII.9, etc., etc.

The Rākṣasas routed by Rāma, the deities inform Īśvara, have sought safe sanctuaries as the mice tuck in their holes to save their skin. Others have perished like the darkness at the sun-rise :

श्रीराघवेन्द्रेण जिताः प्रविष्टा
रक्षोऽधमा मूषकवद्बिलेषु ।
सूर्योदये सन्तमसं यथैव
तथैव ते दूरत एव नष्टाः ॥ XXV.5

While the liberal use of Upamā in the poem bespeaks the author's penchant for this most lovely figure of speech and mustering appropriate standards of comparison, in an odd case there appears to be some incongruity. The comparison of Laṅkā with *prāṇa*, the life-breath, in the context of its protection, might have been prompted in all likelihood in completely owning it. The *upamāna prāṇa*, however does not agree with Laṅkā, the *upameya,* in gender. However, no umbrage can be taken against the wide array of other *upamānas* that have been admitted in the poem with fruitful results. The author has also not hesitated from inducting more than one *upamāna* for some of the *upameyas*, a phenomenon that forms the basis of Mālopamā. The stanzas that follow are charming illustrations of it :

(1) वात्येव घोरा रजनी तमिस्रा
भयङ्करेवापदिवापतत्सा ।
तथा समन्तात्क्षतविक्षतोऽपि
धैर्यं स नो धैर्यधनो मुमोच ॥ XIV.7

(2) प्रविलोक्य बभूव तत्क्षणा-
दतिविच्छायमुखो रघूद्वहः ।
उपरक्त इव क्षपाकरो
हिमविध्वस्त इव द्रुमोऽथवा ॥ XX.35

The episode of Suvarṇamatsyā which is one of the most charming of the portions of the poem throws up some of the finest of the instances of the Mālopamā where one Simile follows the other in quick succession and with a compulsive flow:

सौन्दर्यमद्भुतमनिन्द्यतमं जगत्यां
वर्णः सुवर्णमिव कोकिलवत्स्वरश्च ।

भृङ्गावलीव ननु कुन्तलराजिरस्याः

कं वा नहि प्रमदयेत् प्रमदोत्तमैषा ।। XII.45

Arthāntaranyāsa, based on the reinforcement that the general statement lends to the particular and vice-versa[128], is the other *alaṁkāra* to have been championed in the poem with gusto. It is in tune with the poet's wont as it displays itself in his works. By its very nature, the Arthāntaranyāsa ultimately results into the emergence of crisp *subhāṣitas* that impart beauty and variety to the poem, and settle down as wise sayings. That perhaps accounts for the devotion with which the author has prosecuted the Arthāntaranyāsa in the *RKM*. Both of its varieties have been used in the poem with equal effect. It is however in upholding the particular expression with its general counterpart that the poet excels.

Śurpaṇakha persuaded herself to believe that Sītā was solely responsible for frustrating her advances to Rāma, and as long as she (Sītā) lived she had no chance to succeed in her mission. Her thinking has been clothed in the Arthāntaranyāsa. Here a popular saying has been skilfully exploited to buttress her contention. Two women, she mused, could not claim Rāma at the same time. The sheath after all cannot hold two swords :

एषा नु यावद्ध्रियते न ताव-

द्रामानुकूल्यं मयि सम्भवि स्यात् ।

नैकत्र कोशेऽसियुगं सह स्या-

दित्येवमात्मन्यधि सम्प्रधार्य ।। VI.9

Rāvaṇa, in his arrogance, misconstrued the wise advice his younger brother Vibhīṣaṇa had tendered him to ensure the safety of the Rākṣasa-race. He came to suspect his loyalty and threatened to banish him unceremoniously in case he himself did not leave. The rotten part of the body, howsoever valuable, has to be chopped off to pre-empt its evil effect on the body, the demon thundered :

वस्तु सत्यं मयि न सुतरामर्हसि त्वं विमूढो

निर्गच्छेतो स्वयमहमुत त्वामहं शत्रुपक्ष्यम् ।

---

128. सामान्यविशेषकार्यकारणभावाभ्यां निर्दिष्टप्रकृतसमर्थनमर्थान्तरन्यासः ।
Alankārasarvasva, Kāvyamālā 35, p.139.

लङ्कापुर्याः पृथगनुचरैः सावमानं करोमि
स्वाङ्गं चेत्स्याद् वपुषि गलितं तद् बहिष्कार्यमेव ॥ IX.18

Rāma was delighted to discover that the hermit-boy, pitted against him, was none else than his own son Maṅkuṭa. When he learnt that Sītā, whom he had presumed to be dead all these years, was also alive, his joy transcended all bounds. He was simply thrilled. Joys indeed come in a train :

सीताऽपि जीवतीत्यस्य भूयसीं मुदमावहत् ।
सानुषङ्गाणि सन्त्येव कल्याणानि महीतले ॥ XXII.80

These illustrations should suffice to highlight the quality of Arthāntaranyāsa in the poem and the author's expertise to handle it with verve. For other illustrations reference may be made to IX.1, 48, XIII.49, XVII.40, XX.13, 60, XXII.76, XXIV.27, XXV.22.

The Arthāntaranyāsa has been instrumental in throwing up a string of lovely *subhāṣitas* which tend to lend the poem an element of eternity. The *subhāṣitas* are the general statements that are intended to reinforce or are, in turn, reinforced by the specific observation on which rests this loveliest of the *alaṁkāras*. In this respect the *RKM* stands closer to the *Bodhisattvacaritam* rather than the *IC,* which, in view of its factual narrative, is not amenable to such finesse. The eternal truths enshrined in these wise sayings lend the language an aura of serenity. Some of the *subhāṣitas* are listed here to enable the reader to evaluate the author's keen perception wherefrom they emanate :

1. मत्ताः प्रमत्ताः किमु वा न कुर्युः । VIII.10
2. स्वरक्षणान्नास्ति परो हि धर्मः । XII.25
3. सौम्याकृतिः प्रत्ययमादधाति । XIV.15
4. विकत्थना नैव भवन्ति शूराः । XIV.56
5. वेद कः कपटिनां खलु वृत्तम् । XVII.40
6. विधाता दुष्टानामपि हि साहाय्यकृतिभाक् । XX.13
7. असम्भावितसम्प्राप्तिः कस्य मोदाय नो भवेत् । XXII.76
8. सानुषङ्गाणि सन्त्येव कल्याणानि महीतले । XXII.80

Of the Arthālaṁkāras, Rūpaka is the only other *alaṁkāra* that has claimed serious attention in the poem. It consists of imputing the *aprastuta* on the *prastuta* to drive home the close similarity that implicitly exists between the two[129]. The author has no fascination for its complicated varieties. As employed in the *RKM*, it is free from ambiguity and is marked, by pleasing simplicity. In the instance reproduced below, the imputation of *megha* on *udvega* has been prompted by the *āropa* of *antarikṣa* on *hṛdaya*. In the parlance of the poeticians it is known as Paramparitarūpaka.[130]

अनेन तस्या हृदयान्तरिक्षमुद्वेगमेघान्तरितं बभूव । V.6

The *aprastutas* that the author has sought to impute on the *prastutas* are tellingly precise and go far to heighten and strengthen the impact of the figure of speech. The following illustrations would bear it out :

1. अवमतिशिखिज्वालया दह्यमानः । IX.19
2. वैलक्ष्यशल्यं हृदये दधानः । IX.39
3. (मा) दशास्यवह्नौ शलभायितो भूः । IX.47
4. विपद्वारिराशौ निमग्नं विदित्वा । XVIII.14
5. रोषात् पुरा संशयशूकदष्टः । XXIII.4
6. ----कुतर्कवीचि प्रेङ्खोलिता । XXIII.9
7. दुःखाम्बुदाच्छन्नमभिप्रपश्यन् । XXIII.10

The rest of the *alaṁkāras* encountered in the poem have been used sparingly. The *RKM* is the only work of the author which seeks to press into service Aprastutapraśaṁsā as well. The variety that has met his approval is the one wherein *prastuta* is implied by the *aprastuta*. The method is evidently aimed at making the *prastuta* more comprehensible. Beñjakayī's headlong fall for Hanumān has been brought into relief by an attractive Aprastutapraśaṁsā. Here *latā, nadī* and *prakṛti* stand for the demon-girl. *Taru, jaladhi* and *puruṣa,* on the other hand, are intended to imply Hanumān :

---

129. रूपकं रूपितारोपो विषये निरपह्नवे । *SD.*, X.28

130. तत्र कस्यचिदारोपः परारोपणकारणम् ।
तत्परम्परितं श्लिष्टाश्लिष्टशब्दनिबन्धनम् ।। *SD.*, X.29

यदि याति लता स्वयमेव तरुं
यदि याति नदी च तथा जलधिम् ।
नहि तत्र विचित्रमिति प्रकटं
प्रकृतिः पुरुषं स्वयमेति यतः ।। X.28

In this first encounter with Rāma the hermit boy Maṅkuṭa unequivocally told him that his edict was unacceptable to him. Submission is repugnant to the Kṣatriya-warrior. This has been sought to be conveyed through two imaginative *aprastutas* : *megha* and *śarabha*. Here the thundering of the cloud, obviously represents the vaunt inherent in Rāma's edict and the *śarabhas* seek to imply the intrepid warriors like Maṅkuṭa :

न मेघगर्जनं सह्यं शरभाणां कथञ्चन । XXII.67

While, unlike the Aprastutapraśaṁsā, the Atiśayokti is not peculiar to the *RKM*, its variety based on the simultaneity of cause and effect is not met with in any other work of the author. This is the only form that has been used in the poem. The phenomenon is intended to project the rapidity that marks the accomplishment of the task. Of the two examples yielded by the poem, the first is mingled with a lively streak of Arthāntaranyāsa :

यदैव दृष्टौ रघुनन्दनोऽस्याः
पपात विद्धा ह्यभवत्तदैव ।
पञ्चेषुबाणैरसुराङ्गना सा
रामे न कस्याभिरमेत दृष्टिः ।। VI.5

यावदेव गिरस्तस्य निस्सरन्ति मुखादिमाः ।
उत्पुप्लुवे तावदेव हिमवन्तं गिरिं कपिः ।। XV.47

When the same object forms the subject and object of comparison, it amounts to Ananvaya[131]. The author has resorted to this in the following verse that emerges as its sole example in the poem. While describing the sacrificial horse, let loose by Rāma, its rarity is sought to be highlighted by comparing it with its own self :

---

131. उपमानोपमेयत्वमेकस्यैव त्वनन्वयः । *SD.*, X.26

स्वेनैव लोके सदृशमश्वमेधाय पार्थिवः । XXII.15

Viśeṣokti is found in the description of Rāvaṇa's encounter with Jaṭāyu, the mythical eagle, who gave the demon tough fight before he fell to his sword. At the early stage of the combat, Rāvaṇa could not overpower or kill it though he made the hardest effort for it. Here the cause is described to have ended in a smoke without reaching culmination in its effect[132]:

यत्नं श्रयित्वाऽपि दशाननस्तं
दिशां विजेता न शशाक हन्तुम् ।। VI.29

In the hemistich, reproduced below, the cause again fails to attain fulfilment. Though Hanumān was tired to the bone, the fatigue did not induce him to sleep. It has been sought to be strengthened by a general statement that lends it an aura of Arthāntaranyāsa. The two join to form Saṅkara:

श्रान्तोऽपि भूयो न ययौ स निद्रां
धीराः स्वकार्यैकपरा भवन्ति ।। XII.1

Sahokti constituted by the simultaneity of two distinct actions[133] is found in the work at two places. Sītā and Jaṭāyu are described to have acted simultaneously in shedding tears and life respectively :

विदेहजास्रैः सममेव हन्त
प्राणान् प्रियान् स्वान् विमुमोच धीरः । VI.33

On upturning the bed the portrait of Rāvaṇa drawn by Sītā and her heart fall simultaneously :

परिवर्तनकाल एव तद्
दशकण्ठाकृतिचित्रमापतत् ।
सममेव विदेहजाहृदा
ननु वैकल्यभृतेन सत्वरम् ।। XX.34

The negation of the *prastuta* followed or preceded by the attribution of the *aprastuta* is what makes Apahnuti. It has been used only thrice in the *RKM*. The two of its illustrations do not differ in substance. Here agony is sought to be concealed

---

132. सति हेतौ फलाभावे विशेषोक्तिस्तथा द्विधा । *SD.*, X.27

133. सहोक्तिः सहभावश्चेद् भासते जनरञ्जनः । *Kuvalayānanda*, 58.

by projecting the torrent of tears as *aprastuta* :

तस्यास्तदा दुःखभरो बभूव
बहिर्गतो ह्यश्रुभरच्छलेन । XXI.2
दुःखौघमेषाऽगलयच्चिरोत्थं
स्वकीयमस्रौघमिषेण तत्र । XXIII.31

Viṣama (IX.15,22,47, XVII.22, etc.), Virodhābhasā (XXI.12, XXIV.25, etc.)and Utprekṣā (XXII.4,79, XXIV.22) are the other figures of speech that have been used in the poem. Some of the *alaṁkāras* tend to mingle to form Saṅkara[134].

METRE

Metre is so close to the genius of poetry that like the figure of speech it cannot be dismissed as a mere outward trapping. The imaginative use of metre serves to heighten the charm of the *prabandha* as a whole[135] and thereby ensures for it wide acceptance. The theoreticians are emphatic that to serve its purpose, the metre has to accord with the spirit of the sentiment and keep pace with the changing contours of descriptions in the poem.[136] The *RKM* concurs with his other writings in testifying to the author's skill in handling the metre. Contrary to the *Indirāgāndhīcaritam*, the number of metres in the *RKM* has dwindled to fifteen. However, it agrees with the *Bodhisattvacaritam*, which is likewise couched in fifteen metres. The metres that the *RKM* has claimed are : Upajāti, Anuṣṭup, Praharṣiṇī, Indravajrā, Vidyunmālā, Puṣpitāgrā, Drutavilambita, Mandākrāntā, Mālinī, Toṭaka, Bhujaṅgaprayāta, Vasantatilakā, Svāgatā, Śikhariṇī and Viyoginī. With a wee less than half of the verses to its credit, Indravajrā, Upendravajrā and their mixture Upajāti stand out as the dominant metres in the poem. This is in keeping with the author's pronounced predilection for them, which, in consonance with their variegated character, measure well with the variety of functions they are called upon to discharge in the poem.

The metre, as employed in the *RKM*, adheres to the norm. Each canto is dominated by a single metre which changes towards the close[137] its cadence. It is a

---

134. IV. 35, VI. 3, 5, X. 22, XII. 42, XIV. 48, XXV. 28, etc. etc.

135. सुवृत्तैरिव शोभन्ते प्रबन्धाः सज्जना इव । *Suvṛttatilaka,* III.12

136. काव्यरसानुसारेण वर्णनानुगुणेन च ।
कुर्वीत सर्ववृत्तानां विनियोगं विभागवित् ।। ibid., III.7.

137. एकवृत्तमयैः पद्यैरवसानेऽन्यवृत्तकैः । *SD.*, VI.320

measure of the fancy that the author has taken for Indravajrā and Upajāti – Upendravajrā is not shown separately from Upajāti on account of its rather microscopic existence that they emerge as the chief metres in Sixteen (II,IV, V-VIII, X, XII-XIV, XVI, XIX, XXIII-XXV) of the twenty five cantos of the poem. Some of these cantos (IV, X, XII, XXV) have received a modest sprinkling of other metres, but their dominance remains intact.

Anuṣṭup emerges as the chief metre in four (I,III, XV, XXII) cantos. While Canto Three closes with Indravajrā, it is substituted by Indravajrā and Upajāti in the Twenty second. In Canto One Upajāti has claimed the first five besides the last four stanzas. It (Upajāti) together with Indravajrā seems to rise above the ancillary status in the Fifteenth Canto, a sizeable segment whereof (68-87) has been composed in them. The Second Canto opens with Anuṣṭup (1-2) and closes with Praharṣiṇī (18-19), the rest of the verses having been claimed by Indravajrā and Upajāti.

Apart from Cantos Nine, Eleven, Seventeen, Eighteen and Twenty, the rest of the poem is dominated by Indravajrā and Upajatī. Cantos Four (1-2), Thirteen, Sixteen, Twenty-one, Twenty-three and Twenty-four end with Anuṣṭup. The first twelve verses of the second part of Canto Four have also been couched in Anuṣṭup . The Fifth Canto closes with Vidyunmālā to be replaced by Puṣpitāgrā in the next. Svāgatā ends the Seventh Canto while Drutavilambita concludes the Eighth one. Canto Ten ends with Toṭaka (24-29), Mālinī (30-31) and Upajrāti (32-34). Indravajā and Upajāti also dominate the Twelfth Canto with the difference that while it begins with Anuṣṭup (1-6), Vasantatilakā (41-50) and Anuṣṭup form its concluding meters. Canto Sixteen opens and closes with Anuṣṭup. The Nineteenth and Twenty-fifth Cantos end with Vasantatilakā and Praharṣiṇī respectively. The latter begins with Indravajrā. Verses 28-30 are couched in Svāgatā. In Canto Nine the author has mustered longer metres as well. While the resonant Mandākrāntā forms its major metre, the canto concludes with the tender Mālinī. Indravajrā and Upajāti turn out to be the close second with twenty two verses (32-53). Cantos Eleven and Eighteen bear testimony to the author's ingenuity in handling the difficult Bhujaṅgaprayāta. While the former (XI) ends with Upajāti which also forms the metre that clothes verses 18-20, the intervening stanzas (21-23) have claimed Anuṣṭup which is also the metre with which Canto Eighteen ends. Upajāti (32-33) forms a brief interlude between the chief metre and the concluding Anuṣṭup. It is again the difficult metres, Śikhariṇī and the half-equal Viyoginī that form the basis of Canto Twenty. The first sixteen stanzas in Śikhariṇī are followed by Viyoginī, which being the major metre, has been used for the next sixty three verses (17-79). Upajāti (80-83) wraps up the Canto. The Seventeenth Canto has Svāgatā as its prominent metre. The closing thirteen verses (52-64) are composed in Anuṣṭup. Canto Fourteen also ends with Svāgata. Anuṣṭup has claimed the intervening ten stanzas.

While the metres in the *RKM* do not follow any set pattern, some of the cantos (XXI, XXII), not unlike the trend in the *IC*, begin with the metre that concludes the preceding canto. The author seems to have been rather demanding on Indravajrā and Upajāti. He has called upon it to be an effective medium for a wide spectrum of subjects, emotions and situations. It is a tribute as much to the author's skill as to the vitality of Indravajrā and Upajāti that the ubiquitous metres have been equal to such diverse subjects as exile, abduction, combat, love, hatred, Vātsalya, journey, conspiracy, stratagem, estrangement and rapprochement. The Anuṣṭup, on the other hand, has been used to deal with situations that demand speedy disposal or are narrative in character. That is why it has been picked up as the dominant metre in Canto One, Fifteen and Twenty-two which abound in minute deatils, being mainly narrative in nature.

It is a tribute to the author's sense of discrimination that he employs Viyoginī metre in describing a situation that is to result in the *viyoga*, separation, from Rāma of Sītā. It is again a tribute to his flair for choice of metre suiting a particular situation that the happy denouement of the union of Rāma and Sītā, a source of joy for everybody he has described in Praharṣiṇī metre which means the joy-giver.

The approaching of Hanumān and Aṅgada to Gopura and their being welcomed by him is appropriately described in the Svāgatā metre which carries incidentally, the maximum rhyme and alliteration. The heaving up and down which goes with Svāgatā and which the metre imparts to the vocables, invests the verse with unique charm. It is again a tribute to his skill in Prosody that a rather difficult *ardhasama*, (half-equal) metre like Viyoginī (its difficult nature can be guaged from the fact even a poet like Kālidāsa has employed it as a major metre only once in his Nineteen-Canto *Raghuvaṁśa)* is carried on to a considerable length covering as many as sixty-three stanzas.

The *RKM* has the distinction of being the sole Sanskrit Mahākāvya to present the Rāma-story in its foreign (non-Indian) setting. The appellation suggests its close adherence to the *Ramakien*, generally believed to owe its origin to the Sanskrit word *Rāmakīrti*. It is a happy coincidence that named as *Rāmakīrtimahākāvyam*, it ends with the word *kīrti.*[138] With the *RKM* the author's poetic achievements touch a new high. Because of its multitudinous excellences, the *RKM* adds a new dimension to modern Sanskrit literature.

---

138. लोकेऽस्मिन्विमलतमामवाप कीर्तिम् । *RKM,* XXV. 31

CHAPTER THREE

KHAṆḌAKĀVYAS

(i) BṚHATTARAṀ BHĀRATAM
(ii) ŚRĪGURUGOVINDASIṀHACARITAM
(iii) ŚARMAṆYADEŚAḤ SUTARĀṀ VIBHĀTI
(iv) THAIDEŚAVILĀSAM

BṚHATTARAṀ BHĀRATAM

In consonance with the author's predilection for unconventional subjects, the *Bṛhattaraṁ Bhāratam* (*BB*)[1] addresses itself to capture, in a century of verses, the glory of what was proudly termed as Greater India; with Cambodia, the ancient Kambujadeśa included therein stealing the thunder. The poem is divided into two broad sections (*aṁśas*), the latter being again split into four well-marked sub-divisions. The first section purports, for all practical purposes, to be a prologue to the drama that unfolds itself in the subsequent verses. Girdled by sea, the host of islands such as Yava, Bāli, Suvarṇa, Kambuja, etc. that Greater India was composed of, are loosely designated as Indian Colonies in Southeast Asia. On closer consideration, however, they appear to have been cultural outposts inasmuch as the islands were annexed not by imperialistic forces with pronounced territorial designs but by bands of cultural crusaders who left the Indian shores, in the fourth or fifth century A.D. with the sublime aim of civilising the islanders so that they might be brought into the dominant cultural stream that flowed forth at the time. That convincingly accounts for the feat that brought them under the umbrella of Indian culture without shedding so much as even a drop of blood. By all accounts, it was *dharmavijaya* as enjoined upon by ancient theoreticians of the land. The mission of the Indian crusaders met with quick success (*prayatnasambhārah phalegrahir abhūd iti,* 4). The implications of this *dharmavijaya* should be obvious from the fact that the religion and culture of these lands bear remarkable resemblance with the Indian way of life:

आचारश्च विचारश्च धर्माचरणमेव च ।
भारतीयेन संवादि द्वीपस्थानामसंशयम् ॥ 5

Sub-section one (15-32) of the second part of the poem sets forth, in brief, the various considerations that might have actuated the enterprising Indians to embark upon the adventurous voyage. In a way, the segment amounts to a recapitulation of the different views on the issue. While, as the author avers, it is difficult to pinpoint any single reason, the missionary zeal (*dharmapracāra* ,14) seems to have been the factor that set them on the perilous journey. Earlier Aśoka the Great had despatched to these islands missionaries to spread the message of Buddhism. It is the result

---

1. *Sārasvatī Suṣamā*, Sampurnanand Sanskrit Vishvavidyalaya, Varansi, Vol.XII. No.1. Saṁvat 2014.

of such concerted efforts that the impact of Indian religion and culture is perceptible on many walks of their life. A corpus of Sanskrit inscriptions, heaven-kissing temples and monasteries, mostly in ruins now, mural paintings, and dance and music bear testimony to the profound influence that India has exercised on these islands. They also share with the Hindus such personal names as Rāma, Kṛṣṇa, Sītā, Sarasvatī, etc. Notwithstanding their conversion to Islam, the stories from the Indian epics and Purāṇas are woven into their social fabric. So are a host of Sanskrit words that have permeated their language, with slight modifications. Some Vedic and Buddhistic rites and Saṁskāras are also observed.

The next segment (33-81) is by far the longest unit of the poem. As revealed by its title Kambujadvīpavarṇanam, it describes the history of Kambujadvīpa, the present-day Cambodia. It is a measure of the author's acquaintance with the history of the land and his undoubted mastery over Sanskrit verse that the entire history of Cambodia, with its glory and decline, has come to vibrate with life in less than sixty verses, in a medium that deserves the connoisseur's encomia. It was the unnamed ruler of the Kuṇḍina dynasty, who, fired with a zeal to broaden Indian cultural umbrella, sailed to the distant Southeastern countries, in the third century A.D. He married a Cambodian princess and set himself upon taming the Cambodian people who "bereft of virtues were one with the beasts and roamed naked promiscuously" (36-37). Some of his successors annexed to their country the neighbouring Laos, Malaya and parts of Indo-China. These early rulers were first to establish diplomatic relations with Indo-china that brought them mutual benefit. In the sixth century A.D. there ruled a king Jayavarman by name. His son Rudravarman and his wife Kulaprabhāvatī had won many a laurel. Their inscriptions are remarkable in preserving the complete account of the dynasty (*varṇanākhilā*,41). Jayavarman of this dynasty was viewed as a virtual deity on account of which his regime was undoubtedly the golden period of Cambodian history. The extremely exquisite mansions of his period bespeak the grandeur and affluence that characterised his rule. Jayavarman II was followed by Yaśovarman. True to his name, he was an embodiment of glory (*yaśaḥ*). Yaśovarman was a colourful ruler with many-sided personality. He represented a unique mix of a powerful but benevolent ruler, great warrior, patron of arts and letters, a great grammarian and a gifted architect. He is known to have written a perceptive *Vṛtti* on Patañjali's *Mahābhāṣya*. His building-activities are reflected in a series of temples, hermitages and monasteries (52-53). He is credited to have built a second capital, Kambupurī by name that came to be subsequently called Yaśodharā. A religious man, he was committed to the weal of his people. These multiple qualities earned him immaculate fame that permeated with its aroma the whole earth (*suvāsyate 'dyāpi hi sāgarāmbarā*, 54).

He was succeeded by Sūryavarman I. He assimilated into his empire countries like Śyāmadeśa that had not been conquered by his predecessors. His successor was Sūryavarman II. A powerful ruler, he founded Angkorvat. He raided Champa but died in the midst of the operation. Subsequently the naval forces of Indraka, the ruler of Champā, razed his capital to the ground. After him, his son Jayavarman VII ascended the throne. He was a man of action. It was he who brought Champa under his control and annexed several other countries. Under him the kingdom registered great expansion and alround progress. He built the capital city of Nagardom that surpassed in excellence even the mythical Alakā. Nagardom was encircled by a stout rampart of stones. Around it, he built a moat ten miles long and hundred yards wide. Jayavarman was a deeply religious and generous monarch. In generosity he is said to have surpassed the famed Śibi. He invested generous amounts for the administration of the temples. He appointed thousands of Brāhmaṇas to conduct daily service in the temples. One of his inscriptions reveals that he had been instrumental in building 798 temples and two hundred other places of worship. Always enterprising, he constructed many a road-side booths for public use. With Jayavarman closes the line of the Kambuja rulers. Cambodia fell on evil days in the fourteenth century. The country that once reigned supreme fell to the French and lost its glory.

The next part entitled Śailendrarājyavarṇanam is the shortest unit in the poem. It consists of mere nine verses. Since it encompassed many a Southeast Asian country, the Śailendra empire was so extensive that it took one at least two years to circumambulate it in a swift ship. Powerful neighbouring countries maintained diplomatic relations with the Śailendra empire. The ancient inscriptions also testify to its unprecedented glory. Though the powerful empire disappeared in due course a band of rulers continued to rule in Yavadvīpa. Their account is to be found in the poem *Nāgarakṛtāgama*.

The sub-section captioned Bālidvīpavarṇanam forms the closing part of the poem. Overwhelmed by the Muslims, the ruler of Yavadvīpa, alongwith his people, shifted to the Bālidvīpa (Borneo) in the 15th century. Bāli still preserves a host of vestiges of Indian culture and Hindu religion.

CRITIQUE :

Though written in the Śataka tradition, it widely differs from the earlier writings. Contrary to most of the Śatakas, it is thematic in character. It is doubtless divided into certain units, but the common thread of the history of Greater India binds them together with the result the *Bṛhattaraṁ Bhāratam* is an integrated poem that does not lend itself to fragmentation. Nor do its verses, like the muktakas, stand in isolation. Despite its independent units, the poem is marked by cohesion.

The treatment of the subject is uneven. With the Kambujadvīpa claiming the better part of the poem, the other settlements have been disposed of rather hastily.

Perhaps, it is difficult to be exhaustive in the narrow limits of mere one hundred verses. The description of the Śailendra empire, "which became the dominant power both on sea and land in the whole of Malaysia by the eighth century, and at the height of its power included Malaya, Ceylon, Sumatra, part of Java, Borneo, Celebes, the Phillipines and part of Formosa, and probably exercised suzerainty over Cambodia and Champa"[2] leaves much to be desired. While the Arab historiographers are a reliable source of its history (84), the Indian accounts cannot be dismissed as inconsequential. The poet alludes, rather vaguely, to the vastness of the Śailendra Empire (85), its conflict with the Cholas of South India that had been chiefly instrumental in wrecking its dominance,[3] is inexplicably omitted. The Majapahit Empire, that owes its name to the city of Majapahit founded in 1292, grew at its expense, the Javan state having already thrown away the yoke of the Śailendras in the ninth century[4].

It is the description of Cambodia (Kambujadvīpa) that forms the heart of the poem. In view of the great cultural and architectural boom that it registered in the four hundred years of its existence under a succession of brilliant rulers, the poet has rightly apportioned the major part of the poem to its description. But for the vagueness that marks its early history, he has been specific and exhaustive in detailing the tremendous strides that it took in various fields including art, culture, literature and architecture. All this is couched in such a chaste and lucid language that the splendour and wealth of Cambodia have come to be invested with life that one can assuredly feel. Yaśovarman emerges as the best of the Cambodian rulers. He was a great warrior, powerful ruler, imaginative builder and a mighty scholar. His *Vṛtti* on the *Mahābhāṣya* is unfortunately lost. No less conspicuous were the achievements of Jayavarman VII. Besides building a new capital, he expanded his empire at the expense of Champā and other neighbouring countries. The author has depicted the achievements of the two rulers with a totality that seeks to project them in their multi-focal splendour. The stanzas, reproduced below, forcefully highlight the different aspects of Yaśovarman's dynamic personality :

पवित्रचर्येऽथ जनानुरञ्जके जनाधिनाथे पृथिवीं प्रशासति ।

प्रजा बभूवुः सकला निरामया बभूव राष्ट्रं सकलं निरीति च ।। 46

---

2. *Discovery of India*, 1969, p.205
3. ibid., p.206
4. ibid.

न केवलं तस्य रणेऽतिपाटवं जनाधिनाथस्य बभूव विश्रुतम् ।
कलासु दाक्ष्यं सकलासु तास्वपि जहार चेतांसि भृशं मनस्विनाम् ।।
कृतश्रमः शास्त्रचये विचक्षणो विलक्षणः प्रौढिमवाप्य निर्वृतः ।
सदा कवीनामुपजीव्यतां गतो दिगन्तविश्रान्तयशा बभूव सः ।।
पतञ्जलेर्व्याकरणेऽतिविश्रुता कृतिर्महाभाष्यमिति प्रसंज्ञिता ।
नृपेण सूक्ष्मेक्षिकया युतेन सा स्वकीयवृत्त्या समयोजि हृद्यया ।।
स वास्तुविद्यानिपुणो जनप्रियो बहूनि देवायतनानि निर्ममे ।
तदीयभक्त्या दिवि भक्तवत्सलाः सुराः प्रसेदुः परया महौजसः ।।

The following stanza, on the other hand, sums up the character of Jayavarman VII :

प्रशस्यचर्यो गुणिनामपश्चिमो जयाभिधानः खलु राजसत्तमः ।
अधर्मभीरुर्दृढभक्तिसंयमः प्रदानशीलो ननु शालते नृपः ।। 72

The author has referred to the various possibilities that might have led to the 'extraordinary expeditions across perilous seas'. Though broadly non-committal, he expresses himself in favour of the supreme zeal of the Indian people to carry the message of their religion and culture to the distant lands of Southeast Asia that drove them to undertake hazardous sea-voyage[5]. It however appears to be the half truth. Jawaharlal Nehru seems to be more convincing in the belief that "trade and adventure and the urge for expansion drew them to these eastern lands which were comprehensively described in old Sanskrit books as the Svarṇabhūmi, the land of Gold.....It was only (later) that the political element came from India, some Kṣatriya princes, cadets of the noble families, in search of adventure and domination[6].

The *Bṛhattaraṁ Bhāratam* is written in a verse that is characterised by lucidity, sweetness and natural flow. However, occasionally there appears to be a deliberate effort to incorporate learned forms of grammar, which is undoubtedly the poet's first love. कामयाञ्चक्रिरे (13), कैमर्थिकीम्, पारेसमुद्रम् (16), प्रथमे तितीर्षवः (18), आलोकमालोकम् (28), नृपाः ----पराजिग्यिरे (91) are some such forms.

----

5. *Bṛhattaraṁ Bhāratam*, 15-22
6. *Discovery of India*,op.cit.,p.203

The *Bṛhattaraṁ Bhāratam* is, in essentials, a 'matter of fact' poem. The narration of history does not lend itself to poetic flourishes or niceties. However, it is a measure of the poet's equipment that his narrative perforce mustered certain figures of speech, both of word and meaning. As attested by the author's other poems as well, alliteration is his favourite *alaṁkāra* which he has used in the *Bṛhattaraṁ Bhāratam* with effect. Not unoften, the alliteration here has resulted into sweet *padalālitya*. The following verse forms perhaps the best illustration of both the Anuprāsa and *padalālitya* :

प्रजास्तस्य साम्राज्यविभ्रंशदूनाः श्रिया नाम हीना गुणैर्जात्वहीनाः ।
स्वपुत्रैः कलत्रैः सुहृद्भिः समेता उपेतास्ततो द्वीपकं बालिसंज्ञम् ।। 98

Vibhāvanā is reflected in the feat of the Indian settlers who had gained victory over the islands without battle, weapon and army :

विना युद्धं विना शस्त्रं विना सेनाश्च भीषणाः ।
विना नीतिं पुरा द्वीपा भारतीयैर्विनिर्जिताः ।। 12

Simile is found in the description of Yaśovarman. After his victory he shone forth like the sun at the disappearance of the clouds :

रराज सोऽपि प्रथमो जयैषिणां घनव्यपायेन गभस्तिमानिव ।। 47

The collapse of the Bali kingdom is depicted with Dṛṣṭānta :

सुखं प्राज्यराज्ये चिरं संस्थितानां नृपाणां निपातो ध्रुवोऽस्तीति विद्धि ।
जगद् भानुभिर्भासयित्वा प्रकामं रविः श्रान्तकायोऽस्तमद्रिं प्रयाति ।। 94

Virodha (18) and Kāvyaliṅga (48) are the other notable *alaṁkāras* in the poem. A poem like the *Bṛhattaraṁ Bhāratam* does not provide the author many occasions to display his skill in handling various metres. He, however, has sought to relieve the monotony of the narrative by inducting new metres at appropriate places. In all he has employed here five metres. They are as follows : Anuṣṭup, Upajāti, Vaṁśastha, Vasantatilaka and Bhujaṅgaprayāta.

The *Bṛhattaraṁ Bhāratam* is perhaps the solitary Śataka on the subject that is at once novel and refreshing. The sweetness of Sanskrit verse heightens the grandeur that Greater India represented. Like the *SGGSC* and *Tdv.*, the *Bṛhattaraṁ*

Bhāratam may be rated as a historical poem. It is not the poetic flights but the novelty of the subject and its imaginative presentation in a blemishless medium that account for its worth.

ŚRĪGURUGOVINDASIṀHACARITAM

True to M. Winternitz's observation, the Sanskrit language includes in its ambit all that stands for literature. As a truly representative national language it has never known, down the ages, any ethnic or sectarian barriers. While even some of the hostile Muslim rulers extended liberal patronage to Sanskrit for no apparent advantage to themselves, the Sanskritists, on their part, reciprocated the generosity by culling their themes from a wide range of sources without distinctions of religion or language whatsoever. The Sikh history has claimed the sweet medium of Sanskrit from quite early times. Dr. Satya Vrat Shastri's *Śrīgurugovindasiṁhacaritam* (*SGGSC*)[1] is the solitary versified biography of Guru Gobind Singh that he was drafted to compose on the tricentenary celebration of the birth of the tenth Guru by the Guru Gobind Singh Foundation, Patiala, the other work being Pandit Shruti Kant's translation into Sanskrti of Sardar Harbans Singh's biography of the Guru in Punjabi. It was indeed laudable on the part of the Foundation to have thought of tendering homage to the Guru in Sanskrit, which symbolises the very soul of the nation. It was all the more worthy in view of the fact that the Guru himself was a great scholar and patron of Sanskrit. It is doubtless more in tune with the genius of the language to opt for the Sanskrit verse, a medium that was zealously espoused by the Guru.

SUMMARY :

Divided into four cantos and composed of 366 verses in different metres, the SGGSC, would be rated as a *Khaṇḍakāvya* technically though in performing the prohibitive task of dealing with the Guru's chequered career in its entirety and not being confined to any of its facets (*ekadeśa*) it could be rated as a Prabandha Kāvya. Canto One compresses in 89 verses the events from Gobind Singh's birth at Patna to his assuming the stewardship of the community as the tenth pontiff, at Anandpur. Born while his father Guru Tegh Bahadur was on a missionary work in Assam, the child's brief sojourn at Patna under the fond care of his pious mother and grandmother besides his maternal uncle Kripal Singh, served to establish him in a variety of ways as a man of God (*Brahmamayaḥ pumān*, I.6). His loss of the birth place at the age of six was substantially offset by his union with his great father at Anandpur (*ānandapūraṁ janake vitanvan,* I.41). However, much suffering awaited him there. The child had to undergo harrowing agony in the brutal beheading of his father at Delhi under orders of the bigot Aurangzeb, on the Guru's refusal to embrace Islam. The supreme sacrifice that the Guru made was to uphold all that he cherished

1. Guru Gobind singh Foundation, Patiala, 1967

justice, freedom and human dignity. Tegh Bahadur's ghastly murder was frowned upon by the divine forces as well. Delhi was rocked to its moorings by a terrible storm (*bhīmarūpaś cacāra vātyāmiṣato nabhasvān*, I.64). The ninth Guru's venerable head that rolled on the earth was surruptitiously removed by one Jeta to Anandpur at a lightning speed (*vidyugatiś cāpasasāra tasmāt sthānāt tathānandapuraṁ ca sa prait*, I.66). While the child Gobind Singh received and consigned to sacred flames his father's head with rare equipoise, a Labana trader removed his trunk (*kabandha*) to his house and in a rare act of devotion set his house aflame to escape the royal wrath (*śiṣyas tato 'yaṁ svagṛhaṁ dadāha*, I.69). At the request of the concourse, the followers of his father, Gobind Singh assumed the leadership of the community. He was consecrated the tenth Guru on the first day of Vaiśākha at Anandpur with the coconut and five paise that his father had got despatched to him prior to his sacrifice. Guru Tegh Bahadur had sufficiently roused his people against the religious oppression and bigotry. The new Guru launched upon the task of firing the community with the spirit of sacrifice and fight against persecution of all hues with right earnestness.

With Canto II the scene shifts, albeit temporarily, to Nahan, the lovely hill-resort in the Shivaliks, which Guru Gobind Singh visited at the invitation of its ruler. It was there that he married at the age of nineteen, Sundari, the comely daughter of Bhikha. True to her name, Sundari belied the odium heaped on the creator for bringing about, more often than not, unequal marriages. At the irresistible insistence of his kith and kin he married next year, the lovely Jito. However, he declined to accept Sahib Diwan (*Kaur*), the daughter of one of his close disciples; but in view of her unflinching devotion to him, he admitted her to his fold to become the Mother of the Khalsa Panth that he founded subsequently. He was so fascinated by the exceptionally serene and lovely bank of the Yamunā that he founded thereon an impregnable citadel and named it Paonta. The citadel became for quite some time the hub of his manifold activities. He invited a galaxy of fifty two scholars to instruct the people in ancient śāstras and Purāṇas. He himself learnt quite a few languages including Sanskrit, Persian and Brajabhāṣā from them and thereafter embarked upon the literary spree. It was at Paonta that the Guru composed his famous Hymn to Caṇḍī, *Caṇḍī dī var* and the *Akāla Puja* and a host of other works. The *magnum* opus, written by the 52 scholars was unfortunately swept away by the current of the Yamunā in flood. After his two meetings with his grandfather Rama Raya, followed by the latter's death, the Guru returned to his base at Anandpur. The return of the Guru inspired confidence in his people. Soon thereafter Bhim Singh, the ruler of Bilaspur waited upon him to request for military help against the Mughal Governor Mian Khan, who was threatening him with dire consequences through his commander Alif Khan. The Guru readily accepted his request for it was his mission to help the people against the tyrants (*satāṁ hi rakṣā paramaṁ vrataṁ naḥ*, II.42). The terrible blow of their joint forces at Nadon put Alif's hordes on their heel *(raṇājirād eva palāyatāśu*, II.46). The defeat of the Mughal army infuriated Aurangzeb. He ordered his commanders in Punjab to ask Gobind Singh to behave. The Guru treated the message with contempt. He geared up his forces to meet the impending attack. Under his command the Sikhs concentrated at Anandpur. That added fuel to Aurangzeb's wrath (*krodhena sammūrchitaḥ*, II.54). Under his orders Dilawar Khan, the governor of Kangra, sent an expedition under his son against the Guru. He had planned to take the Sikhs by surprise in a nocturnal operation, but the presence of mind and timely action of the Sikhs struck terror in the Muslim forces to the extent that they fled away like so many rabbits (*palāyanaṁ cāpi hi sāmpratam me,* II.60). The humiliating conduct of his forces enraged Dilawar Khan into undertaking a swifter operation. He despatched another expedition, this time under his commander Hussain. While he subjugated the other hilly rulers, Gopal, the ruler of Guler, in alliance with Ram Singh of Jaswal challenged the Muslim forces. In the terrific battle that ensued Hussain's band of hire-lings tumbled under the combined attack and perished like a ship caught in a storm (*vātyeritaḥ pota ivāmbujrāśau*, II.68). Hussain was killed, so was his ally, the ruler of Katoch. The Guru blessed the victorious forces of Gopal and Ram Singh. Though humbled time and again, Aurangzeb decided to fight it out once more. Ill-luck awaited him this time also. His army was badly mauled by the doughty combatants of Jaswal (*tām āpatantīṁ tarasā 'dhvanīnāṁ vidhvaṁsayāmāsa bhaṭaiḥ svakīyaiḥ*, II.74). In a final bid the Mughal emperor sent his son Muazzam to Punjab to suppress the Sikhs once for all. Muazzam put up his camp at Lahore. While planning operation against the Guru, the prince was advised by his minister Nand Lal not to burn his fingers with the Guru, an ascetic and saint as he was. The advice had the desired effect. Muazzam decided not to desecrate the holy resort of the Guru. Relieved of the impending danger, the Guru retreated into meditation.

Canto III describes in essentials the founding of the Khalsa. Sure of peace, at least for the present, the Guru engaged himself in literary pursuits. While he composed his autobiography, the *Vicitranāṭaka*; his literary circle (*Paṇḍitamaṇḍalī*), translated a lot of Sanskrit classics into vernacular. However, perhaps as a reflex to the preceding military engagements, the Guru was constantly grappling to charter for himself a pious path (*puṇyamārga*) to protect the honour and identity of his people. After considerable deliberation he evolved the Khalsa Panth on the Baisakhi day at Anandpur and initiated into the new order five of his devoted disciples who came to be known as Five Dear ones (*Pañcapriyāḥ*). At the behest of the Guru the newly initiated disciples, in turn, initiated the Guru in the order (*dīkṣayatādhunā mām*, III.41). The organisation of the Khalsa infused new life into the harried community. It evoked wide following. People irrespective of caste, creed and sex joined the Panth in thousands. While all this brought glory to the Guru, it served to inflame the malice of the hill-rulers. They formed a confederation and attacked the Guru a number of times but were uniformly beaten back (*jetuṁ guruṁ jātu śaśāka nāpi*, III.49). Frustrated in their designs, they sought the help of the Mughal emperor Aurangzeb to achieve their nefarious objective. Their forces intent upon destroying it as storm does the tree or hail-balls the crop, besieged the Guru's citadel like a mighty river. So complete was the siege that the town was left with no food and drink. While the Sikhs themselves were deliberating the escape to a safer haven, Aurangzeb offered to lift the siege in case the Guru agreed to vacate the town along with his concourse. Though not unaware of the evil stratagems of the wicked Mughal, the Guru saw merit in shunning resistance and conducted his people out of Anandpur with a heavy heart. The sacred town was overwhelmed with the enemy.

Canto IV, as it rings curtain on the poem, is full of an overabundance of details. True to apprehensions, the Muslim forces swooped on the retreating Sikhs and inflicted heavy losses on them. A number of Sikhs were swept away by the swift current of the Sirsā, while trying to cross it in the nocturnal darkness to save themselves from the pursuing Mughals. Others ran helter-skelter. The Guru was reduced to such straits that he had to seek refuge in a mud-house at the Chamkor village alongwith a posse of his soldiers. The Muslims chased them to their hideout. It was the heroic battle that the Sikhs, merely forty in number, fought with the numerically superior army of Aurangzeb at Chamkor. When half of the Sikhs had fallen, Ajit Singh, the young son of Guru Gobind Singh darted forward with the blessings of his father to spell doom on the enemy. Unable to withstand the ferocity of his arrows, the peers of the dreadful tongues of Kālī, the enemy took to heels. However, he was soon surrounded by the Mughal soldiers and like Abhimanyu he died a hero's death on the battle-field. The Guru's second son Jujhar Singh also met the same end. Finding his stay at Chamkor fraught with dangers, the Guru, at the intercession of his followers, slipped out of the village with three of the five Sikhs who had survived the combat. The two who stayed back fell fighting the wicked enemy. In this hopeless situation the age-worn mother of the Guru alongwith his two young sons unluckily fell into the trap of one Gangu, who, under the guise of providing her succour and shelter robbed her of her valuables and reported their whereabouts to the ruler of Sirhind. The sons were immediately captured and thrown in the prison. When all persuasions, inducements and threats failed to break their iron will and they persisted in their refusal to embrace Islam, the brave boys were put to sword by the bigot ruler of Sirhind (*bhṛtyās tayor hā śirasī akṛntan*, IV.74). The Guru received the terrible news with an equipoise that is associated with a man of God (*tvayy arpitam, me 'sti na ko 'pi khedaḥ*, IV.76). While he was camping at Dina Nagar along with his three disciples, the Guru received an invitation from Aurangzeb to come to the south for working out a treaty of peace with him, which he declined firmly (*nāgantum īśe diśi dakṣiṇasyām*, IV. 82) but offered him, if he so desired, to meet him at Kangra in Punjab. During his stay at Damdama (*Lakhijangal*), the Guru revised the holy Granth. When his message did not evoke response from Aurangzeb, he, on his own, proceeded to meet him but returned on hearing of his death. Muazzam (Bahadur Shah) sought and got the Guru's help in the fratricidal war with his brother Kam Baksh. Muazzam came out victorious and expressed his gratitude to the Guru. He also accompanied Muazzam to the South to put down a rebellion by his governor. The two became intimate friends. At Nanded the Guru baptized Madhavadas Vairagi into his order and christened him Banda Bairagi. The Guru sent him to Punjab to punish the tyrant rulers there. While there he sustained stab wounds inflicted by the two Pathans, the secret agents of the ruler of Sirhind, in a nocturnal operation. Though the two were put to sword immediately, the Guru succumbed to the wounds. Before breathing his last, the Guru asked his disciples to treat the holy Granth their Guru because it was his soul and body. While singing the glory of Khalsa, he attained fusion into Brahman.

FORMAT OF THE POEM :

In the poeticians's jargon, the *SGGSC*, as observed earlier, is a Khaṇḍakāvya, though, in defiance of his injunctions, it details, albeit briefly, the Guru's life in its entirety. The eventful career of the Guru marked by an exuberance of vicissitudes, thrilling and elevating, forms a subject for a Mahākāvya. While in its present form, the poem seems to be weighed down with abundant details, the Mahākāvya would have provided the author with a wider canvas to deal with the varied events in the Guru's career in greater details.

However, it would be idle to visualise for the *SGGSC* a format that it does not profess to have. It should be dispassionate to evaluate the poem as it stands. And the fact of the matter is that it describes, in brief, the variegated career of the Guru in verses that are at once elegant and elevating. it is doubtless intended to be a versified biography of the great Guru. This is what the name of the poem suggests and the author candidly admits[2] with equal certitude that it may be called a historical poem. As a biography it exemplifies the modern concept of biography. And contrary to the ancient Caritakāvyas its narrative is not shrouded in the overgrowth of conventional trappings, which, whatever their poetic worth, form insurmountable hurdles in its smooth flow and tend to undermine the worth of the biography by the frequent digressions that they essentially constitute. Here the narrative flows uninterrupted by prolix descriptions. Whatever descriptions we have in the poem are invariably brief and seem to be skilfully interwoven in the texture of the narrative. The

---

2. *Śrigurugovindasiṁhacaritam* (*SGGSC*), Preface, p.1.

frame of the poem is undoubtedly fragile to sustain the massive narrative enlivened by the equally tremendous personality of the Guru. But it is the brevity of the expression that turns out to be its asset. Obviously the poet has no fascination for the conventional descriptions that overwhelm the narrative in the Caritakāvya and thereby turn it into fiction rather than history. It is precisely because of the balanced conception of biography that the poem emerges as an excellent historical Kāvya and thereby seems to debunk the unkind charge that Sanskrit language cannot claim genuine history to its credit. The *SGGSC* is as good a historical poem, as interesting as a biography as it is a poem. The blend of poetry and history makes it out as one of the best biographies/historical poems in Sanskrit verse. The *SGGSC* is as readable a biography as Louis Fisher's biography of Mahatma Gandhi or Frank Morase's biography of Nehru, with the added sweetness of Sanskrit poetry distinguished by dynamism and piousness of the Guru that it seeks to delineate in inspiring tones.

GURU GOBIND SINGH AS PROFILED IN THE POEM :

The profile of Guru Gobind Singh, as attempted in the poem, does not differ from what we know of him from other sources including his own writings. To be sure, like all great men the Guru was endowed with a multi-dimensional and dynamic personality. As a man of action and as a godhead he does not differ from Lord Kṛṣṇa as he is projected in the *Gītā*. Like him he was the Supreme light, the embodiment of bliss (I.14), the great God (*Prabhur eṣa sākṣāt* I.26) who had descended on the earth with the specific mission of upholding righteousness, destroying wickedness and defending the values that usher in social discipline. The poet has sought to capture the totality of the Guru's personality in two beautiful verses :

धर्मस्य गोप्ता सुजनस्य पाता
गोब्राह्मणानां परिरक्षिता च ।
विद्वन्मनोमोहयिता गुणैः स्वै-
र्दुष्टस्य यो दण्डयिता जनस्य ।।
यन्नाममात्रश्रवणेन सद्यः
सैन्यं रिपूणां बिभयाञ्चकार ।
कोपारुणाक्षः स्फुरिताधरो यः
साक्षादयुग्माक्ष इवाबभासे ।। I.23

The poem leaves little doubt about he divinity of the Guru. He is called the man of God (*brahmayasya puṁsaḥ,* I.5). His body exuded an aura of divinity. (*divyaṁ vapuḥ kāntim atho ca divyām*, I.26). He represents the refulgence of the sun and charm of the moon (*sa tejasā sūryaśatapratāpaḥ kāntyā tathā cenduśatābhirāmaḥ*, I.14). The Upaniṣadic simile that is whipped up to illustrate the impossible phenomenon of a child playing on the laps of two mothers, also bears testimony to his divine character (*yatha śaśī krīḍati khe jale ca, tathaiva saṁkrīḍam atra me,stu,* I.37). It was his objective to eradicate from the world evil of all hues and thereby contribute to the weal of the society (*lokasya kalyāṇam abhīpsur eṣaḥ,* III.4).

As a defender of faith, the Guru geared himself, rather the whole community, to meet the tyranny and oppression that the Mughal emperor Aurangzeb and his agents and allies had unleashed on the hapless people to force them to submit to Islam. He was convinced that it was difficult to protect the faith without imparting martial orientation to the movement (*kṣātreṇa dharmeṇa vinā nahi syāt svadharamarakṣā,* I. 79). He equipped himself in warfare to ultimately emerge as an embodiment of martial powers (*savigrahaḥ Kṣatriyadharma eṣaḥ,* I.82). But he was in search of a permanent antidote to tyranny and evil. That he found in the organisation of the Khalsa. The dramatic manner in which he chalked out the holy path (*puṇyamārgaḥ*) at Anandpur Sahib, fired the oppressed people into unprecedented zeal to uphold the noble principles for which the Khalsa was founded and stood. Dr. Raghavan has tellingly recapitulated the circumstances that led to the birth of Khalsa. As observed by him, "the fifth Guru Arjun was executed by the Mughal ruler and the indignation at this led to the sixth Guru Har Gobind giving the first martial orientation to the movement. In the same manner the ninth Guru Tegh Bahadur made at Delhi the greatest sacrifice with his life for the cause of the Hindus and this led his son, successor to the Guruship at the age of ten, to organise the Sikhs as a military community with the mission of protecting the people from the oppression and atrocities......The Sikhs (the disciples) he made into Singhs (lions). It is not a transformation of the religious into the military but an integration of the spiritual and the active."[3]

The Khalsa that the Guru founded was intended to defend the faith as much from the external threats as from the internal accretions that threatened to sap it dry. In order to ensure human brotherhood that the Khalsa espoused, the Guru did away with all distinctions of caste, creed and religion (*na dharmabhedo na ca jātibhedo, na deśabhedo na ca varṇabhedaḥ,* III.46). It was again to remove all distinctions in the form of worship that the Guru enjoined upon his disciples to worship only one

---

3. ibid., Foreword, p.iv

God, the Akālapuruṣa, beyond time and space and not to bow before any image, idol, sepulchre or grave. With a view to giving still more practical shape to his ideals of equality and commonness, the Guru introduced the institution of community kitchens in which people from all strata of society took meals together without so much as even an iota of complexes (*āryā anāryā mṛtapās tathā ca... samāśanaṁ cakrur atīva modāt*, I.85).

As a man of God, Guru Gobind Singh was blessed with an exceptional equipoise which did not yield to the gravest disasters. The siege of Anandpur and the unequal battle at Chamkaur were events that could have worn down even a man of steel.The Guru withstood them with rare fortitude. The equanimity with which young Gobind Singh received the severed head of his father and the poise with which he consigned it to the sacred flames are associated with super humans alone. Likewise the Guru's controlled reaction to the beheading of his young sons by the cruel ruler of Sirhind (*tvatto hi labdhaṁ jagadīśa sarvaṁ tvayy arpitaṁ me 'sti na ko'pi khedaḥ, IV.76)*, could have emanated from a *vītarāga* only.

Another aspect of the Guru's personality that is equally winsome is that he combined his multifarious preoccupations with a love for poetry and literature. Amidst the tumult of military engagements and a series of adversities he pursued his literary activities with amazing devotion. He was not only a polyglot but a great poet and patron of letters. His poetry tends to break down narrow sectarian barriers. While he was deeply impressed by the philosophical contents of the Upaniṣads. the *Devī-māhātmya* inspired him to write his *Caṇḍī dī Vār*. With equal devotion he sang the glory of Viṣṇu in his different incarnations.

Thus it is the rounded profile of the Guru that emerges from the poem. He was indeed a pious man, a *Karmayogī*, fired with the zeal to stamp out evil to establish an orderly and ethical society.

POETIC MERITS OF THE *SGGSC*

(i) As a biography that approaches close to the modern concept of the term, the *SGGSC* is dominated by the narrative. And in comparison to it, all else seems to sink into paleness. However, next to the uninterrupted flow of the narrative, shorn of literary gimmicks, it is the poetic excellences that contribute to the success of the poem. While it differs from the modern biography in the poetic medium, from the ancient *Caritakāvyas*, like the *Vikramāṅkadevcarita, Navasāhasāṅkacarita, Harṣacarita*, etc., it differs in pruning, if not mopping down, the accretions and aberrations that beset these so-called biographies and more often than not, are instrumental in pushing the narrative into oblivion. In the *SGGSC* the verse is essentially the vehicle of the narrative which is rich in varied details. The verse in the *SGGSC* reminds one of the *anyūnānatiriktamanohāri-*

ṇyavasthiti of the word and meaning as enjoined upon by Kuntaka. The sublimity of the subject-matter is matched in the poem by the elegance of the expression. Nowhere do the two fall apart. It is this concurrence of the narrative with the medium that raises the poem to a commendable level. The verse in the *SGGSC* is distinguished by chastity and serenity. The limpid flow of its verse is in no way inferior in swiftness to that of a hilly brook. It is capable to carry the variety of situations with effortless ease.

Being chiefly narrative in character, the *SGGSC* does not admit of the type of descriptions one is wont to expect in a Sanskrit Kāvya. Herein the descriptions are reduced to the barest minimum both in number and size. However, despite their slimness in size, they are rich in contents. With his poetic skill, keen observation and sensitive mind the author is well equipped to capture the essence of the situation in pithy verses. The poem is replete with an abundance of situations, both noble and ignoble, elevating and frustrating, sublime and banal. The author has depicted them with such an ease and effect that they are invested with lifelike precision. Aurangzeb's bigotry and brutality, the dreadful appearances of the royal executioners (I.61-65), Guru Tegh Bahadur's supreme sacrifice, the fearless stand of Guru Gobind Singh's young sons in the face of lurking death, military engagements, Guru's poise, scenic beauties-- all this and much else has been briefly described in elegant verses, in a manner that the varied descriptions have come to vibrate with realism. The tyranny and iconoclastic zeal of the wicked Mughal emperor Aurangzeb are vividly depicted in a solitary verse :

स ब्राह्मणान् हन्ति हिनस्ति गाश्च
भनक्ति देवप्रतिमाश्च दुष्टः ।
ददद् बलाद्यावनधर्मदीक्षां
स्वमाततायित्वमथो व्यनक्ति ।। I.45

The verse that follows tellingly highlights the fearsome mien of the executioners. With their dark complexion, burning eyes and sharp weapons they seemed to be the embodiment of cruelty and sinfulness :

राज्ञो वधाज्ञामुपलभ्य हिंस्राः
कालायसप्रख्यरुचो नृशंसाः ।
आरक्तनेत्रा निशितासिहस्ताः

पापौघरूपा वधका नृपस्य ॥ I.60

The spirited reply of the Guru's young sons to the order of the ruler of Sirhind to accept Islam or face death and their consequent beheading is set forth in inspiring tones :

पिता स्वयं धर्ममुपादिशन्नौ
माता ददौ नौ पयसा च धर्मम् ।
धर्माय नौ जीवितमत्र विद्धि
तं धर्ममावां हि कथं त्यजाव ॥ IV.60

आकण्ठमग्नावपि भित्तिमध्य
इस्लामधर्मे न मतिं व्यधत्ताम् ।
दिवि स्थिता देवगणा अपीदं
लोकातिगं कर्म तदभ्यनन्दन् ॥ IV.72

क्रूरोऽतिकोपात्सरहिन्दराजो
वधं तयोस्तूर्णमथादिदेश ।
आदेशमात्रप्रतिपालकाश्च
भृत्यास्तयोर्हा ! शिरसी अकृन्तन् ॥ IV.74

The battle of Chamkor that threatened to be a unilateral affair was converted into a fierce engagement by the resistance the doughty Sikhs put up to the numerically superior Mughal forces. The three verses reproduced below capture the furiousness of the Guru at the treacherous swoop of the enemy and the havoc that he did to him by pressing into service his skill in archery :

समापतन्तीमिव तां स्रवन्तीं
त्रिंशच्च शिष्या दश चैव धीराः ।
वीरातिवीरा रुरुधुर्बलेन
सर्वं तदाश्चर्यकरं बभूव ॥

गुरुस्तदा रुद्र इव प्रजानां

संहारकाले भयमादधानः ।
बाणान् प्रवर्षन् परितः प्रसर्पन्
चञ्चद्द्विजिह्वानिव भीमरूपान् ।।
एको बहूनात्तधनुर्मनस्वी ।
व्यनाशयत्तीव्रबलेन वीरः ।
गाण्डीवधन्वेव रिपोश्चमूनां
चकार घोरं कदनं स तत्र ।। IV.15-17

The poise that Guru Gobind Singh maintained in the face of grave peril and disaster has been delineated in sombre terms. This is how the Man of God reacted to the news of the assassination of his two young sons by the fanatic ruler of Sirhind, close on the heels of the loss of his two other sons in the battle :

वृत्तं यदा दारुणमेतदाप
गोविन्दसिंहो दशमो गुरूणाम् ।
न विव्यथे तस्य तदान्तरङ्गं
हिमालयस्येव भृशं दृढस्य ।।
त्वत्तो हि लब्धं जगदीश ! सर्वं
त्वय्यर्पितं, मेऽस्ति न कोऽपि खेदः ।। IV.75-76

The beauties of nature represent a pole apart from these harrowing happenings. The description of the dense forests in the vicinity of the Yamunā is marked by a sort of verve that is reflected in the swift cadence of the verses. The thrill that the Guru experienced on seeing them is reproduced in the following stanzas. The description is more impressive than the complicated jugglery attempted by many a worthy poet :

एकान्तरम्यं वनखण्डमाराद्
दृष्ट्वा स हृष्टोऽजनि सौम्यदृष्टिः ।
अदृष्टपूर्वा प्रकृतेर्मनोज्ञा
छटा बलात्तस्य जहार चेतः ।। II.13

क्वचिच्च गुञ्जद्भ्रमरौघदृश्यं
क्वचिच्च कूजद्विहगौघदृश्यम् ।
पपौ मनोज्ञं प्रकृतिप्रियोऽसा-
वुपोषिताभ्यामिव लोचनाभ्याम् ॥ II.15

It hardly brooks repetition that as a biography the *SGGSC* is dominated by the narrative. It does not therefore lend itself to the treatment of the sentiments (rasas) in the traditional style. But since it concerns itself with the man, who, though God (*śrīprabhurūpa* eva, I.24), had incarnated himself to root out the evil and establish righteousness, the poem, not infrequently, dwells upon his physical and moral powers in a variety of ways. The depiction of his two-fold valour in the poem culminates in the Virarasa which may be accepted as its chief sentiment (*aṅgīrasa*). The *vīratā* of the Guru, unfolds itself in many hues and contours. His whole life is a saga of heroism. Besides the physical bravery, the Guru is equally rich in *dharma* and *dayā*. All the three aspects of heroism have found vigorous expression in the poem though, due to the limitations imposed on him by its size, the poet could not have been exhaustive in portraying them. The *SGGSC* therefore, bristles with the Guru's *dharmavīratā and dayāvīratā* as well.

The *dharmavīra* aspect of heroism is evident in the poem, from the outset. As a matter of fact, the Guru had taken birth to protect the *dharma* against the onslaughts of fundamentalism let loose by the tyrant rulers. It was again his *dharmavīratā* that galvanised his great father to make the supreme sacrifice in order to ensure the freedom of religion :

तत्क्रोधवह्नौ शलभायते चेद्
भवेत्स्वधर्मस्य ततोऽभिरक्षा ॥ I.46
कोऽन्यो धरायां त्वदृते ऽस्ति तात !
यो दुष्करं कार्यमिदं विदध्यात् ॥ I.47

The unusual composure that he displayed in the face of the heaviest odds, speaks volumes of his moral strength. Neither the severed head of his father nor the loss of his four sons --two in the battle and two to the sword of the beastly ruler of Sirhind--sent him into hysterical wailings. He took it all as the divine verdict, unshaken and unmoved :

कृत्तं शिरस्तज्जनकस्य दृष्ट्वा
न विव्यथे नापि चचाल चित्तम् । 1. 72

वृत्तं यदा दारुणमेतदाप
गोविन्दसिंहो दशमो गुरूणाम् ।
न विव्यथे तस्य तदान्तरङ्गं
हिमालयस्येव भृशं दृढस्य ।।

त्वत्तो हि लब्धं जगदीश ! सर्वं
त्वय्यर्पितं, मेऽस्ति न कोऽपि खेदः ।। IV.75-76

The help that the Guru extended to Muazzam, the son of Aurangzeb who had done the worst to his father, in the fratricidal war and in accompanying him to the south to quell the rebellion may be interpreted as the *dayāvīra* form of his heroism :

म्वजम्समाख्यस्य सुतस्य राज्ञो
निमन्त्रणं प्राप्य तमभ्युपेतः ।
शिष्यैः स्वकैर्वीरवरैस्तदानीं
गुरुर्व्यतानीद् बहु साह्यमस्य ।। IV. 90

सिंहासनारोहणतो बहादुर्
शाहेति नूत्नं भुवि नाम बिभ्रत् ।
निमन्त्रयामास गुरुं सहैतुं
स चापि हर्षेण तमभ्युपायात् ।। IV. 94

The series of battles provide the alluvial soil for heroism to bloom. While the encounters with the hill-rulers, though no less fearsome, were skirmishes of sorts, it is in the unequal battle of Chamkor that the Vīrarasa reaches its denouement. The doom spelt by the Guru, the peer of Śiva, Rudra and Arjuna, reminded one of the destruction of the aeon (*saṁhārakāle bhayam ādadhānaḥ*, IV.16; *Gāṇḍīvadhanveva ripoś camūnāṁ cakāra ghoraṁ kadanaṁ sa tatra*, IV.17).

The most powerful depiction of the Vīrarasa, however, is found in the encounter that Ajit Singh had with the Mughal forces. The enemy had no answer to the young warrior's skill in archery and thought it wiser to take to heels :

करालकालीरसनेव बाणान्
चिक्षेप चण्डाकृतिरात्तधन्वा ।
तं तेजसां राशिमशक्नुवाना
सोढुं प्रदुद्राव चमू रिपूणाम् ॥ IV. 23

Pathos is touchingly evident in the old lady's cursing her lot and wailings at the forcible seizure of her grandsons by the minions of the Sirhind-ruler. That was a prelude to their execution soon thereafter :

सा वेपमाना कदलीव वाते
स्वं भागधेयं च विगर्हमाणा ।
शोकेन दुःखेन च तप्यमाना
मम्लौ द्रुभङ्गे पतितेव वल्ली ॥ IV. 53

The inhuman skinning of Mati Das and Dayalu and their throwing into the boiling water, to break down Gūru Tegh Bahadur is as ghastly as powerful it is in expressing the Raudrarasa :

आशीर्षपादं प्रविदार्य काय-
मार्यस्य दीप्तं मतिदासनाम्नः ।
दयालुसंज्ञस्य निचिक्षिपुस्ते
तप्तोदकुण्डे सुदृढं शरीरम् ॥ I. 56

A glimpse of the Vātsalya is had in the childhood sports of Gobind Singh. The depiction, though subdued, is pleasing :

स बाललीला विविधाः प्रकुर्व-
न्नावर्जयन्नात्मजनस्य चेतः ।
पक्षे विपक्षे व्यभजत्स मित्रा-
ण्यथाकरोत् कौतुकयुद्धमेभिः ॥ I. 20

(iii) The language of the poem is imbued with a refreshing lucidity. That indeed is the hallmark of the author's poetry. However, the *SGGSC* has received a heavy sprinkling of recondite grammatical forms, while it was neither surprising nor unnatural for a grammarian that the author basically is. Some of them seem to have been purposely flung into the poem to overwhelm the reader with his unquestioned equipment in grammar. The number of such learned forms runs into eighty eight. The author is especially fond of the aorist, though some of the forms ending in *kvasu* are equally profuse. It is precisely because of this that at places, they overburden the verses with their complexity. Some of the more complicated forms may be reproduced here. प्रासोष्ट (I.13)T अचीक्लृपत् (I.39); सम्प्रैरिरत् (I.53); समार्पिपन् (I.81); आसीषदत् (II.35); सङ्ग्रहीष्ठाः, कृथाः, सम्बूबुधः (II.49); बिभयाम्बभूव (II.59); अवधिष्टाम् (II.70); मा स्म दत्थाः (II.81); अवातनिष्ट (III.26); प्रार्तथत (III.39); पुरा मारयति श्वमारम् (IV.58); प्रास्थित (IV.93); निजशात्रवाणाम् (IV.30); अवतस्थिवत् (IV.41); बम्भ्रम्यमाणः (IV.83); धर्मविरोधि विद्वान् ----- चकार मायां बहु तत्र विद्वान् (IV.101).

The *SGGSC* is embedded with a number of expressions drawn from the earlier texts including the Upaniṣads. The maximum number of borrowals are from Kālidāsa, the author's favourite classical poet. Verses 63 and 64 of Canto Four are undoubtedly inspired by the *Kaṭhopaniṣad* (I.24-25). The famous line from the *Īśāvāsyopaniṣad – kavir manīṣī paribhuḥ* (VIII) has been slightly modified to highlight the Guru's literary equipment (*gurur manīṣī paribhuḥ*, III.2). The well-known *subhāsita* from the *Mṛcchakaṭika : chidreṣv anarthā bahulībhavanti* (IX.26) is incorporated in IV.120 with a view to stressing the unending nature of the Guru's sufferings. Other such expressions are listed below alongwith their original sources :

Expresions	SGGSC	Source
प्रवर्तितो दीप इव प्रदीपात्	I.4	*Raghuvaṁśa*, V.37
शमीमिवाभ्यन्तरलीनपावकाम्	I.9	*Raghuvaṁśa*, III.9
समानयंस्तुल्यगुणं वधूवरं	II.4	*Śākuntala*, V.15
उपोषिताभ्यामिव	II.15	*Raghuvaṁśa*, II.19
समुद्रमापः प्रविशन्ति यद्वत्	III.9	*Bhagavadgītā*, II.70
चित्रार्पितारम्भमिवावतस्थे	III.19	*Raghuvaṁśa*, II. 31 *Kumārasambhava*, III.42
क्षतात्किल त्रायत इत्युदग्रः	IV.19	*Raghuvaṁśa*, II.53
त्वं रक्ष कल्याणपरम्पराणाम्	IV.34	*Raghuvaṁśa*, II.50
प्राणैरुपक्रोशमलीमसैर्वा	IV.65	*Raghuvaṁśa*, II.53

त्वमस्य विश्वस्य परं निधानं

त्वमव्ययः शाश्वतधर्मगोप्ता IV.76 *Bhagavadgītā,* XI.18

(iv) The narrative in the *SGGSC* is enlivened by the figures of speech, both of word and meaning. Of the *śabdālaṁkāras*, the author has decided predilection for alliteration which indeed is his forte. He has employed it with such frequency that the poem may be justifiably be said to be brimming with it. Lines like *dharmyāsu dhuryā gurudharmapatnī* (I.13), *diśaḥ praseduḥ pradiśaḥ praseduḥ* (I.15), *ākarṇya vācaḥ sa pituḥ pravāco, nisargabhāvāc chiśur āha vācaḥ* (I.47) abound in the poem.

In view of the elegance and sound effect that the Antyānuprāsa lends to the verse, the author has pressed it also into service with some frequency. The following verse forms perhaps the best illustration of this :

धर्मस्य गोप्ता सुजनस्य पाता

गोब्राह्मणानां परिरक्षिता च ।

विद्वन्मनोमोहयिता गुणैः स्वै-

र्दुष्टस्य यो दण्डयिता जनस्य ।। I.2

Equally interesting is –

शास्त्राणि नित्यं परिशीलयन्ती

पुराणमाख्यानमथो वदन्ती ।

दृश्यं मनोज्ञं च निभालयन्ती

दुर्गेऽवसज्ज्ञानमसौ दिशन्ती ।। II.19

Yamaka by its very nature tends to rob the poem of its clarity and thereby blurs the understanding thereof. The poet has therefore used it very sparingly. However his Yamaka, whenever it occurs is as lucid and sweet as is his alliteration. The following verse would bear it out :

समुदितो मुदितः स गुरुर्गुणैः

सुरहितो रहितो निखिलैर्मलैः ।

अविकलं विकलङ्कमथोज्ज्वलं

रसमयं समनं गमयन्नभात् ।। I.89

The author is equally at home in handling the Simile. He has culled his *upamānas* from a variety of sources including mythology and the Purāṇas. The Simile is resorted to in order to drive home the point with precision. That in turn depends on the aptness of the *upamāna* (standard of comparison). The author's wide learning and penetrating insight have enabled him to muster the most appropriate of the *upamānas*. The following verse exemplifies what may be called "Double Simile" on the cruel officials of Sirhind detaching her grandsons from her proximity, the old lady trembled like a plantain tree in a strong gale and withered with anguish like a creeper fallen from the tree. The two *upamānas* bring into relief the fear and agony of the hapless grand-mother, held in the iron-clutches of the enemy:

सा वेपमाना कदलीव वाते
स्वं भागधेयं च विगर्हमाणा ।
शोकेन दुःखेन च तप्यमाना
मम्लौ द्रुभङ्गे पतितेव वल्ली ।। IV.53

The stanza reproduced below also uses the Simile twice in its body. Of the two *upamānas*, the first is drawn from mythology, the other is too banal though the comparison of arrows with the furious serpents tellingly conveys their virulence. In the unequal battle of Chamkor, the Guru played havoc with the enemy as does Rudra at the end of the aeon :

गुरुस्तदा रुद्र इव प्रजानां
संहारकाले भयमादधानः ।
बाणान् प्रवर्षन् परितः प्रसर्पन्
चञ्चद्द्विजिह्वानिव भीमरूपान् ।। IV.16

By comparing him in the next verse with Arjuna, the wielder of the mighty Gāṇḍīva bow, the poet has again sought to underline the heavy losses he inflicted on the enemy-forces :

गाण्डीवधन्वेव रिपोश्चमूनां
चकार घोरं कदनं स तत्र ।। IV.17

Some other Similes also merit attention because of the aptness of the *upamānas* and the way they contribute to the clarity of the subject. The Guru's son Ajit Singh fought valiantly like Abhimanyu in the Great War (*yathābhimanyuḥ kuruyuddhamadhye*, IV.21). He shone forth in the midst of the enemy-forces like lightning in the layers of the clouds. (*ghanāvalīmadhyagateva śampā*, IV.22). The standard of comparison *śampā* the lightning, forcefully stresses the heroic lustre of the young boy. Banda mopped down the enemy's soldiers as storm strikes down the trees (*vātyeva vṛkṣāṁś ca bhaṭān ripūṇām*, IV.112). For other examples of Upamā reference may be made to the following verses, I.19; II.43, 54,68; III. 6, 9, 54, 61, etc.

At one place the *upamāna* used in the poem lacks precision. Water as a standard of comparison for the blood gushing from the Guru's wounds could have drawn a better *upamāna* unless it is presumed to have been used to highlight the swiftness of the flow of blood, rather than its colour :

दीर्णव्रणेभ्योऽस्रवदस्य रक्त-

धारा यथा प्रस्रवणेभ्य आपः । IV. 123

The following verse is characterised by Mālopamā. The Mughal army hastened to destroy the holy town of the Guru as the storm destroys the tree or the hail-storm batters the crop :

वात्येव वृक्षं करकेव सस्यं

संहर्तुकामा प्रचचाल वेगात् ।। III.54

Virodhābhāsa is found in the description of the Guru's glory that emanated from his organising the Khalsa. While it pervaded the heaven and the earth and was both delightful and pleasing, it inflamed jealousy in the heart of hill-rulers :

कीर्तिर्गुणैर्द्यामिथ गां स्पृशन्ती

लोकस्य हृद्याऽपि प्रियङ्कराऽपि ।

मात्सर्यवह्निं गिरिराजहृत्सु

प्रोद्दीपयामास भृशं तदानीम् ।। III. 48

The two verses quoted below form beautiful illustrations of Arthāntaranyāsa. Herein the respective ideas have been reinforced by upholding the particular statements with the general expressions :

कृत्तं शिरस्तज्जनकस्य दृष्ट्वा
न विव्यथे नापि चचाल चित्तम् ।
गोविन्दसिंहस्य कुमारकस्य
धैर्यं हि यत्सा प्रकृतिर्गुरूणाम् ।। I.72

सम्प्राप्तमात्रे स्वपुरं प्रवीरे
प्रजा ननन्दुर्जहसुर्जगुश्च ।
इष्टस्य पुंसः पुनरागमो हि
दिव्यं कमप्युत्सवमादधाति ।। II.34

The author has not used many metres in the *SGGSC*. Here Upajāti is his favourite metre that he has uniformly employed in all the four cantos, varying it only towards the close of each canto. The last verses of the first three cantos are couched in Vaṁśastha, Svāgatā and Śārdūlavikrīḍita respectively. In the Fourth Canto, the metre changes in the last two verses. Verse130 is in the Śārdūlavikrīḍita metre followed by Mālinī in the last.

These elaborate investigations to which the *SGGSC* has been subjected from various aspects, reveal beyond doubt that it represents a happy blend of a biography, historiography and an elegant poem. All the three command equal attention. No wonder, it was honoured by the Sahitya Akademi as the best writing in the year 1968.

ŚARMAṆYADEŚAḤ SUTARĀṀ VIBHĀTI

Though fabulously rich in almost all the conceivable genres of literature, both sacred and profane, the Sanskrit language suffers from a curious paucity of *ātmavṛtta* and *yātrāvṛtta*[1], autobiography and travelogue, believed to be comparatively modern in character. Dr. Satya Vrat Shastri's *Śarmaṇyadeśaḥ Sutarāṁ Vibhāti*,[2] a century of verses in different metres, is intended to make up for the deficiency in a convincing way. The poem purports to be a perceptive record of the author's brief though extremely rewarding visit (June 17-25,1975) to the Federal Republic of Germany, the country "which has contributed the maximum to the study and interpretation of ancient Indian wisdom".

Sponsored by the German Embassy in Delhi through the courtesy of Ms. Duckwitz the visit took the author, on June 18, to the lovely city of Frankfurt the starting point of his visit. However, the poem opens with a graphic general description of the country, which, in the body of mere five couplets, captures effectively its material prosperity, landscape, scenic beauties, vibrance of the people who had suffered the most in the last global war. On arrival at Frankfurt, the author was received at the airport by Mrs. Krüger, the official representative. A considerate lady, Mrs. Krüger conducted him to Hotel Frankfurt, and after a hearty lunch escorted him by train to Marburg. The author was simply thrilled by the beauty of the German land. The heavy rain and lush green countryside contributed immensely to make the trip all the more pleasant. The villages, en route, with their double-storeyed elegant houses, spacious roads, modern amenities not precluding cars and inhabited by well-dressed people would put the cities elsewhere to shame. The visitor like the author, was certain to mistake them for well-spruced towns (17-23). At Marburg, the author met the well-known scholar, Prof. Wilhelm Rau and his colleagues at the Indologiche Seminar and had with them a frank exchange of notes on academic activities (24-25). After the three-hour encounter that included discussion on Śastric topics (*śastracarcā*), he returned, delighted, to Frankfurt.

---

1. Chuni Lal Soodan's *Kāśmīraviharaṇam* (Saharanpur, 1976) and Pt. Naval Kishor Kankar's *Yātrāvilāsam* (Jaipur, 1983) are two other worthy travelogues. However, on account of its pedantic style weighed down by an endless string of recondite grammatical forms, the *Yātrāvilāsam* sinks into a prose romance.
2. Akhil Bharatiya Sanskrit Parishad, Lucknow, 1976

Early the next day he left for Göttingen to reach there within an hour and a half. The Buddhist scholar Gustav Roth, whom he had met earlier at Turine received him with a smile. He introduced him to the other scholars of his Seminar. At the instance of Prof. Roth, a number of snaps were hurriedly taken (30). What the author saw at the entrance of the Seminar building was something to be treasured in memory for life. He found inscribed there a *mantra* from the *Atharvaveda* and a few lines from an inscription of Aśoka. That was naturally taken by him to reflect the Germans' devotion to Sanskrit and Buddhism (31-32). What filled him with amazement were the beautiful verses composed by Prof. Waldt Schmidt to felicitate his teacher Prof. Sieg on his 80th birthday. The author was so charmed by them that he could not resist the temptation of obtaining a photostat copy of the verses. Thus ended his second day in Germany.

The next day brought him to Bonn, the capital of the country. At Bonn he saw without loss of time Prof. Hahn. He was greatly impressed by his (Prof. Hahn's) gentle nature and sharp mind (40). Situated on the banks of the river Rhine, Bonn is a veritable feast for the eyes (41). With its grassy highlands, rich gardens, boat-like houses, energetic people devoted to various chores, the capital city has a magnetic pull (42-45). It's famed thirty-three storeyed sky-scraper stirred the poet's imagery to describe it as the forehead of the town (46). A boat-trip upto Ankle was arranged for him which he enjoyed to his heart's content. The imposing building of the Ministry of Post and Telecommunication, on the banks of the Rhine, has five statues on it, representing the five continents (51). At Stuttgart he was received by a representative of the German authorities. The next day was earmarked for visiting Heidelberg. There he gave a lengthy talk on modern Sanskrit literature which evoked spontaneous applause from the audience (57). After the speech, Prof., Aithal, his Indian friend, stood him a sumptuous lunch at his home (58). The day ended with the author's return to Stuttgart (59).

His visit to the Indologische Seminar at Tübingen, the following day, was by far the most conspicuous and fruitful. He came together there with Professor Paul Thieme and other scholars. In a departure from the pre-announced subject, the author talked on Sanskrit synonyms, on which he had done a lot of research and thinking. Documented with a plethora of excerpts from an equally vast array of ancient texts and commentaries, the talk left the audience thrilled at the depth of the author's grasp of and investigation into Sanskrit semantics. Both Prof. Thieme, who presided over the Seminar and Prof. Stietencron were full of praise for the originality of the subject and its lively presentation.

Prof. Paul Thieme is a senior German scholar, now retired. The author had met him earlier at Delhi when he had come to participate in Max Müller's 150th Birth Anniversary Celebration and was the guest of honour on the last day of the Drama

Festival organised by the Department of Sanskirt, University of Delhi on the occasion. He delighted everybody with his Sanskrit. Prof. Berger had also graced the occasion. That the two scholars still carried the fond memories of the Festival gave he author immense delight.

The visit to the famous Black Forests, the next day, marked the finale to his sojourn in the Śarmaṇyadeśa. With a two-day halt at Rome, he returned to India, his home country, to the delight of his kinsmen.

The *Śarmaṇyadeśaḥ Sutarāṁ Vibhāti,* besides being one of the few travel-accounts in Sanskrit, seeks to perpetuate the Śataka-tradition, initiated by masters like Bhartṛhari, Amaru and others. However, unlike most of the earlier Śatakas, it is not a conglomerate of a series of *muktakas*, self-contained verses, on a variety of subjects with each unit standing apart. It is a well-knit poem with a single thread running into its warp and woof. Being descriptive for the most, it does not lend itself to tender fancies or gorgeous imageries. Still, even the matter of fact description, emanating as it does from a gifted poet, exudes sweetness. The poet's keen perception coupled with an innate proclivity to muster the most appropriate phraseology, invests his account with tender beauty and forceful vibrance. There are occasions when the travelogue writer tends to yield to the poet. The rounded description of the Republic as a whole, at the outset, has the undoubted merit of driving home the various facets of the country and its energetic and vivacious people:

योरूपभूमण्डलमध्यवर्ती
पारं समृद्धेः परमभ्युपेतः ।
नानानदीप्रस्रवणैः सुरम्यः
शर्मण्यदेशः सुतरां विभाति ।।

अकृष्टपच्यं खलु यत्र सस्यं
हृद्यास्तथा शाद्वलभूमिभागाः ।
दीर्घाश्चकासत्यथ दीर्घिकाः स
शर्मण्यदेशः सुतरां विभाति ।।

तरुप्रतानैः समलङ्कृतानि
प्रतानिनीभिश्च विभूषितानि ।

श्यामाख्यया लोकसुविश्रुतानि
श्यामायमानानि वनानि यत्र ।।
देशानुरागं परमं वहन्तो
मनस्विनो नित्यमुदात्तचित्ताः ।।
हृष्टाश्च पुष्टाश्च भृशं च तुष्टा-
स्तरस्विनो यत्र जना विभान्ति ।। 6-9

The description of the expanses of the Black Forests bears testimony to the poet's love for nature and his skill in detailing its beauties with warmth and effect. With imaginative daub of *padalālitya*, the alliterative account of the Black Forests tends to capture their different aspects in their entirety :

दीर्घाणि दीर्घैस्तरुभिर्युतानि
ग्रामैः पुरैश्चान्तरितानि तानि ।
विश्रामकामैः श्रमकर्शितैर्वा
नानाजनैश्चापि समाश्रितानि ।।
झरैश्च रम्यैरनुनादितानि
सुखं गँवाध्यासितशाद्वलानि ।
जलप्रवाहैः परिशोभितानि
स्रोतस्विनीभिश्च विभूषितानि ।।
बहूनि तावत्खलु योजनानि
विस्तीर्णतामापतितानि तानि ।
नेत्रद्वयासेचनकान्यभूव-
मालोकमालोकमहं प्रहृष्टः ।। 89-91

Within the narrow limits of the poem, some of the imageries engage attention by virtue of their freshness and aptness. Happy is the conception of the skyscrapers as so many bridges linking the earth with the heaven :

अभ्रंलिहाग्रा बहुभूमिकाश्च
भूमेश्च खस्यापि च सेतुभूताः ।

अट्टालिकालीरवलोक्य यत्र
जनः परं विस्मयमभ्युपैति ।। 10 ।।

The famed thirty-three storeyed sky-scraper of Bonn seems to have stirred the poet's imagery rather heavily. Not only is it viewed as the forehead of the town, but also as one fired with the zeal to transport the glory of the town to the heaven and meet its denizens :

चकास्ति तत्रैव महाविशालं
शालद्रुमाकारवदभ्रचुम्बि ।
द्वात्रिंशता भूमिवरैरुपेतं
भालं पुरस्येव नितान्तशोभि ।। 46

राईनवातानुपभुज्य शीतान्
नभःस्थवातानुपभोक्तुकामम् ।
भूमिष्ठलोकानवलोक्य कामं
द्युलोकजालोकनकौतुकार्थि ।।

पुरस्य शोभामिव वीक्षितुं वा
तत्कीर्तिमारोपयितुं दिवं वा ।
तस्यापि खस्यापि च सेतुभूतं
दूराभिलक्ष्यं भवनं सुरम्यम् ।। 48-49

The description of Bonn incidentally emerges as the finest part of the poem.

The *Śarmaṇyadeśaḥ Sutarāṁ Vibhāti* does not afford much occasion to the poet to display expertise in the use of various figures of speech. Svabhāvokti was natural to preponderate in the 'Down to Earth' poem that the Śataka is. The description of the Black Forests, quoted earlier, amounts to be the best illustration of the *alaṁkāra*. The author has again resorted to the Svabhāvokti in describing Bonn, situated on both the banks of the river Rhine :

कूलद्वये तस्य नदस्य तावद्
बॉनाख्यमास्ते नगरं निविष्टम् ।

यस्योपकण्ठे वलया गिरीणां
सौन्दर्यमत्यद्भुतमर्पयन्ति ।। 42

द्राक्षाकृषिव्यापृतकर्षकैश्च
नानाविधोद्योगरतैर्जनैश्च ।
नौकासमानाकृतिभिर्विचित्रैः
स्वल्पाल्परूपैर्निलयैस्तथा च ।।

कार्यं प्रधानं खलु मन्यमानैः
कार्येष्वतः स्वेषु भृशं प्रसक्तैः ।
स्त्रीभिश्च पुम्भिश्च भृतं पुरं तत्
कामप्यपूर्वां सुषमां बिभर्ति ।। 44-45

Alliteration, as borne out by the verses reproduced above, breathes through the poem. Much of the *padalālitya* in the Śataka owes itself to this sweetness of Anuprāsa.

The author has employed only three metres in the poem. While the Pūrvapīṭhikā is written in the Āryā metre, the Uttarapīṭhikā claims Anuṣṭup. The intervening Yātrāvarṇana is couched in Indravajrā and Upajāti, treated as a single unit.

The canvas or horizon of the *Śarmaṇyadeśaḥ Sutarāṁ Vibhāti* is not wide. It is a descriptive poem. This is what a travelogue ought to be. However, charming poetry occasionally breaks through the rugged veneer of the travelogue. And that is a great achievement for the author.

THAIDEŚAVILĀSAM

In view of the amazingly close cultural and religious affinities that it bears with India, the bastion of Sanskrit and Buddhism, the beautiful country of Thailand, the ancient Śyāmadeśa, could have been, at any point of time, a meet theme for the sensitive Sanskritist to deal with it with verve. However, it was left to Dr. Satya Vrat Shastri, undoubtedly one of the foremost Sanskrit poets of the day, to come out, on his first assignment into the Thai country, with the delightful poem the *Thaideśavilāsam*[1] (*Tdv.*), a Khaṇḍakāvya in 121 verses. Notwithstanding its slim girth, the *Tdv.* represents a fine atiempt on the part of the poet to describe, in essentials, all that the Thais themselves believe to be synonymous with the country : the nation, the culture, the religion and the king[2].

SUMMARY :

Though neither demarcated nor intended as such, the *Tdv.* may well be divided into seven segments of uneven size. With its well-rounded resume of the character of the land as reflected in its geographical situation and fertile soil, its expertise in striking fusion between old and new, its perennial fascination for the *Rāmāyaṇa*, the immortal epic of India, and the complete blend that Buddhism has worked out with Hinduism, headed by a benevolent monarch, the peer of Rāma, the first segment (1-12) is intended to serve as a prologue to the poem proper. Segment two formed by stanzas 12-32, is distinguished by a lovely description of the metropolitan city of Bangkok. It is a measure of the author's poetic skill that within the tiny frame of twenty verses the sprawling capital has come to vibrate with life in its entirety and diversity. The Crocodile Farm, the Snake Farm, rich departmental.stores, shops full of gold and jewellery, the Floating Market, the Temple of the Emerald Buddha adorned on its walls with a series of scenes from the *Rāmāyaṇa*, all this, rather nothing worthwhile has escaped the poet's Argus eye. All this has been described with such sensibility and effect that it may justly be rated as poetically the best part of the poem. The picture of the Rājadhānī that emerges from the poem is doubtless of the fairyland full of beauty, charm and pleasure *vilāsadhānī*)

---

1. Eastern Book Linkers, Delhi, 1979. It is interesting to know that the name *Thaideśavilasam* was suggested by Dr. Mrs. Pranee Lapanich, the author's colleague in the Chulalongkorn University, Bangkok.
2. *Thaideśavilāsam*, 61

The third segment (33-61) is devoted to the history of the ruling Chakri dynasty marked by a brief but perceptive account of the earlier rulers. To the founder of the dynasty, belongs the unique distinction of composing in verse the Thai *Rāmāyaṇa*, the *Rāmakīrti,* that stands, till date, as an undying monument to his glory (34-36). What the father had told in detail, Rāma II, his son told in brief to form a handy volume. It is his version that forms the basis of the dramatic representation of the Rāma story, in the Thai country (37-38).

One of his successors Phra Mongkut, popularly known as Rāma VI, continued the dynastic tradition of singing in his speech the divine character of Rāma. As a scholar well-versed in Vālmīki's *Rāmāyaṇa*, he took pains to highlight the divergences between the *Rāmakīrti* and the Indian epic, and used such words as helped bring out many Mudrās at the performance. On account of his manifold contribution to the enrichment of arts and letters, his reign came to be known as the golden era of the Thai history (39-42). He also established the Chulalongkorn University after the name of his father which continues to be the prominent seat of higher learning in the country. Chulalongkorn is known to be the first Thai ruler to have received the western type of education. Under him the country registered such material and educational advancement that it entitled him to be rated as the maker of modern Thailand (45-47). Blessed with abundant qualities of head and heart, the present monarch, Atulyatej Bhumibala, is ninth in the lineage. His solicitude for his people is well-known, so is his equipoise. Of his daughters, Sirindhorn is an earnest student of Sanskrit and is devoted like her father to the public weal. It was in recognition of her administrative and intellectual competence that king Atulyatej Bhumibala, on his fiftieth birthday conferred on her the high-sounding title of Mahachakri. The occasion was greeted with prolonged festivities (52-61).

The scene in the next segment (62-91) is transferred to Ayodhyā, the history whereof forms the contents of this part of the poem. Ayodhyā had the singular distinction of having served as a seat of power for four hundred and seventeen long years, covering the reign of as many as thirty three Thai rulers. Founded by king Ramadhipati, it was devastated by the marauding hordes from Burma, who captured Thailand and raised in Ayodhyā a column to symbolize their victory over the country (88). Ayodhyā is dotted with archaeological remains and such other religious and secular monuments/palaces as have been instrumental in turning it into a rendezvous of the connoisseur. The Elephant Enclosure (81), Phra Mongkol Bopitr Monastery (82), the Chedi of the brave queen Suriyothai who laid down her life to save her loving husband in the battle-field (83-86), the lofty Stūpa Wat Phu Khao Thong, built by king Buronguong of Burma (87), the old palace with its Trimukha pavilion (90) and the Candrakasem Palace which was built by Naresuan the Great during his heirapparentship (91), claim notice.

Consequent on the destruction of Ayodhyā, Taksin founded the city of Thonburi on the bank of the Chao Phaya river which continued to be his capital for fifteen years. The valour of Taksin is still celebrated in the Thai legends (62-64). The glorious but woeful tale of Taksin, who valiantly redeemed the national honour by freeing the country from the clutches of the Burmese but was subsequently put to death, when he went mad towards the close of his reign, is told in sedate tones (68-76). The poor general mounted the throne with a bang but ended in a whimper.

The fifth segment (92-99) is by far the shortest. It details the romantic story of king Ekathasarot, who, in a dramatic meeting with 'In' yielded to her captivating charms but respected her love by putting the son Prasatthong, begotten on her, on the royal throne.

The sixth segment (100-116) details other places of interest in Thailand. The Pattaya and Phuket beaches that attract people from far and wide, are a joy to behold. In the Coral Island one is struck with wonder on seeing the corps of aquatic beings reflected in a mirror. Chiengmai is the bright gem of the northern Thailand. Its Umbrella Village is equally striking. Of its many monasteries Doi Suthep, adorned with a golden pagoda, deserves special mention. The figures of two dragons in stone, at the start of its flight of steps with their tails extending upto the hill-top fill one with amazement (114). The beauties of the Thai women are also duly noticed. Slim and fair, they charm one and all (115-116).

The last five verses form the epilogue with a prayer to Lord Śiva to bestow happiness on all (121).

CRITIQUE :

Written in chaste and fluent Sanskrit the *Tdv.* comes as a gush of fresh air in the literature dominated by traditional themes. It is uniquely distinctive in making the history and culture of a foreign land, its subject matter. The *Tdv.* may therefore be justly rated as a historical poem which widely differs from other Kāvyas of its genre, wherein the historical account is overladen with the overgrowth of fiction to the extent that, more often than not, the latter sucks history into its orbit. It is a tribute to the author's equipment in Thai history and his unquestioned poetic talents, that in the body of mere 121 verses The Thai history from the earliest times, with its grandeur and foibles, has been skilfully interwoven to form an integrated texture. Here the Thai history is narrated in such neatly chiselled stanzas that nowhere does one suffer the tedium or grotesqueness associated with history. Rather, the elegance and sweetness of the diction eggs on the reader to proceed uninterrupted to ultimately discover that what is projected as Thai culture which bears deep imprint of his own social milieu. The glories of Ayodhyā and its subsequent destruction, the founding of the Chakri dynasty, the love-affair of Ekathasarot, the valour of Taksin and his ignoble end, the supreme sacrifice of the brave lady Suriyothai, the benevolence of the present ruler coupled with the beauty and affluence of the country invite one's attention like a scroll of graphic paintings attempted by master painters. The *Tdv.* alongwith the companion monograph[3] serves to establish the author as an authority on Thai history and culture, a feat that he accomplished in an incredibly short period. Though the poem is primarily intended for the cultured Sanskritist, it may well serve as a tourist guide, so wide is its sweep. And that is something that the Sanskrit language can be legitimately proud of.

As a gifted poet, the author comes to grips with the subject right from the start. In keeping with his wont, the *Tdv.* is marked in its inception by a rounded description of the Thai country that serves to project, in relief, the character of the land in its varied aspects :

श्यामेति नामातिपुराणमस्य
ख्यातं पुराणादिषु यद्विहाय ।
थाईतिजात्यध्युषितत्वहेतो-
र्यं थाइलैण्डं कथयन्ति लोकाः ।। 2

उच्चार्यमाणानि पदे पदेऽत्र
विहारभूमिष्वितरत्र चापि ।
वमन्ति शाक्यस्य मुनेर्वचांसि
पीयूषधारां श्रुतिशष्कुलीषु ।।
रामायणे दृष्टिपथं प्रयाति
रुचिर्जनानां प्रबलाऽत्र चित्रम् ।
तस्य प्रयोगा अतिकौशलेन
कर्षन्ति चेतांसि बलाज्जनानाम् ।। 8-9

The author had clear vision of the type of language that he wanted to employ. By its very nature, the *Tdv.* could ill-afford the luxury of high-flown language or laboured style. The poem is couched throughout in a lucid medium marked by what in the poetician's parlance is known as *mādhurya* to the extent that nowhere does

---

3. *Studies in Sanskrit and Indian Culture in Thailand*, Parimal Publications, Delhi, 1982

the language fall out of step with the modernity of the subject. Rather, its glamour is enhanced by the grace of the classical speech. The poem attests to the poet's capacity to deal with the whole spectrum of subjects in their diversity and complexity, in corresponding phraseology. How far his language accords with the variety of situations that abound in the poem is borne out by his descriptions of the military engagements, serene monasteries, bewitching beauties of the sea-beaches, physical charms of the Thai women and tender love-scenes.

The two successive verses that describe respectively the heroic fight and fall of the legendary queen Suriyothai and the pall of gloom cast by her death are distinctively marked by *ojas* (vigour) and *śoka* (grief) :

पुंवेषधृत्सा युयुधे बलेन
रिपोर्भटैर्भर्तृहिताय वीरा ।
तत्रैव युद्धे प्रहृता च गाढं
सा वीरलोकोचितमाप लोकम् ॥
तद्भस्म संस्थापितमत्र चेद्यां
तच्छोकतप्तेन तदीयभर्त्रा ।
आगन्तुका यां प्रविलक्ष्य सत्यं
म्लानानना दुःखभराद् भवन्ति ॥ 85-86

Tenderness besides lucid phraseology characterises the description of Ekathasarot's loss of self-control at the sight of pretty In. The two were locked in love with productive results :

हृतोऽस्या अनिन्द्येन रूपेण चापि
स्त्रिया रूपवत्याः स इन्नामिकायाः ।
प्रभुर्नो बभूवात्मनः सत्प्रजानां
प्रभुर्हन्त ! चित्रो विलासो विधातुः ॥
स तां रात्रिमेतां स्वदारांश्चकार
कणेहत्य रेमे तया चापि सार्धम् ॥ 96-97

The beauties of nature are represented by the description of the sea-beaches of Pattaya and Phuket (100-104). Pattaya seems to steal march over the others. The charms of its sandy expanses attract people from far and wide. The blissful experiences that they undergo there tend to make them forget all else, even themselves :

यद् द्रष्टुमापतति सर्वत एव लोको
यद्रामणीयककथाश्रुतिसम्प्रणुन्नः ।
यत्सैकते विलुठितुं च मुदाभिलष्य-
त्यन्यच्च सर्वमपि विस्मरति प्रसन्नः ।। 10

Contrary to these, mundane serenity reigns the sacred precincts of the Emerald Buddha monastery. The calm poise of the Buddha's image stirs the devout down to their heart :

शान्ताकृतेः शाक्यमुनेरपूर्वां
मूर्तिं शुभां मारकतीं दधाना ।
भक्तैर्भृता सन्ततमेव सद्भि-
र्विराजते यत्र विहारभूमिः ।। 19

The *Thaideśavilāsam* bears testimony to the poet's keen observation, alert mind and sensitive ear to whatever he comes across. The inquisitiveness that the poem betrays, compares favourably with that one notices in Bāṇa's *Harṣacarita*. It is a measure of his keen sensitivity that he can describe even such trite subjects as the Crocodile Farm, Rose Garden, Floating Market and affluent departmental stores with such warmth and precision that they are catapulted to poetic heights. While describing the Crocodile Farm he says that with the large number of crocodiles reared in the farm, it is a true *makarālaya* but the appellation can hardly be applied to it as it is restricted to the sea alone :

जलाशयो यत्र विभाति यस्मिन्
सम्पुष्टिमाप्ता मकरा लसन्ति ।
याथार्थ्यतोऽयं मकरालयः सं-
स्तन्नामतो वक्तुमशक्य एव ।। 22

The Floating Markets that deal in a variety of wares imported from different countries are a treat to the eye :

पण्यस्य नौभिः क्रयविक्रयाभ्यां
कुल्यासु दूरादुपसम्भृतस्य ।
जलेचरा यत्र च पण्यवीथ्यो
नेत्रद्वयासेचनकीभवन्ति ।। 21

It is these Svabhāvoktis that turn out to be the best specimens of his poetry in the poem. It is again to the Svabhāvokti of all the *alaṁkāras* that the poet resorts to describe the various situations and events that abound in the poem. The figure Svabhāvokti is intended to depict an object in all its hues and contours[4]. Therein rests its relevance. Besides the two quoted earlier, the Svabhāvoktis reproduced below focus on the totality of the objects under description :

सरीसृपाणां परिपालनार्थं
यत्रास्ति केन्द्रं बहुजातिकानाम् ।
विषं विनिकृष्य यतस्तु वैद्याः
प्रयुञ्जते रोगचिकित्सिकायाम् ।। 24
नृत्यानि वाद्यानि च गीतिकाश्च
दीक्षा च भिक्षोरथ मुष्टियुद्धम् ।
निस्त्रिंशयुद्धं च समस्तमेतत्
सन्दर्श्यतेऽत्रानतिविस्तरेण ।। 29

Alliteration is the other *alaṁkāra* that carries the palm. It spills over the better part of the poem's phraseology and imparts to it pleasing *padalālit*ya and thereby lends added charm to the verses like :

---

4. स्वभावोक्तिरसौ चारु यथावद्वस्तुवर्णनम् ।
Kāvyadipikā, Motilal Banarsidass. Delhi, 1985, p. 140.

रामेति सीतेति सुदारुकेति
शोभेति शान्तीति वरेति वापि ।
नामानि रम्याणि जनो दधानो
हर्षप्रकर्षं हृदि वर्षतीह ॥ 11

अनुत्तमं काव्यमिदं विशालं
रामाधिबद्याख्यनृपस्य दीर्घाम् ।
कीर्त्यस्य सत्यं धुरि सत्कवीनां
यशःपताकां विधुनोति दिक्षु ॥ 36

which pulsates throughout the poem. The author's predilection for Antyānuprāsa, as noticed earlier, is deep and unmistakable. Besides pretty *lālitya*, it invariably results in soothing rhythm. The author is one of the few poets to have exploited it to admirable advantage. The following verse represents by far its best illustration :

राजा प्रजारञ्जनमादधानः
सर्वात्मना बुद्धवचःप्रमाणः ।
अतुल्यतेजःपदवीं दधानः
प्रशास्ति यं भूमिबलाभिधानः ॥ 3

No less remarkable is

लोकाभिरामो नवमोऽस्ति रामः
क्रोधस्य यत्रास्ति सदा विरामः ॥ 49

Equally happy are the author's imageries (Utprekṣās). While the sprawling capital Bangkok shines forth with its grandeur like a pearl-necklace, as it were, around the neck of the Earth-maiden, the Chayo Phya river is visualised as offering watery homage to the seat of power. And the Grand Palace is looked upon as a lustrous piece of the heaven fallen below (26) :

देशस्य तस्यास्ति भृशं विशाला
कण्ठे भुवः शुभ्रतरेव माला ।

ऐश्वर्यसौन्दर्यविलासधानी
बैङ्काकनाम्नी खलु राजधानी ।। 13

चायो-फयाख्यां समया निविष्टा
स्रोतस्विनीं पूः सलिलौघहृद्याम् ।
तरङ्गहस्तैस्तरसा ददाति
या पाद्यमस्यै परयेव भक्त्या ।। 32

The Simile is an index to the fertility of the poet's imagination. It has been used in the *Tdv*. rather infrequently. The few that are found are marked by the aptness of the *upamānas*. The Burmese hordes descended upon Ayodhyā to raze it to ground like swarms of so many disasters :

तामेकदा सम्प्रतिपन्नशत्रु-
भावाः समेता विपदामिवौघाः ।
ब्रह्माभिधानान्निकटस्थदेशा-
दाक्रान्तवन्तः प्रबला जनौघाः ।। 66

Virodhābhāsa is reflected in the behaviour of king Ekathasarot, who, though controlling the destiny of his people, lost self-control at the mere sight of the lovely In :

प्रभुर्नो बभूवात्मनः सत्प्रजानां
प्रभुर्हन्त ! चित्रो विलासो विधातुः ।। 96

The daub of Arthāntaranyāsa reinforces the Virodha.

While the author is doubtless capable to handle the literary motifs, he has resorted to them rather sparingly. The poem does not offer him many opportunities to parade his learning. However, the forms like— राजाऽत्र रामात्प्रति राजमानः (10), आविरस्ति (12), नेत्रद्वयासेचनकीभवन्ति (21), निपाठं निपाठं (35), कणेहत्य (97) bear the stamp of a grammarian.

The poem echoes quite a few of Kālidāsa's ideas that invariably add to its effect. The famed *subhāṣita purāṇam ity eva na sādhu sarvam, na cāpi kāvyaṁ*, नवमित्यवद्यम् (*Malv*. 1.2) is reproduced, almost verbatim, in the *Tdv*. (5). Some of the imageries from the *Meghaduta* have also been exploited to profitable use. The grandeur of Ujjayinī leads Kālidāsa to fancy it as a refulgent segment of the heaven, brought down by its own denizens.[5] Our author too could not resist the temptation of viewing the Grand Palace of Bangkok as *divaś cyutaṁ kāntaṁ khaṇḍam* (26). The markets of Bangkok like that of Kālidāsa's Ujjayinī, with its overabundance of jewellery, serve to reduce the seas, the mines of jewels (*ratnākaras*), to mere reservoirs of water (*toyaśeṣāḥ*,14), the mass of jewels having been drained off to the respective markets. *āgantukānāṁ ramayanti cetaḥ* (4) is but a doctored version of Kālidāsa's *āgantūn ramayati janaḥ*.[6]

The author's equipment in metrics is obvious from his skilful handling of the different metres. He has sought to relieve the monotony of the same rhythm persisting throughout by varying the metre at the appropriate place. However, he has been chary not to disturb the sequence of the descriptions by needlessly inducting the new metre midway. It is only after the description concludes that a new metre has been introduced. Altogether nine metres have been employed which include Indravajrā, Upendravajrā, Upajāti, Bhujaṅgaprayāta, Vasantatilakā, Āryā, Vidyunmālā, Anuṣṭubh and Drutavilambita. It is interesting to know that of these the first seven are found in the Thai poetry under the names Indrawong, Upendrawong, Upachāt, Phūchoṅkhaprayāt, Vasantatilok, Pathyāvat and Vicchummālā respectively.

The *Tdv.* emerges as the sole poem to deal with alien history and culture, howsover close they might have been to the homeland of Sanskrit. Despite its brevity, it has sucked into its limited range all that is projected as the soul of the Thai country. The poet's susceptibilities coupled with his deep study of the Thai history and keenness of observation has worked out a happy blend of the old and the new, that Thailand represents. The author's Herculean efforts, vividly reflected in his sweet, limpid verses, have indeed gone far to bring the two friendly countries still closer.

---

5. *Meghadūta* (Ed. S.K. De), Sahitya Akademi, New Delhi, 1957, verse 30
6. *Meghadūta* (Part I), Ed. Sansar Chand and Mohandeva Pant, Moti Lal Banarsi Dass, Benaras, 1951, verse 32

CHAPTER FOUR

CORPUS OF LETTERS

CORPUS OF LETTERS

The letter is the humblest means of communication. Despite the availability of sophisticated alternatives, it continues to retain its utility, almost intact. Its mode of delivery has undergone tremendous changes, down the years, no doubt. While before the introduction of the well-organised postal system, humble couriers or birds were employed to deliver letters to distant places, it is postman now who is eagerly awaited every morning. The letter was primarily intended to convey one's well-being and other related message. How dearly was it prized should be obvious from the fact that the message communicated by the letter was considered only a wee less comforting than the actual union with one's dear one : *kāntodantaḥ suhrdupanataḥ saṅgamāt kiñcid ūnaḥ* [1]

Letter-writng is a social necessity. Everyone, howsoever small or great, educated or uneducated has to fall back to the letter to exchange information and thereby keep oneself abreast of what transpires in distant corners. It is a tribute to the vitality and pervasive influence of the letter that even the latest electronic gadgets have not been able to supplant it or wear down its usefulness. While all write letters, the letters of the great personages are not mere missives. As men of culture and competence, they express in their letters their considered views on a wide range of subjects that throw welcome light on many a thorny issue, with the result that they come to acquire historical value. How Nehru's famous letters to his daughter deal with the whole spectrum of history, is so well-known as to need no emphasis. His political letters coupled with those of his contemporaries like Sardar Patel, Subhash Chandra Bose and others give a connected account of the struggle the country waged to throw away the yoke of British imperialism. These letters command wide respect and are avidly read. Likewise the letters of the litterateurs add up as literary documents that are profitably referred to by all serious students of literature. Even when they deal with lighter matters, they make delightful reading.

Letter writing in Sanskrit is perhaps as old as the language itself. Its style and objective might have been different but it has always been an important vehicle of communication among the cultured Sanskritists. Versified letters are perhaps a recent phenomenon, tlhough verse has been closer to the genius of Sanskrit since times immemorial.

A gifted poet as he is, the author has written, over the years, hundreds of letters

---

1. S.K.. De (ed), *Meghadūta,* Sahitya Akademi, New Delhi, 1957 verse 97.

in Sanskrit verse to his Sanskritist friends and acquaintances, both Indian and foreign. Taken together, they form a sizable volume[2]. The sweet medium of Sanskrit verse has raised them to poetic height. As a matter of fact, some of them have been conceived, both in contents and style as mini Kāvyas. That adds a new dimension to the trite practice of letter-writing. The author's letters, as they stand, may be classified into three categories : personal letters, literary letters and felicitative letters though occasionally the three tend to intrude into each other's domain. Whatever their class, they invariably bear the stamp of the poet. Not unoften the letter-writer yields to the poet in the author. This is what turns them into Kāvyas and merits critical evaluation as poetic pieces.

The personal letters deal with matters connected with the writer or the addressee. They cover a wide spectrum of issues ranging from expressing thanks for congratulations or others in a variety of ways. It is, however, a different matter that even the 'down to earth' matters are discussed or described so poetically that they come to be invested with a wealth of poetic flourishes. The first two letters addressed to his great father are very personal in nature. While in the first he expresses his joy at the latter's condoning his unspecified lapse, in the second he has requested his father to remind Ācārya Vishva Bandhu of the work he had already spoken of to him because the final decision rested with him (*sarvaṁ hi manye tadadhīnam eva*, II.5). The letter also carries a brilliant pen-sketch of the learned Ācārya. Composed of mere two Svāgatā verses, the first letter is the shortest of the lot. The second runs into six stanzas. Written to Ācārya Vidyanidhi, the third letter also belongs to this category . The Ācārya is reminded that the time to fulfil the promise he had made earlier has come now; though he regrets the distraction it might cause, engaged as he was in constructing the house. The letter is marked by an intimate inquiry about the well-being of the Ācārya's kinsmen. The fourth letter is addressed to the noted linguist, Dr. Suniti Kumar Chatterji. Herein expressed is the author's regret for the delay in sending the paper he had sought. The letter makes deservedly flattering references to Dr. Chatterji. It also evidences the high regards that the author has for the mighty colossus (*bhavdbhyaḥ sveṣṭadevebhyaḥ śraddhānaivedyam arpyate*, IV.8). The next three letters represent the mix of the personal and the literary. Letter No. 6 was written to congratulate Dr. Krishna Lal on his recent Kāvya. The seventh letter is meant to convey gratitude to the veteran Sanskrit scholar, Ācārya Viśhvanāth

---

2. To be sure, all the letters written by the author are not traceable. What is preserved with him is only a part of the whole corpus. The letters presently available with him number seventy. They have been serially numbered by us to facilitate ready reference.

Shastri for his liking the author's newly-published Khaṇḍakavya *Śrīgurugovindasiṁhacaritam* and to request the Ācārya to send him a copy of his commentary on *the Tarkasaṅgraha.* By letter No. 8 the author seeks to assure Dr. D.K. Gupta of Patiala that he would speak to the unnamed scholar of Kāśī for his work and hints at its sure success. Since it was written after the author's return from Ranikhet, it includes, perhaps by way of contrast, a graphic description of Delhi's blistering heat. The next four letters are intended to convey thanks to his well-wishers for the felicitations they had extended to him on his elevation as Professor in the Department. One of the personal letters (No.48) informs his German friend Mr. Alois Payer of the award of twenty five thousand rupees conferred on him by the Government of Uttar Pradesh. Another letter (No.34) addressed to Vidyāvācaspati Mani Nath Jha, concerns itself with expressing the author's gratitude to the veteran savant for felicitations on President's Award to him .

Some of the personal letters have public overtones. The lettter (No.18) written from Bangkok to Dr. Krishna Lal on September 25, 1978, for example, expresses the author's anxiety on the reports of the havoc the floods had wrought in certain parts of Delhi (*tatrāplāvo bhūyān āstetyetaccintā sarvatrāste*, 18.4). The letter that the author wrote, on his return from Tübingen, to his German friend Alois Payer on November 11,1984 besides thanking the Payers for the love and care they had showered on the author and his wife during thier stay there, alludes to the ghastly murder of Indira Gandhi and thc pall of grief it had cast on the entire nation (*kṣubdhamānasatarаṅgadolitāḥ, santi na kṣaṇam apīha sakṣaṇāḥ* , 31.9). The succeeding letter (No.32) was written on the following day (Nov. 12,1984) from Puri to Dr. Krishna Lal. It mentions the loot and arson that followed Indira Gandhi's assassination in many parts of the country including Puri and Delhi *(agnidāhādikaṁ kutsyaṁ vṛttam atrapi dāruṇaṁ diliyāṁ tu bhuyas tad abhūd iti cintā garīyasī, 32.6).*

The most touching personal letters are those which were written in response to the condolence messages on the demise of his father Prof. Charu Deva Shastri. The poet and son in the author were so deeply stirred by the departure of the mighty scholar that it found expression in some of he chillingly pathetic verses. All the five letters (Nos.38-42) are so sentimentally couched that they amount to miniaturised Kāvyas replete with Karuṇarasa. The letters are slightly repetitive in contents, but that does not rob them of their poetic merits. "The scholar who had throughout his life adored the Śabdabrahman has ultimately attained fusion with Him. Forlorn is the Sanskrit- world, forlorn is the goddess of learning, scholarship and intelligence have been rendered destitute. The sun has repaired to the Western mount and the world is merged in darkness", this is what he wrote to Ācārya Divakar Datta Shastri of Shimla, on April 24,1987 :

यावज्जीवं समाराध्य शब्दब्रह्म विशेषतः ।
तातपादा अन्तकाले तत्रैव विलयं गताः ।।
अनाथं संस्कृतजगदनाथा च सरस्वती ।
अनाथं चापि वैदुष्यमनाथा प्रतिभाऽपिच ।।
तादृशेऽथ महाभानावस्ताचलमुपेयुषि ।
तामिस्रमिव भात्येतज्जगत्कृत्स्नं चराचरम् ।।

The literary letters touch upon or otherwise deal with a plethora of issues of academic and literary interest. They encompass in their sweep such wide-ranging matters as encouraging the younger scholars in prosecuting their literary activities, brief reviews of the recently published works, the author's own literary and creative pursuits including his visits to foreign Universities and resume of the Sanskrit studies as they are conducted there. It is interesting to note that most of the literary letters have been claimed by Dr. Krishna Lal, the author's pupil and colleague in the Department at Delhi. For instance, letter no.17 written from Bangkok on August 24,1978 urges him to complete the Dictionary of Vedic Etymologies. That was bound to bring name to him also (*śiṣyaprakarṣo yaśase gurūṇām*, 17.8). It also carries a lovely description of the rainy season at Bangkok and additionally informs the addressee that his (the author's) latest Kāvya the *Thaideśavilāsam* was in the press. Another letter included in Miscellaneous Verses (7) purports to be a brief review of Dr. Pushpa Trivedi's Kāvya *Agniśikhā*. He praises the poem for its elegant language and sweet diction (*mādhvīkamādhuryadharā manojñā*, 3). The letter (No. 13) written to Pandit Durgadatta on September 30, 1970 is also intended to convey the author's appreciation of his two Kāvyas *(ojasvinyā girā baddham ūrjasvi ruciraṁ tathā arthagauravayuktaṁ cāpy alaṁkārair alaṁkṛtam*, (13.7). The letter to Prof. Stietencron, written on 7.3. 1985, acclaims his deep grasp of Sanskrit semantics. The Professor's Sanskrit writings including some in verse, have also evoked the author's appreciation. He is frank in his opinion that while the German Indologist's intelligence and learning are beyond question, he needs more of *abhyāsa* (practice). That besides *pratibhā* and *vyutpatti* are viewed, collectively, not individually, by the poeticians as the genesis of poetry :

शक्तिश्च नैपुण्यमथापि लोक-
शास्त्रादिकावेक्षणतः प्रजातम् ।
काव्यज्ञशिक्षाभ्यसनं च विज्ञाः

काव्यस्य हेतुं समुदीरयन्ति ॥
एषु द्वयं वर्तत एव सत्सु
श्रमस्तृतीये तु चिकीर्षितः स्यात् ।
सङ्कल्पमारुह्य तदर्थमाशु
प्रवृत्तिमन्तोऽत्र भवन्तु सन्तः ॥ 33.5-6

This again is the view he communicated to Dr. Krishna Lal (*śaktyā sahaivāhur amandam āryāḥ, kāvyasya hetāv abhiyogam eva*, 50.4), while congratulating him on the prize his daughter secured in a competition. Letter No.19 details the author's trip to Canada, America, Japan and his meeting with the noted Indologists in the respective countries besides the lectures he delivered in different Universities on a number of subjects. The next letter, again addressed to Dr. Krishna Lal from Bangkok, apprises him of the publication of the author's papers in various journals and his visit to a number of ancient temples, monasteries and other places and objects of archaeological interest which he soon hopes to subject to critical evaluation. The letter also canveys the information that the *Thaideśavilāsam* was to be released shortly. The graphic description of the interesting festival Songkran, that is celebrated for three consecutive days in Chiengmai in North Thailand, forms the contents of the succeeding letter (No.21). The letter that follows was written to Dr. Brahmachari Surendra Kumar of Muzaffarpur. It gives details of his assignment as Visiting Professor in Thailand. The author informs the Brahmachari that while in Thailand he taught Sanskrit to princess Sirindhorn, composed the Khaṇḍakāvya *Thaideśavilāsam*, wrote eighteen papers on Thai history, culture and religion and discovered/obtained several Sanskrit inscriptions which he means to study ere long. Letter No. 27, written on 24.4.1984 from Puri to Dr. Krishna Lal runs into thirty two Anuṣṭup stanzas. Because of its size and contents it is as good as a mini Kāvya. While pointing out the benefits that accrue from *deśāṭana*, the author describes in brief the history of the installation of the images of Jagannātha, Baladeva and Subhadrā in the famous shrine of Puri, one of the most sacred centres of pilgrimage. The next letter informs Mr. Alois Payer of the Rathayātrā festival of Puri. Letter No. 36 written to Shri Keshava Sharma of Shimla refers to the Seminar on Aesthetics to be organised at Puri in the last week of September.

The last four of the literary letters (49-52) all addressed to Dr. Krishna Lal, form a well-knit series They are thematic in character as they deal with the history of Thailand and its national epic, the *Ramakien* (*Rāmakīrti*). All sizably lengthy, the bunch includes a letter (No.51) that may be rated as one of the longer of the letters, it running into forty one well-chiselled stanzas. Besides the personal touch it acquires in informing the addressee of his frozen shoulder and pain in the spine which the doctors opine, cannot be wholly eliminated (*na mūloccheda eteṣāṁ sambhavīti cikitsakāḥ*, 51.7), the author has herein given Sanskrit version of two of such episodes– Anomatan upākhyāna and Beñjakayī upākhyāna – of *Rāmakīrti* as are found neither in Vālmīki's *Rāmāyaṇa* nor in the *Rāmacaritamānasa* of Tulasīdāsa. The chaste language and swift flow of the verses raises the letter to appreciable heights.

Letter No. 49, written from Bangkok, throws valuable light on the nomenclature and history of the capital of Thailand. Popularly known as Bangkok the world over, the Thais themselves have no fascination for the name. Krungthev is the appellation they apply to the metropolis. Krungthev represents a queer mixture of Sanskrit and Thai languages. While the word Krung is of Thai origin, theva is clearly a corrupt form of Sanskrit 'deva'. The word therefore means Devasthāna', the abode of gods. It was founded, more than two hundred years ago, by the founder of the present Chakri dynasty, who wrote the *Ramakien* which the Thais believe to be a matchless epic, the like of which was neither heard nor seen elsewhere.

In fulfilment of his promise made in the earlier letter (*tadrasaṁ pāyayiṣyāmi kalayā bhavato 'py aham/svapatramādhyamenaiva tatkāvyam upavarṇayan*, 49.19), the author apprises Krishna Lal in his next letter (No.50) that the basic structure of the Thai *Rāmāyaṇa* is not different from that of Vālmīki's. But the Thais take the *Rāmāyaṇa* to be their preserve and as such have introduced into it, over the years, a number of new episodes that tend to impart it a new form (*Rāmāyaṇasyānyad iva svarūpam*, 50.10).

The last letter takes the trend to its culmination. It breaks the happy news that the author was engaged in translating into Sanskrit verse, the episodes peculiar to the Thai *Rāmāyaṇa*. The work has already touched four hundred verses and it is bound to swell further. It may be named *Thairāmāyaṇamañjarī* after Kṣemendra's *Bṛhatkathāmañjarī*.

The felicitative letters stand on a different footing. These were written on different occasions, to felicitate some of the most outstanding personages from different walks of life. They include stalwarts like Dr. C.D. Deshmukh, Dr. C. Sivaramamurti, Prof. Dharmendra Nath Shastri, Prof. Stietencron, Prof. Sarup Singh, Pt. Kamalapati Tripathi and Princess Sirindhorn of Thailand. Some of these write-ups are not in the form of letters. They have been included in the category because of the similar strand of contents. They are of moderate size, the lengthiest being of ten verses. The felicitative letters focus on the chief traits of the person and the contribution he made to the enrichment of his field of activity whichentitle him to elevation. Some of them add upto charming pieces of poetry.

CRITIQUE

The documents under study are doubtless letters. The medium of Sanskrit verse, however, has invested them with unusual charm. While the longer letters, as indicated earlier have the flavour of the Kāvya and are marked with the trappings associated with it, the shorter ones too are not shorn of poetic beauties. Rather, some of the shorter pieces occasionally steal the thunder. After all, they all have emanated from a highly talented poet. The author has been liberal in pressing into service the various *alaṁkāras* including the Arthāntaranyāsa and Anuprāsa which have resulted respectively in a wide variety of *subhāṣitas* and an abundant quantum of pleasing *padalālitya* flowing into them. They also betray a wealth of poetic flourishes. The author has not hesitated in taking recourse to the time-worn gimmick of the Citrakāvya. True to the poeticians' precepts a substantially large number of letters are composed of a wide range of lively descriptions. They are not wanting in *rasa* as well though it would be futile to expect in such writings an interplay of various forms of them. Like the longer poems, the letters are also dotted with a host of recondite grammatical forms, which however odd for the letters are not surprising in view of the form the author is eager to invest them with. Thus the posse of letters is armed with practically all that entitles a writing to the status of a Kāvya. This in fact is what they essentially are.

The letter may not be a suitable medium for lesser persons to delve into profound issues. However, the author has seized upon the opportunity offered by some of the letters to set forth his views on the theory of poetry. According to him, poetry, in essence, is a charming expression distinct from the beaten track,[3] Vakrokti as Bhāmaha holds it to be[4]. Language is the outer frame that sustains the Kāvya. It should be couched in forceful language that imparts it grace and vigour. It should be invested additionally with profundity of meaning and embellished with a variety of *alaṁkāras*[5]. Lucid expression lends it additional charm[6]. It is such a Kāvya that is easily acceptable to the connoisseur and evokes his esteem[7]. The author in his letters

---

3. उक्तिविशेषः काव्यं भाषा या भवति सा भवतु । Abhibhāṣaṇapadyāni, 8.9
4. सैषा सर्वैव वक्रोक्तिरनयार्थो विभाव्यते ।
   यत्नोऽस्यां कविना कार्यः कोऽलङ्कारोऽनया विना ॥ *Kāvyālaṁkāra*, 2.85
5. ओजस्विन्या गिरा बद्धमूर्जस्वि रुचिरं तथा ।
   अर्थगौरवयुक्तं चाप्यलङ्कारैरलङ्कृतम् ॥ Corpus of letters, 13.7
6. प्रसन्नपदाक्षरम् । ibid., 20.1
7. काव्यं सहृदयैरुक्तं हारि सुग्राह्यमेव च । ibid., 12.13

as elsewhere has made a vigorous effort to live upto his ideals.

DESCRIPTIONS

The rhetoricians have laid down varied descriptions as essential concomitants of the Kāvya[8]. These notwithstanding the impediment they created in the flow of the theme, established themselves as a powerful motif, eagerly exploited by the successive generations of poets. Whatever the distraction they might cause, these descriptions have been instrumental in ushering in variety and diversity in the theme that otherwise could have weighed down under insipid uniformity. The lettter is not the alluvial soil for the descriptions to sprout. But as a sensitive poet with keen insight into what transpires around him, the author has given his letters a sprinkling of varied descriptions besides brilliant pen-sketches of some of the eminent scholars of the day. By far the most important letter from this point of view is the one sent to Dr. Krishna Lal from Bangkok on 23.12.1978 where he mentions some of the Japanese Indologists whom he had met in Japan on the way back from his marathon tour of the U.S.A. and Canada which had taken him to as many as fourteen Universities therein, from the Columbia University, New York on the East coast to the University of California, Los Angeles on the West coast. In Japan the author had met Prof. Hajime Nakamura, Prof. Takakasi, Prof Sengaku Mayeda and Dr. Akira Yuyama for whose scholarship he has fulsome praise :

निवर्तमानो यात्रातो जापानेऽहश्चतुष्टयम् ।
विद्वत्सङ्गसुखाकृष्टः प्रमना व्यत्ययापयम् ।।
तत्र दृष्टा मया नाकामूरेत्याख्या विपश्चितः ।
ताकाकासीति चाप्यन्ये मायेदाख्यास्तथाऽपरे ।।
यूयामेत्यपरे चापि प्राच्यविद्याविशारदाः ।
अधीतिनः शास्त्रचये सर्वे पण्डिततल्लजाः ।।

प्रवृत्ता शास्त्रचर्चा तैः सह बहुमनेहसम् ।
वाचामगोचरश्चित्ते प्रमोदो जनितो यया ।। 12-15

The author was Visiting Professor for some time in the Catholic University, Leuven, Belgium. In a letter to Dr. Krishna Lal sent on 1.8.1987 from there he recounts the history of Sanskrit studies in that ancient seat of learning referring also to the large number of publications of the scholars there in the field :

8. *Sāhityadarpaṇa*, VI 322-324

सम्प्रत्यहं बेल्जियमाख्यदेशे
कृताधिवासो गमयामि कालम् ।
अत्रत्यविद्वत्प्रवरैः समेतो
निरन्तरं शास्त्रचये प्रसक्तः ।।

देशेऽतिरम्येऽत्र चकास्ति विश्व-
विद्यालयः ख्याततमो जगत्याम् ।
कैथोलिकाख्योऽतिपुरातनो यः
समेधितः सूरिपरम्पराभिः ।।
गीर्वाणवाणीपरिशीलनार्थ-
मप्यर्जितं येन यशोऽद्वितीयम् ।
अध्यर्धशत्यां नियमेन यस्मिन्
गीर्वाणवागध्ययनं प्रवृत्तम् ।।

ग्रन्था अनेके रचिता इहत्य-
विद्वत्प्रवेकैर्महता श्रमेण ।
उद्घाटयन्तो गहनं रहस्यं
विभान्ति ये संस्कृतवाङ्मयस्य ।। 44.3-6

In a letter sent to Mr. Alois Payer on 1.2.1984 the author mentions the names of these scholars :

गिल्बर्ट्पालेट्समाख्याता एगर्मण्टाभिधास्तथा ।
कैलिवार्तेत्यभिख्याश्च प्राच्यविद्याविशारदाः ।।
ख्यातिं परामधिगता विराजन्ते बुधा इह ।
यत्सङ्गमात् परां कोटिमानन्दस्याहमश्नुवे ।। 26.6-7

These descriptions form integral parts of the letters and do not seem to have been forcibly imposed upon them. They stem from the context and serve to provide pleasing diversion to the reader. The salubrious and comforting climate of the hills provides happy contrast to the heat of the plains in the summer. While writing to Dr.

D.K. Gupta on his return from a holiday at Ranikhet, the author was provoked to describe the blistering summer of Delhi. The scorching sun and searing winds spell misery all around, compelling the people to stay, as far as possible indoors :

तपत्यजस्रं बलवद् भगवान् तिग्मदीधितिः ।
उष्णाश्च वायवो वान्ति सर्वलोकस्य कष्टदाः ।। 8.3

The pithy depiction forcefully brings out the rigours of the summer.

The rains bring welcome relief to the harried peole. Next to the winter it is the most comforting season. When reminded by Dr. Krishna Lal of the rainy season at Delhi, the author was quick to describe back the rains at Bangkok. Within the space of two Svabhāvoktis he has captured the substance of the season. "Here also the rainy season is in full swing. The sky is overcast with clouds for the better parts of day and night. The cool breeze blows incessantly and torrents of rain continue for long. The tanks, now full of water have lotuses in full bloom. Everything appears to be washed de novo. The trees, bushes and creepers have donned the attractive robe of foliage":

अत्रापि वर्षाः प्रकटाः समन्ताद्
व्योमाम्बुदैरावृतमस्ति चापि ।
निरन्तरं वाति च शीतवातो
धाराश्च वर्षस्य पतन्ति भूयः ।।
सरांसि पूर्णानि जलस्य चापि
विकस्वराब्जानि सुखावहानि ।
वृक्षाश्च गुल्मानि च वीरुधश्च
नवाम्बरत्वं दधते सुपत्रैः ।। 17.5-6

In a personal letter to Mr. Alois Payer from Delhi on July 1,1988, the poet could not again resist the temptation of describing the rainy season that had just set in. "Now the season here is pleasing. The cool Zephyr comforts the people oppressed with heat. The torrential rains have resulted into vegetation all around which is a treat to the eyes. The clouds shedding continuous showers impart immense joy :

ऋतुः सुखो गन्धवहः सुखश्च
वर्षा इदानीं प्रकटप्रकर्षाः ।।
हरीतिमा सम्प्रति सम्प्रवृत्तो
नेत्रद्वयासेचनको विभाति ।
जलस्य धारा विसृजन् पयोद-
श्चामन्दमानन्दमवातनोति ।। 43.4-5

The letter (No.21) written to Dr. Krishna Lal from Bangkok on April 24,1979, carries a graphic account of Songkran (Saṅkrānti) festival celebrated in Thailand in the beginning of the month of Vaiśākha. It is essentially a water-sport. Men and women, without any distinction or hesitation, throw water on each other with gay abandon. Young girls also join the fun with gusto. It continues for three consecutive days without intermission. No immodesty or rudeness is involved in it. People sing, dance and laugh heartily. Lakhs of People throng Chiengmai to witness the fun. It appears to be an inflated but colourless version of our Holi :

सौङ्क्रान्समाख्योऽद्भुत उत्सवोऽयं
थाय्याख्यदेशोत्तरदिग्विभागे ।
रम्ये स्थले चांग्मइनाम्नि लोके-
नोत्साहपूर्वं क्रियतेऽतिभव्यः ।। 21.5
दिनत्रयं यावदयं प्रवृत्तः
शुभोत्सवो लोकमुदे प्रवृद्धः ।
नृत्यन्ति गायन्ति हसन्ति यान्ति
प्रोन्मुक्तभावेन जनाः समेऽत्र ।।
जलं तथाऽन्योन्यमिह क्षिपन्ति
दिनत्रयं यावदनारतं ते ।
असंस्तुतं वाप्यथ संस्तुतं वा
जलेन कामं स्नपयन्ति हृष्टाः ।।
स्त्रियः पुमांसश्च समं समेऽपि
क्रीडन्ति मोदात्सलिलेन कामम् ।

नारीति तेषां नर इत्ययं वा
विशेषलेशोऽपि न लक्ष्यतेऽत्र ।।
न शीलभङ्गो न च वृत्तभङ्गः
स्वप्नेऽपि तेषां परिकल्पनीयः ।
क्रीडेति सर्वे परिहासहेतोः
सामान्यभावेन जलं क्षिपन्ति ।। 21.7-10

Another letter (No.27) addressed to Dr. Krishna Lal on April 28, 1984 from Puri details the fascinating history of the installation of the images in the famous shrine there. "Once Indradyumna, the king of Ujjayinī saw three logs of wood floating in the sea. One of them bore the four emblems of Viṣṇu. Indradyumna alongwith his queen Guṇḍicā came to Puri. While he was thinking as to how the image of the great god was to be installed an aged Brāhmaṇa came to him and offered to fashion three images out of three logs on the condition that none would see him working behind closed doors. He set about his job in right earnest. Once the sound of carpentery suddenly ceased. The queen, in contravension of the stipulation, opened the door only to find the incomplete images. The Brāhmaṇa had mysteriously disappeared. He was actually the divine architect who had descended in the garb of the Brāhmaṇa. Indradyumna had the three icons of Kṛṣṇa, Baladeva and their sister Subhadrā installed in the shrine at Puri :

अपूर्णा मूर्तयस्तत्र तिस्र आसन् स्थिताः पुरः ।
तासां निर्माणकर्ता तु नैव कुत्राप्यदृश्यत ।। 27.26
अहो स्वयं विश्वकर्मा निर्ममे प्रतिमा इमाः ।
दारवीरिति हृष्टेन भक्तिप्रह्वेन चेतसा ।।
निश्चिक्यतुर्नृपश्चापि तत्पत्नी च सुलक्षणा ।
देवालये स्थापनीया विधिवत्प्रतिमा इति ।।
एवं निश्चयमास्थाय स्थापयामासतुस्तदा ।
तिस्रस्तौ प्रतिमा दिव्याः पुरीक्षेत्रेऽतिपावने ।। 27.28-30

A reference to the Rathayātrā festival of Puri is made in the next letter (No. 28) which also reminds the addressee Mr. Alois Payer that last year they were there to see for themselves the grandeur of the festival (28.3-4).

Some of the letters are punctuated by pretty penpictures of a number of mighty scholars of the day. These are not extravagant pieces to humour the person but are realistic sketches that encompass in their sweep the varied qualities of the scholars that elevate them to the status they hold. It is to the credit of the author that at his masterly touch the entire personality of the person comes to peep out of the stanzas, their brevity notwithstanding. This is how Pt. Mani Nath Jha is sketched in one of the letters (No.34) :

अधीतिनः शास्त्रचये पाण्डित्यं परमं गताः ।
जङ्गमान्येव तीर्थानि भवादृक्षा बुधोत्तमाः ।। 34.2

The sketch of Ācārya Vishva Bandhu has claimed a longer metre that has enabled the poet to be a bit more elaborate though, in essence, the two do not differ much :

वैदुष्यविभ्राजितदिग्दिगन्ता
विद्वत्समभ्यर्चितपादपद्माः ।
सुव्यक्तावाचो मम कोविदाग्र्या
आचार्यवर्याः प्रणतिं निवेद्याः ।। 2.4

The description of the Ācārya is doubtless more alliterative, poetic and forceful.

The author seems to be at his best in depicting the multi-dimensional personality of his father. It is doubtless characterised by greater warmth, but those who have known Prof. Charu Deva Shastri would bear it out that the mini-thesaurus of his myriad virtues that the son has attempted here does not suffer from exaggeration. He was an embodiment of erudite sholarship and saintliness. And this is what the author has sought to project in the two verses :

ह्रीरार्जवं सत्यमुदारता च
वाचां रहस्याकलने च वृत्तिः ।
अनेकशास्त्राविरताभियोगः
सूक्ष्मेक्षिकाऽन्यत्र सुदुर्लभा च ।।
परार्थचिन्ता मृदुभाषिता च
स्नेहस्तथा बन्धुजनेषु गाढः ।

दिगन्तविश्रान्तयशस्सु येषु
गुणा अनेके स्थितिमन्त आसन् ।। 41.5-6

The Anuprāsa and *padalālitya* combine to add charm to the sketch.

RASAS

Though it is not hard to come across letters surcharged with sentiments unlike the Kāvya they are scarcely amenable to the inter-play of the various emotions that criss-cross the tender mind. As a sensitive poet attuned to the throbbings of human heart under joy and sorrow, the author has utilized to the utmost the opportunity offered by the letters to depict some of the *rasas.* Incidentally Karuṇa (Pathos) emerges as the chief of the sentiments that found place in his letters.

The assassination of Prime Minister Indira Gandhi was a national shame and calamity. It had left the nation aghast. The spirit of India was struck in the heart. In a letter to his German colleague , Mr. Alois Payer, the author has tellingly depicted the grief that the tragedy had cast on the nation. The people were violently agitated at the macabre way they were robbed of Priyadarśinī, they loved so intensely :

नूत्नया घटनया सुदुःखिता
वज्रपातसमया समे जनाः ।
क्षुब्धमानसतरङ्गदोलिताः
सन्ति न क्षणमपीह सक्षणाः ।।

सर्वमेव परिवृत्तमिहास्ति
भारतं हृदि हतं न चकास्ति ।
यन्न चिन्तितमभून्मनसा त-
ज्जातमस्ति खलु दैवविपाकात् ।।

ख्यातेन्दिरा या प्रियदर्शिनीति
प्रियं न तद्दर्शनमद्य लभ्यम् ।
इत्येव शोकाकुलितान्तरङ्गः
सर्वो जनो भारतदेशवासी ।। 31.9-11

As indicated earlier, the letters (Nos.38-42), written in response to the condolence messages on the death of the author's father, are replete with Pathos. The letter addressed to Ācārya Divakaradatta Sharma stands out as the best piece of the lot. It is poignant in thrust and forcefully underscores the void his father's departure had left behind. *Jagajjīrṇāraṇyam* is what one cries in anguish at the fall of the colossus :

यावज्जीवं समाराध्य शब्दब्रह्म विशेषतः ।
तातपादा अन्तकाले तत्रैव विलयं गताः ।।
अनाथं संस्कृतजगदनाथा च सरस्वती ।
अनाथं चापि वैदुष्यमनाथा प्रतिभाऽपि च ।।
तादृशेऽथ महाभानावस्ताचलमुपेयुषि ।
तामिस्रमिव भात्येतज्जगत्कृत्स्नं चराचरम् ।। 38.3-5

It is Pathos again that dominates the letter to Pandit Pinakapani Madhyandina to condole the death of his father Pt. Sthanuddatta Sharma. "Being a devotee of Sthāṇu, he has gone to the abode of Sthāṇu. As a sublime soul he is not to be grieved at all. It is out of infatuation that we are overwhelmed with sorrow ":

स्थाणुदत्ताः स्थाणुभक्ताः स्थाणुभूयं गता ननु ।
अशोच्यास्ते, वयं मोहाद् भवामः शोककर्शिताः ।।
पितृशोको मयाऽप्यूढो भवद्भिरपि चेत्यतः ।
समदुःखौ स्थितावावां पितृव्यसनपीडितौ ।। 45..6

The sudden disappearance of the Brāhmaṇa engaged in fashioning the images of Viṣṇu and others, occasions Adbhutarasa. The moment the queen Guṇḍicā opened the door of the room, she found, to her amazement, neither the Brāhmaṇa nor any one else, but only the icons :

अपावृते पुनर्द्वारे नैव कक्षे ददर्श सा ।
विप्रं वाऽन्यं जनं वापि परं विस्मयमागता ।।
अपूर्णा मूर्तयस्तत्र तिस्र आसन् स्थिताः पुरः ।
तासां निर्माणकर्ता तु नैव कुत्राप्यदृश्यत ।। 27.25-26

It is interesting to note that of the two *rasas* depicted here, Karuṇa is held as the chief sentiment (*aṅgīrasa*) by Bhavabhūti[9], while the same status has been accorded to the Adbhuta by Nārāyaṇa Paṇḍita.[10]

FIGURES OF SPEECH

The *alaṁkāras*, according to Daṇḍin, heighten the beauties of the poem.[11] The judicious touch of an *alaṁkāra* purges the bald expression of its grotesqueness and imparts it uncommon lustre and effect. It is such a piece that meets the approbation of the connoisseur. The author has pressed into service several figures of speech, both of word and meaning to enliven his expression. However, the *alaṁkāras* to him are not an end in themselves but only a means to attain poetic excellences. His letters owe their charm, in no small measure, to the prudent application of the various figures of speech.

As evidenced by his other works the Anuprāsa (alliteration) is his favourite *alaṁkāra*. He has employed it liberally with fruitful results. It has invested his verses with sweetness and cadence, besides pleasing sound effect. The unusual flow that marks the innocuous query directed to Ācarya Vidyanidhi emanates from the graceful Anuprāsa it is clothed in :

कच्चित्सुखं कर्मसु सज्जमाना
रंरम्यमाणा गृहवाटिकासु ।
पितुः प्रहर्षं परिवर्धयन्तः
सर्वे सुपुत्राः कुशलोपपन्नाः ? ।।
कच्चित्सुखं तिष्ठति गेहके सा
पूज्या ममाम्बा गृहकार्यदक्षा ?
अन्येऽपि ये ज्ञातिगणा भवेयु-
रनामयं ते कलयन्ति कच्चित् ? ।। 3.4-5

The sweet *padalālitya* in the description of the scholarly attainments of Dr. Suniti Kumar Chatterji also owes itself to Anuprāsa :

---

9. *Uttararāmacarita*, III.47
10. तस्मादद्भुतमेवाह कृती नारायणो रसम्।
Sāhityadarpaṇa, Lucknow. v.s. 1978, p.64
11. काव्यशोभाकरान् धर्मानलङ्कारान् प्रचक्षते । *Kāvyādarśa*, II.1

हृद्यानवद्याखिलविद्यमान-
विद्याभिविद्योतितमानसानाम् ।
दिगन्तविश्रान्तयशोविलास-
विराजितानां तपसोज्ज्वलानाम् ।। 4.2

The following verse that seeks to felicitate Dr. Dharmendra Nath Shastri on his seventy-fifth birthday forms one of the most graceful illustrations of alliteration. It goes to the credit of the author that he has ably sustained the thrust of Anuprāsa even in a long metre like Sragdharā :

लोके यस्य चकास्ति हारि चरितं सौजन्यजन्यं यशो
यो धत्ते, मतिवैभवस्य सुतरां यश्च प्रमाणे स्थितः ।
सोऽयं तर्कशिरोमणिर्निशितधीर्धर्मेन्द्रनाथाभिधो
विद्वान् शास्त्रसुमालिसन्ततलसत्सत्स्रग्धरो[12] वन्द्यते ।। 53.1

Anuprāsa attains culmination in its refined version, popularly known as Antyānuprāsa, which has the added merit of lending rhythm to the verse. As is amply borne out by the *Śrībodhisattvacaritam* and *Śrīramakīrtimahākāvyam*, the author has unmatched expertise in exploiting it (the Antyanuprasa) to yield soothing sound-effect. The rhyme in the letters manifests itself in substantially different forms. While occasionaly all the four lines rhyme with each other, for the most it is confined to three or two lines only. It is a tribute to the author's skill that even in such writings as the letters he has whipped up the Antyānuprasa with considerable frequency. The verse, reproduced below, which forms part of the felicitative letter to Dr. D.N. Shastri, represents perhaps the most exquisite admixture of both the varieties :

प्रतिभाप्रतिभानभृतः सुभृशं
स्वयशःसुरभिर्विविधं विबुधः ।
स्पृहणीयचरित्रतयाऽद्य जग-
त्यविगीतनिपीतसुनीतिसुधः ।। 53.5

The same phenomenon is highlighted with equal force by the following verse addressed to Dr. C.D. Deshmukh. Here again both the varieties of Anuprāsa are

12. The name of the metre has been skilfully woven here.

interlaced :

शास्त्रेष्वधीती निपुणप्रतीति-

यस्य प्रिया भारतभारतीति ।

प्राचामपाचां विदुषां सुवाचा-

माचामकः प्राग्रहरो विभाति ।। 54.1

Some other verses wherein all the four or three lines rhyme may also be noted here, which, coupled with the earlier illustrations, would attest to the author's undisputed skill in handling this lovely *alaṁkāra* :

विविधशास्त्रचयप्रतिभापति-

र्जगति कीर्तितहृद्ययशःपतिः ।

सफलताधिपतिर्जगतीतले

जयति दिव्यगुणः कमलापतिः ।। 59.1

तस्याधुनाऽध्यक्षपदे नियुक्तः

शास्त्राटवीसञ्चरणप्रसक्तः ।

भक्तः प्रभोर्विज्ञजनानुरक्तः

श्रीतन्क्रनो विज्ञवरश्चकास्ति ।। 63.6

श्रीपायराख्याय विदां वराय

सौजन्यवैदुष्यगुणाकराय ।

सदा ममान्तःकरणे स्थिताय

शुभाशिषो मे शतशो लसन्तु ।। 48.1

Along with Anuprāsa some flashes of Yamaka can also be seen in letters. Yamaka consists in the repetition of words in the same sequence but with different or no meaning. In the lines that follow, the word *kṛtibhiḥ* is repeated thrice in the same order, but while the second and the third differ in their meanings, the first and the fourth are void of sense :

रुचिराकृतिभिः कृतिभिः कृतिभिः ।

परिपुष्टतमाभिरलंकृतिभिः ।। 15.6

In the following illustrations of Yamaka, culled from the letters, the repeated words have distinct or no meanings though they do not defy the sequence :

नैवं प्रत्येमि सुदृढं भविष्यति भविष्यति ।। 20.4

भवत्युत्सव उत्सवोऽक्ष्णोः । 21.4, 23.2

सन्तो वसन्ततिलकानवधीरयन्तः ।

तान् भारतस्य तिलकान् भवतो वदान्यान् ।। 35.5

माध्वीकमाधुर्यधरा धरायां । 36.4

न क्षणं क्षणमप्यन्यकार्यार्थं लब्धवान् । 49.3

यशःसौरभं सन्ततं सन्ततं स्याद् । 64.8

Of the Arthālaṁkāras , Upamā and Arthāntaranyāsa the author has repeatedly mustered to enrobe his expression. He has been more liberal in employing Upamā (Simile) in his letters than in Kāvyas. By comparing the *upameya* with the appropriate *upamāna*, the Simile seeks to shed the ambiguity that might otherwise stick to the subject. The author's *upamānas* have been drawn from a variety of sources. Some of his *upamānas* may not be novel, but they have been used with telling effect. The full moon or its crescent forms the standard of comparison in quite a few verses. He has used it to express his joy caused by Dr. Krishna Lal's letter. It overflowed his heart as the water of the ocean, agitated by the rays of the full moon, spills over its banks. While happiness has been explicitly compared here with the water of the ocean, the comparison of the letter with the full moon is implicit :

प्राप्तेन रम्येण भवद्दलेन

हर्षप्रकर्षो हृदि मे न माति ।

पयः पयोधेरिव पूर्णिमायां

शीतांशुरश्मिप्रकरप्रणुन्नम् ।। 21.1

Devadatta Bhatti's Kāvya, the author opines, would gladden the heart of the reader like the full moon (*pārvaṇaś candramā iva*, 24.4). The author was convinced that Dr. Krishna Lal's gifted daughter would grow, day by day, like the crescent of the moon (*cāndramasī kaleva* 50.7).

The author has also drawn some other *upamānas* from nature. His heart, he avers, was anxious on not receiving Prof. Stietencron's letter as is the Cātaka bird in the rainy season (*sotkaṇṭhaṁ tena ceto me varṣābde cātako yathā*, 30.2). The fond memory of his German friends was embedded deeply in his heart like the writing on the stone (*nikhāta sudṛḍhaṁ satyaṁ śilālipir ivācalā*, 30.5). In the stanza that follows, natural love has been compared to a hilly brook. True love wells up from one's heart like a cascade from the hill :

स्वयमेव समुद्भूतः पर्वतान्निर्झरो यथा ।

अकृत्रिमोऽनुरागो नो देशकालावपेक्षते ।। 31.7

On hearing the news of loot, arson and worse that followed Indira Gandhi's assassination, his worry increased like darkness in the dark night (*yac chrutvā vardhate cintā tamisrāyāṁ tamo yathā*, 32.2). The author was sure that Siddhārtha, the son of his friend, would blossom into a worthy citizen as the lotus blooms in the morning (*kamalam iva vikāsaṁ prāpnuhi tvaṁ prabhāte,* 57.5).

The verses recited at the All India Oriental Conference, Dharwar (1976), are adorned with two beautiful Similes. Here also the *upamānas* have been drawn from natural phenomena. The assembly shone forth with scholars like the sky with a host of stars or the flowers with the bees (*sada etad vibhāty adya nabhas tārāgaṇair iva// vidvadgaṇābhijuṣṭā yā prasūnālir ivālibhiḥ//* Abhibhāṣaṇapadyāni, 10.1-2). The felicitations extended by his well-wishers on his elevation as Head of he Department were valued by him like an inexhaustible treasure (*akṣayaṁ nidhim iva vidhinārpitaṁ mahyam,* ibid., 4.6). At the Farewell function arranged by Mr. Alois Payer, the author's heart agitated with emotions like a boat tossed by storm on high sea (*āndolitaṁ bhāvanayā ca bhūyo, vāteritaḥ pota ivāmburāśau* (Prakīrṇapadyāni, 4.8). Kālidāsa's genius has been compared with the *dīpaśikhā* that dispells darkness from everything wherever its light descends (ibid.,9.6). In the first of the preliminary verses of his planned poem *Viśvamahākāvyam,* the author has compared the earth decorated with various countries with the ornamental design on the body of an elephant (*aṅge gajānāṁ raciteva bhaktir vicitrarūpā jagatı vibhāti,* ibid., 12.1). While addressing his colleagues on assuming the reins of the Department, he exhorted them to unite like gems strung together in a garland[13]. With the measures he outlined, he was sure, the research-work in the Department would acquire lustre like a gem polished on whetstone.[14]

13. दृढं संग्रथिता भूत्वा सूत्रे मणिगणा इव ।

Abhibhāṣaṇapadyāni, 3.13

14. शाणोल्लीढो मणिरिव भूयो भूयः समुज्ज्वला भविता । ibid., 3.27

The author has also pressed into service the Mālopamā or the Simile wherein the *upameya* is compared with more than one *upamāna*. While congratulating Princess Sirindhorn of Thailand, one of his brilliant pupils, the author has compared her with the morning (*prabhātavelā*), tide of milky ocean and the all-bearing earth. The three *upamānas* serve to unravel three distinct aspects of the Princess's personality :

प्रभातवेलेव विभासितार्था
क्षीरोदवेलेव विशुद्धरूपा ।
सर्वंसहेलेव दृढा स्वमार्गे
जीव्याः सुखं त्वं शरदां शतानि ॥ 65.1

In the following verse that seeks to underscore the efficacy of the blessings, the author has compared them with the clouds laden with water and the mountains pregnant with a variety of minerals :

तोयगर्भा यथा मेघा धातुगर्भा यथाद्रयः ।
कल्याणगर्भा विदुषां तथैव ह्याशिषो मताः ॥ 11.2

Arthāntaranyāsa is the other *alaṁkāra* that the author has resorted to with some frequency. The general statement whipped up to strengthen the particular erxpression and vice-versa results in the emergence of Arthāntaranyāsa. It invariably ends up in a wise saying, the *subhāṣita*. How a series of *subhāṣitas* has flowed from it would be noticed later. The skilfulness with which the author has worked up Arthāntaranyāsa in his letters is indeed laudable. The verse reproduced below, purporting to thank his father for overlooking his lapse, is clothed in a beautiful Arthāntaranyāsa. Here the particular statement is sought to be reinforced with a general one. Even when violently shaken by the storm, the trees shed only flowers:

बालचापलमभूदिह यन्मे
क्षान्तमेव तदिति प्रमुदे मे ।
वायुनापि बलवत्प्रविधूताः
सङ्किरन्ति तरवः कुसुमानि ॥ 1.2

It is a measure of the fancy the author has taken for it that even such an innocuous matter as acknowledgement of a letter has been invested by him with the frame of Arthāntaranyāsa. The following illustrations would adequately exemplify his fascination for this figure of speech :

यत्सत्यमद्य प्रचुरप्रमोद-
वारांनिधावस्मि कृतप्रवेशः ।
चिराय लब्धा नहि किं प्रवृत्तिः
प्रियस्य बन्धोः प्रियमातनोति ।। 3.1

प्राप्तं पत्रं प्रेषितं यद् भवद्भि-
र्हृष्टश्चाहं प्राप्तमात्रेण तेन ।
बन्धूनां सत्प्रेमगर्भा गिरो हि
कल्याणानामर्पयित्र्यो भवन्ति ।। 10.1

The stanza that follows forms part of the letter, written from Bangkok to Dr. KrishnaLal and is intended to apprise him of the author's wellbeing. At the touch of the Arthāntaranyāsa, however, it comes to vibrate with poetic charm. Here again the general statement serves to uphold a particular one. With well-wishers like you praying for our happiness, we could not have been otherwise. How can the darkness threaten to overpower light when the sun is shining in full blaze :

सर्वत्र नो वार्तमवैत विज्ञा !
भवच्छुभेच्छासु कुतोऽन्यथा स्यात् ।
सूर्ये तपत्यावरणाय सत्यं
भवेत्प्रकाशस्य कुतस्तमिस्रा ।। 17.2

Dṛṣṭānta has also contributed its mite to raise the poetic excellence of the letters. It seeks to illustrate an assertion or statement with appropriate example, the two being in the *bimba-pratibimba* relationship. In the letter (No.15) to Ram Krishna Mishra of Bulandshahar, the author's statement that a creative writer in Sanskrit does every one proud is sought to be illustrated with the statement that the spread of moonshine is an unfailing source of joy to the Kumuda-flowers, which, in essentials, boils down to an example :

गीर्वाणवाणीरचनाकरेण

सत्यं भवेत्सर्वजनस्य मोदः ।

इन्दोः कराणां प्रसरेण विष्वक्

स्यादुत्सवः कैरवकाननस्य ।। 15.5

In the verse reproduced below, the statement and illustrative example again stand in the relationship of *bimba* and *pratibimba*. The argument that felicitations to a respected person are meaningless, is fallacious. Is not the sun, who is an embodiment of light, worshipped with lamp and incense ?

सम्मानितस्याथ जनस्य मानः

कैमर्थिकः स्यादिति नैव वाच्यम् ।

प्रकाशरूपो नहि तिग्मरश्मि-

र्दीपेन धूपेन च पूज्यते किम् ? ।। 64.5

For other examples of Dṛṣṭānta one may profitably turn to 35.3, 56.1, 60.7, etc.

While the letters are interspresed with Svabhāvokti, one does not encounter the Atiśayokti so frequently. The Svabhāvokti amounts to a versified replica of the subject the poet seeks to describe. Most of the descriptions in the letters are based on Svabhāvokti. The description of the Catholic University of Belgium and the Indological studies conducted there is likewise enrobed in the Svabhāvokti. It again forms the basis of the description of Tübingen, "Perched on the hill-slope, on the bank of the Neckar river, the lovely town of Tübingen is embellished with vistas of trees and pastures. Its sky-scrapers are a treat to the eye. Its pleasure-groves are strewn with flowers. The trees laden with a variey of bloom and fruits appear in majestic glory. Within the space of three Upajāti verses the author has sought to describe in totality the beauties bestowed on the town by nature :

विराजमानं गिरिमेखलासु

सौन्दर्यमत्यद्भुतमादधानम् ।

नेकारनद्या निकटे निविष्टं

ट्यूबिंगनाख्यं पुरमस्ति तत्र ।।

विराजितं पादपराजिभिर्य-

द्विभूषितं श्यामलभूमिभागैः ।
अभ्रंलिहाग्रैर्भवनैरनेकै-
रलङ्कृतं नेत्रसुखं ददाति ॥

आकीर्णपुष्पस्तबका वसन्ते
दीर्घा अपूर्वां सुषमां दधानाः ।
पूर्णैः फलानां तरुभिः प्रपूर्णा
विभान्ति यत्रत्यविहारवीथ्यः ॥ Prakīrṇapadyāni, 11.2-4

Of the several varieties of Atiśayokti, the one based on the absorption of *prastuta* into *aprastuta* is perhaps the most fascinating and poetic. It is this variety that has caught the author's fancy. While describing the death of his father he avers in one of his letters (No.38) that on the departure of the mighty sun to the setting-mountain, the world seems to have sunken into cussed darkness. Here the sun and the western mountain stand for his father and death respectively. The imagery in the second hemistich lends lustre to the Atiśayokti. Both combine to result into a happy idea :

तादृशेऽथ महाभानावस्ताचलमुपेयुषि ।
तामिस्रमिव भात्येतज्जगत्कृत्स्नं चराचरम् ॥ 38.5

Elsewhere also the author has resorted to this. In the address to his colleagues on assuming the stewardship of the Department, he described it as a garden. The students are the flowers, the teachers fountain (-heads of knowledge) and its fame is the divine fragrance. The *aprastutas* have so thoroughly swallowed the *prastutas* that the latter are hardly discernible to the reader unless he is aware of the context:

उद्यानमिदमस्माकं नानापुष्पैः सुशोभितम् ।
नानाप्रस्रवणैश्चापि दिव्यगन्धि मनोहरम् ॥ Abhibhāṣaṇapadyāni, 3.14

In the hemistich reproduced below, the cause *pratīkṣā* has not resulted into the meeting of the author with the addressee which should have been its natural sequel. It is Viśeṣokti :

प्रतीक्षमाणावन्योन्यमप्यावां नैव सङ्गतौ 16.4

Virodhābhāsa has also claimed quite a few verses. The apparent contradiction involved in it disappears on deeper consideration. What the author wrote to his German friend Mr. Payer adds up to reflect Virodhābhāsa. "Though bodily far removed, I am close to your heart."

दूरस्थितोऽपि कायेन मनसा निकषाऽस्मि वः ।। 25.2

The author has again used it effectively to detail the characteristics of Kālidāsa's style.

वेगाद्वहन्ती च न चोत्तटा च ।

गम्भीरभावा च न चाप्रसादा ।। Prakīrṇapadyāni, 9.5

LANGUAGE

Conceived as Kāvya, the letters are distinguished by a language that is fully worthy of a Kāvya. It is as chaste as the language of an enlightened grammarian can be. And it is as lucid as can emanate from a sensitive poet. Its chastity is not limited to mere adherence to grammatical requirements. It is rich in idiom. In fact, the letters are couched in a language that should be current coin among the *śiṣṭas,* the cultured. *acirāyiṣi yad bandho patrapratīvacasy aham* (20.2); *kṣamāpayāmi svam ato bhvadbhyaḥ* (21.3.); *pravartayiṣye na cirād vimarśaṁ teṣv iha sthitaḥ* (22.10); *putrīyāmi priye tasmin* (37.5); *atratyā devabhāṣāyāḥ śikṣakā mayi hārdinaḥ* (Prakirapadyāni, 3.3), etc. are such expressions that bespeak the author's mastery over the nuances of Sanskrit semantics besides his equipment in grammar. In his scheme of things, lucidity of language is the hall-mark of poetry (*prasannapadākṣaram*, 20.1). This is what makes the Kāvya graceful and acceptable (*kāvyaṁ sahṛdayaiḥ uktaṁ hari sugrāhyam eva ca*, 12.13). Lucidity, however, is not synonymous with shallowness (*gambhīrabhāvā ca na cāprasādā*, Prakīrṇapadyāni, 9.5). *Prasāda* (perspecuity) and *arthagaurava* (profundity of meaning) is what characterise the corpus of the author's letters. Sweetness of diction is the natural concomitant of lucidity. And the letters abound in sweetness of phraseology (*padalālitya*) which, as hinted earlier, has emanated from the abundance of alliteration that, in a way, forms the corner-stone of the edifice of the author's poetry. The craftsman in him is adept in spinning out with ease the unending strings of alliteration that invariably result into *padalālitya*. It is not the product of any deliberate effort on his part. It is inherent in his muse. This effortless ease adds grace to his alliteration and sweetness to his phraseology.

The author has indeed an inexhaustible repository of graceful phraseology. He can conjure it up at the slightest instance, almost out of nothing. The joy on receiving his father's letter has spurred him to shower elegant verses marked by sweetness and unhindered flow. One of them merits reproduction :

सम्प्राप्य तूर्णं प्रणयेन पूर्णं
दलं सरागं भवदीयमद्य ।
वाचं स्वकीयां विसृजामि सद्य-
स्तुष्टोऽस्मि हृष्टोऽस्मि सुखं स्थितोऽस्मि ।। 2.1

This is how he sought co-operation from his colleagues on assuming the charge of the Department. The verse is brimming with *lālitya* :

रुचिराकृतिभिः कृतिभिः कृतिभिः
मम साह्यमिहास्तु कृतं कृतिभिः ।
सुरवाचमिमां प्रति सर्वनृणां
रुचिरा रुचिरारचितास्त्वचिरात् ।। Abhibhāṣaṇapadyāni, 3.11

Some more instances of *padalālitya* are reproduced here to drive home the author's skill in the art :

(i) आशीर्वचो हि भवतां भवतापहारि
यत्प्राप्तमद्य मयका परमोपकारि ।। 11.1

(ii) माध्वीकमाधुर्यधरा धरायां
गीर्वाणगीर्यद्ध्रियतेऽधुनापि ।
सदा तदर्थं विहिताभियोगा
भवादृशा एव निबन्धनानि ।। 36.4

(iii) गुण्यः शास्त्रसुमालिसन्ततलसत्सत्स्रग्धरो वन्द्यते ।। 53.1

(iv) अविगीतनिपीतसुनीतिसुधः । 53.5

(v) प्राचामपाचां विदुषां सुवाचा-
माचामकः प्राग्रहरो विभाति ।। 54.1

Not unlike his longer poems, the author's letters are also padded with a fairly large number of intricate grammatical forms. These are evidently out of tune with the letters, but seem to have been prompted by the author's eagerness to establish them as worthy pieces of poetry. The forms span almost all the prominent parts of Sanskrit grammar including frequentatives, denominatives, compounds, complicated usages of kārakas, forms ending in primary and secondary suffixes besides aorist which seems to be the poet's major weakness. Some of the learned forms may be listed here to give an idea of the author's equipment in grammar :

रंरम्यमाणाः (3.4), चेखिद्यते (18.3), तन्तनीति (67.2), पार्वतीज्ञानिः (6.2), पारदृश्वा (4.7) अरुन्तुदः (20.20), पाठं पाठम्, पायं पायम् (49.18), पद्यरूपैः (49.16), काशिकान् (8.6), दारवीः (27.28), अध्यत्र जने, ईश्वरेऽधि (17.12), अधीतिनः शास्त्रचये (19.15), गृहमावसन् (49.4), प्रतिसङ्किरन्ते (3.3), व्यलम्बिषि (4.4), अपपारम् (13.2), प्रत्यैक्षिष्ट (16.4), अचिरायिषि (20.2), आसीषदम् (22.1), अध्यजीगपम् (22.6), व्यरीरचम् (22.7), अलेखिषम् (43.1), अध्यवर्तिषि (47.3), अशकम् (49.1)

प्रकीर्णपद्यानि-- हार्दिनः (3.3), जन्मान्तरीणः (3.6), विद्वान् (12.6), सुदुःसाधम् (12.6).

While the *padalālitya* in the letters has stemmed from the judicious application of Anuprāsa the plethora of *subhāṣitas* that embellishes the language have their genesis in the exuberance of Arthāntaranyāsa the author's skill in handling which is admittedly superb. That has resulted into the emergence of a number of *subhāṣitas* which shine like jewels scattering lustre all around. These have been instrumental in warding off the monotony that could have otherwise tarnished the language. They testify to the author's keen mind, penetrating observation and wide learning. An idea of their grandeur can be had from some of the more exquisite of them listed below :

(i) वायुनापि बलवत्प्रविधूताः
सङ्किरन्ति तरवः कुसुमानि । 1.2

(ii) बन्धूनां सत्प्रेमगर्भा गिरो हि
कल्याणानामर्पयित्र्यो भवन्ति ।। 10.1

(iii) दिव्यं निधिं नु समवाप्य न कः प्रहृष्येत् ।। 17.1

(iv) सूर्ये तपत्यावरणाय सत्यं
भवेत्प्रकाशस्य कुतस्तमिस्रा । 17.2

(v) चिरं गुरो ! कार्यविधौ न कार्यम् । 17.9

(vi) निगूढमन्त्रणानां हि सर्वं चित्तेऽवतिष्ठते । 20.13

(vii) नाग्निना शाम्यति ह्यग्निः क्रोधः क्रोधेन नैव च ।
परस्परविरोधो हि परस्परविनाशकृत् ।। 32.5

(viii) यशोधनानां हि यशो गरीयः । 33.3

(ix) अनौचित्यकृता दोषा उद्वेगायैव केवलम् । 49.2

(x) शरीरकष्टं कष्टाय भवेदिष्टस्य सर्वथा । 51.3

(xi) चन्द्रस्य कान्तेः प्रसरेण विष्वक्
स्यादुत्सवः कैरवकाननस्य ।। 56.1

(xii) भावो जन्मान्तरीणो हि स्थिरः सम्बन्ध उच्यते । Prakīrṇapadyāni, 3.6.

(xi) पुस्तकीभवति पण्डितः । ibid., 4.3

(xiv) न साहसानाश्रयिणो जनाः स्युः
कल्याणभाजो जगतीतलेऽत्र ।। ibid., 12.7

The language is further embedded with a number of expressions from ancient texts. This is the wont of the author which he has kept up in his letters also. These borrowals represent universal ideas that are bound to occur to the modern writer. They should not be construed to diminish the originality of the author; they rather lend grace to his phraseology. The borrowals fall into two categories. While some of them have been bodily lifted from their sources; others have been modified/altered to suit the context and the metre. *āsīn mahīkṣitām ādyaḥ praṇavaś chandasām iva* (51.15); *nakṣatratārāgrahasaṁkulāpi jyotiṣmatī candramasaiva rātriḥ* (60.7); *purāṇam ity eva na sādhu sarvaṁ na cāpi sarvṁ navam ity avadyam* (ibid., 11.4): *prābhāmahatyā śikhayeva dīpaḥ, trimārgayeva tridivasya mārgaḥ* (Prakirṇapadvāni, 9.2) belong to the first category. The other parallels are listed here alongwith their originals :

(i) कश्चित्स्नेहमयस्तन्तुरन्तर्मर्माणि सीव्यति । 31.3
स हि स्नेहात्मकस्तन्तुरन्तर्मर्माणि सीव्यति । *Uttararāmacarita*, V.17

(ii) नास्ति येषां यशःकाये जरामरणजं भयम् । 39.3
the same, *Nītiśataka*, verse 42

(iii) संविभक्ततया जातं मद्दुःखं सह्यवेदनम् 41.9
संविभक्तस्य दुःखस्य सह्या स्याद् वेदनेति यत् । 42.3

स्निग्धजनसंविभक्तं हि दुःखं सह्यवेदनं भवति ।

Abhijñānaśākuntala (AS), p.147

(iv) सर्वं शून्यमिवाभाति तदभावे जगन्मम । 42.6

शून्यं मन्ये जगत् *Uttararāmacarita*, III.38

जगज्जीर्णारण्यं भवति ibid., VI.38

(v) स्नेहप्रवृत्तिरेवैवंदर्शिनी । 42.6

स्नेहप्रवृत्तिरेवंदर्शिनी । *AS*, p.240

(vi) लब्धः पत्रेण कुशलोदन्तः प्रियजनस्य हि

किञ्चिदेव भवेदूनः सङ्गमादिति सूरयः ।। 44.2

कान्तोदन्तः सुहृदुपनतः सङ्गमात्किञ्चिदूनः ।। *Meghadūta*, 97

(vii) मोदमानौ दमे स्वस्मिन् क्रीडन्तौ पुत्रनप्तृभिः । 46.2

क्रीडन्तौ पुत्रैर्नप्तृभिर्मोदमानौ स्वे दमे ।।

Ṛgveda, X.85, *Atharvaveda*, XIV.1.22

(viii) अनिशं पालयन्तौ च कुलधर्मं सनातनम् । 46.5

कुलक्षये प्रणश्यन्ति कुलधर्माः सनातनाः । *Bhagavadgītā*, I.40.

(ix) चेतःप्रसादः सुतरां मत आवश्यको यतः ।

प्रसादे सर्वदुःखानां हानिर्जीवस्य जायते ।। 52.16

प्रसादे सर्वदुःखानां हानिरस्योपजायते ।

प्रसन्नचेतसो ह्याशु बुद्धिः पर्यवतिष्ठते ।। *Bhagavadgītā*, 2.65

(x) काष्ठं च काष्ठं च यथा पयोधौ

संयुज्यते चापि वियुज्यते च ।

तथैव लोकः स्वयमेव लोके

संयुज्यते चापि वियुज्यते च ।। Prakīrṇapadyāni, 4.6

यथा काष्ठं च काष्ठं च समेयातां महोदधौ ।

समेत्य च व्यपेयातां तद्वद्भूतसमागमः ।। *Rāmāyaṇa*, II.105.26

Mahābhārata, XII.28.36

(xi) अथ योगवियोगभागयं

शुभमाध्याय विसृज्यतां जनः ।

निजदेशमुपैतुमर्थ्यतां

त्वरितं नोऽस्तु च सङ्गमः पुनः ।। Prakīrṇapadyāni, 4.11

पुनरस्तु त्वरितं समागमः ।। *Naiṣadhīyacarita*, II.62

(xii) स्नेहप्रवृत्तिरेवैवंदर्शिनीति भवेन्ननु ।। 42.6

काश्यपः - स्नेहप्रवृत्तिरेवंदर्शिनी । *Abhijñānaśākuntala,* Act. IV

(xiii) चिन्तामणिश्चिन्तितमेव सूते ।। 54.3

चिन्तामणिश्चिन्तितमेव दत्ते

सतां हि सङ्गः सकलं प्रसूते ।। An old Sūkti.

METRES

The letters, the addresses and the messages sent by the author provide wide avenues for him to employ a fairly large number of metres, based on both *varṇas* (syllables) and *mātrās* (instants). While Āryā is the only *mātrāvṛtta* pressed into service, the other variety includes half equal metres (*ardhasamavṛttas*) as well. Besides the favourite Upajāti which dominates almost all his works, the author has also come to grips with demanding metres like Toṭaka, Bhujaṅgaprayāta and Rucirā. He has taken recourse to the mighty Śārdūlavikriḍita and Sragdharā as well. All these combine to bear testimony to the author's equipment in prosody. His skill in metrics also unfolds itself in his incorporating in the body of the verses the names of the metres used therein[15]. In all the author has used here twently one metres which are as follows: Anuṣṭup, Indravajrā, Upendravajrā, Upajāti, Śālinī, Rathoddhatā, Svāgatā, Bhujaṅgaprayāta, Vidyunmālā, Drutavilambiṭa, Toṭaka, Dodhaka, Praharṣiṇī, Rucirā, Vaitālīya, Viyoginī, Vasantatilakā, Mālinī, Śārdūlavikriḍita, Sragdharā and Āryā.

The author's letters thus have all the trappings of a Kāvya. It is these that elevate these 'matter of fact' writings to poetic heights. One can assuredy browse through them with fruitful result.

---

15. (i) गुण्यः शास्त्रसुमालिसन्ततलसत्सत्स्रग्धरो वन्द्यते । 53.1
(ii) शोभां वसन्ततिलकादधिकां दधानः । 59.4
(iii) स्वच्छन्दं विचरन्नमन्दमतनोच्छार्दूलविक्रीडितम् । 59.5

CHAPTER FIVE

MISCELLANEOUS WORKS

(i) ṢAḌṚTUVARṆANAM
(ii) NAPUṀSAKALIṄGASYA MOKṢAPRĀPTIḤ
(iii) KO 'HAM
(iv) MAHĀKAVIKĀLIDĀSĀṢṬAKAM

ṢAḌṚTUVARṆANAM

As the name implies, the *Ṣaḍṛtuvarṇanam* (*SRV*)[1] amounts to be a brief account of the six Indian seasons. These seasons with their diverse characteristics and shifting phenomena, have exercised down the ages, powerful fascination for the Sanskrit poets to describe them with gusto. Beginning with Vālmīki, the successive generations of poets have vied with each other to describe the beauty, hospitability or ferocity of different seasons of the country. With the classical authors, it established itself as one of the essential motifs of a Mahākāvya. Our author's *SRV* forms a link in the long chain of *ṛtuvarṇanas.*

No poet, howsoever gifted, can afford to be exhaustive in detailing, with poetic trappings, the six seasons in the diminutive frame of fifteen verses. Unlike in Kālidāsa,[2] the poem opens with spring. It has claimed three stanzas, which notwithstanding their traditional tenor, capture in no small measure, the maddening charm that the *ṛturāja* unleashes all around. The host of cuckoos, black bees, salvan zephyr, the mango-blossoms, etc. may seem trite to the modern reader but these are what form the essential ingredients of the spring and lend it charm and meaning (1-3).

The next two verses, devoted to the description of the scorching summer, constitute poetically the best part of the poem. The wild fire which reduces to ashes everything that comes into its sweep, the burning sun and dusty storms present the true picture of the Indian summer. While some of the birds, gasping for breath, struggle to beat the heat in the waterbasins, others retreat to the somewhat cosy holes of the trees, with their young ones tucked under the protective umbrella of their wings (4-5).

The author has been generous in apportioning five of the fifteen verses to the rainy season. It is the rains that provide relief from the oppressive heat. The hovering dark clouds with frequent flashes of lightning, torrents of rain, the captivating cooings of the peacocks, rumblings of the clouds and croaking of the frogs and delightful winds not only afford contrast to the heat and dust of the summer but also usher in a phase that brings cheer and comfort to parched earth and harassed people (6-10),

---

1. First published in the *Saṁskṛta-Ratnākaraḥ,* Jaipur, Vol. IX, No. 4, November, 1962. Reproduced later in *Bhāratī*. Vol. VII, Caitra, Saṁvat 2013.
2. The *Ṛtusaṁhāra* begins with the description of summer.

The autumn adds new dimension to the phenomenon. The *kāśa* flowers sprout all around, the quarters are purged of darkness inflicted by the rainy season, the crops, ripe for harvesting, generate infinite hope in the farmer and the clouds shed their darkness and assume whiteness (11-12).

The poet does not seem to be much fond of Hemanta. It has been curtly disposed of in a solitary verse. After all, it is the Hemanta that causes the greatest grief to the *cakravākas* (13).

The last two verses seek to describe the Śiśira. With everything withered, it is the most desolate season. The trees are denuded of their leaves, the creepers lose lustre and the lotuses are burnt with frost. The whole earth bears the appearance of a woman in tattered rags.

The *SRV* cannot lay claim to originality, so far as the ideas are concerned. It follows the similar description of the ancient poets. Some of the ideas bear striking resemblance with what we find in Kālidāsa's *Ṛtusaṁhāra*[3] or Vālmīki's description. It is the lucidity and chastity of language that turn out to be the hallmarks of the poem As it is basically descriptive, the *SRV* does not admit of tender imageries or highflown fancies, though the *ṛtuvarṇana* is not unworthy of such flights and flourishes. Besides alliteration, it is the Svabhāvokti that is the chief characteristic of the poem. Some of the Svabhāvoktis are simply superb because of the way they bring out the varied traits of the different seasons. The description of the summer in the following two verses has the merit of capturing the distinguishing situations in their totality. The summer is enlivened here with all that is harshly associated with it :

वृक्षसंघट्टजन्मा दवाग्निर्महान्
दन्दहीति द्विजान्श्वापदांश्चाकुलान् ।
जाज्वलीत्यन्तरिक्षं दिशो धूसरा
रंहसा वान्ति वात्या रजोविक्षिपाः ॥

घर्मक्लान्ता विवृतवदना आलवालेष्वजस्रं
चङ्क्रम्यन्ते विकिरनिकरा उच्छ्वसन्तस्तपर्तौ ।
क्रोडीकृत्यापिदधति शिशून्शाखिनां कोटरेषु
पित्सन्तोऽन्ये क्वचिदपि वने छायया पर्यटन्ति ॥ 4-5

---

3. cf. SRV., IV; *Ṛtusaṁhāra*, 1.25-26

The relevance of the Svabhāvokti ies in the precision with which it highlights the subject under description. The description of the rainy-season, reproduced below, has the merit of encompassing the various traits of the season in their entirety. That indeed contributes to its elegance :

नरिनृतति मयूरा गर्जितं खे निशम्य
परिरटति च भेकः कूर्दमानः सहर्षम् ।
परिसरति बलाका मेघसंसर्गकामा
वहति च पवमानश्शाखिनः संधुनानः ।। 9

The following description of the autumn is marked by Arthāntaranyāsa. Here a particular idea is sought to be reinforced with a general statement. The rains have resulted in rich harvest. Having done their duty, the clouds have now assumed white colour. Those who seek the solicitude of others always beam with happiness :

जीमूताः कृषिषु चिरं विमुच्य तोयं
क्षेत्रौघान् सपदि विधाय सस्यपूर्णान् ।
शुभ्रत्वं दधति कृतोपकारभारा
दीप्यन्ते न भुवि परार्थसम्पदः के ।। 12

With everything shorn of charm in the Śiśira, the earth seems, to be clad as it were, in rags. It is Utprekṣā :

गुल्मिन्यो विगतंप्रभा विटपिनो विष्वग्विलुप्तच्छदा
हिम्येनापि नभस्वता वनभुवां शादाः समुज्जासिताः ।
पद्मिन्यो विरसास्तुषारमथिताः खेदाय नः साम्प्रतं
विश्वस्तेव च हन्त ! भाति वसुधा शोकेन शीर्णाम्बरा ।। 15

In the last line of the stanza above there is Virodhābhāsa in that the earth is said to be *viśvastā,* reassured, which does not go well with its description *śokena śīrṇāmbarā*, in tattered rags with *śoka*, sorrow . The Virodhābhāsa, however, is resolved with the help of Śleṣa, *viśvastā* having the other meaning, though not so familiar, of widow, vide Amara: *viśvastāvidhave same.* For a widow to be enveloped in sorrow would be quite understandable.

The descriptions of the seasons does not occasion many a grammatical nicety. However, the author's predilection for grammar shows itself in some of the learned froms. These may be detailed here- दन्दहीति, जाज्वलीति (4), चङ्क्रम्यन्ते, (5), काल्यम् (6), वर्षुकः (7), नर्तं नर्तम् (8), नरिनृतति (9), समुज्जासिताः (15).

Curiously enough, the poet has been at pains in demonstrating in this small poem his skill in metrics. He has used fourteen metres in fifteen verses including the not-so-familiar Mattamayūra and Bhramaravilasita. Verses two and three are couched in Upajāti. The other metres employed are (1). Vasantatilakā, (4) Sragviṇī, (5). Mandākrāntā, (6) Śālinī, (7) Rathoddhatā, (8) Mattamayūra, (9) Mālinī, (10) Hariṇī, (11) Bhramravilasata, (12) Praharṣiṇī, (13) Vaṁśastha, (14) Toṭaka, (15) Śārdūlavikrīḍita.

The *SRV* is a welcome addition to the literature on the description of Indian seasons.

Incidentally, it is the first poem available in print of the author. It was published when he was hardly twelve. The editor of the magazine where it had appeared as early as 1942 in his editorial Note has mentioned the fact of his age. Coming from a boy of 12, the poem shows remarkable maturity. It looks quite strange that he should have developed even at that young age such a thorough grasp of prosody to try his hand at a variety of metres, some of them rather complex and intricate as also develop the sense of the appropriateness of their use. He has described Vasanta in Vasantatilakā, the dancing peacocks, the *mattamayūras*, in Mattamayūra, the leaves falling from the trees; there being *viyoga*, separation of them from the trees; in Viyoginī. Such kind of uncanny insight into the connection with meaning of the names of the metres and the subject-matter described is rare even in a grown-up poet, not to speak of in a budding one. But then Pratibhā is something inborn and is one of the first prerequisites of poetry.

The poem under reference is a proof positive of the author having been born with that. It unfolded itself later in the form of a number of Mahākāvyas and Khaṇḍakāvyas making him a front-ranking creative writer in Sanskrit of the present century.

NAPUMSAKALINGASYA MOKṢAPRĀPTIḤ

The short play *Napuṁsakaliṅgasya Mokṣaprāptiḥ* (*NMP*)[1] serves to unravel a different aspect of the author's equipment. It humorously attributes the unhappy plight of the Sanskrit language to the controversy that has raged down the ages, about the uncertainty of the nature of the masculine and neuter genders in the disquisitions on grammar and actual practice.

The masculine gender finds Sanskrit dismayed over the people's aversion in contrast to their whole-hearted devotion to it in earlier times. On finding that the predicament, on the festive day of Holikā, emanates from the conflict in which the neuter gender is locked with it, the masculine vows to destroy the former. Soon the neuter alongwith the host of his allies like Liṭ, Leṭ, etc., is arrayed against the masculine and boasted of his glorious lineage. After all, it is a scion of Śikhaṇḍin, who, though impotent, had killed Bhīṣma in the great war. The masculine sticks to his guns and musters ancient texts to uphold the existence of only two genders--masculine and feminine and thereby makes a cogent case against the neuter : *tatra bhagavatā bhāṣyakāreṇāpi āvirbhāvarūpaḥ pumān, tirobhāvarūpā ca strīti lakṣaṇa-svīkārāt mama ca striyāś caivāstitvaṁ svīkṛtam. Helārājo 'py evam āha....evaṁ ko 'vasaro yan napuṁsakaḥ syāt* (p.98). The allies of the neuter assert its unmistakable existence, between man and woman. It provides the masculine an opportunity to ridicule it as a Triśaṅku and warn it not to oppress Saṅskrit in any way. The neuter reminds the masculine of the greatness that the grammarians have bestowed upon him in maintaining that when the two clash it is the neuter that survives : *napuṁ-sakānapuṁsakayar napuṁsakam avaśiṣyae* (p.98). In fact, the masculine (puṅliṅgam), he taunts, smacks of the neuter. That cuts the masculine to the quick. He asserts that he is puṅliṅgaḥ and not puṅliṅgam, but in the process does not refrain from pouring scorn on Pāṇini. Even the poets, he avers, did not shun to have a jibe on the great grammarian for the intricacies with which is padded his text so far as the neuter gender was concerned. He holds Pāṇini responsible for inventing the demon in the form of the neuter. As the neuter protested, the puṁliṅga threw it, alongwith its cohorts, in the leaping flames of Holikā. While the masculine and his allies congratulated the Sanskrit language for the riddance she had thus achieved, Napuṁsakaliṅga attained emancipation from worldly bondage. After all, this is what Pāṇini had predicted and what Śrīharṣa had visualised :

---

1. *Bhāratī*, Jaipur, Vol. IV, No. 3, Saṁvat 2010.

उभयी प्रकृतिः कामे भवेदिति मुनेर्मतम् ।
अपवर्गे तृतीयेति क्लीबो मोक्षमवाप्नुयात् ।।

It is scarcely possible to put the *NMP* under the umbrella of any of the ten traditional forms of Rūpaka. It may however be loosely designated as a One Act Play, though the tiny frame hardly entitles it to the appellation. It evidently lacks the frame-work that is needed to sustain that variety of play. The *NMP* has neither the desired canvas of the story nor the accompanying charm of verses to be placed in the tradition of One Act Plays of the ancient masters. Nevertheless, it marks a novel experiment in the stage of Sanskrit drama. The *NMP* is perhaps the sole play to have been based on what is otherwise deemed as a taboo to the playwright – the *śabdaśāstra* (grammar). With its abstract characters it may also be called an allegorical play. The two prominent dramatis personae, (the masculine and neuter genders) alongwith their friends Liṭ, Luṭ, Leṭ, etc. and their wives Yaṅluṅanta and Phakkikās are as shorn of concrete personality as the characters in Aśvaghoṣa's unnamed allegorical play or Kṛṣṇamiśra's *Prabodhacandrodaya.*

The *NMP* is rather intended to pour ridicule on the uncertainty that attends the determining of the gender in general and resolving the clash between the masculine and neuter with respect to the adjectives in particular. It was natural for a grammarian like the author to pick up such a knotty issue of Sanskrit grammar for dramatic representation. With the masculine determined to black out the very existence of its foe, the two genders are viewed here as two arch rivals. The two pit their forces in battle-like formations. The arguments against neuter are doubtless picked up from authoritative texts like the *Mahābhāṣya* and the *Vākyapadīya*. With equally sound logic the neuter, on the authority of Pāṇini, (*Napuṁsakānapuṁsakayor napuṁsakam avaśiṣyate*), counters the masculine and drives him into a tight spot by reminding him that his very name puṅliṅgam owes itself to neutrality. However, the masculine has the last laugh, but not before taking a dig at Pāṇini. The master grammarian has done havoc with the loving-folk, who, in a way, have been cheated of their heart :

नपुंसकमिति ज्ञात्वा प्रियायै प्रेषितं मनः ।
तत्तु तत्रैव रमते हताः पाणिनिना वयम् ।। पृ0 99

The playwright has been rather harsh in denouncing the poor neuter. In bragging of its noted lineage, the neuter unwillingly brings itself into pungent disrepute :

अभूत्पुरा वीरवरः शिखण्डी
जघान भीष्मं निशितैः शरैर्यः ।
तस्यैव वीरस्य कुले प्रजातो
नपुंसकोऽहं समुपस्थितोऽस्मि ।। पृ0 98

Worse is the position that is assigned to it midway between man and woman. The graceful hair and well-shaped bosoms distinguish a woman. The distinctive mark of the man is the manly hair on the body. The *napuṁsaka* (impotent) lacks both. It is neither man nor woman :

स्तनकेशवती नारी लोमशः पुरुषः स्मृतः ।
उभयोरन्तरं यत्तु तदभावे नपुंसकम् ।। पृ0 98

The language of the play is lively and blemishless, fully worthy of the stage. No lengthy dialogues or verses hamper the flow of the theme. By all accounts it is a lively play, the peer of modern humorous skit.

JAYA DEVI SVATANTRATE

Composed of five verses in free metre, the tiny poem, 'Jaya Devi Svatantrate[1]' unravels the author's commitment to patriotism and freedom that he cherishes with unbounded devotion. It was inspired by the Pakistani attack on our beloved motherland in 1965. Though carried out with the heinous design of dismembering the country, close on the heels of the death of the first Prime Minister, Pandit Jawaharlal Nehru, the attack ended in a fiasco thanks to the mature leadership and skill and sacrifices of our armed forces.

The poem is addressed to glorify the Goddess of Freedom with assured verve. It was after a prolonged, grim struggle that freedom was achieved at great cost. Many doughty fighters laid down their lives with a smile so that the subsequent generations may breathe in freedom (*sāhasikajananijaraktavandite*, 3). That is why the country cherishes it beyond measure and would make any sacrifice to defend and preserve it (*asaṅkhyakoṭikaṇṭhastute*, I; *Bhāratabhūmivīrāgravandite*, 2). The poet makes a fervent appeal to the Goddess of Freedom to bring about the destruction of the enemy and grant victory to the country, so that it may live in peace and glory. He is conviced that the Goddess would assume the role of Caṇḍī in sapping the deceitful enemy dry (*atyācāraparāṇāṁ piba raktaṁ danujānām*, 5).

Written with patriotic fervour, the poem is not intended to reflect the author's talent or equipment. It is marked by vibrant nationalism, and is imbued with the mission to uphold the morale of the people that is likely to spill under such like strains. As a matter of fact, the poem represents the fight that the litterateur carries from off the battle-field to frustrate the enemy. It also serves to belie the charge that the modern Sanskritist has not shed his fascination for conventional themes. The author's writings prove it abundantly that he is abreast of the changing milieu. The Sanskritist of the day is doubtless well-equipped to meet the challenge that the relentless march to development poses. The present poem is an added proof thereof.

---

1. *Divyajyotiḥ*, Vol. X, No.2, Saṁvat 2022 .

KO'HAM

Written in eight delectable verses in the Śārdūlavikrīḍita metre, *Ko'ham*[1] purports to be revolutionary poem inasmuch as it effectively voices the modern thought, in its myriad ramifications, in a medium that is supposed to be the vehicle of only the conventional themes. It gives powerful expression to the mental conflict that afflicts a modern man and the hypocrisy it entails, besides his heartless aversion to social and moral norms. And all this has been done with such lucidity and keen perception that the language that is believed to be shackled by grammar, breathes freshness and buoyancy.

The first stanza stirs the eternal issues that have tormented the sensitive mind, down the ages, and have led to the birth of philosophic speculations in all times and climes. Who am I, whence did I come , what is my objective, what values I cherish and how relevant is my existence ? – – these abstruse problems terribly churn the human being and alas he has no cogent answer to them. He is a stranger to himself (*ātmā me sutarām asaṁstuta iti prāpto'smi citraṁ daśām,* 1).

The hypocrisy of life is underscored with extreme pungence in the second verse. The stanza forms a gloss of sorts on Bhartṛhari's dictum *manasy anyad vacasy anyat karmaṇy anyat.* This trifurcation of thought, word and deed spells doom to the practitioner of the dubious game. Neither his thoughts find fair expression, nor does he stick to his convictions convincingly. The shattered mentality results in the loss of his peace and harmony (*vipratipannamānasatayā no śāntim āpnomy aham*, 2).

The third stanza adds up to a pathetic depiction of the helpless person vacillating between the two poles of attatchment and detachment . While possession (*parigraha*) robs one of peace, dispossession (*aparigraha*) deprives him of what is mistakenly believed to be the colourful facets of life. The conflict thus generated by the desire for worldly enjoyments (*bhoga*) and renunciation (*tyāga*) thereof make him blind to the harsh realities of life.

In the fourth stanza one is encountered with the rather detailed analysis of the wise saying *śāstrāṇy adhītyāpi bhavanti mūrkhāḥ*. Ironically, the line that divides learning from deceit has been blurred, if not altogether obliterated. The so-called custodians of knowledge are master practitioners of fraudulent pratices (*paravañcanādikṛtiṣu svīyā pravṛttiḥ*, 4). The modern scholar is so impervious to the plight of society that even the most heinous of the crimes do not arouse him into

---

1. *Arvācīna-saṁskṛtam*, IX.1, Delhi, 1987

action. The apathy of learning to social evils is a bane to the higher values of life. The supposedly enlightened intellegentsia has lost its *prajñā* and instead has become *prajñācakṣu.*

The conflict between affluence amassed through dubious means with resultant comforts and loss of mental peace that it invariably involves forms the contents of the next verse. Even those who wallow in wealth or are deceitfully perched on prestigious posts, in hours of honest introspection, are stung with remorse. After all, what they possess has accrued to them by divesting its rightful claimants. And peace does not blossom on deceit.

Verse six has pronounced socialistic overtones. It projects the indigence of the proletariat who shed their blood for the bourgeoisie. The hapless working class raises palatial buildings for the rich, but is itself doomed to the hovels, with hardly anything to cover its nudeness (*vāsaḥ parṇakuṭī viśīrṇamalinaṁ vāso mamācchādanam*, 6).

The seventh verse vividly describes the struggle that knowledge has to wage, down the years, with a heartless and exploitive system. Besides that, the stanza amounts to a cruel commentary on the indolence of the Indian people. Once known for their devotion to duty, they are the most lethargic and corrupt people under the sun. Supposed to discipline the nation, the *ācārya* is a prisoner in the corridors of power. The things have degenerated to the level that the doctor is the worst enemy of the patient and the offices (*kāryālayas*) are havens for the dissipation (*laya*) of the work (*kārya*). Bribery has been accepted as the panacea for all the ills that beset society.

Thus disgusted and frustrated, the modern man is stranger to himself, unable to determine his goal. He is groping in the dark, with no light in sight. (*ko'haṁ veti na vedmi hanta kim iti bhrāmyāmi digbhrāntavat*, 8).

Notwithstanding its slimness, the poem touches a high watermark in unravelling the boundless potentialities of the Sanskrit language. The way it has highlighted the complex issues and nagging conflicts and paradoxes of the contemporary society and the restlessness that torments the modern man in forceful terms, is the surest testimony to the virility of the language. The poem is a pointer to the manner how the ancient medium can be exploited to voice the minutest nuances of modern thought. It is, however, true that poets like Dr. Satya Vrat Shastri who can unfold these possibilities, are not many.

MAHĀKAVIKĀLIDĀSĀṢṬAKAM

Mahākavikālidāsāṣṭakam is one of the author's shorter poems which still is in manuscript. It is a bunch of elegant stanzas in praise of Kālidāsa, undoubtedly the greatest poet the country has ever produced. However, it is not a sentimental outpouring in praise of the man, an eulogy, the kind of which one meets with often in Sanskrit literature. It forms a sincere effort to capture in the body of the eight stanzas what, in essentials, accounts for his greatness. The *aṣṭaka* seeks to focus on the various excellences of Kālidāsa's poetry that have ensured him a lofty niche in the galaxy of great poets of the world, though homage to the man was inherent in the process. This the poet has done so adroitly that the poem may be said to be a dissertation of sorts on Kālidāsa's poetry. In order to drive home the various virtues that mark Kālidāsa's poetry, the author has not refrained from occasionally borrowing the phraseology of the master himself. That, however, does not detract from the merits of the poem. If anything, these studied borrowals add lustre to it like gems studded tastefully in gold.

The qualities of Kālidāsa's poetry the author has sought to stress are not novel or unique in any way. It is the manner in which they have been projected as its chief characteristics that invests the poem with worth and beauty.

By common consent, the greatest virtue of Kālidāsa' speech is its diaphanous lucidity and abundance of sentiments. The poet has underscored it by pressing into service the figure of speech Upamā. Kālidāsa's poetry is untainted with blemishes (*śuddharūpāḥ*) like the streams of the river Gaṅgā. Its beauty is like that of digits of the moon (*śaśāṅkalekhā iva kāntimatyaḥ*). It occasions (lit.illumines) the knowledge of new things (*nūtnārthavijñānavibhāsayitryaḥ*) (1).

Kālidāsa's poetic genius has done the country proud. Rarely is such a colossus born. The author has sought to express the quantum of debt the country owes to the master poet with the charming Mālopamā. The fullness of the poetic genius in him shines forth like the sun (*aṁśumālī*) with its multitude of rays (*aṁśuprakarṣa*) or the Himālaya with its masses of snow (*himātireka*) (2).

Kālidāsa represents a happy blend of old and new. He was not illogically enamoured of old nor had unreasonable aversion for the new. He meant to strike a balance between the two. While he did not hesitate to borrow his items from such ancient texts as the Vedas, the epics and the Purāṇas, or imbibe them from other sources what was germane to him, he recast them so ingeniously that they acquire added vibrance and relevance. And the medium that he employed is itself an exquisite amalgam of the natural and the ornamental (*avyājamanohara*). The famed *subhāṣita* from the *Mālavikāgnimitra* : *purāṇam ity eva na sādhu sarvam* was bound to occur to the author to describe the phenomenon (3).

Contrary to the view that either word or meaning form the bedrock of poetry, Kālidāsa held them both as its indispensable pillars. While word and meaning, *śabda* and *artha*, form its (poetry's) frame, *rasa* forms its soul. Kālidāsa is matchless in depicting the various emotions of the human heart to the extent that he is the uncrowned king of *rasa*, especially of the *rasarāja*. It is his espousal of word and meaning as the essential ingredients of poetry, *sāhitya* (which is a short form for *śabdārthasāhitya* that the author uses in the stanza ingeniously explaining adroitly the in-set meaning of the oft-used term) enlivened by the strong current of sentiments that has elevated him to the deified status he holds. The graces of his poetry are indeed winsome (4).

In the fifth verse Kālidāsa's style has been compared with the heavenly Gaṅgā. As the Gaṅgā is full of currents, so is Kālidāsa's poetry full of sentiments, with Śṛṅgāra carrying the palm. In fact, Kālidāsa is a poet of tender love in both its aspects. The author has pressed into service the Virodhābhāsa to highlight some other traits of the master's style. Its ancient moorings do not in any way abridge its excellences. Despite his regard for tradition, his poetry breathes freshness. It is rich in contents (*gambhīrabhāvā*) but is not shorn of lucidity (*na cāprasādā*). Depth and ease are what characterize it (5).

Perhaps as a tribute to Kālidāsa's unmatched expertise in handling Upamā (*upamā Kālidāsasya*), the author has resorted to it in the sixth stanza to bring into relief the splendour of his genius. According to him Kālidāsa's poems bear comparison with *dīpaśikhā*, the flame of the lamp, an *upamāna* already immortalized by him in the *Raghuvaṁśa* (VI.67). The two have indeed much in common. The bright flame of the lamp dispels darkness from all that comes into its ambit. The moment its light descends on an object, it acquires lustre. His string of poems brightened by his matchless genius turn the poems of other poets, though great in their own right, lustreless. It is an acknowledged fact that no Sanskrit poet, however great, comes anywhere near Kālidāsa in excellence (6)

The chief quality of Kālidāsa is his use of soft and comely phraseology (*komalakāntapadāvalī*). Reference is made to it in the next stanza. This phraseology coupled with apt figures of speech make connoisseurs just fall in for it (7).

Kālidāsa's greatness is further sought to be impressed by inducting in the next verse lines from the *Raghuvaṁśa: nakṣatratārāgrahasaṅkulā 'pi jyotiṣmatī candramasaiva rātriḥ* (VI.22). There have been many great poets in the country in ancient and modern times, but none can excel Kālidāsa. After all, the stars cannot have the temerity to beat the moon. The lustre that his genius has lent to poetry is undying.

It will thus be seen that on the tiny canvas of just eight stanzas the author has made an herculean effort to capture all that makes Kālidāsa great. He has brought into focus in each verse the various traits of Kālidāsa's genius, as reflected in his poetry, so ingeniously that they form a perceptive critique on the great poet. His masterly strokes have brought into bold relief Kālidāsa's philosophy of poetry. In a poem on one who is an acknowledged master of Simile, Upamā was natural to dominate. Besides his own, the author has not hesitated in borrowing instances of this from Kālidāsa himself. With the exception of the fourth verse which is in Indravajrā, the rest of the *aṣṭaka* is in Upajāti. Written in chaste and fluent verse, the *aṣṭaka* adds upto a befitting tribute to the great poet.

CHAPTER SIX

SUPPLEMENT TO THE CORPUS OF LETTERS

SUPPLEMENT TO THE CORPUS OF LETTERS

After the volume had gone to the press, Dr. Satya Vrat Shastri wrote a number of letters in Sanskrit verse to his friends and acquaintances. Some of the earlier letters were also retrieved from his archives. Taken together, they form a bunch as poetic and delectable as the posse studied earlier in the body of the work. While it is not possible, at this stage, to assimilate this component in the critique of the Corpus, an evaluation thereof is a desideratum. That precisely is the rationale behind the 'supplement'.

The letters under study also adhere to the pattern set by the versified letters, discussed earlier, and like them, encompass two broad categories. The personal letters concern themselves with issues connected with the author or the addressee, though occasionally they seem to intrude into other domains as well. Thus letter No. 53a, written from Bangkok to the author's friend and pupil, Dr. Krishna Lal, on July 13, 1989, is primarily intended to be a personal document, though it is not shorn of literary and cultural flavour. It effectively brings home the author's perception of how a man of culture should plan out his schedule to obtain optimum return from his time, which otherwise is always under strain. While the wise make most of their time by engaging themselves in literary pursuits, the lesser persons squander it way on frivolous exertions (*kāvyādivimukhānāṁ hi kālo yāti nirarthakaḥ*, 53a. 4). The truth enshrined in the wise saying *kṣaṇaśaḥ kaṇaśaś caiva vidyām artham ca cintayet* (knowledge and wealth are acquired respectively at every moment and in bits) is beyond dispute. Sustained perusal of Kāvyaśāstra alone makes life worthwhile because knowledge knows no limits and human endeavours are no match to its magnitude (*śāstrāṇy anantapārāṇi vayaṁ cātyalpamedhasaḥ*, 53a.7).

The letter also refers to the author's visit, last month, to southern Thailand. Of the two towns he visited, Nagaraśrīdharmarāja is known for two of its temples dedicated to Śiva and Nārāyaṇa. The service therein has unhappily ceased. Even the idols of the deities have been removed to the museum, though they are superbly executed and evoke instant esteem from the sensitive visitor.

The next letter (No.54a), also written to Dr. Krishna Lal, on August 26, 1989, for all purposes, purports to be an extension of the preceding document. It is consciously split into two rounded segments. The first part made up of verses 1-6 is meant to convey the author's congratulations to the addressee on his imminent elevation as Head of the Department. In the second segment comprising the following fourteen stanzas, the author picks up the thread from the preceding letter and goes on to describe the places of archaeological interest in Nagaraśrīdharmarāja. The town is known for the gigantic Buddhist monastery, Wat Mahathat.

Letter No. 55a, addressed to Mr. Alois Payer of Ofterdingen (Germany), consists of mere five verses in the Upajāti metre. Herein the author expresses deep concern over the operation of the addressee's wife and wishes her speedy recovery from the malignant cancer.

The next three letters (56a-58a) have again been claimed by Dr. Krishna Lal, who had been in frequent and intimate correspondence with the author. Not unlike letter No. 54a, the first of the three is divided into two parts while in the first segment the author hints at the line of action to be followed in seeking re-employment in the University and emphasises the necessity of his prolonging the stay at Bangkok to see his *RKM* through the press, the second part details the oppressive summer of Bangkok and the fruits that make their appearance with its arrival. Whereas the sweet and succulent mango is well known in many parts of the world, Maṅkut, Lukgoṅ and Thuryan are peculiarly the Thai fruits. The Maṅkut, evidently an adaptation of Sanskrit *mukuṭa*, occupies a place of pride in the summer fruits and is keenly sought after for its tastefulness and richness in iodine. The interior of Lukgoṅ resembles the Indiaṅ Lichi, though it differs in its outward appearance. The pungent smell of Thuryan is repulsive to the outsider but it is eaten with gusto by the Thais.

Written from Bangkok on May 24, 1990, letter No.57a makes anxious enquiry about the welfare of the addressee, Dr. Krishna Lal about whom the author had seen an evil dream, the other night, and unfolds, in the process, his tender solicitude for his friends and pupils. The author showers on him the choicest blessings and prays for his longevity and welfare. The letter is punctuated with a lively description of the rainy season. It addedly reveals that the Thai translation of his *Rāmakīrtimahākāvya* was ready for the press and it should be out before long.

Dr. Krishna Lal again is the recepient of the next personal letter (No. 61a) in the series. The author informs him that the (unspecified) formal letter is enclosed herewith and directs him to proceed accordingly in the matter. The addressee is addedly informed that he was determined to return to Delhi ere long, the persistent request of the colleagues here for extending the stay, notwithstanding. In view of the poor health, it would be better for him to be with his kinsmen now. The letter closes with a lovely description of the rainy season.

Written from Bangkok on Oct. 8. 1990 to Dr. Sadananda Dikshit of Puri, letter No. 63a is intended to convey the author's appreciation for his unflagging zeal for popularising Sanskrit, and his decision to return to India by the end of the month (*nivartitāhe māsānte mamaiṣo 'sti vinirṇayaḥ*, 63a.4). Addedly the author herein refers to the esteem his *Ramakīrtimahākāvya* has drawn from the Thai Sanskritists. While the rainy season might have ended in India, there in Bangkok, he tells the addressee, it continues unabated. Only two days back the torrential rain had caused heavy floods which had led to the disruption of traffic and other inconveniences. The letter carries a description of the flood.

Letter No. 64a, written from Bangkok to Mrs. and Mr. Payer, on Oct. 23, 1990, represents an interesting admixture of a personal and a literary document. More poetic in tenor, it describes at some length, the peculiar phenomenon of rains at Bangkok, even after the onset of the winter season, which, the author avers, must be harsher in Germany, robbing the country of its sylvan beauties. While expressing the author's happiness at receiving, after long, the letter of his German friends, it pointedly refers to the author's weakness inflicted by old age and his keen desire to return to India to be in the midst of his near and dear.

The next two letters (65a-66a) are again claimed by Dr. Krishna Lal. Besides intimating the addressee in letter No. 65a, that he was forwarding herewith the letter of the lady Head of the Department there in the Silpakorn University for necessary action, he informs him that in view of the pressing request of the university he would have to extend his stay there by a month. The subsequent letter (No. 66a) is meant to confirm that he was addressing a letter to the Joint Registrar so that a favourable decision was taken on time. It also informs the addressee that he was scheduled to return to Delhi on the 6th of January, 1991 to resume work in the university on the 8th.

Written to Dr. Sadananda Dikshit from Delhi, letter No. 69 is entirely a personal document. Hoping that he might have recovered by now from the ailment, the author cautions him against over-exertion (*āyāsaḥ parihartavyas, tathāpīti matir mama,* 69.3). Sound health is the key to all achievements. The adverse effect of over-work has been painfully manifest in his own case.Though repeatedly cautioned to the contrary by his father, he persisted with hard work in the early years and did not heed his wise counsel. The result is now so obvious. The old age has overtaken him swiftly. Though afflicted by many an ailment it is strong will that sustains him now (*dṛḍha saṅkalpaśaktir me tena jīvāmi karmaṭhaḥ*, 69.10). He further conveys to Dr. Dikshit that his *Kālidāsa in Modern Sanskrit Literature* would be out soon. He also means to bring out the Corpus of Versified Letters, written by him, over the years. Comprising more than one thousand verses, they form a unique literature, deal as they do with diverse subjects of interest.

The literary letters in the series number eight. Though worthy by themselves, they are distinguished by one of the bulkiest letters, ever attempted. *Comprising 137 verses, it (No.67a) may well boast of being the longest letter in Sanskrit.*

Letter No. 58a, addressed to the author's friend Dr. Krishna Lal, informs him that the printing of the Thai translation of the *Rāmakīrtimahākāvya* (*RKM*) had begun and the poem should be out by the end of July. Her Highness the Princess of Thailand has contributed an interesting Foreword to it Based on *Ramakien*, the Thai version of the *Rāmāyaṇa*, the *RKM* has evoked spontaneous esteem from the Sanskritists here. The author further informs the addressee that the happy tiding of his invitation to the International Seminar on *Rāmāyaṇa* to be held in Mauritius, had reached him through his son, Sharat Chandra. The conference is bound to serve to resolve some of the tricky problems of the epic besides providing an excellent opportunity of meeting scholars from different parts of the world.

The subsequent letter (No.59a) was written to the well-known Sanskrit poet, Pt. Durgadatta Shastri Vidyalankar, whose prose-romance *Viyogavallarī* has evoked favourable comments from the author (*Viyogavallarīṁ pāṭhaṁ pāṭhaṁ tṛptīṁ na yāmy aham*, 59a.4). The letter further contains the author's views on poetry (*kāvya*) and its purpose (*kāvyaprayojana*). Only the poetry that stems from natural inspiration, meets the approbation of the connoisseur (*antaḥpreraṇayā jātaṁ kāvyaṁ svābhāvikaṁ matam*, 59a.6). Aesthetic pleasure (*svāntaḥsukha*) or *nirvṛti*, as Maṁmaṭa puts it, constitutes the highest purpose of poetry, though the poet craves for fame as well, which is also a potent factor to inspire him. The author informs the addressee that his *RKM* was poised to be released soon. This, he confides, owes its genesis to natural inspiration, not to the desire for name or fame (*na tv eva loke kavikīrtilobhāt*, 59a.14). Though overtaken by old age and the consequent weakness he is preoccupied with literary pursuits wherein a scholar finds fulfilment besides unadulated pleasure (59a. 18-20).

Letter No. 60a is also a literary document of sorts. Written to Dr. Sadananda Dikshit of Puri from Bangkok, on July 16, 1990, it seeks to felicitate him on his annexing the degree of Vidyavaridhi, which, the author avers, marks the fulfilment of his cherished desire to see him honoured with the prestigious degree, besides extending the addressee his warm greetings for his devotion to the cause of disseminating Sanskrit. While others pay lip-service to Sanskrit, Dr. Dikshit, the author is convinced, has identified himself with the cause (*bhavantaḥ Saṁskṛtatmānaḥ*, 60a. 11). Dr. Dikshit is further informed that the *RKM* was now on the threshold of being released.

Letter No. 62a is addressed to Pt. Durgadatta Shastri. The author herein expresses his joy at the bunch of verses sent to him and assures him to do something for his Kāvya after he returns to Delhi.

Written to Her Highness Sirindhorn, the Princess of Thailand, Letter No.68, is purely a literary document, though it has a regal air about it. It dwells upon the universal appeal of the *Rāmāyaṇa*, a seminar on which was organised to synchronise with the completion of the thirty sixth year of the Princess. The popularity of the

Rāma-story is so pervasive that it is viewed even by the alien peoples as their preserve, inextricably rooted in their history and culture. Whether it is the grandeur of the epic story or its ennobling idealism or the profusion of sentiments that accounts for its wide acceptability, cannot be asserted with certitude. But herein is found reflected the wide spectrum of diversity, inherent in man's joys and sorrows, his internal conflict, varied patterns of thought and behaviour, hopes and expectations, in brief, the entirety of human experience. Rāma's equipoise in the face of the heaviest odds, his devotion to his father as much as to his wife, his tireless exertions to retrieve her, all this has enthralled the people in all times and climes. It is the greatness of Rāma that has drawn the people to the epic even in lands that do not subscribe to his divinity. Though time-worn, Rāma story retains its freshness unabated.

The last letter (No.70) in the series, addressed to Dr. Ram Kishore Mishra, may also be rated as a literary piece. Here again the author informs the addressee that his *Kālidāsa in Modern Sanskrit Literature* should now be out by the end of July, and assures him to contribute Foreword to his *Devayānī*, whenever its proof-sheets are sent to him. He also expresses his happiness that Dr. Mishra was currently going through his *RKM*.

Written from Bangkok to Dr. Rama Kant Shukla, on April 26, 1991, letter No. 67a holds a place of pride in the series. Its uniqueness stems as much from its form as from its contents. *In sheer bulk it purports to be the longest versified letter, ever attempted by a Sanskritist.* Composed of as many as 137 delectable verses, the letter may justifiably be claimed to be an independent Kāvya, sustained by an equally interesting theme, which, notwithstanding its different episodes in their diverse versions, is strung together by the ennobling story of Rāma, that has evoked wide popularity in various countries.

The Seminar on *Rāmāyaṇa*, organised at Bangkok, as part of the International Festival, to mark the completion of the thirty sixth year of Princess Sirindhorn, resulted into a profound interaction among the *Rāmāyaṇa*-scholars, drawn from six countries including India, represented by the author himself. While the scholars grappled with some of the knottiest problems of the *Rāmāyaṇa* through a series of learned papers, the Ballet troupes from different countries lent it considerable charm with their exquisite performances. Their presentation of the Rāma-story in indigenous styles held the audience spell-bound. The technique of their presenting the various characters of the *Rāmāyaṇa*, with leather figures, masks and puppets drew spontaneous applause from one and all. While the main group performed the story without uttering so much as even a single word, the singers unravelled the import of their performance through corresponding songs to the accompaniment of music.

The sustained interaction among the scholars, drawn from Myanmar (Burma) Laos, Malaysia, Indonesia, Thailand and India, on and off the venue, contributed to a better understanding of the influence the *Rāmāyaṇa* has exercised on their social and cultural life, and the variations that several well-known episodes of the epic have undergone in these countries. Notwithstanding the uniformity in the broad framework of the main story, it is distinguished, in these countries, by substantial deviations in details.

The letter seeks to detail some such episodes. The well-known episode of *Mārīca-vadha*, as evidenced by *Phalak Phalam*, the Laotian *Rāmāyaṇa*, has therein suffered alterations to the extent that it reflects poorly on Sītā's devotion to her husband. As Sītā, allured by the golden deer, hovering in the vicinity of the hermitage, asked Rāma to fetch it for her, Rāma confided to his younger brother Lakṣmaṇa that he smelt a rat as the golden deer was an utter impossibility. These well-intentioned words caught the ear of Sītā. She was so infuriated at Rāma's supposed defiance that she hastily drew an arrow from his quiver and tried to thrust it in her bosom. Rāma, screaming in fear, assured her that he would retrieve the dear in case she had really taken fancy for it. Rāma chased the deer in the jungle and shot at it an arrow from a convenient distance, The demon, as the deer actually was, cried in anguish Oh ! Lakṣmaṇa, Oh ! Sītā. On hearing it, Lakṣmaṇa concluded that his elder brother was in trouble. He lost no time in joining him. As he found Mārīca still breathing, he also hurled an arrow at him which only resulted in the deer's resuming his original form of demon. It was then that Rāma killed him with the second arrow. Thus in the Laotian version Mārīca took three arrows to be killed finally. The two brothers returned to their hermitage to find it empty, with Sītā nowhere in sight.

The Indonesian version of the episode also differs in some details. There Lakṣmaṇa follows his elder brother, close on his heels, of his own accord and it is at his hands that Mārīca meets his end (*tatrāsti Mārīcavadhaḥ śareṇa saumitriṇāstena sudāruṇena*, 67a.54).

Minor divergences are found in the episode of Kumbhakarṇa, as it is known in Indonesia. According to it, Kumbhakarṇa goes to meet his wife before he joins the battle. She presents him a formal robe. She was so perturbed by his resolve that she covers her face with her hands and it is after much hesitation that she allows him to proceed to the battle-field (*kathñacid evābhyupaiti patyur gamanaṁ raṇārtham*, 67a.47).

The same version would likewise have us believe that the demonesses who mounted guard on Sītā in the Aśokavāṭikā, in Laṅkā, were not ugly but attractive like heavenly nymphs.

Slight variation is also witnessed in what precedes Sītā's abduction. According to the Indonesian *Rāmāyaṇa*, Rāvaṇa, before carrying her away, went to Rāma's hermitage and rained Lathi-blows on trees and bushes in the vicinity, when all were asleep there. This he is said to have done to test his might vis-a-vis Rāma, because the enemy, howsoever weak or unequal, should never be under-estimated, or otherwise taken lightly (*alpo 'pi śatrur na bhaved upekṣyaḥ* 67a.62).

The Combodian *Rāmāyaṇa*, on the other hand, tells us that despite all his might Rāvaṇa could not go close to Sītā because whenever he attempted to do that he felt burning sensation all over his body. Sītā's spiritual might (*satītvatejaḥ*) thus kept him at bay.

In this context one thing deserves special attention. The Laotian *Rāmāyaṇa Phalak Phalam*, written two hundred years ago at Vintienne is available only in Ms., now with the National Library. Bulk of *Phalak Phalam* is in Sanskrit with a small portion in Pali. While the Laotians know Pali, they are ignorant of Sanskrit. They therefore, do not know in full the contents of the epic. The Rāma-story figures in Laos in paintings in temples, monasteries and palaces of Lamprabang, its ancient capital. Hundreds of paintings from the *Rāmāyaṇa* therein fill one with wonder. It is surprising that these captivating paintings have not been photographed so far.

Many a scene from the *Rāmāyaṇa* is also painted in the Prambān temples of Indonesia.

These attest to the wide appeal of the Rāma-story. The people in Indonesia perform various episodes of the epic in their traditional style. The earliest reference to the *Rāmāyaṇa* there is found in an eighth century epigraph. The poet Vākpatirāja wrote in Prakrit, the poem *Rāvanavadha,* based on the Rāma-story. It is Vākpati's version of the story that is popular till date in Bali and Java. The performers in Bali cover themselves with masks to present the Rām *story* in the form of dance-drama, popularly known as Wayang. In Java the Rāma-story is presented through puppets or enacted with the help of masks.

Though a Muslim country, Indonesia has preserved the *Rāmāyaṇa*-tradition. There the Rāma-story is enacted once a month in the capital town of Jakarta.

In Malaysia, the Rāma-story is known only in three parts of the country. They owe their interest in the story to the neighbouring island Java, traders wherefrom introduced the shadow drama which is still enacted, under the name of Wayangkulit, by the roving performers in the midst of rural audiences. It consists mainly of the puppet-dance to the accompaniment of song and music. The *Rāmāyaṇa* in Malaysia is pupularly known as *Hikāyatserirāma*. Islam and Hinduism seem to have worked out a happy kinship there. The Malaysians believe that Rāvaṇa obtained invincibility after obtaining a boon from Allah.

The Myanmar or the Burmese *Rāmāyaṇa* also betrays certain divergences from the known versions of the Rāma story. One or two episodes would suffice to illustrate the point. The first episode concerns itself with the return of Viśvāmitra from Ayodhyā alongwith the two princes to ward off the menace of the demons to his sacrifices. As he arrived at the bank of a tank enroute to his hermitage, he left to perform religious observances, instructing Rāma and Lakṣmaṇa not to enter into the tank under any circumstances. In the meanwhile two sages appeared from somewhere. They too deterred the princes from venturing into the tank. In a surprise move, they threw their clothes in the tank. The garments instantly caught fire and disappeared in a trice. The amazing incident stirred the curiosity of the princes, who, much against the advice of Viśvāmitra and the two sages, plunged into the water. The plunge turned the adolescent princes into youthful men, equipped with choice garments and ornaments.

The other episode pertains to Sītā's *svayaṁvara*, which is both instructing and interesting. While inviting the various kings to the *svayaṁvara,* Janaka sent an invitation with Sītā's replica printed on the letter, to Paraśurāma as well, who, in the Burmese version, was not a sage but the ruler of a country. He was incidentally engrossed in penance on a mountain. He took the invitation as a possible obstruction to his penance and threw away the letter in disdain. It was carried by a strong current of wind to far off Laṅkā and fell in the hands of Rāvaṇa, its ruler who rushed to Mithilā to try his luck with the mighty bow. While he lifted the bow, much to the chagrin of Sītā, he failed in stringing it which brought relief to the princess. Lakṣmaṇa also tried his hand at the bow but alternately succeeded and failed like Rāvaṇa. It was Rāma who not only lifted it but also strung it with 'playful ease' (..... *helayaiva dhanus tad utthāpya cakāra sajyam*, 67.117).

Rāma's alliance with Sugrīva, the monkey-chief, is also described differently in the Burmese *Rāmāyaṇa*. In the course of his vigorous search for Sītā, Rāma was overcome with fatigue and fell asleep, under a tree, on the lap of his younger brother, Lakṣmaṇa. In the meanwhile a fierce wild-fly appeared from nowhere and pierced into Lakṣmaṇa's back to suck the blood. Inspite of being under servere pain, he kept his cool without in anyway lowering his guard. Lakṣmaṇa's devotion to his elder brother filled Sugrīva, who was perched on the tree, with admiration. He contrasted it with Vālin's cruelty to him. As a result of sudden upsurage of emotions, tears dropped from his eyes and fell on Rāma below. That awakened Rāma from the sleep. As he saw the monkey above on the tree, he took up his bow to punish him. Sugrīva was obsequious to him. He explained the circumstances that led to his expulsion from the kingdom. He told Rāma that it was on contrasting it with their profound mutual affection that he was moved to tears. Rāma was convinced of his sincerity. An alliance was struck between the two to bail each other out of the impasse.

CRITIQUE

To be sure, the documents under study form an integral part of the Corpus of Letters, evaluated earlier, and, as such, share with them most of the characteristics that elevate a writing to poetic heights. There can be little doubt about the form they are intended to be invested with.These are essentially poetic pieces, equipped with the concomitant trappings.

DESCRIPTIONS

A substantial number of letters are enlivened with lively descriptions, which, howsoever odd they may sound in such down-to-earth writings, serve to lend variety and vivacity to their otherwise bald contents. They invariably stem from the context and therefore square with the general backdrop of the letters. Contrary to his longer poems, the author seems to have taken here greater fancy for the traditional descriptions, laid down by the poeticians, though he has also kept up his wont of inducting innovative sketches.

The summer and rain, thought diametrically opposed in character and effect, have claimed greater attention of the author in some of the documents. Thus, while writing to Dr. Krishna Lal, in the summer at Bangkok, on March 6, 1990, he, as a sensitive poet attuned to the environment around him, has sought to describe its rigour and contrast it with the sweet fruits that make their appearance with its advent. While he has captured the severity of the summer in a pithy verse with a pointed reference to the oppressingly hot wind, he has been well detailed in highlighting the summer fruits, particularly the peculiarly Thai ones :

अथ ग्रीष्मप्रभावो हि सुतरां परिलक्ष्यते।
अत्युष्णा वायवो वान्ति लोकस्य भृशदुःखदाः।।56.7
आम्राण्यनेकरूपाणि साम्प्रतं पण्यवीथिषु।
विकर्षन्ति नृणां चेतो रस्यानि मधुराणि च।।
अन्यान्यपि फलान्यत्रादृष्टपूर्वाणि भारते।
ग्रीष्मर्तोरनुकूलानि दृश्यन्ते पण्यवीथिषु।।
आम्लं च मधुरं चापि मङ्कुटाख्यं विशेषतः।
समस्तेषु फलेष्वत्र सत्यमेव नृपायते।।
'आयोडीन'-गुणाढ्यं तत्स्वादं स्वादं विलक्षणम्।

मुकुटस्याकृतिं बिभ्रद्रसना सरसायते।।569. a-9
फलेष्वन्येषु 'लुकङौ' इत्याख्यमपरं फलम्।
अन्तर्लीचीसमं तावद् भिन्नं तु बहुशो बहिः।।
थुर्यन्नामापरं तात! फलमत्राभिलक्ष्यते।
तीव्रो गन्धो यदीयो नो नो रोचेत कथञ्चन।।
स्वादु रस्यमिहत्यास्तु फलं तन्नाम भुज्जते।
अतीव रुच्यं तत्तेषां लोको भिन्नरुचिर्यतः।।56a .15-17

As a welcome spell that brings cheer to the people reeling under sweltering heat, the rain have been a favourite theme with the Sanskrit poets. The author has seized upon every opportunity provided by the letters to describe with gusto the most comforting of the seasons. In a letter to Dr. Krishna Lal, his colleague at the Delhi University, while making anxious enquiry about his well-being, the author has broken into a lovely description of the rainy season at Bangkok and the relief and joy it has brought after months of rigorous summer."The rains here are now in full swing. the sky is overcast with clouds for most of the time. The cool breeze provides relief to the harried people. the sustained spells of rain have resulted into vegetation everywhere which is a great source of pleasure. However, whenever the sun breaks through the clouds, it is unbearable as in our own country." The description, though not much different from that attempted in letter no.17, also addressed to Krishna Lal, has a charm of its own.The sweet phraseology, judicious application of Anuprāsa and Yamaka, polished ease and lucidity of style combine to raise it to lovely height:

ग्रीष्मप्रकोपः कलयाऽत्र शान्तिं
गतोऽस्ति शान्तिं जनयज्जनेषु।
साभ्रं नभो वाति च शीतवातो
वर्षा इहातिप्रकटप्रकर्षाः।।57.8
हरीतिमा नेत्रविलोभनीयो
गुल्मेषु वृक्षेषु लतासु चापि।
सर्वस्य भूयो मुदमातनोति
घर्मार्तिहारित्ववशाज्जनस्य।।57a.9

क्वचिद्यदा नाम सहस्ररश्मि-

र्घनावलीमध्यत आविरस्ति।

तदास्य तापः सुतरामसह्यः

स्वदेशवद् देश इहापि भाति।।57a .10

The author is so enamoured of the rainy season that he has embedded another of his letters, addressed again to Dr. Krishna Lal from Bangkok, on Sept. 13, 1990, with a pretty sketch thereof. The description does not differ in substance and metre from the preceding piece and is replete with many a verbal resemblance, but it brooks reproduction as it seeks to capture the essence of the season in merely two verses:

वर्षर्तुवेगोऽत्र भृशं प्रवृद्धो

मेघावृतं तेन नभो विशालम्।

हरीतिमा नेत्रविलोभनीयः

सौख्याकरो दृष्टिपथं प्रयाति।।

ग्रीष्मस्य लेशोऽपि न लक्ष्यतेऽत्र

मन्दाः सुखा वान्ति च वर्षवाताः।

अनेकवर्णाढ्यविकस्वराब्ज-

पूर्णाः सरस्यो मुदमापहन्ति।।61a. 11-12

The description of flood is not common in Sanskrit poetry. It is in a letter written to Dr. Sadananda Dikshit, on Oct. 8, 1990 that the author has incorporated a brief description of the flood and the disruption caused by its ferocity. While rightly hoping that the rains might have receded in India by now, the author informs the addressee that here the reverse seems to be happening. Only two days back there had been torrential rain which had inundated all the roads, streets and vistas besides throwing traffic out of gear :

याते द्वे एव अहनी धारासारैरिहाभवत्

वृष्टिर्येन जलाप्लावः प्रादुरासीदनर्थकृत्।।

मार्गा वीथ्यः प्रतोल्यश्च सर्वा आप्लावमज्जिताः।

यातायाते अभूतां यद्वशाद् रुद्धे समन्ततः।। 63. 12-14

Bangkok seems to have had a prolonged spell of rain last year. The letter addressed to Mr. Alois Payer, is again dotted with a charming description of the untimely heavy rain even after the winter had set in. While the winter might have descended on Germany with its ferocity, denuding the trees of rich foliage and thereby rendering them ugly like a dustladen mirror, here in Bangkok the opposite seems to be true. "The rainy season is very much on the stage. The sky is overladen with massive dark clouds resembling in colour the herd of elephants. Though enveloped in darkness, the quarters are brightened with frequent flashes of lightning. The wind blows with a roaring sound. The thunderings of the cloud remind one of the terrific noise caused by the clash of the mighty winds at the end of the aeon. The ground is under a thick sheet of water. The people are helpless in the situation, awaiting the ordeal to come to an end. In the meanwhile, they have geared themselves to meet it in their own way." In the five delectable verses in Drutavilambita, the author has highlighted with telling effect the vagaries of the rains at a time when it should have been a comforting winter :

ननु भवेद् भुवि शीतलताऽधुना
शरदृतौ भवतो बहुकष्टदा।
हिमहता मलिना इव दर्पणा
नहि मुदे स्युरहो वनराजयः।।
इह पुनर्विपरीतमिवास्ति यद्
उपगमेऽपि ऋतोः शरदो नभः।
परिवृतं जलदैरवलोक्यते
जलभृतैर्द्विरदोपमकान्तिभिः।।
चपलयाऽपलया निखिला दिशः
परिवृतास्तमसाऽपि निरन्तरम्।
प्रवहति प्रबलाऽनिलसंहतिः
प्रलयघोषसमश्च घनारवः।।
प्रवहदम्बुरया सकला स्थली
परुषनिःस्वनजीवचयास्तृता।

विकललोचनलोकविलोकिता

नयनयोरयनं परिगच्छति।।

अथ कदा शममेष्यति वर्षण-

मिह भुवीति भृशं विकलो जनः।

स्वसमयं समयोचितसाधनैः

कथमपि प्रवियापयतेऽस्थिरः।। 64.7- 11

The alliterative phraseology, marked by pleasing *padalālitya* and unusual flow, effectively reflects the ferocity of the unusual rains and tends to raise the description to the level of ancient masters.

As against these conventional descriptions, though imaginatively drawn to invest them with an aura of freshness, some of the letters under study are punctuated with depictions that tend to depart from the norm. The description of the summer fruits has already been noticed. The letter, written again to Dr. Krishna Lal, is enriched with a life-like sketch of the Buddhist monastery Wat Mahathat in the town of Nagarasrīdharmarāja. The gigantic Vihāra has all the characters of the *Rāmāyaṇa* depicted on the columns in its *sanctum sanctorum*. The adjoining chamber is adorned with a massive figure of the Buddha. The monastery has in its front a large flight of steps, flanked at the start by two exquisite figures of the Yakṣas. The steps lead to two remarkable images in a temple, whose identity no one knows. The figures probably belong to the Hindu temples which were subsequently transformed into Buddhist monasteries. It invariably happens when a country switches over to a new religion. This is what happened in our country as well :

वात् महाथादिति थाइभाषया कीर्तितो महान्।

एको बौद्धविहारोऽस्ति तत्र नेत्रसुखावहः।। 54a.9

गर्भगृहे तु वाटस्य नानास्तम्भाश्चकासति।

रामायणीयपात्राणां प्रत्येकं यत्र चित्रणम्।।

अपरस्मिन् प्रकोष्ठे तु राजते सुगताकृतिः।

अतीव विपुला सत्यं तद्भक्तानन्दकारिणी।।

दृश्यते तत्पुरस्त्वेका सोपानानां परम्परा।

यत्पादमूले लसति यक्षाकृतियुगं शुभम्।।

सोपानानि समारुह्य देवमन्दिरवत्स्थितम्।
अगारं दृश्यते यत्र द्वे मूर्ती स्तो विलक्षणे।।
कयोरेते इति मया पृच्छ्यमानेऽपि कोऽपि न।
यथावदशकद्वक्तुं स्वमज्ञानं प्रकाशयन्।।
एवं प्रतीयते तात! नैके देवालयाः पुरा।
बौद्धविहाररूपेण कालेन परिवर्तिताः।।
इदं तावद् भवत्येव सति धर्मविपर्यये।
परिवर्तनमेतादृगस्मद्देशेऽपि दृश्यते।।54a.12-18

The discussion on the descriptions will not be complete if reference here is not made to the description of the Rāmāyaṇic episodes in the longest letter of the Corpus. The descriptions are so vivid and graphic, that the reader feels the incidents taking place before his very eyes. Sītā overhearing Rāma speaking to Lakṣmaṇa about the impossibility of a golden deer which she wanted for herself enrages her to such an extent that she pulls out an arrow from Rāma's quiver. As she is about to dig it into her, Rāma raises an alarm and takes it away from her agreeing at the same time to do her bidding. This scene the poet in the letter-writer describes in the verses:

कृत्वा यदा हेममृगस्य रूपं
 रामाश्रमाभ्याशमुपैति यावत्।
मारीचनामाऽसुरपाश एष
 तावत्स सीताक्षिपथं प्रयाति।।
विलोक्य तं विस्मितमानसा सा-
 ऽऽनेतुं तमाह स्वपतिं विमुग्धा।
असम्भवं हेममृगस्य जन्मे-
 त्यवोचदेषोऽवरजं च विद्वान्।।
तद्वाक्यमस्या अपि कर्णमापद्
 यत्क्रोधमस्या ज्वलयाम्बभूव।
स्वेच्छाविघातात्कुपिता स्वभर्तु-

स्तूणीरतोऽसौ शरमाचकर्ष।।
वक्षःस्थलं विध्यति यावदेषा
तेनातिघोरेण शरेण तावत्।
चुक्रोश रामः सुतरां भयार्तः
शरं च तस्याः करतोऽपनिन्ये।।
अत्याहितं भोः किमिति त्वयैवं
चिकीर्षितं चेति वचोऽभ्युवाच।
तवाग्रहश्चेदयमेव ताव-
न्मृगं त्वदर्थं समुपानयामि।। 67a. 44-48

Similarly graphically is described the scene in the Malaysian *Rāmāyaṇa* of the sage Viśvāmitra coming upon a pond on the way to his Āśrama from Ayodhyā bringing with him the two lads Rāma and Lakṣmaṇa. Delivering the warning to them not to enter the pond, that being inauspicious, the sage goes out for his daily ritual. After he leaves, two unknown sages appear there and warn the lads against entering the pond. They throw their upper garments into it which instantly go up in flames and disappear. Inspite of all this, the lads jump into the pond to come out of it in a trice full-grown beautifully-dressed young men with crown and ear-rings in their respective colours. Rāma is green and Lakṣmaṇa is golden. This finds description from the letter-writer, so total and complete, that the reader has the full feel of it :

ऋषिः सरामः सहलक्ष्मणश्चा-
योध्यापुरात्पुण्यनिजाश्रमाय।
प्रतिष्ठमानः समुपैति विश्वा-
मित्राभिधानोऽर्धपथे तडाकम्।।
नेदं शुभं नात्र कदाचिदेव
निमज्ज्यतामित्यभिधाय रामम्।
स लक्ष्मणञ्चापि ययौ महर्षिः
पूजादि निर्वर्तयितुं यतात्मा।।
अत्रान्तरे तत्र ऋषी कुतश्चि-

त्समागतौ, द्वौ निषिषेधतुस्तौ।

बालौ प्रवेष्टुं सरसि प्रमाथि-

न्यनिष्टसम्भावनया प्रणुन्नौ ।।

स्वे अङ्गवस्त्रे क्रमशः सरोऽम्भ-

स्युभौ ऋषी चिक्षिपतुः क्रमेण।

क्षणाच्च ते संज्वलिते अदृश्ये

बभूवतुश्चेत्यतिचित्रमासीत्।।

मायासरस्यां प्रविलोक्य दृश्यं

रोमाञ्चकार्येतदतीव भीतौ।

नहि प्रवेष्टुं मन आदधीतां

द्वयोस्तयोस्ताविति बुद्धिरासीत्।।

ऋष्योस्तयोस्ताववमत्य विश्वा-

मित्रस्य वाक्यं च प्रविष्टवन्तौ।

तस्यां सरस्यां तत उत्थितौ च

क्षणेन तावद्युवतामवाप्तौ।।

किरीटिनौ कुण्डलिनौ सुवेशौ

स्वं स्वं च वर्णं प्रविधारयन्तौ।

हरीतिमा सम्प्रबभूव रामे

सुवर्णवर्णोऽथ च लक्ष्मणोऽभूत्।। 67a.94-104

The Burmese *Rāmāyaṇa* mentions Paraśurāma as a king who is described practising penance on a hill top. Janaka wants him too to attend the *svayaṁvara* of his daughter and for this purpose sends him invitation with the figure of Sītā on it which he, Paraśurāma,. throws away taking it as an obstruction to his austerities which then having been carried away by strong wind to far away Laṅkā falls into the hands of its ruler Rāvaṇa who, attracted by Sītā's figure goes to Mithilā and attends the *svayaṁvara.* He is able to lift the bow, much to the consternation of Sītā, but not to string it. It is Rāma alone who does the impossible :

देशस्य कस्यापि बभूव राजा

रामः प्रतापी भुवि जामदग्न्यः।
ऋषिर्नहीति प्रतिकूलरूपा-
ऽऽस्ते ब्रह्मदेशीयकथा विचित्रा।।
सम्प्रेषितं भूमिपतौ बभूव
निमन्त्रणं स्वं मिथिलाधिपेन।
यदा तदाऽयं क्वचिदद्रिशृङ्गे
चर्तुं तपोऽभूत्समभिप्रवृत्तः।।
निमन्त्रणार्थं प्रहिते स्वपत्रे
सीताकृतिं तज्जनकोऽङ्कयद् या।
अशोभयत्पत्रमवर्णयच्च
सीतास्वरूपं परिणेतुमिच्छून्।।
आसाद्य पत्रं जनकेन सृष्टं
रामस्तपस्वी किल जामदग्न्यः।
साक्षात् तपोविघ्नमिवाकलय्य
दूरीचकारैतदनादरेण।।
तद्वायुवेगेन हृतं तदा सल्-
लङ्कापुरीं नीतमभूज्जवेन।
विधेर्वशात्तत्पतितं च हस्ते
तच्छासितू रावणनामकस्य।।
आलोक्य सीताकृतिमेष लुब्धः
स्वयंवरार्थं समभिप्रतस्थे।
कालेन रम्यां मिथिलाभिधानां
स राजधानीं जनकस्य चाप।।
आप्त्वा च तां चापलसम्प्रणुन्नः
स रुद्रचापोद्धरणे प्रवृत्तः।

उत्थापने तस्य बभूव शक्तो
ज्यारोपणे नैव तु यत्नतोऽपि।।
उत्थापयन्तं प्रविलोक्य चापं
विदेहपुत्रीं भयमाविवेश।
दुष्टस्य हस्ते खलु मा स्म पप्तं
दुःखाय मे तत्सुतरां भवेन्नु।। 76a.107-114

The descriptions may justly be compared with lovely pastures, shedding cool comfort all around. These have been chiefly instrumental in warding off the monotony that could have otherwise crept into the letters.

LANGUAGE

Not unlike their counterparts studied earlier, the letters in question are couched in a language which is distinguished by rare chastity and flow. To the author chastity of language is not merely synonymous with grammatical correctness. It is the idiomatically vibrant expression, sanctioned by the *śiṣṭas,* that makes it an unblemished medium. And this is what the author has espoused in all his writings, including the matter of fact documents like letters that are in fact studded with some of the choicest expressions which may well be the envy of the ancient masters. *vinivedyātrabhavatsu* (54a.20), *kāryabhāro mahān eṣa niyatyā pātito mayi* (58a.7), *tasmin prasaṅge bhṛgunandane 'pi, samprāpayāmāsa nimantraṇaṁ saḥ* (67a.106), *videhaputrīṁ bhayam āviveśa* (67a.114) *prāṇaih paritrātum asau pravṛttaḥ* (67a.125), *dhairyād rahayāmbabhūvātmānam* (68.13) are some of the expressions, which alongwith those noticed earlier, set the norm in idiomatic speech. The letters share with the earlier part of the Corpus an abundant measure of lucidity. The language of the letters is well abreast of the ideas and situations that find expression therein. The undercurrent of lucidity flows unabated through their length and breadth. The author has sought to give expression to various thoughts in accordant phraseology. His anguish at the serious illness involving an operation on Margerita, the young wife of his German colleague Mr. Alois Payer, and his prayer for recovery have been enclothed in such an appropriate phraseology that it alternately exudes worry and solicitude :

सम्प्रेषितं स्विटज़रलैण्डदेशात्
पत्रं समासाद्य ममास्त चेतः।

चिन्ताभरेणामथितं नितान्तं
तान्तं तथाऽशान्तमतीव दुःखात्।।
कष्टं महत्सोढवती प्रिया मे
पुत्री शुभा मार्गरिटाभिधाना।
अल्पे वयस्येव तयाऽनुभूता
शल्यक्रिया हन्त! विधेर्विधानात्।।
सम्प्रार्थयेऽहं प्रभुमीशमीड्यं
निरामयत्वं सुतराममुष्याः।
सम्पादयन्ती सुखिनी गृहस्थ-
विधिं प्रजीव्याच्छरदां शतं सा।। 55a.1-3

The lucidity of expression marked by charming Anuprāsa and flow goes far to heighten effectiveness of the sentiments expressed here. The same phenomenon is perceptible in the depiction of Lakṣmaṇa's equipoise in the face of severe pain caused by the bite of the menacing wild-fly. Though the fly had pierced his back to suck the blood, he kept his cool. He not only stood the ordeal with courage, he sustained his brother dutifully without so much as even a flutter :

पीडामसह्यामनुभूतवान-
प्येषोऽतिधीरो विचचाल नैव।
न विव्यथे वा न च वा चकम्पे
सर्वं तदाश्चर्यकरं बभूव।। 67.122

The lucidity of expression, coupled with effective use of Anuprāsa has resulted in sweet *padalālitya* flowing into the letters, which incidentally is the author's forte. The instances listed below drive home effectively the author's expertise in the art :

1. तान्तं तथा ऽशान्तमतीव दुःखात्।। 55 a. 1
2. काव्यक्रियायां स्वमनःप्रियायाम्। 59a. 10
3. विकललोचनलोकविलोकिता। 64 a. 10

4. साभ्रं नभो वाति च शीतवातो
वर्षा इहातिप्रकटप्रकर्षाः।। 57a . 8

5. वृत्ता मे चिन्ता चित्तार्तिकारिणी। 57a . 4

6. रामाभिरामचरिते रमते जनौघः। 67a. 137

While the *padalālitya* has emanated from skilful handling of the Anuprasa, the number of *subhāṣitas* that adorn the language of the letters owe their genesis mostly to the Arthāntaranyāsa, though occasionally Dṛṣṭānta has also contributed its mite. The following *subhāṣitas*, culled from the letters under study, strengthen and enhance the worth of their counterparts :

1. सत्सङ्गतिः पुण्यवशेन सत्यं
सञ्जायते दिव्यसुखप्रदात्री। 58a. 15

2. विपश्चिदुद्धैः सह तात! चर्चा
प्रवर्तिता ज्ञानचयं तनोति।। 58a. 16

3. क्षमाशीला हि साधवः । 59a. 2

4. विपश्चितां कामदुघा मताऽऽशीः। 59a. 23

5. सङ्ग इष्टैर्जनैः सत्यमुत्सवायैव केवलम्। 61a. 4

6. तृप्तिर्भवेच्छ्रेयसि नैव कस्यापि।। 67a. 37

7. अल्पोऽपि शत्रुर्न भवेदुपेक्ष्यः। 67a. 62

8. हरति रुचिरगन्धा केतकी लोकचित्तं
न तु सुरुचिररूपः किंशुको गन्धहीनः।। 70.3

As against the tenderness and charm inherent in the *padalālitya* and *subhāṣitas*, the author, true to his equipment in grammar, has used in the letters complicated grammatical forms. They are doubtless odd with the nature of the present writings, but they have uniformly been an integral feature of his works, The learned forms inducted here, pertain to all departments of Sanskrit grammar, though aorist has been the author's major weakness. These may be noted here to reflect the author's equipment in grammar :

अध्यगायि, अवापि (53a. 1), असूसुचन् (56.2), प्रत्यपीपदन् (58a.4), व्यरीरचत् (58a.9), असुसूचत् (58a.14), अशकम् (59a.1), अचीक्लृपत् (63a.6) उपास्थिषि (68.2),

आपत् (68.13), अज्ञासिषम् (69.2), मा स्म पप्तम् (67a.114), अजिघृक्षत् (67a.226), व्यचिचिन्तत् (67a.124).

आत्मनीनः (53a.6), आलोकमालोकम् (53a.15,67a.73), स्वादं स्वादम् (56a. 12), स्वादुंकारम् (53a.15), नृपायते (55a.11), सरसायते (56a.12), स्वस्तिकाम्यया (57a.13), निविवृत्सा (16a.9).

एता (57a. 13), गमयिता (64a.5), प्राप्तास्मि (61a.9), सङ्क्रन्ताहे[1], लब्धाहे (61a.4), निवर्तिताहे (63a.4), स्वभार्यां समया[2] (67a.56), आत्मन्यधि[3] (76a.62), मह्यं द्रुह्यति[4] (67a.125), परम्पराप्राप्तपथेन[5] (67a.76), भोयेतादृशः[6] (67a.95), प्रतिष्ठमानः[7] (67a. 98).

The author has kept up his practice of mustering choice expressions from ancient texts to impart grace and force to his language. The letters are embellished with a number of such borrowals. They usually fall in two categories--those lifted bodily from their sources and those modified to suit the context. *kṣaṇaśaḥ kaṇaśaś caiva vidyām arthaṁ ca cintayet*[8] (53a.50), *avaśyaṁ yātaraś cirataram uṣitvāpi viṣayāḥ*[9] (53a.8) *nahi kastūrikāmodaḥ śapathena vibhāvyate*[10] (53a.5), *athavā śreyasi kena tṛpyate*[11], *asambhavaṃ hemamṛgasya janma*[12] belong to the first category. The second group is made up of the following :

1. यात्येकतोऽस्तशिखरं यदि धर्म एक-
स्तत्स्थानमापतति निश्चितमन्य एव।

1. Ātmanepada by Pāṇ. समो गम्यृच्छिप्रच्छिस्वरत्यर्तिश्रुविदिभ्यः (1.3.29)
2. द्वितीया by Vārttika अभितःपरितःसमयानिकषाहाप्रतियोगेऽपि under Pāṇ. उपान्वध्याङ्वसः (1.4.48),
3. With कर्मप्रवचनीयसंज्ञा (by Pāṇ.) अधिरीश्वरे (1.4.97), सप्तमी by Pāṇ. यस्मादधिकं यस्य चेश्वरवचनं तत्र सप्तमी (2.3.9).
4. चतुर्थी by Pāṇ. क्रुधद्रुहेर्ष्यासूयार्थानां यं प्रति कोपः (1.4.37).
5. समासान्त अ by Pāṇ. ऋक्पूरब्धूःपथामानक्षे (5.4.74).
6. य् by Pāṇ. भोभगोअघोअपूर्वस्य योऽशि (8.3.17).
7. Ātmanepada by Pāṇ. समवप्रविभ्यः स्थः (1.3.22).
8. An old *subhāṣita*.
9. *Vairāgyaśataka*, Verse 12.
10. *Kuvalayānanda*, Nirnaya Sagar Press, Bombay, 1931, p.54.
11. *Śiśupālavadha*, I29.
12. *Hitopadeśa*, Mitralābha, verse 27.

धर्मद्वयस्य युगपद् व्यसनोदयाभ्यां
पूर्वस्तिरस्क्रियत इत्यतिकष्टदायि।। 54a19.

cp यात्येकतोऽस्तशिखरं पतिरोषधीना-
माविष्कृतारुणपुरःसर एकतोऽर्कः।
तेजोद्वयस्य युगपद् व्यसनोदयाभ्यां
लोको नियम्यत इवात्मदशान्तरेषु।।

Abhijñānaśākuntala, IV.2.

2. अतिस्नेहो ममैवायं पापशङ्की भवत्सु यः। 57a.6
अतिस्नेहः पापशङ्की।

Abhijñānaśākuntala, Act IV, after verse 18

3. राजन्तां सर्वथा स्वस्था मोदमानाः स्वके दमे। 57a.7
cp क्रीडन्तौ पुत्रैर्नप्तृभिर्मोदमानौ स्वे दमे।

Ṛgveda, X. 85.42; *Atharvaveda*, XIV.1.22

4. क्लेशः फलेन तनुते नवत्वम् 157a.13
cp क्लेशः फलेन हि पुर्ननवतां विधत्ते।

Kumārasambhava, V.86

5. सत्सङ्गतिः पुण्यवशेन सत्यं
सञ्जायते दिव्यसुखप्रदात्री।। 58a.15
cp. सतां सङ्गः सद्भिः कथमपि हि पुण्येन भवति।।

Uttararāmacarita, II.1

6. मित्रभावेन सग्धिं च सपीतिं चापि कुर्वते।। 67a.18
cp. सग्धिश्च मे सपीतिश्च मे

Vājasaneyisaṁhitā, XVIII.9: *Maitrāyaṇīsaṁhitā*, II.1.4, 141.17

7. दृढं रामकथासूत्रं तेषां मर्माणि सीव्यति। 67a.16.
cp. स हि स्नेहमयस्तन्तुरन्तर्मर्माणि सीव्यति।।

8. तृप्तिर्भवेच्छ्रेयसि नैव कस्या-
पीत्यत्र सन्देहलवो न कश्चित्।। 67a.37

cp. अथवा श्रेयसि केन तृप्यते।।

Śiśupālavadha, I.29

9. अल्पोऽपि शत्रुर्न भवेदुपेक्ष्यः 67a.62

नोपेक्षितव्यो विद्वद्भिः शत्रुरल्पबलोऽपि सन्।

Cāṇakyarājanīti ,The Adyar Library, Vol.92, verse 126.

10. इच्छाभिपूर्तौ दनुजस्य तस्याः
सतीत्वतेजोऽभवदन्तरायः।। 67a.65

cp स्याद्रक्षणीयं यदि मे न तेज-
स्त्वदीयमन्तर्गतमन्तरायः।।

Raghuvaṁśa. XIV.65

11. नान्यत्र देशे परिलक्ष्यते भो-
येतादृशो भूषणभूष्यभावः।। 67a.94

cp अन्योन्यशोभाजननाद्बभूव
साधारणो भूषणभूष्यभावः।।

Kumārasaṁbhava, I.42.

In short, the author has taken recourse to many a device to make his language effective enough to convey various shades of thoughts and situations.

LITERARY ISSUES

In keeping with the trend as it obtains in the earlier bunch, the author has expressed, in some of the letters, his considered views on issues of literary interest. Thus, according to him, only that can be rated as true poetry which emanates from natural urge *(antaḥpreraṇayā jataṁ kāvyaṁ svābhāvikaṁ matam,* 59a.6). Such a Kāvya alone meets the approbation of the connossieur *(rañjayet sutarāṁ cetas tat kavitvavidāṁ dhruvaṁ,* 59a.6). Well-equipped poets, aware of their duty to society, are difficult to come across these days (59a.7). Nor are there well-intentioned readers and critics to evaluate poetry dispassionately (*alpīyāṁsas tu ye santi viśuddhahṛdayā bhuvi*, 59a.9).

The author concurs with the ancient critics in admitting unadulated pleasure as the dominant purpose of poetry (*svāntaḥsukhaṃ yady api mūlam asti kāvyakriyāyāṁ svāmānaḥpriyāyāṁ* 59a.10). *Svāntaḥsukha* is synonymous with *sadyaḥ-paranirvṛti,* as Mammaṭa puts it. But the poet is not a recluse. The longing for fame is as strong a factor as any other consideration to drive him to poetry (*sarvair api prārthyam ihāvadātaṁ vidagdhagoṣṭhīṣu yaśo garīyaḥ,* 59a.11).

His view on how a litterateur should plan his schedule to obtain maximum return from the time, has been well set forth.

FIGURES OF SHEECH

Imaginative application of the *alaṁkāras*, both of word and meaning, has been the convenient device with the Sanskrit poets to lend clarity and effect to expression. The author has pressed into service almost all those figures of speech that were effectively used by him in the earlier part of the Corpus. Anuprāsa, however, is his favourite *alaṁkāra*. He has exploited it to the utmost to impart sweet rhythm to the expression. The letters bristle with strings of lovely Anuprāsa, some of which, besides those already quoted, may be listed here to drive home the author's skill in handling it :

1. मनसि मोदभरो नहि माति मे। 64.1

2 प्रवहति प्रब्रलाऽनिलसंहतिः
प्रलयघोषसमश्च घनारवः।। 64.9

3. रुचिं रामायणे राजकुमार्या अभिलक्ष्य ते। 67.4

4 स्वस्मिन् स्वस्मिन् यथा देशे स्वरूपं प्रविलोक्यते। 67.6

5. काव्यक्रियायां स्वमनःप्रियायाम्। 59.10

6. स्वसमयं समयोचितसाधनैः। 64.11

The elevated version of Anuprāsa, popularly known as Antyānuprāsa, has been espoused by the author in his writings with sustained vigour. However, in the letters under study it has been employed only once. The author's solicitude for Mrs. Payer is enclothed in this :

वयं तु तस्याः सुतरां स्मरामो
गुणांश्च तस्याः परिकीर्तयामः।

तस्याः सुखं नित्यमथो लषामः

दीर्घं तदायुश्च सदाऽर्थयामः।। 55.5

The Simile also has been used with equal frequency. The appropriate *upamānas*, drawn from various sources, tend to purge the ideas under description of haze and thereby lend it clarity and easy comprehension. Even the repeated perusal of the prose-romance *Viyogavallarī* did not satisfy the author as a thirsty man is never tired of drinking cool water (59a.4). The motherland is dear to the author like his own mother (68.20). Shorn of their foliage in winter, the vistas of trees in Germany look ugly like the dustladen mirrors (64a.7). Sapped of strength in old age, the author avers, he resembles a field with its stock of grain eaten away by the birds (69.9). The performing artists from six countries he likens to the six Rasas (flavours) (67a.34). The metaphor of stream he puts on the Rāma story and then compares it to the stream of the celestial river (the Gaṅgā in the heaven) (67a.80). Janaka's invitation for Sītā's *svayaṁvara* is taken as an obstruction incarnate to his penance by Paraśurāma (67a.110). The different versions of the various episodes in different countries strengthen the basic Rāma-stroy, as the water of various rivers serves to swell the ocean further (67a.136) :

नद्यो यथा विविधदिग्भ्य उपस्रवन्ति

वारांनिधिं च सलिलेन समेधयन्ति।

देशान्तरेषु विततानि कथानकानि

पुष्णन्ति रामचरितं महितं तथैव।। 67.136

Next in importance to Simile in the letters is the Arthāntaranyāsa which has been employed with fruitful results. Based on the general statement upholding the particular one and vice-versa, it has invariably led to the emergence of the pretty *subhāṣitas.* The author's contention, in the following verse, that his *RKM* would evoke approbation from connoisseurs has been sought to be strengthened with the general statement that it was the fragrant Ketakī that captivates the heart of the people, not the Kiṅśuka, which though lovely in form, is void of smell :

सहृदयहृदयं चेत्काव्यमेतन्मदीयं

हरति सफलता स्यादस्य सत्यं तदैव।

हरति रुचिरगन्धा केतकी लोकचित्तं

न तु सुरुचिररूपः किंशुको गन्धहीनः।। 70.3

For other examples of Arthāntaranyāsa, reference may be made to 58a. 15, 58a.16, 59a.2,59a.23, 61a.4, 67a.37, etc.

Rūpaka (64a.3, 57a.8), Dṛṣṭānta (60a.17), Virodhābhāsa (59a.13), Svabhāvokti (57a.8-10, 64a.7-11) are some of the other figures of speech that the author has resorted to.

METRES

As against the twenty one metres in the Corpus of Letters studied earlier, the author has used here only six, which, besides his favourite Upajāti and Anuṣṭup include Vasantatilakā, Toṭaka, Mālinī and Drutavilambita.

APPENDIX

TEXT OF THE SHORTER WORKS

बृहत्तरं भारतम्

प्रथमोऽशः

अस्ति दक्षिणपूर्वस्यां दिशि ऋद्धिं परां गता ।
समुद्ररशना भूमिः ख्याता रामायणादिषु ।। 1 ।।

भारतीयोपनीवेशा इत्येवं सम्प्रकीर्तिताः ।
यवस्वर्णादयो द्वीपाः पुरा तत्र चकाशिरे ।। 2 ।।

द्वीपस्थानभिलप्यन्तो विनीतान् संस्कृतानथ ।
पुरा भरतवर्षीया देशात्त्वस्माद् विनिर्ययुः ।। 3 ।।

तेषां प्रयत्नसम्भारः फलेग्रहिरभूदिति ।
नात्र कस्यापि सन्देहः पौर्वापर्यं विजानतः ।। 4 ।।

आचारश्च विचारश्च धर्माचरणमेव च ।
भारतीयेन संवादि द्वीपस्थानामसंशयम् ।। 5 ।।

पुरा तेऽभिविनीताः स्युरार्यैर्वर्षात्समागतैः ।
पारेसमुद्रंगंयातैर्लोकानुग्रहकाङ्क्षिभिः ।। 6 ।।

चक्षुरुन्मीलयेमैषां ज्ञानाञ्जनशलाकया ।
धर्मं वा ग्राहयेमैतानिति बुद्ध्या प्रचोदिताः ।। 7 ।।

चतुर्थ्यां हि शताब्द्यां ते पञ्चम्यां वा विपश्चितः ।
परिहाय निजां भूमिं द्वीपानेतान् समभ्ययुः ।। 8 ।।

यद्यप्युपनिवेशत्वमेतेषां परिकीर्तितम् ।
ऐतिह्यविद्भिर्विद्वद्भिस्तथापि नहि तत्तथा ।। 9 ।।

अद्यत्वे ह्युपनीवेशा देशा येऽमी प्रकीर्तिताः ।
साम्राज्यवृद्धिमिच्छद्भिः शासकैस्ते विनिर्जिताः ।। 10 ।।

परं भरतवर्षीया न शस्त्रेण जयं पुरा ।
अरोचयन्नतस्ते नो बलाद्देशान् विजिग्यिरें ।। 11 ।।

विना युद्धं विना शस्त्रं विना सेनाश्च भीषणाः ।
विना नीतिं पुरा द्वीपा भारतीयैर्विनिर्जिताः ।। 12 ।।

किं मुधा रक्तपातेन किं वा नो भूमिकाम्यया ।
इत्येवं धर्मजिष्णुत्वं कामयाञ्चक्रिरे हि ते ।। 13 ।।

अत्र केचिन् महाभागाः शास्त्राध्ययनचुञ्चवः ।
उपन्यस्यन्त्यभिप्रायं स्वीयं युक्तिविभूषितम् ।। 14 ।।

द्वितीयोऽशः

धर्मप्रचारो नहि केवलः स्याद्धेतुः पुरा येन गता भवेयुः ।
सहस्रशो भारतवासिनः स्वं देशं विहायापरदेशपूगम् ।। 15 ।।

नैषोऽत्र हेतुः प्रतिभाति साधुर्हेत्वन्तरं किञ्चन मार्गणीयम् ।
कैमर्थिकीं सिद्धिमपेक्षमाणाः पारेसमुद्रं भरता गताः स्युः ।। 16 ।।

वाणिज्यहेतोर्धनसिद्धिहेतोः साम्राज्यहेतोर्भ्रमणस्य हेतोः ।
देशात्स्वकाद् दिग्विजयस्य हेतोर्गताः पुरा स्युर्वद कस्य हेतोः ।। 17 ।।

क्व वा समुद्रो गहनो गभीरस्तरङ्गमालापरिवेल्लितश्च ।
क्व वाऽप्रगल्भाः प्रथमं प्रयातास्तथापि तेषां न विचारणाऽभूत् ।। 18 ।।

परैर्हृतायां निजराजलक्ष्म्यां तिरस्कृता बन्धुजनैः स्वकैर्वा ।
गताः पुरा जन्मभुवं विहाय वीराः कुमाराः किमु राजवंश्याः ।। 19 ।।

दुर्भिक्षवृष्ट्यादिपरम्पराभिः कदर्थिताः प्राणपरीप्सवः किम् ।
याताः स्वदेशात् परकीयदेशानितीव नाना विदुषां वितर्काः ।। 20 ।।

इत्थं विवादे प्रबले प्रवृत्ते न शक्यते निश्चयतः प्रवक्तुम् ।
तथापि वच्मोऽवितथं निरुक्तं सर्वं वचः संभविकार्थकत्वात् ।। 21 ।।

नैकोऽत्र हेतुः परिकल्पनीयो न हेतुनैकेन प्रसिद्ध्यतीदम् ।
तथापि वाक्ये प्रथमे य उक्तस्तमेव हेतुं प्रथमं गृहाण ।। 22 ।।

स्वं स्वं चरित्रं भुवि भूमिदेवाः प्रशिक्षयन्तः किल सर्वपुंसः ।
पुरा प्रयाता इहदेशजाता यवादिदेशान् दिशि दक्षिणस्याम् ।। 23 ।।

तथा नियुक्ताः प्रियदर्शिना प्राक् सम्राडशोकेन सहस्रशो ये ।
शाक्यस्य सन्देशहरा मुनेस्ते द्वीपान् यवादीन् मुदिताः प्रयाताः ।। 24 ।।

अतो दरीदृश्यत एव भूयान् द्वीपेषु सर्वेषु समः प्रभावः ।
प्रमाणितो भारतवर्षजस्य धर्मस्य शीलस्य च संस्कृतेश्च ।। 25 ।।

गीर्वाणवाणीग्रथिताभिधेया उत्कीर्णलेखाश्शतशश्शिलासु ।
अभ्रंलिहाग्राणि सुविश्रुतानि ध्वस्तावशिष्टानि च मन्दिराणि ।। 26 ।।

नृत्यानि गीतानि दिगन्तरेषु ख्यातानि माधुर्यरसाप्लुतानि ।
चित्राणि वा भित्तिसमर्पितानि प्रौढैः कलायां कृतिभिः कृतानि ।। 27 ।।

दूरङ्गतानामिहदेशजानामाख्यापनान्यूर्जितगौरवस्य ।
आलोकमालोकमिमानि भूयः संजायते चेतसि हर्षवर्षः ।। 28 ।।

अद्यापि सीतेति सरस्वतीति प्रभावतीति श्रुतितर्पणानि ।
रामेति कृष्णेति सुदर्शनेति स्वरन्ति नामानि मनोहराणि ।। 29 ।।

अद्यापि धर्मान्तरसंश्रयेऽपि द्वीपेषु बालिप्रमुखेषु हन्त !
पुण्याः कथाः संकथयन्ति लोका रामायणाद्वाऽपि पुराणतो वा ।। 30 ।।

अद्यापि यातेषु शतेषु वर्षेष्वहो महान् संस्कृतशब्दराशिः ।
ध्वनेर्मनाक् सम्परिवर्तनेन प्रयुज्यमानो मुदमातनोति ।। 31 ।।

अद्यापि पूर्वविहिताः कलनाः समस्ता
आर्षेषु शास्त्रनिवहेष्वथ सौगतेषु ।
आजन्ममृत्यु कलया परिपालयन्तो

धन्या नरा नयनयोरयनं प्रयान्ति ।। 32 ।।

कम्बुजद्वीपवर्णनम्

बभूव धीमानिह नीवृति द्विजः कुले प्रसूतः प्रयतेऽतिविस्तृते ।
स कुण्डिनानां यशसा महीयसां चिचिन्त नित्यं भरतप्रपञ्चनम् ।। 33 ।।

इदं परं सुष्ठु विधाय मानसं विहाय देशं प्रणयैकभाजनम् ।
स्थितान्समुद्रात्परतो दवीयसो जगाम देशान्प्रथितान्स कम्बुजान् ।। 34 ।।

यशूमसीहस्य स जन्मनः परं तृतीयके हायनसङ्गते शते ।
उदुह्य राज्ञीं विधिवत्तदीश्वरां शशास राज्यं शमितारिसंहतिः ।। 35 ।।

गुणैरुदारैर्विकलाः प्रियङ्करैर्वनस्थसत्त्वैरथ साम्यमागताः ।
अनावृताः स्त्रीपुरुषा अपत्रपा विचेरुरत्र प्रकटं सहेतरैः ।। 36 ।।

क्रमेण तत्र स्थितिकामुकैर्जनैरुपागतैरार्यकुलोद्गतैस्तथा ।
स्वयं विनीतैर्विनिनीपुभिः परान्विनिन्यिरे कम्बुजवासिनो जनाः ।। 37 ।।

ततः परैः कैरपि शासकैः किल लओस-मुख्या मलयावसानकाः ।
सदेशदेशास्तरसात्मसात्कृताः सुहिन्दचीनाः कलया च निर्जिताः ।। 38 ।।

अमीभिरेव प्रथमैः प्रशासकैर्नयज्ञधुर्यैरपि चीनभारते ।
सुदौत्यबन्धेन दृढेन योजिते श्रियोऽभिवृद्धेरुभयत्र कामुकैः ।। 39 ।।

वियत्सु ऋत्स्वब्दशतेषु यीशुतः शशास पृथ्वीं जयवर्मसंज्ञकः ।
स रुद्रवर्मा च कुलप्रभावती सुतः कलत्रं च कुले स्म विश्रुतौ ।। 40 ।।

शिलार्पिता अद्य तयोर्द्वयोरपि प्रशस्तिबन्धा विलसन्ति भूरयः ।
यतोऽस्य वंशस्य च वर्णनाऽखिला प्रतीयते नीप्यजनस्य हर्षदा ।। 41 ।।

इहैव वंशे जयवर्मनामकः परोऽपि भूपः कृतलक्षणोऽभवत् ।
गुणातिरेकात्खलु यत्र दुर्लभात् प्रजाजनः पश्यति देवरूपताम् ।। 42 ।।

असंशयं तस्य महात्मनः कृतैः प्रवृत्तिमान्स्वर्णयुगस्तदाऽभवत् ।
तथाहि तादात्विकसम्पदो विभोः सुरम्यसौधानि निबोधयन्ति नः ।। 43 ।।

ततो हि राज्ञो जयवर्मणः परं ततोऽधिकं स्फीतपराक्रमो बली ।
शशास भूमिं यशसाऽन्वितो नृपो यथार्थनामा स हि वर्मणा युतः ।। 44 ।।

यदा यशोवर्मनृपो यशोऽन्वितः स्वराज्यगुर्वीं धुरमाधितात्मनि ।
तदा बभूवुः सकलाः प्रजा अपि प्रसन्नचित्ताः परिवृद्धिकामुकाः ।। 45 ।।

पवित्रचर्येऽथ प्रजानुरञ्जके जनाधिनाथे पृथिवीं प्रशासति ।
प्रजा बभूवुः सकला निरामया बभूव राष्ट्रं सकलं निरीति च ।। 46 ।।

बभुश्च तत्रत्यभटा रणोद्धटा निरीक्ष्य तं दिग्विजयार्थमुद्यतम् ।
रराज सोऽपि प्रथमो जयैषिणां घनव्यपायेन गभस्तिमानिव ।। 47 ।।

रणेऽप्रधृष्यः खलु शत्रुयोषितां विधाय वक्त्रं च्युतपत्रकाङ्कनम् ।
स मन्यमानः कृतकृत्यतां स्वकां मुदः परां कोटिमथाश्रितोऽभवत् ।। 48 ।।

न केवलं तस्य रणेऽतिपाटवं जनाधिनाथस्य बभूव विश्रुतम् ।
कलासु दाक्ष्यं सकलासु नाम्यपि जहार चेतांसि भृशं मनस्विनाम् ।। 49 ।।

कृतश्रमः शास्त्रचये विचक्षणो विलक्षणः प्रौढिमवाप्य निर्वृतः ।
सदा कवीनामुपजीव्यतां गतो दिगन्तविश्रान्तयशा बभूव सः ।। 50 ।।

पतञ्जलेर्व्याकरणेऽतिविश्रुता कृतिर्महाभाष्यमिति प्रसंज्ञिता ।
नृपेण सूक्ष्मेक्षिकया युतेन सा स्वकीयवृत्त्या समयोजि हृद्यया ।। 51 ।।

स वास्तुविद्यानिपुणो जनप्रियो बहूनि देवायतनानि निर्ममे ।
तदीयभक्त्या दिवि भक्तवत्सलाः सुराः प्रसेदुः परया महौजसः ।। 52 ।।

सदा यतीनां सुखचिन्तने रतो बहूनि चैत्यानि मठांस्तथाऽऽश्रमान् ।
स कारयामास वशी नराधिपस्ततः परं किञ्चिदभून्न तत्प्रियम् ।। 53 ।।

स धर्मकृत्याकुशलो हिते रतः प्रजानुरागोद्धुरकन्धरो नृपः ।
ततान तां कीर्तिमहो यया पुनः सुवास्यतेऽद्यापि हि सागराम्बरा ।। 54 ।।

न राज्यसादृश्यमिहास्ति मे पुरे रमेय येनात्र कृतारिशातनः ।
इतीव मन्ये मनसा विचिन्तयन् स राजधानीमपरां विनिर्ममे ।। 55 ।।

चकार तां कम्बुपुरीतिनामिकां स कम्बुजानां विजयी नराधिपः ।
ततोऽतियाते समये कियत्यपि यशोधरेति प्रथिता पुरी बभौ ।। 56 ।।

प्रवर्तकोऽनूकविशेषकस्य यः स सूर्यवर्मा प्रथमश्चकास्ति नः ।
अयं स्वराज्ये परमेऽन्तराणयदवाक्स्थिताञ्छ्यामभुखान्प्रदेशकान् ।। 57 ।।

अनन्तरं सूर्यसमानसंज्ञकोऽपरो हि सम्राट् परशक्तिकोऽभवत् ।
स वाटमंगस्थमथाकरोत्प्रभुस्ततोऽस्य कीर्तिं प्रजगुर्दिगङ्गनाः ।। 58 ।।

चिरं च चम्पामभियोधयन्नृपो दिवं गतः सोऽनवसाय्य विग्रहम् ।
ततश्च चम्पाजननाथ इन्द्रकः समुद्रचम्वाऽस्य पुरीमलुण्ठयत् ।। 59 ।।

ततः प्रतीतो जयवर्मसप्तमः क्रमागतं प्राप्य च पित्र्यमासनम् ।
ग्रामादिसंज्ञैर्गुणिभिः समादृतैः श्रियोऽभिवृद्धिं व्यदधाच्च साधनैः ।। 60 ।।

अथारिवर्गस्य स भीतिदो नृपः क्रियाभिरामः सुविदूरदर्शनः ।
पुराणविद्भिः कथितां सचम्पिकां चिरं स्वतन्त्रां वशमानयत्प्रभुः ।। 61 ।।

युधां विजेता स शिरांसि दुर्हृदां लुलाव काण्डानि च हेलया यथा ।
अनामदेशं च चिराय योधयन्नवाक्प्रदेशान्स्ववशे निनाय सः ।। 62 ।।

अभूदपूर्वा ननु राष्ट्रविस्तृतिर्वृहत्तरा श्रीरपि सर्वतोमुखी ।
प्रशासके तत्र नृपे जनप्रिये नवं हि सर्वं प्रबभूव शर्मणे ।। 63 ।।

स राजधानीं परया श्रिया युतां विनिर्ममे नागरधामसंज्ञिताम् ।
अतीत्य या पुण्यजनैरधिश्रितां स्थिता पुरी तामलकाभिधानिकाम् ।। 64 ।।

इयं हि तेनाश्ममयेन प्रांशुना बलीयसा सालवरेण योजिता ।
अमुं च सालं परितो भविष्णुना नवापि काचित्परिखा विनिर्मिता ।। 65 ।।

प्रमाणमस्याः कथयामि तच्छृणु भवेन्नु जिज्ञास्यमिदं सखे तव ।
विशेषतोऽर्थेऽविदिते नृणां ध्रुवं कुतूहलिन्यः खलु चित्तवृत्तयः ।। 66 ।।

शतं गजान् दाशतयेन संयुतान् निशामनीया परिखा सुविस्तृता ।
तथा च मीलान् दश सा परायता समासतो मानमिदं विदाङ्कुरु ।। 67 ।।

निरुक्तपूर्वे वरणे विरेजिरे ह्युदग्रकायानि सुगोपुराणि ।
अमीषु पञ्चस्वपि पञ्च जज्ञिरे महापथास्ते शतफीटविस्तृताः ।। 68 ।।

इयं महापूः समपार्श्वकैर्युता रराज मीलद्वयसंमितैः शुभैः ।
सुवास्तुविद्याप्रविचक्षणा हि तां वितेनिरे शात्रवरोधकाम्यया ।। 69 ।।

इदं परं नु श्रुतिपेयमस्ति ते बयोन-देवायतने पुरि स्थिते ।
अमी च चत्वार इहाभिकीर्तिता महापथाः सङ्गमलिप्सया ययुः ।। 70 ।।

अदश्च देवायतनं परिस्थितं निकर्षणे विद्धि महाप्रमाणकम् ।
हितोपदेशा अपि राजदेशना विशब्दिता यत्र चकाशिरे जनैः ।। 71 ।।

प्रशस्यचर्यो गुणिनामपश्चिमो जयाभिधानः खलु राजसत्तमः ।
अधर्मभीरुर्दृढभक्तिसंयमः प्रदानशीलो ननु शालते नृपः ।। 72 ।।

अलं बहूक्त्वा विततां वदान्यतां ययाऽतिशेते स शिबिं महीपराट् ।
कृते स देवालयसंविधेः सुधीर्महान्तमर्थं विनियुक्तवान्प्रभुः ।। 73 ।।

न्ययुङ्क्त धीरः किल देववेश्मनि स केवलेऽस्मिन्नुपसप्त तान्यहो ।
द्विजन्मनां सौम्य सहस्रकाण्ययं कृतप्रसङ्गानि च देवतार्चने ।। 74 ।।

इहाङ्करामार्णवसंमिता द्विजा पुरा खमुन्यङ्कगुरूनुपासते ।
अमी च सर्वे तत एव लेभिरे ससत्क्रियां वृत्तिमलन्तरां नृपात् ।। 75 ।।

इदं च लेखादपरं शिलार्पितात्प्रतीयते मोदकरं सतां नृणाम् ।
वसुग्रहर्ष्यङ्कितदेवतालया विरेजुरत्र द्विशतं क्रियागृहाः ।। 76 ।।

स एष राजा जयवर्मनामकः क्रियासु दक्षः सततं समुत्थितः ।
विनिर्ममे लोकहितान्यनेकशो गृहाणि मार्गान्तरसंश्रितानि च ।। 77 ।।

अयं स राजा महतां महीभृतां सुकम्बुजानां चरमः किलाभवत् ।
अतः परं वृत्तपरम्पराविदः प्रचक्षते नैव तदाश्रयं क्वचित् ।। 78 ।।

चतुर्दशे सा यशुजन्मनः परे सुकम्बुजश्रीर्ह्रसिता शताब्दके ।
निवेशनान्यस्य च यानि सन्निधौ स्थितानि देशस्य विनष्टयेऽभवन् ।। 79 ।।

पुरा प्रकर्षं परमं जगाम यः शशास राज्यानि समृद्धिमन्ति यः ।
स सम्प्रति फ्रांसजनैरधिष्ठितः प्रहीणतेजाः परमं च सीदति ।। 80 ।।

अहो विधेश्चित्रविचेष्टिता बत स यो विधाता सदयः स शोभते ।
कथं स दत्त्वा स्वयमुन्नतिं परां पुनर्हरंस्तां विषमीभवत्यहो ।। 81 ।।

शैलेन्द्रराज्यवर्णनम्

शैलेन्द्रराज्यमभवत् प्रथितं पुरा यत्
स्वर्णे यवे मलयदेश उतापरेषु ।
देशेषु तस्य नहि वर्णनमस्ति शक्यं
शक्तो नु केवलमिहास्ति सहस्रजिह्वः ।। 82 ।।

दिव्यस्य वा सुचरितस्य हि पुण्यभाजां
संकीर्तनं किमपि पुण्यमथातनोति ।
एवं यतेन मनसा प्रविचिन्त्य चिन्त्य-
मस्मिन् वयं सुखदकर्मणि सम्प्रवृत्ताः ।। 83 ।।

अर्वाभिधे प्रथितदेशवरे प्रजातै-
स्तात्कालिकैः कृतिवरैरितिहासविद्भिः ।
शैलेन्द्रनाम्न इति वृत्तमलेखि राज्य-
स्यास्ते तदेव खलु नः परमं प्रणाणम् ।। 84 ।।

पोतेन तीव्रगतिनाऽपि कथञ्चिदेव
वर्षद्वयेन परितो भ्रमणं भवेन्नु ।
साम्राज्यमेवमभवत् सुतरां विशालं
यद्वैभवस्य तुलना भुवि नो बभूव ।। 85 ।।

चीनादिराष्ट्रपतयोऽपि च चोलपाला
अन्ये च येऽपि प्रतिवेशिनृपा बभूवुः ।
दूतादिप्रेषणपराः सममानयंस्तान्
ते चापि भूमिपतयः समभावयंस्तान् ।। 86 ।।

कालेऽम्बु वर्षति सदा भुवि वारिवाहो

देशोऽपि चास्ति सकलो बहुसस्यशाली ।

एवं पुरा बहुविधं समभिष्टुताऽभूत्

शैलेन्द्रराजकुलजा महती समृद्धिः ।। 87 ।।

द्वीपेषु तेषु च शिलासु समर्पिता ये

लेखाः पुराणपुरुषैः शतसङ्ख्यकास्ते ।

अद्यापि साग्रहमहो प्रथितामपूर्वा-

मृद्धिं पुरा पिशुनयन्ति जनस्य दिव्याम् ।। 88 ।।

कालेन शक्तमपि ऋद्धमपि प्रसिद्धं

शैलेन्द्रराज्यमभवत् खलु नामशेषम् ।

माजापहीतमभवत्तदनन्तरं च

द्वीपे यवे नृपतिचक्रकमद्वितीयम् ।। 89 ।।

दण्डेन शत्रुशमनं प्रविधाय तत्र

शान्त्या सुखं नृपतयो वसुधां शशासुः ।

तेषां च नागरकृतागमनाम्नि काव्ये

सौराज्यवर्णनमभूदनवद्यहृद्यम् ।। 90 ।।

वालिद्वीपवर्णनम्

ततो याति काले कुतोऽप्यागतेन मुसल्मानधर्मप्रियेणाप्रियेण ।

नृपाः शान्तिकामाः पराजिग्यिरे ते न साम्येन तिष्ठत्यहो कश्चनापि ।। 91 ।।

चतुःसागरावेष्टिताया शुभायाः गतायाः परां कोटिमृद्धेर्जगत्सु ।

बलेनैव बाह्वोः सुखं निर्जिताया अभूवन् पुरा ये भुवः शासितारः ।। 92 ।।

गतास्तेऽपि देशाच्च्युतास्तेऽपि राज्याद्धहा पश्य चित्रं विलासं विधातुः ।

प्रतापेन येषां बभुर्दिग्दिगन्ता गतास्तेऽपि कष्टां दशां मन्ददिष्टाः ।। 93 ।।

सुखं प्राज्यराज्ये चिरं संस्थितानां नृपाणां निपातो ध्रुवोऽस्तीति विद्धि ।

जगद् भानुभिर्भासयित्वा प्रकामं रविः श्रान्तकायोऽस्तमद्रिं प्रयाति ।। 94 ।।

ततस्तत्र कालात्परीवर्तशीलान् मुसल्मानधर्मावलम्बिप्रचारः ।
प्रवृत्तः समस्तेषु देशेषु वेगात् स्रवन्त्या यथा वारि कूलङ्कषायाः ।। 95 ।।

कथं धर्मरक्षा भवेन्मेऽधुनेति नृपोभूत् पुरा यो यवद्वीपशास्ता ।
स संचिन्तयामास दीर्घं न चापि विवेदाभ्युपायं विना विप्रवासात् ।। 96 ।।

स्थितोऽहं यदि स्यां स्वके देश एव ध्रुवो म्लेच्छसम्पर्क इत्याकलय्य ।
स पञ्चाधिकायां दशम्यां शताब्द्यां श्रितो बालिदेशं नृपो धर्मभीरुः ।। 97 ।।

प्रजास्तस्य साम्राज्यविभ्रंशदूना श्रिया नाम हीना गुणैर्जात्वहीनाः ।
स्वपुत्रैः कलत्रैः सुहृद्भिः समेता उपेतास्ततो द्वीपकं बालिसंज्ञम् ।। 98 ।।

अथाद्यापि रामायणादेः पुराणीर्महाभारताद्वा पुराणादिकाद्वा ।
कथाः श्रोतुकामाः पुमांसः स्त्रियो वा समेत्य व्रजन्ति प्रगे मन्दिराणि ।। 99 ।।

पुराणं स रक्षन् जगत्यां प्रसिद्धं सुशर्मैकहेतुं निजं हिन्दुधर्मम् ।
सुखी बालिदेशो भुवो मण्डलस्याखिलस्यावतंसः श्रिया मोमुदीति ।। 100 ।।

षड्ऋतुवर्णनम्

कूजन्ति कोकिलकुलानि कलं वसन्ते
गुञ्जन्ति मञ्जु कुसुमेषु च षट्पदौघाः ।
वान्त्यद्य दक्षिणदिशः सुभगाः समीरा-
श्चेतोहराः सकलिकाः सहकारशाखाः ।। 1 ।।

अनोकहानां स्तबकाचितानां
नवैः पलाशैरुपशोभितानाम् ।
वीनां विरावैः कृतकौतुकानां
विलासिवृन्दैश्च सनाथितानाम् ।। 2 ।।
आकृष्टरोलम्बकदम्बकानां
प्रतानिनीभिः समुपाश्रितानाम् ।
वातेन मन्देन च वेल्लितानां
हरन्त्यभिख्याः सुमनोमनांसि ।। 3 ।।

वृक्षसंघट्टजन्मा दवाग्निर्महान्
दन्दहीति द्विजान्श्वापदांश्चाकुलान् ।
जाज्वलीत्यन्तरिक्षं दिशो धूसरा
रंहसा वान्ति वात्या रजोविक्षिपाः ।। 4 ।।

घर्मक्लान्ता विवृतवदना आलवालेष्वजस्रं
चङ्क्रम्यन्ते विकिरनिकरा उच्छ्वसन्तस्तपर्तौ ।
क्रोडीकृत्यापिदधति शिशून्शाखिनां कोटरेषु
पित्सन्तोऽन्ये क्वचिदपि वने छायया पर्यटन्ति ।। 5 ।।
प्रावृट्कालः काशते सर्वदिक्षु
कादम्बिन्यो द्यामलं भूषयन्ति ।
दृष्ट्वा काल्यं वारिदं मोदमानाः

शब्दायन्ते चातका वारिलुब्धाः ।। 6 ।।

पुण्डरीकसुषमोज्ज्वला भृशं
पुष्करे पतति सारसावलिः ।
द्योतते हि चपला क्षणे क्षणे
वर्षुकः स्तनति भीतिदोऽम्बुदः ।। 7 ।।

रम्येऽरण्ये सप्रमदं काममटन्तो
मन्द्रध्वानान्वीक्ष्य पयोदान्दिवि रम्यान् ।
नर्तं नर्तं चारुकलापा मुदमाप्ता
रोरूयन्ते 'मत्तमयूरा' अविरामम् ।। 8 ।।

नरिनृतति मयूरा गर्जितं खे निशम्य
परिरटति च भेकः कूर्दमानः सहर्षम् ।
परिसरति बलाका मेघसंसर्गकामा
वहति च पवमानश्शाखिनः संधुनानः ।। 9 ।।

नवजलधरा वृण्वन्त्यद्य क्षितिं तमसा भृशं
सुरधनुरिदं सर्वाशानां महन्ननु भूषणम् ।
रचयति शिखी सङ्गीतं स्वं वनेषु ससंमदो
भजति भुवनं भूयान्मोदो विहाय वियोगिनः ।। 10 ।।

हृद्यः काशो लसति शरदृतौ
काष्ठाः सर्वा विजहति मलिनम् ।
चण्डः सूर्यः प्रतपति गगने
पङ्कं सर्वा जहति सरणयः ।। 11 ।।

जीमूताः कृषिपु चिरं विमुच्य तोयं
क्षेत्रौघान् सपदि विधाय 'सस्यपूर्णान् ।
शुभ्रत्वं दधति कृतोपकारभारा
दीप्यन्ते न भुवि परार्थसम्पदः के ।। 12 ।।

यदातिदीर्घाः क्षणदाः क्षणप्रदा
　　रथाङ्गनाम्नोस्तु युगस्य दुःखदाः ।
कदर्थिकाश्चापि विनेयसंहतेः
　　स एष हेमन्त उपस्थितः सखे ! ।। 13 ।।

शिशिरः पवनो विपुलाः करका
　　विकिरन्पवते तरसा शिशिरे
जननी स्वशिशून् सविकम्पतनू-
　　न्समया ज्वलनं परितो नयते ।। 14 ।।

गुल्मिन्यो विगतप्रभा विटपिनो विष्वग्विलुप्तच्छदा
　　हिम्येनापि नभस्वता वनभुवां शादाः समुज्जासिताः ।।
पद्मिन्यो विरसास्तुषारमथिताः खेदाय नः साम्प्रतं
　　विश्वस्तेव च हन्त ! भाति वसुधा शोकेन शीर्णाम्बरा ।। 15 ।।

नपुंसकलिङ्गस्य मोक्षप्राप्तिः

(एकस्मिन् गृहे किञ्चित्खिन्नमनाः संस्कृतभाषा पुंलिङ्गस्त्रीलिङ्गाभ्यां

कृत्तद्धिताभ्यां च स्वसहायकाभ्यां परिवारिता तूष्णीं तिष्ठति । तां तूष्णीकामवलोक्य चिन्तितं पुंलिङ्गमेवं भणति ---)

पुंलिङ्गम्--देवि सुरभारति ! अद्य होलिकावसरेऽपि किमिति विवर्णेव लक्ष्यसे । अस्माभिः समेतापि न जल्पसि। न हससि न वा प्रसीदसि । कोयमस्थाने शोकोदयः ?

संस्कृतभाषा -- भ्रातः पुंलिङ्ग ! अद्य चिराय लोकेन परित्यक्ताया मम कीदृशं सुखम् ? आसीत् सोपि कालो यदा सकलोऽपि लोको मामेवाश्रयत् । सर्वस्मिन्नपि च कार्ये ममैव प्राधान्यमभूत् । परमद्य तु मम स्थानं भाषान्तरैर्गृहीतमिति भृशं परितप्यामि। हीना च दीना चाहं कथं जल्पेयं कथं वा हसेयम् ।

स्त्री (लिङ्गम्) -- सत्यम् । (स्वगतम्) किन्नु खल्वेतस्यां लोकापरागकारणं भवेत् ? भवतु, पृच्छाम्येनाम्। (प्रकाशम्) -- देवि, कथय कुतस्त्वय्यपरक्तो लोकः ?

संस्कृतभाषा -- बहूनि तत्र कारणानि । आद्यस्तावत् त्वयि च त्वत्प्रतिद्वन्द्विनि नपुंसके च लोकस्यानिश्चयः, ततश्च बहुलो व्यत्यासः । भाषान्तरेषु च स्त्रीपुंसयोरेव सद्भावात्सौकर्यमनुभवति लोकः। द्वितीयस्तावत् । ------

पुंलिङ्गम् -- आः ! मयि स्थिते केयं दास्याः पुत्रस्य नपुंसकस्य चर्चा ।

अहं च स्त्रीलिङ्गं चाचिरेणैव तं कवलीकरिष्यावः ।

(नेपथ्ये)

नपुंसकलिङ्गम् -- कोयं भोः ! क एष साहसिकधुरन्धरो मां (कवली) कर्तुमीहते । पश्यामस्तावत्। भो भोः ! आत्मनेपदादयः सखायः उच्यतां लिट्लुट्लेट्प्रभृतिभ्यः सुहृद्भ्यो यच्छीघ्रमेव स्वभार्याभिर्यङ्लुगन्तप्रक्रियादिभिः समेता इहोपतिष्ठध्वमिति । अयं पुंलिङ्गो नाम मुमूर्षुमामपवदतीति ।

सर्वेपि समवेताः -- इह स्मः । प्रतिष्ठतां तावदार्यः ।

(सर्वेऽपि तत्रागच्छन्ति यत्र पुंलिङ्गादयस्तिष्ठन्ति ।

नपुंसकम् -- (सबाहुक्षेपम्)

अभूत्पुरा वीरवरः शिखण्डी
जघान भीष्मं निशितैः शरैर्यः ।
तस्यैव वीरस्य कुले प्रजातो
नपुंसकोऽहं समुपस्थितोऽस्मि ।।

पुंलिङ्गम्--(किञ्चिद्विहस्य) साधु वीरशिरोमणे साधु । सत्यं वाचि शूरोऽसि ।

नपुंसकम्--कथं वाचि शूरः, शास्त्रशूरोप्यस्मि । पश्य इदानीमेव स्वकीयया सेनया त्वामितो द्रावयिष्यामि।

पुंलिङ्गम्-- अलं विकत्थनेन । किं त्वादृशा नपुंसकाः करिष्यन्ति । वीरत्वं हि पुंसां धर्मो न नपुंसकानाम्। किं च लोके द्वे एव लिङ्गे श्रूयेते स्त्री च पुमांश्च, पुरुषश्च प्रकृतिश्च । त्वं पुनः कुत आगतोसि । तत्रभवता भगवता भाष्यकारेणापि संस्त्यानप्रसवौ लिङ्गमिति वदता आविर्भावरूपः पुमान्, तिरोभावरूपा च स्त्रीति लक्षणस्वीकारान्मम च स्त्रियाश्चैवास्तित्वं स्वीकृतम् ।

वाक्यपदीयटीकाकारो हेलाराजोऽप्येवमाह-- तथा चाविर्भावतिरोभावयोर्व्यापकत्वात् सर्वत्र स्त्रीपुंलिङ्गयोगः। एवं कोऽवसरो यन्नपुंसकः स्यात् (3.13.16)।

नपुंसकम्-- रे पुंलिङ्ग, किमन्धोऽसि न मां पश्यसि त्वत्पुरतः स्थितम्। रे रे फक्किकादयः सखायः लोडादयश्च सहायकाः किन्न मां पश्यथ।

(आत्मनोऽङ्गानि स्पृशन् सरुदितस्वरम्) किं ममास्तित्वमेव नास्ति।

(सर्वेऽपि नपुंसकसहायकाः सस्वरं वदन्ति)

कथं नास्तित्वं श्रीमतः? श्रीमान् हि स्त्रीपुंसयोरुभयोरपि गुणैर्विभूषित इति शास्त्रकारैरपि स्वीकृतम्। तथा चोक्तम्--

स्तनकेशवती नारी लोमशः पुरुषः स्मृतः।

उभयोरन्तरं यत्तु तदभावे नपुंसकम्।।

पुँलिङ्गम्-- (विहस्य) तद् भवानुभयोरन्तरे स्थितस्त्रिशङ्कुवत्। वरं स्थीयतामन्तरैव। न पुनर्वराकी संस्कृतभाषा स्वेन च स्वकीयैर्बीभत्सैरेभिः सहायकैश्च कदाचित्पीडनीया । यूयं शीघ्रमेव मुञ्चतैतस्या पिण्डम्। मा स्मेयं वराकी भवादृशानामनुकम्पाभाजनं भूता शीघ्रतरं मडमडायेत्।

नपुंसकलिङ्गम्-- कथं त्रिशङ्कुरिति । मम शक्तिं नैव जानासि दुर्बुद्धे। तव तु नामैव खलु मम माहात्म्यस्य प्रत्यक्षमुदाहरणम्। पुंलिङ्गमिति नपुंकलिङ्गश्शब्दः। किञ्च, मम माहात्म्यं मुनिना पाणिनिनापि स्वीकृतम्।

अत एव स आह-- नपुंसकमनपुंसकेनैकवच्चास्यान्तरस्याम्, नपुंसकानपुंसकयोर्नपुंसकमवशिष्यत इति । तव च मम च सङ्घर्षे ममैव विजयः हो हो हो

पुंलिङ्गः-- पुंलिङ्गमिति रूढिवशाल्लोकाः कथयन्ति । वस्तुतस्त्वहं पुंलिङ्गोऽस्मि पुंसो लिङ्गमस्येति व्युत्पत्तेः । यत्तु पाणिनिमुनिवचनमुदाहरस्तत्र त्विदमेव विवक्षामि यत् त्वादृशानां सृष्टिं कुर्वता तव पाणिनिना यादृशोऽनर्थः कृतो न तादृशोऽन्येन केनापि । पाणिनिमुनिविषये तु सत्यमेवोच्यते कविवरैः--

नपुंसकमिति ज्ञात्वा प्रियायै प्रेषितं मनः।

तत्तु तत्रैव रमते हताः पाणिनिना वयम्।।

किञ्च विचारवान् पाणिनिरेकसूत्रे श्वानं युवानं मघवानमाह। पाणिनेर्बुद्धिवैभवं त्वनेनैव स्पष्टं भवति यत्स भृशं भवतीत्यस्य स्थाने बोभवीतीति द्रविडप्राणायामं करोति, त्वं गृहीतवानित्यस्य स्थाने अजर्घा इति कर्णकटुरूपमेवंविधानि बहूनि कटुविकटानि रूपाणि निष्पादयति।

नपुंसकम्-- धिङ् मूर्ख! शब्दशास्त्रस्य प्रणेतारं भगवन्तं पाणिनिमप्यपवदसि।

पुंलिङ्गः-- अथ किम्। अयमेव पाणिनिर्येन त्वादृशानां ब्रह्मरक्षसां सृष्टिं कुर्वता संस्कृतभाषा दीनामवस्थां

प्रापिता।

नपुंसकम्-- अलं रे अलम्। एतावत्ते साहसं यन्मां ब्रह्मराक्षसं वदसि । तिष्ठ, इदानीमेव त्वां चूर्णयामि।

पुंलिङ्गः-- अलं चापलेन। नो चेत् पश्चात्तप्स्यसि।

(मुष्टिं बद्ध्वा तमभिद्रवति । संस्कृतभाषा भयं नाटयति)

पुंलिङ्गः-- (सवेगं नपुंसकलिङ्गं कण्ठे गृहीत्वा) जाल्म दास्याः पुत्र बहु नाम वल्गसे। इदानीमेव त्वां ससहायं राक्षस्या होलिकया सममेव निर्दहामि।

(सर्वानपि वह्नौ पातयति)

संस्कृतभाषा स्त्रीपुंसाभ्यां कृत्तद्धिताभ्यां च भूयोभूयो वर्धाप्यते। तदनन्तरं सर्वेऽपि सम्भूयोच्चारयन्ति--

उभयी प्रकृतिः कामे भवेदिति मुनेर्मतम्।
अपवर्गे तृतीयेति क्लीबो मोक्षमवाप्नुयात्[1]।।

सर्वेऽपि स्वं स्वं स्थानं प्रतिष्ठन्ते।

पटाक्षेपः

---

1. नैषधकारस्य श्रीहर्षस्यास्मिन् श्लोके परिवर्तितश्चतुर्थश्चरणः।

जय देवि स्वतन्त्रते

शृणु मे रणगानं शृणु चह्वानाह्वानम् ।
असङ्ख्यकोटिकण्ठस्तुते जय देवि स्वतन्त्रते ।।1।।

वितनु विपक्षविनाशं त्वं क्षिप शत्रुषु पाशम् ।
भारतभूमिवीराग्रवन्दिते जय देवि स्वतन्त्रते ।।2।।

शृणु रणभेरीघोषं त्वं कुरु शत्रुषु रोषम् ।
साहसिकजननिजरक्तरञ्जिते जय देवि स्वतन्त्रते ।।3।।

कुरु शत्रूणां कदनं प्रेषय तान् यमसदनम् ।
धार्मिकजनसोल्लाससंस्तुते जय देवि स्वतन्त्रते ।।4।।

अत्याचारपराणां पिब रक्तं दनुजानाम् ।
सन्ततनिजभक्तरक्षणोद्यते जय देवि स्वतन्त्रते ।।5।।

कोऽहम् ?

प्रश्नोऽयं समुदेति मे मनसि भोः कोऽहं कुतस्त्यस्तथा
किं वा नाम करोम्यहं जगति किं कुत्रास्म्यहं संस्थितः ।
किं लक्ष्यं किमु वा महत्त्वमथवा किं वा ममाऽऽस्ते पदम्
आत्मा मे सुतरामसंस्तुत इति प्राप्तोऽस्मि चित्रां दशाम् ।।1।।

यद्यच्चिन्तनमस्ति मे मनसि किं वाचा भवेत् तत् स्फुटं
किं वा कर्मणि तद् भवेत्परिणतं किं वा परेभ्यो भवेत् ।
तत्सम्यक् प्रतिपादितं किमथवा ज्ञातं मया स्यान्नवे-
त्येवं विप्रतिपन्नमानसतया नो शान्तिमाप्नोम्यहम् ।।2।।

किं मे धावनमस्तु वा सुविरतिः कार्यान्तरेभ्यो भवेत्
किं वा तेष्वभिरक्तिरस्तु किमु वा तेभ्यो विरक्तिर्भवेत् ।
चिन्ताचान्तमना इति प्रविततं सर्वं चरं चाचरं
पश्यन् व्याप्तमिदं जगत् किमपि किं नैवाहमालोकये ।।3।।

ज्ञानं मे प्रथितं मया च पठिता ग्रन्था अनेके भुवि
तत्किं मे परवञ्चनादिकृतिषु स्वीया प्रवृत्तिः सदा ।
दीनां दुर्विधतां गतां च जनतां नो वीक्ष्य चित्तद्रुति-
र्मेऽन्धो वा बधिरोऽथवाहमिति मे नैवास्त्यहो निर्णयः ।।4।।

दिव्योऽहं सुविभूषितो गुणगणैर्लोकस्य पूज्यस्तथा
कुर्वन् वैभवशालिभव्यभवने वासं सदर्पं सदा ।
ध्यायन् द्रव्यमुपार्जितं कुसृतिभिर्नैकैस्तथा गर्हितैः
कृत्यैश्छद्मपरैर्नृशंसपरमैः शान्तिं परां नाप्नुवे ।।5।।

आढ्यानामकृतात्मनां बत ! कृते श्राम्यामि रात्रिन्दिवं
नैवाहं च लभे कथञ्चिदपि हा ! स्वीयामभीष्टां भृतिम् ।
हर्म्याणां रचनाविधावनुदिनं श्रान्तस्य मे हन्त भो !

वासः पर्णकुटी विशीर्णमलिनं वासो ममाच्छादनम् ।।6।।

आचार्योऽप्यनुशास्मि नैव सततं राज्ञां नयेऽवस्थितो
वैद्योऽहं परमातुरादिविषया चिन्ता न मां बाधते ।
कार्याणां लय इत्यनेन विधिना कार्यालये कार्यकृद्
उत्कोचादिपरः परार्थघटकः सौख्यं परं व्यश्नुवे ।।7।।

कः पन्थाः किमु मे स्वरूपमथवा कस्यास्म्यहं भूतले
किं वा कर्म करोमि कस्य च कृते भ्राम्याम्यहं सन्ततम् ।
किं वा वच्मि शृणोमि किं किमथवा ध्यायामि यामि क्व च
कोऽहं वेत्ति न वेद्मि हन्त ! किमिति भ्राम्यामि दिग्भ्रान्तवत् ।।8।।

महाकविकालिदासाष्टकम्

गङ्गोदधारा इव शुद्धरूपाः

शशाङ्कलेखा इव कान्तिमत्यः ।

नूत्नार्थविज्ञानविभासयित्र्यः

श्रीकालिदासस्य गिरो विभान्ति ।। 1 ।।

अंशुप्रकर्षेण यथांऽशुमाली

हिमातिरेकेण यथा हिमाद्रिः ।

तथा कवित्वस्य भरेण दिव्ये-

नायं कविप्राग्रहरो विभाति ।। 2 ।।

पुराणमित्येव न साधु सर्वं

नैवानवद्यं च समस्तमस्ति ।

महाकवेः काव्यकलाविलासे

पुरातनत्वं च नवीनता च ।। 3 ।।

शब्दार्थसाहित्यमपूर्वमस्य

काव्येषु पुष्टाश्च रसप्रवाहाः ।

सर्वाञ्जनानुन्मदयन्ति सत्यं

कुर्वन्ति तांस्तद्वशगान् हठाच्च ।। 4 ।।

''वेगाद्वहन्ती च न चोत्तटा च

गम्भीरभावा च न चाप्रसादा ।

रसोत्तरङ्गा प्रतिभा विभाति

महाकवेर्देवतरङ्गिणीव'' ।। 5 ।।

निजाद्वितीयप्रतिभोत्थदीप-

शिखेव काव्यावलिरस्य दीप्रा ।

सम्प्रापयत्यन्यकवीन्द्रकाव्य-

समूहमत्यन्तविवर्णभावम् ।। 6 ।।

पदावलिं कोमलकान्तरूपां
न्यस्यन् यथास्थानमयं कवीन्द्रः ।
ताञ्चाप्यलङ्कारभरेण युञ्ज-
न्नाभाति काव्यज्ञभराभिजुष्टः ।। 7 ।।

कविप्रवेकेषु लसत्स्वनेके-
ष्वनेन भूमिः सविशेषशोभा ।
''नक्षत्रताराग्रहसङ्कुलाऽपि
ज्योतिष्मती चन्द्रमसैव रात्रिः'' ।। 8 ।।

BIBLIOGRAPHY

BIBLIOGRAPHY

Basic Works

1.	*Śrībodhisattvacaritam*	:	Second Edition, Meharchand Lachhmandass, Delhi, 1973.
2.	*Indirāgāndhīcaritam*	:	Bharatiya VIdya Prakashan, Delhi, 1976.
3.	*Śrīrāmakīrtimahākāvyam*	:	Typed copy
4.	*Śrīrāmakīrtimahākāvyam*	:	Moolamall Sachdev Foundation, Amarnath Sachdeva Foundation Bangkok, Thailand, 1990.
5.	*Bṛhattaraṁ Bhāratam*	:	Sārasvatī-Suṣamā, Varanasi, Vol.12, No.1, Saṁvat 2014.
6.	*Śrīgurugovindasiṁhacaritam*	:	First Edition, Guru Gobind Singh Foundation, Patiala, 1967. Second Edition, Sahitya Bhandar, Meerut, 1984.
7.	*Śarmaṇyadeśaḥ sutarāṃ vibhāti*	:	Akhila Bharatiya Sanskrit Parishad, Lucknow, 1976.
8.	*Thaideśavilāsam*	:	Eastern Book Linkers, Delhi, 1979.
9.	*Ṣaḍṛtuvarṇanam*	:	*Bhāratī*, Jaipur, Caitra Sukla Pratipad, V.S. 2013, pp.153-154.
10.	*Napuṁsakaliṅgasya mokṣaprāptiḥ*	:	*Bhāratī*, Jaipur, Vol. IV, No.3, Saṁvat 2010, pp.97-99.
11.	*Ko'ham*	:	*Arvācīnasaṁskṛtam*, Delhi, Vol. IX, No.1, 1987.
12.	*Jaya Devi Svatantrate*	:	*Divyajyotiḥ*, Shimla, Nov. 15, 1965, p.5.
13.	*Kālidāsāṣṭakam*	:	Unpublished.
14.	Corpus of Versified Letters	:	Unpublished.

Secondary Works

1. *Ṛgveda-Saṁhitā* : Vol.1, Vaidika Saṁśodhana Maṇḍala, Poona, 1933.
2. " : Vol.II, ibid., 1963.
3. " : Vol.III, ibid., 1941.
4. " : Vol. IV, ibid., 1946.
5. *Ekādaśopaniṣatsaṅgraha* : Ed. Swami Satyanand, Amritdhara Bhavan, Lahore, V.S. 1995.
6. *The Nighaṇṭu And the Nirukta* : Ed. Lakshman Sarup, University of Punjab, Lahore, 1927.
7. *Vālmīki-Rāmāyaṇa* : (Vol. I-VII) : Gujrati Printing Press.
8. *Adhyātma-Rāmāyaṇa* : Gita Press, Gorakhpur, V.S. 2031.
9. *Ānanda-Rāmāyaṇa* : Pandit Pustakalaya, Kashi, 1968.
10. *Mahābhārata* : Text : (Vol.I-IV) : Gita Press, Gorakhpur, V.S. 2013-2015.
11. *Śrīmadbhagavadgītā* (With Śāṅkara-bhāṣya and Hindi Tr.) : Gita Press Gorakhpur, V.S. 2024.
12. *Bhagavadgītā* (With English Translation and Commentary) : Swami Prabhupad, The Bhaktivedant Book Trust, Philippines.
13. *Arthaśāstra* (Vil.I-III) : Ed. Udayavir Shastri, Meharchand Lachhmandass, Delhi, 1970.
14. *Kāvyālaṅkāra* (Bhāmaha) : Ed. Devendra Nath Sharma, Bihar Rashtrabhasha Parishad, Patna, 1985.
15. *Kāvyādarśa* (Daṇḍin) : Ed. Dharmendra Kumar Gupta, Meharchand Lachhmandass, Delhi, 1973.
16. *Kåvyālaṅkāra-sūtra* (Vāmana) : Ed. Bechan Jha, Chaukhamba Sanskrit Sansthan, Varanasi, 1989.
17. *Kāvyālaṅkāra* (Rudraṭa) : Ed. Ramadeva Shukla, Varanasi, 1966.

18. *Dhvanyāloka* (Ānandavardhana): Ed. Vishveshvara, Jnanamandala Ltd., Varanasi, 1962.

19. *Kāvyamīmāṁsā* (Rājaśekhara): Ed. Kedar Nath Sharma, Bihar Rashtrabhasha Parishad, Patna, 1965.

20. *Kāvyaprakāśa* (Mammaṭa) : Ed. Vishveshvara, Jnanamandala Ltd., Varanasi, 1960.

21. *Alaṅkārasarvasva* (Ruyyaka) : Kāvyamālā 35, 1939.

22. *Kāvyānuśāsana* (Hemacandra) : Ed. R.L. Parikh, V.M. Kulkarni, Mahavira Jaina Vidalaya, Bombay, 1964.

23. *Candrāloka* (Jayadeva) : Ed. V.L. Shastri Pansikar, Nirnaya Sagar Press, Bombay, 1937.

24. *Sāhityadarpaṇa* (Viśvanātha) : Ed. Shaligram Shastri, Lucknow, V.S. 1978.

25. *Kuvalayānanda* (Appayadīkṣita) :Ed. V.L. Shastri Pansikar, Nirnaya Sagar Press, Bombay, 1937.

26. *Daśarūpaka* (Dhanañjaya) : ibid., 1928.

27. *Suvṛttatilaka* (Kṣemendra) : Chaukhamba, Varanasi, 1968.

28. *Vṛttaratnākara* (Kedāra Bhaṭṭa) : Ed. Jagdish Bhatta Shastri, Bharadvaja Pustakalaya, Lahore, 1937.

29. *Manusmṛti* : Nirnaya Sagar Press, Bombay.

30. *Harivaṁśapurāṇa* : Gita Press, Gorakhpur, V.S.2041.

31. *Viṣṇupurāṇa* : Gita Press Gorakhpur.

32. *Saundarananda* : Ed. Surya Narayan Chaudhari, Motilal Banarasidass, Delhi, V.S.2026.

33. *Kumārasambhava* (I-V) : Ed. M.A. Karandikar and Sailaja Karandikar, Booksellers Publishing Co., Bombay, 1950.

34. *Raghuvaṁśa* : Ed. Narayana Rama Acarya, Nirnaya Sagar Press, Bombay, 1948.

35. *Meghadūta*	:	Ed. S.K. De, Sahitya Akademi, New Delhi, 1957.
36. *Kirātārjunīya*	:	Haridas Sanskrit Granthamala, 105, Varanasi, 1968.
37. *Śiśupālavadha*	:	Vidyabhavana Sanskrit Granthamala Benares, 1955.
38. *Naiṣadhīyacarita*	:	Ed. Shivadatta Sharma, Nirnaya Sagar Press, Bombay, 1933.
39. *Hammīra-mahākāvya* (Nayacandra Sūri)	:	Ed. Muni Jinavijaya, Rajasthan Oriental Research Institute, Jodhpur, 1968.
40. *Pārśvanāthacarita* (Hemavijayagaṇi)	:	Ed. Velasimha, Varanasi, 1916.
41. *Bharata-bāhubali-mahākāvya* (Puṇyakuśala)	:	Jaina Vishva Bharati, Ladnun, 1974.
42. *Śatakatrayādi-subhāṣita-saṅgrahaḥ* (Bhartṛhari)	:	Ed. D.D. Kosambi, Singhi Jaina Granthamala, 23, Bombay, 1948.
43. *Nītiśataka* (Bhartṛhari)	:	Ed. Roop Narayan Tripathi, Adarsh Prakashan, Jaipur, 1989-90.
44. *Puruṣārthopadeśa* (Bhartṛhari)	:	Ed. K.V. Sarma, Vishveshvaranand Institute, Hoshiarpur, 1969.
45. *Svapnavāsavadatta*	:	Ed. Rama Chandra Sharma, Dhanpat Rai and Sons, Jalandhar.
46. *Cārudatta*	:	Ed. C.R. Nagpal, Jalandhar, 1975.
47. *Mālavikāgnimitra*	:	Ed. M.R. Kale, The Standard Publishing Co., Bombay, 1918.
48. *Vikramorvaśīya*	:	Ed. Charudeva Shastri, Lahore, 1929.
49. *Abhijñānaśākuntala*	:	Ed. M.R. Kale, Gopal Narayen and Co., Bombay, 1934.

50. *Mṛcchakaṭika* : Ed. R.D. Karmarkar, Poona, 1937.

51. *Ratnāvalī* : Ed. Tarinisa Jha, Allahabad, 1975.

52. *Veṇīsaṁhāra* : Ed. K.K. Tripathi, Meerut, 1983.

53. *Mudrārākṣasa* : Ed. Ashvini Kumar Bhattacharya, Calcutta.

54. *Uttararāmacarita* : Ed. M.R.Kale, Gopal Narayen and Co., Bombay, 1924.

55. *Daśakumāracarita* : Ed. M.R. Kale, Motilal Banarasidass, Delhi, 1966.

56. *Kādambarī* : Ed. Kasinath Pandurang Parab, Nirnaya Sagar Press, Bombay, 1932.

57. *Pañcatantra* : Ed. Jwala Prasad Mishra, Shri Venkateshwar Steam Press, Bombay, 1923.

58. *Hitopadeśa* (Mitralābha) : Ed. B.L. Sharma, Ajmer Book Company, Jaipur, 1985.

59. *Hitopadeśa* (Mitralābha) : Ed. Babu Ram Tripathi, Mahalakshmi Prakashan, Agra, 1988.

60. *Bhāminī-Vilāsa* : Ed. Jibananda Vidyasagara, Calcutta, 1963.

61. *Siddhāntakaumudī* : Ed. Vasudeva Laksmana Sarma Panasikara, Meharchand Lachhmandass, Delhi, 1985.

62. *Laghusiddhāntakaumudī* : Ed. Parameshvaranand, Meharchand Lachhmandass, Lahore, V.S. 1992.

63. *India As Known to Pāṇini* : V.S. Agrawal, Prithvi Prakashan, Varanasi, 1963.

64. *The Rāmāyaṇa – A Linguistic Study* : Satya Vrat, Munshi Ram Manohar Lal, Delhi, 1964.

65. *Essays on Indology* : Satya Vrat Shastri, Meharchand Lachhmandass, Delhi, 1963.

66. *Studies in Sanskrit and Indian Culture in Thailand* : Satya Vrat Shastri, Parimal Publications, Delhi, 1982.

67. *Kālīdāsa in Modern Sanskrit Literature* : Satya Vrat Shastri, Eastern Book Linkers, Delhi, 1991.

68. *Rāmāyaṇa-Kālīna Saṁskṛti* : Shanti Kumar Nanu Ram Vyas, Satsahitya Prakashan, Delhi, 1958.

69. *Rāmāyaṇa-kālīna Samāja* : ibid., Delhi, 1964.

70. *Indirāgāndhīcaritam : Eka Samīkṣātmaka Adhyayana* (Ph.D. Thesis : Typed Copy) : Indira Kant Pathak

71. *Saṁskṛta Vāṅmaya meṅ Indira Gandhi* (Ph.D. Thesis : Typed copy) : Kanak Mathur

72. *Principles of Literary Criticism* : Ed. R.C. Dvivedi Motilal Banarasidass, Delhi, 1977.

73. *Alaṁkāra-mīmāṁsā* : R.C. Dvivedi, Motilal Banarasidass, Delhi, 1965.

74. *Saṁskṛta Kāvyaśāstra kā Itihāsa* (Hindi Tr.) : P.V. Kane, Motilal Banarsidass, Delhi, 1966.

75. *A History of Sanskrit Literature* : A.B. Keith, Oxford University Press, 1953.

76. *A History of Sanskrit Literature* : A.A. Macdonell, Motilal Banarasidass, Delhi, 1962.

77. *Saṁskṛta-kavi-darśana* : Bhola Shankar Vyas, Chaukhamba Vidya Bhavan, V.S. 2012.

78. *Saṁskṛta Vāṅmaya kā Vivecanātmaka Itihāsa* : Suryakant, Orient Longman, 1972.

79. *Jaina-Saṁskṛta-mahākāvya* : Satya Vrat, Vishva Bharati, Ladnun (Raj.), 1989.

80. *Prācīprabhā* Perspectives in Indology : Delhi, 1989.

81. *Ratnacandrikā* Panorama of Oriental Studies : Delhi, 1989.

Journals

1. *Annals of Bhandarkar Oriental Research Institute*, Poona.
2. *Journal of Oriental Research Institute*, Baroda.
3. *Vishveshvaranand Indological Journal*, Hoshiarpur.
4. *Punjab University Research Bulletin*, Chandigarh.
5. *Bharātīya Vidyā*, Bombay.
6. *Sambodhi*, Ahmedabad.
7. *Jain Journal*, Calcutta.
8. *Mysore Orientalist*, Mysore.
9. *Journal of Haryana Studies*, Kurukshetra.
10. *Proceedings of the Second International Rāmāyaṇa Conference*, 1986, Bangkok.
11. *Arvācīna-saṁskṛtam*, Delhi.
12. *Bhāratī*, Jaipur.
13. *Viśvasaṁskṛtam*, Hoshiarpur.
14. *Sāgarikā*, Sagar.
15. *Sārasvatī-suṣamā*, Varanasi.
16. *Divyajyotiḥ*, Shimla.
17. *Svaramaṅgalā*, Jaipur.
18. *Saṁvid*, Bombay.
19. *Sarasvatī*, Allahabad.
20. *Saptasindhu*, Patiala.

ERRATA

Page	Line	Incorrect	Correct
5	27	distinguish	distinguishes
29	30	had	Delete it
36	3	of	or
41	1	dominant	dominant sentiment
45	24	echo	echoes
47	20	knee	knees
49	1	fold	folk
51	21	them	theme
52	18	frost	forest
60	31	in the canto IX	in canto IX
77	12	, surely	. Surely
86	3	gaity	gaiety
87	18	bycott	boycott
87	39	foreigh	foreign
88	4	prisoh	prison
92	28	them	him
95	38	mainly	many
97	4	, the	. The
102	11	electricity	alacrity
111	27	after	afar
132	8	try with	try conclusions with
137	20	the	The
146	22	the author	The author
147	26	While	Delete it
160	24	armours	armouries
160	36	source	course
161	13	couldron	cauldron
161	21	warrior	warriors
161	32	*śibiram*	*śiviram*
166	17	He	, he
167	38	to people	to the people
169	13	story that	story. That
169	35	injunctions Daṇḍin	injunctions of Daṇḍin
170	2	potential in	potential of
170	27	shows	turns
172	25	differs	differ
172	29	score	scores
176	26	anoher	another
177	19	theroriticians	theoriticians
181	21	With	with
193	16	in purview	in its purview

Page	Line	Incorrect	Correct
195	22	in joy	in the joy
196	13	invests	invest
200	19	exchange	exchanges
201	7	Unlike	like
201	22	as gullible	as a gullible
205	13	Kuśa	Lava
209	27	befall to Kaikeyī	befall Kaikeyī
215	18	subjects in	subjects enumerated in
216	10	to demanding	to the demanding —
217	9	, the	. The
218	5	serve	serves
223	23	realise in	realise
224	4	clothed	clothed in
224	7	language not	language which is not
224	8	subject	subjects
227	24	vile	wile
231	13	it	It
256	12	in completely	by completely
256	15	hesitated from	hesitated in
262	20	its	their
262	26	its cadence	Delete the words
276	14	Granth their	Granth as their
276	15	into	with
276	16	poeticians's	poetician's
276	28	admits with	admits. With
276	28	that	Delete it
277	8	interesting as	interesting it is as
277	9	as it is a poem	Delete the words
287	6	may be	may
288	7	Double Simile on	Double simile. On
299	35	Which	Delete it
302	8	mundane	Delete it
304	9	pulsates	pulsate
306	5	its	their
306	25	has	have
309	30	times	time
310	9	merits	They merit
310	12	or...ways	Delete the words
335	14	embellishes	embellish
343	25	on	at
347	2	to be	to be a
350	3	form	forms
350	33	make	makes
369	10	Malaysian	Burmese